Dedicated to the memory and work of Dorothy O. Johansen, 1904–1999.

Contents

COMRADES OF THE QUEST

COMRADES OF THE QUEST

An Oral History of Reed College

JOHN SHEEHY

Oregon State University Press

Corvallis, Oregon

ISBN 978-0-87071-667-6
Cataloging information for this title is available at the Library of Congress.
First published in 2012 by Oregon State University Press.
Printed in the United States of America.

The paper in this book meets the guidelines for permanence and durability of the Committee on Production Guidelines for Book Longevity of the Council on Library Resources and the minimum requirements of the American National Standard for Permanence of Paper for Printed Library Materials Z39.48-1984.

 Oregon State University Press
121 The Valley Library, Corvallis, Oregon 97331
www.osupress.oregonstate.edu   541-737-3166

PART FIVE: RADICAL TRADITIONALIST, 1989–2011
Page 458

EPILOGUE
Page 516

Comrades of the Quest

In the drama of college-building on the American stage, Reed appears as a heroic actor, propelled to the front of the stage by its pure expression of widely admired purposes. But the character of the college has been complex and double-edged, and we understand it well when we comprehend how much pain resides behind the noble face. If this college is a bold figure in American higher education, it is one that has steadily courted tragedy. The willingness to take that as part of the price, to continue on a high road of unbound danger, is the final indication of the intensity of the institution.

  —Burton R. Clark, *The Distinctive College*

INTRODUCTION

In every round-up, the finest steers are always outside the bunch.
   —David Starr Jordan, president of Stanford University 1891–1913,
      at the laying of the Reed College cornerstone, June 8, 1912

As Comrades of the Quest, we have set out, as President Foster has expressed it, "to
do something significant in the realm of Higher Education." We do not feel that our
enthusiasm and purpose are commonplace or ordinary, and we shall not be satis-
fied with mediocre results.
   —*The Reed College Quest*, June 16, 1913

"Communism, atheism, free love" is not a slogan that would have met with the approval of Reed College's founding president, William Trufant Foster. A righteous young man with an electrifying, stentorian style, Foster did not believe in "isms," or in labels of any kind, finding them far too confining for his uncompromising brand of intellectual freedom. "Comrades of the Quest"—the rallying cry Foster adopted when the college first opened its doors in 1911 in Portland, Oregon—better captured the crusading spirit he had in mind. Foster set out to make critical thinking the holy grail at Reed, and, in doing so, sought to create an "ideal college" that would revitalize the liberal arts while preparing its graduates for the ever-widening dimensions of the modern world.

   Although Foster's quest quickly earned Reed College national recognition as a promising new educational model, it also generated local derision. In the words of founding philosophy professor E. O. Sisson, "There seemed to be no bounds to the public misunderstanding and misrepresentation of an institution that ventured to break the hard crust of custom and orthodoxy." Portland critics, alarmed by Foster's progressive challenges to their city's social and political status quo, attacked the college for its supposed embrace of "communism, atheism, and free love" during the Red Scare that followed the First World War. The pejorative stuck, but, with a playful sense of subversive irony, the Reed community appropriated the slur as its unofficial slogan, acknowledging both the cocky arrogance of Foster's quest and the frictions inherent in its implementation.

Although Reed's educational model would serve as an inspiration to other colleges in years to come, the principles intrinsic to Foster's institutional design—intellectual freedom, academic rigor, and egalitarian democracy—insured that Reed College would forever remain an iconoclast in higher education. As pillars of Foster's vision, these three principles were intended to operate interdependently: intellectual freedom was the desired state of being; academic rigor the path to attaining that state; and egalitarian democracy the environment necessary to supporting and enhancing that attainment.

Much of Foster's design for Reed, however, was pragmatic, stemming from the immediate challenge of making a liberal arts college relevant in an era dominated by specialized research universities and pre-professional training. To achieve this, he believed it essential to impart to students the most rigorous set of intellectual skills and attitudes possible for informing every area of inquiry in a rapidly changing world. Students and professors were encouraged to study together in a collaboration unbound by custom, tradition, or codified rules of behavior, tempered only by an "Honor Principle" of individual restraint that Foster chose not to define lest it become sclerotic. To maintain the highest standards of intellectual purity, Foster imposed a number of curricular hurdles, including a thesis and oral examination in a student's senior year. To ensure small, intimate classes, the student-faculty ratio was set at ten-to-one, and professors were directed to focus on teaching, not research. To instill self-discipline and discourage students from working for grades instead of for learning, professors issued no grades except upon request after graduation. To cultivate egalitarianism and inclusiveness, Foster banned fraternities, sororities, honors, and awards, as well as what he considered the sideshow amusements of intercollegiate sports. To promote a democratic community, he offered the faculty a share in governance and students an unprecedented degree of autonomy. All of these features quickly came to define Reed, and remarkably have remained largely in place throughout the college's first century.

As a result, Reed was distinguished not by just a few educational improvements but by genuine innovation. Within a few years of opening its doors, the school was hailed in *The New York Times* as an intellectual powerhouse and one of the most demanding colleges in the country. By the 1930s, Reed was generating the country's highest percentage of Rhodes Scholars and of graduates going on to earn advanced science degrees. By the early 1950s, the college was reputed by *The Saturday Evening Post* to have the "smartest body of undergraduates in America," an assertion echoed by *Time* magazine in the early 1960s. As recently as 2006, *The Princeton Review* declared Reed College to be the best academic experience for undergraduates in America.

But while Reed served as a groundbreaking new model for the liberal arts, a series of paradoxes in Foster's institutional design created inherent tensions—both internal and external—that over the years would serve to keep Foster's ideals vital but that also repeatedly threatened the college's stability.

The first of these paradoxes stemmed from Foster's belief that intellectual freedom was dependent on rigorous Socratic discipline. In a place where everything was open to question and no topics were off the table, unthinking conformity to conditioned beliefs, status quo conventionality, or ideology of any sort was regarded as a hindrance. Foster's academic rigor was a process of completely grinding down such hindrances and replacing them with a pragmatic method of thinking that ideally acknowledged no boundaries, in which people had the freedom and capability to think anything and everything. Nothing was considered sacred except the right to free inquiry. Such intellectual freedom required intensive attention to training the mind to think about thinking itself. It was by its very nature stressful and painful. There was no easy way through it. Absent the positive feedback and quantifiable rewards of grades, honors, and awards of distinction, the training at Reed became an existential end in itself. The hyper-intellectual environment it fostered—unrelieved by such traditional features of college life as intercollegiate sports and fraternities and sororities—resulted in a great deal of student anxiety and relatively low participation in extracurricular activities. The demands placed on students by their studies created a culture of time scarcity. For many, there was simply no end in sight to the work itself.

A second paradox was the pairing of such a disciplined academic program with a laissez-faire social structure. Unlike the first paradox, in which discipline was believed to lead to the attainment of intellectual freedom, in the social realm the paradox was reversed. Here, social freedom led to the establishment of community norms.

Foster, by nature anti-traditional and anti-authoritarian, wished to see as few regulations on campus as possible. Independence was to be the context for community at Reed, with self-reliance and risk-taking the intended outcomes. Foster's adoption of the ambiguous Honor Principle in place of hard and fast rules meant that students were responsible to each other for conducting themselves honorably. The non-codified nature of the Honor Principle placed it in a difficult and complex middle ground between rules and no rules, incorporating both but not abiding in either, requiring that its agency be continually reëxamined in times of crisis and so remain relevant to the changing mores of the campus community. "What is the Honor Principle?" became Reed's version of a Zen koan. To attempt to define it was to violate it. Foster hoped that a community that valued independence would naturally rely upon mutual self-restraint as a means of protecting that value in the community.

In practice, however, adherence to the Honor Principle was complicated by the rebellious nature of students, whose idea of social freedom often appeared most pronounced in reaction to a perceived threat of repression. While students took vigorous action against behaviors such as cheating and stealing, they were reluctant to intervene in the ways other students conducted their social lives, especially with regard to sex and the use of intoxicants, instead adopting a laissez-faire or even libertarian attitude. By the end of Reed's first decade, students' protection of their social freedoms came to outweigh their enforcement of a community-wide ethos of honor, becoming a constant point of friction with the college administration.

The larger challenge for many students, though, was balancing their social independence with the college's rigorous and structured academic discipline. That became apparent as the student attrition rate rose within the college's first few years to between 50 and 60 percent, a level at which it remained for most of the next eighty years, into the 1990s. High attrition distinguished Reed from other selective, academically demanding liberal arts colleges whose average attrition levels ran between 20 and 30 percent, earning the school a reputation as an "intellectual boot camp," and reducing its potential applicant pool to largely a self-selecting lot.

A third paradox in Reed's design arose from Foster's pursuit of egalitarian democracy. Reed's constitution, which provided an unprecedented share of power to the faculty and of autonomy to student government, was ideally meant to encourage both self-reliance and ongoing innovation within those bodies, without the constraints of executive, top-down administration. To Foster's surprise however, the checks and balances inherent in such a democratic structure made developing the overall college a slow and messy process, and soon led to a general conservative posture on the part of both faculty and students—supported by an ever-increasing cadre of alumni—a conservatism that manifested itself as an allegiance to what commonly came to be called the "old Reed." Instead of continual bold innovation, Foster instead found himself wrestling with the faculty in an effort to find the right power-sharing balance to keep the college moving forward, foreshadowing decades of governance impasses and crises.

Ideally, the three paradoxes in Foster's design would have prevented Reed from becoming too fixed in its ways, maintaining the college's original pioneering spirit while reinforcing its ability to adapt to advances in higher education over time. In fact, Reed's academic model would continue to occupy the leading edge of the American educational vanguard for the next fifty years, thanks in large part to the adoption of a general education humanities program implemented by Foster's successor, Richard Scholz, in the early 1920s. That, however, would be the college's last major innovation. As multiculturalism began reshaping the academic landscape in the second half of the twentieth century, and as pre-professional training once again gained dominance, Reed became reactionary, stubbornly holding onto its Western humanities program and its commitment to training in critical thinking for the sake of critical thinking. In so doing, the college once again challenged the educational status quo, only now, ironically, as a nonconforming traditionalist. Part of this conservative stance, aside from normal institutional inertia, rested on a reluctance to alter the fundamental workings of a proven educational model whose causal factors were not fully understood by its practitioners.

By embedding paradoxes in his institutional design—whether wittingly or unwittingly—Foster ensured that his ideals would live on with what he hoped would be a "deathless spirit." These paradoxes also, however, established a creative tension that continually placed the college in a precarious state of discord regarding its own nature and purpose. In the repeated patterns of conflict that emerged at the college, it became clear to successive generations of the Reed community that with the good of each of Foster's ideals came some bad, but that trying to eliminate the bad effects also risked losing some of the good. Working with the paradoxes held promise that the college would maintain a level of excellence and a certain distinctiveness; attempting to diminish or eliminate them would leave Reed in peril of conformity and mediocrity. Despite periodic upheavals, the only way forward appeared to be in protecting Foster's ideals.

Like most nonconformists, Reed's identity in the world at large turned in part on being misunderstood. The perception of the college as an iconoclast played out repeatedly in town-and-gown clashes with the surrounding Portland community. In particular, the social freedoms and self-governance exercised by students came under consistent attack with complaints ranging from the lack of compulsory chapel services in the 1910s, women students smoking in the 1920s, political radicalism in the 1930s and '40s, premarital sex in the 1950s, countercultural behavior in the 1960s, nudity and other hedonistic activities in the 1970s and '80s, drug use in the 1990s, and the adjudication of allegations of sexual assault in the first decade of the twenty-first century. The college's stand on academic freedom—most notably during times of national hysteria such as the Red Scare of the late 1910s and McCarthyism in the early 1950s—also stirred up local suspicion and fear.

The result was an erosion of local financial support that began during Reed's first decade and continued through the 1980s, sending the college to the brink of financial collapse on four separate occasions. Ironically, the need for frugality served to reinforce Foster's insistence on independence from the influence of outside moneyed and political interests; self-reliance became a proud core value of the Reed community. The chronic lack of funding also precluded the college from expanding its curriculum too far astray from its primary goal of training students in critical thinking. For better or worse, focusing on doing one thing well—

and incurring the sacrifices that that standard required—became Reed's credo.

Shortly before his death, William Trufant Foster returned to the campus one last time to give the commencement speech to the graduating class of 1948. The title of his speech that day perhaps said it all: "Pay the Price and Take It." The story of the Reed community's struggle over the course of the college's first century to follow Foster's iconoclastic vision is the subject of this book.

The Reed Oral History Project was initiated in 1998 to capture and preserve the experiences of the college's community during its first century. Over a thirteen-year period, 125 Reed alumni, trained in oral history techniques, interviewed nearly four hundred former students, faculty members, administrators, and trustees. More than a thousand other individuals participated in facilitated group interviews or storytelling sessions. Added to the collection were dozens of legacy interviews conducted between 1935 and 1992, primarily by noted Northwest historian and longtime Reed professor of history Dorothy O. Johansen '33. *Comrades of the Quest* is composed of excerpts from transcripts of those interviews, supplemented with passages from various published and unpublished memoirs, letters, public addresses, and student theses, as well as articles from newspapers, magazines, and college publications.

Unlike many college histories that address only institutional development, this book was assembled on the premise that what distinguishes a college is not its physical campus, facilities, or sports teams, but the community it creates. If there is such a thing as the "Reed experience," this book attempts to explore it via the interplay of community members—presidents, professors, trustees, staff, and students—through their own recollections and in their own language.

In that spirit, I chose not to insert interpretations or summaries from an omniscient historical narrator into the text. Short introductions provide basic directional context for each chapter, as do testimonials interspersed throughout the book from three former Reed history professors—Dorothy O. Johansen '33, Richard Jones, and Chris Lowe '82—as well as from a handful of alumni who made parts of the college's history the focus of their student theses. Otherwise, community members are left to express their own histories through the recounting of their personal experiences, insights, and understandings. While this approach may present a challenge to readers accustomed to more traditional linear histories with ample historical analysis, my intention is for the reader to experience the stories as directly as possible, without mediation and from multiple perspectives, much as one experiences a group storytelling session.

At the same time, I set out to highlight through the stories certain themes and patterns in the community's development. Since the stories collected in the Reed Oral History Project were often told in fragments or discrete episodes, attempting to weave them into a coherent whole meant creating something of a synthetic literary work. By juxtaposing differing accounts of the same event, or allowing one narrator to amplify or expand on the partial tale of another for the sake of either completeness or ambiguity, I have sought to bring a number of individual vocal performances together into a chorus, usually melodious, sometimes dissonant. That chorus, it should be noted, is lacking many voices, due to the fact that a number of people chose not to participate in the oral history project, or were overlooked in being interviewed due to the limitations of outreach, time, and money, or simply had their stories left out of the book due to space constraints. As with any such undertaking, a valid question can be raised as to whether the voices that are included in the book adequately support the full telling of Reed's story.

Ultimately, of course, the story these voices tell in their totality expresses my perception of the community's history. I picked out the stories that appealed to me and chose how to piece them together. My methodology, which is perhaps closer to that of a documentarian than to a traditional oral history rendering, has undoubtedly created perspectives and contexts that individual narrators may be unaware of, or might even disagree with. Nevertheless, my intention was to preserve each narrator's voice and language as much as possible while also aiming for clarity and readability. That effort included editing out false starts and repetitious statements, tightening up narrative structure, combining related or similar references made in different parts of an interview into one segment, standardizing verb tenses, and clearing up idiomatic phrases or awkward syntax. I applied the same approach to the selections included in the book from written memoirs and letters. If there are errors, lapses, inconsistencies, words used out of context, or unintended meanings, I accept full responsibility. I hope that readers and narrators will forgive such shortcomings.

Finally, there is the matter of oral history itself. As an area of academic study, oral history got its start in 1948 when historian Allan Nevins founded the oral history office at Columbia University. The field took off during the 1960s and early 1970s, with the emergence of the civil rights and feminist movements, as a means of documenting and giving voice to groups that had often been pushed to the margins of society. While oral history enjoys increasing popularity today, many academic historians continue to view it with suspicion. It is easy to see why. The human memory is wildly selective. After a passage of years, most of us honestly believe the things we think we saw, despite our muddled chronology and lack of complete context. Our memories are also subject to change as we learn more about our past, the knowledge of which reshapes our memories going forward. When it comes to oral history, it may be as Emerson famously observed, that "there is properly no history, only biography."

Oral history's current popular appeal may indeed be one part nostalgia and another part the love of a good yarn. "No good story is quite true," remarked

Leslie Stephen, the Victorian creator of Britain's *Dictionary of National Biography*. And yet, while reality in oral history may be a subjective, slippery concept—particularly as no two people tend to have the same recollection of the same event—beneath the hypothetical narratives of what happened runs the deeper purpose of memory, that of making meaning of our lives. Oral history theorist Alessandro Portelli maintains that while memory may be the last place one hopes to find eyewitness accounts that are either true or false, the themes and structures that memory imposes offer ways of getting at the meaning of what actually happened.

"Memory is not just a mirror of what has happened," notes Portelli, "it is one of the things that happens, which merits study. Oral sources tell us not just what people did, but what they wanted to do, what they believed they were doing, and what they now think they did."

Oral history differs from other forms of memory recollection—such as memoir or journal writing—in that it arises from a dialogue between an interviewer and an interviewee. That dialogue turns on inquiry and recall. In the case of the Reed Oral History Project, the interviewers sought a connection between an individual's personal biography and his or her role in the college's collective history. They approached individuals with a list of open-ended questions designed to explore personal, cultural, academic, and institutional experiences at Reed. They were, however, trained to follow whatever memory stream the interviewee chose to pursue. Portelli calls this process "history-telling"—a cousin to storytelling—because of its thematic scope and dialogic nature.

The French sociologist Maurice Halbwachs, who coined the term "collective memory"—understood to express some essential truth about a group—pointed out that collective memory is more about the present than about the past because it is integral to how a group currently sees itself. Since a majority of the Reed interviews were conducted over the same thirteen-year period, Halbwach's observation may explain some of the consistencies with which individuals from different generational cohorts expressed their identification with Reed. However, conducting the interviews with people from different generations over the same time period also introduced other variables. For example, an event recalled sixty years after its occurrence may differ in perspective, shape, and detail from one recalled after a passage of only six or sixteen years. In particular, as people's narratives draw closer to their recent past, the ability to see that past in clear historical perspective becomes more challenging. The historian Eric Hobsbawm calls this obscurity and fuzziness the "twilight zone between memory and history"—between the open, dispassionate record of the past, and the past as a remembered part of one's own life. This zone, along with the different communication styles of different generations, has undoubtedly influenced the content and narrative flow of the book, particularly in the final chapters.

College stories are of course a recognized genre in themselves, with specific motifs, themes, and mythic roles that are the stuff of films, biographies, and literature: the stern but nurturing professor, the student's coming of age, the raucous parties, the triumphant breakthrough of intellectual discovery. But oral history, in that it plumbs the personal experience, often serves to feature other roles and motifs that are similar but less commonly recognized. Reed College, with its idiosyncratic lack of fraternities and sororities, posted grades and awards, and intercollegiate athletic teams and homecoming events, provides for a unique collective memory that is perhaps well served by the benefits of oral history.

"I think one should work into a story the idea of not being sure of all things," advises writer Jorge Luis Borges, "because that's the way reality is." To that point, this book is not an institutional history of hard facts and precise details. It is more a memory play, which, like most memories, follows a stream full of little whirlpools, each filled with past incidents caught up in a circular pattern of repeated stories that reinforce a set of underlying convictions or beliefs. In the case of the Reed community, many of those convictions and beliefs emerged in response to the vision of an ideal college set down in 1911 by William Trufant Foster.

By paying close attention to these stories, it is my hope that we may recognize not only the themes, mores, and patterns that have shaped this particular community's story, but also something of the forces that have shaped our own individual narratives. As Steven Falk, Reed class of 1983, aptly put it, "In listening to other people's stories, I heard my own."

PROLOGUE

The pressure cooker that I experienced at Reed, beginning as a naïve, intelligent, gutsy, arrogant person with no background, made my life complete. There's no other way to say it.

The first two years of the Reed system, that of knocking the arrogance out of you, really worked for me. I went from thinking I was the smartest, strongest person to being completely open to learning because I knew that there was so much I didn't know, that I would never know, no matter if I studied a lifetime.

In your junior year the message was, "You know nothing. You are absolutely stupid. You have to take this junior qualification exam, but don't think you're going to pass it, you're so bad." Then they tell you that you passed and you're good enough to go on. Pat you on the head. In your senior year it's, "You can learn anything. There are so many things to learn."

But after your thesis and your orals, it's, "You don't know anything now. Go to graduate school. Go out and live. Go forth from here and enjoy life. Learn life. Manipulate life. You have the skills. You can do anything. But you've got to work at it. You really don't know it now, but you can learn it."

The kind of adult that system produces is one who is strong but who is also compassionate, who knows there are many ways to the truth, and that he or she can learn new things. That's what Reedies do. If they try this or that and they don't like it, then they try something else. They go back to the earth and live on the farm and grow buffalo, or they invent a company, or they blend in enough to be the president of a university or the head of a law firm.

There's something different about Reed that appeals to what is inside you. It is like falling in love. Then you have to decide if you can take the boot camp. Reed students who survive the process of being torn down, built up again, and then taught to learn that you will always learn, go out from Reed and keep that attitude of learning and of seeing the possibilities of life. That going through the fire marks the passage from a young person to a real adult.

—Mertie Hansen Muller '56

PART ONE

PART ONE: RADICAL UPSTART, 1911–1920

RADICAL UPSTART, 1911–1920

The sideshows have swallowed up the circus.
　—Woodrow Wilson, president of Princeton University 1902–1910

Reed College was launched in 1911 as an innovative experiment to restore relevancy to the liberal arts in an age dominated by science and industry. The antebellum American college—a model heavily influenced by Oxford and Cambridge with their religious affiliation, devotion to character development and civic responsibility, and use of classical curricula emphasizing ancient languages and mathematics—had lost its primacy to newly established land-grant colleges, research universities, and professional schools, all of which appeared to be more tailored to meet the specialized, utilitarian needs of the increasingly secular, industrialized age.

To compete for student enrollment, liberal arts colleges had resorted to relaxing their curricular requirements, downplaying religion, and encouraging vigorous spectator-sports competition at the expense of their primary missions, inadvertently aligning themselves with social climbers and purchased degrees. The time was ripe, many believed, for a new kind of college that would give renewed relevance to the liberal arts while preparing its graduates for the ever-widening dimensions of the modern world.

This belief particularly resonated with adherents of pragmatism, a distinctly American philosophy that flowered at the beginning of the twentieth century. Advanced largely by the efforts of philosophers John Dewey, Charles Pierce, and William James, pragmatism had as its essential premise a skepticism toward ideologies. Ideas were to be viewed not as immutable truths but as contingent and adaptable responses to the environment—tools that people could utilize in coping with the world around them. The pragmatists' skepticism served as a personal safeguard against an increasingly impersonal mass society undergoing rapid

William Trufant Foster surveying Crystal Springs Farm, the future site of Reed College, 1910.

industrialization. Skepticism also proved to be well-suited to the entrepreneurial spirit of the times, helping to fuel the constant change and disruptive innovation that industrialized capitalism depended on. But perhaps most important, skepticism and its accompanying spirit of inquiry had a liberating effect on a generation of jurists, journalists, policy makers, and academics who comprised the progressive movement. Freed from fatalistic nineteenth-century determinism, progressives sought to apply scientific methodology to social problems in a universe that they viewed as still in play, where people interacted with their environment as agents of their own destinies.

This progressive spirit was embraced by Thomas Lamb Eliot, a Unitarian minister who for forty years had waged a moral and cultural crusade in the frontier town of Portland, Oregon. The descendant of a distinguished Boston Brahmin family of ministers and educators, Eliot was regarded, by the turn of the twentieth century, as Portland's most eminent citizen. He held a liberal Christian's belief in free inquiry, maintaining that a liberal education freed people to discover truths on their own. But that discovery was not to be an end in itself. Education, like wealth, was for Eliot a measure of responsibility to God, best borne by the assumption of moral and intellectual leadership in the community. While Eliot himself modeled such leadership in Portland, his most influential role was brokering the philanthropic activities of his wealthy parishioners with worthy social and civic causes. In the 1880s, he suggested to two members of his congregation, Simeon and Amanda Reed, that they use their riches for the betterment of Portland by establishing an institute for lectures and the arts.

Consequently, when Simeon Reed died in 1895, he designated that a portion of his fortune, made in river transportation on the Columbia River, go toward furthering the cultural advancement of Portland. Amplifying his wishes, his widow, Amanda, specified that the Reed estate be used to establish an institution of learning. At her death in 1904, her will named a board of five trustees with Eliot as chair, and assigned them the task of creating the Reed Institute. Aside from an insistence on equality and freedom from sectarian influence, the terms of Amanda Reed's will left the exact nature of the institute somewhat ambiguous. It was to be devoted both to the "increase and diffusion of practical knowledge among the citizens of Portland," and to the "promotion of literature, science, and arts." While Eliot favored pursuing the latter, one of his fellow trustees, Amanda Reed's nephew and business manager, Martin Winch, strongly insisted that the intention of his aunt and uncle was to create a vocational or technical school. Like his uncle Simeon Reed, whose view of education was that children should be taught "useful industry" and kept in school for fewer hours, Winch had received only a meager academy education to prepare him for a career in business. The rift between Winch and Eliot would plague the college for decades, and would haunt Thomas Lamb Eliot to his dying day.

To break the impasse, Eliot convinced the other trustees to seek the views of leading educators around the country as to what kind of school to establish. Most influential of these advisors was Wallace Buttrick, the secretary of the General Education Board. Formed in 1902 with a $180 million grant from John D. Rockefeller, the General Education Board encouraged experimentation in higher education, supporting new, pacesetting institutions in underserved regions of the country, including black schools in the South. Eliot also sought the advice of his cousin, Charles Eliot, who had just joined the General Education Board following his retirement from Harvard University after forty years as its president.

Harvard had been the birthplace of the liberal arts tradition in America upon its founding in 1636, originally as a training ground for gentlemen clergy. By the time Charles Eliot took the helm in 1869, Harvard's student enrollment, like that of most colleges across the country, was on the decline. The popularity of the German university model, with its emphasis on specialized research and professional training, was rendering the small and religiously affiliated liberal arts college an anachronism. Studies that emphasized ideas rather than things such as technology and engineering had no place in the German university. In that model, contributing to the growth of new knowledge was more important than training new leaders in civic affairs through the study of what English poet Matthew Arnold described as "the best which has been thought and said in the world." The fact that popular professional schools, such as those teaching medicine, law, divinity, and science, did not at the time require entering students to have a bachelor's degree made a liberal arts education seem even more irrelevant.

Charles Eliot set about changing that, first by reshaping Harvard into a premier research university, and next by making entrance to its graduate school dependent on four years of liberal arts education, free of technical or vocational training. College was to be about learning for the sake of learning, with graduate school to focus on specialized training. By establishing a period of broad immersion in the liberal arts prior to the pursuit of professionalization, Charles Eliot sought to better prepare students to cope with the rapid pace of technological, economic, and political change underway in the late nineteenth century. He believed that a useful education entailed not only training for a profession, but a commitment to public service and a capacity to change and adapt. To that end, he opened Harvard to student self-direction, employing a new free-electives curriculum developed at Cornell University, which provided students with unrestricted choice in selecting their courses of study. Freed from the dogmatic authority of the antebellum prescribed curriculum, and left to take charge of their own thinking, students would, Charles Eliot believed, be better able to discover their own natural bents, which they would pursue later in specialized graduate education. Although slow to take root in the face of strong resistance, his innovations offered new purpose to the traditional function of the liberal arts college.

Upon review of the Reed Institute's predicament in Portland, Charles Eliot and Wallace Buttrick recommended that the trustees establish a college of arts and sciences. They also recommended that one of Charles Eliot's former students, William Trufant Foster, be appointed the school's first president.

Like his mentor, William Trufant Foster was not so much an originator of new ideas as an aggregator of emerging trends and an aggressive implementer of pragmatic educational reform. Critical of prescriptive classical curricula for making professors lazy and students passive, Foster proposed that Reed College adopt Charles Eliot's elective curriculum to capture students' intellectual enthusiasm and to emphasize that the subject studied was not as important as the student-teacher relationship, nor was the corpus of knowledge as important as learning how to go about acquiring knowledge in the first place. Foster insisted that students avoid the narrow utilitarian approach of the research universities, and "specialize in the humanities," advocating the view that no field of inquiry could be understood except in relation to other fields.

Foster, like Charles Eliot, had a pragmatist's preoccupation with the present. For pragmatists, the sort of historical and theoretical knowledge that a liberal arts education provided was valuable in exposing the contingency of current arrangements in the world around them. Understanding that contingency allowed pragmatists to recognize a priori assumptions and to think for themselves outside the established status quo, ideally making enlightened contributions toward advancing the common good. At Thomas Lamb Eliot's request, Foster sought to involve Reed College directly in social and cultural reforms around Portland. In this way—combining philosophical pragmatism with direct community service—both Foster and Eliot felt that they were serving the intentions of Amanda Reed's will for the improvement of local culture, as well as bringing a new ascendancy to the liberal arts.

Under Foster's leadership the new college—unburdened by a past and armed with Simeon and Amanda Reed's generous $3 million endowment—quickly rocketed into the top tier of national higher education, producing four Rhodes Scholars from its first six graduating classes and establishing itself as a promising new experiment in liberal arts education. Its heterodoxy and progressive nature, however, quickly led to a conservative backlash in Portland, where the school was denounced as a hotbed of godless radicalism, diminishing local financial support. Then, in the mid-1910s, Reed's endowment, held mostly in real estate, was decimated by a recession. Attempts to raise funds from the community were damaged by resentment over the college's zealous reform efforts and William Trufant Foster's pacifism during the First World War. At the end of its first decade, Reed College would find itself dangling by a thread.

CHAPTER 1

The Founders

You are working in the same fashion as I and with like aims. If anybody tempts you to found a university, pizen yourself, Tommy. Certainly your present work is large enough and good enough.

— William Greenleaf Eliot, in a letter to his son, Thomas Lamb Eliot

There is danger in breaking away from the bondage of narrow sectarianism, in that one may go adrift upon the sands of infidelity.

— Cyrus Dolph, trustee

In the early 1850s, Massachusetts-born Simeon and Amanda Reed, both in their twenties, settled in pioneer Portland. Simeon prospered with the growing city, making his fortune in the heyday of river transportation and becoming part of a small group of businessmen, among them William S. Ladd, Henry Failing, Henry Corbett, and Captain John Ainsworth, who led Portland's early economic development. Having no children of their own to inherit their wealth, the Reeds agreed, under the guidance of their minister, Thomas Lamb Eliot, that it should be used after their passing for the "intelligence, prosperity, and happiness" of the city's inhabitants. The circuitous route those expectations took following their deaths led to the creation of an institution that many of their friends and family members believed was completely contrary to the couple's wishes.

SIMEON GANNETT REED: I was born in East Abington, Massachusetts, on the twenty-third of April, 1830. I married Amanda Wood on the seventeenth of October, 1850. I came to California via the Isthmus of Panama, and then to Oregon in 1852. I built a store in Rainier on the Columbia River, and engaged in general merchandising. At the time they were raising lots of potatoes and onions along the river and they were running a steamer twice a month down to San Francisco, so I thought Rainier would be a good shipping point and subsequently a good place for a store. I eventually sold out the business, and moved to Portland to take a position with William S. Ladd, who was then Portland's mayor, in general merchandising. I remained with Ladd until he started in the banking business. While clerking for Ladd I had bought an interest in the Columbia River Steam Navigation Company, eventually buying out the balance of the company. I had about as much to do with bringing about the organization of the Oregon Steam Navigation Company as perhaps any one person.

The condition of the steamboat business at the time was one steamboat operator running between Portland and the Cascade Rapids, another between the upper Cascades and The Dalles, and a third being built on the upper Columbia. It occurred to me that consolidation of these different interests could be brought about on suitable terms with proper management. Now, this was easier said than done, getting these conflicting interests together. Not being a steamboat man myself, being rather engaged in the mercantile business at the time, these people would each one come and talk matters over with me in sort of a confidential way. Each one seemed to be afraid of the other. Finally, it developed into the fact that the different interests could be brought together providing the terms were satisfactory, and a board of directors and managers could be agreed upon. The Oregon Steam Navigation Company was formed.

The company prospered and so far as steamboat interests were concerned, everything ran smoothly. In May 1862, we purchased the Cascade Railroad Company, which then consisted of a short tramway on the Washington Territory side of the Columbia River. The company then negotiated for the railroad on the Oregon side, giving us practically the control of both sides of the river. We also commenced building a portage railroad from The Dalles to Celilo. I was elected vice-president, and devoted my entire time to the business of the company and its management.

The growth of the country kept us pretty busy in keeping up with our facilities. At the time the population of Portland was 4,057. The population of Walla Walla, Washington, was five hundred. When the company was first formed, the business was principally government business—transportation of troops and supplies. Then after that came the farmers from the Willamette Valley, sending some of their boys up there with young stock to fatten on the bunchgrass. Early settlers in eastern Oregon, Washington, and Montana were nearly all from the farms of the Willamette Valley. We took them up pretty low and charged them pretty well for then bringing them down again.

Then they began to make mining discoveries. The big rush was during the Salmon River excitement in the summer of '62, when our facilities were taxed to their utmost. We held the position of a monopoly, occupying the key to the Columbia River portages at the Cascades. We always tried to help the farmers so they would make more money. The merchants and storekeepers could take care of themselves.

In those days, we three men—myself and two partners—were personally acquainted with the majority of people throughout the Willamette Valley. We had no red tape in our company. We were more interested than anybody else in promoting the growth and prosperity of that country. Business was very successful. In 1879 a syndicate purchased the stock of the company, leaving us with a 30 percent interest in the new Oregon Railroad and Navigation Company, which was eventually sold to Union Pacific Railroad.

During the steamboating, we occasionally took a fly outside. I took an interest in a mining enterprise in Baker County, and built the Auburn ditch some thirty miles long for placer mining. In 1871, in connection with William S. Ladd, I purchased thirteen improved farms in the Willamette Valley. The largest of these farms contained more than three thousand acres. After I got the farms, I thought I would do a little farming and get some fine stock on it. I went east and brought out five carloads of imported short-

Amanda and Simeon Reed in 1854, soon after their arrival in Oregon.

horn and Ayrshire cattle, Clydesdale horses and mares, Cotswold and Leicester sheep, and Berkshire pigs. While there was no great amount of money in it for me, it did the country some good. Our Clydesdale horses and our shorthorn cattle improved in the climate over the original stock.

In 1882, I bought a controlling interest in the Oswego Iron Company, and began the Oregon Iron and Steel Company for the manufacture of pig iron, nails, and bar and plate iron on a large scale. The company owned about a hundred acres of city property, with stores and hotels being built, about 683 acres of iron ore land, and about thirteen thousand acres of timberland in close proximity to the furnace. We also had eleven thousand acres on the lower Columbia. We had water power and dams, and two and a half miles of narrow-gauge railroad from the ore mines to the works. We proposed to supply the whole coast with what pig iron they could use.

LLOYD LYMAN '48 (Reed thesis): Simeon Reed was the product of his age, a successful pioneer capitalist. As his experiences proved, anyone with a reasonable amount of luck and perseverance might expect to become rich. So many opportunities were presented to anyone with capital that it was difficult to discriminate between a good and a bad proposition.

Reed was essentially a doer rather than a thinker. One of his foremost characteristics was the industry and thoroughness with which he attacked every problem. He also possessed a great deal of pride in his property. Everything he owned was of the best quality that could be purchased.

As with most successful businessmen of his age, Reed was essentially an optimist, a believer in progress. He engaged, however, in numerous practices that by the standards of our day would be considered dishonest. That which was most expedient was often deemed to be most right. In fairness, such methods were also employed by his opponents.

MORTON ROSENBLUM '49: While doing research as a student for a study of Simeon Reed's farming practices, I came upon a receipt from the Pinkerton Detective Agency that acknowledged Reed's payment to the Pinkerton for bribing an Idaho jury on a mining case.

MARY LADD, daughter-in-law of Reed's business partner, William S. Ladd: The Reeds lived on First Street in Portland. They lived not only comfortably but luxuriously for that time. They had a whole block and the house was up high, with a driveway winding into it. Opening out of the sitting room was a conservatory full of plants and birds.

They had a great number of paintings, copies of things that they had seen in Europe, but their art education had not gone very far, and they were not people of cultivated tastes. Mr. Reed's tastes were always for the gaudy, and he liked display.

He was a rotund and jolly man, with very curly hair and quite a bit of color in his face, full of fun and life, always with a cigar in his mouth. It was a very interesting life for young men and women like the Reeds and his partner, William S. Ladd, and his wife. In everything they did they laid foundations for the future, and there was an adventurous spirit about life in general. They did things in a lavish, wholehearted way.

The Reed home on Southwest Front Avenue between Montgomery and Harrison streets, circa 1885.

PART ONE: RADICAL UPSTART, 1911–1920

William McEldowney, foreman at Reed Farms: Mr. Reed was open and generous, and liked to do things in the right way. He was also restless, interested only in the stock and seeing that his farms were neat and that the managers were accomplishing something. The farms never paid out while they were devoted to raising stock. The farmers were not very interested in Mr. Reed's efforts to raise better stock. Money was made in the racehorses Mr. Reed raised and raced. In the early days Mr. Reed was a fine rider in his high-top boots. He was also a good marksman.

Ella Dehart, Reed family friend: The Reeds came into my life when I was five or six. I was taught to call them Uncle Sim and Reedie. They were both very hospitable and loved to have company and to have young people with them. When we spent the day with the Reeds, we really spent the day. They were both very musical, and sang in the choir of the Unitarian Church. Mr. Reed liked to tease. Mrs. Reed was nearsighted. She wore very heavy glasses, and didn't read much.

Lloyd Lyman '48 (Reed thesis): Simeon Reed was fussy about his clothes and tended to be a flashy dresser. On Sundays he drove to church with his wife in a smart landau behind high-stepping matched horses in silver-mounted harnesses. He also liked bourbon whiskey and was not a stranger to the wines that go with good living. But his passion seemed to be for expensive cigars that he bought in lots of five hundred and smoked constantly. Among his acquaintances he was known for his easy good nature and superlative hospitality. He seldom missed an opportunity to play genial host to a houseful of visitors.

Reed showed his wife the utmost devotion and respect. Such treatment was partly engendered by her fiery disposition. Despite having the appearance of a prim and docile wife, Amanda was strong willed. If the situation warranted, she was capable of displaying a temper that her husband described as "swearing mad." She also possessed an astute and capable mind that Simeon trusted in both domestic and business problems.

It is an irony of fate that in the midst of all the luxury and plenty that money could produce, the only barren things were Reed and his wife. Undoubtedly it was this frustrated desire for children that prompted Reed's interest in the education of young people.

That the Reeds chose the Unitarian faith is very possibly the result of Thomas Lamb Eliot's influence. This gifted Unitarian pastor became a great friend of both Simeon and Amanda. Closely associated with Simeon Reed's religious activities were his philanthropies. Here again the influence of his wife and of his minister is clear. Money was given at various times to Dr. Eliot for charitable purposes in Portland.

Henrietta Eliot, wife of Thomas Lamb Eliot: Mr. and Mrs. Reed were Universalists when they came out here, but they were brought into the Unitarian church of my husband, Reverend Thomas Lamb Eliot, and became faithful members. Mrs. Reed was a woman of relatively simple tastes given her affluence. There was nothing ostentatious about her at all personally. She did not seem to realize that she was a very rich woman. She was a person of great poise and dignity, and, in a quiet way, of leadership.

Ernest Boyd "E. B." MacNaughton, trustee 1919–1941, 1955–1958, president 1948–1952: Simeon Reed was independent in his politics. He was a Republican back in the 1860s and 1870s when all of his business associates were Democrats at the time, although he wasn't a firm Republican. In the political parades he used to march with the Democrats down Third Street, and then turn around and march with the Republicans back up Second Street. He was independent and very anxious to be well thought of by the right people. He was likewise independent in his actions. When Thomas Lamb Eliot first came to town, Simeon Reed joined with him as an early supporter, and then stuck firm. There was some tie there from Quincy, Massachusetts, where his wife Amanda was from.

DOROTHY JOHANSEN '33, history professor 1934–1969, archivist 1969–1984: Thomas Lamb Eliot had roots that went deep into New England ministers and educators. His father, William Greenleaf Eliot, had moved from Boston to the frontier town of St. Louis in the 1830s, where he became the first minister of the Congregational Society and a founder of Washington University. Thomas graduated in the university's first class, and then went on to Harvard Divinity School. He accepted an invitation to serve in Portland as pastor of the Unitarians, and from the time of his arrival in 1867 he was to this pioneer town what his father had been to St. Louis—its educational guide and its social conscience. In short time he became Portland's most eminent citizen.

CHRIS LOWE '82, history professor 1991–1996: Eliot's commitment to education extended back to his arrival in Portland to establish the First Unitarian Church. Up until then, local Unitarians and Universalists in the area attended the fairly liberal First Congregational Church headed by Reverend George H. Atkinson. Atkinson was known as "the father of Oregon schools" for his efforts to create public schools in the state. He also helped to found in 1854 the Congregationalist-affiliated Pacific University in Forest Grove, about thirty miles outside of Portland. Until Reed was established in 1911, Pacific University was the nearest institution of higher education to Portland.

When Eliot arrived on the scene roughly half of Atkinson's congregation went over to Eliot's new Unitarian church, but the two men became friends anyway. Eliot followed Atkinson as su-perintendent of Portland public schools from 1872 to 1875, and the two allied to defend public education in 1880 against an attempt to cut funds entirely for the public high schools in Portland.

DOROTHY JOHANSEN '33, history professor: In 1875, Reverend Eliot suggested to the Reeds in an admonitory ode celebrating their twenty-fifth wedding anniversary that, as "stewards of His bounty," they should use their riches for the betterment of society. From the substance of Simeon Reed's will drawn up three years later, one could infer that his words took root. In a birthday wish Eliot sent Simeon Reed in 1887, he urged his friends to go further.

THOMAS LAMB ELIOT, trustee 1904–1924, letter to Simeon Reed, October 17, 1887: Simeon, there is always something to busy us, always something to develop. I want you to celebrate some of these birthdays by founding a Reed Institute of lectures and art and music and museum. It will need a mine to run it.

SIMEON REED, "Last Will and Testament": Feeling as I do, a deep interest in the prosperity of the city of Portland, Oregon, where I have spent my business life and accumulated the property I possess, I would suggest to my wife that she devote some portion of my estate to benevolent objects, or to the cultivation, illustration, or development of the fine arts in the city of Portland, or to some other suitable purpose, which shall be of permanent value and contribute to the beauty of the city and to the intelligence, prosperity, and happiness of the inhabitants.

ELLA DEHART, Reed family friend: After Mr. Reed's health broke down, the doctor wanted him to go to a warmer climate. The Reeds traveled all over southern California and finally settled in Pasadena with plans to build a garden estate called Carmelita. But Mr. Reed was quite ill by that time, and in 1895 he died in Pasadena. Mrs. Reed then built Carmelita there.

DOROTHY JOHANSEN '33, history professor: After her husband's death, Mrs. Reed husbanded all the income from the estate, of which she was the executrix, to fulfill the suggestions of her husband's will. When she began to draw up her own will, she asked Thomas Lamb Eliot's advice, and he hastily sketched for her what he thought was the need of Portland—an institution along the lines of popular education.

Amanda Reed died in 1904 and by her will left to Eliot and four other men the trusteeship of the Reed estate for the establishment of an institution of learning. The trustees then had the burdensome task of deciding what would best fulfill her intentions. When it was disclosed that the estate was estimated to be worth about $3 million, national newspaper headlines heralded Portland's good fortune. But Amanda Reed's disappointed relatives immediately filed suit to break the will.

AMANDA WOOD REED, "Last Will and Testament": It is my desire and intention that the institution so founded and established shall be a means of general enlightenment, intellectual and moral culture, the cultivation and development of fine arts, and manual training and education for the people. And I desire and direct that it forever be and remain free from sectarian influence, regulation, or control, permitting those who may seek its benefits to affiliate with such religious societies as their consciences may dictate.

CYRUS DOLPH, trustee 1904–1914: In my endeavor to draft the will of Mrs. Reed, I sought to put into intelligent and legal phrase my conception of the distinction between dogmatic, denominational sectarianism and the gentler doctrine of the Redeemer of Mankind, upon which

I conceive the true religion is founded. The former was an abhorrence to Mrs. Reed. Of the latter she seemed to me to be the embodiment. My own position is that there is danger in breaking away from the bondage of narrow sectarianism, in that one may go adrift upon the sands of infidelity.

JUDITH STRASSER '66 (Reed thesis): Thomas Lamb Eliot had resigned his ministry in 1893 and devoted himself to civic activities, including helping found the Portland Art Association, the Portland Library Association, and the Oregon Humane Society. He had also served as superintendent of schools, and helped to develop a comprehensive system of Portland public parks as a park commissioner. When, upon Amanda Reed's death in 1904, her will named him as one of the five trustees of her estate, he was the logical and unanimous choice for president of the new college's Board of Trustees. Eliot saw the will through a five-year legal contest with Amanda Reed's family in the courts, and in 1909 took charge of the effort to determine the nature of the Reed Institute.

Eliot himself found optimism in various progressive reform movements of the times, but his opinions on issues of social significance derived from his Unitarian beliefs. Unitarianism was influenced in those days by the high social and economic standing of many of its members. It maintained a moderate noblesse oblige attitude, emphasizing the need for wealthy men to take active interest in social reform in order to prevent revolution. Progressivism, on the other hand, was a righteous and morally indignant movement that was gaining support from ministers accustomed to preaching the Social Gospel, which took account of conditions in an increasingly industrialized America. The Progressive Party movement became a veritable religious crusade.

In education, Eliot combined his sense of noblesse oblige with a Christian liberal's belief in free inquiry. A liberal education freed a man to discover truths on his own. But this was no end in itself. The educated man, especially one of wealth, bore the responsibility of moral and intellectual leadership. Eliot never condemned the amassing of wealth. He himself invested profitably in Northwest real estate. Wealth for him, however, was a kind of power, and power of any kind for Eliot was a measure of responsibility to God. The wealthy man who understood his responsibility undertook the difficult course of philanthropy, which required unusual moral courage to overcome both his acquisitiveness and his sense of pleasure and power.

Eliot proposed that the Reed trustees invite views from leading educators as to the best methods of establishing the Reed Institute. Among those was Wallace Buttrick, secretary of the General Education Board, founded in 1902 by John D. Rockefeller. Later merged with the Rockefeller Foundation, the General Education Board encouraged experimentation in higher education and supported institutions that would set the pace in underserved regions of the country. Eliot also sought the advice of his cousin, Charles W. Eliot, who had joined the General Education Board following his retirement from Harvard University after forty years as its president.

After spending several weeks in Portland, Wallace Buttrick determined that Oregon and the Pacific Northwest were well supplied with trade and technical schools. Along with Charles Eliot, Buttrick recommended that a liberal arts college would best serve the needs of Portland and Oregon in keeping with Amanda Reed's will.

The trend at the time in higher education was toward impersonal, democratic, research-oriented universities. Reed, on the other hand, as envisioned by the General Education Board, would be a small college, but in a new tradition that did not yet exist. It would serve its community as did the land-grant universities, but it would view the individual's education as the

Reverend Thomas Lamb Eliot, circa 1913.

primary goal of higher education. While other schools opened their doors to all, it would welcome only the academically talented and intellectually committed. Where the heterogeneity of the large university and the demands of naturalism and positivism were pressuring religion out of higher education, it would maintain a religious, although nonsectarian, bias.

THOMAS LAMB ELIOT, trustee, in the *MORNING OREGONIAN*, January 1, 1910: The college's service will be for every citizen. Its influence is not for a day, nor a year, nor decades only, but for centuries, as a source, a promoter of high intelligence, and inspiration to the body politic, a provider of the highest forces of civilization, it ought to be and will be the crowning pride of this great metropolis. Its promise should be, and is, that the poorest boy or girl within our gates shall have an equal opportunity with the richest to gain the very best education, equipping them for efficiency, leadership among men, and a realization of the highest manhood and womanhood.

E. B. MacNaughton, trustee: Dr. Eliot's congregation had a little wooden church building on Broadway and Yamhill streets in downtown Portland. He used to tell me that there were times when he was treated in Portland just like a pariah. He said the funerals that his Unitarian church held were too often for men who had never been in church anywhere else, and would perhaps have a difficult job of getting a burial anywhere else with a Christian minister speaking. His congregation was small. I used to go there, and they didn't aggregate more than fifty or sixty people. Thomas Lamb Eliot bulked large in the community of the unflocked, and also with church people who had every confidence in him and would accept him when he took a stand on something. That didn't add to the happiness of the fundamentalists around town.

In the early beginnings of Reed College, there was a lively interest in town sparked from the sincere regard with which Dr. Eliot was held. Anything that he was willing to sponsor was sure to have a friendly audience and local support. Most of the early Board of Trustees members, with the exception of Amanda Reed's nephew, Martin Winch, had complete confidence in him. When he expressed his thoughts about the direction the college should take, they accepted it, not realizing the full import of the thing, and they stuck with it. Among the other trustees were C. E. Wolverton, a federal judge; Cyrus Dolph, a prominent local attorney; and William P. Olds, the owner of Olds & King, the largest department store in Portland. Olds never cracked a book in his life, although he bought them by the yard for their bindings. When he died they found his whole house stocked with them.

When the lawyer Cyrus Dolph died in 1914 his spot on the board was filled by James B. Kerr, a big corporate attorney, and one of the finest Christian gentlemen who ever walked in shoe leather, but at the same time a straitlaced and staunch Presbyterian. He and the other men on the board gulped many times during Reed's early development, but they were willing to play the thing out and see how it would unfold.

Dorothy Johansen '33, history professor: Among the five trustees, Martin Winch was greatly disturbed by the course of events. The son of Amanda Reed's sister, Winch had served as business manager for Simeon Reed. He and his young son, Simeon Reed Winch, were surrogate offspring to the childless couple. By virtue of his special relationship with the Reeds, Winch thought of himself as their chief spokesman. He himself was not college educated. His experience was limited and he was strongly drawn toward the practical, especially the manual arts. At the time Amanda Reed's will was contested, he did not consider his own interests, which would have been better served if he had joined in the suit with other family members. His health, never robust, was broken during the years of litigation and disrupted family relations.

Winch felt that in allocating the trust fund solely to support a college of arts and sciences the board was ignoring his aunt's intentions of establishing a vocational or technical school. The trustees reached a conciliatory agreement with him that the foundation of a college did not exclude fulfilling in time his interpretation of his aunt's intentions. This agreement, however, did not relieve the other board members of their anxiety that creating a liberal arts college would be construed as contrary to Amanda Reed's intentions, a charge that would plague the college for decades to come.

For reasons of health, Martin Winch resigned from the trustee board in June 1910. To replace him, Eliot recruited William Mead Ladd, the son of Simeon Reed's longtime business associate and former Portland mayor William S. Ladd.

A graduate of Amherst, William Mead Ladd was a prominent banker and extremely religious and conservative. Earlier in the spring of 1910, the board had accepted from the Ladd Estate Company's extensive land holdings a gift of forty acres of farmland in southeast Portland platted for residential development. Ladd candidly admitted that having a college in the neighborhood would enhance his real estate development.

With a building site established, Thomas Lamb Eliot concentrated on finding a man who could create a college with no prototype and no pattern to follow.

JUDITH STRASSER '66 (Reed thesis): The trustees first offered the presidency to James Hayden Tufts, a professor of philosophy at the University of Chicago and a colleague and close friend of John Dewey. Tufts' major focus was with the development of a better society. In this both he and Eliot agreed. But where Eliot held that men, through experience and education, grow to a knowledge of existing and eternal Truth, Tufts disagreed. Like Dewey and other fellow pragmatists, Tufts rejected eternal truths and the idea of the moral as something already existing and waiting to be discovered. In his book *Ethics*, written with Dewey in 1909, Tufts emphasized that the moral was an evolutionary, ever-changing process, which involved looking at each ethical act from a multitude of angles before making any choice—a constant process of forming and reshaping ideals and of bringing them to bear upon conditions of existence. He believed that only in society, where we can use our intelligence to "try on" the perspectives of others, does moral progress exist.

Like Dewey, Tufts emphasized in education the development of the individual's ability to interact with other people in society. Such education focused on the cultivation of individuality and on learning through experience to direct the course of subsequent experience. When Tufts called for a spirit of inquiry, he asked for the discovery of a true unknown. His idea of a research-oriented university, closely bound to its community, provided an atmosphere in which, ideally, anything went. Such an institution could not concern itself with building the characters of future leaders capable of mediating the extremes in society and resolving its social conflicts, as Eliot sought to create. Ultimately, Reed's financial limitations kept Tufts from assuming the presidency. The trustees could not commit themselves to an establishment of the twenty-five buildings and athletic fields that Tufts considered necessary for a true university. While the trustees apparently never understood the magnitude of difference between their educational goals and Tufts', they did profit from his ideas in shaping their vision for the college.

DOROTHY JOHANSEN '33, history professor: Eliot's experience with James Tufts was of great value, in that it enabled him to define more accurately what the scope of the new institution should be. He also learned that it was far more advisable to take a man from a small college, providing that its atmosphere had been progressive.

Wallace Buttrick at the Rockefeller General Education Board and former Harvard president Charles Eliot recommended a young lecturer at Columbia University named William Trufant Foster. The trustees invited Foster to Portland in June 1910. After discussing with him his ideas for the establishment of a college, they immediately offered him the presidency. On his return east, Foster stopped off in Chicago to discuss the position with James Tufts, who reported back to Eliot his own favorable attitude toward the candidate. To his wife, summering in Maine, Foster wired the simple message, "Elected President." When it came to her it read, "Electric President." There was prophecy in this error, as the trustees and the city of Portland were soon to realize.

CHAPTER 2

The Visionary

The story of Reed College is fired with the zest of pioneers. We thought our adventures were bold and inspired. Fortunately so. We live by vision and by faith.
  —William Foster, president

Foster painted the prospect in glowing colors—faculty houses, no fraternities, no intercollegiate athletics, small classes, real faculty government, and above all, a spirit of teamwork. A fine bill of goods!
  —Arthur Wood, sociology professor

Reed's founding president, William Foster, was the quintessential young man in a hurry. New England's youngest full professor at twenty-seven and already a published authority on debate and argumentation, he was also the youngest college president in the country when appointed to Reed at thirty-one. His rapid rise in academia, coupled with his aversion to orthodoxy, tagged him as a brilliant upstart. The same reputation would soon be attributed to Reed, largely as the result of Foster's gifted promotional efforts. In the compelling vision laid out by Foster, Reed College would bring new relevance to the liberal arts, revolutionize higher education, and become first rank among academic institutions. Foster's exaggerated claims almost ensured a cocky start-up with unrealistic expectations.

WILLIAM FOSTER, president 1910–1919: In June 1910, at the close of my nine months at Columbia University's Teachers College working on my dissertation, I was asked by telegram to go to Portland, Oregon, to consider building a college from the ground up. That was the first time I heard of Reed College. I learned later that Charles W. Eliot, the former president of Harvard, where I had been an undergraduate, and Wallace Buttrick, head of the Rockefeller Foundation's General Education Board, had taken chances, independently, on recommending me.

I was excited. Traveling as far west as Oregon—to say nothing of staying there—seemed an adventure. I had been "west" only once, and then only as far as Chicago. In the venerable *Boston Transcript* I had seen a headline, "Far Away from Home but Doing Well," which referred to the adventures of a Boston boy who had gone all the way to Worcester Massachusetts Academy. I laughed at that, yet I myself was as provincial as the *Boston Transcript*. I had some of the worst if not some of the best traits of proper Bostonians. To my wife, the frontier also seemed adventurous. She was also provincial, having always lived in Maine.

On arrival in that faraway town, I learned that the trustees had accepted from the Ladd Estate Company a gift of forty acres. Forty acres of land, five trustees, and one endowment estimated at $3 million. That was all there was of Reed College. Three million dollars now seems a trifle, but in that day it seemed like a lot of money. I was president of a college with no students, no faculty, no classrooms. Worse still, no grandstand and not even a college yell.

I climbed through the fence of the pasture and walked among the twenty-five blooded cows of Ladd's Crystal Springs Farm. With tassels and blue ribbons they could have made a bovine show as colorful as an academic procession and as self-satisfied, though not perhaps as funny. I began to plan the building of a college there. In effect, the trustees had said to me, "You have been complaining loudly that colleges in the East are shackled by traditions. Here in the free and open West you can try out your theories. If they don't work, blame only yourself."

No traditions! How I rolled that morsel under my tongue. Reed College was to be neither hampered nor hallowed by traditions. A hundred colleges seemed to me to be hallowed by petrified errors. "Reed College," David Starr Jordan, Stanford's founding president, said at the laying of Reed's cornerstone, "is the only college that has no graduates of whom it is ashamed, the only college which has made no mistakes."

Promptly I made mistakes, so that distinction was gone. How should we use our freedom? Many colleges would gladly make radical changes were it not for their own history. Traditions are hard to cope with when they are glorified by graduates who wish to keep dear old Alma Mater exactly as it was in their youth and by professors who find that the easiest thing to do. During my first year I visited fully a hundred colleges across the country. Nearly everywhere was much discontent and little study. Could a college be built upon intellectual enthusiasm? If the worst influences were kept out, might not teachers and students *study together* with spontaneous delight? A naïve fancy, some men surmised, born of inexperience and idealism.

The college pledged itself to make scholarship not only respectable but necessary, and not only necessary but attractive. Nothing whatever would be sacrificed in the interests of mere numbers. Intercollegiate athletics, fraternities, sororities, and most of the diversions that men are pleased to call "college life," as distinguished from college work, would have no place in Reed College. Those whose dominant interests lie outside study should not apply for admission. Only those who wish to work and to work hard would be welcomed.

All this pioneering on paper would have stayed on paper had we not found men and women with the vision, enthusiasm, brains, and daring to try to make the dream come true. To find them was not difficult; the dream was attraction enough. With the average age well under thirty, the faculty was the youngest in the country, possibly the youngest in history. There were no leftovers, no teachers who had grown old and tired in one place because there was no other place to go. Before Reed College had graduated its fifth class, many men called us "cockeyed." Other men called the teachers "rambunctious." If the college were not "cockeyed," it was at least cocky.

Unfortunately, I took with me to Oregon the good and the bad of my New England inheritance. Chiefly the bad, it sometimes seems. I was born a rebel. For many years I did not know what was the matter with me. Then I began to realize that my New England ancestors made me a cantankerous nonconformist, scowling at contented men and women, and warning them that whatever they were doing, they should be doing something else. To reform the world—and quickly—I mounted my horse, spear in hand, and rode forth in all directions at once. High medical costs, false medical advertising, degrees in dentistry awarded after three months of training, the conspiracy of silence in matters of sex, silly motion pictures, injustice to the unemployed, billboards on the Columbia River Highway, intercollegiate athletics, the chaos and waste of English spelling, the low level of so-called "higher" education—these were among my targets.

I mention the belligerent orator who shouted, "I want tax reform! I want suffrage reform! I want money reform!" And the heckler who cried, "You want chloroform!" I do not blame those who felt that way about me. I hoped, however, that Reed College would continue to stand staunchly—and if necessary, stand alone—for whatever Reed College considered right.

RALPH HETZEL, University of Oregon administrator: I was fortunate enough to be one of a party, led by Dr. William Foster, that tramped across what seemed to me an endless lot of open country and finally arrived at a large pasture in Eastmoreland where a number of Mr. Ladd's splendid cows were grazing. We climbed over fences and logs, shielding the ladies from vicious animals in the pasture.

Under these discouraging circumstances, Dr. Foster set forth in his very vivid style a vision of a beautiful campus, magnificent buildings, splendid faculty—an institution that would give out tremendously valuable service within the very near future. It seemed like a dream to me at the time. It was only the tremendous enthusiasm of

Looking across the Willamette River toward Portland's West Hills from Crystal Springs Farm, 1908.

Dr. Foster that made us believe that it was going to be a reality.

VICTOR CHITTICK, English professor 1921–1948: In 1910, I was a graduate student at Columbia and president of the English Graduate Club, when we invited William Trufant Foster, who was taking his Ph.D. at Teachers College, to the club to speak. I was fascinated by what he had to say and by his personality. He was the kind of a person in those days that we would call sharp. He had a reputation as a brilliant exponent of academic ideas, and his manuals on rhetoric and argumentation were widely used.

After he left Columbia that year, Foster went west to set up Reed. One of the first things he issued was a pamphlet that gave a short biography of the staff he had assembled. A copy of that came into my hands and impressed me tremendously. There was an evangelism about Foster's ideals that appealed to me, a defiance of tradition and general sentiment about what should go on in the college, specifically that the level of scholarship should be high or the student shouldn't be there.

A few years after that, I came west to teach at the University of Washington. The university was celebrating its semicentennial and they had big shots from all over the American educational world assembled up on the platform. Among them was Foster. At thirty-one he looked so young that we called him "the boy president." In the course of the remarks being made, he sat there with his head dropped in his hand, looking intensely bored. This visibly annoyed the oldsters. Then, when he got up to speak, Foster electrified everybody in talking about what Reed College was doing.

FRANK LOXLEY "F. L." GRIFFIN, mathematics professor 1911–1952, president 1954–1956: All those old-timers on the platform became infuriated. Foster was pointing out what a sham many of the pretenses commonly being given to intellectual matters in higher education were. The audience was deliriously happy. Someone said that his remarks came like a breath of fresh air in a stuffy room.

WILLIAM FOSTER, president: The first and often the only question asked about any college was, "How large is it?" Never how large is its vision, but always, how large is its student body? We thought there was no great need for one more college run on the assembly line, or loudspeaker, or sheep-dip method of education.

F. L. GRIFFIN, mathematics professor: Very few men contributed as much as Foster to correcting the imbalance in American education between educational matters and recreational activities. He fashioned Reed not as a savings-bank college, where a student would deposit some course credits and then draw out a diploma, but as a coherent educational enterprise. The student would graduate only when he could show by a satisfactory thesis and all examinations that he possessed some well-organized knowledge. Foster knew the inequalities inherent in most grading systems. He corrected the worst of these and allowed extra credit toward graduation for work of a high quality. The grades, however, were administered without disclosure to the students, so that their usual role as instruments of motivation largely disappeared.

LINDSLEY ROSS '15: One thing that griped me was Reed's grading system. Almost nothing specific was told to us about how it operated. Mysterious things were mentioned such as "norm curve," "credit for quality," and "skewed curve because of selectivity," but questions such as "How many credits for how much quality?" or "How hard would one have to work to get an A rather than a B?" were never resolved. I worked out my own solution. Although I had been at

William Foster, Reed's founding president, circa 1912.

the top of my high school class, I was in a bigger pond now with a lot of smarter frogs. So I quit trying to get As after the first year and loaded myself up with extra courses. I was thus able to finish Reed in only three years.

Dorothy Johansen '33, history professor 1934–1969, archivist 1969- 1984: Though Foster said at one time that he would like to make Reed the "Harvard of the West," he disliked Harvard because he had suffered there a great deal as an undergraduate, finding his college years a "burden anxiously to be endured." Poverty contributed to Foster's discontent. He was the youngest of three children and the only son. His father died before he was two years old. The family income was meager, and his childhood was never without anxiety. He worked at all kinds of jobs to supplement the family income, and before he

left high school he was fully self-supporting.

He entered Harvard expecting to sit at the feet of inspiring teachers. Instead he had classes from graduate students who did not know how to teach. Traditional subjects were taught as if their content was remote from actual experience. The formalities of lecture hall and classroom ignored both his talents and his interests.

Foster worked his way through school tutoring and doing odd jobs. He also wrote for newspapers and magazines and published the *Harvard Athletic Album*. He was not a member of any social club, though he was elected president of the Senior Senate. Under Harvard's free-elective system, he ranged over a wide variety of courses. In preparatory to teaching, he concentrated on English as well as argumentation and debating, becoming president of the debating club. Argumentation provided the training he wanted in systematic thinking, and in debate he found an outlet for his pent-up wrath.

WILLIAM FOSTER, president: At Harvard there was still the inheritance of boys who came from the right families and the right schools and whose fathers provided them with enough money to wear the right clothes, live in the right buildings, and pay their bills without resort to tutoring or other socially incorrect forms of self-support. Lacking such inheritance, no boy in my day could make the social clubs by distinction in scholarship. My experience as a student and later as a teacher at Bowdoin and Bates affirmed that there was little intellectual enthusiasm among students, that the amount of study was discreditably small, and that the constantly increasing confusion of incidental amusements tended to make the serious central purpose of the curriculum of minor interest to the student body.

DOROTHY JOHANSEN '33, history professor: In his dissertation at Columbia University's Teachers College under the influence of John Dewey, Foster placed the blame for this situation upon college administrations, and proposed remedial measures. Published in 1911 as a book called *Administration of the College Curriculum*, Foster's dissertation was a polemic against malpractices of higher education. The closing chapter, "The Ideal College," was characteristically Fosterian in offering a constructive counterview. He had presented its essential features to the Reed trustees at his first interview. It is, in a very real sense, the intellectual charter of Reed College and the principal instrument in creating its identity.

WILLIAM FOSTER, president, "The Ideal College": The Ideal College is a college free to pursue its mission with unobscured vision of the truth, and power to proclaim the truth without fear or favor of politicians, or religious sects, or benefactors, or public cries, or its own admin-

istrative machinery. A college that mistakes not bigness for greatness, open only to minds capable of good scholarship, and ready, if not eager, to make the sacrifice it involves. It is a college that shuts its doors promptly on idlers by means of a discipline from which there is no escape.

It is a college that never permits growth beyond the possibility of daily, vital contact between each student and inspiring teachers. It is a college that sees the folly of putting large sums into fine buildings and small sums into strong men, that pays professors enough to leave them free to put their life blood into their daily work.

It is a college that gives comparatively few courses, but gives them honestly and thoroughly; that puts a further premium on sound scholarship by making quality as well as quantity of work count toward graduation in a definite way.

Finally, it is a college imbued with that kind of democratic spirit that cooperates for the common good with all the agencies of social progress; a college with a view of its responsibility that is not shut off by campus walls; a college that is religious without being sectarian; a college that, with all its idealism, makes daily, practical contact with the many-sided life of city and state, here and now; a college that is changing because it is living; that looks forward oftener than backward, yet seeks the wisdom of organized experience to light the path ahead, thus supplanting the blind guidance of tradition by the safer guidance of scientific insight.

JUDITH STRASSER '66 (Reed thesis): For Foster, the major dissatisfaction with liberal arts colleges at the time was not due to too much liberal education, but rather to too little of it. Too many of the modern attachments in higher education served as serious hindrances to a truly liberal education that specialized in the humanities.

DOROTHY JOHANSEN '33, history professor: Few, if any, of Foster's attributes of the ideal college could be ascribed to him as uniquely his own. One can find among them echoes of the ideas and the criticisms of contemporary educators and of spokesmen for the reform-bent Carnegie Foundation and Rockefeller General Education Board. What was unique was Foster's skill in drawing from them and from his own personal and professional experiences a positive program without obvious internal contradictions, and presenting it with evangelical force and conviction.

HARRY TORREY, biology professor 1912–1920: I was teaching at Berkeley when President Foster visited the campus, talked with me, and put into my hands a copy of his book, *Administration of the College Curriculum.* I was impressed with the liberal spirit of both his talk and his book. Here was the opportunity for constructive pioneering in education and its administration, and for a laboratory for testing the unimpeded application of new views and methods. To me, Reed was conceived from the beginning as a dynamic center with a minimum of pattern and a maximum of opportunity for constructive thinking and doing, and for creative discovery.

ARTHUR WOOD, sociology professor 1911–1915: Foster was an able, shrewd, resourceful man. He had no speculative interests at all. Like the Romans, he was a very good man for building roads. He was hard, practical, and opportunistic. Yet his personality was somewhat schizoid. He could be charming and lovable, but he could also be arrogant, morose, and domineering.

Reed attracted the first-comers on the faculty because it was a new and promising venture in education. Foster painted the prospect in glowing colors: faculty houses, no fraternities, no intercollegiate athletics, small classes, real faculty government, and above all, a spirit of teamwork. A fine bill of goods! Some of us had had the normal academic experience in other institutions

of double-crossing, discouragement, and frustration. All of us who came to Reed came with high hopes.

DOROTHY JOHANSEN '33, history professor: Foster was an impatient rebel, but in every instance of rebellion he was the advocate of a constructive alternative to the status quo. His conception of education admitted every experience that had a personal or social value and contributed to growth. It was ultimately a practical education that followed Dewey's approach for enabling people to meet new situations or crises, analyze them, discover the issues involved, and then develop new solutions. The teacher directed the rational, inquiring mind of the student not to the extension of knowledge but rather to the formulation of questions based upon knowledge, and to the exploration of besetting human problems. Scholarship was not to be an end in itself for Foster. It was the application of a process of mind by which socially useful ends could be achieved. In that sense, it implied a new role for the liberal arts college.

The trustees—especially Eliot—found great satisfaction in Foster's conception of scholarship and also in its application to the local situation. They were in need of a man who could resolve conflicting theories about college education and at the same time resolve their private problem of justifying a liberal arts college within the terms of Amanda Reed's will. Confident that they had found such a person in William Trufant Foster, they committed themselves to follow his direction. The main difference between the trustees and the president at this point was one of age. At thirty-one, Foster was a man of such great energy that he had to drain it off in action—sometimes before he had convinced others of the wisdom of his acts. The trustees, in their fifties and sixties, moved slowly and deliberately. Experience and age had dimmed their faith that an ideal could be realized immediately.

CHAPTER 3

Breaking Ground

There seem to be no bounds to the public misunderstanding and misrepresentation of an institution that ventures to break the hard crust of custom and orthodoxy.
—Edward Octavius "E. O." Sisson, philosophy professor

The community was not ready to absorb what Foster and the faculty wanted to unload on it. They did seize hold of anything and blow it up.
—Victor Chittick, English professor

For teachers at his dream college, William Foster recruited to Portland an idealistic group of young men and women, many of whom were from elite schools in the East. With an average age under thirty, they were the youngest faculty in the country. Foster made it clear that the focus of their mission was to teach not only the students on campus but also the citizens of Portland. This was in accordance with Thomas Lamb Eliot's desire to employ the college in extending social and cultural reforms to the local community.

Accordingly, social service became a strong component of the college's early self-image. However, unlike Eliot, who had carefully woven himself into the fabric of the city, Foster and his band of reformers descended upon provincial Portland like foreign crusaders, quickly developing a reputation in conservative quarters for their arrogant self-righteousness and radical social reforms.

JEAN WOLVERTON PETITE '15: The opening date of the college was set for September 18, 1911. Two lecture rooms, two small classrooms, an assembly hall called the chapel, a small library, and an office for the president and secretary comprised the temporary physical plant at Eleventh and Jefferson streets. At nine o'clock on the given day, a few guests, the students, faculty, and three trustees picked their way through building debris to the small assembly room, which their number filled to overflowing. The ceremony took thirty minutes. Thomas Lamb Eliot gave the invocation, a student sang, Professor Arthur Wood read from the Scriptures. Then, our president stood before us with the message of his ideals for our life at Reed College.

WILLIAM FOSTER, president 1910–1919, opening day speech: This day is pregnant with meaning. The future of this institution is, in a peculiar sense, in our hands. Our sense of the future is committed to our care. Our devotion to worthy ideals should create for Reed College a deathless spirit.

FRANK LOXLEY "F. L." GRIFFIN, mathematics professor 1911–1952, president 1954–1956: Arriving in Portland in 1911 I saw the large farm area of forty acres in Eastmoreland that had been donated to Reed College by the Ladd Estate Company. To prepare for the first year's instruction, the trustees had erected a building on the corner of Eleventh and Jefferson streets in downtown Portland, while the permanent buildings were being erected on the Reed campus. One was simply called the Arts Building, later renamed Eliot Hall in honor of Dr. Eliot, and the other the Dormitory Building, later referred to as the Old Dorm Block.

The cornerstone of the Arts Building was laid in a very interesting ceremony of the Knights Templars, and the cornerstone for the Dormitory was appropriately laid by some students of the first entering class.

BEATRICE OLSEN MILLER '24: The buildings at Reed were designed by thirty-four-year-old Albert Doyle, as a modification of the finest collegiate-gothic style, largely characteristic of the Tudor reign of the fifteenth and sixteenth centuries, although their style cannot be attributed to any one period. The design of the chapel, for example, dates back to the tenth century, while its open timber ceiling survives from the seventeenth century, and the stairway leading up from the south entrance is copied after the spiral stairs used prior to the Elizabethan era. Gray stone and red brick were the materials chosen, patterned after the style of Oxford University. The best materials were used, and the foundation was built to last forever, in accordance with

Opening day, September 18, 1911, in the college's temporary quarters in downtown Portland. President Foster is at the far right.

Students from the first entering class lay the cornerstone for the Dormitory Building on June 8, 1912.

Dr. Foster's frequent reference to the thousand-year future of Reed.

The seal of the college was placed on the oriel above the door to the chapel. It includes a fleur-de-lis taken from the coat of arms of Dr. Thomas Lamb Eliot's alma mater, Washington University in St. Louis, and thirteen stars taken from the family crest of Amanda Reed's distant relative from Quincy, Massachusetts, President John Adams. A deep red Richmond rose was added for local symbolism, representing Reed as the college of Portland, the Rose City. The dominant feature of the seal is the griffin, taken from the coat of arms of Simeon Reed's family. With the head, shoulders, and feet of an eagle, and the body of a lion, the griffin in early times symbolized a guardian and protector of man and the beasts of the earth. It was also connected in mythology with Apollo, the sun god, whose chariot was supposedly drawn by one. In its capacity as the servant of light, the griffin became the enemy of ignorance.

The dormitory building was based on old English manor houses, with a sally port in the middle adopted from old French medieval gothic. In the days when every man's home was his castle, the sally port was a place from which to dash forth in defense. The statues of the beavers atop the dormitory were chosen, not as a cynical reference to the activities of the students, but as symbols of Oregon, the Beaver State.

HARRY TORREY, biology professor 1912–1920: Before my actual coming to the Reed campus, the plans for the Arts Building were sent to me. I designed the rooms for the biology department on the first floor in the belief that the building was to sit on the level ground. To my horror when I arrived, I found the first floor was quite underground in the basement, including my office.

MARGARET MCGOWAN MAHAN '24: My father, Howard McGowan, was hired to be the first business manager of the Reed Institute in 1908.

PART ONE: RADICAL UPSTART, 1911–1920

He had been working for Sam Winch, Amanda Reed's nephew and the brother of Martin Winch. I went down with him to the opening of the college on Southwest Eleventh and Jefferson streets. My father worked on the campus construction with the architect, Albert Doyle, who also built our family house in Eastmoreland, which was just then being developed. I used to go to Prexy, the president's house, with my father for very dressy social affairs attended by Thomas Lamb Eliot and William Foster, who was a very strong person, opinionated and forceful.

The campus remained a working farm when the students came. It was called the Ladd and Reed Farm Company. My dad had charge of running it. He parceled out parts of the campus to Italian truck farmers. They were allowed to grow vegetables there in exchange for maintaining the grounds. At the college my father was responsible for all the business.

DOROTHY JOHANSEN '33, history professor 1934–1969, archivist 1969–1984: Tuition was set at fifty dollars per semester, which the Board of Trustees assessed on the grounds that people were inclined to appreciate what they had to pay for. It was also board policy that no qualified student be denied because of the tuition fee. This was one of Foster's conditions for making Reed a social democracy. For most students who applied, Reed offered an opportunity they might not otherwise have had. At least half their number came from local families of low incomes that precluded expense of travel and living away from home.

ELSA GILL PERROW '15, administrative staff 1917–1919: I had been out of preparatory school for a year and was sort of at loose ends. It was my father who knew about Reed. He had an idea that this was a good opportunity to go into college while living at home in Portland. He presented my credentials to President Foster with-

out my knowing it. I went in a little bit under protest because I didn't know quite what I was getting into. Of course, after I had been there a year, wild horses could not have got me away from Reed College.

We were very much indoctrinated by President Foster and the faculty with the idea that we were sort of special, and that we had to more or less be an example and prove the theory that academic integrity was the outstanding and important thing. The faculty instilled in us a feeling of not being too acquiescent. You think for yourself, make your own judgments. That started very early, and created a certain amount of revolutionary feeling on campus. I suppose we did think of ourselves as something rather special, in fact, we used to refer to ourselves as the "hand-picked bunch." The class in general was chosen by their high academic careers in high school. I felt kind of a little bit of an outsider in a way because many of the others had striven and tried in every possible way to get in, and thought it was a tremendous achievement that they had managed to be accepted. I felt a little bit as if I had gotten in under false pretenses.

We started off in the storefront building on Eleventh and Jefferson, just four classrooms and very limited faculty, with a student body of about fifty, evenly divided between men and women. In the first year the only courses available were math, English, history, German, and a course called College Life. It was kind of an orientation course to give high school students an idea of what they should be like and how they should conduct themselves as college students. It was quite illuminating.

WILLIAM FOSTER, president: Of 263 applicants, fifty who seemed most likely to become co-workers in our adventure were taken into the first class. My own schooling had convinced me that the usual entrance examinations neither opened the gates to all those who were best fitted, nor kept out all those who were unfit. Far from it. So, from the beginning, the chief tests at Reed were interviews with applicants, parents, teachers, and employers. The aim was to find out whether the applicant had good health, capacity for work, earnestness, and right habits. Entrance was easy for the strong man with irregular preparation but impossible for the weakling who had been "pulled through" the conventional courses. High school graduation, whether or not from a so-called "preparatory" course, was not enough. The college did not require that the schoolwork be done in the usual time, manner, or subjects, and there was no minimum age for entrance. The first year no students were admitted from other colleges. It seemed best not to have anybody on the campus telling us how things were done elsewhere. Some mistakes were made, but the few students who failed to pursue their studies for the love of the pursuit, without prodding of teachers or the lure of credits, soon became dissatisfied with themselves or with the college.

To explain what kind of college we were trying to create and why, we gave a course called College Life in which we discussed the history of colleges, the aims of Reed College, the curriculum, methods of study, use of the library, the Honor Principle, mental recreation, health, athletics, social affairs, student government, vocations, and the chapel.

EDITH MCDONALD '19, William Foster's personal secretary 1917–1923: I graduated from high school in North Spokane, Washington. I had taken a commercial course there, and I did not suppose any college would let me in without Latin and other preparatory courses.

But Dr. Foster said they were more interested in where you stood than what you took. He first offered me an opportunity to come and work in the office when I finished high school. Then, he gave me a scholarship, and I began with the second class of 1916.

I had interruptions. I had a nervous breakdown. I went home and was in bed for a month. Dr. Foster sent for me and said he wanted me to come back and work in the office for no more than an hour a day, and to have corrective exercises. They assigned Annie Osborne, the physical education professor, to me. Gradually, I increased the amount of time I could put in at the office, and began taking courses again.

In the office I worked mainly on Dr. Foster's correspondence. Many an hour I sat beside his beautiful mahogany desk and filled up shorthand books. There was a big picture hanging in his office of Alice Freeman, who was named the president of Wellesley at age twenty-seven. Sometimes I got my inspiration from that while I waited between dictating sessions.

ARLIEN JOHNSON '17: The year I was graduating from Washington High School in Portland, William Trufant Foster came to address the assembly. I don't recall all of what he said, but it impressed me tremendously. Reed had a different program from the ordinary liberal arts college. There was a stress on learning how to think as well as remembering what to think. I went home that day and said to my family, "I want to go to Reed College."

The college had some rather remarkable faculty, people who later became quite well-known in their fields away from Reed. The one that meant the most to me was William Fielding Ogburn, the sociology professor with whom I had my major. We would come out of his classes so excited that we would go out on the lawn to eat lunch and continue to talk about the things we were learning. Ogburn exposed students very early to the theory that human nature is slow to change but that material culture, often through inventions, changes rapidly and unevenly, with the reality that the cultural lag will cause social maladjustments, sometimes neuroses and functional psychoses. That was enlightening.

The Arts Building—now Eliot Hall—nearing completion in the late summer of 1912.

WILLIAM FOSTER, president: I found as my first hire a young man at Williams College whose ideas about teaching mathematics seemed as "cockeyed" as the rest of the Reed program. When he came to us I told the people of Portland we had the best teacher of mathematics in the country. They smiled indulgently. College presidents are ex officio liars, everybody knew that. In any event an entirely new kind of textbook produced by that young man was later adopted by several hundred colleges. Much later, the Rockefeller Foundation decided to send four graduate students somewhere to study the best methods of teaching mathematics. These four prospectors went to Reed College, having passed several hundred older and bigger institutions on the way. They had to travel three thousand miles to find Frank Loxley Griffin.

F. L. GRIFFIN, mathematics professor: In the autumn of 1910 Dr. Foster called on me, among others, at Williams College. He asked me whether I would be interested in going to Reed. I said, decidedly, "Yes." First, my wife's people lived in Portland and to visit them we needed to cross the continent. But more important, I saw the rare opportunity to experiment with establishing new types of courses in math—something hardly possible at Williams. Shortly after my acceptance, I received a very gracious letter from Dr. T. L. Eliot, which said in part, "The Board of Trustees are very much pleased that our first appointment after president has fallen on someone so closely aligned with the president's educational philosophy." Naturally, that gave me much joy.

When the faculty assembled the first and second years in Portland, everyone else seemed interested in education experimentation. So much so that Dr. Kelley Rees, who made Greek civilization come alive in his classics classes, said to me one day, "Griffin, this whole faculty is crazy." Then he looked at me, and I at him, and he said,

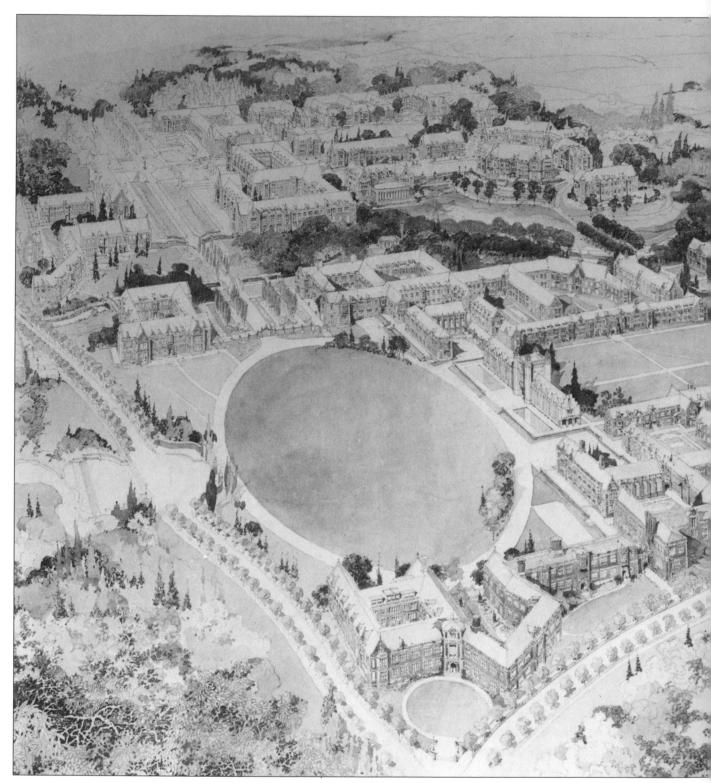

An aerial perspective of the future campus plan approved by the Board of Trustees in 1912 following construction of the Arts Building (Eliot Hall) and the Dormitory Building (the Old Dorm Block). Drawn up by the firm of Portland architect Albert Doyle,

Reed College
Portland Oregon

Doyle Patterson & Beach
Architects

the layout is based upon the quadrangle concept of St. John's College at Oxford University and incorporates the Tudor Gothic style of architecture then in vogue. This grandiose vision conveys the heady optimism that pervaded the college during its early years.

"All but you and me of course." But he and I were just as crazy as the rest. I was setting up a mathematics course for freshmen in which for the first semester they got a substantial bit of differential and integral calculus. That was radically different from what was customary. In the sophomore year they came back for much more complicated calculus. The physics people were very happy, because they could make use of calculus methods very early.

There was a period of some twenty-five years that a higher percentage of Reed graduates obtained doctorates in science and math than from any other college or university in the United States. In one period of ten years the number of Reed graduates in mathematics who went on to get a doctorate was higher than the percentage from all but about four or five of the largest universities.

Instructors at Reed were free to use their own teaching methods and held accountable only for results. President Foster used to say that when a person, however young, is appointed as instructor, we assume until we get evidence to the contrary that he is competent to teach his own courses in his own manner, and without some department head telling him what to do.

Among the members of the first faculty was Foster himself, who gave public lectures and did some teaching in English composition. Mr. Foster was also an expert debater, and under his tutelage Reed's debating team beat several university teams. Working with Foster was an excellent registrar and secretary, Miss Florence Read, who relieved Dr. Foster of a great deal of needless responsibility.

DOROTHY JOHANSEN '33, history professor: Twenty-six-year-old Florence Read, a graduate of Mount Holyoke, operated with absolute devotion to Foster and his program. "Flotilla," as she was known to faculty and students, organized and kept the necessary machinery of ad-ministration running smoothly for the first ten years of the college. With only untrained student help, she was also registrar, recorder, director of extension services, and, after the first year, admission officer. After leaving Reed, she went on to serve as president of Spelman College for twenty-six years.

MAIDA ROSSITER, librarian 1912–1918, women's advisor 1936–1937, dean of women 1937–1942: I had been at Stanford for seven years as reference librarian, most of which I considered utter tragedy. One day I was out walking to lunch when I came upon the head of the education department and a strange gentleman who turned out to be Mr. Foster. That was the beginning of it. In the course of time Mr. Foster came down and talked to me about a job at Reed. I decided to stay in California because my father was ill. Later Mr. Foster telegraphed me that he would be in Oakland. I went up there and we talked it over again. It was before Christmas, and I had a sort of after-Christmas realization that I could go.

The joke of it is that I didn't go to library school! Miss Isom, who ran the Portland Library Association, made it very clear to Mr. Foster that she was greatly displeased at my appointment. She was steely, carrying the flag. I wasn't prepared for such unfriendliness in the Portland library world. It seemed to me very unprofessional and disturbing, but at the same time, I had a little common sense and so just plugged along. Over time Miss Isom grew warmer. I suppose I wore her down.

HAROLD MERRIAM, English professor 1913–1918: Since the library was starting from scratch, it had first to acquire standard works and general works such as encyclopedias and other reference books. Foster encouraged building up a collection of "living" books, by which he meant avoiding useless books. I think he was influenced by his experience with New England college libraries that contained many shelves of useless books by retired ministers.

Librarian Maida Rossiter was a woman of a fine practical nature, and relied heavily on the recommendations of the professors in building up the library. Both Frances Isom at the Portland Library Association and Cornelia Marvin at the state library were experts in their work and no doubt found Maida Rossiter a strange appointee. They considered the decision favored by her attractiveness. She was a woman who seemed to appeal strongly to men, and William Foster was not wholly beyond such appeal. However, she was taken from Stanford Library, and so could not have been totally without library experience.

WILLIAM FOSTER, president: Edward Octavius Sisson found his way from the Kansas frontier to Harvard Graduate School in that school's "Golden Age," and there acquired under William James, Hugo Munsterberg, George Herbert Palmer, and Josiah Royce not only the degree of doctor of philosophy but, far more important, a zest for adventure on the frontiers of thought.

When he first heard of the Reed project he asked—"unblushingly," he said—for an opportunity to have a part in it. That meant leaving the headship of the department of education at the University of Washington, an established institution with three thousand students, where he was clearly headed for the presidency, and starting all over in an embryonic college that had only freshmen and sophomores and not two hundred of them. That, too, was bold pioneering. From the outset no one had a surer grasp of our aims or greater enthusiasm for them. Before he left Reed in 1913 to become president of the University of Montana, he had made a profound impression on the college. A decade later, in 1921,

Librarian Maida Rossiter in the college's first library, in the Arts Building (Eliot Hall), circa 1915.

he returned to Reed, his first love, and there he remained until he retired at seventy.

EDWARD OCTAVIUS "E. O." SISSON, philosophy professor 1911–1913, 1921–1939, 1945–1946: The most essential fact about Reed is that from the outset it was mutation rather than a mere variation. Like every innovating scheme, it was ceaselessly subject to forces dragging it away from its peculiarities and back to "normalcy." It seems almost a miracle that Reed has been able to maintain its variant course without grave departure through so many vicissitudes, both within and without. That conservation has been nothing static, no mere preservation of something laid down once and for all. Such static continuation was out of the question for anything so diverse from orthodox tradition as Reed. Especially when there seem to be no bounds to the public misunderstanding and misrepresentation of an institution that ventures to break the hard crust of custom and orthodoxy.

WILLIAM FOSTER, president: Another Harvard alum, Eleanor Rowland, was as able a teacher of psychology for undergraduates as I have ever known. She devised for the guidance of Reed students the first set of psychological tests ever used for an entire student body. As the first dean of women—referred to by one of her enthusiasts as the "Woman of Demons"—she played an essential part in making a success of our student government.

SIMON WOODARD '10 (Reed thesis): Eleanor Rowland arrived at Reed from Bedford Hills State Reformatory for Women in New York, where she had been conducting psychological tests on delinquent girls. Rowland continued intelligence testing at Reed, undertaking pioneer work with the Binet-Simon intelligence test, later known as the Stanford-Binet test. She was perhaps best known for her work at Reed on Portland's "feebleminded" population, including intelligence testing of delinquent girls and unemployed males. Her book, *Life Among the Lowbrows*, was considered one of the most popular of the pedigree literature.

ELSA GILL PERROW '15, administrative staff: Eleanor Rowland was outstanding, not only as a woman psychologist, but as a psychologist in general. She had studied with William James at Harvard. She introduced us to Freud, who was just becoming known, and brought us reproductions of Cubist paintings, which had just hit this country and were causing a sensation at the time. We were terrifically lucky to have such close association with her, and with the other professors, as classes were small and there was personal contact with faculty all the way through.

MAIDA ROSSITER, librarian: I liked Eleanor Rowland very much. We respected her. Eleanor and her mother lived next door to me in the large apartment on the third floor of the dormitory now called Abington. Eleanor was kind of an aloof person with a lot on the ball, although always easy and pleasant to get along with. She had a great love affair with one of her students, Harry Wembridge '16, and one night eloped with him.

In the first few years it was a happy place, except for Harry Torrey, the biology professor, who had frightful attacks. Oh, the headaches we used to have from those faculty meetings! There were all-night sessions, and great unhappiness. Harry Torrey used to talk about "divine discontent." He was the oldest member of the faculty, and more romantic than we younger ones. He would pace up and down all the time at the meetings, interjecting "Mr. Chairman this" and "Mr. Chairman that." I went back to my room after one faculty session and found a note that said, "We took your pint of whiskey. We had to go out to dinner, and we had headaches. We can't stand any more!" Downtown they used to call Mr. Torrey's wife the woman who wants her husband to be president of Reed. She was very attractive, as he was too. But that temper of his!

DOROTHY JOHANSEN '33, history professor: Harry Torrey was very much on the problem-orientation basis, as much of the college has always been. If you asked him a question, he wanted you to find out what the answer was even if you had to spend some time researching it. The students came in one day after a rain shower and said that the walks of the campus were covered with rain. Using the old Oregon phrase, one student said, "It's been raining"—not cats and dogs but—"raining worms." Professor Torrey said, "Let's find out why." That led to a paper that was published on the activities of worms, on why worms come out in the rain. Those were the days when people weren't asking questions like that and solving them in biology classes.

ARTHUR WOOD, sociology professor 1911–1915: In the second year there came to Reed a group of hard-boiled materialists in science—William Ogburn in sociology, Harry Torrey in biology, and Conger Morgan in chemistry—all capital fellows. Although Ogburn was a sociologist he thought of himself as a scientist. He thought all social truth was subject to measurement, a doctrine with which I heartily disagreed. But I never knew a mind more avid for the truth. At all events, these men and others that followed gave Reed a start toward her eminence in science. They attracted the best students to their courses.

Meanwhile, a subtle cleavage developed between them and some of the other faculty, especially the evangelistic trio of Norman Coleman, E. O. Sisson, and William Foster. Curiously, despite my reasonably strong religious convictions, I was more inclined to flock with the pagan group, who subsequently came to my defense when Foster eventually gave me the "go" sign.

HARRY TORREY, biology professor: I was attracted to the old Ionian Anaximenes, who viewed individuals as part of and continuous with what we call the environment. The astronomer who observes and ponders a galaxy millions of light years away in space and time senses that a dynamic fossil—such as the ammonite that I, surrounded by a small group of Reed students in the summer of 1913, dug out of a shore cliff on San Juan Island—is just as much a part of his experience as the galaxy of stars. That fossil on San Juan Island had lived millions of years ago, but it was still a part of those Reed students' environment when they looked at it with understanding. On that same day, Harry Wembridge '16 found pecten fossil shells twenty feet above the waterline that were indistinguishable from those of the species living in short water. It was an experience that had an effect on his thinking, behavior, and self-definition.

What then is Reed College? To some it is a stimulating, productive teacher. To others it is the views of the president, or a group of administrative regulations, or a school preparatory to Oxford, or a way toward postgraduate distinction, or an opportunity for excellence, an atmosphere for achievement, a freedom to seek reality, broadly, basically, with expert and imaginative guidance. But always, it is a center, part and continuous with its environment, not a self-defined compartment with sharp boundaries.

I see in my inner eye the collecting of students from far and near, scattered peripherally, drawing together radically as they approach the college. There they find chosen curricula, aims, and policies already pointing the way, current practices that may pass from the superficial into characteristic controlling rituals. Rituals have a way of substituting doctrine for discovery, of narrowing and confining the mobility of thought. For example, there is a specialization that becomes an end in itself. But this should not be confused with specialization that focuses attention for the purposes of investigation. Here is the creative process that broadens, deepens, enriches living. A friend of freedom.

FLORENCE RIDDLE '51: My parents met at Reed and were very excited by Dr. Torrey. They ceased to be interested in the Episcopal Church, but considered Dr. Torrey, and themselves, very religious people. They practically made their religion according to his world view. For my father, Matthew Riddle '17, who went on to teach biology at the college, Reed defined his ideals, his concept of the sacredness of life, and his religious orientation, the kind of new-age religious ori-

entation such as you experience when you read about the intersection of Eastern spirituality with quantum physics.

ARTHUR WOOD, sociology professor: Billy Foster had long been a friend of mine. We went to the same high school in Boston, and were helped financially through college by the same teacher in that school. I had often camped with him and taught with him in summer tutoring schools. When Billy received his Reed appointment, he thought of me as a teacher and as one who could take general charge of the college chapel. I had just finished seven years at Harvard—four at the

President Foster with the early faculty in 1914. Front row (left to right): Josephine Hammond, Charles Botsford, Florence Read, William Foster, Doris Foote, Eleanor Rowland, Max Cushing, Maida Rossiter. Second row: Norman Coleman, F. L. Griffin, Harold Merriam, Harry Torrey, William Ogburn, Frederick Weber, Hudson Hastings, William Morgan, Kelley Rees, Stanley Smith. Back row: Bernard Ewer, Karl Compton, Arthur Wood, Jasper Stahl.

college and three at the divinity school, which in those days had a very liberal outlook. I spent my evenings working at a settlement house, trying to keep young fellows away from saloons and bawdy houses. It was a painful experience trying to integrate the two worlds, the slum and the ivory tower, but I went all out for the Social Gospel, which was in vogue in those days.

I started teaching English composition at Reed my first two years, and then moved over to social ethics, a very dubious field. The first students at Reed were a wholesome, unsophisticated lot, very pious and fundamentalist in their religious outlook, and they demurred at my liberalism. Even Dr. Eliot—a Unitarian!—warned me to go easy. Then came Professor Norman Coleman, a Methodist evangelist in temperament, and the students drank in his biblical outpourings with enthusiasm. From then on, my being in charge of the chapel was illusionary.

F. L. Griffin, mathematics professor: Among those who caught the Foster vision very early was Norman Frank Coleman. Shortly after being appointed professor of English at Reed, Coleman wrote a very warm and discerning letter to the young students who constituted our first freshman class, calling them "comrades of the quest." The phrase struck fire at once and gave rise to the name of the college paper, the *Quest.*

Comradeship was the thing that was greatly prized in those early years. Coleman was especially able to foster it with his own students. He was a much admired and a greatly loved professor whose advice on many matters beside academic affairs was eagerly sought. His talks in the chapel services were exceptionally stirring with deep insight, and his course on the Bible was greatly appreciated. Kelley Rees, our professor of classics, asked me one day, "Griffin, who is the ablest preacher in this town?" I said, "You tell me." He said, "Norman Coleman, of course."

Harold Merriam, English professor: What Foster accomplished during the first two years at the college brought me to the point of writing a letter to him asking for an appointment to his faculty. He never really forgave me for applying and being appointed. He once said to me, with some slight rancor, "I find my faculty. I never appoint a person who applies. You are the exception." He outlined the normal procedure to me many times—he traveled to universities and colleges and visited classrooms. If, after inquiries, he judged the instructor one that he wished to have at Reed, he made an offer that was so attractive as to seem irresistible.

I was appointed as the second man in the English department—to work with Norman Coleman, whom I had worked under at Whitman College. When I arrived I found that Josephine Hammond had been appointed to that position as assistant professor, and that I was to be an instructor. When I complained to Mr. Coleman, he told me he had not known about her appointment himself, and that I should ignore the situation as much as I could. Foster maintained that no one was department chairman, but the title of professor was assuredly the top man. Perhaps it was a malicious rumor, but the report was that Miss Hammond was an old flame of Mr. Foster's. She did not approve of either Mr. Coleman or me, and I thought her a poser.

In spite of all that, when I arrived on the Reed campus I found a community of interests—faculty and students working familiarly and friendly together. The faculty members respected one another and accepted this newcomer warmly. Mr. Foster, in spite of his faults or shortcomings, had a genius for establishing community feeling. He took his faculty into administrative matters through the policy and budget committee, of which I was a member. I began to feel that a college could be what the British had taught me as a Rhodes Scholar at Oxford—a community of scholars. Foster was a man of high-flying ideals and his charm of personality made them contagious. The early years of Reed was a bed of them, with conspicuous success in putting some of them into operation.

It was only when Mr. Foster became overworked and harassed by a shortage of money and when his faculty came to distrust his sincerity that unrest developed. He was frank and courageous and indefatigable, but he was also impulsive and he forgot on one day what he had said the day before.

WILLIAM FOSTER, president: Our first professor of physics, Karl Compton, lacked means for his researches in atomic energy in his basement laboratory at Reed. He left us after two years and went on eventually to the presidency of MIT. When he left us, there was a physicist named Knowlton at the University of Utah who, along with three other teachers, had just been dismissed for disloyalty to the university president. In protest of his firing, fourteen members of the faculty had resigned.

I went to Salt Lake City and spent a day finding out what had happened, at the end of which I asked Knowlton to join us, assuring him that he would not be required to be loyal to the president at Reed. Many years later, a study of graduates of colleges throughout the country showed that Reed College headed the list in notable physicists graduated per thousand male students. Not only that, but Reed had more than four times as high a rating as such distinguished colleges as Haverford, Wesleyan, and Amherst. The achievements of Knowlton and of his students are exactly the kind we dreamed of when we made those promises of devotion to scholarship.

F. L. GRIFFIN, mathematics professor: When Compton left, Foster, with his characteristic readiness to meet any situation, went over to the brawl at the University of Utah and grabbed A. A. Knowlton, popularly known as Tony. Tony wasn't a nickname for Anthony. That's not how he got his nickname. One time on an outing trip several of the science staff were dressed in rough outing togs, and a professor looking at Knowlton asked out loud, "Doesn't Knowlton look like a British Tommy?" Well everyone thought that was appropriate, so his close friends began calling him Tommy Knowlton. Many, hearing "Tommy," misunderstood and thought it was "Tony." It's strange how things get started.

Speaking of nicknames, the first year on campus we also had the wonderful luck to get a rare director of physical education, Charles Selwyn Botsford, almost universally known as "Bots."

HAROLD MERRIAM, English professor: The college put an emphasis on study and encouraged independent thought, but what I learned at Reed was that a student—under expert guidance—really educates himself. I was in sympathy with adult education, and Reed was admitting older persons of intelligence who had had little formal education. One of our assistants in English, William Boddy '15, was a minister with only an eighth-grade education. One man in my freshman class was the head of an office in Portland with forty employees. Reed was also conducting adult education in Portland with lecturing by the faculty.

ARTHUR HAUCK '15: Beginning in the fall of 1911, the college provided a series of free extension lectures annually. These courses were intended for Portlanders who desired serious and sustained opportunities for intellectual and moral enlightenment. The lectures were held at the Central Library and the East Side Library, and the conferences were held at the college. The first course was twenty-four lectures and conferences on modern English prose writers. It drew 3,360 people. By 1917, annual attendance in the extension courses had grown to fifty-five thousand.

Participation of the Reed faculty and students in community affairs was not confined to these courses. There were frequent requests for public lectures on varied subjects. In 1915, for example, 149 public addresses were given aside from the extension lectures. Reed students also did pioneering work in Portland on the problem of unemployment, demonstrating that in the Northwest it was not altogether the result of shiftlessness but rather an outcome of the large number of seasonal industries in the area. At the request of the mayor, they also issued a report on the influence motion picture and vaudeville theaters in the city were having on young people.

PAUL DOUGLAS, economics professor 1917–1918: We had a desire to share educational experiences with the community. We did not feel that we were there to lay down the law, but merely to bring them developments in the fields of science, economics, literature, and so forth, and then to cooperate with people in the community who were interested in intellectual and cultural things. As with every new college, distinct tensions developed between the college and the community. Perhaps we young folks were not always tactful. Perhaps the community was excessively critical. Despite those tensions, the time I spent at Reed was to me one of the most thrilling that I have ever had. The world has too much of the false stuff and too little of the real. Reed was always genuine and vital. I never found a better group of students or a more balanced community of scholars.

I suppose we were influenced by the progressive movement in politics and economics, which had come to its peak in Oregon around 1912. There was also a touch of the so-called "Social Gospel" of Walter Rauschenbusch in our activities. John Dewey was a permeating influence as well, both with professors E. O. Sisson and Joseph Hart. I had never studied under Dewey but I knew what his ideas were, and in general I approved of them, especially his famous observation, "Education is not a preparation for life; it is life itself."

ARTHUR WOOD, sociology professor: Each spring we had somewhat hilarious civic conferences, with townspeople roaming all over the place. There were charts and graphs on all sorts of civic problems, with speeches that gave the last word on what to do and why. I was head over heels in civic affairs as a member of the committee that drew up the Oregon minimum wage law. I also worked with a civic committee on the problem of the unemployed lumberjacks.

When we secured the Gypsy Smith Tabernacle downtown to house the unemployed, the business leaders rose up in angry protest, preferring that the fire department turn the hoses on the idle workers to drive them out of town. Foster was furious at me. Then I took students to the shelter and gathered information about the workers. I testified before a federal commission, which liked my stuff and wanted to publish it, and offered me a fellowship at the University of Wisconsin. Whereupon Foster, seeing the light, insisted that I give it to him for publication in the *Reed College Bulletin*. O tempora, O mores!

JUDITH STRASSER '66 (Reed thesis): The first annual spring conference held at Reed in May 1913 concentrated on the "conservation of human life." Subjects discussed included organized efforts to abolish war, venereal diseases, child labor, obtaining pure foods, preventing tuberculosis, promoting temperance, improving conditions of labor, safeguarding men at sea and on railroads, bettering the living condition of prisoners, juvenile offenders, solving the housing problems of cities, and health problems of immigration. The sex ed course involved twelve lectures, focusing on one of Foster's pet projects, social and sexual hygiene. The course attempted to meet the problem of misinformation about

Conference on the Conservation of Human Life
at Reed College, May 9, 10 and 11, 1913.

OPEN TO THE PUBLIC ALL THREE DAYS.

SEX HYGIENE SECTION.

1. **Exhibit of the Oregon Social Hygiene Society.**

   An entire room will be given to this exhibit, which is shown at this Conference for the first time. It will show by means of tables, pictures and other displays present conditions, causes of sexual immorality and proposed remedies in the field of education.

2. **Four Addresses.**

   May 10, 12:15 P. M.—Medical Aspects..........L. W. Hyde, M. D.
           2:00 P. M.—Pedagogy of Sex Hygiene..E. O. Sisson, Ph. D.
           2:50 P. M.—Moral and Religious Aspects............
           ....N. F. Coleman, A. M.
   May 11   —Education of Children in Matters of Sex..
           ....W. G Eliot, Jr., A. B.

3. **Other Addresses Related to Sex Hygiene.**

   Park Plans....................................L. H. Weir, A. B.
   Playgrounds..............................Miriam Thayer, A. B.
   Amusements...................................A. E. Wood, A. B.
   Recent Legislation.......................Calvin S. White, M. D.
   Child Labor...........................Mrs. Millie Trumbull
   Mental Deficiency.....................Stevenson Smith, Ph. D.
   Juvenile Courts........................Lilburn Merrill, M. D.
   Care of Delinquent Girls...................G. A. Thatcher
   Psychological Tests for Delinquents........Eleanor Rowland, Ph. D.
   New Problems of Rural Life...............E. P. Cubberley, Ph. D.

OTHER SECTIONS.

Dealing with Conditions of Labor, Parks and Playgrounds, Rural Life Problems, City Life Problems, Pure Food and Water. Exhibits, May-Pole Dances, Out-of-Door Games.

REDUCED RATES ON ALL RAILROADS
ASK FOR CERTIFICATE WHEN BUYING TICKET.

For full program, address **REED COLLEGE**, Portland, Ore.

Poster for Reed's first civic conference, May 1913.

sex by explaining to adolescents the physiological aspects of reproduction and the moral and religious aspects of sexual intercourse. Foster later edited a book about sexual and social hygiene called *The Social Emergency*.

SIMON WOODARD '10 (Reed thesis): Two of Foster's closest colleagues and mentors, former Harvard president Charles W. Eliot and Stanford chancellor David Starr Jordan, were also educators with a passion for social hygiene. Along with Foster they served as executives of the American Federation for Sex Hygiene, and its successor, the American Social Hygiene Association. Foster led the formation of the Oregon Social Hy-

giene Society in 1911 in the wake of the largest sex scandal in Oregon's history. It began when police apprehended nineteen-year-old Benjamin Trout for a minor offense. Trout confessed his crime, then continued, for no obvious reason, to describe in detail the existence of a clandestine homosexual community in Portland. An ensuing citywide hunt resulted in the arrests of dozens of men—including many prominent doctors, lawyers, and businessmen—allegedly engaged in sodomy and other indecent acts in various dens across Portland, the most egregious of which was determined to be the YMCA. At the time, the president of the YMCA was William Mead Ladd, a trustee of Reed College and a member of one of Portland's foremost elite families. The Oregon Social Hygiene Society, which Foster became president of in 1914, was regarded as the last hope by Ladd, the YMCA, and Portland's prominent civic leaders to manage the scandal, and they threw much of their weight behind it.

William Foster attributed the failure of Portland social agencies to address sex properly as the result of a "conspiracy of silence," a pernicious vestige of Victorian-era morality that entailed suppressing sex information in the name of purity. The same-sex scandal in Portland shattered this silence and cast sexual immorality into the open for all to see, hear, and discuss. The mission of Oregon social hygiene reform shifted at that point from targeting venereal disease and prostitution to the diagnosis and treatment of a more broadly defined, socially transmitted "disease," that of sexual corruption, subsequently leading to a symbiosis of eugenics and social hygiene in Oregon social reform.

The Oregon Social Hygiene Society responded to the scandal by creating a plan to protect Portland's youth from the spread of homosexuality and other harbingers of sexual degeneracy. During Foster's years as Reed's president, Reed students and faculty shaped much of their work at Reed around public service, including many projects that served the goals of social hygiene, explicitly or implicitly.

The most widespread was in Reed's extension courses and conferences, where the frequent occurrence of social hygiene and eugenics in the curricula began in 1912 and increased over subsequent years. There were public lectures and extension courses on sex hygiene and eugenics education in schools, segregation and treatment of the "socially inefficient," marriage laws and other legislation, censorship of the content of films and vaudeville shows, and psychological testing of the "feebleminded." The rich curricula for these courses and the reform zeal exhibited at Reed's annual conferences brought to life a college doubling as an organ of reform.

HARRY TORREY, biology professor: We took an intimate and helpful interest in the life of the city. Math professor F. L. Griffin used to go to political meetings and speak at times. He also taught mathematics to elementary students with such brilliance that one of his blackboard demonstrations moved a student to tears of high emotion born of excellence. Sociology professor Arthur Wood and his students used to arrange for the feeding and housing of loggers and other seasonal workers who were out of work in the winter. I was asked to speak to a large group of the unemployed on eugenics! Which I did, and never have I had a more attentive and well-behaved audience, bristling with questions that kept me well into the night. An anti-fly campaign was mounted by some Portland women to rid the city of a real plague. I furnished speakers from among the students. Sixty schools were addressed in a single day. Several of us were in the Oregon Social Hygiene Society. We supplied lecturers to the Women's Club, and we talked to socialist meetings, and preached sermons in Eastmoreland churches! I found myself talking one night about a collage of pictures exhibited at the Portland Art Museum.

WILLIAM OGBURN, sociology and economics professor 1912–1917: I went to Reed because of the prospects of shaping a college that had no traditions. This motive was not restricted to me. There was a feeling of dedication on the part of the teachers, and it was very marked in the president, as it was in Mr. Eliot of the trustees. The faculty worked extremely hard and conscientiously at their tasks, and were particularly successful in developing student-teacher relationships. I kept the door of my office open a quarter of the time so that the students could come in whenever they wished.

My irritation at Reed mainly centered upon two points. One was the tremendous pressure I felt to teach, to see students, and to take part in city affairs. I recall that one fall I made forty-five speeches in the city in addition to my full classroom work, and I was instrumental in founding the Oregon Civic League. The second irritation turned on the fact that my duties were so pressing that I had little time for research or for keeping up with the scientific literature in my field. Thus I began to feel frustrated and hemmed in.

VICTOR CHITTICK, English professor 1921–1948: I had known William Ogburn as a graduate student at Columbia. I was teaching at the University of Washington when he arrived at Reed. We talked about his experience there. He said that all of the work on the extension classes in Portland was overtime. Everybody was overworked, but everybody tried to give the program their level best, and consequently overdid it. He also said that this wide contact with the Portland community had been dangerous too. The community was not ready to absorb what Foster and the faculty wanted to unload on it. They did seize hold of anything and blow it up. The accusations of being radical began in those days.

MORNING OREGONIAN, "Academic Freedom," June 30, 1915: Shall a board of trustees remain quiet where an instructor enunciates revolutionary doctrines or fathers socialistic heresies and economic absurdities? No, never.

If our opinion were to be asked, we should say that too little, and not too much restraint, is placed upon some college professors we know.

F. L. GRIFFIN, mathematics professor: On one occasion a trustee sharply criticized a member of our faculty for having participated with an Episcopalian rector in drawing up and signing a report designed to curb one of the social evils in Portland. Mr. Foster looked this trustee in the eye and said, "It was his duty to sign it." Mr. Foster's job was not worth so much to him that he would fail to defend any proper action on the part of faculty members.

He stood for freedom of speech, for our right to express ideas as they came to us. But he also expected common courtesy and consideration for the feelings of others. I recall one occasion in a faculty meeting where Mr. Foster rather gently but firmly pointed out the inappropriateness of the action of a professor. "I am not opposed to critical analysis of any ideas," Foster said, "particularly when the other person has a chance to hear the statement and to answer. But I am opposed to treating anyone's serious beliefs derisively." He just wanted consideration all around.

One time Mr. Foster went down and gave several lectures at the Socialist Hall, for which he was roundly criticized by some people in town for allegedly showing personal interest in socialism. In fact, he went down there to tell those boys that they had only part of the story. That was what he was there for, not to prove to them how good a socialist he was. Though there would have been no particular harm in that if he had wanted to be one.

WILLIAM FOSTER, president: There is no reason why independent thinking, tolerance of opposing views, free speech, and the highest community regard for the speaker cannot go together. Without freedom of speech there can be nothing worth the name of "college." With freedom of speech there are sure to be statements from some teachers with which some men disagree. From students, too. In a public address at Reed I said that if any professor were so farsighted as to be able to tell us what actually would happen in the next generation, he would be condemned by some men as a starry-eyed idealist, by others as a communist, socialist, pacifist, or whatever happened to be the favorite epithet of the day.

The large and unending mission of higher education is the pursuit of the truth. Under my leadership the five trustees created that as a tradition at Reed. We loathed traditions but we loved that one. During my years at Reed not once was there interference with freedom of teaching or freedom of speech. Even under sharp provocations, even with the lure held out of much-needed money, not one of the five trustees ever flinched. Again and again the trustees were urged either to muzzle some member of the faculty or to get rid of him.

One was Paul Douglas, professor of economics. Some influential citizens objected to him because he had helped to get the minimum wage for women in Oregon placed higher than eighteen cents an hour and because, as advisor to the Oregon Grange, he had advocated a program in some respects like that which a generation later came to be known as "The New Deal." The trustees listened to complaints about him but said nothing to me. I thought of that when, shortly after the outbreak of the Second World War, Paul, asking no favor except that he be sent into combat, left his chair at the University of Chicago and at age fifty enlisted as a private in the marines. I thought of that again when Paul, twice wounded and decorated for bravery, came home as a lieutenant colonel and was elected U. S. Senator from Illinois.

F. L. GRIFFIN, mathematics professor: Foster's uncanny success in selecting outstanding young teachers is attested by the renown he subsequently won. Out of a faculty of sixteen in those early days, there were seven who later became college presidents. Mostly Foster chose young men and women who desired to try pioneering educational experiments not feasible in older institutions. He sought teachers who would actually enjoy the difficulties to be surmounted in creating a new college. That included Robert Leigh, who joined Reed to teach government. He did a very fine job for Reed for a couple of years, then left, eventually becoming the first president of Bennington College, where he carried out a good many of Foster's ideas. Here and there across the continent are several hundred colleges that were modeled after ones in New England. Reed is perhaps the only college in the West that has a New England college modeled after *it*.

THOMAS BROCKWAY '21: I met Professor Robert Leigh in his last year teaching at Reed, when I was a freshman. He was a kindly man who walked rather nobly with his head high. Years later, when Leigh was appointed the first president of Bennington College, I joined his faculty right after the opening. One or two other Reed people were already there. Wilmoth Osborne '18 was director of health. Harold Gray had previously taught English at Reed. Lewis Jones '23 taught economics, and years later became the second president of Bennington when Leigh resigned. So we had a little Reed cluster. Everybody soon got very sore at President Leigh for always saying, "There's a little college in the West that does it this way." People would say, "For God's sake, forget it."

ROBERT LEIGH, political science professor 1915–1918: I find everywhere among graduates and ex-faculty members of Reed a kind of loyalty far different from the primitive tribal emotion that the average college engenders. It appears as an abiding loyalty to some very true and significant ideas in higher education. It is the loyalty of an intelligently accepted idea. I wish some sort of "Order of Purgatory" might be established for those of us who have left Reed but whose heart is still there.

KENNETH LATOURETTE, history professor 1914–1916: I had been convalescing from an illness that brought me home to Oregon City from missionary work in China. By the summer of 1914 I was able to do part-time work, and so I went to see President Foster. I told him my situation, and he took me on as an instructor in history out of the kindness of his heart. The European war had broken out, and he said, "Come to campus, you can have a room here and you can give a course on the history of Europe since 1870 one semester, and the history of the Far East the second semester." He told me that I could also give a series of public lectures under Reed's auspices at the downtown public library on the European background of the war. All of this for working quarter time!

I found Reed to be the most exciting place intellectually that I had ever been. We were all young faculty, bristling with ideas, and encouraged to express them and try them out. When we got together for lunch it was really a seminar. And the faculty meetings were really seminars on education. The sparks flew, in a good way. The members of the faculty had been attracted by the vision that Dr. Foster laid before them individually and later collectively. The attitude toward any new idea was, "Let's think about it, perhaps try it out." They were doing extraordinary good teaching. You heard about that in the sessions and living among them in the dormitories and playing with them on the tennis or handball courts. It was an education in itself just to be with them. Ogburn was the most stimulating teacher on the faculty, and the most popular.

His was the social approach, getting the students interested in the voting habits of people on the hill versus those down in the flats. The student body partly shared in the feeling of adventure.

I for one had the feeling of being a "comrade of the quest." As a part-time professor, I could find time to write, unlike the other faculty members who were too busy. My lectures on the Far East grew into a textbook titled *A Short History of the Far East*, which established me as one of the early pioneers of Far Eastern study. I could name on the fingers of my two hands all the men in academic circles at the time who were doing any work on the Far East. After leaving Reed, I eventually went to Yale as professor of missions and Oriental history, thanks in large part to Mr. Foster's counsel.

E. O. SISSON, philosophy professor: There is an old academic conundrum that asks, "Why is it that a professor reading examination papers is like a wiener dog eating sausage?" The answer is, "Because he is consuming his own substance in mangled form."

At Reed, a professor would occasionally get mangled, but in a very different manner—the student would be making hash of the professor's views! The Reed student was expected to speak out when he disagreed with any statement or idea, no matter whose it was. Only in that manner could a student really practice the indispensable art of thinking for himself, of examining critically the data, and arriving independently at logical conclusions.

WILLIAM FOSTER, president: After our experiments had been tried for five years, every member of the faculty recorded his judgment concerning them. Those teachers, having studied at thirty-seven colleges and universities and taught at thirty-three and having thus observed the results of other policies, unanimously favored every one of the Reed College departures from

tradition. At the same time the Student Council endorsed every phase of our program and pledged the continued support of the students.

Elmer E. Brown, the U.S. Commissioner of Education, said that Reed's large-minded and penetrating views gave it a national reputation of very high and enviable character. G. Stanley Hall, president of Clark University, said that Reed College had solved more problems in college education than any other institution. Charles W. Eliot, former president of Harvard University, declared that the college had achieved within a few years a standing in the country of decided advantage. The *New York Times* gave the college two full pages heralding the success of its unique experiment in higher education.

Reed had escaped assembly-line and loudspeaker education. Reed teachers did not pontificate, they guided—and they did not always win arguments with students. Reed students, conversely, could not parrot an instructor or memorize a text. If they were to survive, they had to engage in that most painful of all human activities—thinking. They also learned from the first day that, while Reed is eager to guide them in learning, they are on their own to a degree previously unknown to most of them. The responsibility for class attendance was theirs, not their teachers'. The responsibility for honesty in examinations and in the library was theirs. The responsibility for decency and order in campus life was not theirs alone, but at Reed it was a *community* responsibility.

As one who has luxuriated on campuses known for their country-club way of life, I know of no college where students had a better time than at Reed. The difference was they did not let the sideshows get in the way of the main event. Many distinguished scholars came to teach at Reed and remained there at financial sacrifice simply because they knew that on Reed's campus, scholarship and the search for truth have the right of way.

Chapter 4

Early Community

The community at large has from time to time been disturbed or even perturbed over the extent to which students are given responsibility and control over their own life on campus.
— Edward Octavius "E. O." Sisson, philosophy professor

I know of no college or university in the United States in which the faculty has had so much power to shape its destiny.
— Charles McKinley, political science professor

Lacking the traditions of college life facilitated by intercollegiate sports, fraternities, and sororities, students and faculty began experimenting with innovative ways to fill the vacuum. Perceptions about religion, women's rights, and egalitarianism began to shape campus culture. Student self-governance, centered around the uncodified Honor Principle, was established in the college's second year as part of a student constitution drawn up by students and faculty.

Academically, the college soon ascended into national prominence as a promising new experiment in liberal arts education, issuing four Rhodes Scholars from its first six graduating classes. The *New York Times* noted that, while a handful of other colleges had adopted one or two of the innovations seen at Reed, none had done so with such a spirit of "religious enthusiasm."

During this period of institutional experimentation, William Foster extended to the faculty an unprecedented right to democratic power sharing with the president. In practice, however, the experiment proved problematic. Foster's genius for inspiring others with his lofty aspirations fell short in the daily give-and-take of running an institution, where his hard-driving, stubborn, and impatient personality tended to hinder the collaborative environment he espoused. An unexpected decline in the value of the Reed Institute's financial holdings further frustrated Foster's efforts, exposing the fault lines of a new college suddenly finding itself overextended in pursuing its dream plan.

EDITH McDONALD '19, President Foster's personal secretary 1917–1923: The whole educational world was interested in the college. I used to have some very interesting times guiding visitors around campus. They were intrigued with the fact that there were no fraternities or sororities, and no intercollegiate athletics. The educational people were without exception tremendously interested in an institution starting that way, but nobody thought it would stick.

EDWARD OCTAVIUS "E. O." SISSON, philosophy professor 1911–1913, 1921–1939, 1945–1946: I can see three distinct but interrelated factors in the dominant pattern of the college that might be considered the essence of Reed, all of which were present at the very outset. The simplest and clearest is a devotion to intelligence—to the intellect, if we take that word with great caution. The second is an insistence upon making the college a shared experience of all its members, a joint activity among all. The third is a refusal to shut out from the college any aspects of the outer world—facts, interpretations, or proposed solutions—that belong to the subjects the student is dealing with. For short, we might call these intelligence, democracy, and freedom of learning.

The best proof that the college has been peculiarly devoted to these three aims is that it has been gravely misunderstood and often seriously condemned on account of each and all of them. That the college is too intellectual—too "highbrow"—is probably the charge that has been made oftener than any other. In itself the accusation is most flattering. But still, we must remember that the cure for overintellectualism is more intellect, not less.

WILLIAM FOSTER, president 1910–1919: When I was young, I so warmly believed in coeducation that I pursued knowledge not only at Harvard College but also at Smith College. One of my courses at Smith required canoe trips with one girl after another on Paradise Pond, from which we could see the adjoining insane asylum. The mother of one girl, I was told, drove to the wrong gates. "Madam," said the guard, "This is not Smith College. This is the insane asylum." "Well," said the lady, seeking to cover her embarrassment, "There is not so very much difference." "Oh, yes, there is," answered the guard indignantly. "To get through this institution anyone has to show considerable improvement."

From the outset at Reed we held that men and women of college age could and should do more than simply hand back what they had heard in lectures or read in books. We believed that if we selected the right students and expected and encouraged them to do original work, at least some of them would do it as undergraduates. That was one reason why, from the beginning, we required concentration on a major subject and a thesis and a final oral examination that included examiners who were not members of the faculty. It did not seem too much to require that a student should know something when he or she was graduated.

Deep was my satisfaction when, before we had graduated our first class, Karl T. Compton, our professor of physics, put two theses on my desk and said: "Either of these would be accepted at Princeton for the degree of doctor of physics." These theses and others were published in leading journals of physics, whereupon the undergraduate authors began to receive letters addressed to "Professor" so-and-so.

RICHARD JONES, history professor 1941–1982, 1985–1986: Foster was determined that the new college should establish its own curriculum and instructional methods free of the restraints imposed by tradition. Specifically, he substituted the elective-course principle that he had studied under at Harvard for the traditional course of study. Each student worked out with a faculty advisor an individual program that had only three requirements: one, about 30 percent of the elections must be in one department; two, in the last semester of residence a student must take a seminar in the major subject and prepare a thesis in connection with the seminar; and three, every graduate must pass a final oral exam. A one-semester orientation course called College Life and two semesters of English composition were virtual, if unofficial, requirements for the freshman year. There were no others. Even the number of courses taken was indefinite. Among Foster's innovations was differential credit for course work depending on the quality of performance. To graduate, a student had to acquire one hundred units, accumulated through a combination of quality and quantity of work.

Foster conceived of all courses as having common liberal education objectives. Accumulation of specialized knowledge was truly valuable only if it was instrumental to development of the processes of critical thought. The teaching function had to always stress interaction with students and critical analysis, not the transmission of lore or rote skills. Emphasis was placed on participation as opposed to instruction.

Foster asserted that courses in liberal education provided the best foundation for professions such as law, politics, medicine, ministry, teaching, social service, journalism, and business, and suggestions were offered as to which courses of study were most useful in pursuing particular professions. For example, study of modern foreign language was considered to have practical utility for journalism and medicine, but not for engineering, law, or business administration. Course choices were few, and emphasis was largely ahistorical, reflecting Foster's preoccupation with the present. Although Latin, Greek, and history were offered, they found little place in the pre-professional recommendations.

DOROTHY JOHANSEN '33, history professor 1934–1969, archivist 1969–1984: Early on, Reed's highly selective admissions policy and tough-minded scholastic rigor became major factors in student pre-selection. Aside from the first two entering classes, which saw 60 percent of the students graduate, class retention dropped to under 40 percent in succeeding years, and remained at that level for the first four decades, indicating that the cause of high attrition was inherent in some institutional characteristic. The high standards that attracted some students kept others from applying. Reed's reputation for being different or radical excluded the unadventurous and those whose families were offended by such reports.

WILLIAM FOSTER, president: It was the conviction of the faculty that, if a student's intellectual enthusiasm does not become evident by the middle of the second year, it is not advisable for him to remain. Students who had no great difficulty in getting what might be called passing grades were dropped from the college merely because they had shown no evidence of an overpowering desire to do their best in something intellectually difficult.

WILLIAM OGBURN, sociology and economics professor 1912–1917: I did not consider the students as having unusually high IQs. They were average or might have been a little lower, but they had a fervor and ambition that was particularly responsible for their success after they were graduated from Reed.

Another reason for their success was the part that intellectual interests played in the community life on campus. What is ordinarily called "college life" was extremely meager at Reed— no intercollegiate sports, no fraternities, no sororities—but a sort of social invention filled the vacuum. This was the clustering of students in groups around either an intellectual idea or the personality of an instructor, or both. They were thought of as clubs, for instance, the Biology Club. There were probably a dozen such groups—a science group, a psychology group, a social science group, a group interested in social work, another in political activity. One or more teachers was always a leader in these clubs. Those who could have a meeting without refreshments had a slightly higher prestige than those who felt they had to have cakes and tea. The loyalty and devotion to these clubs seem to me to be perhaps a little extreme though probably not fanatical. They served to give tremendous drive to intellectual interests. This intellectual interest showed itself in the classroom and laboratory, where the discussions were very lively and interesting.

Harry Torrey, biology professor 1912–1920: The laboratory became a place where we thought constructively. Any place adapted for such thinking was, for us, a laboratory. I took the opportunity to emphasize biology as a humanly cultural discipline. There was a time when it was said that to major in biology at Reed, one must subscribe to the Portland Symphony! The symbol might just as well have been the Museum of Art. So far as I was successful, my students were humanists.

Lindsley Ross '15: I chose Reed because it was located in my home town of Portland, but also because of the challenge, the "spirit of the quest," a phrase that meant something different to each of us, but seemed to catch on and fire up everyone's enthusiasm. Some were strongly dedicated to social service and uplift, like William Boddy '15, who was a minister and may have swept a few others along with him. There were several students dedicated to teaching as a form of social service. As for myself, and I think most of the rest of them, the emphasis was strongly on rigorous scholarship. But we all had a good time. Usually a campus dance or another social event was held once or twice a week. Campus Day meant an opportunity to do the college a good turn by sprucing up the grounds. We had lots of fun with

various quartets and choruses under our music leader, Howard Barlow '15. It was far from being all work and no play.

Elsa Gill Perrow '15, administrative staff 1917–1919: The one intercollegiate activity that happened at Reed was debating. President Foster was very big on debate and he built a strong debate club. Our team challenged the University of Washington to a debate in the chapel, and just completely knocked them out. They just didn't have a look in. It was a tremendous victory. Afterwards, we had a rally and marched around the gym. That was the beginning of short-lived intercollegiate activity.

Physical education was required. The girls had their gym and basketball teams, but of course we had to appear in bloomers. Bloomers were not allowed outside the gym, not even on the tennis court, let alone walking back and forth between the gym and the dorm. I don't know how we put up with it. When we went down to swim in the lake, we had to wear raincoats over our bathing suits, but once we got into the lake we were more or less free to wear Jantzen suits—no bloomers or skirts there. I don't know who set these rules, but they were more or less just accepted as the way things were done.

Frank Loxley "F. L." Griffin, mathematics professor 1911–1952, president 1954–1956: Mr. Foster carried out a policy of athletics for all. He saw no reason why all the athletic facilities of an institution should be placed at the disposal of a few selected individuals who least needed physical development, ruling off from the playing field or court the people who needed it most. Foster himself was an excellent man on first base. In the early years the faculty baseball team, which included several former university lettermen, was too much for any student team. But the friendly rivalry on the playing field built up a fine feeling of comradeship.

Arthur Wood, sociology professor 1911–1915: Portland was a pious conservative community at the time, and Reed got the reputation of being indifferent to religion. The minister of the Unitarian church in Portland, Dick Steiner, confirmed this to me by pointing out that a privately endowed college has a duty to give students a sensible orientation to religion, which Reed failed to do. Some mamas looked upon Reed as subversive and wouldn't let their little ones go there.

Bessie Foster, wife of William Foster: My husband was religious and made chapel a compulsory part of the daily routine at the very beginning. Chapel was one of the most delightful factors at Reed.

Kenneth Latourette, history professor 1914–1916: One of the accusations made against the college was that it was disseminating atheis-

tic or at least agnostic views. It was anything but that! Reverend Eliot, the president of the Board of Trustees, was liberal but in the manner of what could be called a conservative Unitarian, no Congregationalist certainly. They were liberal Christians at Reed, and that, to a conservative Portland, was just this side of atheism.

Maida Rossiter, librarian 1912–1918, women's advisor 1936–1937, dean of women 1937–1942: Mr. Foster was an officer in the National Spelling Reform Society, and Simplified Spelling was one of his pet causes. It was an efficient phonemic spelling system where alphabetic script was matched closely to spoken sound, substituting one letter in place of two letters that represent a sound, such as "f" for "ph" in "alfabet," or dropping surplus letters such as the "e" at the end of "examin." It was solemn business, used in all the college publications. Some were dedicated

Campus Day was set aside every spring for the entire Reed community to devote to cleaning up the campus grounds. Students and faculty members gather in front of the Dormitory Building's sally port in 1913 following their day of physical labor.

Early students used the lake in the Reed canyon as a swimming hole.

to it, and some weren't. A few of us came in with a sign for the entrance to the driveway that read "DRIV SLOW AND CAWSHUSS."

WILLIAM FOSTER, letter to Lindsley Ross '15, December 31, 1912 (using Simplified Spelling): This is my greeting to you for the New Year: may it be the best year of your life so far! And if you hold the same wish for me, let us be really "Comrades of the Quest." How much that may mean in fellowship and idealism, I have tried to tell you from time to time.

In the first place, our Quest must be for higher things. The dramatic opportunity of beginning a new year calls us to burnish our old ideals, and add new ones with a faith that will make them potent. Tho we may not hitch our wagon to a star, we must look high—we must venture upon the glowing promis of the new year with aims that are adequate challenges to the strength of

our youth. And in all good things we must work together. That is our second necessity: that is a part of comradship. I must be of greater help to you; you must be of greater help to me; and together we will make a college that commands our loyalty unto the end. For loyalty is at once the price and the reward of our highest life together; that, too, is part of comradship.

F. L. GRIFFIN, mathematics professor: Foster was much devoted to promulgating Simplified Spelling, about which he got a good deal of good-natured and sometimes caustic ribbing. I just didn't like the stuff. I said to him a bit unkindly, after he had been badgering me a lot, "Well, William, I haven't taken up Simplified Spelling, but the point is I learned to spell when I was young." He didn't like that at all. The college catalog had some announcements that looked a little bit puzzling in Simplified Spelling. I noticed on the galley proof a course in the English Bible that read, "The greater part of the King James version is red." I teased him about it until he changed the line to "Reading of the greater part of the King James version."

DOROTHY JOHANSEN '33, history professor: Simplified Spelling did as much as anything to damage Reed's early reputation in many people's minds. There were criticisms on editorial pages of local newspapers and complaints to the Board of Trustees about queer spelling at Reed College. Such people ignored the fact that Harvard Law School had adopted Simplified Spelling for the *Harvard Law Review.* Reed eventually found it to be too much of a battle for what it was worth, and eventually, after a few years, resorted to common spelling.

MARGARET MCGOWAN MAHAN '24: They stopped using Simplified Spelling the year I started, thank goodness. Try playing Scrabble with it sometime.

Edith McDonald '19, William Foster's personal secretary: Mr. Foster had an appreciation for anything unusual. He also admired intellect wherever he found it. He had a genius for recognizing possibilities and an uncanny ability of seeing potentialities in people. There was a student who had had some hard sledding—a rough, difficult childhood that had left its mark. Mr. Foster saw the makings of something there, and saved the man with the opportunities that were given to him at Reed. He also had an appreciation of the benefits of work, and a great sympathy for anyone who wanted an education and had to work hard for it.

He took great pride all of his life in any of the people who had been at Reed. William Boddy '15 went on to get his doctorate and work at Hull House in Chicago. I went to work for Dr. Boddy in the 1920s, and lived with the Boddys in their house in Chicago. Mr. Foster came to visit and we went to church one Sunday where Dr. Boddy gave the sermon. Mrs. Boddy said that when they stood up to sing after the sermon, the tears were coming for Mr. Foster.

Kenneth Latourette, history professor: Foster had this dream of the college administering to social change, but he was essentially interested in the students. He was very keen on and very kind with counseling people. He gave a great deal of his time to that. He believed in the elective system, and was willing to prick faculty rules and switch hard and fast curriculum requirements to let a promising student do what the student was interested in doing. But the faculty wouldn't let him. They insisted on upholding the standards of the college.

William Foster, president: In our third year of operation a sophomore boy took charge of our music program and made an immediate success of it. All of us were happy with the results. For three years that boy led the music. His thesis in English, however, was not accepted. The hours that he might have spent in writing a thesis he had spent wisely on other work. His achievement in music was perhaps as original and as valuable as any of the accepted theses, but we had no department of music. In vain I urged the faculty to grant the boy a degree. On Commencement Day I presented him with a gold medal bearing the seal of the college. In due course that boy, Howard Barlow '15, conducted the New York Philharmonic Symphony and most of our other major symphonies.

I mention the incident for two reasons—it seems to show how quickly a college faculty, starting untrammeled, lets its own rules prevent it from doing an obviously right thing, and it raises the question of whether we put enough responsibility early enough on our most gifted boys and girls. In 1948, Reed awarded Howard Barlow an honorary LL.D. in recognition of his long career as a distinguished conductor.

Elsa Gill Perrow '15, administrative staff: Arthur Hauck '15 was the most popular man in the whole student body because of his genial personality and delightful way of dealing with people. He became eventually the president of the University of Maine. At Reed he was our student body president. I got to be vice-president. The women were always vice-presidents, you never got as high as president. But it so happened that Hauck finished his required units halfway through his senior year, and then had some job off campus for spring semester, so I had to conduct student body meetings as vice-president. As I walked up the aisle in the chapel where we had all assembled for our first meeting, I could hear the male portion of the community muttering, "petticoat government." That was the beginning of the women's movement at Reed, I suppose.

The first freshman classes were initially divided into male and female classes. After we moved onto campus in 1912, they became more mixed because of the interests of both sexes. In the dining room, which was then in a portion of the dormitory now known as Winch, the women and men sat separately by choice at the tables, and didn't mingle.

My senior year I lived on campus and a group of the men, wanting to be revolutionary, decided that they would start a mixed table. Four of them, including Stephenson Smith '15, who became Reed's first Rhodes Scholar, asked me and Marian Alhans '17 to become the female portion of the mixed table. I think they did it more or less to tease the girls, but Marian and I decided that we were not going to be put upon in any way, and that we would hold up our end. The result was that we were such a hilarious table and did so many crazy things that the waitresses practically had to push us out of the dining room. After that, the mingling of the sexes increased. It was a real revolution at the time.

Not that there was ever any confrontation, but I always felt that there was an automatic division between the women. The intellectual side of the women, particularly the scientists, psychologists, and mathematicians, was all behind Eleanor Rowland, the professor of psychology. She was also dean of women, so all the problems came to her. When you talked to her you came away feeling, "What a brain. What a woman. How marvelous she is, and how insignificant and ignorant am I."

The women who were interested in literature, poetry, and the arts more or less worked with Josephine Hammond, who taught English and was in charge of drama. When you had an interview with her, she would say, "Now, you are just the person I want in this certain part in my play." You went out feeling on top of the world, as though you were really somebody. With the men, it was the same. The scientific men thought that there was nobody like Eleanor Rowland, while those interested in literature, poetry, and the arts worked with Josephine Hammond.

MAIDA ROSSITER, librarian: Josephine Hammond could do things awfully well. She was a little ahead of anything they had around town. There is no doubt she was a good teacher, but she was a very vigorous slave driver. Extraordinary things would happen in the last rehearsals before the big productions she put on. One time she was very discouraged with this young man's performance and she just turned around and said: "Oh, take the fool out."

ELSA GILL PERROW '15, administrative staff: Josephine Hammond not only put on small dramas, she staged a presentation of *Antigone* in Greek, and following our senior year she staged her own pageant play, *Everywoman's Road*. It was a tremendous affair based on *The Summoning of Everyman*. The cast included the entire woman student body. There was this big set with terraces and upper-level entrances. Everywoman herself appears with a book and handcuffs. The Spirit of Truth, played by Josephine Hammond herself, appears on stage to tell Everywoman where her heritage is and what she has ahead of her. The main scene was about women throughout the ages, and particularly their downtrodden condition. This long procession, featuring every kind of occupation that women have had through the ages, beginning with cave women and going through the Greek slaves and medieval times, up to modern stenographers and teachers, and even prostitutes, stretched from the back of the theatre all the way down the aisle and across the stage. Then came women in literature and art as they appeared at different periods, from biblical Ruth, Brunhilda, Shakespeare's Beatrice, a Browning character, and on through. I played Joan of Arc, which was one of the few characters the audience recognized, so I always got a good hand when I walked across the stage. It was quite a spectacle. The underlying theme was the emancipation of women, which was just beginning to take place at that time. Of course there were many parodies of this thing afterwards, which we had good fun with. Everything was parodied sooner or later at Reed.

MORNING OREGONIAN, "Reed Co-eds Tell Taste in 'Hubbies,'" February 28, 1916: Countering a national survey of co-eds that ranks income as the first requirement of a sufficient man, Reed co-eds rank intellect first, with income a second requirement. Furthermore, the man must be a feminist, but not the lace handkerchief and ruffles about the bottoms of his trousers kind. College education is not essential but desired. Self-made men are in some respects to be more desired than those with inheritance. At the start of marriage the husband need not provide all of the income, as she would help until they started a family. "Dreamy dancers" must have other qualifications. Smoking is welcomed, and slight drinking tolerated. Musical ability preferred. Must be one who will stand for equal rights.

MAIDA ROSSITER, librarian: The whole faculty group at Reed was so young it was crazy. I was thirty when I came to Reed. Once in a while, Jacob Stahl, the German professor, who was twenty-six and had studied under Mr. Foster at Bowdoin, would say, "Don't you think it would be nice if we got dressed up for dinner tonight?" We would put on our best bib and tucker for dinner in the Commons, and then I would go back to the library and Jacob to his office, and we would plug along until past nine o'clock and then go and dance. Such dances! I used to dance a great deal with Howard Barlow '15, who didn't want to tie in with any of the girls, as I was available and had no beau.

F. L. GRIFFIN, mathematics professor: We had no artificial distinctions for people to belong to restricted groups on the Reed campus. If anyone was better there than someone else, it was because of his personal qualities, not because

Josephine Saunders '17 appearing as the Flame of Life in drama professor Josephine Hammond's pageant play Everywoman's Road. *Wrote Portland theatre critic Keone Cass Baker, "Feminists will love this play. It is a trumpet call to women to tell them of the equal heritage they share with men."*

of his membership in any organization or his wealth or anything else. We owe to Mr. Foster that great social homogeneity. We also owe to him the sense of community responsibility. He gave students a voice and a part in community government. He treated the faculty likewise.

DOROTHY JOHANSEN '33, history professor: The notion of being free from the distinctions of belonging to a fraternity or sorority was so protected at Reed that there was a feeling of reluctance to even name the residential houses in the dormitory for fear that it might mark the beginning of an identification with a group that was not collegewide and not intellectually oriented. So they named the houses by alphabetic letters originally, and then shifted people from house to house so that they didn't develop an identification of them with a secret sorority or fraternity.

GRIFFIN yearbook, 1920: Among the women's houses in the dormitory, way down in House A the popular indoor pastime is reclining deep-pillowed in divans, singing and playing jazz. House B is noted for its marble games played with the toes. House C amuses itself in the dangerous art of matrimony, containing married people, engaged ladies, single ladies, and faculty with children. House D, the "anylitical," bandies the latest scandal about with utter sangfroid. Among the men's houses, House F is far-famed for its noise and for being the honored guests at the women's House D tea. House G covered itself with glory at the Junior weekend canoe carnival. House H, the "silent house," is a refuge for those seeking the "larger life," and its members are lineal descendants of the First Class. It has sponsored the International Moppers' Union, to alleviate the tyranny of Herr Brunner the janitor, and the Anti-Bachelors' Club, to protect Cupid and preserve cherished traditions. Every bureau boasts a girl's picture.

House distinction was rife when men's House F, preceding its annual dance, proudly placed a large stone owl on the roof over their entrance. There it sits in silent mystery, for it holds a story with an unsolved past. Of course, it was rather a challenge, so one dark night, before the House F dance, the owl flew off. "F" knew not where. A most diligent search was made, but all to no avail. Sunday, the wise owl appears again, but over the women's House D instead of "F." Well, it caused considerable excitement, but everything smoothed out beautifully when "D" invited "F" into a box of "Owls" and an informal tea. There may be some who are chuckling villainously, but to most Reedites the restored owl carries a deep riddle in its stony head.

WILLIAM HELMS '23: In my sophomore year I moved into a three-man room in House G, which housed a group of male students who had no common interests and had no recognition on the campus. House F was the largest house and it boasted a more positive image. Their emblem was a stone owl, about thirty inches in height and weighing perhaps two hundred pounds. This was perched on a parapet on their house.

The newly born House G would have liked to have that owl, but it was closely guarded. However, one of us sighted an exact duplicate of that owl on a gatepost of a fine home in Portland. It was not hard to figure where the House F owl had come from. I don't remember just how it came about, but owl number two came to perch on the parapet outside House G. From then on it was war. House F could not tolerate another owl on the campus and we finally lost it. Rumor had it that owl number two ended up in the bottom of the Reed lake.

E. O. SISSON, philosophy professor: The community at large has from time to time been disturbed or even perturbed over the extent to which students are given responsibility and con-

The men of House F proudly display their stone owl, stolen from a neighborhood lawn in 1919.
This totem would go on to have a long and colorful history at Reed as the "Doyle Owl."

trol over their own life on campus. Having had a fairly close watch on it from the beginning, I have no question that the order and morale of the college has always been higher and more wholesome than it could have been under the traditional police system of control.

DOROTHY JOHANSEN '33, history professor: Foster wished to see as little making of rules on the part of the administration and as much on the part of the students as was possible. He preferred to see the development of strong moral character come from the development of self-reliance and independent government, of learning through experience. At his suggestion, a group of students and faculty drew up a constitution of the student body in 1912 that allowed the Student Council to regulate and control student activities, including adjudicating differences among student organizations.

By later standards, the whole atmosphere of the campus in the 1910s was extremely puri-

tanical. Men callers, except fathers and brothers, were to be received only in social rooms, and fathers and brothers were allowed to visit girls' rooms only on Sunday afternoons and only when accompanied by their wives. The Student Council resolved in 1914 that the tango and all other dances of questionable character would be prohibited. A woman member of the Student Council and the dean of women, Eleanor Rowland, had to rebuke two freshman girls for over-familiarity with boys, for loud and silly talk, and for dancing outside the circle in the Paul Jones dance.

In 1911, the honor concept was initially applied by the college to unproctored examinations. A year later, the Student Council agreed to extend it beyond exams. The Honor Principle was deliberately left undefined to evolve as a community ethos, incorporating not only the concept of personal honor but also other accepted principles of social behavior, infractions of which, such as misconduct at social affairs and in the dormitories, had the potential to bring ill repute to the college. In honor cases, the Student Council acted with Rhadamanthean severity, in several cases recommending suspension and dismissal.

STUDENT COUNCIL, minutes, May 31, 1912: The Honor System should not be limited by a specific definition of what it covers since our conception of the ideals of the college make it unnecessary.

REED ANNUAL yearbook, 1915 (using Simplified Spelling): Interesting results wer obtain from a list of questions given to the members of the senior clas. Of the forty-eight members of the clas, thirty-three answerd these questions. . . . Twenty-four considerd the working of the honor system satisfactory, while eight wer somewhat doutful. Several suggestions for improvement wer made. Some thought the students should take more personal responsibility, while some thought it was not emfasized on freshmen enuf by upperclasmen. One would not call it a system. . . . About three-fourths of those who exprest themselvs on the woman question wer in favor of absolute equality of the sexes, while only three entirely disapproved. Twenty-eight of the thirty-three dance. Two regard dancing as immoral, although eight wer doutful on the moral side. Seventeen hav not changed their ideas on dancing since coming to college, and one has become more firmly opposed to it. Twenty-five ar members of some church, Methodists, Presbyterians, Baptists, Christians, Episcopalians and Congregationalists being wel represented.

DOROTHY JOHANSEN '33, history professor: By the academic year 1914–15, the financial situation at Reed was not as rosy as it had once been. There were signs that Portland's boom days were on the wane, though no one anticipated the length of the coming recession or the relatively low point of its leveling off. During the first decade of the new century Portland had experienced remarkable growth and prosperity, more than doubling its population to over 250,000 people. Many Portland fortunes made in navigation and trade, like Simeon Reed's, had been profitably invested in real estate. Simeon Reed's pride, the Abington Building, completed in late 1887, was Portland's first office building to be equipped with an electric-powered elevator and given over entirely to office occupancy. It was also the Reed Institute's chief source of income. Located near the Willamette River waterfront on Third Avenue between Washington and Stark, it was in the heart of the business district in 1900.

Unfortunately, as river bridges replaced ferry traffic and street railways moved the city center away from the riverfront, the business district moved further west, and the annual net rents from the Abington Building dropped from $12,560 in 1914 to $2,740 in 1918. Price fluctuations, overproduction, and competition from producers outside the area had overtaken the lumber and agricultural industries, the staples of the regional economy. The consequences of more than a decade of overbuilding and of unreal values created by speculation depressed the spirits as well as the economy. The real estate holdings of the college, initially valued in the neighborhood of $3 million, had a more realistic valuation of about $1.2 million by the mid-1910s.

Shrinking income negated Foster's plans for sabbatical leaves, retirement pensions, and scheduled salary increases, and delayed plans for development of four-year curricula in the various fields and the establishment of new departments in the arts and music, Amanda Reed's will having specifically mentioned "galleries of art and lecturers in music and art as well as literature and science."

ROBERT LEIGH, political science professor 1915–1918: The failure to give art, music, and drama their proper place at Reed was quite noticeable. Foster was a puritan at heart, and believed that these subjects were ornaments, not essentials. Reed had almost an ascetic system of education—big requirements of reading, listening, talking, writing, and thinking on abstract subjects—mollified wisely by some participation in Portland's community activities. The usual correctives to intellectual absorptions elsewhere, such as competitive social life and intercollegiate athletics, were taboo, so there was a considerable vacuum. Work with one's hands and body and brain together, such as that normally carried out in studios, workshops, and theatre, was not developed. The emphasis in the college community on theoretical mental training at the expense of artistic and creative elements was a gross distortion of our essential task of education.

DOROTHY JOHANSEN '33, history professor: When, in February 1914, the Board of Trustees formally put all faculty, old and new, on one-year appointments for the year due to financial concerns, even those who had had reason to assume indefinite tenure were gravely concerned.

WILLIAM OGBURN, sociology and economics professor: A year or two after the first faculty assembled, a marked factionalism developed, with a majority of the faculty on one side and with the president and a smaller number of faculty on the other. I am not sure why this cleavage occurred. Many of the faculty were ambitious and came with great expectations. The same was true of the president.

But there seemed to develop a great deal of criticism of Mr. Foster. My impression of him is that he had very little sense of the rights and aspirations of others. He seemed to think that the loyalty and sacrifices on the part of the faculty should take precedence over any material or personal ambition. This blindness towards the rights of others was accompanied by a considerable selfishness on his part.

KENNETH LATOURETTE, history professor 1914–1916: Mr. Foster had very great kindness for me, and I liked him very much, but some of the faculty were very antagonistic toward him. The first month I was there I went on a hike with Professor Conger Morgan in chemistry and he spent most of the hike telling me that Mr. Foster was a liar. Among the faculty there was a feeling that there must be greater faculty governance because Mr. Foster was too dictatorial. I was never with Foster that much, but I could see how some people might resent him.

When he first came out to Oregon, talking about how Reed was going to be, the other colleges around the state thought he was just high hat. Foster did give the impression of being high hat, but I think that was pretty superficial. Essentially, he was a humble man. He had ideas and profound convictions, and great enthusiasm for those ideas. He did sometimes however seem to put himself forward as though the idea was "his" idea. In that way, he could be seemingly high hat, proud, and reserved.

ERNEST BOYD "E. B." MACNAUGHTON, trustee 1919–1941, 1955–1958, president 1948–1952: One of the great mistakes Foster made was to bluntly tell members of the University Club, then a small but potent downtown membership organization, that Portland was a backward area. To the people that lived there, that was just poison. It put them on edge against him. Some of that feeling was overcome in the early years as the faculty began to participate in community endeavors.

But Foster's new ideas, such as Simplified Spelling, were ahead of their times, and those ideas and the attitudes of the faculty toward the community were difficult for self-satisfied Portland to accept. Foster quickly got opposition from the leading newspaper, the *Morning Oregonian,* and they were merciless in their criticism of this brash young man from the East. He also told his colleagues at the other colleges in Oregon, including the small but growing University of Oregon and Oregon State College, that they were back numbers and behind the times. His capacity to say things in a sharp, cutting, vinegary way lost him all their good will.

HARRY TORREY, biology professor: When Foster tried to practice the art of stroking us all the right way, it was with an unpracticed hand, activated by a profound lack of knowledge as to how the fur actually does run.

F. L. GRIFFIN, mathematics professor: In 1915, President Foster appointed a faculty committee—the Committee of Five, of which I and Norman Coleman were members—to draw up a constitution that provided for faculty participation in the administration. Foster believed that such a system avoided the two great opposing evils of administration—an executive vested with autocratic power and an executive vested with so little power that he could not be held responsible.

The Reed constitution obligated the president to consult an elected Faculty Council before sending his recommendations on budgetary and faculty personnel matters to the Board of Trustees, thus letting the board know whether or not the recommendations had the approval of the faculty committee. Beside this advisory role, the Faculty Council had the right to refer for discussion any proposed recommendation about which there was grave disagreement to a joint welfare committee comprised of trustees and faculty.

CHARLES MCKINLEY, political science professor 1918–1960: I know of no college or university in the United States in which the faculty has had so much power to shape its destiny, where the president has available to him so much candid and constructive faculty advice and willing administrative help, and where the Board of Trustees may so quickly and fully learn the essential value of the college process and its problems. Of

the many educational experiments tried at Reed, this was one of the most valuable and unique.

DOROTHY JOHANSEN '33, history professor: A sense of humor is seldom characteristic of a rebel-reformer. Even a strong sense of humor rapidly erodes in a college president. Foster had a genius for organization and for inspiring others with the vision of his aspirations. A master in the art of argumentation and rhetoric, he was extraordinarily successful in communicating his own ideas. On the platform, he was reported to have "shone like a new-day sun."

In the daily administration of the community, where effective communication was a two-way operation, the sun did not always shine. Foster's confidence in the rightfulness of his own ideas sometimes blinded him to others' aspirations and achievements and, under stress, tended to undermine his capacity for leadership. What he justified as promotion of the college and a crusade for reform in higher education, some cynics interpreted as self-advertising with an eye toward offers from larger and richer institutions.

The pressures under which Foster worked caused the trustees to wonder whether he could continue the pace without a breakdown. His schedule of addresses and lectures on the East Coast and in California, speaking at educational conferences, recruiting staff, keeping in touch with various foundations, and generally spreading the word about the college, were grueling. Usually optimistic, generously and impulsively sympathetic, amiable—even charming and lovable, according to his critics—he was prone to headaches, and under stress could be arrogant and domineering, morose, unpredictable, and irascible. Frustration and impatience honed his already sharp tongue to a bitter cutting edge.

Still, Foster held to his course in the face of personal animosity from some of the faculty, little encouragement from the board, and a growing hostility of public opinion in Portland.

CHAPTER 5

Foster's Dream Collapses

Where everyone thinks alike, few are doing any thinking at all.
　—William Foster, president

As [Reed] unfolded, it was like the fall of a comet in the community.
　—Ernest Boyd "E. B." MacNaughton, trustee

Within six years of its high-profile launch, Reed found itself in crisis. The college's endowment, held mostly in rent-generating real estate in Portland's waterfront business district, plummeted to half its value during the Northwest recession of the mid-1910s, the severity of the losses due in part to businesses moving away from the river. The consequent budget cuts and salary reductions intensified the frictions between President Foster and the faculty, resulting in the departure of a number of promising professors.

Meanwhile, Reed's progressive and unorthodox nature led Portland conservatives and the local press to label it a hotbed of radicalism, eroding any substantial local financial support. Foster's outspoken opposition to America's entry into the First World War in 1917 further inflamed public sentiment. The war itself provided the final blow, dramatically reducing student enrollment and diminishing the faculty to a skeleton staff. While Foster struggled to be responsive to changing circumstances, his efforts were overtaken by events beyond his control.

ROBERT LEIGH, political science professor 1915–1918: Portland would not come to the financial support of Reed College and make it in reality a local institution. This was not due to the failure of the college. Many of the businessmen of the Northwest were of an older generation that placed a high premium on social correctness, size, display, and money traditions—the first leisure class group of the frontier. They were the products of luck in buying real estate, physical prowess in mastering the log drive, and the successes of initiative and native shrewdness. They did not yet see the value of locally trained, scientific, industrious students as Reed might furnish them, as the older industries in the East did in turning to their local colleges.

ERNEST BOYD "E. B." MACNAUGHTON, trustee 1919–1941, 1955–1958, president 1948–1952: I became attracted to Reed College at the time of its launch because I had been born in Cambridge, Massachusetts, although on the wrong side of Mt. Auburn Street, in the river wards. When word came that there was going to be a new college in town and that a man from Harvard named William Foster had been invited to start it, I went around to a series of meetings and lectures that Foster was holding. Foster was a youngish man, full of vim and vigor, looking to enact a concept of a new educational unity that had been developing in his mind. He talked in a Bostonian accent that I understood, and as I became exposed to the new concepts he was attempting to develop, I liked them.

As his dream college unfolded, Foster ran into trouble for numerous reasons, some of which were not of his making and others that stemmed from his complete inadequacy to cope with the circumstances he confronted. Portland was an easygoing community when Foster came to town, with many of the fixations and inhibitions that anyone from New England would have recognized. It had been developing for half a century before Seattle began to show rapid growth following the discovery of gold in Alaska in the 1890s.

The people who went to Seattle in the late 1890s were full of enterprise, and not afraid of going into debt in order to make money. They hocked their shoes to build buildings and to develop projects in the city. By contrast, in Portland at that time there was hardly a business property that had any debt on it. People lost caste if they borrowed money for purposes of that kind. In its first half century Portland had accumulated wealth and a fixation that it was the destined city of the Pacific Northwest. A large number of citizens had made a great deal of money and lived in fine houses but showed little in the way of public spirit. It was not difficult to guess that

their money had been made almost exclusively in trade without competition.

Mr. Foster came out to this community under a full head of steam to create a college that would set new stakes in the field of education. He had no money sense, but he had plenty of energy to develop what he thought was the answer for higher education not only in the Pacific Northwest, but as a pilot plant in the country. As the plan unfolded, it was like the fall of a comet in the community. It resembled nothing that had been there before. The language and the thoughts were completely different, and as a result there was no basis for communication. The emphasis from the start was put upon the superior student, with the product to be produced so wonderful that it was looked upon as aloof.

The college flaunted a disregard for the things that made college life alluring elsewhere, like intercollegiate athletics and fraternities and sororities. As a result, high schools in the area and their students' parents came to avoid it. Those who went to Reed were what they called "greasy grinds" or something worse, always with their noses in a book. The physical location of the college, accessible only by streetcar, also made it remote from downtown Portland.

As the college became involved in the products of its labors, it lost contact with the community, and the community deliberately cut loose from the college. Anybody who had anything to do with it was viewed as the same kind of freak as its president, William T. Foster. There was nothing I or any of my friends downtown could do in those early days to lessen the breach or bridge the gap. It developed faster than anyone could have realized. The attitude the faculty expressed, either openly or silently, was, "The downtown folks are a bunch of nincompoops, they don't understand us out here and we don't care."

Then the college began running into financial problems. Its endowment as left by the Reed family was predominately in Portland real estate with an initial appraised value of $3 million. Amanda Reed's will specified that only $150,000 of that was to be used for construction of the college's buildings. During the period that her will was challenged in the courts, income had accumulated in the endowment, which, along with the gift of forty acres in Eastmoreland from the Ladd Estate Company, made it possible to construct the first two buildings on campus. The college was then left utterly dependent upon the income from its endowment, as generated by its real estate holdings. Most of those holdings were located on the west side of Portland between the riverfront and Third Street. There were also some parcels of land on Jefferson Street between Tenth and Fourteenth streets that Simeon Reed allegedly won in a poker game. It was on some of that land that the first temporary campus building had been built to hold classes in 1911.

DOROTHY JOHANSEN '33, history professor 1934–1969, archivist 1969–1984: Unlike other private institutions, all financial matters and the administration of college funds at Reed rested solely in the hands of the trustees. The president had only a consultative role. With the exception of Thomas Lamb Eliot, who cherished hopes of increasing the endowment and made gentle overtures to potential donors, the board as a whole conceived of their duty as primarily conserving the endowment and maximizing income from it, not fundraising.

The college maintained a business office of which Eliot, as president of the board, was executive head. Alex McGowan served as business manager. McGowan had been Martin Winch's bookkeeper for the Reed estate and inherited some of Winch's attitudes toward the college. He looked upon the college as part of a business enterprise that was not paying its way because of

The migration of Portland's downtown business district away from the Willamette River frontage where many of the Reed Institute's real estate investments were located cut the value of Reed's endowment in half, creating a financial crisis for the college.

the peccadilloes and financial ineptitude of the Institute's employees. While his loyal services to the college spanned thirty years of its history, the first three presidents of the college looked upon him as one of the frustrations of their office, as they could never get a figure as to what might be expected in terms of available funds. On several occasions during Foster's regime, either Eliot, informally, or the Board of Trustees, formally, had to spell out McGowan's duties relative to those of the president. McGowan often failed to fill requisitions from the president's office if he thought them unimportant, such as an order for a library book, or if they overran a specific budget allotment.

FRANK LOXLEY "F. L." GRIFFIN, mathematics professor 1911–1952, president 1954–1956: Alexander McGowan was a very canny Scot if there ever was one. He showed me the liquid assets that had accumulated during the several years of litigation with Amanda Reed's relatives over her will. It looked like a collection of J. Pierpont Morgan's favorite assets—stocks and bonds. He also showed me a list of the parcels of real estate held by the Reed Institute. The trustees held nearly all those parcels and sold the liquid assets to finance the first two buildings on campus. In the long run their firm faith in Portland real estate proved to be an unfortunate circumstance. About three years after Reed opened, the taxes on our numerous holdings of realty parcels were so large they took 41 percent of the gross income of the Reed Institute. There was little after that to pay for the operating expenses of the college.

BESSIE FOSTER, wife of William Foster: Mr. Foster could see that he was going to run short of money despite the trustees' promises when he came to Reed that they had $3 million and he would not be required to raise funds. At the time there was a very real obstacle in the collection of funds for the college. Mr. Foster was serious-

ly hampered by the mistake of being identified with William Z. Foster, the head of the American Communist Party. People labeled Reed "communistic," which could not have been further from the truth, but the stigma stuck.

EDITH MCDONALD '19, William Foster's personal secretary 1917–1923: No one was antagonistic until the college began getting into money difficulties. Then you had conflicts about what went where. By 1917, the budget had to be cut very radically. Mr. Foster reduced his salary from $6,000 to $4,000. Coincidentally, that was the year he was offered a job at both the University of Minnesota and Colorado College as their president, but few people knew that. He asked me if I would go with him, and I said, "What would Reed do without you?" Out of loyalty to Reed he ended up staying. He would have had it easier if he had left, because after that things got tighter and tighter.

DOROTHY JOHANSEN '33, history professor: In the midst of financial difficulties, Foster did not recommend, nor did the trustees consider, raising student tuition. To do so would have reversed their policy that no qualified student would be denied admission for lack of tuition fees. But the college was not exactly flooded by applications for admission either, given its rigorous reputation. However, the fivefold increase in student enrollment between 1911 and 1915 that resulted from the rollout of the college's four-year program came at a price, as new faculty hires were curtailed due to the college's developing budget limitations. The college's ideal ten-to-one student-faculty ratio rose to fourteen-to-one in 1914 and to sixteen-to-one in 1916. This added to faculty discontent and notably lowered the college's avowed standards.

HUDSON HASTINGS, economics professor 1911–1920: There was a marked decline in the standards of Reed during my final years there. Men and women who had come to teach there with high ideals, a clear vision, and a determined purpose to make real progress were largely replaced by teachers who either lacked these high qualities or unfortunately did not have the necessary personal qualities to impart these ideals to students.

HARRY TORREY, biology professor 1912–1920: From the beginning, my Reed salary was not a living wage, so it wasn't the money that attracted me to the college. But the lack of it that soon developed not only made it difficult to attract experienced and forward-looking academics, but led to the engagement of young and inexperienced teachers in need of jobs, and materially delayed Reed's realization of its earlier anticipations. This was a failure of opportunity that made it easy for other institutions to attract away talented faculty such as William Ogburn in sociology, Paul Douglas in economics, and Karl Compton in physics. I myself accepted an invitation to the University of Oregon, where both my opportunities and salary were enhanced far beyond anything Reed could offer.

BESSIE FOSTER, wife of William Foster: During the early years my husband would pass off frequent complaints from members of the faculty with a laugh. It was all part of the wonderfully challenging game of starting a college. The vibrant atmosphere that pervaded the place was due to the youth of the faculty. There was no "dead wood" around. When Karl Compton decided to go back to Princeton, and I expressed my regrets, W. T. said, "I don't want people nobody else wants." He had a great gift of picking men and women and the record shows that somebody wanted them. The presidents of the University of Montana, Bard, Bennington, MIT, and Spelman College were culled from Reed's early faculty, and Paul Douglas and William Fielding Ogburn went on to fill important chairs at the University of Chicago.

DOROTHY JOHANSEN '33, history professor: The dilemma of an intellectual community based on independent thinking and free, critical inquiry was becoming apparent at Reed, as the true functioning of such a utopian community began to undermine the consensus essential to maintaining it. That such a place can be tentatively a community is dependent upon the cooperation of its members, arrived at through the processes of discussion, consultation, mutual give-and-take, and eventual agreement and cooperative action. Under stress these processes tended to focus internally on definitions of conflicting interests and their jurisdictions rather than upon solving the substantive problems the community had been set up to solve. Externally, they were met by the growing hostility of the local society that they ideally sought to serve.

Reed's governmental crises, and there have been many, have occurred when the college's overriding purpose has been threatened or when its component interests have hardened into factions and parallels of strategic conflict. Such situations have not been unique to Reed, but because the obligation to act upon democratic principles has been so great at Reed, the extent and intensity of involvement in the crises may well have been uncommon.

WILLIAM FOSTER, president 1910–1919: During World War I, a few excited Reed students, following certain newspapers in doubting the patriotism of everybody but themselves, circulated a petition in favor of the expulsion of all "Bolshevists" from the college. What should be done about it? "In the first place," I asked, "if a man really is a fool, is it not better to provide him a platform on which to announce the fact than to make a martyr of him? In the second place, why not urge every student to ask for a definition of terms before he signs the petition?" It seemed to me that if there were students with scant knowledge or twisted thinking, the college was a good place for them. The petition found few signers.

About that time a wealthy Portland manufacturer said to me, "If I had my way, I would close Reed College and all other colleges until there were enough 100 percent Americans for teachers. Colleges are centers of every foreign 'ism'!" Our critic overlooked the fact that even manufacturers could not agree on what they meant by a term apparently as exact as "100 percent American."

On the eve before the United States declared war on Germany, I presided at a meeting in Portland at which I introduced David Starr Jordan, the founding president and chancellor of Stanford University. The war, I said, would settle nothing. The First World War would lead directly to a second world war and that to a third world war, unless we formed a world government with power to stop wars. I scorned the notion that the war would "make the world safe for democracy." We had a mission at home, I said, to make democracy safe for the world. My efforts were not fully appreciated. The *Morning Oregonian* said I was an enemy of the Republic. Despite the criticism, Reed's trustees stood their ground for freedom of speech. They knew that a college must either require its teachers to put their opinions on and off as the wind blows and a newspaper directs, or suffer occasional discomfort. They knew, moreover, that where everyone thinks alike, few are doing any thinking at all.

MORNING OREGONIAN, "Pacifists are Put Down as Traitors," February 28, 1917: William Jennings Bryan, William Trufant Foster, Dr. David Starr Jordan, and Miss Grace DeGraff were named and classed as "traitors" by former state senator Dan J. Malarkey in an address before the luncheon meeting of the Lawyer's Auxiliary to the Naval Militia. He was backed up by the speakers who followed, in the assertion that the extreme pacifists were no better than the I.W.W. and were working to the detriment of the government. When the wild applause that followed this remark had subsided, Malarkey continued: "No matter what motives actuate them, they could serve our enemies no better. We must combat these spineless pacifists and I glory in the answer that our Mayor Albee gave them when they attempted to get him to join them in the peace-at-any-price movement— national honor first, peace second."

MORNING OREGONIAN, March 2, 1917: William Foster and his pacifist professors are not in accord with the patriot sentiment of America. They are among the socialist sowers of class hatred and the secret champions of Germany. Neil Malarkey, a student at Reed and the son of Dan J. Malarkey, the head of the local patriotic movement, deplores the attitude of individualism that puts personal safety and comfort before the needs of society and the nation. On the Reed campus Neil Malarkey is leading a recourse to arms to defend the country's honor by enlisting in the Oregon National Guard.

MORNING OREGONIAN, letter to the editor from S. M. MEARS, March 3, 1917: Mr. Foster and his fellow pacifists should be made to take the front line in the military mob that we would have at the start so that they would be sure to be in the slaughter.

MORNING OREGONIAN, letter to the editor from H. H. WARD, March 3, 1917: Reed seems to have the earmarks of being a hotbed of Socialism, if we are to judge it by some of the utterances of its president and some of its professors.

F. L. GRIFFIN, mathematics professor: Mr. Foster was greatly interested in pacifism, and bitterly opposed to the idea that we should get into the

First World War. He brought down upon himself and upon the college a lot of sharp criticism
because of certain statements he made and certain actions he took. But once we went to war,
Mr. Foster carried on a very vigorous and effective campaign of war work at Reed. When the
first draft came along, 73 percent of Reed male
students who were physically fit had already enlisted voluntarily.

WILLIAM FOSTER, president: When war was
declared in April 1917, I reiterated my previous
unwavering loyalty to President Wilson, whom
I knew from his days as president of Princeton
University. I had personally assured him that
should the country decide to go to war, he would
have my support.

It was soon clear that the country had no plan
for using our colleges. All at once students and
teachers began more or less hysterically enlisting in the army or navy or rushing out to do anything, anywhere, that sounded like war work,
especially if a uniform went with it. The Reed
College faculty was hard hit. It was clear that our
colleges should be used in the best possible way,
and equally clear that our young men would stay
in the colleges only under government orders
and in military uniforms. I was asked by a committee of the Association of American Colleges
and Universities to write a report urging that the
army make provision for using our colleges to
meet the need for trained experts. I then accompanied the committee to Washington to present
it to Secretary of War Newton D. Baker.

Baker agreed with us. More than that, he publicly urged all students as a patriotic duty to continue their studies unless called into military
service. He warned the country against sending too many college students to the front, thus
cutting off the future supply of trained leaders.
Partly as a result of this report the Student Army
Training Corps was organized in hundreds of
colleges. This corps was hastily planned and far

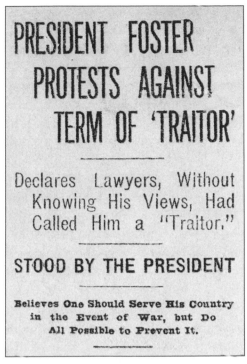

PRESIDENT FOSTER PROTESTS AGAINST TERM OF 'TRAITOR'

Declares Lawyers, Without Knowing His Views, Had Called Him a "Traitor."

STOOD BY THE PRESIDENT

Believes One Should Serve His Country
in the Event of War, but Do
All Possible to Prevent It.

*President Foster's outspoken opposition to Amer-
ica's entry into the war in Europe led local patriot
groups to brand him a traitor.*

from perfect. It was a first step, however, toward
better solutions of the problem.

Authorization for a branch of the training
corps was received at Reed College two weeks
before classes were to begin in the fall of 1917,
but there were no barracks and no authority to
build them. That same day I asked our superintendent of buildings to go across the river to the
army base in Vancouver and borrow blueprints
for the army barracks there, and begin the construction of identical barracks on the Reed campus. In three weeks the barracks were completed
and filled with young soldiers.

BESSIE FOSTER, wife of William Foster: When
war broke, my husband's stated conviction that
it was wrong to become involved provoked critical comment, and yet, nevertheless, when the orders came for him from Washington to review
the Red Cross operations, he went off to Europe

without hesitation. He and Kansas governor Henry Allen and the Pulitzer-Prize–winning journalist William Allen White were asked to determine how the responsibilities should be divided on the war front between the American Red Cross and the YMCA.

ELSA GILL PERROW '15, administrative staff 1917–1919: In August 1917, President Foster was sent to serve as a member of the six-person American Red Cross Commission in France for almost three months. He traveled through the war zone vested with an American military rank, and with aides and facilities for investigating every condition that the Red Cross work touched. It gave him a chance to see the war as it really was, not just in one place, but all along the line, and to go places where no one else was allowed, meeting the important people and asking all the questions he wanted without being told to "mind his own affairs." He was able to mingle with the soldiers on the front line, and to talk to the girls nursing in the field.

When he got back to campus, Mrs. Foster invited the faculty and staff over to their house on campus, where Mr. Foster showed us the pictures he had brought back, along with the French posters and things like French war bread. The following week he began a course of lectures in Portland. The Lincoln High auditorium was packed with a couple thousand people. He gave an eyewitness account of his experiences of the terrible atrocities of the war.

BESSIE FOSTER, wife of William Foster: As soon as he returned from Europe in 1917, W. T. was asked by the government to go to California to raise funds for the Red Cross. I went with him and saw with what effort he raised thousands of dollars in the few days we were there. This task, however, caused him immeasurable nervous damage, for it forced him to talk about the terrible things he had seen at battlefield hospitals, including surgery without anesthetic. He became nervously debilitated.

MORNING OREGONIAN, December 11, 1917: Upon returning from Europe, William T. Foster,

President Foster reviewing Reed cadets in the Student Army Training Corps. The SATC, which Foster helped to created in 1917, was a forerunner of the Reserve Officers' Training Corps (ROTC).

PART ONE: RADICAL UPSTART, 1911–1920

one of the ablest public speakers in the Northwest, has begun a tour across the country, giving 150 talks in 50 cities on matters pertaining to the Red Cross and what it is accomplishing for the wounded, sick, and destitute in war-ridden countries in Europe.

ELSA GILL PERROW '15, administrative staff: There was a scarcity of men on campus during the war. While working at the college I drew up a list of Reed students and alumni on military duty and was surprised to see that there were seventy-five. I remember coming across a picture in a newspaper of American aviators at Oxford and seeing the familiar face of James Barrie Rogers '19. Jimmie had been making a name for his young self ever since he enlisted. He passed highest in his class at the California aviation school, and was given charge of the rest of the men in his bunch who were to go to England. He had passed highest in his exams at Oxford, and was made first lieutenant. Just three years before he was the most mischievous monkey in the college.

Reed had its finger in the pie of war work. In the spring of 1918 a class of Reconstruction Aides started at the college. They were a group of young women taking a course at the college under the direction of the surgeon general, which fit them for providing remedial exercise, massage, corrective gymnastics, and the like to wounded men incapacitated for work by the war. Reed was the only institution in the West selected for this training. Almost a hundred women applied to take the spring course. More than two hundred enrolled in the second course in the summer. They came from all over—California, Washington, Idaho, Colorado, the Dakotas, Utah, and farther east. They were a lively looking lot, with a good many schoolteachers of the wide-awake sort, a lot of physical education people, and a scattering of older married women and young girls. They had to take a government exam at the end of the course, and then they were subject to call for going to France in the fall. Another course was also started on campus in the Red Cross' Institute for Civilian Relief.

It was a lot of extra work, but we didn't object. If I could help turn out a group of women who were prepared to put wounded soldiers back on their feet again, I wouldn't feel that I was entirely a slacker in the war effort.

CORA HOWES '18: Dr. Foster studied the methods and equipment of physical reëducation when he toured the front lines in France with the Red Cross. In 1918, he launched the reconstruction course at Reed. Prior to the war, Bertha Stuart, head of physical education at Reed, had instituted corrective exercise for spinal curvature, foot defects, and other pathological conditions as part of the curriculum for Reed students, so the college was already oriented toward reconstruction. Stuart volunteered for service in the Red Cross, and left the college for duty in France during the war.

I was among over two hundred women trained in physiotherapy skills to serve in the forty U.S. Army hospitals around the country, helping restore the wounded soldiers to their fullest capacity for a useful life. Many of these women became charter members of the American Physical Therapy Association, organized in 1922. The association recognized the course at Reed as the first organized credited school of physical therapy in the United States. It was said that physical therapy was born on the battlefield.

JOSEPHINE FELTS '21: It was a morning in autumn on the Reed campus. I was a newcomer and no one had paid any attention or even spoken to me. We were, some of us, rather snobs in those days. I was sitting under one of the big firs, reading. Across the grass walked a young man in tight trousers. He sat down beside me. "I'll remember you," I thought, "whoever you are.

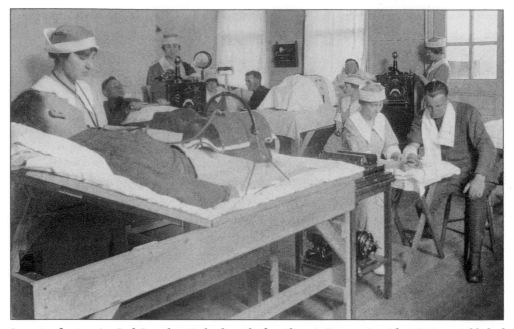

In 1918, after touring Red Cross hospitals along the front lines in Europe, President Foster established a training program at Reed for Reconstruction Aides to learn physical therapy for injured veterans.

You're nice." He was Glenn Chesney Quiett '20. He had started Reed in 1915, but had taken a year off for service in World War I. He was gassed there and had lost one lung. Back from the war, he had not too many years to live. The Glenn Chesney Quiett Health Center at Reed was later named in his memory.

DOROTHY JOHANSEN '33, history professor: By the fall of 1918 many of the older students and younger faculty were in the military or other war services. Foster was more than ever absent from the campus. Foster's secretary, Florence Read, about whom all matters of daily administration centered, was off on war duty. The administration was in the hands of a faculty committee of two, Conger Morgan, professor of chemistry, and Hudson Hastings, professor of economics. The college was so disrupted that it was not known for certain how many students were enrolled at a given time.

In the winter of 1918 there was an honor case that had tragic consequences, resulting in the suicide of a student because of delays in handling the case and failure to recognize symptoms of a serious imbalance in the student.

The following March, upperclassmen, including some members of the Student Council, invaded and "stacked" the furniture from freshman rooms outside while the freshmen were at their annual party. Furniture was damaged. The Student Council assessed the damages and the students responsible paid. But the faculty's administration committee asked for an investigation on Honor Principle grounds as well as for penalties. The student uproar that followed over this perceived threat to student self-governance was almost as disruptive as the war abroad. Stung by the faculty's request, the Student Council investigated the case, suspending fifteen offenders for a month. Council members who had taken part in the melee resigned.

Faculty and students then agreed to amend the Student Council's constitution to facilitate procedures of consensus between the two bodies. A new constitution retained a Student Council, equally divided between men and women, but made its recommendations subject to the approval of the Faculty Community Affairs Committee. If the faculty committee disapproved, the Student Council's action would be referred to a joint meeting of the two bodies for adjustment. With modifications and amendments, this would remain the fundamental constitution of the student body until 1963.

Under the new constitution, the Student Council was to control student conduct as far as possible by the application of the Honor Principle, which was to be based on the assumption that students would be guided and governed by their "own knowledge of right and reason." In those few words, the earlier conception of the Honor Principle as a pervasive community ethos by which the individual judged his actions was changed to an equally idealistic conception of an individual ethic, self-critical and community-oriented.

RICHARD JONES, history professor 1941–1982, 1985–1986: As Foster turned his energies and the facilities of the college to activities in support of the war effort, courses like philosophy, psychology, and religion ceased to be taught, and history offerings were reduced in quantity and quality. In April of 1919, students petitioned for a redress of the imbalance favoring the natural sciences over the social sciences, and for the establishment of offerings in philosophy and religion. Matters got so bad that the college briefly entered into intercollegiate sports.

OREGON JOURNAL, December 19, 1919: Dr. Foster's personal direction of the destinies of the college began to lapse, it is said, with the entrance of Reed College into intercollegiate sport, a definite departure from Foster's policies, and the beginning of the end of his personal direction arrived.

WILLIAM HELMS '23: Prior to my arrival, the college had shunned intercollegiate athletics and stressed intramural, class teams. But in 1918–19 Reed decided to play with other colleges under coach Harry Dorman.

I was drafted onto the football team. I played right guard but spent 90 percent of my time on the bench. As might have been expected, we took some cruel beatings from other small colleges. After two disastrous seasons, Reed went back to class teams. Had we stuck with it another year, the story might have been one of spectacular success.

That fall a handsome young man named Harold Grunland entered Reed as a junior. No one knew much about him, but "Gummy," as he was known, was a phenomenal athlete. Our class teams swept the gridiron clean that fall. Gummy was everywhere, running, kicking, passing. He was also a natural expert at billiards. Gummy disappeared as suddenly as he had appeared. We never heard of him again.

HAROLD MERRIAM, English professor 1913–1918: By the end of the war, Mr. Foster had lost the loyalty of most of his original faculty. Dwindling income accounted for some of the losses. Several faculty members left for what they considered larger jobs and what they knew to be larger salaries. Disillusionment in the president caused other departures.

In spite of his faults, Mr. Foster accomplished many excellent ends. He certainly laid out the foundations that still underlie Reed College, and he did so with great energy and courage. Some of his odd commitments worked against him, like Simplified Spelling, his preoccupation with sex hygiene, and his tolerance of unpopular social thinking. They gave the college a notoriety unacceptable to Portland leaders.

There were elements of greatness in the man that he could not or did not develop.

DOROTHY JOHANSEN '33, history professor: The first effects of the war were a tightening of the money market, further dislocation of the already precarious local economy, and an increase in the cost of living in Oregon. In this predicament the Board of Trustees in the spring of 1917 sought expert advice from a committee of local businessmen headed up by E. B. MacNaughton, a local property manager. The committee was charged with selling or remodeling the forty pieces of real estate left by the estate of Amanda Reed in an effort to increase the revenue generated by the Reed Institute's endowment. Early in 1917, with the consent of but without any notable encouragement from the board, Foster launched an emergency drive for $50,000. By 1919, the total subscription on the drive was up to $49,390.

WILLIAM FOSTER, president: I began four or five years before the war to earnestly urge the attention of the trustees to the financial crisis that was surely coming. I predicted almost to the dollar the situation we would be in by 1919. The trustees never showed any disposition to face the issue. They merely postponed and delayed and temporized and referred matters to committees that never reported, and even forgot that they existed. When I was offered the job as president of Colorado College in May of 1917, the trustees were aroused for once, and came out to the college in a body and spent hours urging me to remain. It was the first time they spoke confidently about the future, and gave me the impression that they would take the initiative promptly and vigorously in going after the needed funds. They did almost nothing.

After the war, and mainly as a result of the war, income from the endowment fell close to the vanishing point. Taxes on our forty-one real estate properties were up, receipts from all sources were down, and inflation was rife. The result was that in purchasing power, income from the endowment was only about one-seventh as large

as it had been when the college admitted its first class. Teachers who had served the college loyally and ably for years were receiving far lower real wages than when they began their work, and they were learning from the butcher, the baker, and the electric-light maker that the purchasing power of a salary is its only charm.

I had accepted the post at Reed, naïvely, with the understanding that I should not have to raise money. During the war, I had succeeded in collecting a substantial sum in gifts for emergency use. In this new financial emergency after the war, I obtained from the Rockefeller General Education Board an unusually generous offer of $300,000 toward a $1 million fundraising drive for the endowment. Month after month, however, the trustees declined to authorize an attempt to raise such a fund, partly perhaps because four of the five trustees were aged and ill.

DOROTHY JOHANSEN '33, history professor: The board had its reasons for stalling. With the exception of Thomas Lamb Eliot and William Mead Ladd, the trustees had lost confidence in Foster's leadership, and they were reluctant to admit publicly that the college's financial embarrassment was more than temporary. Publicity and the possibility of failure in the fund drive were hazards too great for them to risk.

WILLIAM FOSTER, president: When the trustees declined to try to raise a million dollars, I urged them to find a president who could and would add at least a million to the endowment. Then I resigned in order to leave the way open for the right man. I was not the man. One trouble among many was that I had been a leader in too many off-the-campus fights, too many for the good of Reed College. Another trouble evidently was that I came from "cold roast Boston." I had the courage of my convictions—foolhardy courage at times—but I lacked the courage of my emotions. William Mead Ladd, one of the trustees, said to me, "There are many men in Portland who would like to know you, but you won't let them." By my aloofness I failed to gain support for the college. I made few friends. It was my fault. Still another trouble was that my lifelong headache had become persistently worse. Twice during the war I had resigned. This time I made the resignation stick.

The trustees were gracious and generous. They suggested that I take a long ocean trip for my health. When I declined to do that, they provided full pay for a year. In ten years at Reed College I had saved nothing from my salary. Part of it I had returned to the college. I took a month of rest in the Ojai Valley of California, but the headache did not rest.

E. B. MacNaughton, trustee: In effect, Foster was licked before he started. That is regrettable because his ideals were of the highest, his purpose was sincere, and he had a devotion that couldn't be equaled, but he did not have the know-how, the human touch, and the patience to develop things more slowly. He had what might be called a low flash point, and when he was opposed, his friction areas became more and more exposed, and trouble came. One of the big causes of his undoing was that he gave the business community the hard sell, and it didn't take. They locked up against him. At one of the very early meetings on the new campus, I saw W. B. Ayer, the president of Eastern & Western Lumber Company and a patron of the Portland Art Museum, in the audience. We were both members of an informal social group in Portland called the "Deep Think Club." I said to him, "I kind of take to this thing because I came from New England." Ayer said, "I did too, but they are feeding it too fast and the people won't take it."

The people who built Portland came out West in an era before anything else was there, and by bull strength and persistence, they developed their community. They didn't like people—smart alecks as they called them—coming in and pointing out their deficiencies. If you came to town as a raw newcomer, you had to give them the pleasure of looking you over for a few years, before you began to smell right. As

Reed briefly fielded an intercollegiate football team in 1918–19, while President Foster was away on war duty.

Harvey Scott, the *Morning Oregonian*'s longtime editor, said, "A characteristic trait of Oregonians is a self-satisfied pioneer spirit. They want to be left alone."

PORTLAND TELEGRAM, December 23, 1919: Before the college opened, Dr. Foster made it known that he desired only leaders as students. His ideal was that Reed should turn out nothing but leaders. He wanted to create an intellectual aristocracy far removed from the masses. Through this un-American policy he alienated several hundred university men and women in and near Portland. They are normal men and women—some of them have attained leadership—to whom the idea of an intellectual aristocracy is intensely repugnant. In the tradition of all universities worthy of the name, Foster was an apostle of academic freedom, but he permitted the preaching of radicalism by some members of the faculty in a way that had a pernicious effect upon the minds of immature students.

OREGON JOURNAL, December 19, 1919: During the early days of the war Foster exercised his oratorical abilities more or less promiscuously. His outspoken pacifism at that time, contrasted with the radical change in his attitude subsequent to his visit to the fighting front lines, were taken at face value by the trustees. In accepting Foster's resignation, they announced that the college will no longer be molded about the individuality of one person's theories of education but guarded over by a new body of regents.

BESSIE FOSTER, wife of William Foster: In the last year, Mr. Foster could see nothing ahead for his beloved college, or for that matter, for his family. He had been unable to save anything for his four children because of the never-ending personal expenses of the college. He believed that his dream college was being destroyed—lost after all the apparent success. He fell into a profound melancholy and was no longer able to carry a banner for Reed. It was evident that his mental depression rendered him no longer useful and the trustees asked for his resignation.

I suppose some people thought this debacle was due to his being a visionary with no ability for business management. This was not so. He was the sort of man who, if dropped into a desert, would find some way to earn a living. He had supported himself, without help, since he was thirteen years old, and he had infinite resources.

In 1920, his depression ended and health returned when he became interested in forming the Pollack Foundation for Economic Research. His salary was three times what it had been at Reed, and we were able to save enough for the education of our children.

EDITH MCDONALD '19, William Foster's personal secretary: After Mr. Foster resigned, his secretary, Florence Read, was appointed, along with Professors Norman Coleman and Hudson Hastings, to run the college as an administrative committee until a new president could be found. Miss Read left shortly later to work for the Rockefeller Foundation in New York, and then, a few years later, assumed the presidency of Spelman College in Atlanta. I went to work for her there after she was hired.

I think Mr. Foster rather hoped that Reed would be the Harvard of the West. But there was a great lull when Portland wiped its hands of things. It didn't appreciate Reed. After Mr. Foster left the college, he was ill for the first year. I had gone home to Spokane, Washington, with plans to then go on to Hawaii and start a trip around the world with a classmate. Mr. Foster had many opportunities to go back into the academic world but he became interested in economic work with the Pollack Foundation, set up in Boston by a wealthy businessman named Waddill Catchings, who was a friend of Mr. Foster's from Harvard. The foundation was named for a fellow Harvard classmate of theirs who had died. They were joined by Hudson Hastings, who had been at Reed as a professor of economics. Since money was the matter that had caused Mr. Foster concern at Reed, he was going to find out about money. The job paid well, and it took the family back East and gave them the advantages of an education for their children, who were just coming of age. Mr. Foster came to Spokane with Mrs. Foster for dinner and asked me if I would go with him to Boston. I never made it to Hawaii.

JUDITH STRASSER '66 (Reed thesis): In his work with Catchings, Foster presaged and advocated many of the tenets of Keynesian economics. Their books popularized the concept of the circuit velocity of money, later called the "income-flow" approach. Sustained production depended largely on consumer expenditures, which in turn depended on consumers' incomes. These, in turn, depended on the amount of money in circulation, and on the lapse between the time that money, once spent for consumption, was returned to the consumers for repurchasing. During the Depression, Foster and Catchings advocated the government's use of fiscal policy to achieve a balance in the economic system.

EDITH McDONALD '19, William Foster's personal secretary: I was with Mr. Foster in Boston as his personal secretary until 1923. Mr. Foster never said anything outright about his experience at the college, but from Mrs. Foster it was clear he was hurt, tremendously hurt. Many years later, he was invited back to Reed to speak. This was the first time he had ever wanted to accept an invitation to go back. Right before the trip, he had a breakdown of sorts—he couldn't remember anything. Everything had to be cancelled. The next day he was better and wanted to go ahead with the schedule. He went on, first stopping to give a talk at the University of Chi-

cago, and then on to Reed. The reception he got there helped a great deal. I think it did something very real in terms of helping him overcome his hurt.

ELLEN KNOWLTON JOHNSON '39, recorder 1945–1962, registrar 1962–1981: Mr. Foster returned to the college one last time in 1948 to give the commencement address, entitled "Pay the Price and Take It." He died in 1951. Mrs. Foster came out to Reed from the East Coast with Mr. Foster's ashes. It was during the summer, so there weren't many students around. There was no formal ceremony. She didn't want that. Dr. F. L. Griffin, reciting poetry that he felt to be appropriate, scattered the ashes along the canyon.

WILLIAM FOSTER, president: As I look back at Reed, I see that we were not so bold as we thought. We boasted of freedom from tradition but we lacked the sense to take great advantage of that freedom. We denounced intercollegiate athletics, but events of the decades that came after prove that our indictment was too mild. We thought that we were adventurous in leaving students in control of their own conduct. We were merely facing facts. We also felt adventurous in allowing individual students to devise their own plans of study—plans that were not neatly classified and hedged in by our catalog. Now we see that gifted students should be given even greater freedom. Since then bolder institutions have shown how far short we fell of reaching our own ideals. We congratulated ourselves on breaking loose from fixed methods of counting up credits for admission, but we did not go far enough, as the University of Chicago has since proved. We seem to have been restrained by the old adage: "be bold, be bold, be not too bold." In few of our departures from established routine were we bold enough. We did, however, have but one answer to our question, "Should students study?" Yes.

PART TWO

PART TWO: THE GOLDEN AGE, 1921–1945

The Golden Age, 1921–1945

To understand is to unify.
    —Alexander Meiklejohn, president of Amherst College 1913–1923

Reed began its second decade broken in both spirit and pocketbook. Thomas Lamb Eliot, at age seventy-eight lacking the energy to revitalize his dream, handed the reins of the Board of Trustees to James Kerr, a prominent Portland lawyer who had joined the board in 1915 upon the death of Amanda Reed's lawyer, Cyrus Dolph. On December 19, 1919, the same day that William Foster resigned his presidency, the board created a separate Board of Regents comprising the five trustees and six younger business and civic leaders of Portland, among them Reed College architect Albert Doyle and property manager E. B. MacNaughton.

In accordance with Amanda Reed's will, the members of the Board of Trustees continued to manage the finances of the parent organization, the Reed Institute, while the eleven members of the Board of Regents assumed oversight of the college's operations, including final say in determining the college's curriculum and educational policy, so that the college would never again be "molded around the individuality of one person's theories." This new authority proved to be an ineffectual safeguard, however, as the regents soon found themselves enmeshed in a new pedagogical experiment driven by another visionary leader, Reed's second president, Richard Scholz.

Outgoing and personally engaging, Scholz at age forty-one stood in complete contrast to the aloof, hard-driving, evangelistic Foster. While Reed's devastated state might have deterred others, Scholz, a history professor from the University of Washington, recognized an opportunity to rebuild the college around an idea he called "new humanism." Intended to be a "unified reinterpretation of the whole of existence," new humanism was Scholz's antidote to the disillusionment and disintegration left in the wake of the First World War. Scholz's key challenge

The Arts Building (Eliot Hall), circa 1921.

at Reed was grafting his concept of new humanism onto the rootstock of academic rigor, intellectual freedom, and egalitarian democracy instilled by Foster.

While the two men shared a broad conception of education—accepting any experience of personal or social value that would develop critical thinking—Scholz envisioned a teaching framework much different from Foster's. Where Foster had employed the open-electives curriculum of his mentor Charles Eliot at Harvard, believing it created an environment of intellectual freedom, Scholz felt that integrating the facets of a broad liberal education was too important to be left to students. He proposed a curriculum of common studies, the heart of which was to be a humanities course extending from antiquity to the twentieth century.

Scholz's vision in 1921 was in the educational vanguard of the time. A "neo-humanist" movement, spawned at the beginning of the century by followers of English poet and cultural critic Matthew Arnold and his influential book, *Culture and Anarchy*, set out to counter the open-electives curriculum Charles Eliot had established at Harvard with a model of moral rigor that promoted a harmonious, secure, and politically stable culture. Grounded in the classics of Greece and Rome, their aim, as Arnold put it, was "to see life steadily and to see it whole." The neo-humanists were bolstered in their efforts by a rising concern over the influx of immigrants to America, and by the desire among some educators to foster a homogeneous citizenry. This aim gave rise to the development in higher education of the general education course.

Columbia University led the way, establishing in 1919 its famous "Contemporary Civilization" course, an amalgam of modern economics, government, philosophy, and history, which was required of all freshmen. Dartmouth and Stanford both instituted similar courses with a strong civics focus, which they called "Problems of Citizenship." Amherst College, under the leadership of Alexander Meiklejohn, attempted to evolve its elective curriculum into a uniform core curriculum based around philosophy and the social sciences.

Scholz's proposed humanities curriculum was by far the most comprehensive of these new programs. With the exception of a "Great Honors" program instituted for honor students at Columbia in 1920, the other general education courses focused primarily on contemporary material. During its first ten years Columbia's Contemporary Civilization course, for example, covered no material before 1871 and restricted students to reading textbooks. Scholz's freshman humanities program offered parallel courses in literature and history that extended from the ancient Greeks to 1763, and relied heavily upon the use of primary texts.

Although Scholz's own training had been as a historian of antiquity, his approach to humanities differed fundamentally from the neo-humanists' valorization of Greece and Rome. For Scholz, the classics provided students with not only a common cultural heritage—read because they had always been read—but also a common language for understanding historically the cultural forces at work in the current society. Scholz set out to construct at Reed a Socratic "think-shop" that took all of human experience, past and present, into some sort of unified understanding. His proposed program revolved around a conception of the human experience unfolding in time. While freshmen were to start with the Greeks and study the evolution of man and society up through the Age of Enlightenment, sophomore students focused on the problems of the contemporary world. A student's last two years were to be devoted to specialized fields of study, with a required course in the junior year on citizenship and international relations, followed by a senior colloquium that encouraged students to formulate their own unified perspectives on the world.

Scholz felt that such a broad and socially minded context—combining neo-humanist values with social relevancy—would promote students' future civic involvement as responsible citizens, and would help them attain the art of living fully with their hearts and minds. He also believed that a prescribed curriculum would instill a social bond among students, which he thought vital to staying human in an increasingly impersonal, materialistic, and mass-oriented society.

Upon Scholz's appointment, Reed received a modest infusion of funding from its new regents, as well as a financial boost as a result of doubling its tuition fees to $200 per year. Better management of the endowment investments also increased operating income. Scholz employed the new funds to build up academic strength in the humanities, adding six full professors in literature and the social sciences. These six men—Rex Arragon, Barry Cerf, Victor Chittick, Bernard Noble, Benjamin Woodbridge, and E. O. Sisson—along with a handful of professors remaining from Foster's administration, would all come to play central roles in carrying forward Scholz's vision during the years between the two world wars, which came to be known as Reed's "Golden Age."

With the announcement of Scholz's bold new curricular experiment in 1921, Reed returned to its original role as an innovator on the national stage. However, as Scholz began rolling out his program at Reed, he encountered fierce opposition from the science faculty, most of them Foster appointees, forcing him to make a number of compromises to his original goals. More compromises followed upon the end of Scholz's administration in the mid-1920s, as Reed's curriculum underwent yet another stage of development, this one led by the faculty, who consolidated selective elements of Scholz's core curriculum and Foster's rigorous approach into an academic program devoted to a life of the mind. Its purpose was not to reform the world or to train students to be good citizens, but to pursue learning solely for the sake of learning.

In this third major curricular development, Reed continued to play a leading role in the evolution of general education programs nationwide. Spawned largely by an impulse toward order, these programs grew rapidly during the international political upheaval of the interwar years. The neo-humanist movement, having been attacked by critics as ignoring contemporary social realities, gave way to the apparently ideologically neutral "Great Books" tradition. Columbia's General Honors course evolved in the 1930s into the "Colloquium in Important Books," and then in the 1940s into two humanities courses, one on Western civilization and the other on music and the arts, both required of all students. From Columbia the Great Books tradition then migrated with philosopher Mortimer Adler to the University of Chicago, where Chicago's president Robert Maynard Hutchins made it far more canonical in his effort to "revitalize metaphysics and restore it to its place in higher learning." Hutchins also emulated William Foster's example at Reed by pulling Chicago out of intercollegiate sports and banning fraternities in order to increase the university's focus on intellectual pursuits. In 1937, two of Hutchins' professors, Stringfellow Barr and Scott Buchanan, left the University of Chicago to establish the purest of the Great Books curricula at St. John's College in Annapolis. Also in the 1930s, Stanford broadened its Problems of Citizenship course beyond its initial ethics focus, renaming it "Western Civilization." Harvard followed the trend in the mid-1940s, instituting a Great Books course based on the recommendations of their famous *General Education in a Free Society* (or "Redbook") report.

Reed College's humanities program both informed and supported many of these developments. However, given the unique formulation of its overall curriculum, derived from the divergent visions of William Foster and Richard Scholz, Reed's educational program became an idiosyncratic model not easily replicated elsewhere.

CHAPTER 6

Rebirth

Scholarship, even culture, is not merely a thing of individual minds—both involve membership in a community and are the outcome of cooperative thinking and cooperative living.

—Richard Scholz, president

[President Scholz] would come into the regents meetings and start talking about his hopes for the college, and not stop until he had finished his professorial allowance of forty minutes. No one could understand him because he talked so fast. . . . After the meetings were over, everyone would ask, "What in hell was the man talking about?"

—Ernest Boyd "E. B." MacNaughton, trustee

The defining life experience of Reed's second president, Richard Scholz, had been the three years he spent at Oxford from 1901 to 1903 as one of the first American Rhodes Scholars. It seeded in him a quest to form a unified view of life. Scholz believed that, following the devastation of the First World War, humanity was passing into an age of relationships that required a "reconciliation and synthesis of actual life and the best thought of our time." His goal was to extend to students not just knowledge but also understanding. For Scholz, that meant humanizing the teaching process as well as the educational institution.

Scholz's distinction as a Rhodes Scholar lent him the stature of hero-scholar, an ideal that quickly became the college's raison d'être, in contrast to the crusading, reformist culture inculcated by William Foster during Reed's first decade. Embracing Scholz's new, unifying vision, and stimulated by his sharp intellect and personal charm, the college enjoyed a much-needed but brief renaissance.

CLARENCE AYRES, philosophy and social ethics professor 1923–1925: When Richard Scholz was asked to assume the presidency of Reed in April 1921, the college was in a dying condition. At the college's beginning, the trustees had had the unusual wisdom to bring out a fiery young educator from an eastern college and to stand by while he gathered a group of scientists and teachers that has seldom been equaled in American colleges. They were "young men in a hurry." Young men in colleges frequently differ with old men in business. They are apt to speak out in a meeting. When it happens to be wartime, the effect is something like the escape of high-tension electrical current. All this occurred. The result was an alignment of opposing forces, the final withdrawal of the president, the subsequent disintegration of his faculty, and the passage of the college into a sort of receivership with a tiny residue of the old faculty, decimated, almost bankrupt, and definitely stigmatized among the good people of Portland as pacifist, radical, patronizing, and generally unsound.

Upon this scene entered Richard Scholz to play the part of Prince Charming. His chief immediate qualification for the part was an irresistible smile. The very skill with which he drove his 1918 Buick at brake-demolishing speed through the crowded streets of Portland endeared him even to the traffic police. He made an immediate and complete conquest. It was love at first sight.

RICHARD SCHOLZ, president 1921–1924: My plea is simply the plea not merely to humanize knowledge, but to humanize our institutions and our teaching, so that we may help to make men and women not only of knowledge, but of understanding and good will.

CHERYL SCHOLZ, wife of Richard Scholz, dean of women 1924–1937, history professor 1938–1943, dean of admission 1943–1945: We were in January of our third year at the University of Washington, where my husband, Dick, was a professor of history, when he received a letter from Frank Aydelotte, with whom Dick had been a Rhodes Scholar at Oxford. Frank and his wife were coming to Seattle for one day, just passing through on their way home by train to Boston after a visit to Portland. Frank wanted to spend the day with Dick and the University's two oth-

er Rhodes Scholars. Everyone was highly entertained because they wondered what in the world Aydelotte was doing in Portland, so far away from MIT, where he was a professor of English at the time. Finally, Dick said, "I know. Reed College is looking for a new president. I'm sure that he's been out here being interviewed for it."

The Rhodes Scholars spent the whole day telling Mr. Aydelotte why he should go to Reed College. Here was an opportunity to take a small liberal arts college and really go to town with teaching and the scholarly side of the undergraduate experience. Mr. Aydelotte left that night on the train home. After thinking it over for two days, he wrote the Reed trustees to say that he unhappily could not accept as there were not enough books in the college library to be stimulating to the faculty. But, he said, "The man you want is up at the University of Washington. His name is Dick Scholz, and you should see him." As it turned out, months later Mr. Aydelotte accepted the presidency of Swarthmore College in Pennsylvania, which he transformed over the next twenty years with some of the ideas that the Rhodes Scholars discussed that day.

A few weeks after Aydelotte's visit, James Kerr, who had taken over from Thomas Lamb Eliot as president of Reed's trustees, came to Seattle with two Reed regents to interview Dick. That night, Mr. Kerr came out to the house to get a good look at the wife of the prospect. We were then invited down to Reed for three days in mid-February to be seen and to look the place over. I was pregnant at the time, just out to the point where nothing fit. Even though we had no money, I went out and bought two dresses, a coat, a hat, an umbrella, and a pair of shoes. I said to my husband, "If they don't choose you down there, I'm going to send them a bill for all of this."

The last evening of our visit there was a dinner at the Multnomah Hotel where we were staying, at which Dick made his prospective speech to the trustees and regents and their wives as to what he thought could be done at Reed College. Afterward, Dick and I retired with E. B. MacNaughton's wife, Gertrude, to the hotel mezzanine. Gertrude sat holding both our hands for half an hour while the pros and cons were weighed by the trustees and regents in the banquet room. Finally, they came out and said, "We would like you to come to Reed, Dr. Scholz."

We caught the late evening train to Seattle. I began to hemorrhage right on the train. There wasn't a doctor on board, so I just laid perfectly quiet until we got into Seattle the next morning. Dick called our doctor and he said, "Put your wife in a taxi and take her right home. Keep her in bed for five days and I'll be out." That was it. Everything quieted down, and at the end of five days I got up and we began packing for Portland. Dick wanted to start at Reed on the first of April to get his faculty lined up for the next year.

Meanwhile, somebody informed the regents that Dick had been quite a radical at the University of Washington and at UC Berkeley, where he had taught earlier. During the war, the socialist activist Anna Louise Strong had interviewed Dick for the *Seattle Labor Union Record* newspaper about what was going on in Europe. Dick had been all over Europe during his three years at Oxford. In 1914, we had gone together over to Berlin, where Dick worked under Eduard Meyer, the great German historian of antiquity, and visited his cousins there. Dick had watched the crisis building up in Europe very closely. Anna Louise Strong would come out to the house and take notes while Dick talked about places like Serbia and Croatia. Seattle then was very conservative in its thinking, and everybody was trying to find out who was suspect and who wasn't, even at the beginning of the First World War. Dick didn't care who heard what he said. Then, after the war, there came all the repercussions, including the Red Scare and the Seattle General Strike of 1919. The university was being investigated to no end at that time.

Mr. Kerr contacted someone who had graduated from the University of California and asked him to look into the rumors about Dick having been a radical there. The fellow wrote back a very crisp letter that said, "If the regents of Reed College don't know a scholar and a gentleman when they see one, they don't deserve a good president."

We got to Reed on the first of April. On the nineteenth of the month Dick started east by train to recruit new faculty. One of the first things he did when he got to Boston was to make William Foster's acquaintance. After that, every time Dick went east, he went to see Foster. They became very good friends.

Richard and Cheryl Scholz with three of their children, upon their arrival at Reed in 1921. Dicky, the oldest son, would graduate from the college in 1937.

EDITH MCDONALD '19, William Foster's personal secretary 1917–1923: Mr. Scholz came out to the Fosters' house in Boston for a long conversation about the college. Mrs. Foster later said, "It's just wicked what he's going into in that situation. They haven't even told him anything about the financial condition of the college. They'll kill him. He's an artist."

CHERYL SCHOLZ, wife of Richard Scholz: When Dick showed up as Reed's second president, there was a solid mass of alumni, students, and faculty who did not want yet another new experiment at a college that was just ten years old. They had their backs up before he got there. Dick brought with him an ideology that was totally different from Foster's, though the method was the same. Both of them operated out of John Dewey's textbook: define your problem, explain your terms, choose a course of action, examine the alternative choices, arrive at a conclusion, and act. Foster used this method to go at the here and now, to do what needed to be done in current affairs. For him, history provided some means of giving antecedents to what is happening now, but there was no philosophical scope to be found there. It was a very pragmatic approach.

Dick was not really living in the past; rather, he wanted to make the past work in the present. That was the point. The present was the important thing, but boy, did he know his past. He had been trained as an historian of antiquity, but his greater emphasis was upon modern Europe rather than the classical period. His one insistence in teaching history was, "Don't ever remember *when* a thing happened unless you know *why* it happened."

Dick was a very high-strung person, but he was such a humane person that that side of him never got taken out on anybody. He was very warm and kindly, but at the same time a man of deep emotional intensity, and that made living hard for him.

CLARENCE AYRES, philosophy and social ethics professor: Scholz had suffered acutely from the precision of American education. As a boy, he had gone from his Milwaukee home to the University of Wisconsin with a German zeal for learning. He was naturally bilingual and had taken to his high school classics with avidity. The university presented itself as an endless vista of delightful vocabularies, grammars, and pronunciations. He ate it up. His scholarship was distinguished. Phi Beta Kappa decorated his bosom.

His classical attainments marked him for appointment to the first bevy of Rhodes Scholars, and so he dropped into Oxford, a university without curriculum. It was a soul-blasting experience. The chosen product of the American system could prepare lessons, but he did not know how to read. What to do when there were no syllabi and no assignments was a complete mystery, and an intensely humiliating one. He learned, but he never forgot. From that moment it became his mission to teach his countrymen to study without blinders.

CHARLES MCKINLEY, political science professor 1918–1960: Oxford stood forever in Scholz's memory as his "great experience." It was a blossoming time for him. His mind opened out into all directions, developing a catholicity of interest and seeking a synthesizing view of life, which became a dominant trait of his personality. Oxford also meant the opportunity for travel and to meet the people of many countries and races. His interests in history broadened into the history of human culture, world politics, and the social problems covered by the term "internationalism."

CHERYL SCHOLZ, wife of Richard Scholz: After Foster left, there had been no faculty appointments made for a term of more than one year, so that a new president coming in would have a chance to appoint faculty members of his choosing. That was the saving grace as far as Dick was concerned, since he was able to select the faculty he wanted for his core humanities course. It was one of the greatest opportunities that ever came his way.

Dick's first stop on the train east was to sign up Dr. Edward Octavius Sisson for philosophy. Sisson had been among the founding faculty at Reed and was then president of the University of Montana. Dick continued on to the University of Wisconsin where he signed up Barry Cerf, whose work in the classics he was well familiar with, to teach the literature part of freshman humanitics. He brought Victor Chittick down from the University of Washington to cover sophomore literature for the second year of the humanities. Dick himself planned to teach the freshman history portion of the humanities. Clement Akerman, who had come to Reed from the University of Washington the year before Dick arrived, taught economics. Charles McKinley, a Foster hire, was already on campus teaching political science. He had been brought up at the University of Washington under the great political scientist Jay Allen Smith. Dick also brought in George Bernard Noble to the political science department. There were already very good scientific men on the faculty from the Foster era—Frank Loxley Griffin in mathematics, Lawrence Griffin in biology, Tony Knowlton in physics, and Ralph Strong in chemistry. Dick also brought in Arthur Scott, who would later serve as Reed's president, to work under Strong in chemistry. By that first autumn of 1921, Dick was ready to put together the first humanities course in the country to be required of all students at a college. It was exciting business from beginning to end.

CHARLES MCKINLEY, political science professor: Scholz earnestly tried to find an answer to the question, "What is the purpose of a college of liberal arts and sciences today?" He recognized that it could only be solved by an exacting process of experimentation, what he called a "trial-and-error" approach.

The experiment he proposed at Reed had three cardinal objectives. First, every student must be equipped to play an active and intelligent part in helping solve social problems. This was citizenship in the broadest sense of the term. Scholz felt that, relative to their numbers, college graduates come into possession of more social power than those whose formal education ceased with the secondary schools. They must understand what society is like and what its fundamental problems are. They must become socially minded.

Second, Reed must lay the basis for professional training. One who does not appreciate the social significance of his vocation does not possess a fully professional background for his work. But he must also have a wide knowledge of the relations that exist between his particular work and other types of vocational activity. Otherwise lawyers, doctors, engineers, and teachers are not really professionally minded, they are merely craftsmen with more or less skill.

Last, the college should strive with conscious purpose to give its graduates a keen sense of the richness of life. It should help them at the most crucial period of their lives to attain the art of living fully and richly with their minds and hearts. It is here that the curriculum must go beyond the vocational, beyond civic interests, and offer opportunities for learning those many things that give meaning and significance. Cardinal is that students should learn to understand their own natures. They should acquire habits of critical thinking, reading, intellectual curiosity, play, and wholesome and friendly social intercourse.

KENNETH LATOURETTE, history professor 1914–1916: Dick Scholz was a man of tremendous enthusiasm, with a conviction of what ought to be and a dream of what might be. What happened to Scholz didn't matter to him. It wasn't about him. He had a way of bringing you into it. He never led you on to share his enthusiasm, but frankly I did share it when he was trying to lure me back onto the faculty and he told me what it was he was trying to do. Being a historian, he wanted to get this whole thing centered around the history of what is taking place right now with the human race. His wasn't an enthusiasm for an intellectual experience that was remote from the current human social situation.

CHERYL SCHOLZ, wife of Richard Scholz: We would go out to dinner in Portland at times and hear people say that what Dick was doing at Reed was not the kind of college Simeon and Amanda Reed ever contemplated, that they had wanted a little technical school. Regardless, Dick went over very big in the Portland community. People just loved to talk with him. I always said about Dick that he had no table conversation at all, but all of a sudden you would find a whole dinner table absolutely quiet, listening to what he was saying to his neighbor beside him. Everything he was thinking about was exciting to him, and that made him an exciting teacher.

When Dick taught at the University of Washington, they had had a freshman in the Alpha Phi house one year who came home every noon talking about this course that she was taking. Finally one of the older girls sat her down and said, "I wish you'd tell me about this course. I've never heard of it or of the professor before, and here you come home every noon all lit up about it." The freshman said, "Well, I don't know what it is. The professor comes running into the room and he begins lecturing before he even gets to his desk. He talks for fifty minutes just as fast as he can go, and I haven't the slightest idea what he's talking about, but I just love him."

I always said to Dick that that was the most perfect description of his teaching.

ERNEST BOYD "E. B." MACNAUGHTON, trustee 1919–1941, 1955–1958, president 1948–1952:

Scholz was another man who, like Foster, was on fire with a new concept in liberal arts education, but with no experience with operating costs. He had been a classroom man, a magnetic teacher in his chosen field, but without any previous contact with administrative problems or dollar finance. He would come into the regents' meetings and start talking about his hopes for the college, and not stop until he had finished his professorial allowance of forty minutes. No one could understand him because he talked so fast. He didn't have any idea what the thing he was proposing was going to cost.

There were then two governing bodies at Reed—the Board of Trustees oversaw finances, and the Board of Regents oversaw operations of the college itself—and both were completely out of touch with Scholz's hopes and aspirations. They just didn't understand him. After the meetings were over, they would ask, "What in hell was the man talking about?"

CHERYL SCHOLZ, wife of Richard Scholz: The people on the regents board that were closest to Dick were the people that were more in the arts than in business—Albert Doyle, the Reed architect; Bud Selling, a local physician; and Mrs. Elliott Corbett, a member of a prominent Portland family. They understood him. As did the president of the trustees, James Kerr, who strongly supported Dick.

When Dick and I first came to Reed I felt that it was so small that nothing important could ever happen there, because I had only been to big universities before. But Dick's experience at Oxford had been one where everything was done in a small group—you were never conscious of the university itself at Oxford. It was all small business, conducted in a tremendous setting. That was how he approached Reed.

CHARLES MCKINLEY, political science professor: Oxford had meant for Scholz a time of

PART TWO: THE GOLDEN AGE, 1921–1945

rich and friendly fellowship. He had been something of a recluse at the University of Wisconsin. Compelled to work his way through college, and anxious to make every hour count in mastering the academic tasks set before him, he hadn't had time for cultivating friendships with his fellow students. Playing the piano had been a partial solace for this abnormal life, but it was not enough, and he fell victim to difficulties of health that he never completely shook off. At Oxford he enjoyed the comradeship of boys from all over the world, and came to feel intensely the sentiment of fellowship. Coming to Reed, Scholz wanted to intensify its sense of common life, to keep it small, and never to lose these values he felt to be so precious.

RICHARD JONES, history professor 1941–1982, 1985–1986: Integration was the watchword of the Scholz curriculum. Scholz's original proposed design would have required all freshmen to take six courses under the general heading "Man's Social and Biological Heritage." These were history of civilization to 1763; a course in general literature; another on political, social, or economic institutions; biology; mathematics or language; and then a choice of anthropology-psychology, physics, or chemistry.

Sophomore year would have required enrollment in the second year of the history of civilization since 1763, or in a course in either comparative literature or classical literature, and a set of requirements for literature, history, and social science majors different from those for majors in mathematics and natural sciences.

The last two years were devoted to specialized fields of study, with a required course in the junior year on citizenship and international relations, followed by a senior colloquium dealing with matters of general importance.

Scholz instituted a qualifying examination at the end of a student's junior year, and he carried over from Foster's era the senior thesis and final senior oral examination. He also advocated full-year courses in every field, organized to illuminate problems and issues common to the discipline as a whole rather than to fence off special semester segments for isolated examination.

Another application of the integration concept was the administrative reorganization of the college's departments into four divisions grouped around interrelated subjects: Literature and Language; History and Social Science; Mathematics and Natural Science; and Philosophy, Psychology, and Education. Though degrees continued to be awarded by departments, ultimate jurisdiction over student programs was expected to lie with the division. Course offerings were also subject to divisional discussion and approval, which was an important step in terms of curricular control.

CLARENCE AYRES, philosophy and social ethics professor: The opposition is always with us. For Scholz it was the men of the earlier harvest at Reed, the receivers of the wreck of the first adventure under Foster. After a year of planning, Scholz called a meeting in the spring of 1922 to present his proposals in full, and ran into something like a pitched battle.

The president schemed out his curriculum plan in pictorial form on the blackboard. But what was plain to the eyes of faith appeared loose and formless where inspiration was lacking. Doubts developed. Exposition warmed into heated argument. The chair waxed partisan. At the climax of the proceedings, one of the older men rose and, resolutely wiping the president's inscription from the board, proceeded to substitute his own notion of a properly rigorous education. The result: explosion! The meeting was adjourned upon an open fight.

Subsequently, Edward Octavius Sisson—a professor of philosophy and an academic diplomat with presidential experience at the University of Montana—took the politics out of the curriculum proposal and put it into action for trial by ordeal.

VICTOR CHITTICK, English professor 1921–1948: It was an awful struggle to get the curriculum plan set up, with weeks and weeks of acrimonious discussion. We spent hours and hours of debate, back and forth, with the claims of various departmental interests competing with one another. The science people always felt that they were being nibbled at more thoroughly than the other people. You not only had freshman humanities, but also humanities in the second year, which would take up the extra time they claimed as being needed for the science students. Scholz's idea of all students going straight through the first two years in a uniform enterprise of study was knocked in the head by the differentiation of course requirements in the second year between science and nonscience majors.

ELLEN KNOWLTON JOHNSON '39, recorder 1945–1962, registrar 1962–1981: Scholz did many good things, but he was also responsible for a severe split in the faculty that went beyond just differences of opinion. He very much downgraded the science faculty, and the venomous feelings that were left lasted for umpteen years. Many years later I was talking to Dr. Lawrence Griffin in biology, and he made a comment about Scholz that definitely criticized anything good that the man had done. It was that strong. I asked my father, Tony Knowlton, who taught physics at Reed, about it. Dad thought and thought, and finally he said, very quietly, "I never would have said that, but I cannot deny it."

CHERYL SCHOLZ, wife of Richard Scholz: It's probable that Dick didn't consult with the Faculty Council in the first few months about his curriculum. It was all new. He had talked to the trustees about what he wanted to do and they had said, "Well, you have a free hand." I was very

fond of the president of the trustees, James Kerr, but I can imagine him making a kind of ruthless decision on these matters. I don't think that Dick realized how important the Faculty Council was in the faculty's eyes. There may have been a sense among the faculty that something was being put over through trustee and presidential action.

Once Dick encountered opposition from the faculty, he went about preserving his vision as best he could. In the process there was certainly a gnawing away of his original curriculum plan. Most of it was explained in terms of the requirements of divisions for medical schools and for graduate work, but there may have been some resentment among existing faculty that continued.

VICTOR CHITTICK, English professor: When the curriculum finally was established, it was at the very best a compromise and, like all compromises, it wasn't too solidly welded together. For that reason, it was a little easier to give up this and that. You had two fixed elements to work with, time and staff. But largely, it was a matter of scheduling that did it. Getting enough work done to constitute a major, and also fitting in the teacher training. Reed had a terrific reputation for teacher education. Barring one other place in the United States, Reed at the time turned out more teachers than any other college, including the teacher's colleges for men. One summer someone came from the East to investigate why Reed turned out so many teachers when we gave practically no courses in education.

We gradually lost the outline of the curriculum that Scholz set up initially in 1921 and '22 with integrated courses the first two years and a free-wheeling last two years, although that nibbling took place so gradually during the 1920s that one did not feel particularly concerned with each little bit that went. It just seemed as though one condition after another enforced it, and there wasn't anything else to do.

MICHAEL MUNK '56: Despite Scholz's change in curriculum, Reed professors continued to be involved in local civic affairs, including the establishment of the Portland Labor College, whose mission was to educate workers to be more effective in their unions as well as in the general society. Reed political science professor Charles McKinley was a member of the college's original planning board. Operating out of the Portland Labor Temple, the college provided union workers with an understanding of the political, social, and economic issues of the times. Participating Reed faculty included E. O. Sisson, Clarence Ayres, Victor Chittick, Monte Griffith, George Noble, and Anton Friedrich. Even Richard Scholz taught a course there. Other than being reimbursed for their streetcar fare, the Reed professors all volunteered their time.

DOROTHY JOHANSEN '33, history professor 1934–1969, archivist 1969–1984: The Scholz program placed great emphasis on the development of character in the students. In their examination by the faculty committee, prospective students could be refused on the grounds that their character did not show promise of development.

VICTOR CHITTICK, English professor: Physics professor Tony Knowlton and I were both on the admissions examination committee in the 1920s. Student attendance had dropped off, and Mr. William Mead Ladd, the chairman of the regents board, came around and said we have to have students, so bend over backwards to get them, which we did. There was a disposition to do whatever we could to enroll a student, apart from lowering the standards on the aspects of educational achievements.

Blair Stewart '21, professor of economics, set up a measure of objective achievement for new applicants that gave us something pretty tangible to check them by. I've never been able to figure out, though, why we got an extra percentage of crackpots applying, but there undoubtedly were a number of crackpots among the people who got in.

Another kind of pressure was the Jewish element. They thought that they would feel more at ease at Reed, which had no quota systems like those at many other places. That on the whole was not an undesirable thing. The college was glad, and should have been glad, to get those Jewish students. Very few crackpots among them and a great many good students.

MARTHA POWELL WILSON '25: The first two years we had to take what they gave us, as we had no choice of subjects. Dr. Scholz wanted those first two years to be a whole description of life. Dr. Barry Cerf was head of classical literature. He and Dr. Scholz taught the history of civilization class. Dr. Cerf and Dr. Scholz would each lecture for an hour, and then we would gather in small groups and discuss their lectures. When Dr. Scholz was teaching the class, the bell would ring but no one would get up to leave, he was that interesting. Dr. Scholz could discuss any subject, and he was interested in everyone, not just one person, but everyone. When you talked with him, you realized he was really interested in you. And he played the piano beautifully. He was my model.

Reed was unusual because of the system of holding both lectures and conferences. I don't think there were any other schools that did that then, except for Swarthmore. Dr. Scholz spent six weeks at Swarthmore learning all about the college, and Swarthmore's president, Dr. Frank Aydelotte, in turn spent six weeks at Reed. They had been Rhodes Scholars together at Oxford, and as beginning presidents they wanted to make the programs of their respective schools similar.

There were about three hundred students on campus, a slight majority of which were men, with about 125 students in our freshman class. Four years later, there were only about thirty-five in our graduating class. The intellectual workload was heavy. There was a great percentage of students that didn't come back the second year. They went to bigger schools, or to schools that were not as difficult, like the University of Oregon. Reed wasn't easy. It was an unusual place in that we had professors who made you think, really think—something that you didn't have to do at a lot of colleges. I felt completely at home there. It was, as they say, the "Golden Age" of Reed.

FRANK LOXLEY "F. L." GRIFFIN, mathematics professor 1911–1952, president 1954–1956: You know the old wheeze that in a large institution you go more through college, and in a small institution college more goes through you? Well, it doesn't necessarily do so in a small place unless you give it a chance. Under the conference method that Scholz brought back with him from Oxford, a lot of college had the chance to not merely go through, but into, our students.

We had been a friendly group at Reed during Foster's time, but the sense of community—as having some real unified interest in a group of objectives that we should all be trying to move forward—largely evolved during the Scholz administration. We became what you might call a self-conscious entity. The term "Reed community" was coined by President Scholz.

HELEN THORSEN '24: All my friends from Lincoln High School in Portland who had started with me at Reed dropped out one by one. If you didn't make study your whole life at Reed, you might just as well not even try, because if you tried to do anything else, you were sunk.

We didn't talk about grades at Reed because we didn't see them. But we knew that if we didn't make our grades, we couldn't stay, and that was enough to keep me on the beam. I couldn't do

like I did in high school, where I had just barely squeaked through. There was no discussion of the Honor Principle at all, but we were all aware of the fact that it existed. If anyone cheated, they were out almost immediately.

I went to chapel every day. It was not terribly well attended. I'm not sure how many students were religious, as that was something that was usually a private matter. Someone would come in and read excerpts from the Bible and then give a little talk. A student named Lucille Burton would play the chapel's beautiful pipe organ.

From chapel we would go to lunch in the Commons. They had mostly student help there. Students came from all backgrounds. Some were very well fixed, and some were not. Reed seemed primarily interested in students working their way through. Those that were working their way through were not discriminated against at all by those who were not. One gal, Anna Skinkle Allen '24, had a place at the Ambassador Apartments. She brought her adopted daughter with her and a nanny. She never threw her weight around at all, and was just a wonderful person.

WILLIAM HELMS '23: I went to war right out of high school. When I returned to Portland the state of Oregon was giving veterans $200 for college, which opened my way to go to Reed. At Reed, I shared a dormitory room with another war veteran, John Calhoun Van Etten '21, on the second floor of House H. It had a sleeping alcove and a furnished study with a real wood-burning fireplace. The room rent was ninety dollars per semester. I believe the board in the Commons was six dollars per week. Nice table linen, silverware, and good food. It was the best life I had ever lived.

There was plenty of work for students. I became the operator of the power mower that kept the acres of the campus looking beautiful. The pay was thirty cents per hour. Residents living on the campus numbered about 150, or roughly

Formal dining in the Commons, soon after it was built in 1921. In the mid-1960s this building would become the Student Union.

half of the student body. Many students worked even though they did not need the money. There was a camaraderie that seemed to strengthen by working on the mopping crew of Herr Brunner the janitor or slinging hash in the Commons.

In June 1923, I received my degree. That was a hilarious week with practically round-the-clock celebrating. The big splurge was a trip up the Columbia River to the Royal Gorge Hotel, where we dined and danced.

MARTHA POWELL WILSON '25: Most students lived off campus like me and were called "day-dodgers." It took me about an hour and a half to get to school by streetcar. The people living on campus came from Idaho, Washington, Montana, and California, with only a few from the East.

After my first year, I just couldn't take the long commute, so I moved onto campus. To make money for my room and board I waited on tables in what was then the new Commons building, built in 1921. The servings were made up in the kitchen and put on plates, and the servers, who were called "hashers," carried them out to our assigned tables. They paid us thirty-five cents an hour. That covered dorm expenses and the expense of living on campus. President Scholz always had a dinner party for dorm students and daydodgers on Friday nights in the Commons with a guest speaker. Afterwards there would be dancing.

MARGARET MCGOWAN MAHAN '24: When I first started as a freshman in 1920, there were just three buildings on campus—the president's house, the administration building, later called Eliot Hall, and the dormitory. The dorm block was divided by the sally port, an arched passageway through the middle of the building, with the women housed at one end and the men at the other. The Commons dining hall then was at the end of the men's dorm, House H, now called Winch. Once the new Commons was built in 1921, we all ate there and held dances and social gatherings there. Four houses were built for faculty, also in the early '20s, in the holly grove along Woodstock Boulevard.

BENJAMIN WOODBRIDGE, JR. '36: My parents, Benjamin and Marguerite Woodbridge, came to Reed to teach from Rice Institute in Texas in 1922. We moved into one of the new, brown-shingled faculty houses on Woodstock Boulevard. Two of the faculty houses were double, so

we had six families living in the little complex.

Tony Knowlton in physics and his family had the single house nearest the library. He had three daughters, all of whom eventually attended Reed. One of them, Ellen Knowlton Johnson '39, later became the longtime registrar of the college. The next house was Rex Arragon in history and his family. They had two daughters who both later went to Reed. Then in one half of the next house was Victor Chittick in literature and his wife. In the other half of the house was Clement Akerman in economics and his wife. Neither the Chitticks nor the Akermans had children. Finally, in the big house, was Ralph Strong in chemistry.

Barry Cerf, who taught literature, lived with his wife and three children in one of the dorms on campus. President Scholz, who lived in the president's house, later known as "Prexy," had

Students who lived off campus—"daydodgers"—commuted to the college by streetcar.

PART TWO: THE GOLDEN AGE, 1921–1945

four children. His oldest son, Dick '37, went to Reed. Charles McKinley, in political science, lived nearby in Eastmoreland on Thirty-sixth Street. His son went to Reed. My sister Isabelle '38 and I both attended Reed. All of us kids had the run of the yards around the faculty houses and the holly grove behind it. We made quite a playground of the campus.

CHERYL SCHOLZ, wife of Richard Scholz: When Dick was at Oxford he had met Alexander Meiklejohn, who was there one year studying. They were very impressed by each other and became very good friends, for years following each other's experiments in higher education with great interest. Meiklejohn became president at Amherst College in 1912, but he had a rocky time implementing his innovations there, especially after his initial opposition to the First World War angered Amherst alumni. By 1923, his situation there was blowing up, and he was fired. He spent the next year traveling around the country, visiting colleges that were experimenting with different approaches to education.

In the spring of 1924, Dick invited him to Reed for six weeks to lecture students and to also hold a senior colloquium in philosophy. The colloquium was something Dick and E. O. Sisson, who taught philosophy, had been talking about doing since Dick came to Reed. Dick considered it the capstone of the student's intellectual experience. He wanted everybody to come up through the different disciplines and then get together in their senior year to find out what each one had to add or take away from the others in terms of a personal philosophy.

MORNING OREGONIAN, April 7, 1924: With his golf sticks on one arm and his tennis racket in a suitcase on the other, Dr. Alexander Meiklejohn, educator and author, and ex-president of Amherst, arrived in Portland late last night to begin a six-week visit at Reed College. Ousted from the presidency of Amherst last June because of his ultraliberal thought, Meiklejohn does not believe that the modern college is going to the dogs. He sees a great awakening ahead for education. "You have in this community," he said, referring to Reed, "the best attempt now being made in America, so far as I know, to make the college of tomorrow."

ALEXANDER MEIKLEJOHN, guest lecturer 1924–1925: The old structure of interpretation of human life is wrecked, it has lost its unity, it has lost its power. We don't know what to think about any of the essential features of our human experience. We are lost and mixed up and bewildered, and if you ask what is the matter with our young people, it is just because they know it in their bones, whether they know it with their minds or not, that we haven't got a gospel, a philosophy; we haven't, in the proper sense of the term, a religion to give them. We are lost in the maze of gathering together again the fragments of our experience, the theories of our life, the parts of our knowledge, and making out of them a scheme of life by which people may go on in some command of their old faith.

Our task at small colleges is to engage again the attempt to make a philosophy of life or a religion, if that is what you call it, a scheme of values, a settled belief, a formulation of questions, a feeling of enterprises and appreciations out of which human life may be made a significant and beautiful and splendid thing. A college should be a place in which every member of the community is attempting to understand what goes on in human life. Can we as communities that are engaged in the liberal enterprise of attempting to take all of human experience into some sort of unified understanding—can we take our communities, these little communities of a few hundred individuals, and fuse them altogether into some such single thing by which the whole community is dominated?

One question is how to get unity in the curriculum. A thing is understood only so far as it is unified. It makes no difference how much you carry it in your mind, it makes no difference how much information you have with regard to it, it makes no difference what you know about it. So far as our logicians have anything to tell us about the nature of thinking, their fundamental insight in ancient and modern times is this: To understand is to unify. One thing to be said about our modern curriculum so far as we find it lacking in unity is just this: it is not an instrument of understanding. It has become a thing of shreds and patches, a thing of departments and groups and interests and problems and subjects. A curriculum is a plan of teaching, a scheme of instruction only in so far as it is a unified thing.

CHERYL SCHOLZ, wife of Richard Scholz: As Meiklejohn was leaving Reed, he said to Dick, "You have been able to accomplish more in three years at Reed than I was able to accomplish at Amherst in eleven."

Right after Meiklejohn's departure, Dick's health began to fail him. He had been combating his health problems his entire three years at Reed. The first attack was at a board meeting in May of 1922, the year after he came to the college. Following that, it was pretty much of a struggle to get things done. In May of 1924, Dick had his appendix removed. Just after that, there was an incident that sprung up on campus regarding intervisitation between a boy and girl in the dorms. Boris Krichesky '26 had carried books to the third floor of the girls' dorm for Alice Rothwell '27. The two of them were very much in love, and very soon after that incident they eloped and got married. Dick held a big meeting that Dr. Bud Selling and some other members of the regents board had been invited to attend. In the midst of the meeting, Dr. Selling got up and said, "I'm sorry, I have to leave this meeting to take your president to the hospital."

CLARENCE AYRES, philosophy and social ethics professor: In the spring of 1924, a fundraising drive had been launched, with begging committees descending upon the affluent citizens of Portland. Academic panhandling is a delicate business. At once, the old suspicions of the college began to smolder defensively. It was discovered that certain professors had been lecturers at the Workers' Party Hall. Communism!

REGINALD "REX" ARRAGON, history professor 1923–1962, 1970–1974: The Portland Chamber of Commerce voted to investigate Reed because of lectures given by faculty members to a club with Marxist beliefs at the Workers' Party Hall downtown. A faculty debate was held on the matter, the high point being Professor McKinley's comment regarding those who would welcome the inquiry. "Some gentlemen here wish to clear their skirts," he said. The chamber's inquiry was not welcomed by the college, and the chamber did not pursue the investigation.

CLARENCE AYRES, philosophy and social ethics professor: Another crisis developed that spring of 1924 when some locals declared that female smoking was countenanced at Reed. Tyranny over the young was as remote as Greenland to Scholz's program. He had supported student self-government, but endowments had to be got. He got prematurely out of bed after a major operation, and, sadly, asked the girls to cooperate for the sake of larger things. The girls accepted, but it rankled.

The final crisis that spring came over smallpox vaccination. The heavens thundered that the students must be vaccinated. But to thunder at adolescents is a mistake. It only puts their backs up. And up they went. A situation developed on campus that culminated in a flare of insubordination. The older members of the faculty, always sensitive to "faculty prerogative," pressed the issue. The Student Council, vested with jurisdiction by constitutional right, stood its ground, supported by the opinion of the younger faculty, and what began in casual insubordination ended in a long-drawn battle over the merits of student self-government. The ancient suspicion whirled about undergraduate wickedness as a vortex. Specific charges of moral abandonment were made. The campus seethed. Finally the Student Council completed an encyclopedic and reassuring report upon student morals with a cooperating faculty committee made up primarily of younger professors, and presented it to the full faculty for approval as a fundamental policy in treating the undergraduate as an adult.

President Scholz rose prematurely from a second operation to attend the vote. It was his last important scene. After a brief interval, commencement, and the continuous burden of the endowment fundraising effort, he went back to the hospital for a third operation from which he did not recover.

Richard Scholz's experiment with a new curriculum was cut short by his death in 1924.

MORNING OREGONIAN, July 24, 1924: Dr. Richard F. Scholz, president of Reed college and an educator of national reputation, died yesterday morning at 7:35 o'clock at St. Vincent's Hospital, as a result of a series of diseases and ills that have kept him an invalid for several months. Dr. Scholz was in a state of coma for the greater part of the night.

In poor health for several years, he went to St. Vincent's Hospital for an appendicitis operation, which was performed May 12. Following this came a second operation, then on July 12, a third. The cause of the last operation was obstructing jaundice, according to his family physician, Dr. Thomas M. Joyce. Dr. Scholz sank rapidly after the third operation, then on Sunday commenced to improve. Friends, relatives, and medical men thought that he had a chance for life, but on Monday he suffered a relapse and sank into a state of coma. The direct cause of death, Dr. Joyce announced, was general exhaustion.

ALTA SMITH CORBETT, regent 1919–1939: Some considered Dr. Scholz aggressive or radical in educational matters, but they did not fully understand his attitude. He believed that the student should be well rounded in his equipment, so that when he went out from Reed he would not be "at sixes and sevens" but would be well balanced and able to cope with situations as they arose in the outside world.

CHERYL SCHOLZ, wife of Richard Scholz: A friend of Dick's came to see him between his last two operations in the summer of 1924, when we were home finally. He said it was the most exciting afternoon he had ever spent, because Dick could see way into the future of what he was doing, why he was doing it, and what it could mean to educational values in the world. Dick realized that someone like a Hitler could come about because we had not yet arrived at a humane outlook following the devastation of the war.

CHAPTER 7

The Faculty Takes Control

*Another college has been drawn back from the path of Bolshevism by the enlight-
ened authority of a board of regents.*
—*Harvard Crimson*, January 10, 1925

The trustees failed to advise us of the "kangaroo" status of the Faculty Council.
—Charles McKinley, political science professor

The sudden death of Richard Scholz in 1924 left the college at a critical cross-
road without a leader. The Reed faculty—made up of Scholz appointees and Foster holdovers—was locked in an ideological standoff over Scholz's proposed new
curriculum. Meanwhile, Reed remained in a state of financial uncertainty, its
fundraising efforts hampered by lingering local suspicions of the college as a haven for atheists and radicals. In appointing a new president, the regents and trustees were split over whether to search for another innovative educator to carry
forth Scholz's plan, or to look for a more conventional leader who would attempt,
for the sake of fundraising, to rein in Reed's heterodoxy and move the college toward something resembling normalcy.

What happened next would fundamentally alter the trajectory of Reed College. No longer overshadowed by the visionary personalities of Foster and Scholz,
a cadre of senior professors closed ranks and began invoking the powers over
internal affairs that had been assigned them by William Foster's constitution in
1915. In quick order, they consolidated the innovations of Foster and Scholz and
forged them into a rigorous curriculum and classroom experience that solidified
the college's early promise.

REGINALD "REX" ARRAGON, history professor
1923–1962, 1970–1974: Richard Scholz's tragic
death quickly revived the earlier curricular controversy among the Reed faculty. Informal cau-
cusing for representation on the Faculty Council
began immediately.

Those of us in the Scholz camp, joined by a
number of the students, openly urged the ap-

106   PART TWO: THE GOLDEN AGE, 1921–1945

pointment of Alexander Meiklejohn, the former president of Amherst College, who had generated considerable intellectual excitement on campus earlier that spring as a guest lecturer. The other side was apparently grooming their own candidate, Norman Coleman, a former member of Reed's faculty who had taught English under Foster.

DAVID COLEMAN '60: Norman Coleman, my grandfather, spent several months in the spring of 1924 touring Japan with his family and assessing the sentiment of the Japanese people toward America. My father, Francis Coleman '29, who was on the tour with him, was about to enter Reed that coming fall as a freshman. On July 29, near the end of the long trip, a telegram arrived in Tokyo from the trustees of the college announcing the sudden death of President Scholz. Before even opening the message, Grandfather said to my father, "They will be wanting me to take the presidency."

DOROTHY JOHANSEN '33, history professor 1934–1969, archivist 1969–1984: Unlike the president of the trustees board, James Kerr, who had championed the efforts of Richard Scholz, William Mead Ladd, who chaired the regents board that oversaw the college's educational policies, could never understand the Scholz program. When he first joined the Board of Trustees in 1910, Ladd had told Thomas Lamb Eliot that what the city of Portland would need from Reed College would be generals and leaders. This had been largely why, at the start of the college, William Foster immediately put in the community extension courses around Portland.

The tensions that subsequently developed between the two governing boards and the faculty during the 1920s were borne out in great part by the college's deviation from what Ladd and some board members originally assumed to be the purpose of the college.

ERNEST BOYD "E. B." MACNAUGHTON, trustee 1919–1941, 1955–1958, president 1948–1952: The boards were oftentimes provoked and ruffled, but not being competent to openly oppose the faculty of brilliant teachers at Reed, they thought they had better stay with the ship. As time passed, though, the attitude of the boards hardened into a critical point of view against many of the things that the college did.

RICHARD JONES, history professor 1941–1982, 1985–1986: A few weeks after Scholz's unexpected death, James Kerr led the board to a unanimous vote requiring that whoever became Reed's third president would be bound to carry on the Scholz program. Kerr was sensitive to Norman Coleman's indifference to it, and therefore opposed to his appointment.

After months of a board standoff, regents president William Mead Ladd called for a vote on Coleman's candidacy while Kerr was out of the state on a business trip. Coleman received a majority of votes of the two boards to become Reed's next president. Informed that a substantial majority of the Faculty Council had advised against his appointment, Coleman responded with confidence that he could always deal satisfactorily with colleagues who treated him to such candor. Coleman's appointment was officially announced to the Reed community in the *Morning Oregonian* on December 2, 1924.

CHERYL SCHOLZ, widow of Richard Scholz, dean of women 1924–1937, history professor 1938–1943, dean of admission 1943–1945: The faculty who had come up under Mr. Foster already knew Coleman, but those Dick had brought in were very bitter about his appointment. The thing that devastated them was that all of the work on Dick's curriculum was going to be lost. Having Coleman succeed to the presidency was what they most feared. Then, through a coup announced in the newspaper, they got him.

FRANCES BERRY '24, editorial, *REED COLLEGE QUEST*, December 20, 1924: You wonder, you men of experience and maturity on the regents board, why we of the younger generation in our quest for liberalism and our reëvaluation of old standards so frequently overshoot our marks, and let passion outrun judgment. You wonder why we become what you are pleased to term "Bolshevists." If you will look back over the events of the past week, you will find a clear example of the thing that makes the younger generation distrust the older.

You were taking a step that concerns us—faculty and students—as vitally and intimately as it does you. You were selecting a leader whose success as an educator depends largely on our cooperation. You have assumed that there is only one body deserving of consideration in a liberal college—namely, yourselves. We maintain that there are three—regents and faculty, who are the financial and educational leaders respectively, and the student body, who, in all fairness, should have a share in the formation of the spirit and policies of the college.

On every count except that of money, the opinion of the faculty is deserving of first consideration. It is they who make a college what it is. It is upon their cooperation that the success of the president depends. It is to them that we are indebted for whatever inspiration and leadership we receive. It is in them that we put our confidence and with them that we will cooperate. Therefore a disregard of their wishes and their judgment, is, to us, supreme idiocy.

HARVARD CRIMSON, "Retro Santanas!" January 10, 1925: Another college has been drawn back from the path of Bolshevism by the enlightened authority of a board of regents. The death of Richard Scholz, its late president, gave the opportunity for the business interests of Portland, entrenched in the regents board, to deflect the college from its doubtful toying with ideas. . . .

The new president, Mr. Norman Coleman, was leader of the wartime movement to oust the IWW from mines and lumber camps. He is a stalwart defender of the political and social dogmata of the chamber of commerce, and accepts as his standard the businessman's stamp of OK. His constant care will be to purge Reed College of its liberal fevers. . . .

From henceforth Reed College must play, in the educational sphere, a respectable if uninspired and totally mediocre role.

DAVID COLEMAN '60: Norman Coleman, my grandfather, was born on a farm in Ontario. He earned his undergraduate degree in English literature at the University of Toronto, and then taught high school English for many years in Spokane, Washington, before accumulating enough savings to attend Harvard University, where he earned his master's degree. He was recruited to Reed by William Foster in 1912 from Whitman College, where he was a tenured professor in English literature. After teaching at Reed for eight years, Grandfather left in 1920, shortly after Foster departed, to serve as president of the Loyal Legion of Loggers and Lumbermen in Portland. The "Four Ls," as it was known, was an alliance of timber men in the woods and the mills that tried to achieve labor peace in the turbulent times just after World War I. Although the group was characterized by some as a "company union," Grandfather enjoyed his role as a facilitator and peacemaker. It also gave him the chance to get out into the backwoods of Oregon and Washington, armed with only an overnight bag and a rod for trout fishing.

Over six feet tall and handsome with an olive-colored complexion, Grandfather was "Lincolnesque" in both physique and demeanor, and had a quiet reserve and a cryptic sense of humor. His deep and mellow baritone voice carried well when he taught or presented lectures. He continued teaching during his presidency, offering

PART TWO: THE GOLDEN AGE, 1921–1945

a course in freshman composition, which he had originally established in Reed's first decade. The Reed tradition of writing frequently, particularly in the freshman humanities courses, can be attributed in part to him.

MARTHA POWELL WILSON '25: Norman Coleman was nothing like Dr. Scholz. He wasn't very personal. Not the kind of person you could easily butter up to.

NORMAN COLEMAN, president 1925–1934: Evidence that the mythmaking impulse was already at work, students had begun to talk of the old days of the college when men were of heroic stature. "There were giants in those days." As to whether present-day Reed students were of poorer quality than those who helped to make the earlier history of the college, it so happened that all four Reed students who had been Reed's first Rhodes Scholars were students in my classes in English. I can testify that as undergraduates they showed natural student weaknesses and made natural student mistakes. My impression was that there were students at Reed College in the 1920s of as good ability as they had showed in the 1910s.

Yet there was a difference, a difference unfavorable to the later student generation. It arose not from a decline in individual power, but from a decline in group morale. Students of the '20s were enveloped in an atmosphere of perplexity and disillusionment, very different from the atmosphere of hope and confidence that sustained the students ten or twelve years before.

REX ARRAGON, history professor: Coleman had been president for little more than three months before a crisis erupted over the curriculum. The Faculty Council proposed to create a general science introductory course for literature and social science students. Coleman opposed the initiative, citing budgetary limitations. He also

Former faculty member Norman F. Coleman was appointed president of the college in 1925.

expressed his unwillingness to press the regents for money for other purposes.

Charles McKinley, who taught political science, resigned from the Faculty Council in protest that the council's role in curricular and budgetary matters was being threatened by the president. Coleman—who championed uniformity against the division of Reed into two colleges, arguing that unity was not necessarily unanimity—sought to get McKinley to withdraw his resignation. But since Coleman clearly did not recognize faculty control of curricular policy, McKinley refused. I was then elected to take McKinley's place on the council.

It quickly became clear that there had been a change in the style of the presidency, in both color of language and warmth of personality. Literature professor Barry Cerf gave the baccalaureate address that year. The speech was a celebration of the Scholz catalog, stressing that

Faculty leaders Lawrence Griffin, Tony Knowlton, and F. L. Griffin were aligned with President Coleman, a former colleague from the Foster era, in the curriculum battles that ensued following the death of President Scholz.

success in nonprofessional life—that of the individual with himself, his family, and his community—was the prime object of the liberal college. Cerf called on such qualities as critical spirit and breadth of understanding, with a goal of freedom without license, as unrealizable in full as that might be.

Four days later, Coleman delivered his inauguration address on the topic of the college as a community. He pointed to the cleavages in the faculty as due to specialized training and interests, and noted that his approval of student government and of faculty participation in college governance were both qualified as operating within limits.

NORMAN COLEMAN, **inaugural address, June 11, 1925:** Colleges were originally by their name understood to be communities, groups of colleagues organized for purposes of study. In the twelfth and thirteenth centuries when they were first developed, they were also held together by pressure from without, for there were frequent conflicts of gown with town—in fact, whole colleges often migrated from one city to another

to escape from hostile citizens and tyrannous officials. In modern colleges there is less cohesion within and less pressure without, but the problem of developing real community life is apparent.

The widespread criticism of the college in the present day focuses upon its lack of definite aim and unified effort. In particular, these charges are laid against college faculties. In these days of high specialization, college teachers are specialists, each one devoted to his own department, his own subject, his own branch of his subject. Out of this division flows all manner of interdepartmental jealousy and wirepulling, each department fighting to protect its own territory from encroachment. I recall Balzac's satirical picture of the German scholar who selects one spot in the field of knowledge and proceeds to dig and dig and dig, until, at the end of a number of years, what you find at the bottom of a deep hole is not truth, but one German.

REX ARRAGON, **history professor:** The day after the inauguration a group of us, declaring ourselves "the Diehards," held a picnic. The title was half jocular, but nonetheless significant as a symbol for our loyalty to Scholz and his program. The group was comprised not just of those in letters and social sciences, but also included Ralph Strong and Arthur Scott from chemistry.

RICHARD JONES, history professor: Norman Coleman was a conciliator rather than an innovator, a conductor who sought to harmonize various institutional objectives rather than a leader with a well-defined vision of what the college should be. He wished to inject a dose of piety into what was already known in local conservative circles as "godless Reed."

Faculty opposition to Coleman's initiatives was led by political scientist Charles McKinley, with McKinley emerging at every point the winner. Appointed by Foster in 1917, McKinley's scholarly pursuits and civic interests were precisely those Foster would have approved of; however, he was also captivated by Scholz's ideals, the more so because of his impatience with conventional disciplinary boundaries. Though his battles with Coleman usually concerned budgetary and administrative matters, McKinley's under-

lying objective was preservation of what he considered to be basic to the Scholz curriculum.

Humanists and social scientists on the faculty were generally on his side. The opposition was led by F. L. Griffin in mathematics, A. A. Knowlton in physics, and Lawrence Griffin in biology, whose friendship with Coleman dated back to their time on the Foster faculty. Mingled respect for their opponents and appreciation of effective political strategy encouraged McKinley and his "Scholz block" to always include one or more of the opposition on the Faculty Council through manipulation of the vote, which they managed. E. O. Sisson, who had left the college after serving under Foster and then returned at the request of Scholz, had the position of a sympathetically neutral elder statesman.

REX ARRAGON, history professor: In the spring of 1926 a special committee of faculty—Tony Knowlton, Lawrence Griffin, E. O. Sisson, Charles McKinley, Victor Chittick, and myself—took up the matter of curriculum. We agreed to retain the general framework of the Scholz curriculum, but to make it viable and lasting by

Those opposed to President Coleman—"the Diehards"—felt strongly that the faculty should maintain control over curricular policy. Leaders of this group included Charles McKinley and Rex Arragon. E. O. Sisson, right, functioned as a neutral arbiter.

simplification and flexibility. While the pursuit of a non-science major normally began in the junior year, in the science departments this decision was expected in sophomore year, and sometimes even freshman year. That could result in a more pre-professional tone in the sciences.

The freshman requirements in the history of civilization and its correlative, literature of the ancient world, were consolidated into companion courses with integrated sessions of art and philosophy. A required course in contemporary society was established for the sophomore year. The reading requirement in either French or German was retained. The flexibility was in the science requirement. Instead of a required freshman course in biology, two courses in science were required during the first two years from a list including biology, chemistry, physics, mathematics, and a proposed science survey course, which did not remain long in the curriculum. Psychology was added to the list later, as it was a question at the time whether it was a natural or social science.

Coleman opposed the changes, but withdrew his opposition once the Faculty Council indicated that it was willing to issue a strong vote against him.

MARY BARNARD '32: One thing that I felt was a boon as a student was the general science course. Of course, the science professors all hated it because the only people who took general science were girls who were majoring in literature. I don't think there was ever a time when the subjects of history, literature, and languages were so much women's subjects. Men did take them, or rather they endured them, but they tended to major in science, economics, or political science, all of which were greatly emphasized at the time. There were almost no male students majoring in literature or languages. Literature and poetry writing were more feminine things. Real men didn't do things like that.

MARIAN NEDRA WHITEHEAD '44: They put the science students in the Contemporary Society course, which had so many weeks of sociology, so many weeks of political science, and so many weeks of economics. But instead of having lots of people in the course who were interested in those particular fields, we were all scientists. Which meant that they had a terrible time getting people to talk, interact, or express ideas.

FRANZ FRIEDRICH '50: My father, A. Anton Friedrich, had been recruited to Reed by Richard Scholz to teach economics. He was no flaming radical but he did believe that one could have a rational discussion about alternative economic policies, even with those with whom one disagreed. He assigned his students to do research into the role of labor unions, and not surprisingly, some of them came to the conclusion that President Coleman's former organization, the Loyal Legion of Loggers and Lumbermen, was a "company" union—a union run by a company or the government and not an independent trade union. When President Coleman got wind of this research project, he was so enraged that he was heard to declare, referring to my father, "Either he goes or I go." Needless to say, it was my father who left.

REX ARRAGON, history professor: There was a difference of opinion with Coleman over the roles of the president and the faculty in policy and personnel decisions. A crucial case came up in the spring of 1926 regarding a salary increase for the economics professor Anton Friedrich, who was returning to Reed from a leave for graduate study. The Faculty Council approved it, but the president did not. In accordance with the faculty constitution, we resorted to holding a special joint committee of faculty and regents to resolve the impasse. It was the first time this was done at Reed. E. B. MacNaughton represented the regents. He proposed a budgetary solution, but Coleman refused. MacNaughton naturally accepted Coleman's judgment, but in terms that sounded like a threat to Coleman. He reminded him of his presidential responsibility, adding that if he failed in it, he was out. From that point on, the president's authority was definitely weakened.

RICHARD JONES, history professor: Early in 1927, Coleman felt prepared to make a frontal assault on the faculty with a drastic curricular revision. Groundwork had been laid in discussions of severe budgetary problems, always an influential consideration in determining curricular policy at Reed. Student enrollment, which had hovered around three hundred during the Scholz years, was steadily increasing toward four hundred in the late '20s to generate needed revenue. The student-faculty ratio had risen from the college's ideal of ten-to-one during Scholz's years to nearly eighteen-to-one, with a consequent abandonment of most Independent study offerings, and a quadrupling of the number of graduate assistants.

Under severe budget constraints, Coleman was ready to propose the addition of pre-professional programs as a means of encouraging more applicants for admission and as a measure of fulfilling the terms of Amanda Reed's will, which he felt to be violated by the Scholz design for a liberal college. Under his plan, tuition income would be increased while the college would be restored to its original form and purpose.

REX ARRAGON, history professor: Coleman pointed to the need to "educate" trustee president James Kerr and other board members on his proposal in a regent-faculty committee meeting. At the meeting, Kerr asked if the provision in Amanda Reed's will for the "increase and diffusion of practical knowledge among the citizens" was being lived up to at Reed. Since Kerr was a lawyer, the question of a pre-law pro-

gram at Reed under Coleman's new plan came up. To my surprise, Coleman began to explain that there already was such a program at Reed and tried to describe it, pointing to political science, which could scarcely be called a program. Kerr then asked two of the regents present who were also lawyers what they had majored in at college. All, including Kerr, had majored in literature and languages. Kerr magisterially concluded that there was no problem with the fulfillment of the terms of Amanda Reed's will by the college's current humanistic curriculum. With that, Coleman's plans for pre-professional training ended.

E. O. Sisson and I left the meeting wondering if Kerr had actually set Coleman up just to tease him, since Coleman had not been Kerr's choice for the presidency.

CHERYL SCHOLZ, dean of women: Reed was always understaffed. Besides the janitor, Herr Brunner, and the president, the only administrative officer was the business manager, Alexander McGowan. It wasn't until after the Second World War that the president at Reed College got any administrative help. It was unbelievable what he had to carry. That was hard. There was never enough money for sufficient faculty to make the thing go. And nobody seemed to be very diligent about going out and getting money.

During Coleman's administration, the new president at Carleton College in Minnesota came to visit Reed. He told everybody that the first thing he had done when he got to Carleton was to put the college $100,000 into debt, because he had seen all the things that were needed. The same thing had happened at Dartmouth. These men were unafraid. Everybody at Reed went around with their jaws open for days afterward, because at Reed it was just the opposite. The trustees were all afraid. The college was always in hot water of all kinds with the community, with the old-timers in town sitting back and saying, "Well, this wasn't the kind of thing the Reeds envisaged anyway, so it's all wrong." That was a recurring theme for a long, long time.

FRANK LOXLEY "F. L." GRIFFIN, mathematics professor 1911–1952, president 1954–1956: A student group called "the Hecklers" brought a red-hot Soviet advocate named Albert Weisbord to campus to speak. Weisbord had been the leader of the Passaic textile strike. He ran true to form, declaring: "Democracy is bunk; in Russia we give them what is good for them, and if they protest, we hold a pistol to their head."

Students asked Weisbord what he thought of the Loyal Legion of Loggers and Lumbermen, the organization that President Coleman had headed up to bring understanding and agreement to the lumber industry. Weisbord replied, "We are not interested in conciliation. We want to develop a well-trained army of workers who will know how to run their business through the throats of their oppressors." You could just see the Reed students shrink back in dismay and horror.

Of course Reed was promptly pounced on by people in town for letting an organizer for the Communist Party speak at the college. "The sooner Reed is closed and its endowment is put to some constructive use, the better it will be for Portland," said a prominent Portland capitalist.

E. B. MACNAUGHTON, trustee: At the time of Scholz's unfortunate death, we had an endowment campaign going that had raised $400,000, so we thought we were off to a good start. The feeling on the board was that we ought to have a president who would orient us once again to the downtown community, and who would not try to feed new ideas to them so quickly that they couldn't digest or accept them.

Norman Coleman had been an original member of the faculty, and he had made a pretty good record for himself since leaving Reed as head of the Loyal Legion of Loggers and Lumbermen. He seemed like he might be the man.

Then again, he was an unfortunate choice, because like Scholz he had never been anything but a classroom man—he had never gone through the lower chairs of administrative office in a college operation. He was full of good ideas and high ideals, but as naïve as a babe in the woods about the practical side of creating an atmosphere with downtown Portland.

The Board of Regents had been created by the trustees upon Foster's resignation in 1919 to roll up their sleeves and raise money. We were also naïve, and largely unadvised of the depth of the opposition in the community, which we quickly plumbed and found was serious. One day my fellow regent, Mrs. Elliott Corbett, and I went to call on Eric Hauser, who had come to Portland to live. Hauser had made his money running construction on Jim Hill's Great Northern Railway and the New York subway. He was also owner at the time of the Multnomah Hotel in Portland. Mrs. Corbett and I went to the hotel to see him. He sat in the hotel lobby patiently listening to us. We thought that if we got $1,000 it would be a strike. After we had made our pitch, he just quietly said, "I'll give you $10,000."

Mrs. Corbett and I almost fell out of our chairs! It turned out that Eric Hauser had as his attorney Jim Kerr, president of the Board of Trustees, and Mr. Kerr had been softening him up and sheltering him from the poison that was spread around every corner to prejudice people against Reed.

It did seem to be a persistent campaign, not only among the high-society people, who, as some sort of social prestige, were sending their children back East because they thought it was the only place that anyone could get an education, but also among the churches in town. Hauser's donation eventually grew to $100,000, and went toward the construction of the Hauser Memorial Library on campus.

Librarian Nell Unger, at the desk in the foreground, helped to design the new Hauser Memorial Library, built in 1930.

MARY BARNARD '32: When we received word of Mr. Hauser's gift to build a new library, there was more grumbling than rejoicing among the students. Why, when the college desperately needed money for more important things, did we have to have a "new shack" instead? When the "shack" was finished and opened, we found it rather impressive but unfriendly compared to the former library, which had been on the first floor of Eliot Hall. There seemed to be so much uninhabited, unused, echoing space. The nighttime student librarian, Dorothy O. Johansen '33, soon began entertaining us with stories of a spook who lived in the empty tower room, a Phantom of the Library as it were.

REX ARRAGON, history professor: By the spring of 1928 faculty dissatisfaction with President Coleman's handling of financial matters reached a boiling point. The Board of Trustees, who were the financial managers of the college, usually sent down a maximum budget figure for the Board of Regents and the president with a slight increase from year to year. The president and faculty were to fit the pattern to the cloth with the solace of a possible supplementary budget in the fall if tuition income warranted. Coleman continued in his unwillingness to take an initiative with the trustees and regents for improving the financial situation. The faculty finally took action and drafted a five-year budget, voting to set salaries and pensions as the two main budget priorities. Coleman formally accepted it in principle.

CLEMENT AKERMAN, economics professor 1920–1943: The faculty had their greatest control at the time of Mr. Coleman's administration.

CHAPTER 8

Building the Citadel

"Don't get the crazy idea that because you are graduating and have a thesis, that you know anything. Because you really don't." They went to great lengths to establish that idea by intellectually beating the hell out of you.
—Wilbur L. Parker '36

You were pretty much on your own. . . . I saw situations where kids were really going haywire because they couldn't handle the stress.
—Harold "Jim" Jambor '35

A campaign mounted early in Norman Coleman's administration increased Reed's endowment from $1.2 million to $1.7 million; the financial situation, how-ever, remained dire, exacerbated by the Great Depression. The college's operating budget in the early 1930s was $165,000 for four hundred students. By comparison, Swarthmore College in Pennsylvania operated on a budget of $785,000 for five hundred students. To meet financial demands, the college continued to increase enrollment during the 1930s, further stretching an already thin faculty.

President Coleman offered no new initiatives, programs, or reorganizations after finding his initial efforts at institutional change rebuffed. Instead, thirteen senior professors, out of a faculty twice that size, exerted through force of per-sonality and constitutional right a level of authority over educational program-ming and budgetary matters that exceeded the degree of control exercised by the faculty at any similar college.

Beleaguered by persistent local hostility, this faculty oligarchy turned the college inward, away from the progressive activism of Foster and the responsible citizenship promulgated by Scholz, to a single-minded pursuit of learning for learning's sake. This new purpose showed little interest in student well-being, local issues in Portland, or public opinion. Pressures to accommodate changes from the outside environment, both social and educational, were likely to be viewed as detrimental to the college's academic mission.

CHERYL SCHOLZ, dean of women 1924–1937, history professor 1938–1943, dean of admission 1943–1945: After President Scholz died, Rex Arragon took on teaching his freshman history course as part of the joint history-literature humanities courses so central to the new curriculum. He and Barry Cerf, who taught the literature portion, started out being pretty friendly. The trouble with Rex was that he always began to know the business of others better than they did, and sooner than they did too. He was quite a brilliant person. Before long, he probably knew more about Greek literature than Barry did.

REGINALD "REX" ARRAGON, history professor 1923–1962, 1970–1974: In my taking up Scholz's role of teaching freshman history the rediscovery of the ancient and medieval works brought me back to classical literature, and for the first time to medieval poetry and more gradually to art. For the next quarter of a century, through the late 1920s, '30s, and '40s, I developed more or less consciously my view of learning and of *humanitias.*

MARSH CRONYN '40, chemistry professor 1952–1989, provost 1982–1989: Reed was operated at the time like the British system, with one professor for each of the two required freshman courses that made up the humanities: Rex Arragon in history and Barry Cerf in literature. The other faculty members in the two courses were the equivalent of readers in the British system; Arragon and Cerf gave the lectures and they supervised the conferences.

Dorothy Johansen '33 was my conference director. She was great at facilitating the discussion, taking on compulsive talkers without insulting them or allowing them to keep us from doing our business.

HARLOW LENON '35: In Reginald Arragon's freshman history we started out with Ur of the Chaldees, the town in the Hebrew Bible where Abraham was supposedly born, and we went through all the permutations of Babylon and its various regimes, and finally Assyria, Persia, and then Greece. Arragon was big on Greece, and big on Plato and Socrates and the Stoics. After we got through the Greeks, he brought us into medieval thought and neo-Platonism, a body of knowledge that involved some Plato and a good deal of mysticism. It also gave rise to a medieval controversy over the nature of what were called "universals" in metaphysics—general or abstract qualities and characteristics that individuals may share. Are universals real or are they nominal? Do they actually exist in individuals or are they only in people's minds? We had an enormous amount of stuff like that to talk about and to read about, and we just talked endlessly about notions of that kind.

Barry Cerf was a short little man who had the appearance of a Roman senator, hairstyle and all. He was dynamic, cynical, and eloquent, and he knew most all of the world's literature. His approach was like Arragon's, teaching not just the history of world literature, but the history of Western civilization. We started in freshman literature with the *Iliad* and the *Odyssey*, went through the Greek plays—Aeschylus, Sophocles, Euripides, Aristophanes—then on to Virgil's *Aeneid.* Cerf was good because he apparently believed in nothing, although he enjoyed talking about the Book of Job, which is the book of the Bible that deals with the problem of evil. Our conclusion was that, while Barry Cerf believed in evil, he didn't believe that there was any solution or any way out of it, that this was inherently an evil existence.

After we finished the argument about the nature of morality and the cosmos, Cerf called to our attention the recent discovery by the astronomer Edwin Hubble that the universe was expanding. Up until at least the late 1920s everybody thought that the Milky Way was the entire universe. Nobody knew that there were, in fact, other galaxies, let alone several hundred billion galaxies. Our minds were completely blown by how our conventional notions of religion and destiny, God, and the nature of society had been distorted by the idea of an expanding universe.

DOROTHY GILL WIKELUND '29: Students would take problems of all sorts to the faculty in those days. It really felt as if they were substitute parents, or even closer than parents sometimes, because you talked with them about things that you wouldn't talk with your parents about. It was a very close relationship. In the early years there was always a line outside Barry Cerf's door of students waiting to see him.

MARY BARNARD '32: Sometimes a small group of students would assemble in the evening to hear Barry Cerf read Homer aloud in Greek. I had had no idea of taking Greek until I heard the sound of him reading one line of Homer in his resonant voice. He was an inspiring teach-

Classics professor Barry Cerf taught the literature portion of the early humanities program.

er when he was dealing with the classics, but no friend to modern poetry. I remember that he once lectured on "critical periods" and "creative periods" in literature history. "Now," he said, "we are in a critical period. It is impossible to write poetry today." This was in 1928 when Eliot, Frost, Jeffers, Pound, Cummings, Stevens, William Carlos Williams, and Marianne Moore were all in their prime, and Yeats was writing his late poems.

Victor Chittick, a Nova Scotian with a doctorate from Columbia University, was as tall as Barry Cerf was short, and looked rather like a kindly eagle, very impressive in the evening dress he wore to symphony concerts. His speech was blunt and could be more brutal than he realized. He taught a second-year literature survey course dealing mainly with the romantics. He wasn't an emotional type, but he became very emotional with Keats. He was fiercely on the defensive against critics of the classical persuasion who disparaged romanticism, modernism, and American writing generally. In his modern lit course in the late '20s we were reading Hemingway's *A Farewell to Arms*, Proust, T. S. Eliot, and Ezra Pound.

There was a group called "the Godawfullers" that gathered regularly at the Chitticks' house off campus to share their poetry. It was the first time in my life I encountered other people who wrote poetry. We would meet on Saturday nights about once a month to read our Godawful poetry and our Godawful prose. Appropriate for Portland, we all wore slickers and raincoats, with galoshes and buckles. We also wore berets because Greta Garbo had made them popular in the movies.

VICTOR CHITTICK, English professor 1921–1948: The name "Godawfullers" came about from the fact that, although the students would read to one another with the expectation that the others would criticize what they had heard, a piece read was always, without exception, met with complete silence. I referred to it, in my refined way, as a Godawful silence.

CHERYL SCHOLZ, dean of women: When it got out around town that Victor Chittick was having the young read Thomas Hardy's *Tess of the D'Urbervilles*, it caused quite a stir. Certain parties felt the book was not acceptable. At that same time there was also a storm brewing about the girls parking their girdles somewhere after they left home to go to a dance on campus.

JOSEPHINE LEWIS UTLEY '39: My older sister, Claudia Lewis '30, and her Godawfuller friends made up all these songs about their various professors, and sang them openly. It was the beginning of women's emancipation, and there was a strict rule that boys did not go upstairs in the girls' dorms, and vice versa. Of course many did anyway, and some people advocated to have the rule changed. The dean of women, Cheryl Scholz, was very much against that. There were heated meetings arguing pro and con on the subject. Finally, Victor Chittick said, "Well, why don't you just let them go to the second floor and not beyond?" That became known as the second floor compromise, which the Godawfullers memorialized in song:

> Victor Chittick was a sympathetic soul—
> Dean of women was his favorite role.
> He effected the second-floor compromise.
> Good old Vic, in his red pajamas.
> Good old Vic, cultivating phlox.
> Good old Vic had thirty red-hot mamas
> who sat around and worshipped
> while they darned his socks.

Which they did. The Godawfullers were mostly women. When they would go over to the Chittick house and sit around reading their poetry, Chittick's wife Edna, who gave piano lessons, would always give them his socks to mend. Chittick, by the way, loved that song.

Victor Chittick taught modern literature and also hosted the Godawfullers literary group.

JOE GUNTERMAN '34: There was a hot debate on campus as to whether there was such a thing as progress. Among the literary group, the argument against the existence of progress was laid out by Barry Cerf. The opposing group was led by Victor Chittick.

VICTOR CHITTICK, English professor: The New Criticism, which advocated a close reading of the text as though it were self-contained, had just started up at that time. It was an interest of mine and that of a limited number of other people. The rest were interested in comparative literature. Barry Cerf, who taught the classics, had a philosophy to teach. I didn't. I never thought of myself as a literary man. I tried to make myself a teacher, sharing my interest with students and getting them to develop an interest of their own in what they were reading.

ELIZABETH LAMB TATE '39: Dr. Cerf's philosophy stemmed from the English poet Matthew Arnold, who proposed that the purpose

Women students of House A—later renamed Ladd—together with several faculty members who also lived in apartments in the dormitory.

of culture was to make all men live in sweetness and light. He drilled into us Arnold's touchstone theory, which was to learn the best of what has been said, known, and written, and then do our best to apply it.

BRUNHILDE KAUFER LIEBES '35: There were tea gatherings each week at Anna Mann cottage, a women's dorm. I had never experienced anything like that before. Someone asked me, "How do you like your tea?" "Just fine," I said. But what they meant was, "With sugar or lemon?" That struck me as quite funny.

Girls at the tea had quite nice clothing, and they did their hair up. I didn't care about that. I couldn't afford it, anyway. I did buy a few blouses and things, but I didn't have much of a wardrobe. I had two skirts. One was lighter weight, and the other was really for cold days. I had a number of

sweaters. My father was a small man, so I could wear his shirts underneath a sweater. And I had one pair of shoes. Clothes weren't a big issue on campus. Manners were, though.

JOSEPHINE LEWIS UTLEY '39: Some of us were so poor that we would go to all the different teas that were given, and try to eat enough so that we could get by without paying for supper. At Anna Mann cottage you paid two cents for a rather heavy cookie and tea. The Arragons had a tea at their house every Thursday afternoon, where anyone could come. We sat around the dining room table. If there wasn't enough room for everybody, we took turns sitting there. Mrs. Arragon presided, toasting hamburger buns and calling them English muffins and putting marmalade on them. We spent our time desperately trying to figure how we could possibly get two.

MARY BARNARD '32: I was in and out of the Arragons' house all the time because two of my best friends roomed with them. They helped with the housework, helped them to cook, and babysat. Gertrude Arragon was a New Englander with two degrees from Radcliffe. I went to her teas as much for the conversation as for the scones and marmalade. It was a great experience being treated as a social equal in faculty homes, where we talked about all kinds of things.

One advantage we had was that faculty lived near campus, and their houses were open to us. I think that was an important part of my education. There were student groups who met for discussion or to read their work or to read papers outside class work. My roommate and I were constantly riding downtown with one or another faculty member and their wives for concerts. They took an interest in what we were doing outside the campus.

It was a different world then. Faculty wives on the whole didn't work, and they considered helping their husbands as part of their job. Almost like a minister's wife.

ELLEN KNOWLTON JOHNSON '39, recorder 1945–1962, registrar 1962–1981: Being a professor was considered, for all practical purposes, a two-person job. At our home, Mother would have a party for Dad's junior and senior physics majors two or three times a year. One night I watched a girl crying on her shoulder, "Mrs. Knowlton, I want to marry him, but I don't know anything about physics." Mother said, "Neither do I, but you do learn how to say, 'Oh,' at the proper times. Or 'Tell me.'"

My mother regularly made orange bread and took it down to the physics department. Mrs. Arragon would have English scones one day a week. Mrs. Akerman would entertain one day a week with tea and cookies, as would Mrs. McKinley, and a number of other faculty wives. These were gatherings where you went, one, to get fed and, two, to be taught very gently some manners. That was a very important part of it.

SAM LIU '36, trustee 1977–1981: One thing I liked was that the heads of the departments taught the freshmen, and then second-year and third-year courses were taught by an assistant professor. In your fourth year you went back to the senior professor for your thesis.

Dr. Ralph Strong, who was the head of the chemistry department, was a very good teacher, but very strict and rather stern in his lectures. He had a booming voice, so you couldn't miss what he was talking about. When he taught chemistry, you were more or less on your own. He just gave you a known element and you had to find it.

ELIZABETH HINES HOLZER '29: Alice Tenny '28 was apparently the victim of an accident in the chemistry lab, a very preventable one in which some particular chemical was mishandled, which was the cause of her blindness. Amazingly, we didn't wear masks then in the lab. But Dr. Strong was always very aware of the possibility of danger. He had a list of ten chemicals that each person had to pass a test on before they were allowed to handle them.

Dr. Strong was a very fine person, but a severe taskmaster, and, I would expect, a little difficult to live with. When I studied with him he was a widower with a daughter, Patty. After I graduated, he married a woman from the Country Day School in west Portland. She gave birth to a child, and then committed suicide. I guess she was in a postpartum depression, but this particular event gave people who were opposed to Dr. Strong an opportunity to ask for his dismissal.

CLEMENT AKERMAN, economics professor 1920–1943: Somehow the notion followed that Ralph Strong was connected in some way with the tragic death of his wife. There was strong feeling in town about it. It was said that Mr. Strong must be mentally unbalanced. I felt that the regents and President Coleman were too much affected by that. There was no proof. It was very unfair to a man to have dismissed him without any real investigation of the matter. I think my view in regard to Strong was correct, because he served for years in other colleges afterwards.

JACK BENVENISTE '43: In physics we were relegated to one corner of the basement. We didn't get out to civilization too much. You just didn't see a physics student up above. The physics department was full of all kinds of crazy odds and ends, and cabinets with thousand of drawers that nobody had ever looked in. When you started your thesis, the first thing you did was you went around looking through all the drawers to see if there was something that you could use. For my thesis I settled on measuring the velocity of light using ultrahigh-frequency radiation. At that time, ultrahigh frequency was like four

hundred megahertz, which is peanuts now. But I started with that, and went around looking for some tubes—because we used tubes then—that could generate ultrahigh frequencies. We didn't have any, but we did have some huge bottles. We hooked them up, and played and fussed with them until we finally got them to oscillate.

COLIN HERALD CAMPBELL '33: Bruce Horsfall, Jr., '30 was a physics major and a very serious young man. One day, during the lunch hour, when Bruce was otherwise occupied, some guys got ahold of his Model T car. He had left it parked in front of the Arts Building. They propped open the front doors of the building and took the wheels off the car, because with the old-time hubcaps on, it was too wide to go through the doors. Then they carried it through the doors and up the stairs, and in the center of the hall they put the wheels back on. There it sat, parked inside the building, facing the main entrance.

In the 1930s the chemistry lab was housed in the attic of the Arts Building (Eliot Hall).

PART TWO: THE GOLDEN AGE, 1921–1945

Bruce came out of the Commons after lunch and couldn't find his car. He looked all over campus and it was nowhere to be seen. Finally he went into the Arts Building to report it to somebody, and there it was. He was so furious that he propped open the doors, started the car, and just drove down the steps. But those hubcaps were too wide and they took off both building doors. He had to pay for repairing them.

The next time they played this trick on him was really the crowning blow. Before the college built the outdoor swimming pool, there was a diving board on the dam across the creek that formed the Reed lake. The lake was used then for swimming. The pranksters laid planks on the diving board and rolled Bruce's car out over them. Then they took out all the planks, except the two that the wheels were resting on. They then gently pushed the car off those planks so it plopped down on its axles on the diving board. Bruce Horsfall had to have an auto crane come out and lift it off.

REX ARRAGON, history professor: While freshman history covered the visual arts of the classical world through the Renaissance, the arts themselves were one deficiency in the curriculum. E. O. Sisson and I talked with the Portland Art Museum about creating a combined program between Reed and the Museum Art School, in which students would have an opportunity to earn a teaching certificate in art.

HELEN IRWIN SCHLEY '35: The combined art course took five years. In the first year, I went to the museum school and took just art. We had drawing and painting and an hour of art history a week. The second year I attended Reed. I don't think I saw anything of the museum that year. In my third year I spent half a day on campus, and half at the art museum, drawing and painting.

At Reed, I had quite a bit of independent reading. I had a personal class with Rex Arragon,

studying Romanesque and Gothic architecture. I would go to the library and look up a lot of pictures with architecture. Then I would meet with Professor Arragon once a week. It was a great privilege, although I don't know if he enjoyed it that much. Why would a full professor like Arragon enjoy spending a whole hour talking with me about art and architecture? The combined art program only lasted for about three or four years, because art eventually became a part of the curriculum at Reed.

HAROLD "JIM" JAMBOR '35: We were given a lot of occasion to become skeptical at Reed, to examine whatever was out there and determine if it had validity. The search for truth—in the sense of academically related information and scholarly work—characterized the college. I could never say that I learned anything particular there, but I did develop an almost uncanny ability to get answers to questions, either through the library or in seeking out people who were presumed to have good information.

While Reed stressed development of the intellect, it didn't stress development of the personality. You were pretty much on your own. There wasn't anyone who was like a mentor that you could follow and learn from watching and working alongside of. That was not a part of the scene, nor was counseling. I saw situations where kids were really going haywire because they couldn't handle the stress.

CARL LARSON '27: I really didn't like the fact that they didn't report grades to the students. If you weren't doing well, three or four times a year you would get a white slip in your mail slot, saying either that you were on probation or that you should see your advisor. The first time I got a warning, I thought I had been at the top of the class. I corralled that professor right away. He said to me, "Oh, you can do better." To which I responded, "If you're already doing the best you can, how are you going to do any better?" He said, "Just keep showing up."

JIM JAMBOR '35: The junior qual—God, it was enough to give you ulcers. There were some guys who didn't pass the junior qualification exam. But it was a very private thing. I don't know what happened to those guys. They just didn't come back.

DONALD WHEELER '35: There was a movement to get the junior qual eliminated, but it failed. The faculty said, "We're never going to eliminate the junior qualifying exam; it puts an end to playboys."

ELIZABETH TABOR MULLADY '38: The junior qual for political science majors lasted a whole week. There were no subjects. They could ask you about anything. You could go anyplace to take it, even off-campus. Do anything you wanted to do. Take any books you wanted to read. Nothing would help. If you had asked me my name at the end of it, I couldn't have told you. I was just gone.

My senior thesis was a comparison of labor law in the United States and the United Kingdom, which was a very big subject at the time, given labor relations. My thesis orals, however, were scary. They got a labor lawyer for an outside examiner. Lawyers have a way of asking questions that make you feel like you're a criminal. They get you on the stand and you know you are not a criminal but you act like one to get through it. That's what my oral exam was like.

WILBUR L. PARKER '36: In the senior orals the student had the right to appoint two professors as his defense. The faculty then invited an outside professor, one from another college, to come in and lead the inquiry. The purpose of the orals was to convince you that you really didn't know a damn thing, that you were just getting started

on learning something. "Don't get the crazy idea that because you are graduating and have a thesis, that you know anything. Because you really don't." They went to great lengths to establish that idea by intellectually beating the hell out of you. But if you could defend yourself reasonably well, and give reasonably sensible answers to their questions, you passed.

I knew a superb student in economics. Top of his class all along. But he had gone the communist route. They humiliated him in his orals beyond belief. Just beat the intellectual daylights out of him. As far as they were concerned, in defending Karl Marx he was defending an indefensible type of economics. I saw him when he came out. He was crying. They forced him to go to the University of Oregon to get his degree. They wouldn't let him receive his degree at Reed. They were tough.

BLAKE HOPWOOD '31: At graduation we had a thesis parade, and we threw our papers in a big bonfire. And the first person who finished his thesis got thrown into the lake in the canyon.

HARLOW LENON '35: I took American Political Structure from Charles McKinley. There were many burning issues that were capable of being aired in McKinley's course, and we aired them all. The Depression was reaching its height, Franklin Delano Roosevelt was running against Herbert Hoover, Hitler was becoming chancellor of the Weimar Republic, Stalin was liquidating the kulaks—relatively affluent peasants—in rural Russia, and we were hearing about the expansion of the universe. I came away from Reed recognizing that there was a fundamental conflict between theism—particularly Christianity—and materialism, the notion that there was no God or guiding design.

We had chapel service every day at noon. Most of the time it was run by President Coleman. Unlike many of the other professors, he was a devout Christian. When he conducted the chapel service we sang Christian hymns, and he gave sermonettes about goodness. Those chapel services were not as heavily attended as some of the others. Sometimes there was a recital by a student musician, or classical records were played on a big phonograph, or organ music was played by French teacher Cecilia Tenney '19. Sometimes it was a lecture by a professor or visiting scholar. Attendance then was pretty good. Everybody was trying to soak up culture.

THOMAS LAMB FRAZIER '42: I entered Reed one year after arriving in the States from my native Germany. Although Reed was nondenominational, I knew it had some informal ties to the Unitarian church through Reverend Thomas Lamb Eliot. After graduation, I was drafted and changed my name legally from Ulrich Heinicke to Thomas Lamb Frazier. As I was planning to be a minister, I majored in history and philosophy, although there was nothing spiritual, and certainly nothing religious, in those courses. I decided to cover this lack by founding the Religion Club. We were a group of about six to eight and met regularly. Although our interests were unlike those of the other students, we felt easily accepted, and we tried to address some of the transpersonal aspects of life, which Reed did not offer courses in.

MARGARET CHURCHILL LABOVITZ '30: We didn't talk much about religion at Reed. I don't think anybody went to church that I know of. My friend Eleanor Mitchell Wheeler '30 was pretty free-thinking. She and her husband, George Wheeler '29, had married before they came to college. They were the only married couple I remember on campus.

Together, Eleanor and I started the Atheist Society on campus. We were just being outrageous. Eleanor wrote to the Atheist Society of America under the alias "Elmer Nutshell" for their ma-

A student couple, circa 1930.

terial. They addressed her as "Professor Elmer Nutshell, Department of Atheism." We had a lot of fun with that.

JOSEPHINE LEWIS UTLEY '39: There was a terrible song that my older sister, Claudia Lewis '30, and her Godawfuller friends made up about President Coleman. They sang it openly, although I don't see how they could possibly have dared. It went:

> Norman Coleman was the right hand of
>   God—
> Face like a monkey and eye like a cod.
> He kept an asylum full of idiots and fools,
> and every time he looked at them he said,
>   "My jewels."
> Good old Norm, creaking in his corsets.
> Good old Norm.

It shocks me even now. I had Coleman in conference when I was a freshman. He wasn't a typical Reed type. Old-fashioned and very fussbudgety. Very inclined to correct our language and spelling.

ERNEST BOYD "E. B." MACNAUGHTON, trustee 1919–1941, 1955–1958, president 1948–1952: Coleman was so Christlike that the flaming age of the roaring '20s just couldn't understand him. Also, the college had begun to display some of the characteristics of the F. Scott Fitzgerald age—"let 'er rip and let 'em buck"—and he had trouble coping with that.

REX ARRAGON, history professor: It was discovered in the fall of 1931 that President Coleman had sat on a limited offer from the Carnegie Foundation to help colleges enroll in a new faculty pension plan, allowing the time limit for applying to expire before moving on it.

This latest frustration with Coleman over financial matters was all coming to a head when the regents came to the faculty meeting in early January 1932 and announced that Norman Coleman was resigning as president. Among the reasons Coleman gave for resigning was the problem of raising money, along with his preference to return to teaching as he got older.

It was another two and a half years before a new president was hired, and meanwhile Coleman continued on. That was a period of caution on the part of both the regents and the faculty. The faculty recognized the difficulties of the financial situation, and we were determined to live through it with a feeling of solidarity and strength.

E. B. MACNAUGHTON, trustee: Coleman was just licked from the start. Choosing him to become president was the result of a lack of understanding and knowledge on the governing boards of what the college was trying to do, and their desperation to get the community to back the college once more. It just didn't work.

FRANK LOXLEY "F. L." GRIFFIN, mathematics professor 1911–1952, president 1954–1956: In the nine years that Mr. Coleman served as president, salaries received a considerable increment, a five-year program with the Portland Art Museum was set up, and the library was erected.

He was very active in civic affairs and social-hygiene work, and maintained a keen interest in international affairs, making trips to Europe, the Far East, and India. He made a number of proposals that the rest of us were not quite ready for. One was that the college devote more attention to the Far East, as he sensed that developments in that arena would be of growing importance. The rest of us didn't see this so clearly and nothing was accomplished, although I believe we did have a professor teaching Chinese history at one time.

Coleman never tried to push matters in which he was interested, but relied on discussion and hoped that we would be able to see what he wanted. After leaving the presidency, Coleman continued to teach English at Reed until his retirement in 1939.

CHAPTER 9

"Prex Dex"

It seems to be virtually a universal experience that the hardening of the educational arteries sets in as soon as a new college is born, and makes steady headway until the college has long been dead without realizing it.
  —Dexter Keezer, president

[Reed] was a phalanx of free thinkers who had strong ideas of what they wanted to do academically.
  —Cheryl Scholz, dean of women

By the time Norman Coleman relinquished the presidency in 1934, Reed was settling into the mold that would distinguish its institutional personality for decades to come. It was a personality marked by strong faculty governance, a demanding core curriculum of rigorous intellectualism, a nonconformist student body, and a local reputation for radicalism.

The trustees, still hoping to steer Reed toward a more normal collegiate course, brought in a hard-charging non-academic named Dexter Keezer to replace Coleman as the college's fourth president. A New Deal economist, Keezer's inclinations were more in line with those of the social reformer William Foster than those of the scholarly Richard Scholz. He wasted no time in setting out to end Reed's self-imposed isolation, improve its relations with the Portland community, bring more relevancy to the educational program, and provide more balance in the life of students.

RICHARD JONES, history professor 1941–1982, 1985–1986: By 1934, when Coleman stepped down, the impact of Richard Scholz's vision was readily apparent in Reed's stated aims, as well as its essential character and curriculum. The legacy of William Foster's original plan was still manifested in such things as an emphasis on teaching, selective student admissions, rigorous intellectual discipline, and community government, on all of which Scholz had concurred. And while the course-requirement structure was hardly that of Scholz's original dream, it nonetheless testified allegiance to his unifying principles. Full-year courses were the mode, and the four academic divisions under which the various departments were grouped gave vitality to the principle of interdisciplinary cooperation, as did the parallel history-literature humanities requirement in the freshman year.

Thomas Lamb Eliot, with yet two years to live at the time, remained steadfast in his loyalty to Reed despite serious misgivings about Scholz's curricular transformation, as did William Foster, who continued throughout his life to express good will toward a college that was far more limited in scope than what he had first dreamed. And yet, despite the Scholz rhetoric of the college's catalog, the original vision and the values of Eliot and Foster never completely succumbed. Something akin to them were revived again and again throughout Reed's history, in the form of proposals for expansion, change of direction, or curricular innovation, or as a solution to financial difficulties. One such revival occurred in 1934, when the college welcomed Dexter Keezer as President Norman Coleman's successor.

Keezer was a social scientist, a progressive New Dealer, and a seasoned administrator. He arrived apparently unburdened by any prescribed set of curricular innovations, ready to devote primary attention to strengthening the college financially and developing its national reputation. Keezer hoped to use his eastern connections to solve the financial problems, endemic since Foster's first years and badly neglected during the Coleman regime. These hopes evaporated in total failure.

He then turned to the Portland community as represented by the boards of regents and trustees. His reading of board sentiments, by no means universally correct as events were to prove, was that meaningful local support would be contingent upon drastic changes in the character of the college and reformation in the conduct of its students.

TIME magazine, "Prex Dex," November 11, 1935: Few persons would take Dexter Keezer for a college president. Periodically since his graduation from Amherst in 1920, he has found academic life dull. For a year he was a reporter on the *Denver Times*. He took a Ph.D. in economics at the Brookings Institution but quit teaching after six years. From 1929 to 1933 he was associate editor of the *Baltimore Sun*. In 1933 General Johnson made him executive director of the Consumers' Advisory Board of the National Recovery Administration.

One of economist Keezer's associates on the board was William Trufant Foster, first president of Reed College. After Messrs. Foster and Keezer had been working on the consumers' board for six months, Mr. Foster's old job was offered to Mr. Foster's new associate.

Dexter Keezer arrived at Portland last autumn with his wife and small daughter, sworn to become no stuffed shirt. Students made his acquaintance during the freshman-sophomore tug of war when the victorious sophomores discovered that one of the "freshmen" they had been dragging through the mud was new president Keezer. Subsequently "Prex Dex" attracted even more attention by appearing in bright red duck pants. In the winter he could be seen carrying an armful of wood to heat a cold conference room. In the spring he played tennis and fished with his students, shocked bookworms when he inaugurated a carnival and skiing trips, and reminded them: "You don't live on intellect alone."

In making his annual report, this most unacademic of college presidents viewed his field with an ex-newshawk's eye. Of Portland, whose conservative citizens generally regarded Reed as a hotbed of radicalism, he announced that he was trying to "narrow the distance many Portland people have to travel—sometimes even to the Atlantic Coast—to become aware of the educational strength which Reed imparts to the community."

DEXTER KEEZER, president 1934–1942: One of the problems of creating a healthy institution is providing a sense of cohesiveness and group loyalty on the part of the college community as a whole. On a low intellectual plane, intercollegiate athletics do this. On rare occasion, the same result can be accomplished on a high intellectual plane by educational pioneering that enlists the enthusiasm and devotion of the participants. I'm sure that Reed's pioneering in the early years, coupled with the stimulating tart reception by a considerable part of the outside community, produced much unity and group loyalty. But it seems to be virtually a universal experience that the hardening of the educational arteries sets in as soon as a new college is born, and makes steady headway until the college has long been dead without realizing it.

I found Reed was no exception to this tendency. As its pioneering zest evaporated over the years, the more conventional, institutional devices for stimulating solidarity and concern for the institution as a whole, as opposed to the interests of its diverse and often jangling parts, was lacking. I set out to do a variety of things that would stimulate this joint concern.

ERNEST BOYD "E. B." MACNAUGHTON, trustee 1919–1941, 1955–1958, president 1948–1952: Five months slipped by before we realized there had been no inauguration for President Keezer. One day I said seriously to Reed's new president, "You should know by now that Reed College has been credited with encouraging such unconventionalities as communism and free love, and we haven't yet legitimized your relationship with us and made an honest man of you."

REGINALD "REX" ARRAGON, history professor 1923–1962, 1970–1974: After having struggled against stagnation all through the lackadaisical years of Coleman's presidency and the financial impact of the Depression, upon Dexter Keezer's

New Dealer Dexter Keezer assumed the presidency in 1934.

appointment an evaluation of the academic program was necessary. By January 1935, the freshening of the academic climate was underway with the planning of an educational conference to accompany the president's inauguration in mid-May. Divisions and departments began to examine their objectives, and outside educators were invited to participate.

The upshot of the conference was that the faculty quickly resolved that Reed remain the small liberal arts college it had been. The grading system and its secrecy was examined and retained. The underclass curriculum was studied and confirmed with only slight changes. Semester courses were introduced somewhat reluctantly to those who preferred the year-long courses for purposes of maturation in a field. A lively controversy was stirred up by President Keezer as to whether the treatment of history and the social sciences should be normative or descriptive relativism. But, all in all, despite Keezer's belittling attitudes and comments, the effect was little change.

DEXTER KEEZER, president: I had the feeling that some of the work in the social sciences tended to be too bookish. Perhaps my views in this regard were unduly influenced by what seemed to me the tendency of some Reed College social science majors to be preoccupied with a theoretical approach to their subject, to the neglect of essentially important facts available to them through an examination of the actual life of the immediate community.

CLEMENT AKERMAN, economics professor 1920–1943: Mr. Keezer and I were both economists, but we had rather different views about economics. A New Deal reformer, he was more interested in what he would have called a "normative" approach, that of shaping students' opinions. I was more interested in the scientific study of economics, the descriptive. I felt that it was the business of an instructor to get students first grounded in the principles of the subject and then get them to think instead of trying to propagate my views.

ELLEN KNOWLTON JOHNSON '39, recorder 1945–1962, registrar 1962–1981: Dexter Keezer had a lot of ideas, some of which were good, but he was a brusque person. He wasn't willing to listen. He had a very good wife, Anne, who would smooth corners down for him. She held all sorts of teas, inviting students and faculty over, and really worked hard to make things work.

After his first year at Reed, Keezer changed the names of the dormitories, which followed the alphabet from "A" to "H," to Ladd, Abington, Kerr, Westport, Eastport, Doyle, Quincy, and Winch. He was trying to build up some good will with Portland families like the Ladds and Winches who were instrumental in Reed's founding, as well as to acknowledge things like the Massachusetts birthplaces of Amanda and Simeon Reed, Quincy and Abington. There was a fuss, of course, because it was different, but we all got

used to it pretty fast. Renaming the Arts Building "Eliot Hall" after Thomas Lamb Eliot was one of the easier things to accept, since he had been the guy who planted the idea of the college, and he had just died at that time in 1936.

The financial situation was a little better when Keezer came in, as we were just beginning to come out of the 1929 crash period. There was a little extra money that could be found once in a while. Keezer brought in more students from the East, especially from around Bennington College in Vermont, where several Reed graduates were early teachers and administrators. He also brought in foreign-exchange students, and increased the student body from four hundred to more than five hundred students.

But Keezer's primary focus was questioning the purpose of the college. As far as the faculty was concerned, the basic purpose of the college was to provide for the education of excellent minds at an undergraduate-degree level. I'm not sure Keezer disagreed with that, but he wanted to introduce a more rounded approach.

DEXTER KEEZER, president: Students who are precocious in intellectual pursuits tend to regard them as an end in themselves, and neglect the problem of relating those pursuits to effective, practical performance. If the Reed College buildings were burning and only the top 10 percent of the student body in academic terms were on hand, the job of putting out the fire might have to wait upon the conclusion of a very interesting and stimulating discussion of the effects of fire on wood and brick.

There are few more important indicators of a new president's chances to make a substantial educational imprint on a college than the number of key faculty appointments he will have the chance to make. It was an indicator that I innocently overlooked when coming to Reed. In almost eight years, I had occasion to make only one professorial appointment.

At Reed, the machinery for protecting faculty tenure as well as for providing democratic administration of the college included the Faculty Council, composed of eight members elected by the entire faculty. Its duties were to pass on all faculty appointments, promotions, and dismissals, as well as on the operating budget of the college. If the Faculty Council did not approve of the personnel or budgetary proposals of the president, it was up to the governing boards of the college to resolve the conflict.

The setup was notable for the extraordinary large share of direct faculty participation it provided in college administration, and for broadening the horizons of both the faculty members and the administration by having all points of view represented. One of its weaknesses, however, was a tendency to cloak the personal difficulties of people not liking each other in the raiment of high principle. What followed was a search for principles with which to dress up a decision, such as an attack or defense of something such as academic freedom, the Bill of Rights, or the sanctity of the American home. Objective perspective on the setup was difficult for me, since I was being chopped up by its machinery part of the time.

CHERYL SCHOLZ, dean of women 1924–1937, history professor 1938–1943, dean of admission 1943–1945: Keezer was an able, hard worker, and certainly astute in many ways. But he ran into a tougher situation at Reed than he had expected—it was a phalanx of free thinkers who had strong ideas of what they wanted to do academically. They didn't care to be upset by some young man from the East who didn't know a thing about how they had done things up until that time.

The faculty didn't care to be disturbed on those grounds. It never has.

DEXTER KEEZER, president: Before going to Reed I spent a year as executive director of the

Consumers' Advisory Board of the National Recovery Administration, which made me aware of paying more attention to the consumer. With this in mind, I advocated the creation at Reed of a student committee on educational policy to be appointed by the Student Council to collaborate with the faculty on execution of the educational program at the college. The students on the committee accepted their duties fully and discharged them with a high sense of responsibility. However, as far as I could determine, a comfortable rapport was never established between the student committee and its faculty counterpart. Some members of the faculty regarded even the idea of such a committee as anathema, while others thought it silly to consult students about what should be taught and how it should be taught. But a more prevalent opposition seemed to be an undefined fear that it would articulate student opinion about teaching performance. The fact that the few cases involving faculty performance were handled by the student committee

Dean of Women Cheryl Scholz, early 1930s.

in a helpful way did not eliminate faculty uneasiness about the enterprise.

While I was in complete accord with the American Association of University Professors' efforts to see to it that faculty members had job security consistent with preservation of freedom of research and teaching, it was my painful impression that the AAUP also accomplished much in fortifying mediocrity and incompetence in colleges and universities. It was generally no trick at all to convert a complaint about incompetence into a challenge to proper tenure.

HELEN WHEELER HASTAY '39: Being a member of the Student Educational Policies Committee is the one shame that I have about my time at Reed. I didn't know it, but I was being used. Edward Octavius Sisson was a fine old man who had taught philosophy at the college since 1912. But a young teacher, Karl Aschenbrenner, wanted to take over his classes. I was initially flattered to be put on the Student Educational Policies Committee. I didn't realize then they were using me as a dumb little country girl to vote Sisson out and this young man in. I was influential in that. Mr. Sisson saw me in the hall one day. All he said was, "Why did you do that?"

FRANCES MILLER READ '38: I took educational philosophy from Dr. Sisson and it was absolutely hopeless. He had been troubled, I was told, by a debilitating disease. His thoughts didn't hang together very well, so we would just sit there in class. A friend of mine said, "We've got to take this to the administration." So we did. We formed a little committee, not to criticize Dr. Sisson, because we recognized he may have had a problem, but because he did not seem able to cope with teaching philosophy any more.

REX ARRAGON, history professor: Keezer's general objective in personnel cases was to improve teaching, but his selection of cases and the

subsequent proposals he made seemed to disregard individual contributions, the right of tenure, and promise. In the case of Monte Griffith, who taught psychology, he applied pressure in requiring a Ph.D. for promotion or for continuance among the faculty. In the cases of some longstanding faculty, such as Charles Botsford in physical education and Clement Akerman in economics, he questioned their rights of tenure.

ELEANOR EMMONS MACCOBY '39: Monte Griffith taught psychology. He was a big, big man at three hundred pounds, but still very agile on his feet. He had been a heavyweight boxer and football player. His proper name was William, but he was called Monte because he came from Montana. There was a little group of students, almost all male, who clustered around him and had lunch regularly with him and went to his house. It was macho, the whole thing. Their interests were partly centered on sports prowess. Monte was a raconteur and told sort of off-color stories. He was quite a sexist.

There was a group of us in his class who were very serious students. We formed a little committee that we called "the Student Union" to go and see him. We told him that we thought his lectures were too lightweight, too funny, and not meaty enough, and we weren't learning as much as we should be. He swelled up behind his big desk and said, "Union! You punks. I'm the only union man in this whole place." He pulled out his union card to show us. It turns out that he had worked as a copper miner in between his college years.

Monte was a knocker-down of all kinds of beliefs. My parents belonged to the Theosophical Society when I was growing up. Like most theosophists they studied occult kinds of literature and believed in reincarnation. My mother was the only person I knew who was interested in astrology and who meditated every day. I don't know whether Monte ever knew that I had been

PART TWO: THE GOLDEN AGE, 1921–1945

schooled in spiritualism and things like extra-sensory perception, but he had plenty to say about the things he thought of as popular nonsense misconceptions. He knew how to expose some of the fraudulent stuff that was going on, which previously I probably would have bought hook, line, and sinker.

By the end of my sophomore year I was shaken up, Monte having torn everything down for me. I became actively depressed toward the end of the year, and profoundly skeptical about the things I had grown up with. I developed a rather arrogant attitude toward my parents—how could they have fallen for all of this foolishness? I began to buy into behaviorism, which was what Monte was selling. He had been taught by Edwin Guthrie at the University of Washington. Guthrie was not a reinforcement theorist like Clark Hull or B. F. Skinner, two other influential behaviorists. He had his own particular brand of behaviorism. In my junior year I left Reed and went up to study with Guthrie. I realized some

time afterward that Monte Griffith was one of the best teachers that I ever had.

WILBUR PARKER '36: We had a fine and distinguished professor of sociology and anthropology, Alexander Goldenweiser, who had studied with the famous anthropologist Franz Boas at Columbia. He locked horns with Keezer, who was proposing that Goldenweiser introduce businessmen into his classes. Faculty like Goldenweiser wanted to control their classes, and they weren't too eager to have a class taken over by another, unless it was a scholar whom they admired.

DORIS BAILEY MURPHY '38: When President Keezer refused to renew the contract of Dr. Goldenweiser, even refusing to give him a wage increase—Goldenweiser was unbelievably making only forty-four dollars a month—David Fain '38, Al Fine '37, and I drew up a petition signed by sociology majors and took it to Dr. Keezer's office. We pleaded with him to keep Goldenweiser

Monte Griffith and Rex Arragon serenading Eleanor Emmons '39, circa 1936.

on the faculty. He listened politely and then dismissed us, saying that this was an administrative decision, which he could not change.

ALICE SCHOTT RICHARDS '38: Professor Alexander Goldenweiser introduced me to the work of one of his former students, the anthropologist Ruth Benedict, whose book *Patterns of Culture* questioned the relationships between personality, art, language, and culture, insisting that no trait existed in isolation or self-sufficiency.

I was very much distressed by the idea that most sociologists and anthropologists focused almost entirely on males as defining a culture. There hadn't been much research done then on matrilineal cultures. The Navajo were matrilineal, as were several of the other American Indian groups. But when we studied kinship at Reed, the "ego" was always a male, and then you measured from there. I began to wonder, was it really true, that women are simply adjuncts to the culture — or do they have a key role? I didn't feel that women were necessarily put down at Reed; there was more of a feeling of camaraderie, of equality between men and women, which came from sharing common interests. But there weren't many women professors.

DEXTER KEEZER, president: I found the social setup at Reed strangely out of balance and coeducationally dangerous, both for too-docile young ladies and for the young men who were gaining an altogether false impression of the importance of their opinions. The men on the faculty outnumbered the women by more than three to one. More important, not a single woman held the rank of full professor, and only two women held the rank of assistant professor or its equivalent, dean of women. A coeducational college, particularly a residential college, that does not embrace in its faculty a substantial proportion of first-rate women teachers is not as well equipped to do the educational job it undertakes.

ELLEN KNOWLTON JOHNSON '39, administrator: There was a different generational attitude at the time. Women professors were underclass citizens. Jessie May Short in mathematics was always kept as an assistant professor. I once asked my father, Tony Knowlton, who taught physics at Reed, why that was, and he said, "She didn't need the money. She didn't have a family to support." I said, "That's unfair. That means that for anybody to be promoted is a charitable act, so that they can support their family."

JESSIE MAY SHORT, mathematics professor 1920–1939: In the early years of the college there were several women with professorial rank, all of them good teachers and superior persons. After 1921, all of them had left the college because their positions had been made untenable through reorganization in the interest of men brought to the faculty. From that time throughout the 1930s, no woman was brought to the teaching staff with a rank higher than that of instructor, and only one was advanced to assistant professorship — me — and none to a professorship. During that same nineteen-year period, forty men were appointed to the faculty in positions of professor and assistant professor.

There were two main reasons alleged for appointment and advancement of men to the better positions and high salaries, irrespective, often admittedly, of equal or better qualifications of women in the same field: one, that boys need contact with men, and two, that men carry the family responsibilities and should therefore receive special consideration because of their need for larger salaries.

I resented as unjust the argument that men carry the family responsibilities. I knew many women who carried very heavy family responsibilities on low salaries, and men teachers, often rendering less service to the school and community, on much higher salaries with no dependents. The Women's Bureau of the Department of Labor reported in 1937 that one-tenth of the employed women in the United States were the entire support of families of two or more persons, or in many cases families much larger, and that far more women support their parents, grandparents, and other relatives than do men. According to the National Educational Association, 69 percent of single women teachers in 1932 were responsible for one or more dependents. A study I made of the Depression-era drive for men in the schools indicated that depression years appear to inspire the desire to save education from feminization. When good times arrived there was an exodus of men from the public schools.

KATHARINE BAKER COOKE '41: Frau Marianne Beth taught a course at Reed on the sociology of women that may have been the only one of its kind in the country at the time. She and her husband Eric, who taught math at Reed, were both refugees from Nazi Germany, so we got a background in anti-Semitism along with it.

Back then there were a number of people, particularly in Germany, who were out to get equality for women. Frau Beth knew them all. In her course she covered everybody who was around then. It was fabulous, one of the best courses I took at Reed. It led to my later chairing of the Federal Advisory Council on the Status of Women for the government of Canada.

MILDRED FAHLEN TAXER '42: The low point as far as I was concerned was Frau Marianne Beth. The sociology of women course that she taught just didn't relate to us. Her whole emphasis was on Germany, and her diction was poor. It was difficult to understand what she was saying. I considered it a lost cause.

JANE WILLSON FALKENHAGEN '37: When I got through with college I hoped to get a job with one of the big research labs. Dr. Keith Seymour, who was my advisor in chemistry, said that be-

Math professor Jessie May Short was the only woman to be advanced to the rank of assistant professor in the 1920s and '30s. None were made full professor.

cause I was a woman there was no way I was going to find a job like that. I had better prepare myself to teach chemistry, because there was a great prejudice against women using chemistry in any field except nursing. He encouraged me to take biology, which I didn't want to do, and so didn't. But in retrospect it would have made my choice of jobs after college a little more flexible.

After graduating I applied for various teaching jobs, mostly in smaller towns and cities. I didn't find very many where they were interested in having a woman science teacher. They said, "Well, you probably could run the sewing class or the art class." I had a job interview in Clackamas, Oregon, during which the school-board person interviewing me asked, "Now we know there are radical students at Reed. How many people are that way?" I said, "Well, as far as I know, there's one table in the lunch room that we look upon as being a very radical group." That seemed to satisfy him.

MAUDE CUMBOW MCKINLEY '39: When I was a freshman, I was asked to join a secret sorority at Reed populated by upper-class girls, most of whom had gone to Grant High or Lincoln High in Portland, where they had sororities. When I was initiated, they sliced my finger and bled it well. It didn't take very long for me to decide that this did not belong at Reed College. It was socially selective for one thing. When I was a junior, I accepted election as president of the sorority. I worked then to dissolve the organization.

REX ARRAGON, history professor: One significant change initiated by Keezer was acceptance of Phi Beta Kappa. It may seem ironic that objection to Phi Beta Kappa at Reed was based on it being a Greek letter fraternity, but that objection was less serious than the other ground for resistance, which was the distinction of a few students from all others by a discriminatory honors award. These traditions, originally established by President Foster, were applications of the ideal of equal treatment and opportunity for all students, and of the principle that the motivation for learning should not be grades and awards. An exclusive honors group was thought to offend on both counts.

ELIZABETH TABOR MULLADY '38: Students did not want to have a Phi Beta Kappa chapter. We thought we were all too smart for that. I was gathering signatures on a petition opposing Phi Beta Kappa at Reed. President Dexter Keezer called me in and talked me into stopping it. He said that he knew how I felt, and said he felt that way, too, but that Phi Beta Kappa would really mean a lot for people going on to graduate school.

ELLEN KNOWLTON JOHNSON '39, administrator: After a good year of considerable discussion and student argument for and against Phi Beta Kappa, in 1938 the faculty decided to form a chapter. But where most Phi Beta Kappa chap-

In the 1930s it was suggested to women students who were interested in science that they study biology, given the limited career opportunities that would be available to them in chemistry and physics.

ters are made up of juniors and seniors, Reed decided only to accept seniors once they were through with their studies and ready to graduate, and then only on the very day of their graduation. One of the women who had argued most vehemently in 1937 against having Phi Beta Kappa on campus graciously accepted invitation in Phi Beta Kappa in 1938.

FRED LEITZ '40: Reed didn't measure academic grade point averages at the time. We had a grading system that worked with a set of points from one to ten on a Gaussian curve—a bell curve—with one being highest, ten lowest. Scores were assigned based upon both quality and quantity of work. Nobody got ones. Two was an extremely high grade. And the commonest scores were five and six.

You didn't talk about grade point averages because averaging things when the grades are on a Gaussian curve is semimeaningless—very difficult to rate. It didn't take long to note, though, who the smarter students were. There was about a 60 percent turnover rate.

HARLOW LENON '35: We were immersed in a sea of intellectuality, and talked a great deal. There was just a vast amount of talk. The assignments were enormous. To have kept up with them would have been impossible. There weren't that many hours in the day. We got the idea, which never left me, that all leisure time should be devoted to reading good books.

DEXTER KEEZER, president: The typical liberal arts college tends to float along on floods of words, creating the illusion among students that talk about life is most of its substance. It seemed to me that one antidote for this excessive verbalism was instruction in the fine arts, which disclose to students all sorts of creative possibilities that they perhaps never suspected they possessed.

REX ARRAGON, history professor: President Keezer's most important contribution at Reed was the expansion in the arts through resident artists, part-time teaching appointments, and full-time instruction and direction in performance. By 1941, there were regular programs within the curriculum in music, theatre, and the visual arts, including studio work in painting and sculpture. Thanks to foundation grants, Reed was provided with paintings, reproductions, phonograph records, and the record-playing room called Capehart.

ELLIOTT ROBERTS '39: Capehart instruments were the earliest automatic disc players. They played 33-rpm records with cactus needles that were soft enough to leave the vulnerable vinyl records more or less whole, and at the same time hard enough to produce fairly acceptable levels of true music. Homer Capehart, the "father of the jukebox," was a business executive and later a reactionary Republican senator who donated his record players and a small record collection to colleges.

The Capehart room was located in the Winch social hall. Students were paid thirty cents an hour from National Youth Administration student funds to supervise the playing of the Capehart machine. The jobs were sought after because—hey!—you had exposure to Beethoven's *Grosse Fugue*, various piano sonatas, and Schubert. It was a perfectly marvelous opening of ears to fundamentally instrumental music. Also, the process of overseeing the room gave you a certain social cachet. It was a campus institution: "See you at the Capehart room!"

CHAPTER 10

Where They Came From

When time came for me to go down to Reed, I made a little raft about ten feet across and fifteen feet long. I pushed off from White Bluffs on the Columbia River and rode it down to Umatilla, Oregon, where I left it, and hitchhiked the rest of the way into Portland on a dynamite truck returning from Idaho.
  —Donald Wheeler '35

I once heard a member of the University of Oregon faculty say that Reed College can be very bad for some people because they liked it too well. It was the first place they ever felt at home, and they spend the rest of their life looking for what they had found there and not finding it.
  —Mary Barnard '32

With the onset of the Great Depression, college became a refuge for young people unable to find a job. Enrollments surged dramatically after 1935, when the federal government instituted a work-study program under the National Youth Administration. This program paid students up to forty cents an hour for work on school campuses, thereby providing a way for them to earn their tuition.

Given its relatively small endowment and lack of local financial support, Reed was highly dependent on tuition income to cover operating expenses. Enrollment, which averaged roughly 350 students in the late 1920s, grew to more than five hundred by 1940. Men continued to make up 60 percent of the student body; 60 percent of the graduates, however, were women.

Part of Reed's local appeal stemmed from the fact that Reed and the Catholic University of Portland were the only colleges in the city until the late 1930s, when Albany College, some seventy miles south, relocated to Portland and renamed itself Lewis & Clark College. Reed was consequently an attractive choice for local students looking to save money by living at home while attending college. By 1934, 86 percent of Reed's student body were local "daydodgers," who commuted daily to campus, leaving the dormitories partially empty.

VERA SMITH JACKETS '28: It was through my father that I got my love of learning and of learning about the world. He had only one year of high school up in central Michigan, but he taught eighth grade after that in a one-room school. He was a great teacher because he had so much patience. When I was growing up he was working in Portland as the traffic manager of a big grocery chain. He used to bring home stories about places like Shizuoka, Japan, because that's where he bought the tea for the grocery. He always wanted to do something special, but he was trapped without an education. My mother had a fourth-grade education. She was very interested in learning, too, even though she never had a chance of her own. She wanted me to go to college. She didn't know anything about it; she only knew that she didn't know enough, and that she wanted me to know more.

There was a girl from our little church who went to Reed College, Dana Small '23. She went on to be a high school teacher in Portland and later became the longtime companion of Dorothy Johansen '33, who taught history at Reed. Mother said, "Well, if she can go, you can go too." So I went.

There were quite a number of girls and boys in our class who had been to some private school in Portland. Their education had been much better than mine, and I felt inferior to them. We started out with a class of about 150 but that went downhill quite rapidly. A good many of my first-year friends didn't survive and went elsewhere. But I managed to get through. About forty of us graduated. Several of those had transferred in after the first two years.

It cost me $293 that first year for tuition and books. The first year and a half I was a day-dodger like most of the kids, and went to school by streetcar. There was one room on the first floor of the Arts Building where all the day-dodgers put their coats and hats and lunches. I went to live on campus in the middle of my second year. I decided that if I could pay for my board and room by hashing and working in the library, I could get along. "Hashing" was what we called serving in the Commons. We served two tables, each of which would have six kids. All the boys that wanted to sit at my table would rush in all at once and sit down and then laugh. We brought the food around and then collected the dishes and took them back. I hashed all three meals the entire time I was at Reed. I usually got through with hashing dinner and cleaned up by six-thirty or so, and then went to the social room in Anna Mann cottage, which was a women's dorm. A lot of times there would be a student there playing jazz on the piano, and we would dance to songs like "Bye, Bye Blackbird." Then, at seven o'clock, we were supposed to go up to our rooms and study.

DOROTHY GILL WIKELUND '29: By the time I got to Reed I was showing tendencies of rebellion against my parents' Republicanism. Reed took it from there and really opened me up to the mainstream of liberal thought. The more I studied and read and came under the influence of other students and professors, the more radical I became politically. My conservative family became quite disturbed. Two of the main sources of my acculturation were Maurice Bernstein '27 and Irving Furst '30, who had been brought up in the Hebrew Orphan Asylum in New York City. They were streetwise as well as very intellectual, philosophical, and literary. Both of them were very knowledgeable about radical politics.

There was a critical habit of mind at Reed. It wasn't in the curriculum as such; it was just the mental discipline of the people who were there, part of their mental set. Barry Cerf in literature taught us to discount the bathos and take a pretty hard-fisted grasp on literary things, on the statement of things. You didn't read book reviews, you didn't read critical articles, you read the works themselves. That was very important.

For years at Reed there weren't any black students. There was one black girl when I was there, Geraldine B. Turner '32, and she was a very quiet girl. I believe she was the first African-American female student to graduate from the college. Race just wasn't that prominent in our minds in those days.

People in the East sometimes said that Reed graduates were kind of "hairy," meaning rough in manners and poor in appearance. I sometimes feel that I became unsuited to general social intercourse when I was at Reed, because Reed was so wonderful in that respect. They had higher standards of judgment in just about everything.

CARL LARSON '27: My family moved to Portland from Kansas when I was in the third grade. My parents bought a home in the Woodstock addition about three-quarters of a mile from the Reed College campus. A lady came over to our house with three children in tow and asked if my sister and I would like to go down to the Reed campus with her kids. They had summer classes and games for neighboring children there at the time. That was my first introduction to Reed. My mom, Helen Larson, was working then in one of the hotels downtown as a housekeeper. She got to talking with this lady about working at Reed, and the lady recommended that she go see Cheryl Scholz, the dean of women. When my mom came home, she said, "I got a job. I'm going to supervise girls down at the dorm."

A lot of my mom's job was being like Dear Abby or Ann Landers. She liked working more with the men students than the women because they didn't have so many problems. My mom worked also for Herr Brunner, the janitor, cleaning up Dr. Knowlton's lab in the physics department. Her parents had emigrated from Germany to Kansas, and she could speak, read, and write German. Often, an informal gathering of students interested in German would come

Herr Robert Brunner—here with his student crew, circa 1935—served as Reed's janitor from 1912 to 1956.

to our house for Sunday dinner or some other occasion.

My mom was for getting all the education you could get, and she was pushing me all the time. My dad, though, thought I ought to go to work when I was about fifteen or sixteen, like the other boys in our neighborhood. There were five or six shipyards along the river in Portland, and any kid that was strong enough could get a job. My dad had started out working on the railroad, and had eventually worked his way up to locomotive engineer. That was the path he saw for me. I went to Benson Polytechnic High School in Portland, and so I was deficient in a whole bunch of stuff that you needed for Reed, like literature and history. But Dr. Knowlton in physics told me, "You're far ahead of most of these kids in math and science, and that will save you."

I didn't apply to Reed. The faculty and administrators all knew me, and they all knew my mom. I just signed some papers, paid my fees, and walked in and started school. I made most of my money for college playing baseball. A lot of the Portland businesses sponsored a baseball team in the summer. We didn't get paid for just playing baseball, we also got paid for working at the business that sponsored our team. I played a couple of years for a sawmill that was underneath the Sellwood Bridge, then for two of the banks in Portland, and later for Franz Bakery. I got about ten dollars a game.

MARGARET CHURCHILL LABOVITZ '30: My father was a man of ideas. He didn't do anything very conventionally if he could help it. He had many business ventures, almost all of which failed, including a piecrust factory in Chicago. He perfected a machine that made individual piecrusts. The company was very successful at making them, but they hadn't thought about shipping. This was before frozen foods. The crusts broke in shipping! My father went broke. Then he was given a Buick agency in a very nice

suburb of Chicago called La Grange. That's where I went to high school.

My father's brother was a successful lawyer in Portland. He and his wife came to visit, and thought that I seemed too thin and fragile and tired. They proposed taking me back with them to Portland for a year after I finished high school to build me up. My father had remarried, and I disapproved of my stepmother, so I went to Portland. My uncle and his wife lived in Portland Heights, where you could look out and see Mt. Hood in the distance. My aunt was a very attractive, vivacious person who had gone to Radcliffe College. During World War I she had handled a factory and was kind of an advanced woman for the time. I had a very good year living with them. My uncle was somewhat interested in Reed, and contributed to the college.

A couple of the girls that I met through my aunt had just finished high school and were planning to go to Reed. But I wasn't. I had a scholarship to the University of Chicago for the next year. My aunt, though, thought that I ought to go to an eastern school as she had. Every day I was expected to get up early and study for the college boards. Then I found out that Reed didn't require college boards! Besides, it sounded interesting. So, I ended up going to Reed. In the Portland community the general impression of Reed was that it was a rather wild, radical place, but of high intellectual standards.

MARY BARNARD '32: People now and then say to me, "You know, Reedies have a reputation," and I say, "Reedies have *always* had a reputation!" It has always been the same pretty much. When I was in grade school in Vancouver, Washington, kids said to me, "Oh, you'll go to Reed." It was because I was one of those "booky" people. Always reading. Always writing. I visited the classes at the University of Washington when I was in high school. The girls in the sorority had a small room they shared as the study, presumably, though there wasn't much studying going on that I could see. There was no real academic atmosphere in the sorority houses. It was social life that reigned supreme. Studying was just something that was an excuse for being at the school. Then I went to a poetry class. The young professor was introducing some poetry by a poet who the students had never heard of, A. E. Housman. But I had heard of him, and I was pretty disgusted that nobody else had.

Then I went to visit Reed. There were these roomy dorms, with two girls to a room, and two beds, and a place where I felt I could study. I could learn things. I just liked that. I liked the architecture. I liked the atmosphere of the place. Then I went to a Renaissance lecture by Barry Cerf, and I thought to myself, "This is going to be heaven." It was the atmosphere of books. Books: what an important thing!

In the Portland area Reed was looked upon by the young as a school for dreary drudges because there were no Greek-letter fraternities and sororities and no intercollegiate sports. Parents, on the other hand, viewed Reed as extremely dangerous. It condoned immorality, for one thing, because women students were allowed to smoke anywhere on campus. Also, the Reed dormitories were not supervised by housemothers. And of course the Reed faculty was considered dangerously radical. To cap it all off, the college was nondenominational. There was no compulsory chapel attendance; in fact, no religious services were held in the chapel, only concerts and lectures. Despite the staid gravity of President Coleman, a former clergyman, the rumor persisted that the principal subjects taught at Reed were "atheism, communism, and free love."

The stock market crashed the year after I entered college, and in the following years Reed was nothing like it was before or after, because so many people couldn't afford to go to college. I think they probably lowered their standards to take in more people. Enrollment increased to more than four hundred students, but the number of people living on campus dropped considerably since most people commuted from home. They closed one dorm, and there was just one girl in rooms set up for two. It was just very hard times. Only one man in the previous graduating class had been able to find a job, and he had been taken on as an assistant at Reed for an annual salary of $500.

Even so, we still occasionally went downtown to concerts, most often by entering the auditorium by a back door and sitting under the stage. One fabulous evening, Mrs. Howard Barlow, whose husband was a famous conductor and Reed graduate from the first class of 1915, called the president's office and said, "Send Reed College down." That night we had orchestra seats, and we all took taxis, as there were only two student-owned cars on campus.

ELIZABETH McCRACKEN McDOWELL '34: My dad was a dentist in Portland. Three of his patients were professors at Reed—Barry Cerf, Rex Arragon, and Charles McKinley. I went to the University of Oregon in Eugene for two years, then transferred into Reed as a junior. I lacked the background others got from the humanities courses in their freshman and sophomore years. The freshman class had had about 150 students. Only forty-nine graduated with me, so there was quite a turnover. A lot of that was due to students from rich families in Portland. For students considered too young to be sent away from home, they would send them to Reed for a year until they matured a bit, and then back East to Yale or Harvard or to one of the girls' schools like Radcliffe. That had been done for years.

JOSEPH GUNTERMAN '34: I was born in Calexico, California, on my great-uncle's ranch in the Imperial Valley. When I was in grammar school I was sent, along with two of my brothers, to Kassel, Germany, to live with my grandparents for three years. When it came time to go to college, I went to Pomona College, which seemed kind of dull. It was 1930, and everybody was having a bad time financially, including my father, so I transferred to Santa Barbara State Teachers College, but I was constantly finding fault with things there as well. A liberal economics professor thought I would fit in better at Reed. I had never heard of Reed, but, to my surprise, they admitted me.

While I was in grammar school in Germany, I had made friends with a fellow student, Franz Baumann '35. Franz stayed behind in Germany when I went back to the United States. He graduated from school, and wanted to be a doctor, but things got too rough in Germany for him because the Nazis had taken over. He told me he wanted to come to the United States, and asked if I could get him admitted to Reed College and find some funding for his tuition. I didn't have any trouble with the college. They were ready to admit him. I went to one of the Jewish groups in Portland and got a loan that enabled him to come over and study.

CECELIA GUNTERMAN WOLLMAN '37: I graduated from high school in Santa Barbara in 1933, but because of the Depression I didn't have any prospects. When my brother Joe Gunterman '34 left for his senior year at Reed he persuaded our folks to let me go back with him. It was a spontaneous, last-minute kind of an arrangement. I wasn't actually accepted until I got there and had an interview with President Coleman. He was a very nice man, and very popular. Joe's friend Franz Baumann '35, a Jewish refugee from Germany, also came up to Reed with us on that trip.

I didn't know that much about Reed's curriculum, except that it was a very open school, and that it had high standards. It wasn't "Joe College," by which in those days we meant a college with a high social life focused around football games. We knew that we didn't fit in with

that ambition. There were people at Reed from across the country, but they encouraged mostly the locals in Portland to attend. I think there were four or five of us who came up from southern California in 1933. A few years later a fair number of students came from the East. Instead of having exchange students with Europe, Reed had exchange arrangements with colleges from the East. They would come in and have a year at Reed and then go back to their own school.

HARRY TURTLEDOVE '42: I spent my junior year at Wesleyan University on an exchange scholarship from Reed. Wesleyan had an entirely different scheme. Attendance was taken. If your grade level was high enough, you were allowed unlimited cuts from class. If it wasn't, you could get in trouble by not attending. I found out that I was a rare bird because I was from Oregon, and at Wesleyan they considered people from Ohio to be from the West. That was their western boundary. Occasionally, they got somebody from California, but nobody really knew where Oregon was.

I realized how parochial Reed was. Before I went to Wesleyan, I had only seen one person in my life in a "soup and fish"—formal wear—and that was at a Reed dance. I was amazed that people at Wesleyan attended dances wearing tails and all the accoutrements. Here was a university that was over a hundred years old with New England tradition, and while they really weren't stuffy, they certainly weren't as informal as Reed. They also had fraternity houses, and that was a different world from Reed.

HARLOW LENON '35: My father was a lawyer, and almost wholly self-taught. He had a fragmentary grade-school education. He read books, and so I was raised in an atmosphere in which reading was central. We read out loud. My mother had a little college education. She and my father were both articulate and fairly intellectual. My father was not a very good money-producing lawyer, though. He never sent bills. Being a lawyer was a goal imposed upon me by my father, who was sure from the instant of my sex determination when I was born that I was going to be a lawyer. He never deviated, and I obeyed my father.

I had an interview with Dr. Coleman, who was Reed's president at the time. I told him what my father had told me to tell him, which is that I was going to go to law school, that we couldn't afford a full four-year term, and that I was probably bright enough to take some sophomore courses in my freshman year and junior courses in my sophomore year. Dr. Coleman apparently felt that I would qualify, and I think he was also prompted to take this peculiar arrangement because they needed the tuition money. So I got a special dispensation from Dr. Coleman to take two freshman humanities courses, History 11 and Literature 11, and three sophomore courses. My second year, I took all junior classes.

I was at Reed just two years, with no expectation of staying, but I was taken by it. When I had to quit Reed and go to night law school and be a daytime house painter, I hated it. I just worshipped Reed.

SAM LIU '36, trustee 1977–1981: I was born in southern China, about sixty-five miles southwest of Guangzhou, the capital of the province of Guangdong. My dad was working in the United States, and we were dependent on the money that he sent back every so often. He ran a laundry in Kansas City, not the usual Chinese laundry with handwork, but a regular modern laundry. He came back to China to pick up my brother and me when I was about fourteen years of age. He brought us to Portland. His intention was to have us stay in our cousin's place; we called him "cousin," because he came from the same village where we came from. My father said to my brother and me, "You need to have an education, but I can't afford it. You'll be on your own. I will

go back to Kansas City and then I'll support the family."

The cousin was an herbalist in Portland. He was generous enough to let us stay in his office. I slept in his examining room, on his couch, and my brother slept on the couch in the reception room. We went to school and then we cooked for the cousin's family in the evenings. The herbalist was making good money, because at that time a lot of people believed in Chinese herbs. The herbalist had a lot of orders from outside of Portland. They were all in bottles. I used to carry them to the post office. In the meantime, I also worked in a restaurant, mostly weekends, helping out the busboys, or cleaning up the floor in the evening. Twelve to fifteen hours a day, one dollar a day. When a regular waiter took a day off, I usually took his place. Later on, I got two routes delivering the *Morning Oregonian* newspaper. That meant I had to get up at three o'clock in the morning. My brother and I didn't go to bed until at least ten or eleven o'clock, cooking for the herbalist.

I didn't have the faintest idea where I was going to go after I finished high school. I knew I didn't have the money to get out of Portland. The teachers in Lincoln High School donated the money to establish a scholarship for me to go to Reed. I was still carrying the newspaper route during my freshman year. But over the next summer my brother and I got a job in Alaska working in a fish cannery. I went up there and I made $600, quite a bit of money in those days, enough money to pay for college.

I was interested in chemistry, and I liked medicine, too. There was a program where you spent three years at Reed and then you went straight to the University of Oregon medical school for two years. I thought that was surely the way to go. Eight or nine of us in that program went from Reed to medical school. We were together seven or eight years. We became very close. Because I was enrolled in that program, I escaped having to take the junior qualification exam at Reed, or having to write a thesis. While I was at Reed, I stayed in New Chinatown, at Fourth and Davis streets in Portland. My brother and I lived in a room that was about eight by eight feet. Just enough room to fit a double bed that we both slept in. No heat, only one electric wall outlet, and nowhere to study. I lived there all the way through medical school.

I think I was the only Chinese student at Reed. They accepted me, no discrimination whatsoever. It was a very accepting environment. I don't know what was said behind my back, of course. The majority of my friends at Reed were Jews. I had gone to Shattuck Elementary School in Portland and most of the people who lived in the area around the school were Jewish people, so most of my classmates were Jewish. Some of them came with me to Reed, including Oscar Gass '34, who became a Rhodes Scholar.

DONALD WHEELER '35: I grew up on a farm in a fruit-growing town called White Bluffs along the Columbia River in eastern Washington. We grew apricots, pears, and peaches. White Bluffs was later closed down and bulldozed to make room for the Hanford Project, which was where they made plutonium for the Manhattan Project.

There were six kids in our family. Two boys and four girls. My parents were well read. My older brother George earned enough money when he was fifteen to get electricity put in the farmhouse. It was one bulb hanging down on a string over this great big table. We all sat around in the evening, reading. We had a family bookcase that had more books than any family in town. My grandmother and my mother were both activists in the women's movement and the state women's club. One of their accomplishments was the creation of a traveling library in Washington state. This truck would come up

Students and faculty taking a break from their labors during Canyon Day in the early 1930s.

alongside our front porch with books that we had ordered. We also had a set of encyclopedias, *Webster's Unabridged Dictionary*, and quite a few magazines and newspapers, including the *New York Times* and the *Seattle Union Record*. Some of our neighbors would ask, "How come you spend all that money on daily newspapers?" My dad would say, "Oh, we need them for starting fires." I don't think anyone was convinced by that.

My father was a partial Marxist. His father really wanted him to follow him into the ministry, but he decided to become a skilled worker. I think he was probably one of the very few human beings that ever deliberately decided to go into the working class. He felt that he was one of a united front of workers. So he became a very skilled bricklayer.

The decision in my family to attend Reed started with my eldest sister, Margaret Jean '26. She got into Reed because her grades were very good and she had some excellent references. Then my brother George '29 went to Reed, which made it a pretty well-established thing in our family. When it came time for me to go to Reed, I piloted a boat down the Columbia River with a friend of mine, Robert Nitzsche. Robert built the boat and then he bought a motor from Montgomery Ward with a three-month free trial offer. We put in at White Bluffs and made our way down the river to the banks of Vancouver, Washington. There, Robert gave his boat away to a kid that was playing on the beach, since we couldn't take it back upriver, and we caught a trolley service into Portland, where we took the boat motor back to Montgomery Ward with no questions asked. Then I got a trolley and bus over to the Reed campus.

My second year at Reed, I came down the river by raft. We used to catch a lot of logs at White Bluffs as they were coming down the Columbia. We would spike them together and make a little transport raft, and then ride it down the river over the rapids. When I got to be sixteen, I was the only man alive who had run Priest Rapids, which doesn't exist anymore because they built a dam to drown out the rapids. But that was quite a mark of distinction then. When time came for me to go down to Reed, I made a little raft about ten feet across and fifteen feet long. I pushed off from White Bluffs and rode it down to Umatilla, Oregon, where I left it, and hitchhiked the rest of the way into Portland on a dynamite truck returning from Idaho.

HELEN WHEELER HASTAY '39: The first time I saw Reed was when I was five. My sister, Margaret Jean '26, was living in the dorms, and Mother and I went down to visit. What made me really want to go to Reed was eating in the Commons. They served butter in dishes. I had never seen little butter dishes. Right then, I thought that this was the place that I had to go. Living in the dorm seemed amazing to me. We lived on the farm with no indoor plumbing, so this was my first experience with a bathroom. I saw this great big tub. I went in, locked the door, filled the tub to the top, and started sliding down the back part of the tub. I was never happier. I thought, this is for me. I could hear my sister, Margaret Jean, outside the door, saying, "Helen, unlock this door at once." But I wouldn't do it, I was having so much fun. They finally had to come in through the window. Jean said, "Mother, you have to do something about this child." So they took me away from the college.

I made up my mind that I was going to Reed. That's all. It didn't occur to me that in order to get to Reed I'd have to study really hard. Mother said "You know, Helen, George and Donald and Margaret Jean were all good students and liked to study." She was very gentle about it, but she said, "You have never really liked to study very much." I thought, "Well, big deal." The Depression, which was so hard on everybody, was good for me, because they were accepting a lot of people applying to go to Reed at that time. I knew the reputation Reed had, what with all those false things about Reed being named for the Portland Communist John Reed who had gone to Russia. It would always grate on me when I would hear things that were so totally false. When I was first getting ready to come to Reed, I had never been to a hairdresser, and somebody thought I should have my hair cut before I went, so they provided me with a haircut. This woman hairdresser asked, "You're going to school?" I said, "Yes, I'm going to Reed College." I was so proud. She said, "Oh, that's a military school, isn't it?" That was just about as ignorant as a lot of things I heard said about Reed.

When I got to Reed I had never worked a job, except around the house and on the farm. I thought I was going to live in the dorms. Instead—and I have never quite understood how this happened—I ended up living with Rex and Gertrude Arragon, and being their cook and dishwasher. So here I was, never having worked in my life, never having studied in my life, and I was having to do both. I was just in a turmoil for several months. My brother Donald was a good person to have there for my first year, because that year he was named a Rhodes Scholar, and so I got a lot of fame. They had a torchlight parade all around Eastmoreland and carried him on their shoulders. It was pretty exciting.

EARNEST MOVIUS '37: I was born in Selah, Washington, which is just outside of Yakima. My dad worked as an accountant in a lumberyard. My mother had been a primary-grade teacher in the North Dakota area before she came to Washington, so she saw to it that I did a good bit of homework as a first-grader. After the first year of grade school, my teacher said, "You know, this boy does not belong in second grade, he belongs in the third grade." That became a pattern. I skipped most of fifth grade, and sixth. I didn't know what was going on. I was getting the pinch from behind to do better, to do more, and in the meantime, I was sociologically dropping backwards. I started high school at age twelve. It was a killer socially. I couldn't go to the high school dances because I was too young. At the end of my third year in high school, the teacher said, "Hey, you've got enough credits to get out of this school." So they booted me out and I got my diploma. I was fourteen.

In the meantime, my older sister had moved to Portland to live with my aunt, who taught school in the Sellwood neighborhood. My aunt knew about Reed, and said that you wouldn't find a better school. She offered my sister, Myrta '35, room and board so that she could go to Reed. When I finished high school she offered me the same deal. I was fourteen when I applied to Reed. Lucy Hodgkinson, who worked in the administration at the college, said, "What are you thinking? Go home and develop some social amenities." That stuck with me.

I returned to Selah and got a job as a grocery clerk. I worked in the grocery store for two years and, during the interim, developed some testicles, I guess. I began to be interested in girls. I was a hard character to handle, because I was beginning to date and going to movies and that sort of thing. While I worked at the store, I went to Yakima Valley Junior College for two years. Then I went back to Reed. The interviewer, Tony Knowlton, professor of physics, looked at my grades from junior college and, lo and behold, accepted me as a junior at sixteen. That was two years after they told me I was too young to start as a freshman. My sister was still at Reed. We both lived at my aunt's apartment. She slept with my aunt, and I slept on the davenport.

JOSEPHINE LEWIS UTLEY '39: I first learned about Reed when my older sister, Claudia Lewis '30, entered in 1926. I was ten years old at the time. My sister was very intellectual and very accomplished. As time went on, I didn't think I was really probably suited to be a Reedite. Claudia had had to wait two years to go to college because my father died very young, and we had a big family of five kids. My father had been head of the department of horticulture at Oregon State College in Corvallis, and a very prestigious man nationally. The girls in the family were expected to stay home and help more than the boys; however, my mother was determined that we all go to college, and so she went to work.

When Claudia came home on vacation, she often brought her Reed friends along. My brothers would make fun of them and tease Claudia about the way they acted and the way they looked. There was one girl who giggled all the time, and a boy who would eat his pancakes with one drop of syrup. My brothers thought that these people were sort of freakish and too intellectual. The editor of the *Corvallis Gazette-Times* wrote an editorial about how tragic it was that my sister was going to "a communist school" like Reed, when her father had been such a nationally known person, and so important in Corvallis.

When it came time for me think about college, I thought I should go to the University of Oregon, where my brother was doing so well. He was in a fraternity and having a great time. After having been disappointed in love in Corvallis, and not getting along with the high school boys there, I was longing for a little romance and fun and parties, and I thought that wouldn't happen at Reed. I wanted to go to dances, and not just study like they did at Reed, which seemed too scholarly and rarefied. Claudia, my sister, gave me an examination to see if I would be right for Reed. Based on that, she decided I would pass. I was easily influenced by my sister's judgment and her happiness, so I applied to Reed and was accepted. When I entered, it was an immediate epiphany of wonder. I hadn't expected it to be fun. I thought it was just going to be terribly hard work.

As freshmen, we were all assigned to read Michael Rostovtzeff's *A History of the Ancient World*. Rostovtzeff was very difficult and different from anything I had ever read in history. A real eye-opener. Then, almost immediately, two of the senior boys, Don Wheeler '35 and Bill Maxwell '35, took it upon themselves to tutor us freshman girls living in Anna Mann cottage. Bill Maxwell became interested in me one of the first nights. He became sort of a counselor to my intellect. He told me right away to read Evelyn Waugh's *Vile Bodies*, and D. H. Lawrence, people I had never yet heard of.

The next most wonderful thing was that, after dinner almost every night, we went into one of the men's dorms in House H, now called Winch, and put on records and danced a little while before we went to the library. That was such fun. I happened to be a very good dancer, because my brother was a superb dancer, and he had taught me. So for the first time in my life, men were "fighting" to get to dance with me, whereas in high school, I'd been considered just a drag. There were all these wonderful things happening, intellectual and playful.

RUTH WETTERBORG SANDVIK '38: Mother had a friend whose daughter had applied to Reed and received a scholarship. So Mother got the papers to fill out. They asked for some project that you had accomplished. I said to Mother, "I haven't done *anything*! What'll I write?" She said, "You sewed that gray wool suit. Just write about that." At about that same time, a Presbyterian minister came to our house wanting to offer me a scholarship to Albany College in Portland, which later became Lewis & Clark College. Mother said, "Well, we were thinking of sending Ruth to Reed College." The man said, with great emphasis, "I wouldn't send a dog to Reed College!"

He didn't know the personalities he was dealing with. That remark just made us more eager to apply to Reed. What we knew about Reed was that people in Portland said it was "communistic, and atheistic, and it had free love." Amanda Reed was a Unitarian, but I guess people thought she was atheistic. I've always said that Reed was communistic because we were taught how to think there. Now where I got the idea that communists "thought," I don't know, but I did. And then free love. I always enjoyed saying, "I didn't get any."

DORIS BAILEY MURPHY '38: My family lived in Portland until I was eighteen, and then my parents moved to Phoenix for a year or two. I went to the University of Arizona for one year, played, joined a sorority, did all that stuff. We came back to Portland during the Depression, in 1931. My parents were disappointed in me for almost flunking out in Arizona and weren't ready to send me back to school. My father was an architect with a graduate degree from Boston University, and my mother had graduated from a women's college. They valued education very highly, along with the old Protestant values and hard work.

I was always interested in the arts and in literature, so I started a little magazine in Portland called *The Dilettante*. I met a lot of literary people as a result. After that, I started an art colony down on the west-side waterfront of the Willamette River. We renovated an old building and got the landlord to give the artists low rent. A number of my friends did painting and murals that got hung in public places. Others participated in writing a history of the area for the WPA. Some of these artists were going to Reed at the time; some had been there and graduated. Reed was a popular place for the likes of us, who were both literary and political.

I didn't think I would get into Reed given my terrible grades at the University of Arizona, but I went out to campus and talked to the director of admissions, Mr. James Hamilton. I convinced him to let me write a paper about what I had been doing with the magazine and the art colony, and that impressed him enough to let me start on a probationary basis for the first three months.

My very first class was with Barry Cerf. That was my introduction to the *Iliad*, the *Odyssey*, and Shakespeare. I was hooked. Cerf was such a wonderful teacher. He took an interest in me, because I was on probation to begin with, and also because, at twenty-three, I was older than the other freshman students. My other class was with Dr. Alexander Goldenweiser, who taught sociology. I got hooked on everything about sociology. I wrote a research paper on prostitution. I went to the houses of prostitution in Portland and interviewed the prostitutes. It was so well received that Dr. Goldenweiser said, "This is where you belong." Then there was Lloyd Reynolds. He taught creative writing, art history, and eighteenth-century literature.

With these professors, I had a great time. Students and faculty were very close. Some of the professors we called by their first names, some of them we didn't. We saw them socially, and sometimes we drank with them. But it didn't interfere in any way with our student-professor relationship. None of us took advantage of the fact that our professors were very friendly and invited us to tea or drinks.

Portlanders used to say, "Oh, you go to that college that has free love." Whatever that meant. There was a lot of "coupling," as they say, in the dormitories. It was not frowned upon as it would have been at a different kind of college. Most people knew who was sleeping with whom. They were great times, great times! I often wonder if people who came after us, particularly in the 1950s, which was a more restrictive time, had as much fun as we did.

OMA "AMY" WOODCOCK SINGER '38: I grew up in a little town called South Bend along the Washington coast, where my mother had grown up. She was one-half Chinook Indian and had been sent as a girl to the Chemawa Indian Boarding School down in Salem, Oregon. My father was from eastern Washington. He was orphaned, along with his brothers and sister, and lived a very hard life. He went to Catholic school in Walla Walla and then went on to live on a horse ranch and train horses. He didn't get beyond the fourth grade.

Growing up in South Bend, all of my friends were Chinook Indians. There were eight in my family. My mother loved to read to us when we were little. We didn't have any electricity, so she would light a lamp on the dining room table and we would sit around and listen to her reading. Crossword puzzles were just starting then, and my mother was entranced with them. There was a crossword-puzzle contest that she entered into in Chicago, and she won a set of encyclopedias. We just thought that was heaven!

When my older sister graduated from high school in South Bend, no one would walk across the stage with her at the graduation ceremony. They all said, "We aren't going to walk with an Indian." The Indian boys, who were very good football players, were sought after by the white girls, who wanted to date them. But the Indian girls were never invited for social activities to the homes of the white people there.

My mother decided to send me and my two older brothers to the Chemawa Indian Boarding School in Salem, where she had gone as a girl. It was run like a military school. We marched to our meals. We marched to school. We marched to chapel. We didn't mind it much. It sort of kept things orderly.

There were probably fifteen hundred to two thousand Indian students there from all over the West and Alaska, so I got to meet a lot of very interesting young people, and that was a wonderful experience. They had a lot of programs there for us, but none of them had to do with Indian culture. We had chapel on Sunday night with different ministers who came and talked to the young people. Young Indian people were encouraged to play in the band and to attend the dances, which were waltzes; but there were no Indian dances,

no drumming. If the young people spoke their native language, they were punished.

Chemawa had what was called an "outing" system, where they took young women who were good in home economics and placed them in homes as maids and housekeepers. One day the home economics teacher came to me and said, "There are a number of teachers from Reed College in Portland who have young Indian women working in their homes and, if you want to, we can place you in one of those homes and see how you like it." So in the spring of 1934 I agreed to go up to the Portland home of Larry Hartmus, who was the Latin and Greek instructor at Reed. I worked as a housekeeper and a maid, taking care of the Hartmuses' little five-year-old boy. After I had been there three or four months, and had had a chance to read many of their wonderful books—I especially liked *The New Yorker*, to which they subscribed—Mr. Hartmus came to me one day and said, "Are you interested in going to college? You seem to be able to read and understand most of my books here. You could go to college and continue to work here. Go over to Reed and talk to them."

I went over and I talked to the president, Mr. Coleman. He interviewed me, and then someone from the psychology department gave me a test. They called me back and said I was in the ninety-sixth percentile, which didn't mean anything to me. I had no idea what the word "percentile" even meant. They said if you can get a scholarship, you can come to Reed. I went back and talked to Mr. Hartmus and he said, "I'll help you fill out the scholarship applications." In August 1934, the papers came back, and they said, "Go over and register at Reed College!"

The first month I was at Reed, one of the teachers had talked to somebody from the *Oregonian* and said that I was the first person of Indian background who had ever gone to Reed. The *Oregonian* reporter wanted to interview me. I talked to my advisor about it, and he said, "I don't think

Fall registration in the late 1930s. In the center is history instructor Dorothy Johansen '33.

you should have that in the paper." "Why not?" I asked. "Well," he said, "I don't think it would help you any to have people know that you were part Indian. You don't look Indian. You might not have too many friends if you bring this out. Tell the *Oregonian* no."

I was very much aware that there was prejudice, even amongst educated people. When I got to study sociology with Dr. Goldenweiser in my junior year, we talked about my background all the time. He thought it was terrific that I had gotten to come to college. I greatly admired him. He had worked with Margaret Mead, and a lot of what he covered was interesting anthropology, about things that Mead had been studying in the South Pacific. He had so much information that he could just charm you. Oh, my goodness. That was really, really something. He was an inspiration, Dr. Goldenweiser.

ALICE SCHOTT RICHARDS '38: My parents moved from Santa Barbara to New York City when I was a teenager, and since they didn't like the idea of my going so far away for college, I ini-

tially went to Skidmore College, which was a girls' college in upstate New York, for one year. Then I went to Europe, to Switzerland, for a year. It was a marvelous year. I think it was the high point of my whole academic life. It opened up all kinds of new thoughts to me. After that, I came to Reed for a year, and liked it very much. Partly because I was older at Reed, but also because I had had the experience of living in Europe, I took a greater interest in history and other cultures than I would have had otherwise. I was also concerned with so many people being unemployed and having a very hard time. I was affected by the times we lived in. It was a very controversial period in American life, with the New Deal being attacked by many people who didn't like it. I felt very supportive of what the New Deal was trying to do, and that set me off in a sort of a radical direction. My family was relatively well off and I felt rather guilty about that. It made me want to get to the source material of things very often.

The Reed curriculum was much richer and broader and deeper than what I experienced at either Skidmore or Berkeley, where I went later. I had never been in a classroom where you read original sources or that had anything like the quality of learning about the music and art of different periods of history that we got from the humanities courses. Reed was also more challenging. At Berkeley, classes were so big that you didn't really have much chance for discussions with your professors. The discussions tended to be among the students themselves. Faculty pretty much just lectured.

I got into some personal problems that resulted in me leaving Reed after a year. First, a Reedite caused me a lot of personal distress. He was a married student who fell in love with me, and I was very upset about what I should do. Then, I made the serious mistake of getting married while I was there. My first husband was not a Reedite but somebody I had known for many years in Santa Barbara, and I made the mistake of marrying him. Unfortunately, soon I was pregnant and had to drop out and raise a family.

KATHARINE BAKER COOKE '41: I didn't go to school until I was age nine, and then I went to something called the Spring Hill School in Litchfield, Connecticut. It was based on John Dewey's Little Red School House and was similar to the so-called "progressive" schools. Then I went on as a boarding pupil to the Cambridge School in western Massachusetts, also a progressive school, and very much into social issues. They gave us all sorts of interesting experiences, like going to see the Boston Bruins play hockey, attending the Boston Symphony Orchestra, and listening to Earl Browder, who was then head of the U.S. Communist Party.

My parents wanted me to go to Vassar and learn to be a lady, and I told them to stuff it. The counselor at Cambridge School said that I should go to Reed College. "Goodie," I said. It was three thousand miles away. Wheee! I liked the idea. My family had enough money—not Rockefell-er money—that they could send me where they liked.

Bewilderment! That was my first impression of Reed. It was three thousand miles of difference—a different cultural setup. It was more informal than what I had interacted with back East. You didn't have to be introduced to talk to somebody! Well, that's exaggerating, but the natives were friendly. Even the professors were friendly. While it was a different culture from back East, the dead hand of the past didn't extend beyond about 1908. Someone said, "There's a lovely old building." I said, "Where is this old building?" Someone said, "It says right at the top, '1908.'"

And I thought, Oh! Back in New England, it would have been 1708. I wasn't quite sure what was going on.

ELIZABETH TABOR MULLADY '38: Reed was the only college in town that accepted women. I didn't know how good it was; in fact, it had a bad reputation in my Portland neighborhood as a hotbed of free love and radicalism, neither of which I saw much of there.

I had to live at home. My father had been injured and wasn't able to work. When I got out of high school at sixteen, I knew I had to put myself through school. So I went to Behnke-Walker Business College for a year and learned shorthand and typing. That way I was able to get a part-time job while in college. But it was the Depression and there weren't any jobs when I got out. Even Reed didn't have a job for me when I first enrolled. Then Reed's director of admissions, Dr. James Hamilton, lost his assistant, and I worked for him the rest of my time at Reed, including full-time during the summer.

Since I worked in the admissions office, I could review all the applications. I found out what President Coleman had written about me after my interview: "Strong, keen, independent. Should make a good record at Reed." I saw the application of one boy who was an athlete and sounded so well-rounded. I said to Dr. Hamilton, "Here's somebody who's really normal." Dr. Hamilton said, "If they're too normal, they wouldn't do well at Reed."

ELLIOTT ROBERTS '39: I came to Reed from Wasco County in eastern Oregon. My grandfather, Albert Sturges Roberts, may have been the first white child born in Wasco County. He was considered one of the pioneers in the county and The Dalles society, a position of considerable prestige. Grandfather put together a ranch of about seven thousand acres of dry land with considerable capacity for the production of wheat. It was an absolutely beautiful site, but very dry. He was also a businessman, and later elected to the state senate.

Often, the isolation on the ranch seemed very great because the roads could be hub-deep in mud. The way you communicated with people was you had a crank on every telephone and when you called them, you had to holler, "ARE YOU THERE? CAN YOU HEAR ME?" When the bell rang, it rang on every party's telephone, although with different signals. The signal on the ranch was a long, two shorts, and a long. When that rang, anybody who was interested in what the Roberts families were doing got on the line and listened intently.

When I was seven, my mother's sister, Daryl, who was a teacher in Portland high schools, said, "He'll never get an education in a country school. You've got to send him to stay with me in Portland, where he can get a good education." My father objected strenuously. It had to do with the values that were held by country people in eastern Oregon and those of my Aunt Daryl, a woman who had become thoroughly citified. Until then I had never left the ranch except for very brief visits to nearby relatives. I was a ranch kid. Eventually, I was sent to Portland to go to school. It was a fairly dramatic change. My first years were totally miserable. I did not like the city in

terms of its impersonality, hostility, and capacities for disagreeable surprises and disempowerment, in one form or another. During Christmas vacations, spring breaks, and the summertime, I was back on the ranch, so my identification remained very, very strong with that ranch.

I was just short of sixteen when I graduated from Lincoln High School in Portland. The teachers at Lincoln who made up the scholarship committee decided to offer me a $300 scholarship to Reed College. What I found out a good deal later was that my iron-willed Aunt Daryl had gone to her colleagues at Lincoln and said, "I want him to go to Reed College. Never mind those other also-ran institutions around Portland." The decision was not mine, but I found myself at Reed. It was the old story about the career-directing scholarship: bend the twig and the tree grows in that direction.

Lincoln High in Portland was a public school with many good people in it, but it was very stratified and essentially economic royalty, or at least economic aristocracy. My friend Leonard Rowland came to school with cardboard in his shoes. He was a bright guy but someone caught by the Depression and being squeezed out of shape. I don't know what happened to him after graduating from Lincoln, but he didn't have the Reed experience, the opportunity to grow as I did.

One of the things that I'm deeply grateful for is that Reed gave me some measure of perspective outside of the overwhelming grim reality of the Depression, a time-integrative perspective on how all of these desperate people had fared over millennia. If you don't go to a school like Reed, you don't get that in college. College life gets diverted in various ways, turning into things about the best fraternity or about how to beat the system in taking exams in a class. But Reed College gave me an opportunity—effectively peer-enforced, faculty-enforced—to internalize a set of standards for understanding the nature of mankind.

CHAPTER 11

No Rules, No Regulations

There was lots of questioning about anything and everything. Nothing was out of bounds. You could question anything and talk about it. That was encouraged.
  —Genny Hall Smith '43

Reed students had a libertarian streak. There was a sense that you had a right to decide for yourself, and down with all rules and regulations.
  —Ann Stearns Whitehead '44

During Reed's first two decades, the college's image of academic purity tended to attract intellectually adventurous students. By the 1930s, they also came because of the element of freedom that Reed projected in both its scholarly and social life. Self-selection and socialization on campus were beginning to produce what was to the external community a recognizable Reed "type," one strongly distinguished by individualism, political radicalism, and social nonconformity.

The Honor Principle, which had served as the main means of social control for a relatively homogeneous student body during the first twenty years, began showing signs of being a less pervasive community ethos as students moved toward more personal interpretations of the principle. A laissez-faire attitude of protecting the individual from controls of the community, especially in the case of social freedoms on campus, emerged in its place.

REGINALD "REX" ARRAGON, history professor 1923–1962, 1970–1974: Dexter Keezer brought a fresh breeze to the college that at first invigorated, but then chilled. This was due to a temperamental disposition that made the president difficult to work with, ranging from impatience, petulance, and scolding, to disparagement of individuals, threats, and retaliations.

While Keezer initially raised justifiable questions about the curriculum, individual teaching effectiveness, and student behavior in the dormitories, he could not refrain from antagonizing many of his collaborators. Faculty members, in his view, were unduly sensitive, although he would occasionally apologize for an outburst a day or two later, explaining that he was made that way. This explanation regrettably came to appear true.

Conflict arose over dormitory problems and the authority of the president of the college in relation to the roles of the student-appointed Dormitory Council and the effectiveness of student government.

CLEMENT AKERMAN, economics professor 1920–1943: Mr. Keezer seemed to feel that the students should be guided more in their conduct by the faculty. I felt that students were able to take care of themselves in most ways, and that they should be left alone in their social lives to a great extent, and allowed to form their own methods of governance and entertainment. The students themselves felt very strongly about their self-government, and they resented any efforts to be bossed. If anything seemed to infringe upon their self-government, they were up in arms.

There were a few incidents of students publishing things in the *Quest* newspaper that some members of the faculty felt were not proper, and we had some differences over that. On the whole, though, the student government that was set up seemed to work. We had the Community Affairs Committee, which was composed partly of faculty members and partly of student members, and which handled most of the problems of student administration, including questions of conduct on the part of the students.

WILBUR L. PARKER '36: The Honor Principle worked pretty well. Once in a while, someone would slop over and get pulled up for it. If you got hauled before the Student Council with a charge against you, they were almost sure to say, "Leave the college. You're through." They weren't very merciful. If you pulled some dumb stunt—like one student who stood outside the Commons at a dance one night and obnoxiously offered drinks to everybody—they threw him out. If a girl was

caught in flagrante delicto, they just threw her out. That was it!

ELEANOR MAY '45: There were rules about drinking. You could drink on the campus, but you couldn't drink in mixed company, meaning mixed sexes. Also if you sat together in mixed company on the couch or whatever, you had to keep one foot on the floor.

One time I had been downtown with a fellow. He was twenty-one and I was nineteen. At that time in Oregon, you had to carry your own bottle into drinking establishments; you couldn't just buy a drink over the counter. We had some drinks downtown and there was a little liquor left in the pint bottle. When we got back to the campus, he said, "I don't want to leave this sitting here, let's not waste it." So we drank it in mixed company. I was on the Student Council at the time, and somebody came before us to be reprimanded for having been found drinking in mixed company on campus. I thought, "Oh my God, I did it too." So I told the other members of the Council, and one of the boys said, "Shut up." I did, and never said another word about it.

ELIZABETH TABOR MULLADY '38: My introduction to the Honor Principle was in the intro to biology course. We had to get a bug collection—go out and find bugs. Ever try to find bugs in October in Oregon? There weren't any bugs. I spent every afternoon on the nearby Eastmoreland golf course, running around with a butterfly net. The trouble was, there were swans down there who chased me. So I talked to the athletic director, Mr. Botsford, and got permission to claim as my P.E. activity being chased around the golf course by swans. I actually got in a lot of running, and it was all the gym I needed. I hated gym anyway. But it turned out that several people were cheating in that biology class with the bugs. Whether somebody reported them and they had trials before the Student Council and

Gilbert Prentiss Lee '39 and Mary Kuylaars '39 in a dorm room during intervisitation hours.

were thrown out, or they left voluntarily, I don't know. But they disappeared.

ANN STEARNS WHITEHEAD '44: Reed students had a libertarian streak. There was a sense that you had a right to decide for yourself, and down with all rules and regulations. The Honor Principle was the heart of the whole thing—you were responsible for yourself, and expected to police yourself, essentially. The business that you could take your exam back to your dorm room, but you weren't supposed to look up anything—that was very powerful. It worked. If you broke the Honor Principle there was enormous social disapproval from your peers—tremendous rejection and disgust, which was probably more powerful than anything. But you needed at least a modicum of maturity to handle that kind of responsibility. I saw some people who just went to pieces because they couldn't take charge of themselves and there wasn't anybody to take charge of them.

CHERYL SCHOLZ, dean of women 1924–1937, history professor 1938–1943, dean of admission 1943–1945: I sat on the Community Affairs Committee from 1925 to 1944. Comprised of students

and faculty, the committee served as something of an appeals body for students hauled before the Student Council and found guilty of breaking the Honor Principle. I found that something the young do not care to do is to pass judgment on somebody else. That was the weakness of student government, and it is why a great many colleges in the country won't have it. The pressure on everybody when they are in college is to get through it, and to get some education under their belt. They sometimes do what is expedient, with the justification that they won't cheat later.

DEXTER KEEZER, president 1934–1942: Behavior that the student community generally agreed was dishonorable consistently prompted vigorous corrective action. That seemed to evaporate, however, in dealing with conduct in fields where there was not sufficient agreement among students as to what constituted offensive behavior, such as those involving amorous activities of young men and women and the consumption of alcohol. Indeed, in such controversial fields the Student Council seemed to avoid imposing any government at all. Even the elementary contention that the Oregon state liquor law—which

PART TWO: THE GOLDEN AGE, 1921–1945

contained prohibitions against the possession of alcohol by minors—applied to the college campus was strenuously resisted by a durable element in the Student Council, largely on the grounds that it undermined the more compelling principle of individual self-determination in such matters. It may have been that the Honor Principle, with its compulsions of individual conscience, was hopelessly compromised when absolute regulation was introduced.

That line of argument was well worn by many agents of student government in resisting regulation in closing hours of dormitories and the visiting back and forth between men's and women's residence halls. The resistance enlisted equally enthusiastic support on the part of young men who had earthy objectives, and on a group of young idealists who, proceeding on a high and detached plane, were concerned about "the principle of the thing."

One of the latter put it as follows: "I believe that a functioning, organic group, such as the students of this college, have certain rights of self-determination which are ethically and legally beyond the control of any external authority whatever, faculty or regents. I believe the faculty has certain rights, such as freedom of academic discussion, which are similarly beyond the right of the regents to control. Any contrary doctrine is likely to be based on the pernicious theory of absolute sovereignty—a theory which, clothed in various sorts of mystical nonsense, has done perhaps more damage to modern civilization than any other idea."

This flight inspired one of the more impish of the student champions of social laissez-faire to remark to me, "Gosh, it's great to know that interference with freedom of necking is practically unconstitutional." To others it seemed like a dignified and erudite way of obscuring the fact that, like many of their elders, they did not know what to think or do about standards of social behavior of the sort in question.

I doubted that a police system, maintained by college administration, would be able to enforce standards of social behavior much safer and saner than those that the students involved wanted enforced. If the students themselves tried to do the job—granted, in a way most of their elders would find pretty casual—some important elements of education may be involved. I believed, though, that the administration could still do a great deal to create a social environment conducive to the development of standards of social conduct, apart from devising rules and regulations and policing them.

CECELIA GUNTERMAN WOLLMAN '37: President Keezer wanted us to be more decorous in our lifestyle on campus. Among the many things that came up for discussion with him was whether we were going to have dorm controls, including the business of locking the doors in the women's dorms in the evenings. Intervisitation was another one—whether we could have men in the women's dorms and under what conditions and at what hours. That was very intensely debated.

RUTH WETTERBORG SANDVIK '38: We used to say that for every girl there were seven boys—a woman's dream—but six didn't count because they were buried in their books! There were some bashful young men who were very nice. They were from farm places in eastern Oregon. But they were so bashful that we never got a chance to talk to them. The junior boys would look over the freshman girls and pick out which ones they wanted to be friends with. Wilbur Parker '36 picked me out to be his girlfriend. When I passed the French reading test in my freshman year, Wilbur told me that it was because it was easy that particular year. He didn't want me to think too much of my ability.

KATHARINE BAKER COOKE '41: There was a girl from one of Portland's wealthier families who was supposed to be living in the dorms, but she and her beau had a house. She went off and slept with him at his place. I unmade her bed so it could get made up in the morning by the "harpies," which is what we called the maids who serviced our rooms.

At first, we didn't have any sign-out if you left the dorm at night, but then some parent got agitated because they couldn't find their kid. The other problem was that they started to get robberies in the dorms. So they decided that if you were going to go out for the night, you had to write down where you were going, and then sign back in when you returned. They also decided to have a night watchman. The night watchman had the keys to all the dorms and he would let you in after they were locked in the evenings.

THOMAS LAMB FRAZIER '42: I worked as the night watchman on campus. The job gave me startling views of the extracurricular activities at the college—students coming home at night drunk and getting sick all over the dormitory, or hiding their whiskey bottles in the ivy outside of their dorm room windows. Liquor on campus was against the rules, but very much a part of expected behavior. When I came upon couples in their cars or in the canyon behind Eliot Hall, I was embarrassed.

ANN STEARNS WHITEHEAD '44: I went to enough other colleges to know that Reed was probably the only college at the time that allowed men and women to visit in each other's dorms. There was only one visitation period allowed for men in the women's dorms, and that was on Sundays from two PM to seven PM. But in the evenings we had no hours for women. If you went out, you signed out, so that if you didn't show up when they locked the dorm at midnight or one AM, there would be some record of it. Then, when you came back, at whatever hour, the night watchman would let you in.

PHYLLIS GLASENER WHITMAN '44: The rule in the women's dorms on Sundays was that the men had to keep one foot in the hall all the time. They couldn't go into the girls' rooms. I saw many card games played with the card table right up to the door and the guys sitting out in the hall with the girls playing inside the room.

DEXTER KEEZER, president: I am sure that co-educational college education is relatively desirable, both intellectually and socially, for many young men and women. But I have also seen some fine young women tormented, and perhaps even permanently scarred, by being set down in residence in a coeducational college on the careless assumption that what is good for many girls is good for all.

At seventeen or eighteen many girls, who a few years later will become handsome and well-poised, are gawky and ill at ease in almost any company. In getting across a room they are apt to stumble over their own feet. They have the habit of backing into potted palms. They are helpless and hopeless in the pervasive sort of competition for the attention of young men that a coeducational residential college sets up in some degree. Some remain passively miserable. Others seek to offset their social ineptitudes by various desperate expedients to attract attention, many of them dangerous. Then there is the type of girl who seems to have all the social grace and poise that the gawky ones lack, but who is inadequately endowed with common sense. If they are pretty, as frequently seems to be the case, a combination capable of causing a lot of trouble all around is created.

A few months after I arrived at Reed, the mother of a freshman girl who struck me as both extraordinarily pretty and self-possessed burst into my office to announce that she was withdrawing her daughter from college and committing her to a hospital to recover from complete exhaustion. She said that for weeks her daughter had taken advantage of the freewheeling social system of the college to stay up every night until three or four o'clock entertaining a beau. It seemed to me incredible that any young man would have such a durable passion even for the most fascinating girl. A dormitory mate of the young lady later set me right by explaining that four young men shared in keeping the almost all-night schedule.

SYLVIA CAMPBELL POWELL '42: Ethelwynne Lewis '42 was this wonderful girl from Hawaii. She wasn't native Hawaiian, just a great big gal, and lots of fun. We all thought it would be great to have Ethelwynne run for student body president, since the student body presidents were always men, just as a spoof to show that women could run if they wanted to. She agreed to go along, although we didn't expect her to win, it was just to have fun. We posted flyers and threw a lot of nice parties for her, including shows with Ethelwynne dancing in a shadow scene. We put

a curtain up and put a light behind her dancing so that her shadow was cast on the curtain. Ethelwynne did this hula-dance shadow scene, which was much more sexy than doing it out in front of the curtain. Then, when it looked as though she was going to win the election, Ethelwynne backed out!

VICTOR CHITTICK, English professor 1921–1948: One day, one of the girls who was a faithful student of mine came down the hallway in Eliot Hall where the faculty mailboxes were, in a state of combined amusement and annoyance. An instructor had talked to them about sex relations as they flourished on campus, and she, fairly staggering between those conflicting emotions of amusement and annoyance, said, "I've forgotten more about sex than that man ever knew."

THOMAS J. COAD '42: There was probably no sex on campus, although there was some interest in it. The University of Oregon, Oregon State

Students gathered in the social room of Anna Mann cottage before a formal dance in 1935.

College, and especially the eastern colleges with their fraternities and sororities, were much more open. Things were going on at those campuses that were not going on at Reed. Reed was sort of a puritan college. It had a reputation of being just the opposite, but that was not true. I knew of no girl ever getting pregnant at Reed. There was very little drinking. Once in a while we would go to a tavern on Bybee Boulevard and have a beer, but nothing very serious.

SYLVIA CAMPBELL POWELL '42: You were careful not to do heavy necking, the kind where you would get in trouble. Playing kick-the-can was popular, as it was a chance to go off and smooch a little, and then come back. Smoking together was very common. We could smoke in the dorms, but not in the classrooms, and not in the library. At the library we would all sit out on the steps, a whole gang of us, men and women, and the Philip Morris man would come by and give out samples in little boxes with two cigarettes in each.

MARGARET CHURCHILL LABOVITZ '30: An upperclassman, Evangeline Powell '27, who was very active in the student newspaper, the *Quest*, had taken me under her wing at Reed, and pretty soon I was working at the *Quest* too. There were also three boys working at the newspaper. Two of them, Maurice Bernstein '27 and Irving Furst '30, were great friends who had grown up in an orphanage in New York City. There was a third boy, Paul O'Day '30, who was the brother of a physics professor at Reed, Marcus O'Day. Paul was from a lumbering area in Washington state. He was Irish and had taken part in a bloody strike of the IWW—the Industrial Workers of the World—a left-wing labor group. All three boys tended toward communism. One of the New York boys kept a notebook called "The Red Dawn." This was strong stuff for a rather timid little girl from the Midwest. Two of these boys besieged me. However, I was shy and totally un-

able to deal with them, especially the Irish labor loyalist. He had a wonderful way with language. He wrote me a poem:

> Together we watch the solemn parade
> of lavender clouds across the sky.
> I love you and my rebel's heart
> will be soothed in my bosom until I die.

He wanted to marry me. I didn't know what to do. I didn't want to marry him. It was nice to be wanted. But somehow these older boys didn't seem quite healthy. They were rather skinny and sallow and didn't stand up quite straight. In fact, they had had hard lives without a supporting family like mine. I didn't know what to do. Certainly I couldn't talk to the dean of women, Cheryl Scholz. In our loftiness we didn't feel comfortable going to her with our problems; besides, she was altogether too stuffy for my new, radical sympathies. Instead, I went to Barry Cerf, who taught literature. When I explained, "He wants to marry me," his advice was emphatic: "You must not ruin your young life!"

There seemed nothing else to do. I left Reed College that June and went home to Chicago, and the next fall I entered the University of Chicago.

MARY BARNARD '32: The important thing in dating was that there had to be a meeting of minds. Dating was mostly going to dances. You might go to movies, too. But dancing was the thing. Fox trots, waltzes, and the Charleston. There was a Friday-night dance every week held in the social room of what is now called Winch House in the Old Dorm Block.

ELIZABETH MCCRACKEN MCDOWELL '34: I used to go to the weekend dances with Victor Earll '38. There would be about thirty couples. Each night they would pick a winning dance couple. If you won one night, you were judges the next week. Victor and I often won, and so we would be judges the next week. In the spring, we had a women's-choice dance, where the women had to ask for dates. A lot of women asked boys who had never danced. So we decided to start giving lessons to the boys in midweek.

ETHEL FAHLEN NOBLE '40: There were always the junior and the senior formals, and the Christmas dance was formal as well. Many of the formals, with chaperones, were held down at the Shriners' Temple or in country clubs around Portland.

JEANNE HANSEN GORDNER '46: The faculty members danced with us. They were great friends. This was something I hadn't experienced. There were some love affairs. One of the women instructors in political science fell madly in love with one of the students and they ran off together.

What you wore to dances was a reflection of the movies at the time, especially those of Ginger Rogers and Fred Astaire. Real elegant stuff. Even those of us who were impoverished could always manage to get something together.

JACK BENVENISTE '43: The guys in the physics department were kind of oddballs—we didn't have dates, so we didn't take dates to dances. We all went together. We would stand in a row, watching the people dance, and say, "Okay, why don't you cut in on her?" "No, you do it." That kind of thing. There was one young lady who was a very good dancer. The guys would say, "Come on Jack, go ahead. Cut in on her!" They would push me out onto the dance floor, but each time I would try to cut in, she wouldn't dance with me. She hated me, don't ask me why. Finally, after three or four times, she agreed to dance with me. At the end of the dance, she said, "Wow! Where did you learn to dance?" Then she asked, "Would you play tennis with me?" I said, "Sure, be glad to." When I went back and told the guys what had happened, and they said, "Do you

know who she is?" I said, "No, who?" "She's the state tennis champ." I said, "Oh, God." It never came off. I had no stomach for being beaten by the state champion.

CARLETON WHITEHEAD '41, alumni director 1952–1958, college relations administrator 1959–1983: Social life for freshmen climaxed in something called "Hellbat." This initiation took place in early fall, without any advance warning. It involved upperclass men and women stacking up the belongings of freshman women in the Student Union right before a dance. The place would be really festooned.

JACK DUDMAN '42, mathematics professor 1953–1985, dean of students 1963–1985: One of the saddest things I experienced as student body president was when a couple of male students were involved in an apparently homosexual relationship, and the college was determined to expel them. I didn't have any strong feelings one way or another, except that I thought it was not the college's business to be regulating the lives of students to that degree. I fought the administration, but they ended up being expelled.

ELEANOR MAY '45: In my senior year, I was a resident advisor in the Ladd House. One of the older women came to me and said that there was a lesbian affair going on in Ladd, and if I didn't do something about it, she was going to go to the dean. I was just appalled that she would even care what anybody was doing. But she did care, and so I had to go. It was a terribly traumatic thing for me. I went to Ann Shepard '23, the dean of women, and I just started crying. "Now, now, dear," she said, consoling me, "Don't ever worry about it again." I walked out of there and I never did worry about it again. Nothing happened to the girls that were accused by this other woman. Ann Shepard was able to handle things like that.

KATHARINE BAKER COOKE '41: There was a noticeable proportion of homosexuals on campus. We had this lovely joke about a student who couldn't go with us because he was waiting for his wife. "He is coming on the streetcar," he would say. Well, nobody told me this was irregular, so I thought it was fine.

We were an eclectic bunch. One of my friends did her best to tell me what lesbianism was all about and how it was a good thing, which was fine, except it didn't really mean very much to me, not being my line. Some of the faculty may have lived alternate lifestyles, but they weren't called that. Ann Brownlie '23, who fed us in Commons, was a big, fat, butch lesbian. She was efficient, which was good, and the food was good. Excellent, in fact. She ran a good show.

CARROLL HENDRICKSON, JR. '42: At that time, those who hashed in Commons dressed in starched white mess jackets with detachable buttons like the naval officers' summer-uniform whites. There were six people at each table, and the places were set just the way that they are set in Windsor Great Hall by Her Majesty's henchmen.

During the school year, all evening meals were hashed. We stood at attention, and we served everything from the left side, which Miss Brownlie '23 said to do, because the right hand is busy with the drinking glass or cup of coffee. It was done just the same way it would be in a nice restaurant.

Reed had its own china, with the official Reed seal on it. The dinners would be considered formal now, but they were very relaxed and enjoyable. We did observe nice table manners. Many times at the end of dinner, some tables would break out into glorious song. "The Sexual Life of the Camel" comes to mind:

The sexual life of the camel
is stranger than anyone thinks.

At the height of the mating season
he tries to bugger the Sphinx.

But the Sphinx's posterior orifice
is filled with the sands of the Nile—
Which accounts for the hump on the camel
and the Sphinx's inscrutable smile.

JEANNE HANSEN GORDNER '46: At the first meal I had on campus, I noticed that most of the faculty were there. After we were through eating, people started singing in beautiful harmony:

Violate me in the violet time
in the vilest way that you know.
Ruin me, ravage me, cruelly savage me—
You are the best boy I know.

I looked around, and here were all these sedate-looking professors, singing this song. I thought to myself, "This is the place for me!"

Later, we had some students transfer in from Black Mountain College in North Carolina because their college went broke. The girls wore jeans. This was shocking! Unbelievable. In fact, some of them wore bib overalls. This started a new trend at Reed. One of the Black Mountain girls said she was an Alaskan Native—she may or may not have been—and she wore her hair down in front of her face and always went barefoot, making a great effort to look bizarre.

GENNY HALL SMITH '43: There was no dress code at Reed. You could wear any kind of crazy clothes you wanted, including shorts to class, which most other schools prohibited. There were a couple of very unusual fellows on campus. One saw himself as the young Mozart, and he dressed up frequently in what he thought Mozart would have worn. There was another fellow who was a yoga person. At that time, nobody had heard of yoga. He would sit out on the lawn in strange poses. Nobody paid either of them any attention. They were doing what they wanted to do.

CHAPTER 12

"I'll Meet You at the Barricades"

The streetcar conductor would announce the stop for Reed as "Red College."
—Thomas Lamb Frazier '42

We read and discussed a lot of books on [Communism], but mostly scorned them, because we were sarcastic about pretty much everything.
—Harlow Lenon '35

William Foster's high-minded call to challenge the status quo, both in educational circles and in the local Portland community, had given Reed much of its original vitality. By the 1930s, that spirit of rebellion had become institutionalized at Reed, despite the efforts of President Keezer and the trustees to rein it in. Lacking the traditional sports teams to foster school spirit and unity, the Reed community banded together around expressions of personal freedom and radical dissent as a means of defining themselves in ways antithetical to the outside world.

In keeping with Foster's propensity for debate and argumentation, verbal expression, sharply honed in small humanities conferences with professors employing the Socratic method, became elevated to a performance art on campus.

ETHEL FAHLEN NOBLE '40: President Keezer was faced with a lot of bad press for Reed. Every incident that could possibly imply that Reed had some Communist influence hit the front page of the Portland newspapers. It was "that Red institution."

DEXTER KEEZER, president 1934–1942: A member of the college's governing boards once remarked that, if Reed had retained a master of public relation arts and directed him to use his talents in reverse, Reed could not have succeeded better in presenting itself locally in an unfavorable light. This was not the case, of course, in academic circles in the East, where Reed commonly enjoyed a superlatively good reputation. Nevertheless, it was true among many of the cultural leaders of Portland, and particularly among those who were reputed to have consequential sums of money to spare. In those circles the college enjoyed anything but a glamorous reputation. It was frequently referred to as a "hotbed of radicalism" populated by students who, if not queer to start with, picked up a lot of queer notions en route through the college. Local cynics told me that some conspicuously prosperous citizens worked diligently at fostering a reputation for the college as a shady and subversive place to lower its prospects for getting badly needed financial help.

WILBUR L. PARKER '36: Portland had been a Ku Klux Klan city in the 1920s, very bigoted and prejudiced, and it was just slowly coming out of that in the '30s. The college was suspect. People were always wondering, "What are those crazy kids up to now?" But there were people of education in Portland. When I was a kid growing up there, the town was very dominated by New Englanders—Congregationalists and Unitarians—who were largely intellectuals. They believed in the school. You could be of any religion and go to Reed. That wasn't necessarily the case then for other private colleges in Oregon.

Students at Reed, though, were politically active. In 1935 there was a German training cruiser, the *Emden*, which suddenly came into Portland, uninvited. They had all these handsome young cadets aboard. A bunch of us went down to the moorage with placards that were not very complimentary to the new Hitler regime. The police threw the whole lot of us in jail. It made the front page of the *Morning Oregonian*. When they started checking the names of these kids, they found we were first-time offenders, nothing but a bunch of Eagle Scouts and the sons of some very prominent local people. So they said, "Oh, to hell with that," and kicked us out. They wouldn't even book us!

Later that evening we threw a dance for the German cadets at Reed. Everybody attended and was polite and pleasant. The cadets were handsome, bright, charming young men. There was nothing wrong with them, except that they had a cruel ideology not appreciated in this country.

CHERYL SCHOLZ, dean of women 1924–1937, history professor 1938–1943, dean of admission 1943–1945: The wild '20s had been followed by the depressed '30s, and the young didn't know where they were. There was tremendous growth throughout the country of so-called "radicalism" and "subversive" movements, followed by a terrible backlash. And yet, I thought that this sort of thing was exactly what students should be doing, thinking these things out. There were many at Reed that did. The college was a small place that loved them, and made them think, and was willing to put up with their thinking while they were doing it. It was a very healthy period.

CECELIA GUNTERMAN WOLLMAN '37: President Keezer wanted us to change our lifestyle to get along better with the more conservative Portland community. A significant number of the students were very much against this if it meant having to modify their freedom of behavior. If they wanted to have a demonstration on the campus, they were going to have it. And that went for having the lifestyle of their choosing too. As students, we were concerned with what to do about Hitler, whether to be for intervention in Europe or not. And then the Japanese business—Japan had started spreading herself around Manchuria. We gave up wearing silk stockings so that we wouldn't be supporting the Japanese trade. When we wanted to raise a political point of view, we would "rally at the flagpole" with a demonstration on campus.

OMA "AMY" WOODCOCK SINGER '38: A Japanese ship called the *Norway Maru* docked in Astoria, on the Oregon coast, to buy up scrap steel and iron from Schnitzer Steel. We went down to the docks to protest, carrying signs that said "This Steel Will Come Back in Bullets."

MARY BARNARD '32: We were all militantly pacifist, if that's not a contradiction in terms.

In the 1920s and early '30s we were told that all wars were foisted on nations by munitions makers. No war had ever been fought for a good cause. In England, young men were taking the Oxford Pledge, stating that they would never bear arms in any war, no matter what the ostensible cause might be. Anti-war movies and anti-war books were extremely popular. Any lingering notion that war was romantic could hardly survive a realistic description of life in the front-line trenches of World War I. And then the stories of Allied atrocities began to leak out. Patriotism became embarrassing, perhaps for the first time in American history. We were suffering from the Depression, and we knew that we would be graduating into a jobless world, but we feared war more than anything else.

CHRISTIAN FREER '36: The Oxford Pledge crossed the Atlantic and made its way to some American colleges and universities, Reed among them. Some of us organized a parade of sorts and identified ourselves as members of the "VFW"—not the Veterans of *Foreign* Wars, but rather the "Veterans of *Future* Wars." It was not that we were particularly bellicose, but we naïvely accepted the position that if the United States became involved in a war, it would naturally be a just war and we would be ready to do our duty. I don't believe that any of the Reed signers of the Oxford Pledge held to their pledge when push came to shove, especially after Germany attacked the Soviet Union. Some of us went on to serve long and honorably in World War II, and we took some casualties.

WERNER ZELLER '33: At that time, the Socialist Party and the Communist Party were recognized parties in this country and without any bad connotation to them. When a national election would come around, they would send a representative from the different political parties to give their spiel on campus. The Republicans and Democrats sort of took it as a joke, but the Socialists and the Communists were dead earnest. After listening to all the spiels, the student

Recent University of Oregon graduate (and eventual U. S. Senator) Richard Neuberger addresses a group of Reed students in 1938. Rhodes Scholar Oscar Gass '34 (wearing glasses), is sitting behind him.

body would vote, and it was usually in favor of the Communists. One of my old philosophy professors used to say: "At twenty, if a fellow isn't a socialist, he has no heart. At forty, if he is still a socialist, he has no brain." I think that is true. When I look now at the alumni of Reed College, they are probably the most staid, conservative people in the world.

JACK BENVENISTE '43: Before I went to Reed, my mother took me aside and said, "All right, we agree to let you go to Reed if you promise not to become a Communist."

Of course! That was the easiest promise I ever had to make. But the people in Portland were sure it was a Communist haven. The reason was that there was a John Reed from Portland, a newspaper reporter, who went to Russia and reported on the 1917 revolution in very glowing terms in a book called *Ten Days That Shook the World*. In fact, he is the only American buried inside the Kremlin walls. Around that same time, William T. Foster was president of Reed and a fellow named William Z. Foster was chairman of the Communist Party in America. Now, how about that! I mean, if that doesn't convince you, what will?

TIME magazine, "Nomination," November 16, 1936: At their tables in Commons, students of Reed College sat back after dinner for a pre-election political rally. A Republican, a Democrat, and a Socialist spoke their last-minute appeals. Then arose an individual immaculate in white tie and tails, wearing horn-rimmed glasses and a mossy beard, who had come in with the wife of Reed's waggish President Dexter Keezer. Introduced as "Dr. Myron K. Blackstone, fellow of the North American Institute for Political Research," he was recognized by sharp-eyed diners as Lamar Holt, a student from New York. Said "Dr. Blackstone": "I offer to you, the first audience in the world, the program and the platform

for an entirely new political party with entirely new ideals. Ladies and gentlemen, to be brief: regardless of who gets in the White House, we want an American in Buckingham Palace. Mrs. Simpson for Queen!"

"God save the King!" shouted students planted throughout the room. Rushing out of Commons, Reed College International Chapter No. 1 of the Simpson for Queen Committee boarded a hired truck whose sides were covered with huge signs nominating Simpson for Queen and cruised around Portland all evening.

ARTHUR LIVERMORE '40, chemistry professor 1948–1965: Edward VIII, the King of England, wanted to marry an American divorcée named Wallis Simpson, but was being forced to abdicate his throne to do so. We thought it was stupid for the British not to agree to have Wally Simpson as Queen, so we staged a demonstration downtown, parading up and down Broadway with a banner that read, "We don't care who's President. We want an American in Buckingham Palace. Wally Simpson for Queen."

ELEANOR EMMONS MACCOBY '39: There were quite a lot of left-wing people at Reed. It was the period of the United Front, when communists and socialists and other left-wing people all cooperated. It was also the time of the Spanish Civil War. Isolationists and pacifists in the United States were either aligned or not aligned. I was active in the Young People's Socialist League. We all belonged to the League against War and Fascism. The League supported the Loyalists in Spain, and yet most of us were pacifists, and so we were deeply conflicted about that.

DONALD WHEELER '35: There was a longshoremen's strike in Portland in 1934. I picked up a couple of my radical friends and we went down to the river where the picket lines were formed. I told one of the organizers that we were on the

Reed students paraded through Portland in the fall of 1936 promoting British King Edward VIII's right to marry American divorcée Wallis Simpson.

side of the strikers and would do anything to help, including picketing. He just brushed me off as if I was a nobody. Later I found out that Portland was a dangerously backward part of the longshoremen's union. So we didn't get to picket, but later on we marched in the May Day parade. We had a big banner that said, "Not authorized by Reed faculty or trustees." That caused a scandal back at Reed. When I was scolded about it, I said, "Well, I thought we were doing you justice, because you wouldn't be held responsible for our participation."

MICHAEL MUNK '56: The West Coast waterfront strike of 1934 established one of the nation's strongest unions on the West Coast, and resulted in substantial wage and hour improvements. The strikers got support from college students, including those from Reed, who signed pledges not to scab. Members of Oregon's better-known families, among them four sitting Reed trustees and regents—lumberman Aubrey Watzek, attorney Robert Sabin, *Oregon Journal* executive Simon Winch, and banker E. B. MacNaughton—as well as five future trustees, considered the strike a clear and present danger to the state. Forming the Citizens Emergency Committee, they hired more than a thousand vigilantes—organized into a semimilitary organization—to end the strike, accepting that deployment could lead to bloodshed and perhaps loss of life, which there was.

HARLOW LENON '35: My circle of friends included Oscar Gass '34, Robert Barnard '35, and Don Wheeler '35, all of whom went on to become Rhodes Scholars. Although I didn't know it, Wheeler was at that time a committed member of the Young Communist League. He was very smart, but his family was dirt poor. He came to Reed on a scholarship, and professed to be an anarchist. Being a Communist in the 1930s was not the enormous traitorous sin that it later became, but at Reed it was considered to be a stupid adherence to the doctrines of Karl Marx, about whom we talked and talked. We all thought favorably of the Soviet Union then, although we had no knowledge at that time of the Russian kulaks—middle-class peasants—who were dying of starvation or being massacred. All the news reports and books coming from Russia were favorable. New York journalist Lincoln Steffens said, "I have seen the future and it works."

We read and discussed a lot of books on the subject, but mostly scorned them, because we were sarcastic about pretty much everything. It was the most stimulating intellectual atmosphere I ever occupied. The volume of conversation was enormous.

DORIS BAILEY MURPHY '38: I myself never could quite make that jump to being what we called a "fellow traveler" and join the Communist Party. Many of my friends were upset with me. But something held me back. The American Communist Party was a secret movement in many ways. There was so much that they couldn't tell anybody. I talked about it to my advisor, sociology professor Alexander Goldenweiser. Dr. Goldenweiser was a colorful character who had been born in Russia, and was very left-wing in his philosophy. He said, "I know you, you're too outspoken and you couldn't keep a secret. On that basis, I don't think that you should join." So I didn't join.

There were meetings on campus of the Young Communist League in the old Commons, decades later the Student Union. I went to a few of those meetings along with friends who were not members. There were not a whole lot of people at these student meetings, partly because they didn't publicize them. Word went around by word of mouth, not flyers. I would go and listen to communist theory and what the Communists could do for this country in terms of helping people, helping the poverty-stricken.

My group of friends would often meet at my parents' house. We would just talk and talk. How much we talked! We especially talked politics. Some of us had radical ideals and some didn't. We took sides. Most of those in the literature and sociology departments were liberal left-wingers. People in the sciences and the math department were much more conservative politically, for whatever reason. My friends and I used to say, "I'll meet you at the barricades," meaning there would be a revolution soon.

FRANCES MILLER READ '38: There was a large group of students who couldn't care less. They went about their business thinking that the radicals were a bit crazy. There was a certain element at Reed whose main activity was social. Going to dances, arranging dances, that sort of thing. There were one or two individuals who held forth that what the political students were saying was dangerous and wrong.

Then there was a group of those who were mainly science students—physics, biology, and chemistry. At that time, science classes were held in the basement and attic of Eliot Hall. These people were troglodytes. That is, as things got difficult, they retired and faded away to their basement or attic. Not all, certainly. There was a good deal of ridicule extended—unwarranted, of course—toward the people who refused to realize that the gods of war were descending and it was up to the liberal students to do something about it.

MELVIN H. JUDKIS '39: Those of us in the physics department were sort of isolated. We didn't do much with the other kids, and I guess we were an odd group. Between studying, helping at my mother's dry-goods store, and working as a page at the Portland library on the weekends, I had no time for a social life. There were no women in the physics department, and I didn't have a chance to date. One time there was a peace march on campus. In the physics department we got a little toy cannon. As the students marched by, we would fire this cannon. They sort of ignored us, which was probably a smart move.

BARRY BROWNELL '43: Dr. Frank Loxley Griffin, the math professor, was the head of the Republican group at Reed, a definite minority. There were about twelve Republicans on campus.

ELIZABETH ANN BROWN '40: In the political science department there was a tight group of three of us who were Bernard Noble's students. We held a series of panels on the politics of the Far East, Europe, and Latin America, but students were not terribly interested in international affairs at that time. The great American public certainly didn't think in the national and international terms that people do now. Television did not exist, and newspapers in Portland focused on domestic issues.

In my senior year I wrote my thesis on American isolationist propaganda. The political science department had two senior professors—Bernard Noble and Charles McKinley—who violently disagreed with one another, to the extent that my thesis was considered an insult to McKinley, who was an isolationist, and he refused to attend my thesis orals.

ESTHER DORLES LEWIS '42: A very large percentage of the staff hired at Reed were college students from low-income families working for the National Youth Administration at forty cents an hour. My job was to be the secretary to Bernard Noble. If you worked for Bernard, you were kind of a surrogate daughter. He was the director of a Quaker-sponsored institute called the Institute of International Relations. The institute sent speakers out on the circuit, mostly to give talks to schoolteachers looking for in-service credit.

Bernard was definitely not a Quaker. If anything, he was a prime mover in advancing U.S. participation in World War II. He had been a Rhodes Scholar at Oxford, and had participated as a lieutenant in the American army during World War I, receiving the Distinguished Service Medal and serving at the Versailles conference that created the armistice. Bernard was very knowledgeable about what was going on in Europe and very pro-British. He was always going out to speak to groups about why the United States should get into the war. But he had been gassed during World War I, and so he was also rather frail. His fellow faculty member in the political science department, Charles McKinley, had been a pacifist during World War I and continued to be a pacifist. The two of them were generally at loggerheads all the time. They were scarcely polite to one another.

HUGH MCKINLEY '41, son of Charles McKinley: Every four or five years, my father spent a year working in Washington, D.C., and that sort of kept him up-to-date. He helped write the Social Security legislation, among other things.

DONALD WHEELER '35: Professor McKinley gave me board and room at his home at Thirty-sixth and Tolman during my first year at Reed, and so I came to know him quite well. He was tremendously well versed in local politics all across the United States, but a hangover from the populist trend.

When I took his political theory course he handed out the course bibliography. All the leading historians on the subject were there, including Karl Marx. But it was Marx by way of Harold Laski, the English political theorist. I admired Laski, but I thought we should be reading Marx himself. So in the first class I raised my hand and said, "I don't think Laski is good enough on Marx. Marx and Engels wrote a beautiful short work, *The Communist Manifesto*, which covers the subject." I realized I was taking a risk challenging the professor, and McKinley never forgave me. I learned later, when I was applying for a Rhodes Scholarship and got to see my grades, that McKinley gave me a C in political theory that year.

I ended up writing my thesis with Bernard Noble on contract and status. Status was a typical social instrument of medieval times. There were a lot of bad things about it. For instance, to protect the status of the upper classes, in the fourteenth century it was illegal in countries like Belgium and France for a commoner to wear a hat. The upper classes had a right to do things that other people didn't have a right to do because of their status. With the development of capitalism, however, more and more depended on contracts and agreements. In the market itself, any transaction was an instantaneous contract, so status just about disappeared. But then status came back under Marxist doctrine. The worker's status as a worker is all-important for Marx, and that implies certain protections for maintaining that status.

Bernard Noble was what I would call a "left liberal," but that didn't mean that he was sympathetic to such things as strikes. He didn't approve of my taking part in radical student politics or statewide political efforts like workers' strikes. Reed had no endowment to speak of at that time, and he felt that my political activities were poisoning the college's name with potential big donors. I refused to be influenced by him, and he never quite forgave me. He scolded me severely, and never ceased scolding.

Years later, in the mid-1940s, when I was in Washington, D.C., working for the CIA, Noble came to town for a meeting of the Political Science Association and invited me to lunch. He believed I had thrown away my opportunities as a Rhodes Scholar by getting famous as a radical, and that this was also a reflection on him, because he hadn't been able to guard me against these dangerous, poisonous ideas. At that lunch he excommunicated me from Reed.

ARTHUR LIVERMORE '40, chemistry professor: When Nazi Germany marched into Poland on September 1, 1939, we had a chapel meeting where we listened to Hitler talking on the radio. It was a moving experience. Here was a war

starting in Europe. Everybody, especially the men, was wondering what this would mean. I got married in September of 1940 on a Saturday. The next day President Roosevelt signed the bill that started the draft. So, I was automatically put into a different category than if I had not been married. That was just fortuitous.

Arthur Scott, who had been at Reed as a young chemistry instructor during the early 1920s, was invited back to Reed in 1937, at which point he became my advisor. In the middle of that year, he invited me to be the stockroom manager for the chemistry department. Arthur Scott's wife, Vera, was Czech. Her brother, Frank Munk, was in Czechoslovakia, where the war had already started. Scottie would get packages from him sent to the stockroom, and I would hang on to them. The Munks escaped from Prague by train, posing as guardians for a trainload of children bound for Scandinavia. Frank Munk then came to Reed, where he became a professor of political science.

LAURA TUNNELL GLEYSTEEN '40: In sociology we had two professors who were refugees from Europe, Frank Munk and Frau Marianne Beth. They gave us some intimation of the Holocaust and the horror of the Nazis.

SHIRLEY PETERSON GOLDBERG '45: We had some really remarkable guests come to campus. Paul Robeson, the activist actor and singer, spent a week visiting classes. Every afternoon at three o'clock he sang in the coffee shop and socialized with the students. We had Alexander Kerensky, the leader of the provisional government in Russia for a short while following the 1917 revolution before Lenin took over. We also got to see at that time the films of the Russian director Sergei Eisenstein — *Oktober* and *Battleship Potemkin*. That turned me on to film. I never looked back. We had two young Chinese men, who were part of the peasant revolution in China. This was before the success of Mao's revolution. All those visitors had an enormous impact upon us.

WALLACE MacCAFFREY '42: One morning, Carl Stevens '42 and Thomas Coad '42 put up a large poster on the front of the old Student Union that said: "It May Be God's Duty. It Is Not Ours." Most of the sentiment among the students was strictly anti-war. "Keep out. Not our business." That was a strongly prevailing point of view on campus.

CARLETON WHITEHEAD '41, alumni director 1952–1958, college relations administrator 1959–1983: There was a crisis every spring. It was sort of expected, almost institutionalized. In the spring of 1941, the students invited a man to campus who was recommending that people refuse the draft. President Keezer cancelled this man's speech, and the students started a protest that lasted all day, everywhere on campus. They cancelled classes, and everybody went from meeting to meeting with much milling around and lots and lots of discussion. Everybody was excited.

PATRICIA BECK '44: There was some kind of argy-bargy over the cancelled talk. The student body met in the Student Union to debate the issue. The debate got hotter and hotter, until finally, the president of the student body, Bernard Shevach '41, called out, "Calm down, ladies and gentlemen. Let's clarify matters by putting them in the abstract."

There was a roar of happy laughter. The most wonderful phrase!

DEXTER KEEZER, president: During my time as president at Reed, I interfered with complete freedom of speech and inquiry only once, when I refused to let a man who was awaiting sentencing for violating the Selective Service Act use a campus hall to speak against the act. I took the initiative to save the college from running the risk of being on the wrong side of a contempt-of-court case.

It had quickly become apparent to me, though, that what was mistakenly considered subversive radicalism at Reed was simply a decent regard for freedom of study and discussion of political and economic issues. This open-mindedness was regarded as dangerous by a certain element of the Portland community. To be sure, a few members of the student body would have been pleased to be characterized as flaming radicals, and those few worked diligently for that rating. They reflected both an indigenous type of radicalism encouraged by their having been cuffed around by adversity on the frontier and a newer type imported from eastern metropolitan centers. Even so, they were neither numerous nor cogent enough to provide other than a little leaven for the predominantly conservative student body. That conservatism was matched by that of the faculty. Most of them had no more revolutionary objectives than that of getting the mortgage paid off and themselves safely established as substantial property owners.

However, the most important single explanation of Reed's radical reputation was to be found in the hospitality that the college extended to a constant succession of itinerant peddlers of "isms" of all kinds who sought an opportunity to speak at a college as they trekked though Portland. Almost always these speakers pronounced some kind of doom on capitalist society or offered a drastic remedy for what they proclaimed to be its atrocious defects. That appealed to local newspapers to be worth reporting. As a result, the college was portrayed more or less continuously to the community as being involved in purveying subversive preachments of one kind or another. Its inability to generate news about conventional collegiate matters, such as progress in intercollegiate athletics, tended to make the portrait more stark.

CHAPTER 13

The Championship Season

The attitude at Reed was anti organized athletics.
  —Harold "Jim" Jambor '35

When the Reed team won, they lowered the flag on campus to half-mast.
  —Thomas Lamb Frazier '42

Reed's athletic program was built around the philosophy of Charles Botsford, who joined the college in 1912 and continued as athletic director until 1952. In accordance with William Foster's directive to provide athletics for all, Botsford stressed individual development in sports that were played for fun rather than competitively. Team sports were either intramural and open to all students, or played at an informal club level with other schools who were not members of intercollegiate leagues. Botsford, who had spent his youth as a circus performer, focused on sports that students could play all their lives, like golf, tennis, handball, and squash.

Believing that Botsford's athletic program was too lax, President Keezer promoted competitive team sports at Reed in the hope that they would provide the unifying sense of college spirit that he found lacking on campus.

BLAKE HOPWOOD '31: Some writer discovered that Reed College and some college in Pennsylvania had the longest losing record in football of any college in the United States. The press got ahold of that and really built it up. What would happen if they played each other? Would they each try to lose to set the record? The speculation went on for several months. Then the other college finally won a game and spoiled the whole thing! Reed ended up holding that record.

DEXTER KEEZER, president 1934–1942: The objective in eliminating intercollegiate sports at Reed was not only to give a clearer right of way to academic pursuits, but also to open the way for a program of athletics and physical education in which all students would participate, instead of having most of the student body take its exercise vicariously while sitting in the grandstands watching a small company of experts perform.

It was my observation that much of this was

left undone. Indeed, strolling back and forth from campus to the trolley car was in some cases held to fulfill the physical education requirement. The standard of performance in some games was not only so low as to be painful to behold in some instances, but unduly dangerous to the participants. The first intramural football game I saw at Reed had the novel feature of the college's heating-plant attendant as a backfield star. But it also disclosed an ignorance of the self-protective fundamentals of the game that sent shivers up and down my back for what might happen to the players. This sloppiness seemed to spring from a notion that if a game is played all for fun, it does not make any difference how well or how badly it is played.

Also, by eliminating intercollegiate athletics, the college had eliminated a certain measure of alumni interest and support.

ALMALEE STEWART HENDERSON '47: President Keezer had a real vendetta against the athletic director, Charles Botsford, for some reason. One of the Botsfords' sons, Charles '34, had gone to Reed, but when the younger son was ready the Botsfords felt that they couldn't send him to Reed because of this attitude of Keezer's.

My father, Blair Stewart '21, who taught economics at Reed, had meetings with other faculty at our house in the evenings about what President Keezer was trying to do to make Reed into a more traditional college. It was almost the bane of my childhood, this controversy over Keezer that was always going on. I asked Mama one time why there was such a big fight about this, and she said that if you had worked hard for something all your life and then someone came along and wanted to destroy it, you would naturally be upset and concerned about it.

FRED LEITZ '40: Charles Botsford, who had headed up the athletic department since 1912, was a one-man operation. It didn't take long for

him to get me into squash. Bots was very good at it himself. He would always either win or lose by one or two points, irrespective of how good a player you were. You also knew that if he won by a couple of points, it was because he knew you could take it. If *you* won by a couple of points, it was almost an insult once you got to know him, because you knew he was letting you down easy. He could beat anybody.

ELIZABETH HINES HOLZER '29: Whenever you would go into the gym and people were playing volleyball, Botsford would say, "seven all" or "ten all." It was a random number that he chose. Never anybody ahead. He was a fine influence.

CHRISTIAN FREER '36: At Reed there were no athletics coaches; instead, we had a very amateurish student captain-coach system in which a student interested and somewhat proficient in a given sport became the "master" for that sport. In my senior year there were fifteen masters in men's sports and a dozen in women's, ranging all the way from archery and badminton to volleyball and wrestling. I was the track and field "master."

REED COLLEGE QUEST, **January 18, 1939:** President Dexter M. Keezer, in his annual report to the trustees and regents, believes that the present master system tends to give a "bootless quality to much of the athletic program for young men," and is not altogether satisfactory. However, he states that some steps are being taken to strengthen the athletic program, which can no longer be adequately served merely by "jolly informality and zest for the spontaneous playing of games."

REED COLLEGE QUEST, **February 1, 1939:** The votes last Friday on the athletic policy at Reed were 191 for keeping the present system and 8 for a change. No more need be said on this point.

CHRISTIAN FREER '36: To expand the geographical base of the student body, President Keezer began adding student athletes from abroad. The first foreign student I recall was Otto Urbach, from Vienna. He came in the spring of 1936 and shared the suite Grant McConnell '37 and I had in Eastport dorm, perhaps because he and Grant were both skiers. In my senior year, our skiing team, with Grant as the master and Otto Urbach participating, was one of the best on the Pacific Coast, taking fourth place in the intercollegiate championships at Yosemite National Park.

CORDELIA DODSON HOOD '36: Otto Urbach began teaching skiing classes up on Mt. Hood. After Reed, I went to Europe for grad school. Otto was part of my reason for going. I had also become interested in German as a language. I wound up in Vienna through an exchange-student arrangement, and was there during the Anschluss, when the Germans annexed Austria. In fact, I was at the University of Vienna when the Germans shut it down. One of the students I met there was Otto's brother, Karl Urbach '42. I

Italian baron Emilio Pucci '37 was recruited by President Keezer to lead the Reed ski team.

later helped get Karl and his family out of Dachau before it became a death camp, and then helped bring him to the United States to attend Reed.

ELIZABETH ANN BROWN '40: Keezer recruited Emilio Pucci '37 my freshman year. The story went that Keezer had run across him somewhere on the East Coast. I think the college paid him a modest stipend. He held classes in French conversation, of all things, and also taught skiing. I was a skier, and so I participated. The college would rent a panel truck driven by one of the students, Marsh Cronyn '40, and we would ride up to Mt. Hood on weekends to ski.

MARSH CRONYN '40, chemistry professor 1952–1989: We students ran the Outing Club for hiking and skiing ourselves with no help from anybody. I would rent an empty U-drive truck, put benches in it—not tied down, mind you—and then load everybody on. It cost twenty-five cents to go. People would put the tailgate down and sit on it, laying their feet over the side. Emilio Pucci taught us how to parallel ski, none of that Norwegian stuff.

WILBUR PARKER '36: Emilio Pucci '37, Marchese di Barsento a Cavallo, was an Italian nobleman. He was a stout advocate of the Italian fascist regime. He claimed it was more democratic than our democracy. Of course, he got into hot water on that. Everyone would just look at him and say, "Oh, come on, Emilio, you're full of wet hay!" Or worse. But he was a man of great charm, and oh, boy, did he charm the girls. He was a good fellow around campus, but, politically, everybody thought he was a little bit insane.

ELMER "JIGGS" CLARK '42: On freshman orientation day, I found my mother helping me unpack in one of the dormitories, as she was unwilling to allow me to report to school by myself. While I was stuffing shirts in the bureau drawer,

I watched her analyze a character walking across the campus outside. "Now, there goes the type you gotta watch," she said.

Little did she or I realize that this guy, Emilio Pucci '37, with his Roman nose, and with hair that hung down to his shoulders, wearing a heavy rust-colored turtleneck sweater down to his knees on top of eight-wale corduroy pants, was bringing skiing to Reed. In due time, he became an Olympic participant at Garmisch-Partenkirchen, a brigadier general of the Italian air force when the war began, and a landed baron. His fashion designs later came to be in demand by women all over the world. He also designed a T-shirt for Reed, one with Reed's mascot, the griffin, on it.

BARRY BROWNELL '43: Prior to coming to Reed, I had been in the Sea Scouts rowing team at the Portland Rowing Club. When I became a student I convinced a couple of fellows to start a Reed College rowing team. We had a girl coxswain, Mary Elizabeth Russell '43 from Hood River.

MARY ELIZABETH RUSSELL BAUER '43: Neither my roommate nor I liked organized sports, but we were honor bound to put in so much time a week at physical activity. I don't remember what got us started on rowing, but someone told us about the two-man sculls that we could use down at the Willamette River. We started rowing together, the two of us, and enjoyed that a lot.

The men's crew fixed up one of the longer sculls. They didn't have anyone for a coxswain, which is why they asked me. Of course, the rower, Barry Brownell '43, who was right in front of the coxswain, was the one who set the pace. The coxswain tells him when to pick it up, and the others follow him. The main thing I had to learn to do was to steer.

We raced against the University of Washington freshmen down on the Willamette and won by half a length. That was because I steered quite

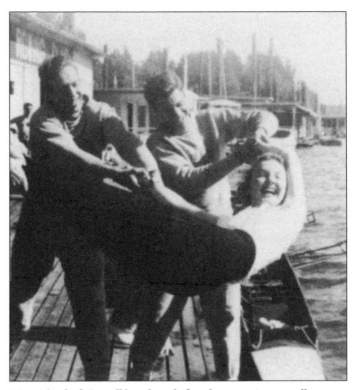

Mary Elizabeth Russell '43, the only female coxswain on a college rowing crew in 1941, being thrown into the Willamette River in celebration of Reed's win over the University of Washington.

close to shore, so we didn't get quite as much current, although it was a little scary because if you get a little too close, why then it's all off.

THE EUGENE REGISTER-GUARD, June 8, 1941: "Get 'em together! Watch that stroke! Digging on the catch! Faster hands! Number 1, you're late! Washing out at the finish!"

These warnings, in a high-pitched voice, are heard almost any sunny afternoon from the wide expanse of the Willamette River, which flows through Portland. They are from the golden-haired, freckled Mary Elizabeth Russell, the only girl coxswain in a college varsity shell. And when Reed College prevails, eighteen-year-old Miss Russell, a sophomore taking a pre-medic course, is tossed in the water in true crew style by the eight perspiring young men who tug at oars.

The crew gave a luncheon in her honor on the campus and presented her with a gold compact engraved with the words: "Mary, from Crew, 1941." "Isn't it wonderful!" smiled Mary Elizabeth Russell. "She certainly is!" chorused the Reed College varsity crew.

DEXTER KEEZER, president: On the whole, Reed's athletic policy was decidedly on the right side. However, the strangeness of the college's athletic setup to much of the local community was driven home to me with tremendous force shortly after I arrived, when I jested at a gathering that Reed was going to hire the services of a football team that would be far and away the best in the Northwest. The team would be housed in a separate building away from the campus lest it get in the way of the main business of the college, and it would have a special faculty whose job was to keep the players eligible.

It did not occur to me that anyone would think that I was speaking seriously, until the following morning when I was aroused from my bed before dawn by a long-distance telephone call. The call was from a football coach in a distant part of Oregon who had read an account of my plan in an early edition of a Portland newspaper, and wished to apply for the position of coach. He was the first of many serious applicants.

ARTHUR CARSON '40: Keezer recruited Alfred Hubbard to the physical education staff, which previously had been almost solely Charles Botsford, to train us. After some training, we went out and played the same local teams—Multnomah College, Pacific College of Newberg— that we had always lost to when we were just a club team with no training and no coach.

We walked through the schedule undefeated, ten straight wins. The famous undefeated Reed football team. But nobody had an inflated idea that we were a good football team. My brother, who was nine years older than me, and who was quite an athlete, came over with a buddy to watch a game. "My gosh," they said, "you guys couldn't beat a good high school team." That was absolutely true.

CHARLES CONRAD CARTER '46: Alfred Hubbard held a rigorous training session every afternoon. We played on Saturday afternoons, and we had two cheerleaders dressed up in cute Reed-colored sweaters and dresses with little beanies. At one game at Pacific College of Newberg we discovered that they had not mowed the grass on the field. The middle of the field was pretty well flattened out, but around the edges the grass was still high. The first play of the game, the Pacific College team lined up, and hiked the ball. Suddenly, up jumped one of their players hiding in the grass on the sideline, and headed downfield for a pass. That was one of the vicissitudes of playing football in rural Oregon in those days.

TIME **magazine, "Husky Reed," December 4, 1939:** Having topped off their five-game season with a six-touchdown victory, Reed became, to the consternation of President Keezer and every self-respecting alumnus, one of the few unbeaten, untied college football teams in the United States.

President Keezer retaliated by barring the team from all college laboratories and libraries for five days (one day for each victory). President and faculty also began to talk darkly of redeeming Reed's scholastic reputation by paying football players not to come to Reed. In his annual report to the trustees, President Keezer grumped: "I would be happier if football were abandoned entirely." Last straw was an attempt to arrange a "Brain Bowl" game between Reed and oft-trounced University of Chicago.

CHAPTER 14

Faculty Coup

Among many of the older faculty members there was a strong sense of community in defense of the Reed they had known and felt should continue.
—Rex Arragon, history professor

The campus wrote off the college's queer reputation as being due to the outside community's inability to comprehend the behavior of the elite.
—Dexter Keezer, president

By 1939, after five years of struggling to bring a more balanced environment to the Reed campus, Dexter Keezer was feeling hemmed in by the intransigence of the institution itself. The key tools of institutional change—unobstructed power and the ability to replace personnel—were not available to him. Tenure and low turnover among the faculty oligarchy made it impossible for him to bring in his own people to advance his initiatives, and the Faculty Council remained a formidable force in protecting the status quo. Keezer's ability to find common ground with the council was limited by his own cantankerous personality, which served in uniting a majority of the faculty and students against him.

MAIDA ROSSITER BAILEY, librarian 1912–1918, dean of women 1936–1942: In the beginning everyone found Keezer attractive and lively, and wanted to go along with him. Things at Reed seemed to be easier, a little gayer and pleasanter, with more money. The faculty did a lot for him, but in the end there was a wall. I never understood what made for the change, but things came to be very different. Keezer started going off on government projects for the Roosevelt Administration quite often. A faculty member who tracked his absences said that one year he was away for seven out of twelve months. He also seemed to consider it his privilege to lose his temper and be disagreeable. I will never forget the way he shook his fist at me one morning and said: "At your peril!" Well, imagine anybody behaving like that! That big hand he had. "At your peril!"

BREWSTER SMITH '39: There was a chant about Dexter Keezer given to the Reed community by a distinguished professor that went:

Caesar, Keezer, Kaiser, Czar—
Who the hell d'you think you are?
Sitting on your horse so high
like a Nazi riding by.

REED COLLEGE QUEST, **January 18, 1939:** President Dexter Keezer, in his annual report to the trustees and regents, accepted the accusation that, as president of Reed College, he has "challenged intellectualism," if, by this accusation, it is meant that he has regarded "intellectualism" as being "by no means the only important concern of the college." His aim during his four years as president, he states, "has not been to change the course on which Reed College after thoughtful consideration was projected twenty-seven years ago, but to bring it back on to that course." The college was originally, and still aims to be, according to Dr. Keezer, "concerned not only with the development of thinking capacity but with the whole personality of students."

CHERYL SCHOLZ, dean of women 1924–1937, history professor 1938–1943, dean of admission 1943–1945: Keezer was being considered for two jobs back East, one at Cornell University, and the other at CCNY in New York City. Sociology professor Alexander Goldenweiser wrote to some friends on the CCNY board of regents to tell them that this man was completely opposed to freedom in teaching. Neither opportunity materialized, so Keezer girded his loins and set about digging in and straightening out this whole situation at Reed once and for all.

The first thing he hit upon was revising the constitution. He wanted to take the constitutional role of the Faculty Council to the Board of Trustees and get a more workable situation between all administrative functions at Reed. Of course, the faculty wasn't ready for that at all. Meanwhile, Keezer was trying to get rid of some longstanding faculty members—Charles Botsford in physical education, Charlie McKinley in

political science, Clement Akerman and Blair Stewart '21 in economics, as well as me as dean of women. There was a whole picture he was working on, because he now had less money to work with. He could have cleared out some of the lower echelons of faculty that were just costing money and not doing a great deal for the college, but instead he went after the higher echelon.

REGINALD "REX" ARRAGON, history professor 1923–1962, 1970–1974: Clement Akerman's crime was that he had attacked the government's first-ever peacetime conscription in 1940. The so-called "Akerman case" turned on the right of free speech on campus. Cooperation between Keezer and the faculty broke down over it, and faculty loyalty was gone for many members after that. Among many of the older faculty members there was a strong sense of community in defense of the Reed they had known and felt should continue. A clean break finally came in April 1941 when the Faculty Council voted against the president's recommendation to move on Akerman. Keezer then renewed his aggressive attitude toward student government, and delayed filling vacancies of the deanships for men and women students, causing increased disquietude.

ERNEST BOYD "E. B." MACNAUGHTON, trustee 1919–1941, 1955–1958, president 1948–1952: Dr. Keezer came to Reed completely untried in college administrative work, but full of the gospel of the New Deal. He hoped that by applying himself to the business of running the college he could advance the new ideas that were being sponsored by President Roosevelt as the best things for the country. He was a likeable fellow, and had a better approach to the Portland community than his predecessors, but it wasn't long before he completely lost the community because he was so intensely pro-Roosevelt. He was invited one day to the Arlington Club, Portland's exclusive businessmen's club started in part by

PART TWO: THE GOLDEN AGE, 1921–1945

Simeon Reed, to attend a talk by Oregon's Democratic governor, General Charles Martin. Keezer had no place on the program. But when Martin made some sharp criticism of Roosevelt's New Deal, Keezer rose from his seat and, defying the whole organization, said, "I'll never come in this place again. I won't have anything to do with it. I won't have such criticism made of one of the people for whom I have the greatest admiration." It was a case of bad taste if there ever was one.

Keezer was always messing around in problems far removed from how to operate a college. The final climax came for me in 1939 when I had to tell the trustees that, as president of the board, it was my judgment that Keezer had lost the support of the student body and the faculty, and that he had also lost the confidence of the downtown community. It seemed to me the only fair thing was to tell him so.

I did not prevail in my opinion largely because Simeon Winch, who had joined the board in 1935, was riding in Keezer's pocket. I knew Simeon Winch very well. He had a persecution complex and was frustrated because he felt that he was always getting bypassed and couldn't get to what he considered a first-rank position. He was intensely proud of his father, Martin Winch—Simeon Reed's nephew and one of Reed's original trustees—who had never rated very high among the important people in the Portland community. Whether it was for his penny-pinching habits, I never knew, but Sim Winch couldn't get over that. When Keezer recruited him to the board, it was Sim's first chance for a place in the sun. The sun proved too hot for him.

After the trustees failed to act on my recommendation regarding Keezer, I resigned from being a trustee. Keezer subsequently kept getting deeper and deeper in crisis. The college was again in Dutch as far as the local community was concerned. It wasn't all Keezer's fault. The students at the time were damned obnoxious in lots of the things they did, and the faculty seemed to take a delight in irritating conservative downtown Portland, not on specific platforms, but by just turning their back to the Portland community and ignoring it.

DOROTHY JOHANSEN '33, history professor 1934–1969, archivist 1969–1984: One reason that Keezer recruited Simeon Winch to the board was as an attempt to rebuild the bridges between the college and the city, an effort he pursued by various devices, all of which were terribly unsuccessful. There was sort of a residual element of distrust in town that the college had not fulfilled Amanda Reed's will. That bothered poor Thomas Lamb Eliot, who died in 1936, to just no end. Among the little scraps of papers found on his desk after his death was one in his handwriting that said, "We have not fulfilled Mrs. Reed's trust. So-and-so,"—just someone's initials—"has made this statement publicly." When Simeon Winch joined the board in 1935, he was carrying the torch of his father, Martin Winch, who felt that his aunt Amanda's will had not been well served by the creation of a liberal arts college.

DEXTER KEEZER, president 1934–1942: I was told by several faculty members that what had originally induced them to join the college was its determination to give studies a clear right of way, without the distractions and obstructions created by conventional athletics and the social setup of fraternities and sororities. This policy also served effectively to attract students seriously interested in the intellectual activities centered in the main tent.

But along with great benefits this policy also introduced a host of institutional problems, one being a reputation as being a very queer place to a substantial segment of the general public. This reputation seemed to complicate the business of securing a well-balanced student body. Often young people are thought to be queer by us more plodding and unimaginative adults because of our inability to appreciate their gifts, perceptions, or fine-grained sensibilities. Sometimes though, they are thought queer simply because they are queer, in the crackpot sense of the term. When there is a college in the neighborhood that also enjoys something of the same reputation, the elements that prompt people to try to effect a union seem to be well-established. It was not infrequent during my travels to hear someone describe in detail a strange sort of boy or girl and then announce with a light of inspiration in his eye, "Why, he or she ought to go to Reed!"

As a rough working rule I thought a college ought to be willing to accommodate about 5 percent of freaks and geniuses in its student body, and not be too much bothered by what they did or why they did it. At Reed it seemed to me that that 5 percent joint classification was exceeded. I also encountered a certain number of students who came to Reed because they distrusted their ability, particularly on the social side, to get along in a standard college setup, as much as they may have liked to do so.

Another factor at play that afflicted a segment of both the Reed student body and the faculty was a feeling of self-conscious intellectual superiority. This feeling had a complex root structure dating back to the college's beginnings, when it was trying to convince the local community that it was a vastly superior enterprise. It at least succeeded in convincing many of those directly participating in it of the idea. The fact that it was small in relation to the immediate metropolitan environment also had some bearing on this attitude, somewhat in the same manner that bantam roosters seem to be affected. The campus wrote off the college's queer reputation as being due to the outside community's inability to comprehend the behavior of the elite.

CHERYL SCHOLZ, history professor: Dexter Keezer was not a coeducational man. He had come out of Amherst, a men's college, and his wife, Anne, had attended a women's college. Coeducation was all new to them, and it frightened them. We had an interesting episode when Cora Anderson '35 collected a group of upperclass girls at her dorm house one afternoon to talk about instituting sex education at Reed. Cora felt that a number of the women freshmen were so young that they came to Reed without knowing anything. There were two girls she was especially worried about, and rightly so. Anne Keezer and I were both there. Anne started the meeting by saying she felt very strongly that anything a girl should know about sex she should learn from her husband when she married him. That clammed the girls up. They didn't know where to go from there, and they never did get the thing started.

I was never Keezer's ideal of a dean because, in his opinion, I was protecting the students, and he was protecting the college. There was a head-on collision between us. Finally, Keezer told me that he wanted me to move into the dormitory. I would have been a single mother, with four children and my mother in her seventies, living in the dorms, busy all day, and busy all night with students. I used to say facetiously that the only reason I survived was that Friday night I was sick of the college, and Monday morning I was sick of the Scholz family. I had all I could take at the time. I told Keezer I wouldn't do it, and that he had to find someone else.

He found Maida Bailey, who had been the first librarian at Reed until she left in 1918. She came back in 1936 as dean of women and moved into the dorms. Then Keezer tried to get rid of me entirely. Someone on the faculty told him that he couldn't fire me, so he sent me on a year's leave of absence. When I came back he assigned me to counseling incoming freshman on their problems. I also began teaching freshman history conferences as an instructor, and, thanks to the faculty, was appointed to the Faculty Council.

Meanwhile, Maida got along quite well. She was a graduate of Cornell and had worked at both

Stanford and Reed as a librarian, so she had a lot of background for the job. On occasion, she toted students off to her ranch near Sisters, Oregon. Then in the early '40s, when Keezer was having trouble with the faculty, he started looking for a new dean of women. I don't know if Maida got fed up and decided to leave, or if Keezer decided he wanted a change. He asked me one day to show this woman from Vassar, Cornelia LeBoutillier, around campus. I found her very entertaining, although I didn't think Reed was up her alley.

ESTHER DORLES LEWIS '42: Cornelia LeBoutillier was brought in by Keezer to make us into ladies. We were to wear dresses to class, and to learn to be polite and have good manners, such as knowing when to wear white gloves and things like that. We had periods where we had to walk with books on our heads to learn to carry ourselves well.

MILDRED FAHLEN TAXER '42: Etiquette. You can imagine how well this went over with Reed students. LeBoutillier was a very handsome lady, and well intentioned, but Reed was not the place to impose superficial kinds of etiquette. Reed students have always been casual in their dress.

Portland, on the other hand, was quite provincial. I worked off campus at the *Oregonian*, and when I went downtown to their decrepit offices to pick up classified advertising for the *Quest*, I had to be attired with a hat, gloves, purse, hose, and shoes.

PATRICIA BECK '44: J. J. Brownlee was night watchman. He detested LeBoutillier as much as I did. We used to have slander sessions together about her. One night he was wreathed in smiles. LeBoutillier had been lurking about, inspecting what everybody was doing. She said to J. J., "Oh, Mr. Brownlee, listen to all those crickets." J. J. said, "Boolyah! Those ain't crickets, those are zippers!" A wise old bird he was.

DEXTER KEEZER, president: Since the college lacked the customary complement of offices to handle straightening out wayward youngsters, the job often devolved upon me. At one time or another I did everything from putting drunks to bed—there weren't many—and breaking up marathon gambling games, to scouring the countryside for a runaway girl at the behest of frantic parents. As I unhappily carried out these extra-curricular activities, I longed for the cooperation of students who felt a special sense of responsibility for those who had gone astray, which the senior members of any Amherst College fraternity during my undergraduate years there would have felt for a fellow member.

Relatively little was forthcoming. In the absence of social organizations, the establishment and maintenance of tolerable social standards also devolved in unusual degree upon the administration. It tended to be a formidable undertaking, both because the college had attracted its full share of students who consciously battled against what they regarded as the oppressive conventions of organized society, and because a goodly number of students had shown up at college from frontier settlements, almost untouched by any knowledge of what these conventions were.

When those who did not conform teamed up with those who did not know how to, no mean force was created for scrapping the standards of social usage established by a stodgy but long suffering society. Sometimes the results were invigorating, sometimes alarming, and sometimes merely uncomfortable. The most consequential result was creating in the minds of many students a feeling that there was a virtue in flouting the conventions of organized society. I spent no time worrying about students with really first-rate heads, but I hated to see the students possessed of no more than run-of-the-mill intellectual equipment complicate the tough road ahead for them in a bootless way, by acquiring the foolish notion that there is some special grace to be gained by being unconventional regardless of whether it makes any sense or not. I am sure that in terms of total environment a substantial proportion of the students would have been better off at some other college of liberal arts and sciences.

CHERYL SCHOLZ, history professor: Keezer and his wife, Anne, had been driving through the West on their summer holiday, and had run into this man on an Indian reservation named Louis Balsam. Mr. Keezer decided Balsam was just the man he needed for dean of men and professor of sociology at Reed. According to the constitution, Keezer needed approval of the Faculty Council for any new appointment. It was summer, and everybody on the council was gone except for me and Monte Griffith in psychology. So he called the two of us over to the President's House one evening and told us that Mr. Balsam was a more Christlike figure than anyone he had ever seen in his life, and that this was an appointment that had to be made right now. So Monte and I said okay. That set the wheels in motion. Everything came apart after that.

REX ARRAGON, history professor: Neither of the deans appointed by Keezer proved to be satisfactory in the eyes of many faculty members and students. Mrs. LeBoutillier, who also taught philosophy, was well-meaning but unfamiliar and unsympathetic with the degree of student freedom from rules and with self-government at Reed. The dean's office in her view was disciplinary, not simply advisory, as had been the Reed practice. This view, backed by Keezer, had been basic to the conflict with the Community Affairs Committee, which I sat on along with Blair Stewart '21 and Cheryl Scholz. LeBoutillier knew that she was unpopular with women students because of her attitude on dormitory regulations and on the role of the student Women's Council, which

oversaw the dorms. More complex was the case of the dean of men. Louis Balsam had been hired in the late summer of 1941. Within months, rumors were abroad that raised serious questions about his suitability as dean.

MALCA KLEINER CHALL '42: I was on the Student Council. The student body president, Patricia Beck '44, and I actually went off campus to the home of one of the trustees, Frederick Harvey Strong, with our concerns about President Keezer, and expressed them to him. It was a rather unusual step for a couple of students to take.

REX ARRAGON, history professor: When the college opened in the fall of 1941, most of the longtime faculty members wanted their loss of confidence in Keezer's administration known to the board. E. B. MacNaughton had resigned the year before as president of the board, in disapproval of Keezer's administration. His successor, lumberman Aubrey Watzek, was a colleague of mine on the board of the Portland Art Association.

With Watzek's advice regarding process, the Faculty Council prepared a statement to President Keezer in October for transmission to the regents. It was the most collaborative document I have ever worked on, and signed by most of the Faculty Council members and full professors. A declaration of lack of confidence in the president, it listed six areas of complaint. E. O. Sisson, who had retired two years before to Carmel, California, came up to Oregon and initiated our contact with Keezer. Sisson issued a letter to Keezer that is the strongest condemnation of an administrator's attitude I have seen.

EDWARD OCTAVIUS "E. O." SISSON, letter to President Keezer, October 19, 1941: Can it be true, as has been charged many times, that you want only yes-men about you? I have fought off such an obnoxious idea and defended you from it. I am regretfully surrendering. I must bear down on my conviction, expressed to you long ago and reiterated yesterday, that you cannot find your fit career in a field which does not command your deepest interest and in which you are not at home and do not wish to be. I must add that trouble lies ahead, even disaster, and perhaps not far ahead, for you and the college.

CHERYL SCHOLZ, history professor: Keezer paid no attention to Sisson's entreaty at all. The fat was in the fire, but he didn't think it counted that the faculty had lost confidence in him.

REX ARRAGON, history professor: Following our meeting with Keezer, our statement was formally presented to four trustees at the home of Simeon Reed Winch. At the request of the board, an uneasy truce was struck with the president. That reigned until December, when the president postponed the election of the Faculty Council, vaguely hinting at constitutional changes.

ROBERT ROSENBAUM, mathematics professor 1939–1942, 1945–1953: One Sunday in December 1941, I was involved with the preparations for an open house at the Eastport dorm, where I was resident advisor. That morning, I was working in my office in Eliot Hall when my wife, Louise, burst in, exclaiming, "The Japanese have bombed Pearl Harbor, and the rest of the campus is attacking Eastport!"

I ran back to the residence hall to find students swarming up the outside walls of the building, aided by ivy, hoping to break through the second-floor windows to capture the Doyle Owl, which was being held there. One Eastport resident who was a well-heeled Anglophile had his favorite record on, "There'll Always Be an England," while he stood valiantly at his dorm window using a stainless steel crankshaft to rap on the knuckles of students that grasped at the windowsill trying to get in.

DICK LEWIS '44: I was in the dorm working my tail off, because I didn't want to flunk out. Suddenly, I heard this thumping. It was some of the upperclassmen. They had a log about fourteen inches in diameter, and they were slamming it like a ram against the door, trying to scare us freshmen! In the midst of the thumping, word that Pearl Harbor had been bombed came over the news, and all that stopped. Everything was still for about an hour.

I was afraid and unbelieving. I had been hardened a little earlier by the death of my father, but what really shook me up that day was looking out the dorm window at all these innocent girls unknowingly walking past outside. As the news spread, three things struck me: one, everyone wanted to call their parents in California or back East; two, there was no joking; and three, a lot of the upperclassmen were crying. After a while, I was too.

ANN STEARNS WHITEHEAD '44: It was a very sudden shift. Here we were, in the midst of this silly play thing, with people climbing up the outside of the Eastport dorm to recapture the Doyle Owl, and then, suddenly, we were at war. That evening everybody in the Commons was singing patriotic songs.

ELIZABETH FUNGE MACAULAY '43: When we came to class on Monday morning, Dexter Keezer called a general assembly of the students. He begged the boys not to go rushing off to enlist but to finish their education or at least go as far as they could.

ROBERT MACAULAY '43: Keezer had volunteered in World War I, and since he came from Colorado, they put him in the horse marines, even though he didn't know anything about horses. He was trying to explain to us that this is what they will do with you. So be careful. Don't go off and enlist too quickly.

JEAN WEBSTER MCNUTT '45: On Monday, December 8, we listened in the chapel to Franklin Roosevelt give his radio address. He said, "This is a date that will live in infamy." We all had very sober faces. We put up blackout curtains right away in all the dorms. That evening the boys came by and serenaded us, so we had all the windows open. It was December and cold, and I caught a really bad cold that night. We felt so threatened after Pearl Harbor that we all started knitting. Girls would be knitting all the way through lectures and conferences.

REX ARRAGON, history professor: In January 1942, F. L. Griffin called for a motion to elect a new Faculty Council, and Keezer, who had managed to postpone the election, made the matter one of confidence in his authority, calling for a standing vote on whether to hold the election or not. The vote was overwhelmingly in favor of Griffin's motion. Elected to the Faculty Council

were only signers of the October declaration of no confidence in the president. The presidential counterattack had failed.

At the end of January, Keezer announced that he was taking leave for a temporary wartime job in Washington with the Office of Price Administration, which had been established to control prices and ration scarce supplies during the war. Arthur Scott, who had taught chemistry since the early 1920s, was appointed to be the acting president in his absence, although most of the faculty would have preferred Blair Stewart '21, from economics.

CHERYL SCHOLZ, history professor: As his final farewell, Keezer called a meeting of the Faculty Council, and asked us who on the faculty we would suggest to serve as acting president. Somebody immediately recommended Blair Stewart '21, who had been back in Washington along with Charlie McKinley on wartime assignment.

President Keezer, second from the right in the back row, following a baseball game with members of the faculty during a more cordial time in the late 1930s.

Keezer said, very sharply, "Oh, no use appointing him, he's just a stooge for Mr. McKinley."

There was a deadly silence after that. Anybody who knew Blair knew he wasn't a stooge for Charlie, and anybody who knew Charlie McKinley knew he wouldn't have a stooge. The whole thing was ridiculous. Then Keezer suggested chemistry professor Arthur Scott. We all liked Scottie very much, but no one thought of him as an administrator. He was articulate when it came to chemistry, but quite inarticulate when it came to saying what Reed was and what it did. He just couldn't put Reed over to other people.

REX ARRAGON, history professor: Before leaving, Keezer submitted a budget that dropped seven junior faculty members, and retained the deans of men and women, who were also part-time teachers in sociology and philosophy. The Faculty Council felt that budget reductions could be achieved by keeping the seven professors but not the two deans. On February 4 they rejected the budget, and, for the second time in my experience at Reed, an ad hoc committee—this time consisting of Blair Stewart '21 and myself—was named, in accordance with the faculty constitution, to discuss an impasse with a regents committee and the president. The regents committee met the next day, and the only reappointment approved was for the dean of women, reflecting perhaps the regents' sympathy with her attempted regulation of student conduct. Aubrey Watzek promptly resigned as president of the trustees in protest of the decision. The next day, unexpectedly, a special inquiry was called for February 7 by John Laing, the chairman of the regents, in the case of the dean of men, Louis Balsam.

The inquiry turned out to be a sort of trial, with Blair Stewart and me serving as prosecuting attorneys, presenting witnesses in support of rumors of impropriety. The inquiry was hard on Balsam and he was not in good defense. At one point Keezer intervened on his behalf to keep Balsam's emotions from getting the better of him. Injudicious and unprofessional dealings with students and faculty members were reported, such as using, in his sociology class, knowledge of student behavior gained in his role as a dean, and making remarks of dubious intent to colleagues. Individually these charges each seemed relatively unimportant, but together they raised reasonable doubts about Balsam's suitability for the deanship. Balsam never came back to campus after the day of the inquiry, and later that month was given a severance package.

Keezer left for his assignment in D.C. in late February. In mid-April, regents chairman John Laing announced that Keezer's return was hoped for and expected. A fresh statement, again collaborative, was prepared and circulated among the faculty for signature, generating thirty-four signatures and nine abstentions. The statement called for the president's resignation for the welfare of the college, and asked for confirmation of the proper distribution of authority to the faculty at the college. On May 5 the regents board refused to ask for the removal of the president, but promised a regents committee to study the distribution of authority between the president and the faculty. Early in June, Keezer came to Portland on government business and requested an extension of his leave. With Aubrey Watzek having resigned from the trustees in February, the only other trustee sympathetic with the faculty's position, Frederick Harvey Strong, was out of town. The three trustees present granted Keezer an extension until October 1. Fred Strong returned the next day and resigned in protest.

The local chapter of the Association of American University Professors took the first step toward requesting an exploratory committee on the matter. A. J. Carlson, an experienced national AAUP hand, observed that the affair was being "superbly handled," and advised the faculty to continue waiting, which we did. In late June, the story broke in the *Oregonian*, and the board issued a statement the next day supporting Keezer. We remained in a waiting mode until August, when Keezer requested another extension of leave until June 1943. This time the board rejected it. Keezer submitted his resignation at the end of the month.

HARRY TURTLEDOVE '42: I find it hard to figure out where Dexter Keezer fit in. In retrospect, one sees that the era of the scholar-teacher college president was coming to an end. But what hadn't developed yet was the college president as front man and money raiser, which is essentially what they are today, with the provost and the deans running the college day to day. Keezer fit somewhere in the middle. He was an economist, but he wasn't an academician. You never got the impression he was exactly happy, although he happily taught one course on the subject of fly fishing, which he conducted in his home. That was apparently his passion. I never really got to know him. I'm not sure how many people did. He always seemed to be a little on the dour side.

REX ARRAGON, history professor: Following Keezer's resignation, the regents agreed to a constitutional review of the roles of the president and faculty, chaired by the son of Thomas Lamb Eliot, regent William G. Eliot, Jr. The findings differed little from the roles traditionally defined at Reed. The faculty's role in the decisions of academic policy and in instructional budgetary actions remained protected. The practice of student government continued as much the same. Procedures involving the joint faculty-student Community Affairs Committee, which reviewed actions taken by the Student Council, however, were made subject to the direction of the president.

In early 1943, the recorder at the college, Ann Shepard '23, replaced Mrs. LeBoutillier as dean. The questions raised by Keezer and LeBoutillier about whether the dean's role was disciplinary or simply advisory—meaning not just advising students but also carrying out the decisions of the Community Affairs Committee—were debated throughout 1943, and culminated by year's end in a clarification of the continued advisory role.

DEXTER KEEZER, president: I stayed at Reed for nearly eight years, which was at least three years too long. After five years in office, I realized that I had accumulated an excess baggage of friction and opposition, particularly by a fine teaching faculty that resented having any president at all. As a result, I was not advancing the good ideas which I suspected myself, perhaps too generously, of still possessing. I did succeed in broadening student interest and involvement in educational policies, developing music and the arts as well as noncommercialized sports like skiing, and rallying the alumni to support the college without resorting to the standard line of sentimental hokum. But I never managed to hit upon the arrangements to generate "college spirit" effectively without introducing elements of whoopla that would detract from the fine atmosphere for study created by the absence of standard school-spirit-rousing machinery.

Before I left Reed I was with a group of students at an outing on the Sandy River. Everybody was yakking about everything. I remarked that what Reed needed was an "Alma Mater" song, and so I composed one right then on the spot:

> On the banks of the Willamette
> where it broadly flows,
> stands fair Reed, our Alma Mater,
> going where, God knows.
>
> Hail to thee, our Alma Mater.
> Hail to thee fair Reed.
>
> Nothing here is ever settled—
> Nothing is agreed.

Although I occasionally sang it, generally in the shower, my song never really caught on.

CHAPTER 15

Wartime

We knew we were living a precious life at college. We knew that. We called Reed "our orchid in a dunghill."
— Sally Hovey Wriggins '44

We were taken to the Portland Assembly Center, a huge barn in the stockyards along the Columbia River. They put up barbed-wire fences and guard posts with machine guns mounted in them. They had searchlights on all night long, to watch for any movement of people.
— Hattie Kawahara Colton '43

In 1942, under interim president Arthur Scott, Reed was forced to shift to a wartime program. Student enrollment dropped from six hundred to three hundred, as the majority of eligible men—and a handful of women—either enlisted in the military or were drafted. Many faculty members were assigned to wartime duty in various agencies of the Roosevelt Administration, leaving behind a skeleton crew of older faculty and women instructors.

One inadvertent impact of the wartime program was the integration of Reed's humanities program. In 1943, under the auspices of the Sixty-Ninth Army Air Force Technical Training Detachment, twenty-five hundred young men were selected to undertake one of the most intensively accelerated courses of study the army had ever offered—the Army Meteorology Program, or AMP—a one-year pre-meteorology course. Reed was among the colleges chosen to provide this training, and nearly three hundred student-soldiers arrived in February 1943 to be taught in special army-only classes by Reed faculty, led by physics professor A. A. Knowlton. The army stipulated that, in addition to science and math, the soldiers be taught history and literature. Due to the limited number of faculty available on campus, Reed's parallel freshman courses of literature and history were combined for the army program, and renamed "humanities." In the fall of 1943, the integrated program was offered to regular students.

CHAPTER 15: WARTIME   187

ROBERT NACE '45: I would like to say that, after December 7, 1941, a somber mood engulfed the nation, but as so often happens in history, we march to war amid cheers, waving, and stirring bands. So it was on campus. We stopped studying. My gang formed a pinochle and whist club. We played pinochle by the hours and talked about which branch of the service we would prefer. The ski troops captured the imagination of a number in our group.

CHARLES CONRAD CARTER '46: The armed forces came on campus and recruited. There were those who joined the navy's Officer Candidate School. There were those who joined the air force to become flying officers. Then the army came along and said, "We want officers who are educated. We don't know how long this war is going to last, but we want you to stay in school and join the Enlisted Reserve Corps so you will be out of the control of the draft board. First, get your education so that you can become a well-educated officer."

Those of us who followed that advice were actually enlisted in the army although we stayed on campus. We didn't have a uniform, but they could do with us what they wanted to do. Over the next six months the army started calling people up by their academic major. The sociologists, literature majors, and psychologists all went first. The last ones left were the physics majors and the pre-med students.

When the physics majors started going, the dean of men, Frank Hurley, who also taught chemistry, went up to the medical school in Portland and said, "I've got a group of twelve pre-medical students at Reed. The army's going to call them up unless you admit them." The medical school was concerned because the armed forces were insisting that their classes be filled, but they were also losing students left and right to the draft. So we were admitted to medical school before our first year as freshmen at

Reed was completed. Lo and behold, one or two weeks later all the pre-meds that weren't admitted to medical school were called up.

GENNY HALL SMITH '43: Women were being recruited to fly airplanes as Women's Air Service Pilots, or WASPs, not in combat, but to ferry planes back and forth when needed. A couple of women quit school to do that. One was Jean Cross '41. At the time I thought, "What a crazy idea. What in the world are they doing that for?" Later, I wondered how I could ever have been so stupid as to pass up an opportunity to learn how to fly!

ROBERT NACE '45: Because of my background as a missionary kid in Japan, I was approached with offers of a commission in the military's intelligence corps. I declined because I was a pacifist. How could you be a Christian or take the Bible seriously, and involve yourself in a military enterprise? That was a central question to me at that point.

We all had to register with Selective Service. I wrote my local draft board explaining that while I was entitled to a pre-ministerial deferment, I was opposed to the war and wanted to be registered as a conscientious objector. Back came my draft card: 1-A, meaning, "You go, now." I learned that the local draft board gave me that classification because they didn't believe that a conscientious ministerial student could be attending Reed College, given its local reputation for "communism, atheism, and free love."

DOROTHY SCHUMANN STEARNS '45: The really ironic thing was that while the war was raging, we were singing traditional German songs on the balcony of the Student Union every week with Heinz Peters, who taught German. Dr. Peters was recruited by the U.S. intelligence agency that was then known as the Office of Strategic Services. His wife, Helga, who was

Male students continued their studies while waiting for their draft notices to arrive in the spring of 1942.

pregnant at the time, took over some of his classes. She was constantly trying to fix me up with a guy who was a German Jewish refugee and an assistant in physics.

MURIEL REICHART WYATT '46: In my sophomore year I took an economics course taught by Professor Robert Terrill. Right in the middle of the course he was suddenly called on by FDR to join the Office of Price Administration. One of the junior students, Gerald Meier '47, realized that the book we had was too difficult for us. So he lectured to us, and pulled us through that course after Terrill left.

JEAN WEBSTER MCNUTT '45: Everybody in the Portland labor pool had gone to work in the shipyards, and the college couldn't get any help. We even lost our beloved "harpies," the women who came in and cleaned our rooms periodical-

ly. We called them "harpies" because they would disturb all our piles of papers. In the fall of 1943, the college started drafting students to work on campus.

ROBERT NACE '45: Overnight, hatred of the "Japs" swept across the country. Almost immediately, the Chinese in Portland started wearing large lapel buttons that said "I am Chinese," to protect them from the anger and hatred. I retained warm childhood feelings from my years living in Japan, where my father had been a missionary, and where I was born.

The Japanese-Americans in Portland were gathered up at the International Livestock Pavilion outside Portland in preparation for their shipment to internment camps. I went with my father, who was a minister, down to the Pavilion, where he was conducting worship for the Christians among them. I found high school friends there from four families, each family crowded into an area that had been the stall for a single show horse only weeks earlier. There was no privacy and there were almost no toilet facilities.

HATTIE KAWAHARA COLTON '43: One day in late April of 1942, six months after the attack on Pearl Harbor, I was coming up the steps in Eliot Hall when Kurt DeWitt '41, a student who was a refugee from Nazi Germany, came running down the steps, saying, "Hattie, I've been looking for you! Your walking papers are posted!" That was how I first heard about the notice. Hastily, I picked up my belongings and headed for the bus stop out on the street. Signs were plastered all over the telephone poles with big headlines addressed to "ALL PERSONS OF JAPANESE ANCESTRY."

GENNY HALL SMITH '43: One of my good friends, Hattie Kawahara '43, came to school one day and said, "We're leaving tomorrow." At the time, the rest of us were all thinking about exams and pretty much concentrated on our work. There were no protests, no big uproar about taking all the Japanese people away. What still bothers me is that I didn't think about it much. It was something that just happened. I mean, yes, Hattie was gone, but I wasn't outraged. I should have been. It was terrible. But it was wartime.

HATTIE KAWAHARA COLTON '43: There were about two thousand Japanese scattered around the Portland area. We were ordered to go to camp on May 4 and given one week to get ready. As soon as the signs went up, various people started knocking on our door, wanting to buy furniture. "I'll give you five dollars for that lamp," that sort of thing.

It was very unnerving. They knew we had to dispose of our things. My brother cried when his favorite lamp went, because he used to like to

Reed's Japanese-American students were pulled out of school and—along with two thousand other Portland residents—held at the Portland stockyards before being sent to internment camps in other states.

PART TWO: THE GOLDEN AGE, 1921–1945

study under it. My father's family were Nichirin Buddhists, so we were able to store some keepsakes, things like old family photographs, at the Nichirin Buddhist Church nearby.

We were taken to the Portland Assembly Center, a huge barn in the stockyards along the Columbia River. They put up barbed-wire fences and guard posts with machine guns mounted in them. They had searchlights on all night long, to watch for any movement of people.

After I got to camp, I petitioned the camp director to be allowed to go back to Reed to take my final exams; otherwise a whole year's work would be lost. That petition was granted. Along with two other Reed students, Ruth Nishino '43 and Midori Imai '42, I was driven to the campus under armed guard in an army car, and dropped off. The soldiers were very sheepish. We went there on two successive days to take exams. After the second day, we were allowed to take our math and economics exams back to the camp with us, and then mail them in to our professors. When we got back to camp there was a problem with where to take the exams. We were being kept in stalls in this huge barn with one common ceiling, and it was so noisy. I petitioned for a place where we could study and then take the final exams. We were given a meat refrigerator where they used to string up the cattle. It was narrow and about twenty feet long. We moved some tables and chairs in there.

The food at the camp was awful. Army rations. A number of Reed classmates came to visit me at the camp, bringing homemade cookies and things like that. Political science professor Bernard Noble came to see me, as did Hazel Johnson, the librarian, because I had worked for her in the library.

LOIS SHOEMAKER MARKUS '45: During the summer of 1943, Father would listen to the war news on the radio in the evening while Mother and I knitted. We heard about the Allied victory over German forces in North Africa, and the landings in Sicily and southern Italy. In the Pacific Ocean, American forces were suffering very heavy losses as they slowly advanced against Japanese soldiers entrenched in the Solomon Islands chain.

Shortly after the fall semester of 1943 began, I was asked to play the organ for a wedding in the chapel. As with so many weddings in wartime, the groom had received permission to take leave on short notice, so, although there were lovely flowers in the chapel, the bride wore a pink suit and hat for the affair and there were no rehearsals.

One day, coming back to my room in Anna Mann, I happened to meet Muriel Reichart '46, who had a room of her own nearby. She was a brilliant girl with delicate, winsome features and an inborn grace of manner. She had just received a packet from her fiancé, Laurence Wyatt '43, which contained an engagement ring. Shyly she showed me her ring, telling me that she felt the stone was small. As Laurence was in the Canadian army, his resources were small, plus jewelry during the war was definitely modest. I asked her to put it on, and then told her that it looked to me like a perfect dewdrop on a rose. She was about eighteen years old at the time.

SALLY HOVEY WRIGGINS '44: My friend Pat Beck '44 and I took a leave from school and to earn money went to work in the shipyards down in Oakland, California. We had a whale of a time. The people running the shipyards were so surprised to see college students that they gave us positions of some responsibility. Pat Beck ran the strap shop, making the little things that hold the cables up on ships, and I ran the rack shop. It was hard to go back to Reed after all that. Our year away had been so exciting that it made Reed seem unreal. We knew we were living a precious life at college. We knew that. We called Reed "our orchid in a dunghill."

BETTY JEAN PERRY FOX '45: Gas rationing kept us on campus most of the time. Daydodgers came to school by bus. There were empty tables in Commons. We turned our wartime ration books over to Miss Ann Brownlie '23, who ran Commons, which allowed her to make us meals with more restricted supplies. As the student body was mostly women, there was little dancing.

LYLE VINCENT JONES AMP '44: A month into my freshman year in 1942 I was approached by math professor Bob Rosenbaum. "You know," he said, "they're going to draft you and send you off to the infantry. But we've got a pre-meteorology program starting this winter at Reed. You might be interested."

So, at the end of the fall semester I went up to Fort Lewis, near Tacoma, donned an army uniform, and became a private in the army. I returned to Reed in uniform as a member of the pre-meteorology program. Once in the program, we were protected from combat in ways that many other draftees or enlistees were not. It was a shock for me though, having to adapt suddenly to a discipline on campus that was extremely different from the total freedom and wonderful liberty I had had as a Reed student. Since I had female student friends from my short time as a civilian student at Reed, I was able to make friends among the army group because I could introduce them to attractive young women.

HARRY BERNAT AMP '44: There were three colleges set up around the country for pre-meteorology training—Colleges A, B, and C. Reed College was College C, for students who had either a year of college or no college whatsoever. We were shipped out from basic training in the Wasatch Mountains of Utah under secret orders, on a train at night so we had no idea which direction the train was going. There were 267 pre-meteorologists, or "PMs" as we were called, at

Reed, and six military personnel who were in charge. We were divided into eight flights. Each flight held all of its classes together and slept in the same barracks. I was in Flight Three. Most of Flight Three consisted of Midwesterners.

We had a horrendous schedule because we were told that we had to do two years' worth of college in one year in order to qualify for the advanced program that would allow us to become weather forecasters. We got up every morning at five-twenty AM with sergeants blowing whistles and pounding on the doors. Then we went outside for calisthenics, after which we had breakfast, and then at seven AM went to our first class. There was a break for lunch, and then we would have classes until about four-thirty. After classes, we would go outside for military drill for about an hour, marching up and down in front of the old dormitories on the main campus. Then we would come in for dinner and go back to class from six-thirty to eight-thirty PM. After that, we would go to our rooms, where we could study until bed check at ten o'clock. After bed check many of us got up and studied until midnight. We did that six days a week. Sundays were our day off.

When we got to Reed, there wasn't room for all of us in the dormitories, so they housed half of us in an old, abandoned Safeway store up the hill from campus. The store had bunk beds about two feet apart to fit everyone in. Every morning we would march in formation down the hill, with somebody calling the cadence: "Hup, two, three, four."

At the end of six months, all the PMs on campus were moved to the old Safeway store, and those who were staying up at the store came down to campus and were housed in the Old Dorm Block. I wound up in the Eastport dorm with four men, two double bunks for four of us, and a cot for the fifth one. We became very close friends because we were together in that room for six months.

ROSEMARY LAPHAM THOMPSON BERLEMAN '48: There were a lot of restrictions on the PMs and they didn't have much free time. A couple of guys showed up in uniform at our folk-dancing class, wanting to dance with me, but I didn't know which one to choose. They looked like they might come to blows if I chose the wrong one. They also came to our chorus rehearsals at night, and we would meet them between classes in the Student Union and have a Coke or two. It made a big difference to all the girls when the PMs arrived, because suddenly we had dates for the dances, plus they looked great in their uniforms. At the same time, there was the undercurrent of knowing that, with the war going on, these boys were not going to be around very long. So it was bittersweet.

JEANNE HANSEN GORDNER '46: The PMs would march across campus to class, counting cadence and singing as they marched:

There are fairies in the garden every night
and they sing and they dance
in the fair and starry light.

When they're sure no one's looking,
then they open every rose
and sprinkle them with the dewdrops—
How they do it, no one knows.

I could never hear them singing the next verse, but everyone in the quad would roar with laughter, so I had a pretty good idea what that verse was about.

HARRY BERNAT AMP '44: Each quarter there were exams called "screeners" that they used to screen out people who couldn't keep the pace. We called them "screamers." Sixty-six of the pre-meteorologists flunked out. The subjects we took varied. We had courses in physics, algebra, complex mathematics, and calculus, all of them very difficult. We also had courses in

Reed housed and instructed nearly three hundred student-soldiers in the Army Meteorology Program (AMP) in 1943–44.

vector analysis, geography, history, literature, and writing.

DALE ENGSTROM AMP '44: At one history conference the professor said, "Well now, let's talk about the reasons why Japan attacked. Did they have any alternative? Do you think that they might have been forced to attack because of the actions of the United States?" We looked at each other surprised. We had a little discussion, and the professor brought up the oil embargoes imposed on Japan prior to the war. He just wanted to get us to think about that larger context of the situation. I learned later that he was told not to conduct such discussions again.

LYLE VINCENT JONES AMP '44: At the end of the year, we learned that we would not be promoted to the next level pre-meteorology course because the army had meteorologists far beyond its need. So we were dispersed into various training programs all over the country.

FRED ROSENBAUM '50, trustee 1984–1996: My humanities teacher, Ruth Collier '32, came into our humanities conference one day looking like she had been crying. She really wasn't paying attention to the conversation in class. At the end of the class, everybody walked out, while I stayed behind. "Are you okay, Mrs. Collier?" I asked. She told me that she had just gotten a letter that day that her son had been killed in the war.

HELEN WHEELER HASTAY '39: One of my favorite courses was Renaissance literature, with Barry Cerf. His classes were some of the most exciting I had ever experienced in my life. But after we took our final exams in his class my junior year, he told us, "I lost the papers of the test I just gave everybody." We were totally dismayed.

MARIAN NEDRA WHITEHEAD '44: Barry Cerf was a great teacher, but he was becoming de-

mented. By the middle of 1943, he was wandering around campus, walking through sprinklers. It was probably Alzheimer's, though he wasn't that old. Not quite sixty.

REGINALD "REX" ARRAGON, history professor 1923–1962, 1970–1974: During the pre-meteorological training course, the army requested that we conduct a joint history-English course. This course combined history, literature, and composition, with lectures, group conferences, and a writing laboratory. In that same year, Barry Cerf, who had conducted the parallel literature correlative to freshman history, was forced by ill health to retire.

With the war on, there was no one in the department with the experience to take his place. The answer was, in light of our brief experience with the integrated meteorology course, to combine the mandatory freshman history and literature courses. For lack of a better name we called it Humanities 11. The course included reading, lectures, and conference discussion on the classical world, the Middle Ages, and the Renaissance.

A few years later, in 1946, sophomore literature and history were also joined together, as Humanities 21.

HUMANITIES ASSIGNED READING LIST, 1943:
Rostovtzeff, *History of the Ancient World*
Code of Hammurabi
Homer, *Iliad, Odyssey*
Thucydides, *History of the Peloponnesian War*
Toynbee, *The Tragedy of Greece*
Aristotle, *Constitution of Athens*
Herodotus, *The Histories*
Aeschylus, *Prometheus, Agamemnon*
Sophocles, *Antigone, Oedipus*
Euripides, *Electra, Medea*
Aristophanes, *The Clouds, Frogs*
Plato, *Apology, Crito, Phaedo*
Theocritus, *Idylls*

LOIS SHOEMAKER MARKUS '45: While our junior exams were underway during the spring of 1944, Allied forces had slowly been struggling up through the southern Italian coastal areas, taking Monte Cassino, and opening up access to Rome, which fell on June 4. Two days later, at the factory where I worked in the summer, I heard the news of the D-Day landing in Normandy. In the Pacific Theater, America was still sustaining great loss of life as troops advanced to Guam and the Philippine Sea.

Dr. Arragon was my thesis advisor in my senior year. I was much in awe of him, but he was not a man you ever crossed swords with. He was very myopic, and wore eyeglasses thickly circled in silver frames that expressed a glacial cold when he was displeased. His outline of my proposed thesis development was of course too ambitious, but he let me proceed in my own fashion. Every night, when I went to bed, all I could think of was one day awakening without thinking about my thesis. The library had a square tower where there were a number of carrells for the exclusive use of senior students. It was always very quiet up there. Each carrell had a green lampshade, and sufficient shelf space for books, files of note cards, and stacks of thesis drafts.

Our theses were due in early May. I was working in a frenzy to feed manuscript to my typist, the wife of art professor Lloyd Reynolds. Both she and I were burning the midnight oil to have the 222 pages, including notes, bibliography, and numerous fifteen-to-twenty-line footnotes complete. Copies went to Dr. Arragon and three other readers for my oral defense.

By commencement day everyone had been so worn out by thesis frenzy that our excitement level was subdued. Just before the ceremony, I learned that I would graduate Phi Beta Kappa. Since we were not a large class and rain had been falling, ceremonies were held in the chapel. My parents were both present. As our names were called, we climbed up the stairs to receive our leather-covered diplomas. Then, after members of Phi Beta Kappa were announced, Acting President Arthur Scott, to everyone's surprise, said that he had another announcement. The faculty had voted to award the Class of 1921 Prize for a Thesis of Outstanding Merit to Lois Shoemaker. I sat stunned. That prize was rarely awarded, indeed, hardly known. President Scott asked me to again come up to the stage and handed me an envelope. I stumbled climbing the stairs, as I was so ashamed of my black, old-lady shoes with a flap covering the laces. Of all things to be concerned about at such a moment!

During the spring of 1945 I had been so preoccupied with my thesis that I barely paid attention to the war or many other events. President Roosevelt had met in February with Churchill and Stalin at Yalta, where they discussed the future of Germany and Europe, as well as the creation of the United Nations. Roosevelt appeared a gaunt and very frail man in the photographs. On April 12 he died in Georgia of a stroke. Harry Truman became President. May 6, 1945, was VE Day, marking the German surrender, and the conclusion of war in Europe. In the Pacific, Allied troops continued fighting their way northward toward Japan, through the Philippines, Iwo Jima, and Okinawa.

Thousands and thousands of men had been killed while I was literally working in my library ivory tower.

PART THREE

PART THREE: THE NATIONAL COLLEGE, 1946–1966

THE NATIONAL COLLEGE, 1946–1966

Education is not a preparation for life; education is life itself.
  —John Dewey

Reed College emerged from the Second World War in poor financial shape and lacking steady presidential leadership. Chemistry professor Arthur Scott, who had successfully guided the college through wartime as acting president, turned authority over to a permanent replacement in 1945, Peter Odegard; even so, Reed would struggle for another ten years with ongoing financial and leadership crises, held together primarily by the persistent efforts of a committed and self-sacrificing group of senior faculty.

Meanwhile, higher education was entering a twenty-five-year period of dramatic expansion initially stimulated by the G.I. Bill, which provided forty-eight months of college tuition for returning veterans. In the late 1940s the program attracted more than two million students—primarily white males—to colleges, quickly overwhelming small, underfunded schools such as Reed. The growth of higher education continued with the intensification of the Cold War in the 1950s, as the federal government began turning to colleges and universities for its scientific research needs. America's postwar economic growth also increased demand for a larger college-educated workforce to meet the sophisticated needs of the modern marketplace.

Following the Soviet Union's 1957 launching of the first artificial satellite, Sputnik 1, and the subsequent passage of the National Defense Education Act of 1958, the U.S. government began directly subsidizing higher education as a means of meeting the technological and geopolitical challenges of opposing the Communist threat across the globe. Then, beginning in 1963, the impact of the postwar increase in the birth rate known as the "Baby Boom" hit college and university campuses. Between 1960 and 1969, undergraduate college enrollments more

Students in an outdoor class on the front lawn in front of Eliot Hall, 1962.

than doubled—from 3.5 million to eight million—prompting parallel growth in faculty hiring and campus construction.

Against this backdrop, Reed strove to maintain its position among the country's top tier of liberal arts colleges. Despite a frugal operating budget and a relatively meager endowment—the college's average endowment per student was only a third that of its peer institutions—Reed managed to excel in both the humanities and the sciences thanks primarily to the sacrifices of low-paid but dedicated professors. Cohesiveness among the faculty was nourished in part by direct and open conflict with the administrations of various presidents and trustees. Between crises in governance—of which there were many—the faculty was instrumental in upholding the norms and principles of the college.

Central to those principles was William Foster's original quest to make critical thinking the holy grail of the liberal arts experience, later institutionalized at Reed in the 1920s by his successor, Richard Scholz, who anchored Reed's rigorous training in a core curriculum intended to provide students with both breadth and depth of knowledge. Foster had believed that if Reed was to be relevant in an educational landscape dominated by specialized research universities, it needed to impart to students the most rigorous possible set of intellectual skills and attitudes for informing every area of inquiry, and outcomes over the years largely supported this belief. A Carnegie Foundation study conducted at Wesleyan University in the early 1950s found that from 1924 to 1934 Reed had the highest percentage of American graduates going on to earn doctoral degrees in natural science, more than double that of its nearest competitor. In another Wesleyan study, the college placed second only to Swarthmore in the percentage of graduates receiving advanced degrees and fellowships in history, economics, and politics. Through the 1940s Reed also produced one Rhodes Scholar for every 147 graduates, beating the averages of Princeton, Harvard, and Yale.

Common wisdom in academic circles held that Reed graduates excelled not only because of such curricular hurdles as the senior thesis, but also because of the college's mandatory humanities program. While general education programs expanded during the 1920s and 1930s, most notably with Western Civilization courses and the Great Books program at the University of Chicago and St. John's College, Reed's approach to humanities was neither a history course, as was the case with many Western Civilization courses, nor a prescribed curriculum of "overriding metaphysics," as John Dewey criticized the Great Books program for being. Humanities at Reed was primarily an exercise in inquiry and in the discovery of a student's critical-reasoning ability, emotional sensitivity, imagination, and judgment, all of these qualities shaped and tested through writing, small-group discussion, and one-on-one meetings with professors.

Rex Arragon, who directed the humanities program from the time of Richard Scholz's death in 1924 until 1962, believed that the program followed John

Dewey's tenet of "learning by doing," employing ideas as instruments to solve problems. Dewey's scientific practice of observation—inquiring and experimenting; then distinguishing, analyzing, and relating ideas; and then drawing conclusions—fit with Arragon's view of disciplined critical thinking as both the means and the significant end of Reed's humanities program. "Doing" was a matter of reasoning. To substitute metaphysics for this scientific method, Arragon argued, was to arrest the rational, intellectual process.

In the postwar environment of government-funded research, which favored well-equipped and specialized university facilities, the question was whether Reed's model would continue to attract highly qualified students in the sciences. Initially it did. Beginning in the late 1940s, Reed developed a reputation as a place for "bright boys" interested in science. By the mid-1950s, natural-science majors comprised 48 percent of the student body, up from 35 percent in the 1930s and 1940s, while majors in literature and the arts dropped from 30 percent to 12 percent. With this shift, the proportion of male students also increased, to 67 percent from 60 percent in the 1930s.

Then, in 1954, Reed became a target of the anti-Communist fury that, spurred by U.S. Senator Joe McCarthy, was sweeping the country. As with the hysteria generated prior to America's entry into the First World War in 1917, the political climate proved to be a near-death experience for the college. In 1956, after the fallout from Reed's bout with McCarthyism, a new president, Richard Sullivan, stepped into the breach. Much like Richard Scholz thirty-five years before, Sullivan saw in Reed's nadir an opportunity for a new round of institution building. He envisioned a growing, first-rate enterprise that could serve as a strategic resource in the Cold War. Sullivan strengthened the college's standards for student admission and teaching performance, and, with major foundation support, considerably expanded the college's facilities, student body, and faculty. The turnaround was dramatic. With renewed vitality, Reed was able to retain its reputation as "having the smartest undergraduate body in the country."

President Sullivan's triumph was not to last long. During the early 1960s, the boom in government and foundation funding began to flow primarily to the public sector of higher education, making the academic marketplace adverse to small, stand-alone liberal arts colleges. The more the rewards of academia swung toward research and publication, the more difficult it became for colleges such as Reed to compete with research universities for talented new faculty. In such an environment, one way for institutions to raise their academic profiles was to add graduate programs. Reed's attempt to do so in the mid-1960s set in motion yet another financial and leadership crisis, one that would destabilize the college for years to come.

CHAPTER 16

The G.I. Bill

There was something very special about the guys that came back from the war. They had a sense of tragedy.
   —Rosemary Lapham Thompson Berleman '48

We were at the end of a real traditional period for Reed students. For people else-where, I don't think the sexual revolution began until the '60s.
   —Nancy Stewart Green '50

With the war ended, in the fall of 1945 Reed College attempted to return to a nor-mal academic program. Interim president Arthur Scott returned to teaching chemistry, relinquishing his presidential duties to Peter Odegard, a former stu-dent of Reed's second president, Richard Scholz, at the University of Washington. Odegard had served during the war as a special assistant to the Secretary of the Treasury in Washington, D.C., and before that had taught at Williams College, Ohio State University, and Amherst College.

The first challenge Odegard faced at Reed was the sudden influx of veterans entering the college on the G.I. Bill. With their government-paid tuitions, the veterans brought in revenue for the cash-strapped college, but they also pushed Reed's threadbare infrastructure and small-conference teaching model to the breaking point. As the bulge of veterans passed through, the size of the student body surged from a prewar peak of just under six hundred students to almost eight hundred by the late 1940s. Reed also went from being a regional college to a national one as the percentage of students from the Northwest dropped to less than 50 percent by the early 1950s; by the 1960s it would be just 20 percent.

The second challenge Odegard faced was the new relevance that the rise of the Cold War gave to Reed's lingering reputation for radicalism. Students contin-ued to invite controversial speakers to campus, and to embrace the leftist activi-ties and bohemian social attitudes that would shortly come to characterize the Beat movement of the mid-1950s.

REX ARRAGON, history professor 1923–1962, 1970–1974: During his war presidency Arthur Scott had had to deal with problems of financial stringency, faculty military service deferments and war leaves, declining enrollment, and accommodation of the army's pre-meteorology program. Scottie was not a born administrator, nor to my mind, an efficient or dependable one. He was good-natured, easygoing, and hard to quarrel with. Relations with him were generally amiable, though he was at times misleading and seemingly evasive on a number of difficult issues. But—and it was a big "but"—he did manage the transition from Dexter Keezer in 1942 to a new president, Peter Odegard, in 1945.

HERB GLADSTONE, music professor 1946–1980: The Reed faculty viewed with suspicion anyone brought in as boss, but Peter Odegard quickly allayed those suspicions. Not long after he arrived, I went up to the registrar's office to get the files on my newly arrived student advisees. Margaret Scott '19, who had served as registrar at the college since 1923, was very defensive of her domain. She refused my request.

I immediately went into Odegard's office to complain. Odegard stood up from his desk, and, turning red, said, "Come on, follow me." He marched down the hall to the registrar's office and said, "Miss Scott, I want you to give Professor Gladstone what he requests." "Mr. Odegard," she said, "it's been the policy of the college not to give information on the students out to employees of the college." Odegard spun around on her. "Miss Scott," he said, "Mr. Gladstone is not an employee of the college. He *is* the college."

REX ARRAGON, history professor: Odegard had an open-door policy for the presidential office. Indeed, the problem was not so much how to get into the office but how to get out of it. He liked to talk about the conditions of the college, both general and particular, with anyone who went in, whatever the occasion for the visit. He handled public relations well, stood his ground on faculty freedom, and good-naturedly parried questions about whether the college had gotten over Communism by comparing that issue to the double-bind question of whether a man had stopped beating his wife. Odegard had one difficulty. He had naïvely accepted the presidency on the understanding that he would not have to raise money.

PHILIP WHALEN '51: Reed was this funny, little, almost invisible college campus, consisting of Eliot Hall and the Old Dorm Block, the president's house, Anna Mann cottage, and the Student Union. Everything else was a mess. There was this huge gymnasium made of plywood that they got from government surplus at some point, which could act as a theatre as well as a gym. Between the gym and the outdoor swimming pool was a funny little building that was the art department. Across the way there was the library and the new chemistry building. Behind that there were these trashy plywood barracks called the Foster-Scholz dorms that they had got from the government after the war. They were for gentlemen students because there was not enough room in the regular dorms for all the vets.

So there we all were, in this sort of rattletrap, half-Tudor, half-plywood layout, out there in the rain and the pretty Eastmoreland woods, milling around in circles, trying to get educated.

JACK BENVENISTE '43: I went to work at the Naval Research Lab during the war. When I came back home to Portland, Professor Knowlton at Reed called me and said he needed help teaching in the physics department. My dad ran a meat market in town. Since he hadn't had a vacation in four years during the war, he asked me to come and work at the market. I taught four days a week at Reed and then worked the weekends at the meat market. I got paid more as a butcher for two days work than I did working at Reed for four days. "What kind of a country is this?" my dad asked. "They think more of butchers than they do of professors!"

ELLEN KNOWLTON JOHNSON '39, recorder 1945–1962, registrar 1962–1981: In the fall of 1945, Reed got its first student under the G.I. Bill. We all thought that was quite something. Then, beginning in 1946, more and more G.I.s started coming. From then on through 1949, they were just pouring in.

PHILIP WHALEN '51: Where I grew up in The Dalles, Oregon, we heard a lot about this phenomenally difficult and high-class outfit called Reed College. It was supposedly very hard to get accepted there, and then, once in, students had to work their asses off, as the place had many requirements to fulfill. It was about fourteen times harder than going to the University of Oregon or Oregon State, and the ones who got out of there became Rhodes Scholars instantaneously. Along with their diploma they automatically got a Phi Beta Kappa key. It was out of this world—just sublime—and the idea of being a student there was unbelievable. I never heard about how it was "Communist Party West."

As it turned out, they were accepting anybody and everybody who came anywhere near the campus at the time, especially veterans since the government would pay for their education. I was among the second batch of students entering on the G.I. Bill in the fall of '46. And then, of course, there were all the youth of America, seventeen years old and very bright indeed, mixed up with this group of ancient-feeling veterans.

WILLIS SIBLEY '51: I started Reed in the fall of 1947 as a seventeen-year-old. Almost all of my male associates were veterans. Those guys were not fooling around. They were old—by my perspective anyway—they were experienced, and

they weren't putting up with any bullshit or any silliness from us young kids. They put us in a terrible spot because in their presence we had to grow up really quickly and become, at least superficially, mature.

During winter break in my freshman year, I stayed on campus in the Doyle dormitory, an all-male dorm. One day the phone in the hall rang. I went out to answer it, and who also should be coming out to answer the phone but a woman in a dressing gown. She was a friend of one of the veterans in the dorm. That was something of an unexpected kind of growing-up experience.

MOSHE LENSKE '50, trustee 1992–1996: The G.I.s had seen what life and living was like close up. They had a different standing with the faculty. When professor Frank Jones gave a humanities lecture in the chapel, the following week one of the student vets was allowed to give a rebuttal lecture on the same subject: "Hell, no!"

FRED ROSENBAUM '50, trustee 1984–1996: When you come back from a war, there's a lot of damage there that others don't see. You don't get off the ship or the airplane and walk into the classroom and take out your notepad ready to roll. Physically you do this, but mentally your mind is totally obscured by other stuff. It takes a hell of a long while to come back into civilian life. Some people can do it fast, but others definitely need help. I wanted to do my best, but I couldn't get it done. I was just a wild guy, and not as focused as I should have been. My experiences through the Holocaust, the Jewish children's evacuation, immigration, and serving in the army during the war had left their mark.

We had some people on campus who were badly shot up. One fellow, Ed Devecka '49, had been shot through the head. He would have spasms and fall down. Those of us who were veterans would kid him and say, "You're drunk again, Ed. Get the hell off the floor." We could do that, but nobody else could. Another student had lost both an arm and a leg. Another was caught panhandling out in the street in front of the college. The police picked up him and took him downtown. A whole bunch of us went to the police station and got him out. He had just gone off his rocker. Those things happened. Some guys had had horrible experiences during the war, and were just happy to be back at school and let it go.

GEORGE JOSEPH '51, trustee 1972–1980: Tom Kelly '48 came back from the service acting very erratic. Prior to the war he had been ranked one of the top ten tennis players in the country. He still played tennis, but he had suffered psychoneurotic damage during the war. Under stress he would get extremely nervous, almost to the point of fainting. He always walked around campus reading a book.

One night he was across the street, at the main entrance to the college on Woodstock Boulevard, waiting for a bus, and reading a book of poems by Percy Bysshe Shelley under the street lamp. In those days, the police kept a very close watch on the Reed campus. During the Red Scare following the First World War, Portland police had formed a "Red Squad" to resist union organizers. In the '40s, a police captain named Bill Brown expanded its power to keep an eye on people he thought suspicious, including students at Reed. The police patrolled around the campus frequently. Well, there was Tom, standing there, under the street lamp, reading.

The police car stopped, and a policeman yelled to him to come to the car and show his draft card as a form of ID. Tom couldn't produce his draft card, and instead just went into a spaz attack. The police threw him into the back of the car and took him down to jail. Four years in the war, and they haul him in for reading Shelley by street lamp.

MORTON ROSENBLUM '49: The next night, February 5, 1947, about twenty girls and boys all

Students gathered on Woodstock Boulevard on February 5, 1947, to protest the arrest of Tom Kelly '48 for reading under a street lamp after curfew the previous evening.

went out to the main college entrance on Woodstock Boulevard after curfew, reading books of poetry under the street lamp. Sure enough a police car came by and stopped. I jumped out with a camera, snapped a shot, and they drove away. It had been a moonless night, so when I developed the photo I dodged in the moon when I exposed the negative, laying down a dime on the paper.

TIME magazine, "Shelley by Moonlight," February 17, 1947: The moon shone bright over Portland, Oregon, and a young man named Thomas Kelly sat on a campus bench reading Shelley by the light of the moon. To the cops who saw him there, this seemed highly suspicious conduct. Kelly didn't think his conduct needed any defense or explanation and he couldn't produce a draft card. So they jugged him. Said one policeman: "See if you can take that, Lord Byron."

In the late 1940s, freshman orientation was held at Breitenbush Lake near Mt. Jefferson in the Cascade Range.

Twelve hours later Kelly was turned loose. The cops had checked up: he was just a Reed College student, a veteran of the Aleutians campaign and a man who likes to read Shelley by lamplight or moonlight.

The next night twenty Reed undergrads, each armed with a volume of poetry, gathered on a downtown Portland street corner by moonlight and solemnly read Shelley together. A police car passed; but no arrests were made.

GALE DICK, JR. '50: For freshman orientation we went on an outing up to a place called Breitenbush near Mt. Jefferson in the Cascade Range. There I met some of the people that I was going to be in college with. I immediately realized—almost in a blinding flash of epiphany—that this was where I personally belonged.

For the first time in my life I was with a whole bunch of people with whom I shared all kinds of interests. Until then I didn't know that there was anybody else in the world who did. I wasn't a misfit or anything, but I was always uneasy. I wasn't where I wanted to be, or doing what I wanted to do. But that day on Mt. Jefferson I had this feeling that Reed was the place, and that I was so lucky to be there. As we came over the ridge, hiking down into the glorious valley of Jefferson Park, I had this intense rush of ecstatic happiness.

GEORGE JOSEPH '51, trustee: I rode up the coast from San Francisco on my motorcycle in the spring of 1949. I knew Portland pretty well, but I had never heard of Reed College. I came out to the campus where I had been told to go see Dorothy Johansen '33 in the admissions office. I went in and here was this very nice woman who, it turned out, was a history professor. What she was doing in the admissions office, I don't know. I hadn't been admitted yet, but we had a nice chat. I thought to myself, perfect, absolutely perfect, this is the place for me. I asked if I could get a cup of coffee somewhere. Dorothy Jo said, "There's a coffee shop down in the basement of the Student Union. Go out the back door, down the steps and you'll see a path that leads to it."

As I walked along that path, a group of fifteen or twenty students was standing on a cement platform, looking down into a wooded area toward the Reed lake. I stood at the back of the group and angled myself around so that I could see too. There was a couple down there doing something I had never before seen done in public. I was fascinated, and so was everybody else. A young woman standing in front of me, turned and said, "Hmmph. They must think there are leaves on the trees." Then she walked away.

I said to myself, "This is the place." I had visited five or six different colleges by that time. I was clearly looking for something. I knew that I had found it that day. It was love at first sight.

GILBERT HART '51: I had not been in a coeducational environment prior to coming to Reed. Prep school, Yale for a year, then the navy for three years: they were all exclusively male. Women were something you spent hours getting your nerve up to call and ask for a date.

The other thing different was that coming from an East Coast, Ivy League background, you automatically counted who was Jewish and who wasn't. It wasn't necessarily anything prejudiced, but if you asked me who in my class at Loomis Chaffee prep school was Jewish, I could list off most of them. I had been at Reed two months when it suddenly occurred to me that I had no idea who was Jewish.

MOSHE LENSKE '50, trustee: We had a little pro-Zionist group on campus that was connected with the Intercollegiate Zionist Federation of America. Every once in a while we would have a meeting at my folks' house. When the establishment of Israel was declared in 1948, the Arab states didn't recognize it as a legitimate state.

They sent seven armies to wipe out the 650,000 Jews that were there. It was a pretty testy time, nip and tuck, and a screaming miracle that Israel didn't get shoved into the sea.

RICHARD ABEL '48: The biggest minority group at Reed was Jewish, and nobody ever gave it a thought. A really Orthodox Jew, like my roommate Elihu Bergman '50, wouldn't eat pork, and he would pass up all kinds of food to continue to observe his rules. He wanted Friday night reserved to himself for Shabbat, and he would drink the wine, take the wafers, light the candelabra and put on the skullcap. It was real for him. He eventually left Reed and went to join the underground in Israel. We had a fellow come in from Israel, Shlomo Efrat '53, who was sent by some Jewish organization to get an American education. He had been, as nearly as he was ever square with us, with one of those really brutal underground groups in Israel.

RUTH CEDERSTROM WOLFE '50: People tried to downplay class differences. My two roommates, both glamour girls when they initially showed up, started dressing much more simply almost immediately. I don't know what the rich people's kids expected at Reed. They liked the freedom, and they liked being out West. Some of them liked being away from anti-Semitism. But they weren't snooty and didn't go around putting people down.

GARY SNYDER '51: It was the first time I had met affluent radicals. I had a hard time putting that together. I wasn't aware of class distinctions— took me years to figure that out. A part of the style of the impoverished intellectual left was that they assumed they were equal to everybody because they had politically correct ideas. Just like Marxists who used to figure they were right. "History is on our side." Part of the confidence of the left in those days was that sense of destiny.

PETER ODEGARD, president 1945–1948: If football great Knute Rockne were to return to this earth, he could not produce a winning football team at Reed. He would not have the material, he would be bucking a hostile atmosphere, the educational process would trap him at every turn, and—for his particular purpose—there would be a lack of money.

While Reed had a sound physical plant, there was not enough of it to permit us to do the job we felt we ought to do. While Reed paid reasonable salaries by the modest standards prevailing in education, it did not pay what an institution of its standing must pay to maintain that position. While our student-teacher ratio of fourteen-to-one was again "reasonable," it fell short of the college's accepted yardstick of excellence—ten-to-one. While Reed's investments, thanks to the acuity of its trustees, yielded an excellent return, they were insufficient to make up the difference between operating expenses and tuition income—and tuition had been increased to a point beyond which equality of opportunity might seriously have been endangered.

A visitor on campus, familiar with Reed's record and standing, was appalled when he learned of some of the gaps in our curriculum. Reed was located on the very rim of the Pacific basin, yet we did not offer courses in Far Eastern affairs or in Oriental languages and culture. We passed on them because we lacked the resources properly to teach them. The average value of the endowment at Reed was $2,974 per student. The average at five eastern colleges of comparative enrollment—Bryn Mawr, Carleton, Colgate, Williams, and Haverford—was $8,943 per student.

ERNEST BOYD "E. B." MACNAUGHTON, trustee 1919–1941, 1955–1958, president 1948–1952: Peter Odegard came to Reed with assurances that money would be raised that would put the college on a reasonable operating budget, and that he wouldn't be under pressure trying to find sup-

port all the time. But the fundraising campaign was a failure. The president of the trustees, Simeon Winch, was unable to get it off the ground. He had left the college way out in left field as far as community contacts were concerned, and it would have taken two or three years on the part of a college president to lay the groundwork before they could go out and ask for money.

Fundraising problems also intensified when Lewis & Clark College, then known as Albany College, was relocated to Portland in the late 1930s from Albany, Oregon. Dr. Morgan Odell was induced to take over Lewis & Clark, then a sinking ship in education. He saw the errors Reed had made and made sure he didn't affront the religious instincts and social interests of the community. For example, one well-known member of the Reed faculty had told his class that a wedding announcement was a public statement that two people were to begin sexual intercourse. That was done! Things like that went through the Portland community like the black plague. Odell made sure Lewis & Clark did everything that followed the traditional college pattern, and so filled in the gaps Reed had left untouched.

REX ARRAGON, history professor: Frustrated by the financial picture, Odegard resigned in 1948 to become chairman of the political science department at Berkeley. He said he wanted to teach, but he became head of a department larger than the Reed faculty, with little opportunity for teaching.

ELLEN KNOWLTON JOHNSON '39, administrator: After Odegard left, Reed found it very difficult to hire someone to replace him at a salary they could afford to pay. Then E. B. MacNaughton, who had been president of the Board of Trustees in the '30s, agreed to step in. MacNaughton had earned the nickname around town of the "great liquidator" during the Depression, because as president of the First National Bank

PART THREE: THE NATIONAL COLLEGE, 1946–1966

he had foreclosed on so many business properties; that had made him in many ways a very hated person locally. But I liked him very much personally. He had lost his wife some years before, and then at the end of the war he married Cheryl Scholz—the widow of Reed's second president, Richard Scholz—who had been dean of women and an instructor at the college.

E. B. MacNaughton, president: The chairman of the Board of Regents, John Laing, asked if I would step in for six months while the search committee went about finding a new president. I accepted his offer, but as soon as I got into the business of the college and saw the state of affairs financially, I knew that no man with a capacity for leadership would, in his right mind, ever come to Reed, because he was licked before he started. He would have to go out with his hat in his hand begging for money before he even got to know his faculty. I told the board I would stay on until I could at least make red turn to black on the financial statements, and also do something to overcome the terrific opposition that had developed in the community because of Reed's alleged pro-Red or communistic tendencies.

One of the smart things I did at the beginning was to make the door to my office open to anyone who wanted to come in with any kick or complaint, and just talk. Before long students and faculty were coming in and there was a free-for-all exchange of letting our hair down and swapping ideas. I liked the faculty although I didn't always agree with them. There was a great deal of friction between the sciences and the humanities. Despite that, and the financial problems of getting money to pay the bills, I never had a better time in my life.

Rex Arragon, history professor: MacNaughton's other jobs—at the First National Bank and the *Oregonian* newspaper—took his mornings. He would get out to the college after lunch. He

was devoted to Reed, and reminisced frequently about his impoverished youth in Cambridge as a poor paperboy outside Harvard Yard.

Jack Churchill '49: There was no question that MacNaughton was a leader. He was very commanding in his presence and in his preciseness. He knew what was going on all the time. You would see him walking around the campus, turning off the light bulbs to save money.

MacNaughton used to go to the bar of the exclusive Arlington Club, the great power center in Portland, home of Republican businessmen and city leaders, and walk down the bar with a picture of a student, saying, "I want you to meet James Jones here. He's a pretty nice-looking guy, and he's got a great future, but he

As Reed president, longtime trustee E. B. MacNaughton prided himself on having an open-door policy for students and faculty members.

needs a scholarship. Would you like to give him $5,000?" Then he would pick out another picture and shop that around the bar. He was quite successful with raising money that way.

HERB GLADSTONE, music professor: E. B. MacNaughton had a great sense of humor but he was also very brusque. He thought the faculty wasted too much time in its meetings, debating things that, after a few minutes of listening, E. B. became a little impatient with. He would stand up and say, "All right, you guys, let's get this show on the road." That cut off debate effectively, which I think most of us found a rather endearing quality. Things improved very quickly under MacNaughton.

THE AMERICAN MERCURY magazine, STEWART HOLBROOK, "The Life and Times of Reed College," October 1950: [Ernest B. MacNaughton is] by all odds the most unconventional big businessman in all the region. He reads books, all sorts of books. The newspaper he heads prints whatever is news, no matter what the economic consequences are to its advertising columns. This head of "atheistic" Reed College is also national moderator of the Unitarian church in the United States.

MacNaughton, who serves at Reed without pay, has stated his position publicly: "I am not an educator. I believe, however, that Reed's methods and attitude have long since passed through the pioneering stage and will, in good time, be largely adopted by all American colleges worth their salt. Most of our big universities have discovered that general education alone can result in dilettantism; and that specialization alone makes for a restricted viewpoint. Science and the humanities must be linked. Reed has been working to this end for nearly four decades."

What most irritates President MacNaughton is the old canard of "radicalism," which is still applied to Reed. "If," he said recently, "we are

to accept a definition of radical as including any defense of civil liberties or expression of opinion not favorable to the existing economic order, then I shall not attempt to defend Reed College against the charge of radicalism. Reed is devotedly all-American to its grassroots."

BETTY ERICKSON TERZAGHI '54: I grew up thirty miles away from Portland in the boondocks, and went to Battleground High School. When it was announced at my high school graduation that I was going to Reed, a woman I had never seen before came up to me and said, "You're going to Reed? You're going to lose your soul!"

JAMES MACQUEEN '52: There was a shadow falling down across the country and closing in on free speech that would culminate in the arrival of McCarthyism in the 1950s. It began in 1948 with the so-called "Hollywood Ten," a group of directors and screenwriters accused of being Communist subversives. The extremes of opinion were being pinched in from both sides. It was the beginning of the Cold War.

GEORGE JOSEPH '51, trustee: Most of the talk on campus was politics, much of it, I'm sure, naïve to say the least. God, it was interesting. The guys there on the G.I. Bill that I knew were very political. They organized a chapter of the American Veterans Committee, which was a distinctly left-wing organization, a sort of anti-American Legion opposed to some of the special veteran privileges the Legion was lobbying for. Ernie Bonyhadi '48 organized the chapter on campus, and they were very politically active.

If there were conservatives on campus, they never spoke out. The only teacher I knew who was an outspoken conservative was political science professor Frank Munk, a refugee from the Nazi invasion of Czechoslovakia, which subsequently was taken over by the Communists in 1948. Munk was, to say the least, immensely disturbed by that. You had to tread easy with him. If you said the wrong thing, you could draw down a firestorm. There were some wonderful debates on campus between Munk, Stanley Moore, who taught Marxist philosophy, and Maure Gold-schmidt '30, who taught political science. The big boys were politically hot, and they held wonderful, free-for-all arguments of a very high level, pulling everybody, including myself, into their debates.

ROBERT SHELLOW '51: Reed maintained—some-what preciously—the image of being a radical, leftist institution, but I don't really think it was one at all. The mistaken impression that Reed was filled with leftist radicals really came from recognizing that there were people there who weren't afraid of ideas. That students could go to Lutz's Tavern or down to the pool hall on Bybee and Milwaukie streets, and play pool while debating Marxist economic theory, was something that was considered by the townspeople to be very shocking.

The majority of students who were not ex-G.I.s came from the Portland region, many of them from very conservative families. They were very focused on their careers, and they went right straight through Reed. It was only the vocal fringe that did their duty to maintain that old image of the school, taking an "in your face" attitude with the townspeople in Portland. They cherished their outlander identity, probably as part of adolescent rebellion.

PAUL ABRAMSON '52: During the presidential campaign of 1948 I was a member of the Young Progressives on campus. We supported Henry Wallace, who was running on the Progressive ticket. Norman Thomas of the Socialist Party came in second in the straw vote on campus—over Wallace and Harry Truman, the sitting Democratic president—because he had spoken there in October just before the election.

RALPH PRATT '50: There were an awful lot of science-oriented students who didn't partake in the big political activities, but who were more conservative in their views. With a couple of friends I started a campus organization known as "the Young Republicans of Eastmoreland." Thomas Dewey, the Republican candidate for president in 1948, won the mock election on campus.

SALLY WATSON '50: A few of us formed the "Young Regressive Party," for fun. We wore gunny sacks around campus and collected slogans like, "Back to a simple food-gathering culture," "The Democrats aren't backward enough: vote Regressive," "Spearhead of the Republican advance backwards."

PHILIP WHALEN '51: With trouble brewing on the Korean Peninsula, the government reared back in 1948 and decided to reinstate the wartime draft, which had come to an end in 1947. A whole bunch of us went downtown to demonstrate. As a protestor you always carried an American flag or else people would get mad and throw rocks at you. So there we were tromping down Broadway with a flag when right in front of one of the big theaters stood Richard Meigs '50, dressed in some mad costume. He had an army helmet liner painted white on his head, and on top of the helmet liner there was a candle. I don't know what he was doing—everybody seemed pissed off with him—but he was very funny.

ROBERT SHELLOW '51: One evening during dinner, I was waiting tables in Commons. People were talking away over the clatter of dishes and silverware, when, all of a sudden, the lights went out. When they came on again there was some loud noise—a trumpet—and Dick Meigs '50 was standing up in the balcony dressed in a uniform with a cloak. He announced that he was staging a military coup, and that everyone should remain in their seats; anybody who didn't would be shot.

After the initial shock wore off, everybody started howling and clapping in great glee.

DONALD GREEN '54: We were immune to the Korean War. There was a draft on, but as students we had student deferments. A few students enlisted, but we were largely insulated. Only poor people went to war in Korea. We were this privileged group.

RUTH CEDERSTROM WOLFE '50: Everybody at Reed considered themselves very broad-minded about other cultures and other races. In some ways they were kind of arrogant in that they thought they were better than other people because they were so broad-minded.

There were a couple of black students on campus, thanks to a special scholarship fund. One of them, Betty Crutcher '50, left after one year, saying that she didn't want to be our pet Negro anymore. We were kind of stung by her criticism. Another black girl, Inez Freeman '48 from Longview, Washington, was very intellectual, and didn't have a problem fitting in. My future husband, Bill Wolfe '51, went up to Longview one time with another Reed student to visit Inez. They stopped at a gas station to ask for gas and directions. The kid working at the station said, "You don't want to go there. That's nigger town." But he told them how to get there anyway. They got there and it was four crossed streets of small, single houses with a white church at one end, all of it out in the middle of a big field with nothing around it. The black men who had bought these houses had come to Longview to work in the mills during the war.

GEORGE JOSEPH '51, trustee: Early on, there was an effort in Portland to get an ordinance against racial discrimination. The City Council wasn't about to pass such an ordinance, so the students at various schools designed a rose decal—Portland being the "Rose City"—and on the rose it said "Fair Rose." If a merchant would promise not to discriminate, they could post the decal. Most of the merchants, whether honestly or hypocritically, readily agreed to Fair Rose, except the Jolly Joan, which was a famous restaurant on Broadway and a very popular hangout for students. We all just stopped going there.

WILLIAM KIRSCH '50: One night we were at the Milbee Club, which was a cocktail lounge students frequented, when Inez Freeman '48 came in with a couple other people, and they refused to serve her. It was a Saturday night and the Milbee Club was packed. Every booth was taken, every barstool. The word went around the bar that they refused Inez, and in three minutes the bar was empty except for one booth. That booth was occupied by four guys, one of whom was the guy who was always with Inez. I said to him afterwards, "Everybody walked out except you and those three jerks." "Oh yeah," he said, "they've all got their own political agenda."

GEORGE JOSEPH '51, trustee: Reed liked to think of itself as the "Oxford of the West." One of the things Oxford was famous for was their debating society, the Oxford Union. Reed had a similar debating tradition, passed down from its first president, William Foster. We formalized that by starting the Reed Union, patterned on the Oxford Union. Jim Walsh '49, who was a philosophy major and later a Rhodes Scholar, was the first president, and Moshe Lenske '50 the second. Any issue could be talked upon. Unions were never just student things; faculty representation was required. They opened with some formality, always a pro position followed by a con, and then it was thrown open to the floor. That's when the fun began. There were some faculty who went at it tooth and toenail.

PAUL ABRAMSON '52: George Joseph '51 was the setup man for the Reed Union, asking lead-

A Reed Union debate in the Commons (later the Student Union building), 1953.

ing questions. Someone like Frank Munk, who taught political science and was on the far right, would start in on the other side. Students would start arguing with him, and then, all of sudden, other professors—Stanley Moore in philosophy, or Dick Jones and Charles Bagg in history— would step in and start cutting him up.

The Reed Union invited Anna Louise Strong, the China expert, to come to campus. There was an objection because she was a supporter of Mao Tse-tung and the Chinese Communist government. President MacNaughton called together a meeting of a committee of four faculty and four students, of which I was one. After long discussion pro and con, MacNaughton agreed that he would abide by a vote among the nine of us, himself included. All of the students voted to invite her, while three of the faculty members and MacNaughton voted not to. Lloyd Williams, professor of math, stood with the students and

broke the deadlock. MacNaughton accepted it, but we were really angry at him.

MOSHE LENSKE '50, trustee: In 1948 a philosophy professor at the University of Washington named Herbert Phillips was canned along with two other professors for being a Communist. He was completely shunned and isolated. His first public appearance after being fired was at a Reed Union. That generated a little publicity. E. B. MacNaughton called me into his office and said, "You know, this is pretty touchy stuff for Reed College. We're in enough trouble already." I said, "Well, it's a student organization. We know how to do it, and we'll do it."

The evening of the Reed Union, while Herbert Phillips presented his side, MacNaughton stood at the door. Afterward, I got a letter from MacNaughton, saying that it had been a very well-run meeting, and a worthwhile thing for the college to have such an open forum. He said to go ahead with other Reed Union events, but, "Whatever you do, don't invite Harry Bridges"—Bridges was the head of the Longshoremen's Union in San Francisco and a pretty radical guy.

RON LAING '56: Harry Bridges wasn't allowed to speak on campus, so his talk was held at the home of Maure Goldschmidt '30, one of the political science teachers, off campus. I went to listen to him. The FBI were walking around taking down the license numbers of the cars parked outside. Based upon his reputation, I expected Bridges to be kind of a rough person, but he wasn't. He was a very erudite, very learned speaker. I was most impressed by what he said.

ROBERT SHELLOW '51: Lutz's Tavern, up the hill from campus, was in full flower. The place had some regular Portland roughnecks, with Reed students mixed in. The owners were a bunch of money-grubbing barkeeps that exploited the hell out of the Reed students, and said nasty things about us behind our backs. Some of them said nasty things to our faces. But because half of us were ex-G.I.s—guys who had been drinking in gin mills around the world—we were used to the culture and knew how to handle nasty bartenders. We were always having an issue of whether we had the nickel or the dime for the beer. Somebody always had to go and see if they could borrow something from somebody to keep the golden juice flowing.

ALICE TIURA MOSS '52: There were two and a half men for every woman on campus at that time. I dated quite a bit. The veterans were a little older, and very serious. They didn't talk about their war experiences really. Men were allowed in the women's dormitories only on Sunday afternoons. They would drop by and we would play hostess, feeding them or giving them a cup of tea. There was very little immediate super-vision. A senior student in our dorm was our housemother, but we never saw her. She stayed out of anything that went on.

NANCY STEWART GREEN '50: There was certainly a whole lot of sexual interest going on, and a whole lot of necking and petting, but who knows how much people were actually sleeping together. I think there was a fair amount of that, but it was very quiet, and not something that everybody knew about. A lot of people didn't do it at all. I knew one couple who lived together off campus, and they were considered quite unusual. Nobody did that. Then, a few years later, everybody did it. We were at the end of a real traditional period for Reed students. For people elsewhere, I don't think the sexual revolution began until the '60s.

ANN SHEPARD '23, recorder 1926–1942, dean of women 1943–1950, dean of students 1950–1968, letter to Barbara Morris Dickey '51, president of the Women's Council, November 18, 1949: It has been reported to me that student conduct in Anna Mann social room does not always follow generally accepted standards of conduct in public places, and that on at least one occasion the cleaning staff has unearthed from under sofa cushions what I shall haughtily refer to as "inappropriate articles of clothing.". . .

Love-making, or petting or necking—whatever term you wish to use—is a language, a way of conveying meaning and is therefore the most essentially private conversation a man and a woman can have. It is not sufficient for a love-making couple to say, "If we don't mind others overhearing us, no one else should."

MICHAEL LOVELL '52: The Pill had yet to be invented. In most of the country, you could purchase condoms, or "rubbers" as they were called, only from behind the counter at gas stations. Some drugstores were reluctant to sell them, and in some states it was illegal to sell any type of contraceptive device. The cost of sexual activity could potentially be very high. If a mistake was made, abortions were illegal and not safe.

DOROTHY MOORE EDLIN '56: All the freshman women on campus were given a lecture by Dean Ann Shepard '23 on how the college was acting in loco parentis. There was a big emphasis on the Honor Principle, and how we had to watch out for the view the local community had about Reed. What she said was ambiguous, in that I took it to mean that the college would not tolerate any appearance of sexual impropriety, but it was only the appearance that really counted. I got the idea that we were being advised to engage in hypocrisy, but I may not have understood her correctly.

We had a guardian, a night watchman we called "Skinny," who took his job very seriously. He had a gun and one arm. We had to sign out of the dorms in the evenings, and then we had to sign back in. We had strict hours—ten PM on week nights and two-thirty AM on weekends—which were actually pretty liberal for those days. Skinny often got angry with the girls and scolded them for coming in late. At Christmas, we always gave him a bottle of booze, so that he would get drunk and then we could stay out later.

MERTIE HANSEN MULLER '56: I had dated very little prior to coming to Reed, other than with older boys who wanted to marry me because they wanted my father's farm. I got my first marriage proposal when I was thirteen. Nobody thought there was anything odd about this except me. I told him to take a hike.

The freshman orientation outing to Breitenbush near Mt. Jefferson was not far from my father's farm outside Salem, Oregon. The first day of the outing I met my roommate-to-be and we went for a hike. I saw a young man, Richard Muller '56, on top of a little foothill with a pair of neat binoculars. I approached him, wanting to borrow them. Well, it turned out that I was what he had been looking at. Three and a half months later, we got married.

RICHARD MULLER '56: In those days, when you fell in lust, you got married. That was the convention. Mertie Hansen '56 and I got married at All Saints Church up the hill from campus. When we told the dean, Ann Shepard '23, that we were getting married, she said, "As soon as you do, you're out!" Married students weren't allowed to live on campus.

CAROLE CALKINS COLIE '54, public affairs staff 1958–1963: Betty Erickson '54 and I roomed in the Westport dorm with a third roommate who was hearing-challenged. She did pretty well for a while, but then the professors weren't willing to turn and speak so she that could read their lips, so at Thanksgiving break she left school. Then Betty and I got a letter from the dean, Ann Shepard '23, that said: "You have done so well with your former roommate that I'm going to ask you to take in another roommate. You are to ask her no questions as to why she is coming from another dorm, but treat her naturally."

We thought that maybe she was friendless or something, so we wouldn't let her alone. We made her go to every movie we went to, we always went to dinner with her, and we were constantly in her face, demanding that she respond to us. Finally, after some months, she told us that she had been moved into our dorm because she and her former roommate had been found to be having a homosexual relationship. Reed had expelled her roommate, but offered to transfer her as long as she promised not to encourage or allow a visit from her partner.

I was more astonished than Betty because I had never even heard the word "lesbian" before. Reed, which liked to present itself as a certain kind of place, was really backward in a few ways, and that was certainly one of them. She was a wonderful person, but she ended up leaving. She went on to commit suicide not long afterward.

GARY SNYDER '51: It seemed to be that you had considerable liberties in your personal life and freedom in dress, as long as you could keep up with the schoolwork. People came to classes barefoot, wore shorts if they wanted to, and entertained themselves however they liked on weekends. There was no code of any kind of proper behavior, except: "Do your work." There was a style that I saw going on with some people—and I'm not including myself in this particularly—of somewhat wild and outrageous behavior combined with excellence in scholarship. Some students couldn't do both, and crashed. Reed had many people that didn't make it, because that combination of freedom and discipline was not easy.

LEWIS LEBER '50: Sandy MacDonald '46 was a brilliant guy who thought of himself as being an eighteenth-century man, although he was actually the son of a big-time lumberman out of Tacoma, Washington. Sandy played the organ and the piano. He put thumbtacks in the piano so it would sound like a harpsichord, and newspapers in the bottom rungs so they would sound like a trap drum, and he would play a whole piece of one of Mozart's operas, singing all the parts.

Sandy would throw parties in which he and his friends would take paper bags and create these curly, white, powdered wigs out of them that they would put on while they drank Madeira wine in the candle light of their dorm room. Sandy was a British loyalist, and would talk on and on about these rebellious nations of America and how they must be brought under control. He would issue ultimatums against the people in Eastmoreland over things pertaining to their duties and obligations as subjects of the Crown. He kept a small cannon that he threatened to use

to "enforce the will of the King." It was a short thing—eight, ten inches—but the shot that he had in it was fairly good size, probably three-eighths of an inch.

He got into some dispute with the guys in Winch dorm up on the second floor. He would send pronouncements up there that they had to agree to abide by the Treaty of Ghent, or some darn thing. They refused to do so. As a consequence, he issued them an ultimatum that they would have until eight o'clock to comply, or hostilities would commence. He and his friends went back down to his dorm room to drink Madeira for a while, and then decided to set up his cannon in the hallway facing the door of the guys on the second floor. He fired it off at a distance of about forty feet. The cannon was slightly off-kilter, and the shot all went into the concrete wall, making a big hole, and fortunately missing the door. After that, the cannon was retired.

Sandy wrote out his thesis in an eighteenth-century script with a quill pen. It was absolutely beautiful. The faculty rejected it because they wanted it typed.

EDMOND MIKSCH '54: One humanities professor said, in his lecture, "I see absolutely no hope for the human race." It confirmed my sense that I had to get off this planet. I spent my years at Reed trying to find an energy reservoir for a good cheap spaceship to create a small pioneering group in outer space. I thought the human race was totally lost.

When I became editor of the *Reed College Science Bulletin*, I started writing about negative mass. I was censored and told that nothing could go off the campus that was as subversive as negative mass. So I wrote my thesis on negative mass. My professors disagreed with it, but they couldn't find anything wrong with it. At the time *Astounding Science Fiction* magazine was collecting a list of "Finagle's Laws," the scientific corollary to the adages known as "Murphy's Laws."

I submitted the following: "If a string has one end, then it has another end." The reason for this pointed to negative mass. It was accepted and published while I was a student.

I went through all four years at Reed, and another five years working on my doctorate at Harvard, with no dates. I was told that that was because one of the questions that I would ask a woman was, "Would you be willing to raise your children on Mars?" But I eventually found a wife. Started a family. A couple of decades went by. I was at work one day and a fellow handed me a little piece of paper from a desk calendar that said, "Miksch's Law: If a string has one end, then it has another end." It turned out that I was world-famous.

GEORGE JOSEPH '51, trustee: I wore my hair shoulder-length before any other kid in America wore shoulder-length hair. Not that I was an avant-garde person, I just happened to like long hair. Many Reed kids had beards. In the public mind at that time nobody had a beard except if they were an anarchist or a Red. We were—and some of us remained—pretty sloppy dressers. We acted as if we didn't care what anybody else thought. We were going to do our thing, our way. That didn't always set well in Portland.

MERTIE HANSEN MULLER '56: All the boys had to learn how to smoke pipes in their first year. They would sit around and talk about tobacco—which was the best kind, where you could get it, what kind of meerschaum pipe to buy. I thought it was the most hilarious thing in the world because it was so affected. You didn't think of Reed students as doing something in fashion. In fact, I didn't realize that the girls were real girls until the first formal dance. Prior to that the girls had not worn lipstick and often didn't wear a bra. Then suddenly at the formal dance these girls appeared with diamonds, makeup, fingernail polish, and high heels.

PATRICIA EAMES '50: Some idiot running the dining room decided there should be a dress code, and that the guys should have to wear jackets and ties to dinner. The first evening the code was in effect, a group of six guys, led by Walter Mintz '50, came marching in wearing jackets, dress shirts, neck ties, and their underpants. They went to the fireplace, and to the tune of "I'm Called Little Buttercup," sang "I'm called little Fauntleroy, dear little Fauntleroy, though I could never tell why." After that, no more was heard about a dress code.

GARY SNYDER '51: My sophomore year a bunch of us focused on finding a place to live off campus. I had enough money from working that summer on merchant marine freighters to pay rent. We drifted over to a house at 1414 Southeast Lambert Street in Sellwood and rented it together. There were students that lived off campus in rented rooms here and there, but I think 1414 Lambert was the first house that was totally taken over by Reed people. It was coed. The college paid no attention to us, as far as I could tell.

That house on Lambert was my first taste of communal life, and it was very workable, economical, and cooperative. We all shared in a lot of good potluck meals together, and we got a lot of study and scholarship done. It was just the right balance. There was a sense of family. We had Thanksgiving dinners together there. We actually maintained a working atmosphere throughout the whole week, as people were a little bit too mature to have gross-out and throw-up drinking parties. It was more adult and that was good. Half the people at 1414 were G.I. Bill people, older people, which was good for me.

ROBERT SHELLOW '51: The coed at 1414 Lambert Street was Carol Brown Baker '52. It wasn't a scandalous situation. Carol worked downtown and had a good job. She used to bring steaks back for us every now and then, and we'd have a meal together, a feast, which was a real treat. Otherwise we lived pretty much on mush and horsemeat. I didn't stay that long at 1414 Lambert, but maybe a semester. It was just too wild. There were comings and goings at all times of the day and night, music and loud talking and some carousing. It was pretty distracting.

PHILIP WHALEN '51: I was not attending class very much, and so I was expelled from Reed for the academic year of 1949–50. I pulled wires, chanted spells, and did dances to appease the gods, and got myself reinstated. During the time I was out of school I was very broke, which is how I came to 1414 Lambert Street. Roy Stilwell '50, who lived there, let me live in part of his room.

GARY SNYDER '51: My first encounter with Phil Whalen '51 was in my sophomore year. He was acting in a play and I went backstage after it was over and we talked. I became aware of his knowledge of literature. He was a fine teacher and conversationalist, already well-versed in East Asian painting and art. We were discovering transla-

tions from Japanese and Chinese poetry about the same time, and quoting them back and forth to each other. I discovered the *Tao Te Ching*. Philip put me onto the *Bhagavad Gita*.

Lloyd Reynolds, who taught art history and calligraphy, hosted the poet William Carlos Williams when he came to Reed. Phil Whalen, Lew Welch '50, Bill Dickey '51, and I went over to Lloyd's house to spend an evening with Bill Williams after he had done his on-campus stuff. Williams became a very strong inspiration or model as a poet, especially for Lew Welch.

DICK POPE '53: The Beat Generation on the West Coast really began in many ways at 1414 Lambert Street. Gary Snyder '51, Lew Welch '50, Philip Whalen '51, and the others who lived there were left-wing but something else was added there that was more important. They were people who were very serious about the environment, very serious about Asian spirituality, and very serious about poetry. There were a lot of dimensions to this, as would unfold in the general culture in the coming years.

Alison Gass '53, Gary Snyder '51, William Baker '50, Carol Brown Baker '52, and David Lapham '60 in Snyder's basement apartment at 1414 Southeast Lambert Street.

CHAPTER 17

Changing of the Guard

The emotion had gone out in the young faculty who came to teach after the war. Their view was that one should not get involved emotionally in anything, especially something that was close to their intellect.
  —Dorothy Johansen '33, history professor

The new faculty made you think of the academics portrayed in the movie Who's Afraid of Virginia Woolf? *They had all been shaped by the Second World War.*
  —James MacQueen '52

Following the war, many of the faculty members who had served during the "Golden Age" of presidents William Foster and Richard Scholz began to retire. Their replacements, hired in the late 1940s and early 1950s, would form the nucleus of a second generation of Reed faculty. Vetted by and under the tutelage of the remaining veteran professors, many of the new generation would provide faculty leadership at the college over the next three decades.

While this cadre generally embraced Reed's traditional core curriculum, they did so with a new, postwar mentality, which favored disinterested research and analytic rigor in all disciplines. They also brought with them an interest in career-related research and publication, particularly in the natural sciences and social sciences, which contrasted strongly with the beliefs of the earlier faculty that the publish-or-perish ethos dominant at most other colleges undermined the primary commitment to teaching.

In 1952, in the midst of these transitions, Reed's interim president, E. B. MacNaughton, turned over the reins of the presidency to Duncan Ballantine, a history professor from MIT. Ballantine generated immediate controversy on campus by questioning whether the college was too intellectual in its orientation, too permissive in its community atmosphere, and too geared toward grooming students for continuing scholarship after graduation, in lieu of preparing them for non-academic fields of employment.

DOROTHY MOORE EDLIN '56: In the fall of 1952, future U.S. Senator from Oregon Richard Neuberger wrote an article for the *Saturday Evening Post* magazine, "The School for Smart Young Things," which identified Reed students as the smartest body of undergraduates in the country. It emphasized that Reed was a school for mavericks—independent-minded nonconformists interested in intellectual development.

Previous to that article most students at Reed had come from Oregon, with a fairly good contingent from California—largely from Unitarian circles—and a smaller group from private schools back East like New Elizabeth Irwin High School in New York and Putney School in Vermont. All of a sudden, there were students from all over the country applying to the college. We called them "the *Saturday Evening Post* kids."

SATURDAY EVENING POST, RICHARD L. NEUBERGER, "School for Smart Young Things," October 25, 1952: The most spectacular recent demonstration of Reed's supremacy in [traditional] fields of scholarship occurred last winter when three Wesleyan University teachers, with the aid of a Carnegie financial grant, completed a study on the origins of leading American scientists during a typical peacetime decade, from 1924 to 1934. As one of their principal conclusions, they wrote: "Reed College, in Oregon, with a total enrollment of only about six hundred students, has been far and away more productive of future scientists than any other institution in the United States."

Specifically, the Wesleyan report disclosed that 132 Reed graduates out of each thousand had gone on to earn a doctor's degree in natural science. The next ranking college, the California Institute of Technology, had barely half the record of Reed, with seventy future doctors of science for every thousand who received diplomas.

Nor is Reed's sole claim to fame its record in the realm of natural science. A later Wesleyan report has revealed that Reed placed second only to Swarthmore in the winning of advanced degrees and fellowships in the social sciences, such as history, economics, and politics. . . . Not too surprisingly, Reed has turned out more Rhodes Scholars than such titans as Columbia, Ohio State, and the University of Chicago. Reed has produced one Rhodes Scholar for every 147 graduates, despite the fact that the national average is one scholar for approximately each 4,500 graduates. Reed's ratio betters even the Ivy League averages of Princeton, Harvard, and Yale. . . .

Ernest Boyd MacNaughton has his own explanation for this: "It's the academic and scholarly atmosphere. We specialize in it as much as West Point specializes in military tradition. The scholar is our hero.". . . President MacNaughton asserts emphatically that Reed College is a living denial of the legend that young intellectuals in America are invariably radical if male and unprepossessing if female. And Reed coeds bear him out. A junior, Anna Lee Bozarth, recently strolled off with a bathing-beauty contest in Central Oregon, winning over several sorority queens from the state university. In 1949, another coed, traveling in Europe with her parents during the summer, slipped into a skimpy swimming suit and won the title of "Miss Capri" from the local talent. And about the same time, a noted Portland artist, Albert Patecky, was saying that the most shapely models to pose *au naturel* for his classes came from the Reed campus.

RON LAING '56: As I read the Neuberger article, there was a paragraph that talked about this orgy they had had on the lawn the previous spring. I thought, "Oh man, that's the place for me. That sounds like a great school to go to." But when I got to Reed, it turned out that I found no orgies ever taking place on the lawn in the spring.

WINIFRED JAEGER WOOD '55: One evening some of us students were fortunate enough to be

SCHOOL FOR SMART YOUNG THINGS

By RICHARD L. NEUBERGER

At Reed College, in Oregon, students take examinations anywhere they please, never get marks, grade their own teachers every year. Their football team is a joke, faculty pay is abysmally low—but this academic anarchy produces more big brains than many big universities.

Some of Reed's girl students take time out from their studies for dormitory capers. There are no sororities at the school.

The campus library is always crowded with students. Reed has produced one Rhodes scholar for every 147 graduates.

FACULTY members at Reed College, in Portland, Oregon, should have known better when they began complaining last spring about persistent student violations of library rules. They might have remembered that they were dealing with what has been called, with considerable justification, the smartest body of undergraduates in the United States.

A group of students promptly dug into the records and announced through their weekly campus newspaper, the Quest, that one faculty member was charged with no fewer than 138 books, while another had eighty-eight in his den, and still another eighty-five. And one had even taken a number of the library's volumes with him on a prolonged leave in Europe. The upshot was not that the students were chastised but that the faculty lost its indefinite-borrowing privileges. Reed's nationwide reputation is, however, based less on such student resourcefulness in extracurricular skirmishes with the faculty than on solid achievement in the more traditional fields of scholarship. The most spectacular recent demonstration of Reed's supremacy in these fields occurred last winter when three Wesleyan University teachers, with the aid of a Carnegie financial grant, completed a study on the origins of leading American scientists during a typical peacetime decade, from 1924 to 1904.

As one of their principal conclusions, they wrote: "Reed College, in Oregon, with a total enrollment of only about 600 students, has been far and away more productive of future scientists than any other institution in the United States."

PHOTOGRAPHY BY GUS PASQUARELLA

Students sun-bathe and study on the campus of Reed College, at Portland, Oregon. The college, founded in 1911, now has an enrollment of about 600 students.

Reed enjoyed national prominence in the fall of 1952 when it was featured in an article in the Saturday Evening Post *that touted the college as having the smartest body of undergraduates in the country.*

invited to a town-and-gown reception on campus. At one point, as I was walking toward the canapés, E. B. MacNaughton cornered me, asking me what my thesis topic was. Then, he sort of looked around the room and said, "You know, I wish I'd done something with my life for education like these professors and some of the Reed graduates who have gone on to great things in that milieu, instead of just making money." I was completely in awe of that comment. Soon after, we heard that he was leaving Reed.

TIME magazine, "Reed's Choice," January 16, 1952: When he took over the presidency of Reed College in 1948, [E. B. MacNaughton] firmly an-

President Duncan Ballantine and Assistant Director of Admission Alyce Jones, wife of history professor Richard Jones, with mail received following the article in the Saturday Evening Post. *Applications from around the country increased enormously, broadening the geographical diversity of the college's student body.*

nounced that he would serve only pro tempore. "I am a businessman," said he. "Any time you find an academic man qualified, I'll step aside." Last week, at a sprightly seventy-one, "Mr. Mac" did step aside. The academic man who takes his place: Duncan Smith Ballantine, forty, associate professor of history at MIT.

Reed searched six months before it decided on Dr. Ballantine, and everyone agreed he should feel at home on the erudite little (six hundred students) campus. A lanky, likeable scholar who got his Ph.D. at Harvard, he served as a wartime logistics expert with the navy, eventually became a top apostle of MIT's experimental general education program.

At Reed, Ballantine will face another sort of problem. In spite of the college's academic standing (among its former professors: U.S. Senator from Illinois Paul Douglas, MIT President Karl T. Compton), it still has more than the usual trouble raising money. Among the reasons: some local citizens, with no justification whatsoever, unfairly suspect its reputation for lively liberalism, and some still labor under the false suspicion that Communist John Reed founded it (Portland steamboat and mining tycoon Simeon Gannett Reed put up the first money) and that its first president, William T. Foster, was really Communist William Z. Foster. In four years, Mr. Mac has succeeded in pulling Reed out of the red, but he has never quite finished the job of pulling its reputation out of the pink. That, says he, will be something for the academic man from Cambridge to do—"And I say to him: snap to it, brother."

RICHARD JONES, history professor 1941–1982, 1985–1986: Within weeks of Ballantine's appointment, one of his former colleagues from MIT, the distinguished mathematician Dirk Struik, had been invited to speak at Reed on mathematics. Struik had meantime been suspended by MIT, pending an investigation of charges of left-wing radicalism. Ballantine, interpreting Struik's visit as an affront to MIT, demanded the withdrawal of the invitation. When it was explained to him the incompatibility of his demand with Reed's long-honored tradition of academic freedom, Ballantine announced that resignation was the only course left open to him. He had been on the campus less than six weeks. The Faculty Council prevailed upon him to reconsider, and in due course the Struik lecture went ahead without incident. But it betrayed a personal insecurity and an astonishing lack of sense of proportion on Ballantine's part.

MICHAEL MUNK '56: The Reed trustees, led by the board's secretary, Portland attorney Robert Sabin, Jr., '15, were afraid that Reed's reputation of harboring social nonconformists, political dissenters, or even "subversives" was putting the college in a very precarious position. After the bulge of students on the G.I. bill passed through in the early '50s, enrollment was dropping. Despite E. B. MacNaughton's efforts, contributions were still hard to come by. The trustees hired Duncan Ballantine to fix that problem by cleaning up Reed's reputation, and thus assuring its continued existence.

RICHARD MULLER '56: Ballantine told us that we had to be more like a little Swarthmore of the West in order to get the rich folks in Portland to give the college money. We resented his effort to try to change us into something we weren't. Reedites basically were real conservatives. We liked the old traditions of Reed. We thought we had the best possible college in the country and saw no reason to make any changes at all.

ELIZABETH WARNOCK FERNEA '49, public affairs staff 1950–1954: Ballantine decided that the junior qual and the senior thesis were unnecessary burdens on students. Well, we all agreed that they were burdensome, but the larger questions were, why were they there in the first place, and were they educationally important?

Ballantine's opinion was that they were not. He basically argued that most of the theses were not worth their weight in paper; they were just juvenile examinations of issues that would not go any further than the library. This point had been raised before, when as a student I was on the Student Educational Policies Committee. Our position then was that the theses were not intended to be great dissertations that would be published. They were to provide students with the experience of putting together an original piece of research. Even though you might never go on to graduate school, the thesis was there to give you an incomparable intellectual experience.

Ballantine argued, "Well, then maybe only the best students should have this experience." We argued that everyone should have the experience. To say that only the best students should do it would mean that we were creating an elite in what was already an elite college. It seemed ridiculous and arrogant. In the end, the thesis was retained.

MARVIN LEVICH, philosophy professor 1953–1994, provost 1972–1979: Ballantine was thought to be in cahoots with the Board of Trustees. He was trying to change the Faculty Council so that it would become less of an independent body.

Very early in my time at Reed, Rex Arragon, who taught humanities, was talking to a group of students, and he said that the faculty was the continuing body at the college. The presidents come and go, the trustees come and go, but the one body that's permanent in a certain way is the faculty. That struck me as being a matter of very great importance to recognize.

RICHARD JONES, history professor: Ballantine wanted faculty involvement outside the curriculum eliminated, and for the administration to take charge of the whole institutional operation and all the personnel policies issues that were then being dealt with by the faculty.

He presented a program for administrative and social reform that involved having five members of the Faculty Council appointed by the president, and three members elected from the faculty at large. With the principal agency of community government thus susceptible to the domination of the president, predisposed by the very nature of his position to be "uniquely able to be detached and tough minded" in matters of personnel and policy, the campus society could be made subject to enlightened regulation and reform. The college, having ceased to be a haven for misfits, a platform for radicalism, and a fertile breeding ground for youthful—and in the case of faculty not so youthful—defiance of moral convention, would gain the support, heretofore withheld, of the larger Portland community.

ELLEN KNOWLTON JOHNSON '39, recorder 1945–1962, registrar 1962–1981: Ballantine was sort of a disaster. He wasn't good at listening. He made up his mind that things should go this way or that way. As a result, there was considerable unhappiness among the faculty. Part of the underlying dynamic, though, was a changing of the guard in the faculty ranks. A lot of the older faculty members, like my dad, Tony Knowlton, who had taught physics since 1915, were retiring.

HERB GLADSTONE, music professor 1946–1980: Some of the original professors hired under Foster and Scholz were still teaching, and staggering into faculty meetings. There was a sense of permanence about these guys—like the New York Yankees, which in those days fielded the same team almost every year.

RICHARD JONES, history professor: No one on the Reed faculty in the following decades would have anything like the prestige in any field that

F. L Griffin had in math, A. A. Knowlton in physics, or for that matter Charles McKinley in political science, Rex Arragon in the humanities, or Victor Chittick in English literature. Each of those people had also been very strong leaders on the faculty.

PHILIP WHALEN '51: The hero of the whole establishment was Reginald Francis Arragon, otherwise known as "Rex." He was "the Man" academically, the father and high priest of the humanities.

REX ARRAGON, history professor 1923–1962, 1970–1974: After the war I became very involved in the national movement for the humanities in general education. Under a Rockefeller Foundation grant I made visits to several colleges in 1947 and 1948, becoming especially close to the program at the University of Chicago. I championed humanistic education in the context of John Dewey's instrumentalism, his learning by doing, which viewed truth as an instrument used by humans to solve their problems. I did not object to an instrumental attitude, as long as it was not treated as categorically distinct from rationality. Emphasis upon reason, upon critical intelligence or cautious thinking, is the chief means as well as one of the significant ends of study.

SALLY WATSON '50: I had Ralph Berringer for two courses, humanities and seventeenth-century literature. Berringer was a short man with a square, mobile face, not at all handsome, but vivid and alive. While other short men tried to compensate by aggression or swagger, he did it by intellect and wit. He was hard. When he handed back a paper or test, his comments on it were practically longer than the paper. And scathing, too, criticizing my spelling, organization, logic, reasoning, ideas, insight, analysis, and evaluation with remarks like "Questionable."

But his humanities class changed my entire

world picture. It was utterly fascinating, and alone worth attending Reed for. We had lectures twice a week from whatever professor was most qualified on the aspect being addressed that week—history, literature, politics, religion, philosophy, music, art, drama. Every aspect of human life was integrated in the humanities course. There were daily hour-long conferences with about fifteen of us around a big table.

Berringer's toe-curling criticism never hit at my opinion, only at my facts, analysis, organization, presentation, and spelling. It was a long, long battle. Every paper or test I'd get back a similar story, often boiling down during my paper conference with him to "You didn't get to where you were going." This was infuriating. "Well, where was I going?" I would demand. But he would never tell me. He would just give an infuriating grin and say comfortably that that was what I needed to find out, wasn't it? It was all I could do to avoid throwing myself off the curb.

I never dreamed, of course, that I was Berringer's special protégé. Even his wife, Betty, who had run the Commons for a couple years before I arrived, was daily posted on my progress, and the entire faculty apparently knew of my struggles and was rooting for me.

Then, one day in the spring, while in a personal conference with Berringer, suddenly I got it. I couldn't put it into words, but I left knowing what he was talking about. And with the next paper, on Chaucer's "Knight's Tale," I knew what I was doing. And I knew that I knew. When Berringer returned it with his usual long comments in his tiny handwriting on the back, he stood and watched while I read the first sentence. "You are beginning to see literature with new eyes. I told you that the unveiling would be interesting." I don't think I came down to earth for days.

DOROTHY MOORE EDLIN '56: A lot of students were scared of Maure Goldschmidt, who taught

Reed's "high priest of the humanities," Professor Rex Arragon, leading a senior symposium at his Eastmoreland home in the 1950s.

political science, because he was so caustic and sarcastic. Sort of witty at their expense, maybe. Well, they deserved it because they didn't do the reading. But I liked him. He was a believer in the thorough study of things, and that appealed to me. We spent almost an entire semester on Alexis de Tocqueville, really parsing every sentence. That was very unusual. It was a big contrast to the style of history professor Richard Jones, who threw fifty books at us each week. Maure kept on the point. He didn't let people just say any damn thing they wanted to. I felt a lot of time got wasted at Reed because of that kind of free expression. There wasn't enough focus. But with Maure there was focus, always.

PHILIP WHALEN '51: The young upcoming humanities hero and crown prince was Richard Jones, who was the pride and joy of Dr. Arragon. You could usually find him in the coffee shop, rapping about one thing or another. He was married to this gorgeous blonde.

JAMES MACQUEEN '52: The new faculty made you think of the academics portrayed in the movie *Who's Afraid of Virginia Woolf?* They had all been shaped by the Second World War.

BERT BREHM, biology professor 1962–1993: The faculty induction process was a real kick. When a newcomer came onto the campus there was an assigned group of faculty to clue the new person in on how to behave. For my induction, I was invited to tea one afternoon at the house of Bud Bagg, one of the senior history professors, in Eastmoreland. About five of the oldest, most well-known, classic Reed professors were there for the tea party. Their "tea" came in interesting bottles, but that was pretty typical of the day.

I sat next to the librarian, Becky Pollock, who was a famous college figure—kind of stern and disapproving—and history professor Dorothy Johansen '33. Dorothy Jo was a genuine Reed

character with a wry sense of humor, and not at all shy in her analysis and criticism of people and events. Becky was smoking cigarettes and Dorothy Jo was smoking cigars. Everybody was blowing smoke.

You had to pick up from them the nuances of how a new faculty member was supposed to respect the traditions of the institution.

DOROTHY JOHANSEN '33, history professor 1934–1969, archivist 1969–1984: The emotion had gone out in the young faculty who came to teach after the war. Their view was that one should not get involved emotionally in anything, especially something that was close to their intellect. They seemed to be the products of large universities with masses of people and all the attributes of the impersonal big school where you make a little group of your own but the school runs by itself. One didn't hear from them an expression of interest in the college as an entity, as something in itself, but rather it was always something that paid them their living or was a good place to teach.

JOHN POCK, sociology professor 1955–1998: I packed a bunch of books into a Pontiac station wagon and drove out to Portland, getting into town about three AM. I drove over to Reed and saw this sign that said, "Chicken manure for sale." It was dark as hell, and I decided that I must have missed a turn and driven into the farmlands beyond Portland. So I parked and went to sleep in the car. In the morning I discovered that Reed College was just beyond this sign.

It was the first week of August, and there was no one around. I saw an announcement of a room for rent just down the street on Reed College Place. I went over and met the two people living there, who turned out to be Rex Arragon and his wife, Gertrude. At the time that didn't mean anything to me. As far as I was concerned, Rex Arragon was just some old fuddy-duddy faculty member. But it was a reasonably good room at a reasonable price. So I moved in with the Arragons, and promptly got into continuing arguments with Rex about the humanities program.

Rex was a stereotypical patriarch, on the surface very affable but underneath it all he had some very rigid ideas about things. He would have rolled over in his grave if he saw the feminist movement or anything like that. I learned afterwards, of course, that he was the power, for all practical purposes, in the faculty, and I didn't quite understand why that should be. But I think one of the reasons was that he had this double ability of being very affable, and then sticking it to you, so to speak. It was better to agree with him, or otherwise you would be dead. Arragon was into everything.

I didn't agree with some of what he was saying about the humanities program, mostly because it was almost totally aimed at the literature of the Hellenic Period and there was a complete absence of science and math. It seemed to me to be a biased view of what all of that was about, and how it was the seedbed for Western civilization.

Students studying in Hauser Memorial Library, 1950s.

PHILIP WHALEN '51: I wrote a paper about how in this so-called "humanities" course there was absolutely no news about the large historical and literary tradition in China, which I found very exciting. I had a meeting with my conference leader, Donald Layman, on this paper, and he said, "Not part of our tradition. Go fuck yourself, Whalen."

Some of us—Lew Welch '50, Ed Danielsen '51, Gary Snyder '51, and I—used to see a guy named Charlie Leong who worked as a cashier in a restaurant in Chinatown called Sinseng. Leong was quite a learned man, probably in his forties. He had been trained in Chinese language in a Chinese school in Portland, and then sent by his parents to stay with an uncle in Beijing and study calligraphy and learn how to cut seals for making impressions.

We would talk to him about Chinese things like Confucius and Chinese poetry. We kept encouraging him to get out of the restaurant and come to Reed. He had been in the army during the war and had the G.I. Bill coming to him. Finally he did. We learned a great deal from him. Charlie Leong '53 was our only China connection at Reed at the time.

MOSHE LENSKE '50, trustee 1992–1996: There was a lot of faculty-student interaction in those days. A number of professors lived in the adjacent Eastmoreland neighborhood and in the faculty houses on campus along Woodstock Boulevard, which are now the language dorms. David French '39, who taught anthropology, had gatherings at his house all the time, including for poker. David studied Native Americans, who, in and of themselves, were big gamblers. Poker was a serious business, and it could go on all night.

GARY SNYDER '51: Dave French '39 taught one course on Far Eastern culture every year or so. I took that and it got me through a couple of good books on Chinese and Japanese history, and it

was one of the early places where I first ran onto the term "Zen Buddhism."

JAMES WALSH '49: David French '39 was a master of coffee-shop pedagogy. I learned as much from him in the coffee shop as if I had taken one of his classes. I ran the coffee shop with Carol Jean Paton '49. There I fell in with another master of such life, philosophy professor Ed Garlan. With Ed, one went from the classroom to the coffee shop and often then on to his home, all the while moving from the great texts to our own life and back again, constantly being asked by Ed in his owlish way, "Well, what do you think?"

JUNE BURLINGAME SMITH '56: The coffee shop was our Round Table. It was dark, knotty pine, and smoky. Everybody, students and professors, met there.

SALLY WATSON '50: You could amble around the coffee shop and listen shamelessly to the various conversations, and join the one you most fancied: the new Mount Palomar observatory, Sartre's existential play *No Exit*, the Harry Hopkins papers, the Arab armies trying to destroy Israel the minute she was voted statehood, new drugs like cortisone and chloromycetin, Alan Paton's South African novel *Cry the Beloved Country*, the unlikely new notion that the universe started with a Big Bang. If there were games going on in the booths, they weren't poker or gin rummy or even bridge, but always chess.

ROBERT SHELLOW '51: Stanley Moore, who taught philosophy, had served as a military attaché detailed to the American Embassy in Moscow during the war. He came back professing that he was a philosophical Marxist. Stanley was kind of an iconoclast. A strange and aloof guy. He was very dashing and looked sort of like a movie star, which made him very popular with the ladies. As a matter of fact, he dated some of

PART THREE: THE NATIONAL COLLEGE, 1946–1966

The Reed coffee shop in the old Student Union building, 1947. Philip Whalen '51 is at the far right.

the students and eventually married one, Laurie Malarkey '53.

Stanley lived in a houseboat down at Weber's Landing on the Willamette River. He would casually mention getting some of the "elements" together and throwing a party, and we would jump into his jeep and drive down to the houseboat, where we would have these long philosophical discussions on every possible topic you can imagine, inevitably accompanied by large quantities of alcoholic beverages. People got rather swacked, and on several occasions would sleep over because nobody wanted to take the chance of trying to step onto dry land.

CAROL CREEDON, psychology professor 1957–1991: Reed had only a few female faculty members. Before I came, there hadn't been any full-time women in psychology since Eleanor Rowland, at the time of the college's founding. Soon after I arrived I discovered that a mem-

ber of my department was already raising some doubts about me, on the grounds that I was a woman with a young child. He told the department head, "Well, we'll never get our money's worth out of her."

The week before classes started, I attended a picnic for new faculty members with some of the regular professors. A fellow came up and sat down beside me, and said, "We've been giving you a hard time, haven't we, this last two weeks?" "No," I said, "everyone's very warm and friendly. I enjoy being here." "Well, I hope you'll be singing that same tune by the end of the semester," he said. "But I want to assure you that the pressure will be much lighter very soon now. You'll just have to put up with us as best you can." I was puzzled by where this conversation was going until it dawned on me that he saw me as a faculty secretary, not as a colleague. It really did not occur to him that there would be any women on the faculty whatsoever.

It was very strenuous teaching full-time at Reed and managing child care. A turning point for me was at a committee meeting that the chair had called on short notice. Leila Birnbaum Falk, who taught music, arrived breathing hard and looking very stressed. Then we got a message that the chair had cancelled the meeting. Leila then began describing what her day had been like finding a babysitter without adequate notice, and what she saw as the total indifference of the college to this situation for women faculty, given that most of the faculty at Reed were males and they had wives for child care, but that faculty women didn't have wives! Her outburst, which continued for quite a while at a considerable volume, made me realize that there was no concern for the plight of women faculty with children.

It was just unconsciousness, I think—all those years in which Reed had been a largely male institution, and then these women started showing up.

NANCY BRAGDON, wife of Paul Bragdon (president 1971–1988): History professor Dorothy Johansen '33 was very sharp-tongued, with a ferocious temper. She went up to the University of Washington and got a Ph.D. in the 1930s, when not a lot of women were doing that.

But she also was not treated fairly by her male colleagues. In the early 1950s, when she published *Empire of the Columbia*, her well-received book on the history of the Northwest, her colleagues were not nice about it. When all of the male colleagues in her department got an increase in salary and she didn't, she went to the president to ask why that had happened. She was told, "You don't have a husband or children." She said, "I'm supporting my mother and my brother." It didn't make any difference. There

An anthropology class in 1947 with Professor David French '39 and students Claire Olsen '48, Ila Clow '49, Carol Jean Walsh '49, and James Walsh '49.

was some bitterness in her about that, but at the same time, she remained intensely loyal to "The College" as she called it.

HERB GLADSTONE, music professor 1946–1980: At the beginning of the '50s, the sciences were overwhelmingly the selection of most of the students applying, who were mostly male. At that time the college had about four hundred boys and two hundred girls. It was a significant discrepancy. I was asked to join a committee to find out what the faculty might do to attract more females, in terms of designing the curriculum. The college felt that smaller departments like drama, music, ceramics, and poetry, as well as art history and music history, would attract females. Nowadays, if you seriously expressed that view you would be called a sexist. But this was something they took seriously then, and probably erroneously, because there were a lot of really good female students majoring in chemistry and the other sciences.

RICHARD JONES, history professor: A Ford Foundation grant allowed the college to conduct an elaborate self-study in 1952–53. While faculty members would have preferred to center attention on the curriculum and the organization of the faculty, President Ballantine chose to concentrate on student life, student attitudes, and student anxieties, looking for clues to address the problem of high attrition at Reed. He had hoped to find confirmation of his opinions that the college was too permissive in its social structure and at once too rigorous and too loose academically. He wanted more regulation of campus life with more clearly defined concrete lessons in the classroom.

The data from the study, however, did not yield quite the results he wanted. It could not demonstrate a relationship between attrition and Reed's high standards or severe grading, nor label the academic requirements as unre-

alistic. It could find no evidence of a desire for more explicit structuring in courses or for more clear lines of authority in either academic life or social structure on the campus.

Ballantine questioned the apparent values implicit in the study's finding that seniors had learned to be more critical of convention than freshmen were. He wondered if they had not been trained to resist authority in any form.

MICHAEL MUNK '56: One of the things Reed tried to figure out in the self-study was why more women than men were dropping out before graduating. The final findings of that part of the study were entitled, "Impact of the College: The Coed."

REED COLLEGE SELF-STUDY REPORT, "Impact of the College: The Coed," 1953: The proportion of female applicants has been declining and the proportion of them who fail to graduate has been increasing since the prewar period. In one sense, this is difficult to comprehend. Considering the sex ratio at Reed, one would imagine the coed's position to be heavenly indeed. The questionnaire indicates that women find it easier to meet members of the opposite sex than do the men, that they date more frequently, that more of them "go steady," and that they more often feel that they have as many dates as they want.

Upon further examination, the coed's position at Reed seems somewhat less enviable. In an environment where intellectual values are primary and where the normal expectation is that college is a step toward graduate school, the traditional interests of females find little expression in accepted norms and goals. Thus far, the college has not attempted to structure its academic and social program to prepare them either for those professions in which women have the greatest opportunities for achievement, or for their adult roles as wives and mothers. Moreover, we have conscientiously avoided those appurtenances of college life, such as sororities and formalized social activities, which prove so attractive to coeds elsewhere. While undoubtedly Reed offers many advantages to women, the fact remains that we are not eminently successful in attracting them to the college nor in keeping them here. . . .

Unfortunately, thus far we have not been able to localize the precise areas of dissatisfaction. . . . It was expected, for example, that women would show a greater lack of self-confidence about their work than men; that more of them would reject the heavy emphasis on intellectual values that characterizes the student group as a whole. Although such differences may exist, the available evidence does not reveal them.

JUNE BURLINGAME SMITH '56: I had a difficult time because I felt that I wasn't heard in the conferences. It was my experience that, consistent-

Students at archery practice on the front lawn, 1946.

ly in these small groups, it was male-dominated thinking. If I came up with something, it just lay on the table and died. The conversation went on, and ten minutes later the same thing I had said was said in the mouth of a man, and everybody was, "Oh! How wonderful!" This was repeated over and over again. I was fairly shy in those days. Reed taught me that I couldn't continue to be shy and polite, that I would have to be more assertive and more insistent and persistent.

RICHARD ABEL '48: Everybody at Reed was really cutthroat, and I think that was a good thing. We had no counselors. We had really very little direction. The college's attitude was, "Hey, this is what we have on offer. If you make it, great, we'll give you a diploma. But if you were frightened out by the workload, frightened out by the conferences and having to constantly debate things, frightened out by the junior qual, or frightened out by the thesis, well, fine, go someplace else. There are other places that'll take you."

I was not terrified by the junior qualifying exam. Most people were. They would drop out in absolute droves. Two-thirds of my incoming freshman class vanished along the way. I always thought that was good. It said something about those of us who had made it. We had finished the obstacle course. The others, for the most part, all wound up at good schools and they got a degree, but it wasn't a degree of the quality we had acquired, one that required the kind of intellectual acumen, resolve, and capacity to think on one's feet that we had demonstrated. We played cards for keeps, we discussed things for keeps, and it was almost literally blood on the floor at the end of the night if you didn't pay attention.

RON LAING '56: History professor Dorothy Johansen '33 gave the introductory lecture for freshman humanities. She got up on stage and started out by saying, "I'd like you to look at the person to the left of you, and the person to the right of you. Only one of you will graduate from Reed College."

JANE CLAPPERTON VAN CLEVE '59, MAT '65: I entered Reed as a third-year transfer from Wellesley, an eastern college deeply committed to the education of women. Was the Reed style "masculine"? Perhaps, but I liked the seriousness associated with men-versus-women at the time. The high visibility of male teachers and students, the emphasis on rational discourse and critical thinking, the confrontational give-and-take of classroom discussions met some real need in me to learn confidence about independent thinking. Reed was good at training students not to be fooled. And certainly I wasn't fooled by the gender discrimination entrenched in the general culture at the time. Reed was hard, but I liked the challenge of meeting tough standards.

CARL WINTER '60: A lot of guys were just out trying to score and keeping score. That was the ethic of being male in the '50s. They didn't regard women as potential equals in either academics or the marketplace, but simply as targets for their sexual energies.

On the other hand, Reed women were bright, competent, and in some cases, well able to defend themselves. Certainly in the classroom they did fine. The amount of cohabitation and general shacking up that was going on at Reed was probably significant, but it didn't permeate the student body. It was just that there were those who were sexually active and those who weren't. Student life was unstructured and unsupervised.

RICHARD UDELL '55: Ballantine started out trying to establish a reputation as a big liberal. In his inaugural address he said that he was going to bring "light, not heat" to Reed. Soon after that, we held a Reed Union where a parent in attendance wanted to know whether, in going to

Reed, his son was going to graduate a scholar or end up as some kind of disgusting, communist rebel. Ballantine leaped up and said, "I want to answer that question!" He made a wonderful speech about the competition of ideas being like the competition of business, in which the best ideas should win, and therefore free speech was necessary. Everyone was very pleased by this wonderful speech.

But then his reputation as a big liberal was lost in a number of incidents. One started when a man and a woman left the campus without her signing out, which women were required to do. They didn't tell anyone where they were going and they left together. Ballantine concluded that they had apparently left on some kind of sexual tryst, and expelled them. He made a speech, the purport of which was that the Honor Principle shouldn't apply to sexual conduct, which should be outside the honor system. It later turned out these two students were vaguely related and had both returned to their home city in California to attend the funeral of a relation who had passed.

ABRAHAM BERGMAN '54: I was on the Student Council at the time. We made a big stand about that, because—what the hell—it was a purview of the students to administer discipline. Our main issue with Ballantine was that he was acting in an arbitrary manner, operating with no process, not discussing the matter with anybody, and making decisions based on morality.

JEAN TIBBITTS THIÉBAUX '57: Ballantine came from a background that was much more administratively authoritarian. He had been at more traditional schools where the president laid things out and people followed behind him. That was clearly not the situation at Reed, which viewed itself as a democratic society where the student body and the faculty were major participants in the formation of policies that governed the college.

CHAPTER 18

Un-American Activities

When the slam-bang tactics of Senator McCarthy and his Red hunt came around, Reed was a sitting duck for anyone who wanted to make charges of that kind.
    —Ernest Boyd "E. B." MacNaughton, former president

In Portland they were making jokes that they wanted to put Reed on a barge and send it down to San Francisco. I wouldn't have noticed if they had. I was totally immersed in my studies. We were, we felt, very protected and safe, in a self-contained bubble.
    —Mertie Hansen Muller '56

In the early 1950s, Cold War tensions fueled fears in America of widespread Communist subversion, spawning a second "Red Scare." Joseph McCarthy, a U.S. Senator from Wisconsin, became the public face of a Congressional effort to ferret out alleged Communist spies and sympathizers in the government and elsewhere.

In 1953, Senator McCarthy turned his sights on academia, denouncing Harvard University as "the Kremlin on the Charles" for its decision to retain three professors who had supported the Communist cause in the 1930s. That same year, the University of Washington fired three tenured academics, and the regents of the University of California at Berkeley discharged two dozen professors who refused to sign a loyalty oath. At the University of Chicago, President Robert Hutchins defiantly resisted a state board's investigation of Communist sympathizers in the university. Among college presidents, his was largely a minority position.

One of the three professors under investigation at Harvard invoked the Fifth Amendment in refusing to answer questions at a congressional investigation about his alleged ties to the Communist Party. The question of whether resorting to the Fifth Amendment constituted grounds of significant misconduct sufficient for termination became a hotly debate topic within academic institutions. Rutgers University and the University of Kansas both ejected faculty members who invoked their Fifth Amendment rights rather than discuss their involvement with Communism. At Harvard, it was decided that no one would be retained who was presently a member of the Communist Party, but no one would be fired for past association with it; use of the Fifth Amendment was determined to be misconduct subject to disciplinary action, but not a matter of "grave misconduct" that would result in termination.

The witch hunt known as "McCarthyism" reached its high-water mark in the spring of 1954 when, during the Army-McCarthy hearings in Washington, D.C., the military was forced to defend itself in televised sessions against charges of being soft on Communism.

In the summer of that year, McCarthyism came to Reed College.

MICHAEL MUNK '56: The FBI first came to Reed in 1953 to interview the faculty and administrators. The main person that they wanted to speak with was the admission director, Bob Canon, who had just been appointed dean of students by President Ballantine in the fall of 1953. They made Canon tell them which other people at Reed were Reds. Canon later told friends and relatives that testifying was the worst thing he had ever done. They believed that he cooperated only because the FBI threatened to expose his homosexuality.

KATHERINE KOLESOFF AVERILL '50: Many Reedites took jobs with the government after graduation, and the FBI was sent out to investigate them. If you came to the registrar's office wanting information, you got it. A lot of what the FBI was doing was simply checking transcripts to make sure the person was indeed a graduate. But the registrar, Maggie Scott '19, would just hand them the person's entire folder, in which she kept everything about every student that ever passed through her hands, including articles from the *Quest* newspaper. I was appalled, but there weren't any privacy laws at the time. I imagine people didn't even think about it until the Velde Committee came through Portland and started subpoenaing people who had been in college with us.

RICHARD JONES, history professor 1941–1982, 1985–1986: Harold Velde was chairman of the House Un-American Activities Committee, or HUAC. The so-called "Velde Committee" came to Portland in the summer of 1954. President Ballantine explained to us on the Faculty Council that it was necessary for us to cooperate because the committee was going to cause us trouble. In fact, it soon became clear that their whole Portland mission had nothing to do with Communism in Oregon, it had simply to do with Reed College. Reed came under attack on the grounds of tolerating Communists, or having Communists who were influential in the faculty, the student body, and the administration.

HERB GLADSTONE, music professor 1946–1980: The issue, so far as we were concerned, was that the government could refuse any financial aid that had been given, even indirectly, to the college. What they meant by that was that Reed, which was filled with students on the G.I. Bill, would find that the government would no longer pay their tuition if the faculty did not sign the loyalty oath. That was the threat.

ABRAHAM BERGMAN '54: There was this pervasive fear around the country in the spring of 1954. Just listening on the radio to the Army-McCarthy hearings investigating Communist infiltration of the military created a fearful atmosphere. The actual Velde Committee hearings in Portland took place during the summer of 1954, when students were not in school. Purposefully, I think.

RUTH CEDERSTROM WOLFE '50: The Velde Committee characterized a certain party at a Reed student's house as having been a Communist recruiting meeting. My husband and I had gone to that party. It was an Easter party. They had Easter decorations and a big jar where they were collecting money to free some liberal person back East who had been jailed. Nobody asked us to become Communists. Nobody said a word about that. I didn't remember it as a subversive occurrence. When I heard the party described at the hearing, I couldn't even recognize it as the party I had attended.

ROBERT FERNEA '54: The question was whether Reed professors had to testify before the committee or not. I was president of my senior class, and rallied the class to sign a letter supporting a professor's right to continue teaching at Reed without testifying. There was a lot of commotion over that. My mother, who lived across the Columbia River in Vancouver, Washington, had garbage thrown in her yard and nasty telephone calls. It was a challenging experience that brought politics down to a local level. It also brought our class together for the first time. Only one person refused to sign the letter.

HARRY JACOB '54: As commencement speaker in 1954, students chose to invite the father of Linda Pauling '54, chemist Linus Pauling. At that time Pauling had been awarded the Humphry Davy Medal from the Royal Society of London, but was denied a visa by the U.S. government because of his political activism opposing nuclear proliferation. His passport was restored not long after he came to Reed, so that he was able to travel to Stockholm to receive the first of his two Nobel Prizes.

LADIS KRISTOF '55: I was born in a part of Austria that became part of the Soviet Union, and in 1939 I was inducted into the Soviet military, in which I served during the whole war from 1939 to 1945. I came to the United States in 1952 and, thanks to a woman I met in Paris, got a job in an Oregon logging camp. I enrolled at Reed in 1953, directly from the camp. Having just escaped from the Communist world, I was on the one hand obviously considered one of the enemy, and on the other hand I was someone who knew something about living under a Communist regime.

On campus there was an unpleasant, ongoing public discussion between Frank Munk and Maure Goldschmidt '30, both of whom taught political science, as to whether a Communist should be allowed to teach at the college. Munk took the position no, on the basis that such a person is really directed by the Communist Party. Goldschmidt took the opposing position, that just because somebody may be a Communist Party member, it does not necessarily mean that he was a tool of the party.

MICHAEL MUNK '56: Homer Owen '50 told HUAC that he was recruited into the Communist Party in 1947 by Reed administrator Bob Canon and a fellow student. He became chair of the Communist Party's John Reed Club, which he said was composed almost entirely of Reed students and their spouses, and later became a member of the central committee of the Oregon Communist Party. After graduating from Reed in 1950, he went on to Cornell University for his master's degree. He testified that he left the Communist Party shortly thereafter.

Along with admission director Bob Canon, Owen was the lead witness in HUAC's Portland hearings. He named twenty-two Reedites and faculty and seventeen other Oregonians as members of the Communist Party. He also named several of his fellow Cornell graduate students as Communists, including Leonard Marsak, who by the time of Owen's 1954 testimony was a history and humanities instructor at Reed.

Owen's wife, Marjorie Emery Owen '49, was a secretary to Bob Canon while she was a student at Reed. According to HUAC, she testified before a closed HUAC hearing in Washington, D.C., that she collected Communist Party dues from Canon and his wife and two Reed professors—Stanley Moore, who taught philosophy, and Lloyd Reynolds, who taught calligraphy and art history—as well as Virginia Reynolds, Lloyd Reynolds' wife.

REX ARRAGON, history professor 1923–1962, 1970–1974: A special trustee-faculty committee was created in the spring of 1954 in anticipation of the approaching Velde Committee hearings, to take up cases arising from faculty taking the Fifth Amendment. The committee drew up a resolution that required substantial evidence of misconduct or concern for the good name of the college before the conduct of any faculty member was examined. While the resolution gave the trustees sole authority to define what was meant by "misconduct" and "the good name of the college," it also specified that the procedure in such cases was to include assistance and advice from the faculty.

When President Ballantine read the resolution at the full faculty meeting, there was a motion by history professor Dick Jones to confirm that by "substantial evidence" the joint committee did not mean gossip, hearsay, or unsupported accusations. Ballantine agreed to this motion, and it was initially recorded in the minutes of the meeting. But later he asked that his concurrence be deleted from those minutes.

The Board of Trustees voted in favor of the resolution on June 4, two days after Reed profes-

sor Stanley Moore, who was on sabbatical that year, appeared before the Velde Committee in Washington, D.C. There he used both the First and Fifth Amendments in his refusal to answer their questions.

On June 19, televised hearings of the Velde Committee took place in Portland. Reed dean Robert Canon testified that he knew of Moore's membership in the Communist Party in 1948. The next day Moore sent an open letter to the Reed community, asking that his conduct be investigated by the college in a public meeting. He also proposed that taking the Fifth Amendment was not evidence of professional misconduct. Ballantine informed Moore that the trustees were undertaking an investigation of the case on the basis of their June 4 resolution, and requested that he return to Portland to discuss the matter. Also on June 19, the Velde Committee in Portland called forward Reed professors Lloyd Reynolds and Leonard Marsak.

ELIZABETH WARNOCK FERNEA '49, public affairs staff 1950–1954: I worked at Reed in public relations when the Velde Committee came to Portland. President Ballantine was unable to deal with it. He was just hopeless. He didn't understand what was happening, or, if he understood, he felt he was in danger, which he was. But he was so immature and childish about it. He locked himself in his office and would not allow anyone but me to speak to the press. He was concerned in some paranoid way with what was going on at the hearings, so I was sent downtown to attend them.

The hearings went on for two days. I had a headache the entire time. It was just unbelievably horrible for everybody, and especially for the faculty members who were being quizzed. There was something about the indignity of it all, and the assumption that all these good people who I had known and respected in college were criminals.

MICHAEL MUNK '56: In his compelled appearance before the committee, art professor Lloyd Reynolds was not in fact asked to "name names," but was asked only whether the testimony of former dean Bob Canon that Lloyd was a member of the Communist Party in 1947 was correct. The absurdity of Lloyd's interrogation was best illustrated by the demands of HUAC's chief counsel, Robert Kunzig, as to whether Lloyd had ever made posters or exhibits for the Communist Party while at Reed. Lloyd stood righteously on constitutional and moral grounds in refusing to answer, as did history professor Leonard Marsak. It turned out that in Reynolds' case, Kunzig's allegation was correct. Lloyd had in fact produced calligraphy for a Portland picnic of the West Coast Communist newspaper, the *Daily People's World*, in the early '50s.

DOROTHY SCHUMANN STEARNS '45: Lloyd Reynolds taught art as a political statement during the war. We all knew his leaning, but we did not find it shocking. America was friends with Russia at the time. Flirting with Communism was common. It was not unusual to have someone ask, "Are you for Trotsky or Lenin?" Trotsky was the right answer.

MICHAEL MUNK '56: The Reed trustees, led by chairman Henry Failing Cabell and secretary Robert Sabin, Jr., '15, decided to punish Reynolds for his defiance of HUAC. Cabell was the grandson of Henry Failing, a pioneer merchant in Portland and an old colleague of Simeon Reed. As a local attorney, Cabell managed the vast downtown land holdings of his grandfather's estate. He, along with fellow attorney Sabin, a member of Reed's first graduating class, had led a group of local business leaders in 1934 to form the Citizens Emergency League as a means of combating the "Red Menace" of the historic longshoreman's strike in Portland.

The day after Reynolds' appearance before the committee, Cabell and Sabin ordered President Ballantine to suspend Reynolds from teaching his scheduled art history class in Reed's 1954

Art history and calligraphy professor Lloyd Reynolds (center) with attorney Kneland Tanner, testifying before the Velde Committee in Portland, June 19, 1954.

summer session. Ballantine enthusiastically carried out the order, and for the first and only time in Reed's history, a professor was barred from teaching his course for political reasons.

Rex Arragon, history professor: Ballantine's suspension of Reynolds immediately created a sharp rift between the president and the faculty. In seeming violation of the resolution of the joint committee of the trustees, Ballantine had failed to consult with the faculty before taking action. His lame explanation of not having time for consultations did not forestall a resolution, carried by the faculty by a vote of thirty-eight to nine, that viewed Reynolds' suspension as a violation of the assurances Ballantine had made to the faculty, and was the sign of a gravely weakening confidence in the president.

Michael Munk '56: The trustees directed Ballantine to conduct interrogations of professors Lloyd Reynolds, Stanley Moore, and Leonard Marsak. Reynolds originally hoped to defy the trustees as well, writing to fellow professor Moore, "It sounds like capitulation to me. I'm no hero, but I hate to get down on my knees unless I'm planting onions or looking for collar buttons."

In Reynolds' case, he was asked to determine whether, to keep his job, he "would extend sufficient confidence to the college" by assuring it that his current political beliefs and affiliations were acceptable. President Ballantine informed the trustees that while he was unable to guarantee that Professor Reynolds had not participated in some recent Communist-front activities, and that he had discovered some evidence of bias in his former courses in eighteenth-century literature, he was able to conclude that Professor Reynolds was not at the time a member of the Communist Party and had not been for some years past, and that he had no sympathy for the Communist Party.

After confessing that the process to which Reed had subjected Lloyd had produced pressures that must be very punishing and had made him sacrifice principles he personally believed to be important, Ballantine recommended to the Board of Trustees that, since Lloyd had confessed his "errors in judgment," he should be allowed to keep his job.

As for the other two faculty members required to pass the trustees' political test, Marsak made assurances similar to Lloyd's, but they were not sufficient to renew his contract when it expired a year later. After that, he was unable to continue his academic career. Stanley Moore was another matter.

Rex Arragon, history professor: After a month of correspondence between Stanley Moore and President Ballantine, Moore, who was away on sabbatical, agreed to come to Portland for a discussion. Ballantine and the trustees held a private hearing with Moore, at which the Faculty Council was present.

Moore refused to disclose any information to the trustees with respect to allegations made before the Velde Committee, and so was charged with failure to cooperate with the board. Whereas Reynolds and Marsak had been hesitant about responding to the trustees, and had struggles with their consciences and pressure from personal and family necessities, Moore was in a more independent position financially. There was no doubt in our minds of his sincerity of principle, nor in the minds of some of the trustees probably. His purpose was not evasive.

Barbara West '64, trustee 1975–1979: The reports presented to the trustees from the faculty and the president regarding Stanley Moore's refusal to cooperate did not favor termination. The board discussed it, however, and decided on terminating him. From what I understand, they felt very frightened for Reed's viability as an institution with Stanley Moore still on the faculty. Their sources of significant donations for the college were pretty much traditional Portland Republicans, industry people, who weren't about to give money to an institution that had, and kept, proven Commies, even though the proof was not there in the HUAC hearings.

ERNEST BONYHADI '48, trustee 1971–1995: It couldn't have been handled worse. Some of it, you were talking conflict of interest. The trustees' chairman, Henry Failing Cabell, was related to Stanley Moore by marriage. Moore had married one of his former students, Laurie Malarkey '53. The Malarkeys were an old lumber company family. They were all very rich, and a number of family members had attended Reed since the early years. Ironically, Moore was married to a Reed gal who could have bought and sold the college.

MICHAEL MUNK '56: Years later, when he was able to resume teaching at UC San Diego, Moore said that in fact he had quit the Communist Party some years before the Velde Commission hearings, and so could have told the trustees what Lloyd Reynolds had told them and kept his job. That confirmed that his defiance was based, as he had argued, on the principle of academic freedom.

MARVIN LEVICH, philosophy professor 1953–1994, provost 1972–1979: The faculty meetings that year were violent, and frightening in character. Frank Jones, who taught English, got up at one meeting and said that he didn't see that membership in the Communist Party was an appropriate issue to be confronted, when you had questions of tenure and teaching effectiveness. President Ballantine, with spittle coming out his mouth, said, "Nobody who takes that position deserves to be on the faculty of Reed College."

I had been hired as a one-year replacement for Stanley Moore while he was on sabbatical. After Moore was terminated, I thought I should resign, because I didn't want to be a replacement for somebody who had been terminated on political grounds. I had no idea where I would go. Stanley Moore called me and asked me not to resign. He felt I could do better if I stayed at Reed and tried in one way or another to fight for the principles that he thought were involved.

ELLEN KNOWLTON JOHNSON '39, recorder 1945–1962, registrar 1962–1981: We lost a good number of students over the Velde investigation. I had students come into the registrar's office and say "I'm leaving because I don't like the things that some of your faculty are teaching." They believed it firmly, because in their opinion Stanley Moore had said something that they thought was anti-American and pro-Russian. Then we had other students, like Michael Munk '56, the son of political science professor Frank Munk, who felt just the other way.

MICHAEL MUNK '56: Moore's firing destroyed my respect for Reed as an institution and provided evidence for my developing Marxist ideology, because I recognized that the trustees' role was not to protect and defend the academic standards and values that the college claimed it championed. They were simply the owners of the property and physical plant, but because of that they had the absolute right to hire and fire any employee. Those trustees during the HUAC investigation imposed their authority and ideology on the academic components of the college because they owned the place.

NANCY NOMLAND BERNHARDT '55: Many people were already unhappy with President Duncan Ballantine, but when he pushed for the firing of Stanley Moore, that did it. There was a big meeting in San Francisco where every Reed graduate that could be gotten ahold of, by jungle drums or otherwise, came. They all signed pledges stating: "We will never give a penny to the school as long as Ballantine stays."

There was a mock Reed Union held by Dick Abel '48, who ran the college bookstore, along with John Scott '55 and Dale Jorgenson '55. Some of the kids realized that this was a phony Union, so they put together signs for a marching demonstration that read "Nepal for the Nepalese," "Brazil for the Brazilians," "Reed for the Reedites, Ballantine Go Home." They marched around campus and then into a private dining room where Ballantine was meeting with some civic leaders.

Then somebody said, "Let's go to Ballantine's house." We all trooped over to his house in Eastmoreland and stood outside with our signs. His little girl looked out the window as if she was saying, "Mommy, what are they doing?" The students turned the "Reed for the Reedites" sign on its side, so that she couldn't see the "Ballantine Go Home" message. I found it very unpleasant. It made me decide that I wasn't a picketer.

HARRY JACOB '54: We held a joint meeting of the Student Council and the Faculty Council. The Faculty Council members were depressingly beaten down. One or two of them were actually in tears. The whole meeting actually turned when one of the Student Council members, Abe Bergman '54, gave this incredibly passionate talk, saying, "Goddammit, it's time for the students and faculty to come together. The faculty's got to have some backbone in this situation." Within five minutes, you could feel that whole room change. The faculty started sitting up and, by God, the tenor of the institution changed based on that one particular afternoon.

RICHARD JONES, history professor: A professor's beliefs, it seemed to me, were absolutely irrelevant. My definition of academic freedom involved the right to remain in an institution so long as one maintained the academic standards of that institution, regardless of beliefs. That made the theoretical question of whether a Communist would be under control of party discipline entirely irrelevant. All you had to do

Philosophy professor Stanley Moore was fired by the Reed trustees for refusing to answer questions from the Velde Committee regarding his involvement with the Communist Party.

was pass the same standard upon his behavior that you pass upon anyone else. If the professor utilized his professional position in an abusive fashion—if he threatened a student to "go this way" to get a good grade, to use a very flagrant sort of example—or if he indulged in the same sort of thing subtly, then you wouldn't have to worry about whether he was a Communist or that Communism was driving him in that direction. You would deal with him in the same fashion as you would deal with someone who abused his position, or wasted the time of his class, or was unprepared, or refused to face the hard questions that his subject matter presented.

MARVIN LEVICH, philosophy professor: It was a period of time in which one could, with a few exceptions, sense the faculty coming together on something that seemed of very great importance: that the business of the faculty was to decide these things, not the Board of Trustees, not the president.

We had meeting after meeting about what position should be taken on this, and what the wording should be of the faculty member who bearded the president. Jim Hamilton '22, who taught education and was also director of admission, took on the job of making this motion at a faculty meeting: "The faculty expresses limited confidence in the president."

ERNEST BOYD "E. B." MacNAUGHTON, trustee 1919–1941, 1955–1958, president 1948–1952: There was a strong feeling of revulsion against the college in the local business community over the Velde Committee turmoil. The situation could have been coped with had not, simultaneously, there developed an almost unanimous opposition on the part of the faculty against the president, resulting in a vote of lack of confidence in him. At the same time the Reed senior class went on a rampage and was at the point of refusing to accept diplomas from Ballantine.

Just how all this eruption came to pass is beyond me. When I left the college in the hands of Dr. Ballantine it was running as smoothly as a Cadillac engine. By the end of the summer of 1954, the president of the Board of Trustees, Henry Cabell, who had been most zealous in his efforts to support Reed and who had, upon Ballantine's appointment, given the college $100,000—the largest individual gift since 1930—told me with definiteness that he would resign. I was sick at heart of the whole business. I put in years working for Reed, gave it a good deal of money, pulled it out of the hole when I took office as president, and served for four years without salary, only to see it slide back into a deeper hole.

MERTIE HANSEN MULLER '56: In Portland they were making jokes that they wanted to put Reed on a barge and send it down to San Francisco. I wouldn't have noticed if they had. I was totally immersed in my studies. We were, we felt, very protected and safe, in a self-contained bubble.

CHRIS MATHEWS '58: One of the first activities we had as freshmen in September 1954, was listening to a welcoming speech by President Ballantine. In his speech, Ballantine expounded on the athletic philosophy of Reed, which emphasized total participation, with winning way down the line of priorities. One thing he said was, "There's nothing worth doing that isn't worth doing badly." The next morning I picked up a copy of the *Oregonian* and read that President Ballantine had resigned.

THE OREGONIAN, interview with Duncan Ballantine, October 2, 1954: Dr. Ballantine said Reed has three good traditions and three bad ones. The three good ones are: its academic quality; its free inquiry; and its honor system. The three bad ones he briefed as: domination of policy and politics by the Faculty Council; individual irresponsibility; and an "intransigent arrogance" toward opinions of the off-campus world. These six good and bad points, he declared, constitute "the history of the college."

RICHARD JONES, history professor: In retrospect, the timing of the Velde Committee episode was unfortunate for the faculty majority. The issues that existed between them and Ballantine prior to the Velde hearings had been on grounds that assured the faculty the support of the bulk of the Reed alumni and of many people interested in Reed. Inspection of the issue of loyalty to the country raised by Velde confused and complicated matters. Even within the trustees, supporters of the faculty's position, who would not have been likely to support chairman Cabell in a head-on collision with the faculty, were dismayed at the prospect of permanent damage to Reed if it became identified in the public mind as a champion of Communists. Some feared that the taint of radicalism might increase agitation for extreme measures such as temporary closure of the college, with reopening delayed until an entirely different social and academic structure had been adopted.

GEORGE JOSEPH '51, trustee 1972–1980: I never liked Stanley Moore. He was arrogant, he was mean, and, if you were not up to his intellectual standards, you didn't count. But still, the way the Reed administration and the Board of Trustees treated him was totally unacceptable to me and most other Reedites, at least those of us who spoke out on such things. That began what turned out to be a thirty-eight-year crusade to rectify the Stanley Moore firing.

ERNEST BONYHADI '48, trustee: I was on the Board of Trustees in 1981. We gave Moore an apology of sorts, but we didn't make it an apology. We passed a resolution basically saying that if the matter had come up before the current board, we would have handled it differently. We

didn't think it was appropriate for us to retract the action that the board took back then.

THE BOARD OF TRUSTEES OF REED COLLEGE, resolution, May 23, 1981: RESOLVED that the Board of Trustees affirms the policy of the College with respect to academic freedom and tenure as stated in the Constitution and Rules of Procedure of the Faculty of Reed College and in the Bylaws of the Reed Institute.

FURTHER RESOLVED that it regrets the action taken by the Board of Trustees which resulted in the dismissal of Professor Stanley Moore in 1954, and welcomes him into the company of former faculty members on the same basis as if his departure had been entirely voluntary. It believes the 1954 action to be inconsistent with the board's interpretation of the principles of academic freedom and with our view as to how these principles should be applied.

TIME magazine, "Reed Tries Again," October 18, 1954: When Duncan S. Ballantine was appointed its president in 1952, Oregon's Reed College got its fifth new administration in just twice as many years. Long noted for its lively liberalism, Reed sometimes seems to carry freedom almost to the point of chaos. Last week, after only two years, Duncan Ballantine had quit.

A lanky, boyish-looking man of forty-one, Ballantine, who has a Ph.D. from Harvard, seems the sort of scholarly man any scholarly college would want. But other colleges do not share Reed's almost fanatical belief in the power of the faculty and the student body. Example: when Ballantine suggested that the faculty council should not have the final say on faculty salaries, his suggestion was rejected.

Last June, without consulting the faculty, Ballantine temporarily suspended an art professor for refusing to answer questions before the Velde Committee. By a thirty-eight-to-nine vote, the faculty passed a resolution expressing a "grave weakening" of confidence in the president.

Last week the trustees picked as president Frank L. Griffin, seventy-three, former mathematics professor. And the question still remains, said Duncan Ballantine bitterly, "Does Reed really want a president?"

JEAN TIBBITTS THIÉBAUX '57: My grandfather, F. L. Griffin, had been the first professor hired by William Foster when the college opened in 1911. Since retiring from teaching mathematics at Reed in 1952, he had been teaching at Wesleyan and then at Washington University in St. Louis. His return as interim president during my sophomore year was hard for me because both the faculty and the students were extremely dissatisfied with the administration of the college under President Ballantine, and they were not of a mind to have someone they regarded as old and conservative come back and take the lead of the college. But I was very proud to see how my grandparents managed to get people reunited in following the founding principles of Reed College again.

FRANK LOXLEY "F. L." GRIFFIN, mathematics professor 1911–1952, president 1954–1956: Though I was a dyed-in-the-wool "Taft Republican," I greatly resented the intrusion of a Congressional committee trying to take over what I considered to be the function of our courts of law.

The trustees put me in office with the objective of clearing up the disagreements with the faculty and serving until a suitable younger president could be found. At the same time they decided to suspend the operation of the constitution of Reed College, which had been in effect since 1915, and authorized me, after suitable consultation with the faculty, to decide what administrative measures could be temporarily put into effect in lieu of the old constitutional measures. My immediate predecessor, Dr. Ballantine, had proposed a

number of modifications to the constitution, but more than a year of ineffectual discussion with the faculty had brought no agreement.

I had been one of the five men who wrote the Reed constitution in 1915, and I had frequently expressed my admiration for many of its provisions. It obligated the president to consult an elected Faculty Council before sending to the trustees his recommendations as to budgetary and faculty personnel matters, thus letting the trustees know whether or not the recommendations had the approval of the faculty committee. Over the years, with the permission or encouragement of several Reed presidents, the Faculty Council came to perform administrative acts that went considerably beyond its original advisory role. Such supplementary functions slightly blurred at times the respective roles of the president and the faculty.

My first step as president was to call together all the members of the faculty and indicate that while I thoroughly believed in the measures of the constitution, I had an open mind with respect to the possible need for changes of some procedures. I gave the faculty a choice between three separate plans of administration. I was very much pleased when they chose, by heavy majority, the plan that appealed most to me. After a one-year trial, there was a full agreement on the general procedures of the new plan.

RICHARD JONES, history professor: F. L. Griffin recognized that the Board of Trustees wanted things to be changed, and that they were going to close the college, literally, if they weren't. Consequently, he went about trying to organize things in such a way as to restore the kind of general conditions that we had had, but also in such as way as to get the board to accept them. He did away with the Faculty Council, substituting in its place a Faculty Advisory Committee, in which five of the members would be elected and five would be appointed by the president.

Griffin was very careful about his presidential appointments. The five faculty members who got the top votes of the faculty were elected. Then, the next five members in the vote ranking were appointed by F. L. This satisfied the people who wanted the change in terms of what the official appearances were, but in action, things were quite the reverse. As acting president his emphasis was on restoring Reed as much as possible to the kind of status and functions that it had formerly had, so that when we got a permanent president, it would be one who would work in those terms.

JOHN POCK, sociology professor 1955–1998: Several of the faculty members had been particularly active in the local ACLU chapter, and the ACLU's position on academic freedom was very close to the ideology of the constitution that we eventually adopted under Griffin. It basically said that the faculty, and not the administration, determined the curriculum, and that the faculty had a right to express their opinions politically outside of the classroom, and, in doing so, were not speaking for the institution.

It was accepted with some compromise. One of the compromises was to give the president the ability to give administrative personnel like the librarian and the vice-presidents faculty status. Many of us felt that this would automatically give the president a block of votes in voting and discussions.

MICHAEL MUNK '56: When F. L. Griffin became acting president, the trustees made him send a questionnaire to every faculty member asking whether they or any of their colleagues had any Communist sympathies. There was also a loyalty oath that the trustees required the faculty to take as a condition of employment.

JOE ROBERTS, mathematics professor 1952– : I initially refused to sign the loyalty oath, the so-called "positive oath." They let that go for quite a while, but then they started pushing it. I went downtown to discuss the matter with an ACLU lawyer. I ultimately did sign it, but it was probably something that I should not have done. I was worried about my family. It's not one of the moments that I feel proud about. Who knows what makes people do things against their grain?

DOROTHY MOORE EDLIN '56: During the time of the Velde Committee, we had started a student club called "FOCUS," which brought leftist speakers to campus. In the fall of '54, right after Duncan Ballantine had resigned, FOCUS wanted to bring folksinger Pete Seeger to Reed. The administration didn't want Seeger on campus. I went to F. L. Griffin's office as part of a FOCUS delegation with Mike Munk '56 and Steve Vause '58 to persuade him to lift the ban against Seeger. Griffin said no, that he had to draw the line because Reed was being threatened with withdrawal of its major supporters. "We almost weren't able to open the school this fall," he told us. "The school is not going to continue if you guys continue your activities." I was sympathetic to his position, but Mike and Steve were not. They weren't going to back down. We finally got permission to bring Seeger here, on the condition that there would be no outside publicity.

The Seeger concert was a big event that packed the Student Union. Everybody was singing. They made a bootleg recording of the concert at Reed, which was put out on a record called *We Sing*.

NANCY NOMLAND BERNHARDT '55: Seeger at the time was included in the *Red Channels*, a booklet that became a blacklist for entertainers. He is credited by some with creating the "college circuit" in his effort to survive. His concert tour was put together by my brother, which was how we got him at Reed. It was blissful, Pete playing in the Student Union surrounded by all these little subverts just cheering him on.

CHAPTER 19

The Sputnik Turnaround

The Cold War between the Soviet Union and the United States turned on science, not guns. Everybody who could add two and two was called upon, out of patriotism, to try to master a scientific education and put it to the use of the country.
  —Michael Nelken '60

Reed discovered money at the end of the 1950s.
  —Leslie Squier, psychology professor

By the mid-1950s, Reed had earned a reputation in the academic world as a "grave-yard for presidents." Including interim leaders, the college had gone through five presidents in the previous ten years, with an average term of two and a half years.

In 1956, Richard Sullivan became Reed's eighth president. A Harvard graduate and World War II veteran, Sullivan had served as executive vice-president and treasurer of the Educational Testing Service in Washington, D.C. He arrived with an informed understanding of the dramatic transformations ahead for higher education in the next decade, driven primarily by the growing demand for college-educated employees, the government's investment in education as a defense strategy in the Cold War, and the coming tsunami of students making up the demographic phenomenon known as the "Baby Boom." Sullivan entered the college with an eye toward renewing its promise by aligning it with these new trends.

His first step was to reposition Reed in the public's imagination as an important asset in the Cold War fight against the Soviet Union, which soon after Sullivan's appointment launched the world's first unmanned spaceship, Sputnik 1. To do so meant modernizing the school's physical plant and its teaching resources. It seemed an impossible task, given that Reed's endowment stood at $3.5 million for seven hundred students, compared with $15 million for nine hundred students at Swarthmore. In a dramatic break from the college's historically prudent approach to financial management, Sullivan convinced the trustees to take a gamble and proceed with a massive upgrade before full funding was secured.

Presidents Richard Sullivan and F. L. Griffin, during the transition from Griffin to Sullivan in 1956.

ERNEST BOYD "E. B." MACNAUGHTON, trustee 1919–1941, 1955–1958, president 1948–1952: Looking back at all of the men invited to the Reed presidency prior to the appointment of Richard Sullivan, the search committees of faculty and trustee representatives chose people on a scholastic basis, dressed up with Ph.D.s, and with noble ideas but naïve as newborn babes in administrative problems. The choice of Richard Sullivan corrected all that. It reflected a change across the whole country in understanding the problems of leadership in academic institutions. A man can have all the doctorate degrees in the world but that doesn't add up to peanuts if he hasn't had experience in the lower echelons of administration and foundation operation, and an acquaintance with the relationships of the large groups—trustees, faculty, alumni, and students—that give guidance to colleges, public relations, and public contacts. That basically was the mistake with all of Dr. Sullivan's predecessors.

ELLEN KNOWLTON JOHNSON '39, recorder 1945–1962, registrar 1962–1981: Starting with

Sullivan, a good part of the president's job shifted to raising money. The academic intellectual stimulation remained there partly, but raising money became a much more important part of the job. Sullivan was able to find money for special projects, and he also got some generous local businessmen and donors on the board of trustees like John Gray, Howard Vollum '36, and Richard Wollenberg, who would prove critical in the decades to come.

My personal feeling was that the whole college turned around thanks to Dick Sullivan. He was intelligent, thoughtful, and kind, but at the same time no easy pushover. He thoroughly believed in Reed, and he came at a time when new ideas about education, especially in regard to national defense, were just fomenting. He picked them up and acted on them. We had a comparatively peaceful, forward-moving time when he was president.

HUBERT CHRESTENSON, mathematics professor 1957–1990: What was Sullivan like? Endless work. When I was serving on the Faculty

Advisory Committee I saw that he would go home with the whole budget of the college, and go over it in detail. He may have had a presidential assistant at some point, but he did a lot of the nitty-gritty work himself.

DOROTHY MOORE EDLIN '56: Sullivan was a fundraiser, but he was very conservative too. I had an experience with him at the first Christmas dance formal he attended. A friend of mine who had left Reed for a couple of years suddenly showed up at the formal. I was thrilled to see him, and we gave each other a very friendly, enthusiastic hug. It just so happened that Sullivan was standing close by. He turned away with a look of disgust, and then apparently mentioned to people that he had been appalled by our embrace. That sort of East Coast snobbery made him a bit of a stuffed shirt to me.

RICHARD SULLIVAN, president 1956–1967: One of the subtle but important needs when I arrived was to create a sense of forward movement at Reed, of moving ahead with confidence that there was a future for the college. After three months, I presented the Board of Trustees with some ideas on budgeting, deficit spending, and risk taking.

These ideas were a shock to many members of the board, because for eight years this kind of approach had not been taken. The college had had conservative management of financial affairs—a balancing of the budget by decreasing expenditures while increasing intake. The restraining effect of this practice, coupled with the prior four years of marking time, made it seem that the only way to make improvements involved money.

You can either wait until you have money and then make some moves, or you can make some moves which essentially help you raise the money. That was the risk Reed had to take as I saw it. The board gulped and went along. We studied long-range financing problems, facilities needed, size of the freshman class, and other interrelated things. It was a strong dose of medicine for the board, but my intuitive feeling was that this was the only way they could act. There were a number of one-man departments at the college, which meant that we had a thin set of upperclass offerings in a number of areas.

There was also a question of balance of faculty and curriculum between science and all the non-science disciplines. Science was strong at Reed and growing stronger than the other fields. Finally, there were poor facilities for the work of a lot of people—labs, faculty offices, the library, and most dramatic, the lack of facilities in the broad fields of the arts.

RICHARD JONES, history professor 1941–1982, 1985–1986: Sullivan's task was eased at the outset by two grants from the Ford Foundation. Together they permitted the college to make unusually rapid progress on faculty salary improvement at a critical time, with a significant advance in faculty morale. Morale was also lifted by a decisive change in relationship between the trustees and the president and faculty. Sullivan instituted a series of informal meetings at which trustees and faculty members could discuss matters of concern to the college and its educational processes. The result was a complete reversal of the suspicious, fearful adversarial relationship that had prevailed more or less since the controversy with President Dexter Keezer in the early 1940s through the presidency of Duncan Ballantine.

Under Sullivan, every department was involved in the process of revision and upgrading. Far more important was the general atmosphere of optimism and the cooperative spirit that permeated every segment of the Reed community. Sullivan's achievement in welding the community together underscored the remarkable capacity of administrative policy, itself directed toward no specific curricular purpose, either to accelerate or dampen curricular progress.

LESLIE SQUIER, psychology professor 1953–1988, dean of students 1955–1962: For a long time the college depended on the long hours of the faculty to make up the difference in financial means. With Sullivan the picture began to change. Reed discovered money at the end of the 1950s.

MICHAEL NELKEN '60: The Cold War between the Soviet Union and the United States turned on science, not guns. Everybody who could add two and two was called upon, out of patriotism, to try to master a scientific education and put it to the use of the country. The laboratories were the battlefields.

RICHARD SULLIVAN, president: The growing public concern for education, coupled with American competition with Russia, especially after the Russian satellite Sputnik launched in 1957, along with predictions for the need for educated manpower in business, government, and industry in the face of technological advance, led to more direct action by the federal government in support of higher education, beginning in the 1950s.

A number of national studies showed that for its size Reed had had the most productive record in educating young scientists of all the colleges and universities in the country. That record had been accomplished literally out of basements and attics on the campus. That could no longer suffice in modern terms.

HERB GLADSTONE, music professor 1946–1980: When chemistry professor Arthur Scott was interim president during the war, he had given a big go-ahead signal to the construction of a new chemistry building. The feeling among some faculty, especially the humanities people,

was that Scottie had railroaded the new building through ahead of other priorities. He also set about getting a nuclear reactor for the college.

THOMAS DUNNE, chemistry professor 1963–1995: Things got hot with nuclear energy right after the war. Arthur Scott was thinking pretty early on about having a working reactor at the college, and during his stint as acting president he set out to get one. A pickle barrel reactor was installed on campus in 1948. It was a rare thing for an undergraduate college to have, and a huge attraction in recruiting the very best science students in the country.

NICHOLAS WHEELER '55, physics professor 1963–2010: Scott raised the money for the nuclear reactor himself from local donors, without the college's assistance. He and his students did some interesting work with it, mainly in connection with off-campus agencies that wanted to do nuclear activation analysis, like the hospitals and

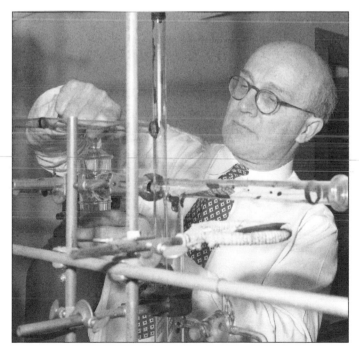

Chemistry professor (and former acting president) Arthur Scott in his laboratory, 1958.

various commercial entities. Reed soon came to have the largest number of student senior reactor operators of any institution in the country.

BERT BREHM, biology professor 1962–1993: Lew Kleinholz came to the biology department at Reed after the war with a level of national recognition that was very influential. Through Lew's influence and stature the biology department obtained a major grant from the Rockefeller Foundation for a new biology building, allowing it to move out of the basement of Eliot Hall.

A strong emphasis on faculty research came to permeate the whole structure and the operation of the department, creating more of a university type of organization than was usually found within an undergraduate liberal arts college. Grants from the Rockefeller Foundation and later from both the National Institutes of Health and the National Science Foundation provided the opportunity for the Reed biology faculty to have one-fourth of their salaries paid from outside money. That allowed us to enlarge the biology faculty and enriched the program substantially, because we could cover more of the spectrum of the biological disciplines. It also meant there was opportunity for faculty members to continue their research at a professional level. Our faculty research labs provided the opportunity to develop students in a much closer, professional scientific relationship as teacher and mentor than we otherwise might. It was a unique arrangement that the college and the department became recognized nationally for.

LESLIE SQUIER, psychology professor: Reed was perhaps the only four-year college in the country that got a federal grant for a new biology building and for research. That provided an impetus for other departments at Reed. In psychology, we were able to get grants from the National Science Foundation and other federal sources that enabled us to mount a really experimental program in behavioral psychology.

NICHOLAS WHEELER '55, physics professor: The psychology department had become strongly behavioral-oriented, and they spent all their time studying rats and pigeons in their laboratory, with little cages and trip levers and blinking lights. They started getting petitions from students who wanted to meet their science requirement by taking a psychology laboratory, on the grounds that it was a laboratory course.

My colleagues in the science division were very unsympathetic to this, arguing that just because you have a laboratory doesn't make you a scientist. They considered what the psychologists were doing intellectually less respectable than what the chemists, mathematicians, physicists, and biologists were doing. There were impassioned debates. The psychologists' effort was

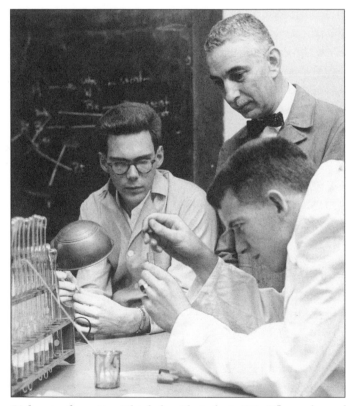

Biology professor Lew Kleinholz with students Otto Pflueger '57 and Paul Burgess '56 in 1955.

to expunge the ghosts from their field—they were coming out of Freudian psychology, where a lot of attributes were attributed to the inner life of the mind, without secure physical basis.

Psychology never did meet any of the science requirements, and the psychology department eventually moved away from strictly behavioral psychology.

HUBERT CHRESTENSON, mathematics professor: The Sputnik era from 1958 through 1964 was the heyday for mathematics and physics. New Math was cropping up.

JOE ROBERTS, mathematics professor 1952– : When I came to Reed in the early 1950s both the freshman and the sophomore math courses were taught out of books written in the '20s by the department's founding professor, F. L. Griffin. They were much more tied to physics and applications, and less to the theoretical side of mathematics. We moved to a more theoretically oriented curriculum, and in the process we stopped using Griff's books.

NICHOLAS WHEELER '55, physics professor: I took the last course F. L. Griffin taught on analytical geometry before he retired. On our first day of class seven or eight of us were sitting there when the door opened and in strode Professor Griffin. He threw open all the windows to the cold February air and said, "Extinguish your cigarettes, gentlemen, and go to the blackboard." He hadn't yet told us anything. No class had taken place, but we were at the blackboard. He asked us to write down an equation with some other terms, and then to draw that figure, and finally to find a change of coordinates that reduced it to a simpler form.

We stood there shivering in the cold at the blackboard. We didn't know how to do any of this stuff. At that moment he was teaching us how much we didn't know, and how much we were going to learn if we paid attention to what he was about to tell us. He humiliated us. I've never seen anybody try anything like that in a class at Reed since. Mathematicians were beginning to look way down their noses at F. L.'s approach because there was nothing abstract in it; it was all procedural, all practical. But it had set a teaching standard across the country prior to the 1950s.

Tony Knowlton, who had taught physics since 1915, had set another standard at Reed. He was a scary, white-haired man who never spoke to any of us. Ann Shepard '23, the dean, once said that she was visited by a Reed physics major who was in tears. "Why are you so sad?" she asked. "Knowlton comes into the laboratory," the student said, "and he criticizes the work of this guy and that guy, but he doesn't say anything to me. He doesn't criticize me at all. He doesn't seem to think that I matter."

In the 1920s Knowlton decided to base an introductory physics course on a single question: how does the sun get its energy? Then, in a Socratic kind of way, the students had to contemplate, well, could it be combustion? If so, what's the physics of combustion? They considered various alternatives and contractions until Knowlton led them to the realization that it had to be the conversion of matter into energy. It had to be $e = mc^2$ in action. First-year physics students in the '20s came to this conclusion before the discovery of the nuclear processes that are responsible for the sun's energy, or indeed, for the energy of stars in general, was made. Knowlton then wrote that approach up as a popular textbook. He was not a very productive physicist by modern standards, but an extraordinarily high rate of people who passed through his classes went on to successful scientific careers.

MICHAEL NELKEN '60: My favorite teacher in physics was Jean DeLord, who had a gorgeous French accent and a French way of life that he

Professor F. L. Griffin, at right, teaching one of his final mathematics classes in the early 1950s.

brought with him as well. He would come to my thesis lab and we would have a glass of wine together and talk about life, but very seldom about physics because we both understood that wine was more important than either life or physics. He gave me a great example of how to balance being a human being with having a career.

NICHOLAS WHEELER '55, physics professor: I was disappointed in my senior year to find that Jean Delord, who was admired as the deepest physicist of the faculty, and the sweetest person, would not be teaching that year. He had taken leave to work full-time at Tektronix, a large electronics company started in Portland by a Reed graduate and longtime trustee, Howard Vollum '36. To fill in for Delord the college hired a Turkish physicist named Asim Barut, fresh out of postdoctoral work at the University of Chicago.

Barut had never taught before, but it became rapidly clear that he knew a lot of physics, and he

didn't realize that we were only seniors. He presented on the blackboard his perception of all basic physics—classical mechanics, electrodynamics, relativity, quantum mechanics, and statistical mechanics—far beyond the normal curriculum, and illegally expanded the course from three hours a week to seven hours a week, which we all faithfully attended. We were a jolly gang. We frequently spent evenings in the heating tunnels that ran from one of end the campus to the other, setting up a table and a bare light bulb down there, and sitting around in 110-degree heat having good times together.

DOROTHY JOHANSEN '33, history professor 1934–1969, archivist 1969–1984: During the 1950s, there emerged a "science image" of Reed, as the college came to represent the scientific goals in not only the natural sciences but also in other parts of the curriculum, including behavioral psychology, analytical philosophy, rational choice theory and other emerging scientific approaches to the social sciences and history, as well as literature with the scientific methodology of New Criticism.

Yet, despite the efforts of various image makers in charge of college marketing and propaganda, the change process of the college was more emergent than transformative in nature, incorporating all that had gone before. The image that the college had projected in its first decade was that of a progressive institution whose graduates would serve society in various ways, including through ministry, social science, law, medicine, teaching, and community service. Following the devastation of the First World War, the image of the college in the 1920s and '30s shifted to what might be called "humanistic," with an emphasis not upon societal obligations but on personal, individualized, and moral obligations derived from classical examples.

With the rise of the "scientific" image in the 1950s, these prior images were not lost. They continued to carry over through the following decades, although not as dominant themes.

BILL PECK, philosophy professor 1961–2002: Philosophy was going through quite a change in the late 1940s and '50s with a new school of thought called "analytic" philosophy, which emphasizes logic and the philosophy of science and related disciplines. It deals with metaphysics and what is called "the theory of knowledge," which are chief categories in philosophy, but in the hands of analytic philosophers those things are treated in the kind of terms that you would expect from people who are immersed in science and the scientific method.

That was not my cup of tea at all. I taught the history of philosophy in the modern period, which many analytic philosophers considered literary, rather than philosophical. My interest in German philosophy separated me from most American philosophers, including my col-

leagues. Marvin Levich, who came to the department in 1953, was part of the new school. He was conscious of being in a vanguard of philosophy reform.

MICHAEL LEVINE '62, trustee 1984–2002: Marvin Levich was a curiously dominating figure. He had a bachelor's degree but hadn't finished his Ph.D., presumably because he couldn't find anything worth committing to. Although he was only about five-four, he was a giant in the sight of the students. His wit was always sardonic. He was careful never to show softness or emotional weakness. He always had an argument, and his arguments always were complex. They all had long prefatory statements. In some ways Levich was terrific, but in other ways he was giving you a picture of the intellectual as a caricature—a person who talked a lot and didn't do much, who could put on a great show in a debate, but who wasn't supposed to have a human side. He would always have a cigarette in his mouth. He would be talking around it and puffing on it, and when he finished one he would immediately pick up another one. It was a little bizarre.

JOHN POCK, sociology professor 1955–1998: In sociology, I felt it was my responsibility to get students to understand that the scientific method could be and was being applied to social issues; not to social problems, necessarily, but to asking the questions: "How does society work? What holds it together?"

If you were interested in talking about current events and social problems, you wouldn't get very much of that in my introductory sociology course, although it was called Introduction to Sociology. What you got instead was an introduction to the idea that the political and the economic aspects of things, along with the ideas of cultural and philosophic belief systems, and finally the social structure were all intermixed and interrelated, and that one could think about a thing like society in the same way as one could think about vertebrae.

PATTY LEAVEY KRISCH '59: John Pock had a guru quality. If you were a freshman taking his introductory sociology-anthropology course, he would encourage you to have lunch with him. There would be was six or eight people at a table, and he would hold forth about sociology at lunch. At first it was very appealing, your professor wanting you to join him for lunch. But when you became an upperclassman, lunch with him became sort of an obligation. It wasn't just the classroom experience we were having. We were having conversation over a meal four or five days a week.

MARVIN LEVICH, philosophy professor 1953–1994, provost 1972–1979: The National Defense Education Act of 1958, which provided funding to education institutions following the Russians' launch of Sputnik, had a mandate that all beneficiaries must complete an affidavit disclaiming belief in the overthrow of the U. S. government.

Despite the fact that Reed's endowment was quite small at the time and so money was scarce, the faculty took the stand that a person's political position was irrelevant to being a member of the college. President Sullivan reluctantly agreed to accept that stand. Reed became one of a handful of colleges in America which refused funds otherwise provided by the National Defense Education Act. Eventually more colleges protested the mandate, and it was overturned in 1964.

It was a very proud thing for Reed to do, but it was partly possible because there was such a strong distinction between public and private colleges at the time. Private institutions, because they were not tax-supported, were considered freer, more independent, and more capable of operating as social critics than was the case for tax-supported institutions. As the decades passed however, private colleges became as dependent on state and federal support as public colleges, which eventually came to mean that there was no chance whatever that an action mandated by the federal government, however heinous and horrible, would be refused by Reed College.

JOHN POCK, sociology professor: Chemistry professor John Hancock and I both arrived at Reed at the same time, and got involved very early on in computers. The government was giving away computer systems, with a requirement for matching funds. John and I tried to get President Sullivan to go in with us on writing a proposal for one of these give-away programs, but Sullivan couldn't because he didn't have any money; and wouldn't because he didn't know the implications of this stuff—and he didn't care. It was also something that the faculty would have had to sanction, and they would never have sanctioned a computer system in those days. Even John had a lot of problems with the people in natural science on this stuff. The mathematicians weren't interested.

We spent about four years of wrangling before we got a National Science Foundation grant to cover the government's requirement of matching funds. With the money we were able to get a rinky-dink IBM computer.

DAVID DIGBY '57: John Hancock was one of a small group of people worldwide trying to create a hydrocarbon molecule they called "dodecahedron" because it was shaped like a dodecahedron—a three-dimensional shape with twelve plane faces. He wanted me to write a computer program to calculate how many different isomers you would have if you put X number of chlorines in place of the hydrogens. At the time I had graduated from Reed and was then a graduate student at Oregon State University. I wrote a program on the vacuum-tube, rotating-drum computer at Oregon State that took up an entire room. It ran about a hundred hours to create a stack of somewhere around seventeen thousand different isomers.

Hancock then wanted to create a machine that would take an arbitrary combination of chlorines and rotate it around to find the one he was after, something he called the Dodecahedron Isomer Machine with Internal Translation, or DIMWIT. He had arranged with the local sheriff, who was confiscating pinball machines from various nefarious characters, to donate a pile of pinball-machine parts. I designed a machine from these parts, and Hancock got his chemistry students to build it. It would only come up with the right answer about one time in ten.

So Hancock got the telephone company downtown, which was remodeling their telephone systems, to donate a big pile of telephone stuff. I designed another version of the same machine using telephone relays this time, and again Hancock's students built it. This machine stood about six feet high, and it went "clickity-clack, clickity-clack," with lights that flashed in the front of it. It came up with the right answer about nine times out of ten.

PETER LANGSTON '68: I saw John Hancock give a talk about FORTRAN computer language and I got all fired up about Reed's computer. It was an IBM 1620, a machine designed for scientific computations. Its memory was cores—tiny magnetic rings—but you could almost see the bits with your eyes. They were that big. The entire memory of the machine was about 16 kilobytes. The console was the size of an upright piano and a half. The computer had a disk drive on it that was the size of a washing machine and contained maybe 64 kb. The printer was the size of another piano. The card reader, which was the size of yet another piano, had an IBM Executive electric typewriter.

I fell in love with that computer. I started spending all my time in the computer center,

Chemistry professor John Hancock with Reed's first student-built computer, the DIMWIT.

working on programs. I wrote programs for music, and actually got a performance on the TV news of one of my music-playing computer programs doing a double violin concerto with a live violinist.

BERT BREHM, biology professor: The biology department was small and exceedingly cohesive. Every Friday afternoon we held seminars where we invited outside speakers with real prominence in the disciplines. We didn't have a budget for entertaining, so we all took turns in hosting the guest speakers. On Friday evenings after the seminar, we invited the entire biology faculty, department associates, and all of our thesis students to one of our houses, and we would make a punch bowl and some inexpensive party food. We always included the wives. It was a very enriched kind of intellectual and social experience.

The other thing that reinforced this cohesiveness was that all of the biology faculty participated in the introductory biology course—Lew Kleinholz, Gabe Lester, Helen Stafford, Larry Ruben, Frank Gwilliam. We all sat in on the whole course. If I was lecturing in biology, all my colleagues would be sitting in the back row. Since we didn't have graduate students and assistants to do a lot of the things like grade papers, the lecturer made up the exam and passed it around to the rest of the faculty for comments and changes. Each person also helped grade the exams. It was a very rich, time-consuming form of total involvement. Just totally absorbing. Most of the time I went home in the evening, had supper, put the kids to bed, then came back to the lab and worked until two AM. There was more activity there at midnight than there was at noon.

MERTIE HANSEN MULLER '56: Sex discrimination was alive and well, in that most of the women in science were biologists. That was an acceptable field for women but not physics. I was the only girl in the physics class. The rest of the physics students had already had trigonometry and calculus before coming to college. I had not. I loved the labs, but didn't understand a lot of the theory, although I learned it quick. Dr. William Parker, who headed up the physics department, definitely wasn't a sexist, but he realized that no matter how good the women students were, we weren't going to be accepted to Ph.D. programs in physics. He advised me to take chemistry.

But being a woman in that field was also sort of a liability at the time. Our class started out with about twenty-five chemistry majors and we graduated with eight, two of us women. One of my classmates, who was top of the class and absolutely brilliant, was offered a job interview in her senior year with a big chemical company back East. They paid her way to go back and be interviewed, but when she got there she found out that they didn't want her as a chemist, they wanted her to run their library. That was pretty typical.

GEORGE ALDERSON '63: The Reed science curriculum prepared you for anything in the sciences. In the introductory biology course, for example, you got a load of genetics, a load of embryology, and just a lot of different components of biology. But it was up to us, the students, to integrate them into our own views of biology. There was nothing in the curriculum that told you, "This is the framework, and this is what you're going to learn, and this is what it all means." It was one of those things typical of Reed—they taught you certain things, equipped you with certain skills, but then it was your responsibility to absorb it and create the framework.

One of the best examples of that was the final exam we were given in one of the upper-division biology courses. The professor told each of us to write our own questions and then answer them, using all the notes and books we had plus any-

Student Paul Burgess '56 (center) with biology professors Helen Stafford and Richard Siegel, 1955.

thing we could find in the biology library. He told us how many questions to write, but the rest was up to us. This was both flattering and challenging. It was up to me to ask myself questions to which I didn't know the answers, and then use what I had learned to figure out the answers.

JOHN GRAEF '60: The way science was being taught had to do with what students could bear. It wasn't about, "Well, we have to do X, Y, and Z in class today." There was not that kind of straightforward rigidity to follow.

The best example was Marsh Cronyn '40, who taught organic chemistry. Marsh was a creative teacher who could take a dry subject and make it come alive. He was famous for never answering a question, instead answering it with another question. You just never knew from day to day how he was going to present the material. But, whatever approach he took, if you stuck with him, the chances were that you would come to make sense of it. At Reed, it was a case of *res ipsa loquitur*—"the thing speaks for itself."

ABRAHAM BERGMAN '54: I took organic chemistry with Marsh Cronyn '40 and worked my ass off, after which he gave me a C. You weren't supposed to know your grades, but of course, you did. I went to him and I said, "What if I don't get into medical school because of this grade?" He looked at me and he said, "How do you think I'd feel if you went to medical school and screwed up?"

You had to be smart to get into Reed, but that wasn't enough. You also had to work hard. We had guys who were more brilliant than the professors, but they flunked out. The fact that the professors knew you and you couldn't BS, that alone was a discipline in critical thinking, of learning to speak your mind, of learning to question everything. "What do you mean?" "Why do

Chemistry professor Marsh Cronyn '40 with Linus Pauling, 1959.

you say that?" "What's your evidence for that?" Those kinds of questions were constantly facing you, and you had to answer them. Thanks to that, you came out of Reed thinking highly of yourself, and you didn't back down from anybody, especially when it came to questioning the conformity of the status quo.

MARSH CRONYN '40, chemistry professor 1952–1989, provost 1982–1989: During the late '50s I went to an educational conference that was all about post-Sputnik—what do we do about education in this country to address it, and so forth. There were people there from colleges all around the country. What they all wanted to know was what we were doing at Reed to graduate all these people who went on to get Ph.D.s. They wanted to know all about the humanities course and the thesis and the junior qual. It was a real eye opener.

CHAPTER 20

Inside a Cultural Bubble

We were conscientiously remote and isolative by explicit wish—almost as a semi-religious devotion.
   —Michael Nelken '60

Reed was ruled by a sort of bootstrap effort of the students.
   —John Graef '60

The intense focus on academic rigor at Reed discouraged the sorts of extracurricular activities that lent balance to student life elsewhere. Students drawn to Reed because of its lack of fraternities and intercollegiate sports also tended to avoid organized group pursuits. Among eight colleges surveyed in a 1960 study at the University of California at Berkeley, Reed students showed the least interest in participating in extracurricular activities or in student government. They also spent the most time per week—thirty to fifty hours—studying outside the classroom. In such an environment, academic hurdles such as the freshman humanities course, the junior qualification exam, and the senior thesis tended to create more of an esprit de corps on campus than any extracurricular activity or even the identification with one's class year.

The college's limited offerings in studio and performing arts did not help to address the imbalance. In the place of structured college programs, students and faculty improvised activities based on shared passions, such as community productions of Gilbert and Sullivan comic operas, which from the late 1940s through the mid-1960s served the purpose filled by "the Big Game" at other colleges.

JIM KAHAN '64: I got on a train, six o'clock in the evening in Los Angeles, bound for Portland. The guy who got on with me was David Kanouse '64, who has remained my closest friend ever since. The overnight train ran up to Oakland where a whole batch of other people bound for Reed joined us in the morning. We basically had a car full of Reedies. We arrived at Portland's Union Station at eleven o'clock at night. Jay Rosenberg '63, who was then starting his sophomore year, came down to the train station in his car to give people a ride to campus. He remained one of my good friends all his life. That was characteristic of Reed—friendships lasted.

I initially got in with a strange group of people on campus who were all different, not mainstream, and I thought, "Oh, these are the weird ones." But it turned out everybody was weird. I didn't fit in, but it didn't matter, because nobody really fit in, which meant that it was okay not to fit in. That was part of the paradoxical magic of Reed.

HARVEY BLAU '63: I grew up in a place called Glendora in the rural San Gabriel Valley of southern California. I had never been outside a sixty-mile radius of town until I left for Reed. We initially went up to Lake Breitenbush in the Cascades near Mt. Jefferson for freshman orientation. The other students were way more talented and knowledgeable of things than anyone I had encountered in my relatively sheltered life. When we got back to campus, I got my first taste of one of the negative things about Reed, which was that some students were not hesitant about putting people down wherever there was a chance to do so.

In principle I had known about the work load at Reed, but you don't really know about it until you're in it. When you've got to read half of the *Iliad* the first week, and the other half the second week, plus all these pages of Greek history and Plato, and then write your first paper the first Friday night because it's due Saturday morning—well, it was quite an eye opener. On Friday nights you could look across campus at all hours of the night and see lights on in the residence halls. Everyone was working through the night. When I first arrived, everyone looked really bright-eyed and clean-cut. By the end of the second week, everyone was wandering around disheveled, unshaven, glazed over, saying, "What is this? Why am I here?"

BERT BREHM, biology professor 1962–1993: Bill Alderson, who taught English and humanities, was known as a ferocious putter-downer. A student got his first humanities paper back from Alderson and looked at the first page, which was nice and clean. The second page was also nice and clean, no comments, no marks, no nothing. "Wow, I must have overwhelmed him," the student thought. Then, on the back of the second page, he found a little comment from Alderson: "This is a wonderful paper. Too bad you had to spoil it by writing on it."

That was the kind of story I heard as a young faculty member from older faculty.

ROY DOOLAN '58: I spent ages five to eight in a Japanese prison camp in Manila. We came very close to starving to death. When we came out, my parents moved to a small town near Chicago, where I started school. The principal said to my father, "We can teach him to tie his shoes, but that's about it. It turns out he has an IQ of forty. We just won't be able to handle that." Several years later we were back in that same principal's office discussing my skipping ahead a grade.

When my letter from Reed came, it said that due to my low SAT scores I was not of Reed caliber. My father then wrote a letter explaining that they should be looking at my grades and not my SAT scores. That letter got me in. I came to Reed with great trepidation about all the difficult people I was going to have to compete with. Then, once there, I found out that all of the problems I was having in a small town with my nerdy behavior and strange beliefs was the norm at Reed. It was wonderful! I said to myself, "I'm home."

HERSCHEL SNODGRASS '59: There was a Reed recruitment film that I saw in high school before I came to Reed. First of all you see a darkened room in the film, and then you see a windowpane with raindrops falling on it. The camera pans the room and there's a light there, a lone light, and there you see a hunched-over figure at an old desk. Then the commentary begins, "At Reed College we study hard. We study hard in the hard, cold rain." That film was just pulling students in.

STEVE MCCARTHY '66, trustee 1988–2009: I had very good grades and very good board scores, and I wasn't dependent on a scholarship, so I could have gone literally anywhere. It was a time when people were often turning down Harvard and Yale to go to Reed. It was not uncommon. Reed offered what I was interested in, which was freedom to think unconventionally and a real focus on studying.

Even though I had done well in high school and loved hard work, Reed was tougher academically than I had expected. I had the same experience that many people did, which was that everybody there was just as smart or smarter than I was. That was an interesting shock. I wasn't able to BS my way through things the way I had done in high school. My career at Reed was a roller coaster of incredible hard work and some accomplishment, and then generally a meltdown of one sort or another, followed by a recovery, more great heights, and then another meltdown.

RICHARD DANZIG '65, trustee 1984–1988: I went to Bronx Science in New York. You needed to take a test to be admitted. It was 98 percent Jewish and quite intellectual, and everybody went to college. In 1961 it was well-known that there were quotas for the Ivy League schools. Harvard took eight people from Bronx Science every year. Yale took three. Princeton took one. The school had a rule that you could only apply to three colleges because they had limited resources to support the applications process. Also, you were automatically admitted to City University of New York if you graduated in good standing. I picked Yale, Harvard, and Reed.

I didn't get into Harvard or Yale, and was disap-

pointed, but happy to go to Reed. I realized how lucky I had been when I came home at Christmas my freshman year and saw my friends who had gone to reputable places across the country but weren't comparably excited about them. They hadn't been catalyzed by college. There weren't any adults on the Reed campus at night, apart from the night watchman, who was a very marginal though congenial figure. Other places were dominated by graduate students or by the faculty or the administration. Reed seemed to me to be of the students and for the students.

HOWARD WOLPE '60: Almost everyone was fresh out of high school. One exception was a thirteen-year-old who arrived in my junior year, Leonard Ross '63. Ross had won $64,000 on the television game show *The $64,000 Challenge*, and another $100,000 on *The Big Surprise*, both on the subject of the stock market. Lenny was remarkable to see on campus. He succeeded to the extent that he ended up finishing his law degree at Yale by the time he was eighteen, then taught at Harvard before going on to work for California governor Jerry Brown and President Jimmy Carter. But he ended up having a tragic psychological illness, and committed suicide some years later.

MICHAEL LEVINE '62, trustee 1984–2002: Perhaps the most remarkable thing about Lenny's gifts and the way he used them was that he was so natural a person, not merely an intellect. You forgot he was fourteen when he was student body president and a big wheel in the Portland-area Young Democrats. And you didn't see him as a freak. Lenny moved among a student body four to eight years older than he was, not as everybody's favorite kid brother, but as a contemporary, and a contemporary leader at that. It never seemed odd that a young kid should be initiating you into life's mysteries, rather than the reverse.

Michael Levine '62, Virginia Oglesby Hancock '62, Peter Stafford '60, and Bill Jarrico '61, appearing on the television game show College Bowl *in 1960.*

VIRGINIA OGLESBY HANCOCK '62, chemistry associate 1963–1980, music professor 1991– : I was on the *College Bowl* team my sophomore year. *College Bowl* was a television quiz show that was very popular for a number of years. They would get four-person teams from colleges all over the country, fly them to New York, and ask them a lot of questions. You earned scholarship money for your school by going and by winning.

I wound up being named an alternate on the team. Then Lenny Ross '63, who was on the team, was kicked off because the *College Bowl* people said he was a professional. One of the other four dropped out of school, which meant that two of us who were alternates got to go to New York. While we were there, we ran into Duncan Ballantine, who had been Reed's president during the McCarthy witch hunt, in the hotel. He was president of Roberts College in Istanbul at that point. Our coach, history professor Dick Jones, had been one of Ballantine's main critics on the faculty. There was an obvious hostility between these two men in the hotel, although we didn't know what was going on.

Then we went on the show. It was, they said, the most exciting game that they had had, with the highest score of any game up to that time. Our opponents were four students from Purdue University, who had been on the show for several weeks already, and they were real pros. Their engineering department back at Purdue had built a mockup of the set, with the buzzers and everything. We had been practicing at Reed by just slapping the table. Still it was neck-and-neck until the tremendously exciting finish. We lost when one of our people was so excited that he jumped in and answered a question out of turn.

LINDA HAMMILL MATTHEWS '67, trustee 2005– : I was a Portland girl from a modest, middle-class background through and through. When it came time for freshman orientation, my mother made me an appointment at the beauty parlor, where I had my hair permed in a very tight, frizzy curl. She bought me a slinky and shiny rayon dress, with a white pleated skirt and a little yellow-and-white-striped top, which I wore to orientation day with stockings and flats. That particular morning, as I walked across campus, I felt like I had gone from Planet A to Planet B. People had long hair. They wore black. Doon Arbus '67, who was in one of my classes, was the daughter of the photographer Diane Arbus. She was the image of sophistication—black boots, black skirt, curly black hair. She smoked cigarettes. It was just a new world to me. There were people from New York City and Los Angeles. I had never laid eyes on humans from these places in my life. I suspect people were looking at me and saying, "Oh my God, where'd you get *that* outfit?"

I went home and told my mother that I wanted a pair of jeans to wear to school. She was shocked—appalled. She said, "You wear jeans to feed the hogs. You don't wear jeans to school."

HOWARD RHEINGOLD '68: It was 1964, and I was looking for a role model and a sense of direction. Jack Kerouac's *On the Road* was the first hint of that. Then I found out that the Japhy Ryder character in Kerouac's book *The Dharma Bums* was based on Gary Snyder '51, who had gone to Reed. After that, I became fascinated by the Beats as a high school student in Phoenix, Arizona. I had choices about college. I was a National Merit Scholar with a near-perfect grade point average. But going to Harvard or Stanford felt like just a really excellent form of brain death. It seemed to me that there was Reed, and then there was "getting with the program." The notion that there was a college where Gary Snyder felt comfortable was irresistibly attractive.

ARMAND SCHWARTZ '60: Freshman humanities was the thing that changed most of us. The course just knocked the pins out of everybody, and we had to rethink who we were, what we were, and where we were going and why. Greek culture was so alien to what we had grown up with as middle-class white Americans, that it started many of us questioning our values. The purpose of the whole exercise seemed to be to take you apart, examine everything, and then put you back together. It was just like rebuilding an engine. Unfortunately, some of the people who got their engines taken apart never got them put back together.

MICHAEL NELKEN '60: Miles Jordan '59 enjoyed humanities so much that he got a seamstress to make him a toga in gorgeous colors—red and blue, with yellow piping—that he wore to class each day. He actually got a job marching around in front of a theater downtown that had a Cecil B. DeMille costume drama playing, trying to get people to come in to the movie.

STEPHEN ADAMS '61: I saw Miles Jordan '59 walking across the campus in a gorgeous, flowing red toga my first day there, and I said to myself, "I am never looking back."

ROGER PORTER, English professor 1961– : After I gave my first humanities lecture, which was on Shakespeare, my students applauded me when I came back to the humanities conference afterwards. I was twenty-five, only three years older than many of the students. I thought it was so wonderful, just a joy to teach them. One of the students in my class that year sailed into a nuclear test zone in the South Pacific. Another went on a cruise in the Mediterranean. It turned out her aunt was Katherine Graham, the owner of the *Washington Post*. "Was it just the family on the cruise?" I asked. "No," she said, "we had a couple of people on board—Adlai Stevenson and Winston Churchill." One student, Jenny Strauss '62, was the daughter of Leo Strauss, a distinguished political theorist at the University of Chicago and the grandfather of the neo-cons. Her roommate was the stepdaughter of Isaiah Berlin, the noted twentieth-century philosopher.

DOROTHY JOHANSEN '33, history professor 1934–1969, archivist 1969–1984: It was assumed that a happy campus was one in which everyone did the same thing at the same time. That was simply not true. Students had individual needs to meet. "Groupness" was not the answer. It was difficult to hold to any traditions of a social or community nature at Reed. In the early days, campus life was geared to activities that had to do with learning. For example, the faculty encouraged and sponsored student clubs—drama, debate, biology, creative writing, etc. In 1915, 252 students had fifteen clubs. By the 1930s, there were more students but fewer clubs. College festivities like the Christmas program, Canyon Day, and Campus Day continued to draw student participation, but those were occasions when the students came together and then quickly separated, going their own way.

The common bond among Reed students was not in their social life, but in their academic life. One reason for discontent on campus from the beginning was that the administrations failed to realized that they should provide for activities in which students would voluntarily engage—which they themselves would create—rather than try to organize activities from above.

PRISCILLA WATSON LAWS '61: Senior theses were due at noon on a particular day at the registrar's office. Jerry Millstein '61 and I decided it was sort of anticlimactic to just slink into the registrar's office, so we typed up a little note, dittoed it, and stuffed it in every senior's mailbox, just twenty minutes before noon on the due date. It said, "Senior parade. Bring your instruments. Be prepared to sing songs. Have your thesis in hand and we will march into the registrar's office and deliver them."

We were met by a large crew of rumpled, barefoot seniors, all of them convened in front of the library carrying their theses and an eclectic collection of musical instruments—an accordion, a trombone, a trumpet, numerous recorders, timpani, a drumhead. Together we marched to Eliot

Hall, playing various unrehearsed tunes. As we paraded up the stairs toward the registrar's office on the second floor, administrators streamed out of their offices and shook our hands.

Dean of Students Ann Shepard '23 had tears in her eyes and she just kept saying, "This is wonderful. I never thought I'd see Reed students doing something like this in an organized manner." After that, the thesis parade became an annual tradition.

BOB CHARLTON '61: I found that Reed stifled creativity. In all fields, it was more interested in criticism than in creation. Its basic approach was to dissect. Very little was constructed. Feeling was considered sloppiness of thought. That overly critical approach to ideas and the somewhat linear approach to thought that Reed fostered were very destructive to any kind of spontaneous creativity. Most creative endeavors were extracurricular, and students who engaged in them suffered heavily in their studies or their sleep.

ROBERT CROWLEY '49, music professor 1969–1970: At Reed, there had always been an exceedingly strong tradition for art as avocation, an attitude which always looked to me as though it came directly out of Aristotle. Connoisseurship was all. Competence was vulgar.

HERB GLADSTONE, music professor 1946–1980: Reed was a very individual-centered kind of school. There was this feeling that you are your own boss and you had to devote your time to your studies primarily, and the extracurricular stuff was just that—extracurricular.

That was an obstacle. If you're a member of the chorus and you've got a paper due on Friday, you skip Wednesday and Thursday rehearsals, with the justification that "I just haven't got the time. I've got a paper due Friday." As a result, studying music was at a real disadvantage with the students. Drama was in the same boat.

Music professor Herb Gladstone conducting a Sound Experiment in the old Student Union in the early 1950s.

But there was student initiative. When I first got to Reed, two students, Bob Crowley '49 and Curtiss Cowan '48, suggested that we give a series of concerts. Curtiss said, "Let's call them 'Sound Experiments.' We can combine all the arts, like dance, and poetry, and put together a program once a month."

Bill Alderson, who taught English, was interested in old British folk tunes, from madrigal singing in the Elizabethan Period to all kinds of Baroque music. In the early Sound Experiments we did a lot of those things, glees and rounds in the British pub tradition, usually for male singers.

ROBERT CROWLEY '49, music professor: For the first Sound Experiment there were English folk songs, as well as a piece that I wrote performed by some jazz musicians with whom I had been playing dance jobs downtown. For the second concert an exceptional pianist, Lloyd Jones '49,

played a Beethoven violin sonata with another student. Herb Gladstone prepared Brahms' *Neue Liebeslieder*, opus 65, with an octet of singers equally divided between students and faculty. The third concert brought madrigals and recorder performances, music for piano and for violin and piano, as well as orchestral music. The last concert in the series featured modern dance.

HERB GLADSTONE, music professor: After that first year, the Sound Experiments really caught on, and eventually became famous, literally—written up in the *Christian Science Monitor*. They went on for at least fifteen years. We would hold the concerts in the old Student Union, located where Vollum Center is now, which unfortunately burned down in 1969. I say "unfortunately" because it had the right atmosphere. We could set up the string quartet on the stage, or, as we often did, light a fire in the fireplace, and put the orchestra before it and the seats in a great semi-circle around them. You could seat about a hundred. In the meantime there were all these delicious smells coming up from the coffee shop down in the basement.

MOSHE LENSKE '50, trustee 1992–1996: Herb Gladstone's annual Gilbert and Sullivan production was sort of like the Reed football game. Everybody—students, faculty, administrators, local Portland musicians—was involved. Because there were so many people in the production, and everybody was always rehearsing, you would hear the songs all over campus, and so everybody knew them. It was very participatory.

HERB GLADSTONE, music professor: The spring of 1947 we put on Gilbert and Sullivan's *The Pirates of Penzance*, and for some reason or other it clicked. The production was popular largely because the faculty members playing the police were so ridiculous. We had all sizes and shapes. They all got together after the first show for an encore, in which they translated the policeman's chorus—"the policeman's lot is not a happy one"—into Latin and sang it with the effect of bringing down the house. That bit later became a tradition. The show got requests to perform around town, all of which we accepted. Carl Johnson, the drama director, finally said, "We've got to stop because, for one thing, the girls' costumes are falling apart." A French student, Lucille Dejardin '49, had designed the costumes. They were brilliant, but almost entirely made out of paper.

The following year we staged *The Mikado*, the most popular of the dozen shows that Gilbert and Sullivan wrote. Lloyd Reynolds, the head of the art history department, was our make-up artist. He got carried away lots of times, but he certainly did a good job on that show. Due to the phenomenal response we received, we moved the production from the old Student Union to Botsford Gym, which seated about six hundred

people. After that we did a different show each spring—*Iolanthe, The Gondoliers, Patience, Ruddigore*. Six Gilbert and Sullivans in six years, and then we started repeating. In 1959, I got the idea of staging a summer season of Gilbert and Sullivan as part of that year's celebration of the Oregon Centennial.

JUDY TYLE MASSEE, dance professor 1968–1998: Herb Gladstone, with the help of Ernest Bonyhadi '48, created the New Savoy Opera Company and performed at the Portland Civic Auditorium as part of the Oregon Centennial celebration. I had just graduated from Portland State, and became Gladstone's choreographer. Herb brought in lead singers from the San Francisco Opera. He chose the very best people he could find for costume work and stage direction. I enjoyed working with Herb so much, but he was a real taskmaster.

Music professor Herb Gladstone directing a rehearsal of Gilbert and Sullivan's The Mikado, *1956*

The summer of 1960 they were renovating the Civic Auditorium, so we performed in the Oriental Theater on the east side of Portland, which was a copy of Grauman's Oriental Theater in Hollywood. It was a huge, gorgeous, fabulous, acoustical setting, and perfect for Gilbert and Sullivan. Every single performance sold out that summer.

HERB GLADSTONE, music professor: We continued to stage that summer show downtown for five years. The last year was one of our most successful, but that year we were hit very hard by the deaths of some of our longtime players, including Bill Alderson, who taught English at Reed, and his wife, Jean Hanslik, a well-known contralto and opera singer and the only experienced professional in the cast. Over the years I had done more than 250 performances of ten different Gilbert and Sullivan shows, and I was getting awfully sick of it, so we brought our productions to an end.

JOHN GRAEF '60: I had come to Reed from a legendary musical prep school, Putney in Vermont. There were two other Putney students at Reed my sophomore year, Helen Pittaway '60 and Susan Homer '61. We began to sing madrigals together, just informally, but fairly regularly. In the fall of 1957 our little singing group—David Mason '58 tenor, myself bass, Betty Strayer '58 soprano, Sue Homer and one other alto—decided to put on a performance. Mark Ptashne '61, who played the fiddle, got together a small string quartet. Chemistry professor John Hancock played the organ. David Rosen '60 played the piano. We put together a little concert of six madrigals and a series of rounds that wasn't more than an hour. It was very participatory and well received. We wound up doing three or four of these concerts that year.

In the fall of 1958, Ginny Oglesby Hancock '62 arrived at Reed along with a group of other fresh-

men who had musical skills, and the group grew a bit. Most of what we sang was seventeenth-century music, but we also put together some barbershop songs and some rounds. Bob Ross '61, who was a freelance artist and our resident Maoist, gave us our name, "Collegium Musicum," and did some wonderful freehand drawings for our programs. Over the next two years, the group grew like topsy, so that by my senior year, seventy-five people auditioned for four places we had open in the group. We were doing five concerts a year, and after that Collegium Musicum became part of the life of the school. It was an example of the way in which Reed was ruled by a sort of bootstrap effort of the students.

LON PETERS '74, economics professor 1980–1981, 2007–2009: The Collegium Musicum singers were directed for years by Virginia Oglesby Hancock '62, who started teaching chemistry at Reed after graduating. Her husband, chemistry professor John Hancock, oversaw the instrumental players. Singers and players each adjourned one evening a week to the Hancocks' living room, a short walk from campus in Eastmoreland. I initially was assigned to play a zink, which turned out to be an especially nasty combination of a French horn mouthpiece and a recorder body. Playing it was just torture. The medieval kazoos, which were called "krummhorns," got all the laughs. Hancock played a post horn, which is sort of a trumpet straightened out into a long, straight horn of about six feet from the mouthpiece to the bell. I quickly beat a retreat to the tenor section of the singers.

The repertoire concentrated on medieval and Renaissance music. Concerts were held each December and April in the chapel, and were always packed with people spilling over to the stairs outside the chapel entrance.

PATTY LEAVEY KRISCH '59: The Christmas dance formal was really special. They would

The 1954 Christmas procession with the traditional flaming boar's head.

make space between the tables and then some guys in long robes would come marching in carrying a flaming boar's head with a choir of ten guys behind them chanting:

> The boar's head, as I understand,
> is the finest dish in all the land.

It was an English tradition that someone had brought back from Oxford or Cambridge.

DUGAN BARR '64: People spent a lot of time playing folk music. It was very important that only true, ethnic folk music be played. You couldn't play commercial stuff. People got in big fights over what was authentic folk music and what was not.

PHIL WILLIAMS '58: There were folk music sessions on the weekends in the social room of the Ladd dorm. We would bring our instruments and sit around and sing. All of us had our *Little Red Songbook*—also known as *Songs to Fan the*

Flames of Discontent—put out by the Industrial Workers of the World, with a red cover no less.

IRENE ASENDORF SCHULTENS '62: The breadth of music at Reed—the choir, the Sound Experiments, the Gilbert and Sullivan productions—was an emotional experience that I was unprepared for. It was all participatory music. When I was growing up such music was a bit demonized because of my family's history in Germany, where the Nazis had misused music to bring up emotional feelings that you aren't quite rational about. But it was Pete Seeger's concerts at Reed that were my leftist awakening. Simply the emotional experience of singing together songs like "Which Side Are You On," or "Let Your Little Light Shine."

CAROL BURNS '62: There were no television sets on campus. There was no influence from any other form of popular culture. Rock and roll and the Beatles were coming along, but at Reed we were listening to classical music and singing folk songs and labor songs like:

Shoeless, shoeless are we—
Just as shoeless as shoeless can be.
Because we don't get money for the labor.

How goofy was that?

Michael Nelken '60: The intrusion of the outside world onto the Reed campus was very, very limited. You never saw a newspaper lying around, you never saw a news magazine lying around, you never heard a radio or television news station playing. We were conscientiously remote and isolative by explicit wish—almost as a semi-religious devotion.

Jerry Case '59: The student radio station, KRRC, was started while I was a freshman. One of the physics majors put together what was then known as a "carrier current" transmitter, which simply fed into the power lines at an AM fre-

Barry Hansen '63, broadcasting from KRRC in the spring of 1960.

quency and could be picked up around the campus. He kept increasing the power input until he finally got a nasty letter from the FCC. After a while, somebody got one of the local Portland stations to donate some of their old equipment to the college. The college applied for an FM license and—voila!—KRRC was born in the basement of the Doyle house. The "studio" was near the washing machines and was covered with scavenged egg cartons for sound deadening. At the time, the station was the only game in Portland for decent classical music and serious talk.

Barry Hansen '63: Despite its meager ten-watt signal, which only went a few blocks into Eastmoreland, KRRC was run like a traditional, educational FM station serving the greater Portland community. We had a meticulously organized schedule of programs offering classical music drawn from the music department's library, with occasional ventures into the spoken arts, and a few public service programs from outside sources, including Radio Moscow. The station's income came from paid subscriptions to a mimeographed program guide that was sold to people living in Eastmoreland.

Chemistry professor John Hancock was the faculty advisor. He was a classical music buff, and he really loved the idea of having a station with a program guide that revealed that they were going to play the *Missa Solemnis* at eight o'clock on Thursday evening. But, after another classical music station started up in Portland, he reluctantly agreed that that model just wasn't really serving much purpose anymore, and that it made more sense to let students play music according to their interests.

We had several people who had nice libraries of jazz and folk music. There was not very much rock and roll. That was partly John Hancock's influence. He just thought it was beneath the dignity of the radio station. He didn't get much of an argument because rock and roll really wasn't that respected even by the students at the time.

I was given a half-hour slot on Friday evening to play blues. My program eventually expanded to four hours on Sunday nights, first as *Folk Music Unlimited*, and then *Music Americana*, since it included many old records that I had dredged up from thrift shops around Portland.

CHILTON GREGORY '60: International folk dancing was a strong element on campus. During the intensity of finals week, people danced until three AM with hopes of sweating out some of the anxiety they had.

JIM KAHAN '64: Pearl Atkinson, director of women's P.E., had a passion for folk dancing that inspired many of us to take it up. It was the single most popular activity on campus, pulling in maybe half the student body on a regular basis. The old Student Union would be packed. The interest was in ethnic dance. Israeli and Balkan dances were popular. There was a group that really liked Scandinavian dances, and another group that liked Greek dances. It was a way of dancing that wasn't the dominant, socially acceptable form at the time, like the Twist. Dancing was also something that many Reed students hadn't done in high school because they were too geeky. There was a large element of that.

BARRY HANSEN '63: Friday night was movie night in the chapel. It was an esoteric program with lots of foreign movies like Fellini, Russian silent films, and old classics. There were two showings, at seven and nine PM. The seven o'clock people would go to the showing and then go out afterwards and party. The nine o'clock people would study in the library until nine, go see the late movie, and then go to bed.

J. D. EVELAND '64: Empire was a political and military strategy board game that began on campus in the fall of 1960. It was provided to us

by my roommate, Dan Drake '64, whose father had created it back in the 1930s. It didn't become thoroughly institutionalized at Reed until the fall of 1963, when the game took on an increasing sophistication, moving from being occasionally set up in various sundry places to a permanent location at a fifteen-foot-long table in the Winch social room.

It was played by an odd and acceptable subculture. We played two games a year, one in the fall and one in the spring. The game sat on the table all semester. Any given player's move took anywhere between an hour and two and a half hours to complete. I built a rather elaborate set of twenty thousand playing pieces for it. A player's turn was indicated by a little Chinese dragon with a baldy head. If you found the dragon sitting in the middle of your country, it was your turn to make a move.

BILL KIRBY '65: Empire was perhaps the most complex non-computerized board game ever developed. To play a round of Empire, which lasted all semester, we had to construct a Mercator map of a mythical planet and put in natural resources, rivers, chemical deposits, timber, and everything else we could possibly imagine in great detail. Then we divided the planet up into mythical, fictional countries, which would immediately start developing their intelligence so they could declare war on each other.

It was interesting that some of the more rabid pacifists on campus turned into warlords almost within twenty-four hours of playing Empire. I myself played the Federation of Albigensian Heretics. Tony Wannier '66, a tall skinny kid who always wore a white leather jacket, played the Kingdom of Pi. His currency was based on the square root of three.

LINDA HAMMILL MATTHEWS '67: Girls did not play Empire. Boys played it, and they had their personas related to the game and they dressed

The Empire game in the Winch social room in 1963, with, left to right, Peter Clark '63, Jim Kahan '64, J. D. Eveland '64, and Alan Arey '65.

for it. The hard-core ones wore black capes with red linings. You could see them walking around campus like demons or vampires, flipping their capes.

JOHN LAURSEN '67: In the Akerman dormitory, where I lived as a freshman, there was a weekly poker game on Friday nights that went on until one or two AM. It seemed as though it was already an institution when I arrived in 1963.

The game was run by a guy in about his midtwenties, Stu Schain '69, who had gone to Reed and then dropped out for a while. It was a table-stakes poker game, which meant that on any given hand people could bet—and potentially lose—however much money they had on the table. It was strictly cash, no IOUs. Schain owned the chips and therefore banked the game and would always "cover the table," meaning that he, in effect, automatically had more chips on the table than anybody else did; this gave him a tremendous advantage and meant that over the course of the evening he almost always won.

We watched this game as freshmen; that's what the big boys were doing, so the younger boys would watch. It was seductive. I became addicted to playing, but addicted to it as a source of income. I never saw it as a thing to do for social pleasure; rather, I liked the money, which as a scholarship student I didn't have any of. It might have been just a lot of testosterone being diverted from its natural course, but I found that I had a natural aptitude for the game and it felt good. At the end of my freshman year I had won $700 playing poker and was owed a couple hundred dollars more.

When I came back as a sophomore in the fall of 1964, poker metamorphosed into a game that was going on every evening, and close to around the clock. It moved over to the laundry room in the basement of the Foster-Scholz dorm. There were twenty-five or thirty people involved at that point. The stakes went up and people started writing IOUs. Stu Schain hit a run of bad cards on a night that I hit a run of good ones. Sometime late in the evening he asked me, "What would you give me for this box of chips?" From that point forward, I was the guy who owned the bank at the poker game. Then the IOUs started escalating. It was like hyperinflation in the Weimar Republic. My single best poker night that year I won $2,500. This was at a time when gas cost twenty-five cents a gallon.

The poker game became a problem because people were flunking out, or were not able to pay their fees at the college. I was clearly known to be the ringleader. Dean Jack Dudman came down to the game and said, "Please stop with the IOUs." He didn't say, "Stop the game altogether," but he did ask, "Why don't you try to get it down to the weekends?" We curbed it back a lot, but several people flunked out and left school.

I went home at Christmas break in my sophomore year planning not to come back, because I wasn't doing very well in my classes at that point. Playing poker from six PM until two AM every night didn't leave a lot of time for studying. Jack Dudman called me at home repeatedly, saying, "Don't leave school. You have great potential, and you should stay at Reed." At that time I was the source of one of his greatest headaches, and he had every reason to want me gone and no reason but his own innate generosity of spirit for wanting to keep me in school.

I came back to Reed and buckled down and discovered that I could apply the same focus to my schoolwork that I had to poker and do just fine academically.

DOROTHY JOHANSEN '33, history professor 1934–1969, archivist 1969–1984: The closest thing Reed had to being in a sorority or fraternity was being custodian of the Doyle Owl. This funny piece of cement in the shape of an owl became the focus of secretive student activity from its first appearance in 1919. A self-perpetuating group of students had had custody of the Owl since the beginning; nobody knew who they were, and nobody knew where the Owl was ex-

cept for one particular group of students at any given time. Part of the ritual was that the group would publicly show the Owl on the campus, sporadically and unannounced, at which point other groups would try to take it away.

LOLINE HATHAWAY '59: I was living in Anna Mann cottage when somebody called an emergency dormitory meeting. There was a woman in the dorm whose aunt in Portland called and said, "The Doyle Owl is in my garage. It's been stored here for a year and a half." The aunt knew how rowdy Reed people got around the Doyle Owl, and she feared for the safety of her house. She implored her niece to please do something to get the thing out of her garage.

The Owl was made of concrete, about three feet tall, and incredibly heavy. We were astounded to see that it was hollow inside. To make sure that people forever after would know that Anna Mann cottage had had its hands on the Owl, we got some hydrochloric acid from the chemistry lab and used it to etch a big "A.M." on the bottom of the Owl. We drove up on the front lawn of the campus where someone was having an open house in the Kerr dorm. It took several of us to get it inside the door there. Right away, some people grabbed the Owl away from us, and took it right out a back window. That was the last I ever saw of it.

RON FOX '64: The Doyle Owl was in the possession of the Haberfeld twins, Steve '63 and Peter '63, along with three other guys who were all members of the football team. They were the biggest and baddest guys on the campus, and in good humor they would often show the Doyle Owl in the Commons during the dinner meal, repelling all attempts to wrest the Owl away.

One evening after one of these failed attempts, I was walking by the library parking lot when I spotted the Haberfelds' car. I broke into the car through an open wing window, and found the

Owl in the trunk. Dwight Read '64 and I then loaded the Owl onto his motorcycle, and took it to a safe place. Dwight eventually drove the Owl down to Los Angeles and got it filmed inside a tank at Seaworld, where he had connections, with sharks and sea turtles. Some months later we secretly spliced this film into the Friday night movie on campus.

JOHN ULLMAN '65: Advance word went out that a Doyle Owl showing would occur during the Friday night movie in the chapel. Owl fanciers showed up in full force. The movie that night was the 1920 German silent horror film, *The Golem*, about a large clay monster created by a mystic rabbi to chastise an anti-Semitic king in Prague. In one particularly suspenseful scene, the king, unable to sleep, walks through his palace and sees the golem standing at the far end of a long hall. The camera, taking the king's point of view, zoomed in for a close-up of the golem's face, but suddenly it became the Doyle Owl's face. Then the camera zoomed out, and the entire Owl was seen underwater at Seaworld with sharks swimming all around it. There was considerable consternation among folks in the audience who had come expecting an epic tussle over the Owl.

KATHLEEN BUCKLIN DAVIES '67: Somehow I got in with a crowd that had possession of the Owl. John Davies '67, who I later married, and Jon Bates '67 were the ringleaders. We publicized a showing of the Owl at the library on such-and-such a date. That day our group displayed the Owl from the balcony rooftop of the library. To get it off the roof, we hired a helicopter to come by with a bunch of rope. The Owl was wrapped up in a blanket and tied to the rope, and then the helicopter took off with the Owl dangling below it.

I was waiting on the other side of campus along Steele Street with someone else in my old purple Chrysler, the "Vomit Comet." The helicopter dropped the Owl off beside the car, but it cracked. A co-conspirator and I dragged it into the trunk of my car, and off we drove.

Tim Custer '70, Jon Bates '67, Tom Weiss '68, and Ian Merwin '69, defending the Doyle Owl from the back of a convertible, October 1966.

CHAPTER 21

Free Love

President Sullivan declared in his speech that sexual intercourse in any Reed dorm, whatever the hour, was a de facto violation of the Honor Principle.
—Barry Hansen '63

At Reed there was an idealistic resistance to the thought that anything so high-minded as the Honor Principle could be connected with things so ignoble as regulations.
—Ann Shepard '23, dean of students

The 1950s shift to a more heterogeneous, national composition of the Reed student body mirrored the growing sophistication and independence among students on college campuses across the country. At Reed, those trends found expression in a desire for greater personal freedom and increased student autonomy. Students began exerting more pressure for a broader role in community governance, free from the oversight of the deans, the faculty, and the president.

As in decades past, these demands were largely played out in debates over the application of the Honor Principle. By the late 1950s the Honor Principle had evolved among students to a state of ambiguity and personal interpretation that seemed at times beyond the reach of rules and regulations. In 1960, the flash point of the debate became the rules governing intervisitation between men and women in the dorms. Meanwhile, as enrollment grew to more than eight hundred students, many of them from outside the Portland area, Reed found itself facing a dormitory shortage. Students began moving off campus into communal houses in nearby neighborhoods, where the rules of engagement between the sexes were more informal. The arrival of the Pill in 1963 further accelerated student demands for the lifting of sexual restrictions on campus.

That year, students dissolved the Student Council in an act of protest, and with President Sullivan's support created a new Community Senate composed of both students and faculty members. One of the first acts of the Community Senate was to relax the rules concerning intervisitation.

DAVID RAGOZIN '62: In the spring of 1960 we had something called the "intervisitation crisis." The mother of somebody living in a girls' dorm stayed there overnight, and came across a young man in his bathrobe in the dorm in the middle of the night. She reported it to President Sullivan, and Sullivan called a big community meeting in Botsford Gym. The buildup was enormous. Sullivan gave an address, and as student body president I gave a rebuttal.

BARRY HANSEN '63: President Sullivan declared in his speech that sexual intercourse in any Reed dorm, whatever the hour, was a de facto violation of the Honor Principle. His reasoning was that such dalliance made it more difficult for him to raise funds for Reed, and therefore harmed the entire community, but many were outraged at this perversion of the Honor Principle's purity. The Student Council was quite busy with sex in the dorms and other intervisitation-related honor cases for awhile.

COMMUNITY AFFAIRS COMMITTEE REPORT, 1960–61: The Student Council reported fourteen hearings this year on potential honor violations, compared with forty-two in 1959–60. Of these, only one resulted in a declaration by the council of an honor violation. The case was that of two students who had stolen cigarettes from the machine. In four other cases the council declined to declare the offenders honor violators, but administered a social probation penalty. The offenses were a serious violation of intervisitation rules, sexual misbehavior on campus, receiving unauthorized aid in paper preparation, plagiarism, and destruction of college property. The council also sent admonitory letters to two students who had failed to sign out of the dorms at night and who had violated intervisitation rules.

In comparison to previous years, this is an astonishingly limited list of actions. Equally notable is the reluctance of the council to deal severely with infractions. A plausible case for leniency may perhaps be made in each individual instance but the entire list of cases reveals an unmistakable preference for softer therapeutic treatment rather than the administration of a community verdict of condemnation.

Is the elective body of the Student Council, to whom the responsibility for the administration of student affairs and the supervision of student conduct has been delegated, operating in the name of the community? Or is it a "shop committee" whose fundamental obligation is the protection of students collectively or individually from the hostile action of the faculty and administration, and negotiation for increased student control of all areas of campus activity?

DAVID CASSERES '65: The Honor Principle occupied a great deal of our imaginations. It was debated endlessly. I served a term on the Student Council where we determined Honor Principle cases. There were three cases in that year. A freshman girl was caught cheating on an exam. She was a confused, troubled girl, toward the end of her first year, who was probably not doing well academically. We debated at great length, and we wound up recommending that she be expelled, and she was. We did not account for the fact that she was very young, and that she had many years of her life before her. I felt bad about it an hour after it was done. It has never stopped bothering me.

We had another case of a freshman girl in what we still called New Women's Dorm, later renamed MacNaughton. It was a triple with two rooms. She was in the outer room when one of her roommates came out of the inner room with her boyfriend still, as her testimony told us, "doing up his pants." This girl was again, very young; she was terribly sexually repressed, and was greatly discomfited by this. It was a serious matter and she brought it first to her dorm mommy, the upperclass student dorm advisor, and then it came to the Student Council. We debated at great length. Our sympathies were very seriously divided. We wound up giving a recommendation that the girl get some counseling, the guy be told not to be so gross anymore, and the roommate be told to be more considerate.

The third case was of a junior who was a premed chemistry major. Before a major exam, the other people in the class went to the library and could not find the books that they needed to cram for the test. It was found that all the books were at this guy's house. He was brought before the Student Council by the faculty. Our feeling was that the wrong could be righted, that he could take some kind of disciplinary action that would perhaps not destroy him, and he would learn a valuable lesson. We gave this back to the Faculty Community Affairs Council and they would not have it. They stepped over the Student Council as the supreme authority in honor cases, and decided that this guy would not be permitted to take the junior chemistry qualification exam, and so could not be a chemistry major. Which meant that he could not go to medical school. He wound up being a veterinarian.

Ever since adjudicating those three cases I have been very suspicious of high principles. I think they have to be examined carefully for how well they can actually be applied to real people.

ANN SHEPARD '23, recorder 1926–1942, dean of women 1943–1950, dean of students 1950–1968: When I entered Reed in 1919, it seemed to me that the Honor Principle was a much simpler, less bewildering principle than it became in the 1960s. It wasn't seen by us as any sort of license to do what we wished, providing only that our actions not hurt another person, but much more as giving us the freedom to behave with honor and judgment without the insult of being told to do so in advance.

Regulations are desirably few, to be made only as needed, and to represent the careful agree-

Dean Ann Shepard '23, talking with a student in the 1960s.

ment of responsible agents of the various parts of the community, but once agreed upon, to be honorably observed. My generation was not sinless and pure. We did stupid things, wrong things, and we broke rules. Freedom was as important to Reed 1920 as Reed 1960, and I hope it always will be. But freedom is not proof against misuse. I believe it to be vital and yet delicate, better earned than given, as I am truly not sure that it can successfully *be* given. It seems to me that freedom for any unit of society inevitably calls for self-denial and inconvenience from the members who belong to that unit and who wish to preserve it. I believe with all my heart that one has to have good and substantial answers to the question "Freedom for what, or to do what?" And that this question is far, far more important than the question "Freedom from what?"

NICHOLAS WHEELER '55, physics professor 1963–2010: As a student, Dean Shepard '23 had been honor cased for roller-skating inside Eliot Hall.

VIVIAN TOMLINSON WILLIAMS '59: The ten PM curfew for girls was ridiculously early. I was in the habit of defying that. During specified times on the weekends, men and women could visit each other's rooms, but the rule was "four feet on the floor" during intervisitation. I was also in the habit of defying that.

DAVID RAGOZIN '62: At the end of the intervisitation crisis we were obliged to hold meetings in each dormitory. In those discussions, the main questions that came up were related to whether there were social pressures, particularly on women, to be involved in sexual activities. In the context of those meetings Sullivan one day asked me how he could be president of a college to which he would not allow his daughter to come. His daughter at that time was a freshman at Swarthmore. Whether life was necessarily much different there, I don't know.

ANNE WOOD TWITTY '59: I transferred in to Reed from Northwestern University in Chicago, which was very much a dating and party school. There was pressure to define yourself in a dating way. The sexual hypocrisy there was quite extreme. Reed was a much more relaxed atmosphere, and offered a very delightful way to be able to be around people and have a sense of community. Somebody said to me, "We don't date at Reed, we have kinship relationships."

At the same time, my women friends and I were quite accepting of the fact that most of the men we knew tended to look down on women as intellectually inferior, but would make exceptions for *us*. We were perfectly happy with that, because if they felt that you were intelligent and interesting to talk to, then you would become a kind of honorary man. It didn't occur to us that this was not a particularly wonderful situation.

RICHARD SULLIVAN, president 1956–1967: One of the justifications for having coeducation rests on the belief that one part of attaining maturity is to find comfort and satisfaction in proper relationships with the opposite sex. If you bring young persons together, but then make it impossible to have any range of perfectly wholesome relationships, public or private, you are contradicting one of the values that led to the very structuring of the institution itself.

You also must face the very troublesome question of how much the institution may invade the private behavior that is essentially the business of the individual, or groups of individuals, with sets of regulations. There is a spectrum of possibilities. At one end you have the spectre that all young men and women are spending an inordinate amount of time sleeping together on college property. At the other end, you have a different situation, as at some coeducational colleges, in which there is no way men and women can see each other except most formally. There are no easy solutions.

I do not think the very heavy hand that is applied in some institutions ordinarily accomplishes what the institutions hope will be accomplished. If we erred at Reed, it was in the direction of considerable freedom of the individual, which was consistent with the general operation of the Honor Principle.

JOHN CUSHING '67: Each of the dorm houses in the Old Dorm Block were self-contained at the time and had access only through their front-door entrances. There was a system of buzzers at the doors of the girls' dorms. Each girl had a different buzzer call, some combination of long buzzes and short buzzes, like dot-dot-dash or dash-dash-dot. There was a list of names beside the door with each girl's buzzer code, and then there was a system of replies.

One buzz-like beep was "Coming." Beep-beep was someone answering for her, "Not here." Beep-beep-beep was "Come on up." Beep-beep-beep-beep was "Come back later." And beep-

beep-beep-beep-beep was "Go away." Occasionally, I would buzz a girl's code and then think, "Oh, shit," and just run away.

JIM KAHAN '64: Leslie Mueller Stewart '64 was fascinated by the fact that there was a lot of sex going on at Reed. She had taken Joe Roberts' math course, in which Joe would talk about a transitive mathematical relationship he called a "diddle": if A diddle B, and B diddle C, then, if it's transitive, A diddle C. Leslie took this to its logical conclusion, and set out to define the diddle relationship between sexual partners on campus. If A slept with B, and B slept with C, then A and C were in a second-order diddle relationship.

Leslie drew up as complete a network map of these diddle relationships as she was capable of based upon her own knowledge, which was extensive. The question was whether it was possible to connect everybody at Reed—virgins excepted, and they were few in number—via this diddle relationship. That was her goal. If you looked at it, the first horrible moment would be when you found out that you were in a second-order diddle relationship with yourself.

SANDY OSBORNE LILLIE '70: I came from a messy background and had been active sexually. I felt that the student body around me, though, had come from pretty protected families in general. They were very sophisticated intellectually but not socially or emotionally. In our freshman dorm all the girls were virgins and they were all determined to lose it by Thanksgiving.

DELLANNE MCGREGOR '71: I was sitting out on the lawn very shortly after the beginning of school. I had taken my shoes off and had my bare feet out on the grass. Some very attractive young man came by and dropped a note in my shoe. I opened the note and it said, "I want to make love to you." And I went, "Oh, what am I going to do?"

A lot of us were in over our heads. We wanted to be sophisticated and up-to-date, and we

Students dancing at the 1965 Christmas formal.

all wanted to have full experiences, but we just didn't have the background to implement any of this at that point. There was a lot of social pressure to lose one's virginity and get on with it.

LUCINDA PARKER MCCARTHY '66: Many of the girls that I knew had abortions. It was horrible because it was the beginning of the sexual revolution, but there was no conscious thought about how to keep yourself from getting pregnant. Abortion was illegal, so if you got one, you had to be picked up by a car, blindfolded, and taken through the West Hills of Portland until you came to the place. You paid a lot of money. Then, if you bled afterwards, too bad for you.

NANCY TESELLE WOOD '66: As a dorm mommy, I had to help arrange an abortion. There was a whole network of people who were aware of what to do. It was done away from campus in a basement on the top of a washing machine, by a woman named Ruth Barnett. There's a book about her called *The Abortionist: A Woman Against the Law.* The person suffered some pain and discomfort following it. It was blooming scary.

BARBARA SMITH-THOMAS '64: With the arrival of the Pill in 1963, you could avoid the consequences of promiscuity. But you could not get birth control from the Reed infirmary. Oh, *goodness,* no! The doctor was Catholic and didn't believe in birth control. He would give you lectures about the rhythm method.

ANITA LOURIE BIGELOW '67: The doctor in the campus health center, Dr. Gregg Wood, gave us a really scary lecture about how if you had too much sex all your parts would freeze up. It was pretty horrifying.

JIM KAHAN '64: The first doctor in the local community who would prescribe birth-control pills in 1963 to unmarried women, and whose practice was very heavily populated by Reed women, had the fantastic name of Dr. Miracle.

JACK DUDMAN '42, mathematics professor 1953–1985, dean of students 1963–1985: I started serving as part-time dean of students in 1963, after psychology professor Les Squier, who had been dean together with Ann Shepard '23 since

Students studying on the campus front lawn in the early 1960s.

the late 1950s, decided to return to teaching full-time. It was the beginning of a period in which a great cultural change occurred in student life. There were changes of attitudes about sexual behavior, drug use, and the appropriate role of a college with regard to control or management of student life and student choices.

Until abortion was made legal in 1973, we were engaged in finding ways of assisting girls who got pregnant, whether they went full-term, put a baby up for adoption, or decided to have an abortion. We had to do all kinds of borderline legal business, like keeping in touch with psychiatrists and physicians who would be able to help a girl who might be psychologically or physically in danger if they were to bear a child, or to find clinics in California, which had a somewhat different system, which would be receptive to a girl in that situation.

Ann Shepard and I were determinedly non-manipulative and non-controlling, reacting as best we could to the needs of individual students. We didn't try to arrange their lives for them or manage the kind of personal choices they made, but react, helpfully if we could, to the difficulties they got into. We dealt with the ordinary kind of academic counseling or assistance, intervening with professors when students' personal difficulties begin conflicting with their academic responsibilities. The more sensational kinds of things were the difficulties that students would get into psychologically, needing technical assistance from counselors and psychiatrists, or difficulties that resulted from their experimenting with drugs, or brushes with the law, such as needing representation in court or help in finding lawyers. All kinds of godawful things you have to do to be of assistance to people in a jam.

RICHARD JONES, history professor 1941–1982, 1985–1986: In 1963, the president of the student body, Tom Forstenzer '65, led a change in the community constitution. The change did away

with the Faculty Community Affairs Committee, which since 1919 had reviewed actions by the Student Council, especially those related to the Honor Principle, and created the Community Senate, in which faculty and students participated together.

Many, like President Sullivan, thought this was a good thing, in that it would create a much closer alliance between the students and the faculty in governing community affairs. In practice however, the members of the Community Senate served as representatives of their respective constituencies, either the faculty or the student body, and consequently created more opportunity for severance and division. Governance then started focusing primarily on who made the rules and who enforced them.

Many of us felt that the thing to do was to get back to the solidity of the Honor Principle rather than to focus on authority.

MARK LOEB '65: The Community Senate that was created had twenty-one members—eleven faculty senators and ten student senators. One faculty senator was elected chairman and had no vote except in the case of a tie, and only in regard to recommendations by the Judicial Board. The Judicial Board was a student committee created to review violations of the Honor Principle and then make recommendations to the Community Senate, to either approve or send back for further consideration.

The Community Senate was given power to formulate community policy in matters of internal community affairs that were not assigned to other constitutional bodies, such as educational policy, admissions, financial aid, and college personnel.

COMMUNITY SENATE REPORT, 1963: Two kinds of behavior are considered anti-social and therefore in violation of the Honor Principle: 1) conduct that causes unnecessary embarrassment,

Students embracing outside of Eliot Hall in the early 1960s.

the classroom. They said that the principle had been abused and demanded that a "dean of discipline" be established at the college. The idea was repulsive to most students and to many faculty members, especially those who were alumni. In the end the motion was defeated.

A large source of the honor cases had been intervisitation, which had been extended in 1961 by the Faculty Community Affairs Committee after the intervisitation crisis, but students generally resented the fact that that committee had been made up of faculty members, the deans, and representatives of the president's office. By virtue of their positions, it was felt they had vested interests in imposing a limitation on intervisitation hours. Under the new community government established in 1963, the role of the deans was drastically limited and the president no longer was a direct participant in student life. As a result, the new Community Senate extended the hours of intervisitation.

discomfort, or injury to another individual or to the community as a whole; and 2) conduct in violation of specific rules that have been developed over the years to meet special conditions in the community.

ANN SHEPARD '23, dean of students: In 1963, the Community Senate reached an agreement that a deliberate infraction of a regulation was in fact a violation of the Honor Principle. The importance of this agreement can be hard to explain to a stranger, but at Reed there was an idealistic resistance to the thought that anything so high-minded as the Honor Principle could be connected with things so ignoble as regulations.

MARK LOEB '65: In the spring of 1964, a number of faculty senators on the Community Senate wanted to suspend the operation of the Honor Principle in the community outside of

GWENDOLYN LEWIS '65, trustee 1994–1998: We had just a single telephone in the dormitory, and all phone calls came and went through that telephone. I was taking messages for other students, and realized that faculty members were calling them not to get a babysitter for their children, but to set up dates. It was before we had rules against professors fraternizing with students, but there just seemed something on the face of it wrong to me, even in cases of a young faculty member trying to date a student close to his own age. It seemed to me like the very needy students were the ones who were getting involved with faculty members.

DOROTHY MOORE EDLIN '56: I was living in two worlds as a student, because my mother was diagnosed with cancer at the end of my senior year in high school. My first two years at Reed, I didn't know whether she would live or die. I found out halfway through my sophomore year that she had very little time left. She died that summer.

I had a romance, a love affair, with a professor who taught humanities and English. He was our first black professor at Reed. It didn't work out, but I thought it was going to. I had a child from that relationship. In those days, it was very, very difficult. My father decided to move to Portland with my younger brother and live with me for a year. We rented the house of philosophy professor Edwin Garlan, who was on sabbatical. I had a hard time that year. I had to withdraw from a couple of classes. Then, after I went off and had the baby, I came back to Reed and graduated. My senior year I lived in Anna Mann, and I was a dorm advisor. I felt pretty old and mature.

ERNEST BONYHADI '48, trustee 1971–1995: Faculty-student affairs were the norm on all campuses at the time. It wasn't just tolerated, it was accepted as no big deal. Ed Garlan married one of his students. Others just had dates; I don't know whether you could characterize them as affairs or not.

BARBARA SERRELL HANSEN '62: I dated faculty, as did a number of the women in my class. Some of them married faculty, others had affairs with faculty or took faculty away from other faculty. For example, one woman took a history professor away from the librarian.

PATTY PARMALEE '62: We were much freer at that time, but we also didn't have as deep an understanding of the power issues that were involved as we do now. It was a double-edged sword.

LINDA HAMMILL MATTHEWS '67, trustee 2005– : The social tone of the campus was set by the male students and the male faculty. You were nobody if you didn't have a boyfriend. Many of my girlfriends went out with their professors. It was very instructive to walk across the campus at seven in the morning and see who the couples were and where they were emerging from. My roommate, Amelia Rosamond '67, married our English professor, Fred Hard.

AMELIA ROSAMOND HARD '67: Fred Hard was my academic advisor in English. I took an independent reading class with him in Spenser my sophomore year. We read the The Faerie Queen together, and got to be friends. There was a whole lot of physical attraction that neither of us was willing to brave censure to do anything about, until the middle of my junior year, when we sort of threw caution to the wind, although we still had scruples about it, and were very discrete. There were a couple of professors who were known for sleeping with students, and it was kind of a given, as I'm sure was true on most college campuses. We were married after I graduated in 1967, and that summer I made that awkward transition from student to faculty wife.

VIRGINIA OGLESBY HANCOCK '62, chemistry associate 1963–1980, music professor 1991– : I went to England for my junior year on a student exchange at Keele University. John Hancock, with whom I had taken freshman chemistry, and who was English, coached me before I went. In my senior year, after I got back, I was in a chemistry seminar that John ran. I would talk to him initially about the class, and then about music, which we shared an interest in. We started dating in the fall of my senior year. We got engaged in February. Everybody seemed to think it was a match made in heaven. Here was the chemistry, here was the music, and how could you do any better? And that's what I thought. I also really liked Reed and, to some extent, didn't want to leave. Marrying into the faculty was a pretty good way of making sure that I wouldn't.

Looking back, it would probably have been a good thing had I said, "This is too soon. I'm not really ready to do this, and I need to go to graduate school on my own and be independent and learn how to do that." We didn't do that in 1962. And so we got married after I graduated.

John had had some involvement with students before. When I was a freshman he was very taken with Jane Shell '59, but that didn't come to anything. She was a senior at that point and went off to MIT. She came back to Reed in 1962 as a faculty member, and wound up marrying a student.

JANET RUSSELL '68: I considered myself the equal of any man and expected them to open doors for me, both literally and figuratively. I was only mildly curious when some of the faculty wives tried to organize a discussion of Betty Friedan's book *The Feminine Mystique*, which had been recently published. They were surprised and disappointed that few of the women students felt that they would be limited by society's expectations. When my thesis advisor in history, David Allmendinger, replaced the nude in his office with a map of colonial Boston and suggested to me a senior thesis topic in women's history, it was I who insisted on writing on a "serious" subject.

JOHN EMERSON '68: There were at least four faculty-student gay relationships at Reed that I knew of. Back in the pre-gay-liberation days it seemed to operate like the nineteenth-century system where if it didn't get in the newspapers or the courts as a matter of public interest, it was okay. I was quite uneasy in my first two or three meetings with one professor, until it got sorted out that I was not interested. He was very gentlemanly about it.

RICHARD CONVISER '65: Although I had a girlfriend in my senior year at Reed, I was aware of being attracted to men and not really being comfortable in knowing how to express that. I've talked to other gay Reed graduates, some a little bit older than me, who had secret trysts with other people on campus or would go off campus and go cruising, looking for sexual pickups in parks and things of that sort. Stonewall—the police riot at a gay bar in New York City that in some ways launched the gay liberation movement—didn't happen until 1969. So sexuality for some people at the time was fairly limited.

RICHARD ENGEMAN '69: History professor Dorothy Johansen '33 was a very special and unusual person. She was somebody that you could talk to about certain personal problems. I think she realized that I was gay before I did. She lived right on the edge of campus, and several times I housesat for her. I would occasionally go to her house and meet her partner, Dana Small '23. Their relationship was easy to put together. For heaven's sakes, they had been living together for many years.

JOHN ULLMAN '65: There was a lot of back-and-forth between Reed and the revolutionary stuff going on at the time down at Berkeley. Peter Bergel '65 and Holly Tannen '68 both went down to Berkeley and got involved in the Sexual Freedom League. The next time we saw Holly she was pictured in *Time* magazine with the head of the Sexual Freedom League, Jefferson "Fuck" Poland. They were nude, liberating a beach somewhere just north of San Francisco.

TIME magazine, "The Free-Sex Movement," March 11, 1966: First it was free speech, then filthy speech. Now it is free love, as students, former students and nonstudents continue to test the limits of the permissible at Berkeley. There have been at least six such orgies, attended by between twenty and forty-five youths each, in the San Francisco Bay area in the past month. All have been held in private residences. Most have included students from Cal and from San Francisco State. . . .

The group's secretary, psychology student Holly Tannen, a bright eighteen-year-old, contends that suppressing sexual expression leads to "pornography and topless night clubs." She concedes she was embarrassed at her first nude party. "I was ashamed of my body," she said. "But I got over that."

RICHARD CONVISER '65: There were all kinds of cracks appearing in the façade of uniformity that had characterized the 1950s—the emerging civil rights movement, the Cuban Missile Crisis, the growing involvement of the United States in the civil war going on in Vietnam. People were just starting to question whether the public positions of elected officials were consistent with more deeply rooted American values, and there were the beginnings of a great deal of social unrest. The Beat era had ended, and on campus we had forerunners of hippies, whom we referred to as "supercools." There was also evidence of drug use on campus.

MICHAEL NELKEN '60: During my tenure as vice-president of the student body, one of the deans, psychology professor Leslie Squier, summoned the Student Council to an emergency meeting to announce that a student was going to be kicked out of school for offering drugs to a girl, who had complained. We were to ratify and endorse this, which we did by unanimous vote. Nobody thought themselves competent to disagree with a faculty member, certainly not with Dr. Squier, on that or on any issue. That student expelled had the distinction of being the first person persecuted for drug use at Reed. The drug in question was *lophophora williamsii*, also known as peyote.

ANNE WOOD TWITTY '59: At the time you could write away to the Native American Church and say that you were practicing your faith, but that you were far away and would they please send you some peyote buttons, which they did. I lived in a house off campus my senior year, and my roommate and another person were chewing peyote. I didn't like the idea of getting sick to my stomach, which is what happens when you chew peyote, so I cleared out that night and left them to whatever experiences they had.

Around that same time, some people were taking acid, which was still legal then. After I graduated, I was at an *Esquire* magazine party in Manhattan, and someone was saying, "Well, you know, the first place people were doing acid was in such and such a place in 1960." A woman stood up and she said, "It was not. It was at Reed College in 1958!"

BARBARA ALEXANDER EHRENREICH '63: I was really an alienated kid. I wanted to go to Reed because I thought that I would be free there from the deadly conformity of high school in Los Angeles. What I found out was that I was not the only one at Reed with that desire. Reed brought together the currents of youthful rebellion in people like me with a feeling of intense intellectual adventure. Everybody there was smart; everybody there was a misfit. What happened was what happens when you get a bunch of very bright misfits together and don't bother them too much with rules, too many rules anyway. There was sex. There were drugs. And there were a lot of motorcycles. I was always attracted to guys with big motorcycles, embarrassingly enough. I managed to straddle both the bohemian culture at Reed and its other side, which was a really hard-working, focused, liberal arts school.

JOHN LAURSEN '67: When I was a freshman, in 1963, I saw a sign in the mail room one day that said, "Legalize marijuana." I sort of vaguely knew what marijuana was, but I had no real desire to know more, nor any interest in legalizing it. I did not know anybody that year who smoked marijuana. It simply wasn't an issue. By the end of my senior year, everyone was smoking it, and many of us were experimenting with psychedelics. It was all very innocent, though, compared to what is now thought of as "drug culture."

LUCINDA PARKER MCCARTHY '66: There was a drug subculture in the early 1960s, but it was more beatnik stuff, attached to people writing poetry and playing music, not so much across the board, with everybody doing it. Then the drug culture got linked up with the whole issue of protesting the Vietnam War. People were also protesting the status quo values of the middle-class by taking risks and using drugs.

In 1966, Steve McCarthy '66, who I wasn't friends with at the time but later married, was on the Student Council. He stood up in a Community Senate meeting and said, "I do not believe that marijuana should be smoked in the library." There was a huge outrage. People tried to recall him as a student senator.

LIZ FINK '67: The campus was divided between the people who did science and the people who did humanities. The science people went into the science labs and stayed there. My science friends didn't take drugs. They were in the biology lab all the time. But everybody in our literature class tried them.

HOWARD RHEINGOLD '68: In 1964, LSD was a frontier. We didn't know what would happen to us or to the world. Much of the subject matter of my early acid trips at Reed was the subject matter of our humanities lectures. Plato's parable of the cave was written just for us! It took a while to sort out.

CRICKET PARMALEE '67: In my freshman year drugs were just coming to campus. One night after folk dancing, I went with some friends to a student house off campus. Somebody had some dope and we all smoked it; me for the first time. One of the folk dancers, a sort of small and boyish fellow, passed out from it. We didn't know what to do. Pot was totally illegal, and so we were put in this dilemma. We could call the college infirmary and ask for advice, and in effect bust him to the school and to his family, or we could hope that this was just something that would pass in a little while. Finally, we did call the infirmary, and he did recover and was all right. What stayed with me was that feeling of our helplessness, of not knowing what to do because on the one hand here was somebody who might get into a lot of trouble because of our seeking help, and on the other hand, for all we knew, he might die.

DUGAN BARR '64: Parties held at student-run houses off campus were usually people playing jazz, or somebody playing the guitar and sing-

An outdoor student concert in the mid-1960s.

ing folk music. Sometimes the music was classical. Typically people would drink some wine or beer, although there were some houses where other substances took their place. Some student houses had semi-permanent residents, and names like "the Pale," "Chelm House," and "the Fishmarket."

JOHN ULLMAN '65: Half a dozen students lived in a house on Long Street and Twenty-eighth Avenue called "the Pale," named after the Pale of Settlement, an area created in 1835 by Catherine the Great of Russia as a zone where Jews would be allowed to live. Some Reedies at the time tried to see how small a food budget they could live on. The students at the Pale got it down to a dollar and a quarter per week per person. The experiment came to an abrupt end when a number of them began to exhibit symptoms of scurvy.

STEVE ENGEL '68: There was a Reed house at Forty-seventh Avenue and Henry Street called "Chelm House," Chelm being the location of a series of Yiddish tales in which everyone is a fool and the wise men are the greatest fools of all. We were sort of a cooperative, although it seemed a little bit like a successful anarchy. But we managed to make it work. We ate a lot of rice and beans and veggies. Most of the people in our household were deeply involved in starting the People's Co-op Market not far from the college.

JAY ROSENBERG '63: Those of us living off campus did a lot of cooking and entertaining. I wrote down a bunch of recipes and bound up copies of them with some very bad amateur calligraphy on the cover, and called it *The Impoverished Student's Book of Cookery, Drinkery, and Housekeepery*. A national literary magazine, *The Saturday Review of Literature*, published a little excerpt from it and said good things about it. Someone from Doubleday Books read that, and got in touch with the Reed Alumni Association, and asked,

"Would you like us to distribute that book for you?" By the early '70s that book had sold more than a hundred thousand copies, and had funded the Rosenberg Cookbook Scholarship Fund.

SANDY CUTRELL '63: In my sophomore year Peter Scheiber '61 and I moved into the Fishmarket together. It was two apartments over two storefronts, one a bar and the other a laundromat, at the corner of Southeast Powell Boulevard and Twenty-first Avenue. Earlier there had been a fish market where the laundromat was.

Reed students had been living there for at least ten years. The other apartment had four people in it, and our apartment had two. Peter created one room that was entirely upholstered in mattresses. We would do our cooking in the other apartment, since Peter had turned our kitchen into a brewery.

JIM KAHAN '64: I only lived in the Fishmarket for a week at the end of my freshman year. In the main social room, which was covered with mattresses, the concept of the Chinese cluster fuck was invented—basically a bunch of people take off their clothes, get into the room, probably drunk, and then just go for it.

ROBERT HORSFALL '63: Peter Scheiber '61 was serving his time as a conscientious objector, working for Goodwill. There he met some Hell's Angels who had been paroled out of San Quentin and had come to Portland. The leader of the pack was a local, Jay Terwilliger, otherwise known as "Lefty." Lefty discovered that we were making beer at the Fishmarket, very high-test and very cheap. Every time we settled down to have a party, he and his Hell's Angels friends would show up. It came just to be expected that if the Hell's Angels dropped in, the police wouldn't be far behind. The Angels would go out the back door as the police came in the front. It became quite exciting, but it made for unusual student housing.

CHAPTER 22

Portland's Academic Gadfly

My favorite Canyon Day activity was the time we painted signs on the asphalt at the entrances to Reed, "Caution: Wildlife Refuge."
  —Richard Conviser '65

The thrust of Communists for Goldwater was to support Barry Goldwater for president, because his election would bring about the revolution that much quicker.
  —Carter Weiss '66

The confident sense of irony with which the Reed community had embraced the derogatory slur of "communism, atheism, free love" in the 1920s, continued to assert itself in students' interactions with the local culture. The time-honored practice of mocking Reed's athletic teams in local competition also served to mock the more conventional college teams Reed competed against, and in turn the significance other schools gave to their sports programs. Even in the arena of political protest, which became de rigueur on college campuses in the 1960s, Dadaist street theatre remained the favored Reed approach, often leaving locals confused and uneasy.

At Reed, nonconformity remained integral to the pursuit of intellectual excellence, and intellectual excellence in turn encouraged the critical thinking that appeared to lead to nonconformity. In the early 1960s inviting controversial speakers and entertainers to campus remained the most effective manner of communicating both Reed's commitment to academic freedom and its adversity to the constraints of the status quo.

ANNE WOOD TWITTY '59: Reed was wonderfully countercultural at the time. Just delightfully funny and laid back and quite the opposite from what was going on in the larger culture around us. There were students on campus whose parents had been involved in the spirit of independence and separateness of that old Wobbly—or Industrial Workers of the World—tradition, which had been so much a part of the Pacific Northwest.

SUZANNE HANCHETT '62: I was what they called a "red-diaper" baby. In my senior year of high school, all my friends ditched me because my father was called up by the House Un-American Activities Committee. That was extremely painful. Coming to Reed, it was wonderful to find that being a red-diaper baby was sort of a status symbol. It was nice to have somebody say, "Wow? Really?! Oh, man!" Reed really wasn't such a radical place, but I liked not being socially ostracized the way I had been in high school.

HOWARD WOLPE '60: We took great pride in our iconoclasm and our openness to having controversial figures come on campus, but there was very little overt political activity on campus itself. The campus was very much inward looking. There was no engagement in presidential elections or local elections. There were a few people who were classically conservative, but most of the student body was progressive and left-wing.

CAROL BURNS '62: We were inspired by the nonviolent civil rights activities taking place in the South, like not giving up your seat on the bus or sitting in at the Woolworth's counter. While our actions were well-organized, they conveyed the idea of spontaneous events. There were demonstrations downtown that drew as many as a hundred Reed students for civil rights, arms control, banning the bomb, and ending nuclear testing.

RICHARD CONVISER '65: Reed seemed like a bit of a womb that provided some protection from the outside world—especially because there was a fair amount of uniformity in the values of students who attended Reed.

Among the solidarity-building activities were Campus Day in the fall and Canyon Day in the spring. On those days, in addition to a softball game between faculty and students, and tugs-of-war in which people wound up getting dragged through the mud and things of that sort, we ac-

tually did some work around the campus cleaning things up. My favorite Canyon Day activity was the time we painted signs on the asphalt at the entrances to Reed, "Caution: Wildlife Refuge," which was literally true, because the Reed canyon had that designation, but it was just another way of demarcating one of the boundaries between Reed and Portland.

JERRY CASE '59: Reedites, particularly ones that came from the East Coast, tended to look down on Portland locals as being provincials, because Portland at the time didn't have much of a symphony, very little theatre, and very little in the way of the arts. A certain contingent of students enjoyed annoying Portlanders. Regardless of the weather, they always carried umbrellas with them when they went downtown and made remarks about supposed attributes of Portland, like its rainyness. They would ride into town on the bus carrying controversial newspapers like the *Daily Worker*. It was a rocky relationship.

HARRY MAKLER '58: A number of Reed students drove old hearses. The hearse contingent walked around campus dressed in black, with hats like undertakers. One day they let it be known that they were going to conduct a public funeral. They got what appeared to be a body, wrapped it in linen, put it into the back of one of their hearses, and drove to the Ross Island Bridge over the Willamette River, led by a motorcycle motorcade. They stopped in the middle of the bridge and solemnly took the body out of the hearse and dropped it over the side of the bridge, down into the river. The traffic was tied up in all directions. The *Oregonian* sold papers about it for weeks. They never did figure out what it was about.

BARRY HANSEN '63: It was during the early 1960s that the transition took place from calling students "Reedites," which had been the term used since the college's beginning, to calling

Students painting the main entry road to Reed campus on Canyon Day, 1961.

them "Reedies." I much preferred "Reedie," in that it rolled off the tongue a lot better.

Look magazine, SAM CASTAN, "Reed College: Portland's Academic Gadfly," March 27, 1962: To a good many people from Portland, Oregon, the twenty minutes that separate their city from the small suburban campus of Reed College aren't nearly enough. Despite a fifty-year record of academic achievement unexcelled by other schools, Reed is still regarded by many Portlanders with vague, unsupportable suspicions. Reed may have a higher proportion of graduates receiving Ph.D.s than any other school in the nation; it may consistently turn out one Rhodes Scholar for every 73 male graduates; it may have, as has often been said, "the smartest body of undergraduates in America." But Reed is "different," and some Portlanders think it is a trifle "too different." They ascribe to the school a marked irreverence for things they consider sac-

rosanct, and their distrust comes easier because Reed doesn't look like what they think a college should look like. It should have a football team in intercollegiate competition. All students should wear shoes. Gentlemen students should not be bearded. Lady students should wear frocks, not blankets with holes cut for the head.

"Reed is about as controversial a place as exists in higher education," says its president, Richard H. Sullivan. "Why fight it? The only thing we demand of our students is a strong intellectual commitment."

This year's freshman class is typical: it is among the top six in the country in average score achieved in College Board aptitude tests. Reed's current sophomore class was among the top 5 percent in its year. Over 70 percent of the members of the last graduating class are now attending graduate or professional school. Over half of them are studying on Woodrow Wilson, Fulbright, National Science Foundation, and other prized awards. "With kids like that," say President Sullivan, "we can afford to leave a good deal up to individual integrity."

MICHAEL NELKEN '60: Nobody was wearing baseball caps on campus or shirts of any kind that identified any player or any team from the professional sports industry. Nobody I knew ever mentioned any sports team winning or losing. Sports, along with all the rest of popular culture—movie stars, politicians, mainstream media—were anathema to Reed in those times.

JACK SCRIVENS, physical education professor 1961–1999: Once I got to Reed, I was really shocked to learn that there was a two-year requirement, four hours per week, for students to take physical education. Freshman all had to take at least half of their P.E. requirement in class. After their freshman year they could fulfill the rest of their requirement independently and fill out activity cards. We checked the activity cards really close, since some students would write in things like "intercourse: three hours." We didn't give credit for that.

JOE WEISMAN '65: There was a lot of stuff you could do for meeting the P.E. requirement. Under the Botsford Gym there was a rifle range. You could get P.E. credit for rifle shooting. We also went a lot to the area around Bend, Oregon, to go caving in the lava tubes there. We got P.E. credit for that. You could get credit for matwork, which was a euphemism for sex. You would just write down "matwork."

MERTIE HANSEN MULLER '56: Reed had a really good rifle team called "the Karl Marxmen."

HOWARD WOLPE '60: I decided to go out for basketball the year that Reed acquired a new basketball coach, Jerome P. Barta. Jerry had not quite absorbed the Reed ethos about athletics. He

actually took this stuff seriously, much to our amazement and disgust, insisting that we have workouts during the week before a game. People were literally throwing up on the floor. None of us were in condition. We used to joke that our practice consisted of "Watch your language."

That year we acquired a transfer from MIT, a six-two center who had played basketball on the junior varsity team there. We also acquired a rather accomplished six-three forward. Suddenly, Reed College became a basketball power. We were finally able to compete with the likes of Oregon Dental and Oregon Medical, who had all these jocks. People started coming out to the games. No one could quite believe what was happening with the varsity.

MORRIS BOL '58: Whenever it was announced at dinner in the Commons that the basketball team had won a game, people would boo!

CHUCK BUCHANAN '58: Under Jerry Barta we won a lot of basketball games in 1956. I was starting guard that year. Years later, one of the new players told me that Richard Sullivan had imported them when he became president. Sullivan apparently was concerned over Reed's image as being very nerdy and not normal enough. He told the players that if it ever got out that he had recruited them, he would lose his job.

ETHAN SCARL '61: The students at George Fox University used to bring their school bell to games and ring it when they won a game, as sort of a taunt. It was enormously heavy, maybe as much as four hundred pounds, and suspended on a big wooden frame on wheels. After one game, we stole the bell. George Fox's president announced that they would be forced to sever athletic relations with Reed College if the bell wasn't returned.

During the next basketball game between Reed and George Fox, Peter Scheiber '61 staged a halftime ceremony with diaphanous maidens dancing and strewing flower petals. George Fox students were presented with the first of ten three-by-five cards, which contained the first clue to a scavenger hunt for their bell. The last clue would bring them to the Hawthorne Bridge over the Willamette River, where they would discover their bell hanging under the bridge. Unfortunately, things did not go quite according to plan.

There were about six of us on the walkway of the Hawthorne Bridge with an array of ropes and a pulley. We were just about ready to get it up in position when George Fox students started appearing. Apparently they got through their scavenger hunt ordeal a little bit quicker than we anticipated. So we raised the bell up, resting it on the metal banister, tightened the ropes and pushed it off. The ropes were supposed to catch it, but there wasn't anything to take up slack and handle the kind of tension that it was going to have. The ropes broke and the thing just went straight down into the river.

I had known someone who was into scuba diving at Franklin High School in Portland, so I called him, and he agreed to dive down and attach a rope to the bell. There was a trucking outfit up at the top of the riverbank, and they offered to hook the rope to a truck and haul the bell up the bank. Eventually, there was a ceremony at George Fox when the bell was returned.

JOHN GRAEF '60: We played six-man tackle football because we couldn't get eleven men out for the team. The freshman team from Oregon State came up to play us on a lark. Their quarterback was soon to be a Heisman Trophy winner. He could throw the ball the length of the field. By the half the score was forty-two to seven. Jerry Barta tried to give us a halftime pep talk. "You know, the trouble with you guys," he said, "is that you're all gutless." Somebody sitting on the bench said, "You're right, coach."

JACK SCRIVENS, physical education professor: We were playing Columbia Christian, and the score was close when we broke at half. All of a sudden we heard this noise coming out of the area past the north end of the field. Then a Reed student on a motorcycle came roaring out of the woods with a young coed on the back of the bike banging garbage can lids. Behind them was a group of students singing a song. As they got closer, we realized it was "Onward Christian Soldiers." In the middle of the group was a young man with long, shoulder-length, reddish-brown hair and bare legs that had cutoff suntan marks. He had a wreath around the top of his head and this great big cross over his shoulders that he was dragging across the middle of the football field from one goalpost to the other.

I looked across the field at the people from Columbia Christian. Their eyes were wide open. They couldn't believe it. Once the halftime entertainment was over, the second half started up. The Reed team started playing some really good football, and we beat Columbia Christian by a couple touchdowns. I went over to talk to their coach afterwards, thinking that I had better apologize for the halftime show. He said, "Don't worry about it, Jack. That's Reed."

MURRAY LEAF '61: The next day the *Quest* newspaper ran a headline, "Athletic Overemphasis?"

CELIA HANSEN MORRIS '64: One of the chants from the sidelines was

Oregon Laundry and Linen Supply!
Oregon Laundry and Linen Supply!

That was the name of the company that did students' personal laundry and linens. It always confused the other team. They had no idea what we were saying.

RICHARD CONVISER '65: Drum major J. D. Eveland '64, wearing a bowler hat and carrying an umbrella, would lead a ragtag marching band of Reedies who would march at halftime in the formation of a cross, probably to get the goat of our Christian-school opponents. There would be an assortment of kazoos, trashcan lids as cymbals, big trashcans as bass drums, and waste cans as snare drums, lending the event a kind of surreal atmosphere. We would clap the players out of their huddle by repeating cheers like:

Schopenhauer, Marx,
Kant, Spinoza—
Come on Reed!
Hit 'em in the nose-a!

Or:

Secant, cosine,
tangent, sine!
Three point one four one five nine!
Come on, Reed—
Hit that line!

If our team should start winning, people would start to chant:

Beware of overemphasis!
Beware of overemphasis!

Another chant we did was:

Atheism,
communism,
free love!

Or just:

Love, love, love—
Free love!

J. D. EVELAND '64: The Reed College marching band had performed one Friday afternoon before Columbus Day at the football game between Reed and Columbia Christian, which the Reed Griffins, under new head coach Jack Scrivens, had by some fluke managed to win. As we were walking back up the hill toward the dormitories, the sky was darkening and the wind was rising and we thought to ourselves, "We've done something to offend the deity here." At six PM the lights went out and the wind began to howl.

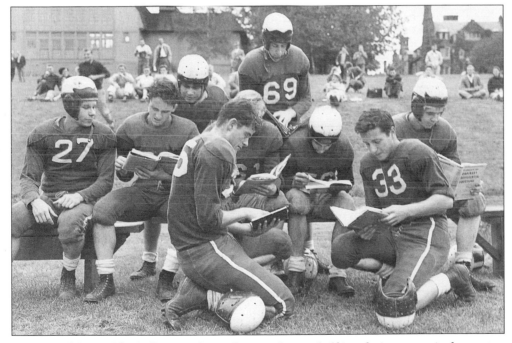

Members of the Reed football team—the Griffins—studying at halftime during a game in the 1950s.

It blew for most of the night and leveled off some time toward morning.

It turned out to be Typhoon Frieda, which was the only category-three hurricane to strike the Pacific Northwest. It was a phenomenal storm that destroyed 11.8 billion cubic feet of timber. The campus was without power for six days. We subsisted on bologna sandwiches because nothing could be heated.

LESLIE SCALAPINO '66: Nobody knew anything about the storm coming. Suddenly it swept down on us. The Commons was packed with students eating their dinner. We looked out the window and the wind simply grabbed this tree with an enormous trunk, tore it in half, and then whisked half of the tree off into the wind. Everyone stood up and went, "WHOA!"

We all ran outside to see what was happening, and it was at that point that the deans showed up, mysteriously, in all of two seconds, and were shouting, "Come back, come back." I was running along thinking, "What's happening?" I had extremely long hair down past my waist, but it was pinned up that day with bobby pins. The magnetic effect of the storm took hold of every single bobby pin and just whooshed them out of my hair in one instant. It was amazing.

MIKE HUMPHREYS '64: The next day Woodstock Boulevard and the campus was blocked with downed trees. People were rescuing books from the fourth floor of Eliot Hall, which had lost part of its roof, cutting downed trees, and working very hard all day.

TOM FORSTENZER '65: During the clean-up, a radio talk-show host in Portland described our clean-up efforts as being way ahead of the city's, and as showing that "those communist, atheist, free lovers can actually work!"

As the proprietor of the college bookstore, the Student Council voted to embrace a sartorial initiative that involved creating a college sweatshirt with a "Communism, Atheism, Free Love" logo on it. That shirt became a perennial bestseller on campus.

CHILTON GREGORY '60: In the Foster-Scholz dorm there was a group of people called the "Foster Boys"—Peter Scheiber '61, John Lovin [James Marsh] '63, Geoff Baldwin '62—who dominated the pranks field. A lot of them were mountain climbers. One of their escapades was downtown at the J. K. Gill stationary store.

A call-girl ring had been uncovered in Portland, and was making headlines in the *Oregonian*. The Gill building had a huge sign that read "CALL GILL'S," with their phone number. One night the Foster Boys came down the side of the building on ropes and changed the sign, but got the spelling wrong. The next morning people in Portland woke to see "CALL GILRS." The *Oregonian* heaped scorn on the Reed students' ability to spell, and they snuck back a few nights later to correct it.

CAROL BURNS '62: In 1962, a big controversy happened, in which our student political organization FOCUS inadvertently functioned as a front for the Communist Party. We had previously had speakers from the Communist Party on campus, but for some reason we decided to sponsor a talk by Gus Hall, the chair of the American Communist Party, at a downtown location, and that raised a big stink in Portland. The downtown location wouldn't let it happen. So we moved it to the Botsford auditorium at Reed. There was a huge attack launched locally on the college. People were calling in to the college switchboard and then just setting the phone down to jam it up.

CAROLE CALKINS COLIE '54, public affairs staff 1958–1963: I was working in the public relations office on campus. The telephones were ringing without pause. Reed had its enemies, of course, but one of particular note was a local preacher of sorts named Walter Huss who ran something in Portland called the "Freedom Center." Huss was an anti-Communist and completely crazed by the Reed students' invitation to Gus Hall. He and his followers picketed Botsford the night of Hall's appearance.

PATTY PARMALEE '62: The *Oregonian* ran a big editorial about everything that was wrong with Reed, noting that "it leans to the left." During Gus Hall's speech, we all leaned to the left in our seats.

RICHARD SULLIVAN, president 1956–1967: There were not many times during my administration when it was necessary to operate by fiat rather than by persuasion. Shortly after Gus Hall's visit, I declared a moratorium on invitations to outside speakers. It was a limited moratorium, much misunderstood at the time, not on the students' rights to invite speakers, but as to whether or not controversial speeches should be open to the public. It gave us a breathing period to examine how we were going to manage the appearance of speakers procedurally.

BARBARA ALEXANDER EHRENREICH '63: The word "intense" doesn't begin to come close to what was going on at Reed. I was being challenged and engaged in every—*every*—direction. Jay Rosenberg '63 would always be in the coffee shop, smoking his five-hundredth cigarette of the day with his cup of instant coffee and waiting like a vulture for somebody to come in that he could engage in a serious and philosophical discussion with. I loved that.

I was a chemistry major, and not a left-winger or a political student. One day another chemistry major asked me, "Barbara, if you were called on to do so as a chemist, would you work on weapons that could be used in war or for mass

destruction?" I thought to myself, "My God, do I have to answer that?" Well, yes, in a world that contained people like Jay Rosenberg, you had to answer that question, you definitely had to.

PETER LOMHOFF '66: In mid-September of my freshman year, 1962, a group of us met with sociology professor John Pock over at his house. He said, "You know, students these days are so conservative. Nobody does anything. Nobody is active in politics. The social attitudes are very conservative. I just hope you guys will begin to change things, and get excited, and get active in life." Then at UC Berkeley a few months later, the free-speech movement happened, and everything totally changed overnight.

WALLY GIBSON '66: There was a lot of activism on campus around the Student Nonviolent Coordinating Committee, or SNCC, between 1963 and 1964. Ray Raphael '65 was their leader. The summer of 1964 was the registration drive of black voters in Mississippi by the Freedom Riders. A bunch of students from Reed went south. I actually considered it at one point. My parents talked me out of it.

JOHN ULLMAN '65: Irene Namkung '65 and I got married at the beginning of our senior year. Irene's father was Korean and her mother Japanese. They didn't have misgivings about an interracial marriage. A lot of their friends were intellectuals and a lot of them were Jews, so I seemed okay to them. In the context of Reed, our being a racially mixed couple was kind of hip. In Portland, though, it was a different story.

Irene and I lived just off campus at this tiny little cabin on Twenty-eighth and Steele. One day, a black family moved into the house across the street. "They won't be there long," a friend told me. "The city will turn off their water and their electricity, and they'll be out of there." By God, in three weeks, they were gone.

To expose this sort of discrimination, Irene and I participated with other students in a civil rights test. If someone was renting a house in a white neighborhood, a white student couple would go up and, after being told that the house was available, they would be shown through it. Then a black student couple would go up and the people would say it wasn't available, that it had already been rented, when in fact it hadn't. Then white students would go up again and be allowed to rent it. Irene and I would go up to see if they would rent to a mixed-race couple. We got a sense of the depths of people's racism in town.

NANCY TESELLE WOOD '66: We were riding our bikes in from off campus, and a little guy in a driveway yelled, "The president is dead!" We said, "What?" And he said, "The president is dead!" And we went "Ha, ha, ha." By the time we arrived on campus, people were all gathered around the few televisions there. I was struck by people who were weeping really heavily. I thought, "Wow, where do they get their passion?"

LAURA STEVENS '67: I went to Sam Danon's French class. Sam came into class very agitated saying, "In France they shoot at people, but they don't mean to hit them." When we came out of class Ron Sharrin '67 was standing there and said, "Kennedy's dead. Now we have this big Southern smiling marshmallow as president, Lyndon Johnson."

JOHN LAURSEN '67: I was in the mail room in the basement of the old Student Union when I heard the news. Everyone was stunned. There was just this kind of hushed silence. There wasn't weeping and gnashing of teeth, but everyone was in shock. That afternoon I left with a group of people to drive down to the Bay Area for Thanksgiving. We drove through the night listening to intermittent reports on the radio stations fading in

and out about the hunt for Kennedy's assassin—they think they know who it is, no they don't, they think they've caught him, no they haven't, that sort of thing. It was a completely eerie and disconnected experience.

CARA LAMB '66: That night, we had a wild party. We played *The First Family* album, which was a comedy record by Vaughn Meader making fun of the Kennedys.

JOHN LAURSEN '67: My freshman year was transformative for me in every way. My family was politically conservative, and although I would be a political science major I had come to Reed with really no understanding of politics or of history. I came out of my dormitory room one day early on wearing a Barry Goldwater sweatshirt and one of my dorm-mates just burst out laughing. Everyone I encountered at that point came from an entirely different political perspective from the one I had grown up with.

LIZ FINK '67: Barry Goldwater, who was running for president on the Republican ticket in 1964 against Lyndon Johnson, was speaking at the Convention Center in Portland. Bob Gottlieb '65 and Jeff Sachar '66 had just come back to campus from working for the Student Nonviolent Coordinating Committee on Freedom Summer, where civil rights activists had gone down to Mississippi to register as many black voters as possible. Bob and Jeff showed up wearing their Mississippi SNCC dungaree outfits, and started organizing a demonstration of "Reed College Communists for Barry Goldwater."

PHILIP WIKELUND '69: Communists for Goldwater was an attempt to turn things around in terms of the way the media was seeing them, a sort of reverse street theatre. The focus was Goldwater, but instead of being against him, we came out for him, trying to get as much media attention as possible, both with TV crews and news reporters. The media didn't know how to take it, and were very tentative in their coverage, reporting things on a strictly factual basis. They really couldn't grasp the idea.

CARTER WEISS '66: The thrust of Communists for Goldwater was to support Goldwater for president, because his election would bring about the revolution that much quicker.

JIM KAHAN '64: The Young Democrats' beer blast was held at a Reed house called "the Faucet," at Fifty-fifth and Woodstock. The juniors and seniors at the house were dedicated beer brewers on a massive scale. In the spring they threw a party that was free for Young Democrats, and a dollar and a quarter for everybody else. Or you could join the Democrat Party at the door for a dollar. It must have been half of the campus that went up there, including six of the eight Young Republicans, and of course everybody joined.

Chapter representation in the state convention of Young Democrats was not just the function of your absolute numbers, but of your market penetration on campus. So although Reed didn't have the absolute number of Democrats compared to the University of Oregon or Oregon State University, we had a market penetration that couldn't be topped because of the beer party. That gave the Reed Young Democrats delegation a tremendous amount of power, and things like anti Vietnam-War resolutions were passed in the organization because of that.

MASON DRUKMAN, political science professor 1964–1970: Having recently come from graduate school in Berkeley to teach at Reed, I formed a group on campus called "In Support of FSM," the free-speech movement. We got the faculty to pass a resolution condemning the police presence on the Berkeley campus, and then we

got President Sullivan to write a letter to Berkeley doing the same. It was regarded as a quasi-academic position, defending academic freedom from interference.

LIZ FINK '67: The minute I got to Reed, I had contact with the members of the Communist Party. My parents were members. Helen and Bill Gordon were two Portland activists who brought together young people in town whose parents were Party members.

In the spring of '64, a Senate committee called the Subversive Activities Control Board, which had been established during the McCarthy era, subpoenaed members of the Communist Party in Portland, among them a Reed alumnus, Don Hamerquist '62, who put out a local newspaper that I always read verbatim. The SACB came to town and the newspaper was shut down. The SACB was here for two weeks, and the demonstrations were huge.

LINDA HAMMILL MATTHEWS '67, trustee 2005– : Walking into Commons my first day of school I saw calligraphed posters, including one that said, "Don't wait. Escalate." It was in beautiful calligraphy, but it had a picture of an atomic explosion on it. I had no idea what was being referred to, and after weeks of pondering this I asked somebody. They looked at me like I was from Mars and said, "It's referring to the war in Vietnam. Haven't you heard about the war in Vietnam?"

Well, no, in fact, I hadn't. I had come from a very protected background in Portland. I didn't know anything about Vietnam, I didn't know anything about civil rights. I didn't know anything about any larger issues in the world. That quickly changed. The social and political aspects of Reed provided an awakening for me.

PETER LOMHOFF '66: As the Vietnam War developed, it put the campus very much at odds

Student body president Tom Forstenzer '65 addresses protesters outside a hearing of the Subversive Activities Control Board in downtown Portland in the spring of 1964.

with most everybody in Portland, and for that matter, most everybody in the country, many of whose opinions were reflected by the conservative William F. Buckley, Jr.

DEBORAH ROSS '68: In the fall of 1964, there was a debate at a high school downtown between philosophy professor Marvin Levich and William F. Buckley, Jr., on whether internal security legislation was consistent with the principles of a democratic society. The place was jammed. Levich and Buckley each gave opening arguments, and then started getting into it. Levich, who was used to giving an hour humanities lecture that used maybe three sentences—all grammatically correct—went to a great deal of trou-

ble breaking down his sentences so they would be comprehensible. We watched the expression on Buckley's face as he was trying to follow these sentences, and you could see how confused and frustrated he was getting.

ROBERT REYNOLDS, physics professor 1963–2002: Marvin essentially demolished every single point that Buckley tried to make. There wasn't any beating around the bush. He made his points, and they were strong points. Buckley got up at the end, looking sort of forlorn, and tried to save face by saying, "Well, it's important that we discuss these things, because really, all that we have are our minds." As he said that, he raised his arms into a sort of cruciform position.

MARVIN LEVICH, philosophy professor 1953–1994, provost 1972–1979: The debate was exhilarating, as long as it lasted. Afterwards, we had cocktails at history professor Dick Jones' house, and Buckley came over. Where I felt that Buckley went wrong was that he was partly untrue to his own conservative principles; if anybody should be involved in the business of conserving the rights of people and preventing government from having the power to examine their beliefs, it should be a conservative.

TOM WEISNER '65: The famous Gulf of Tonkin Resolution, which authorized Lyndon Johnson to take military action in Vietnam without declaring war, was being voted on in 1964, and only two members of the U.S. Senate voted against it. One was Wayne Morse from Oregon.

Senator Morse drove over to Reed in his car by himself, and gave a lecture. I was among the students who organized his visit. We sat in a small room and talked with him about the Tonkin Gulf Resolution for two hours. It was an intense discussion, with Morse being grilled by all these Reed students. He had an intellectual grasp of the topic, and he also had his own personal values. It cost him to have taken that vote. He lost his seat when he ran for reëlection.

MARJORY FRANKLIN LUXENBERG '66: I felt we were politically ahead of the rest of the world. UC Berkeley was first. Whatever Berkeley did, we were doing three to six months later. When they started protesting the Vietnam War, we became very serious about joining in. A bunch of us spent a couple of nights over Thanksgiving weekend 1965 on the steps of the post office in downtown Portland with our sleeping bags and our signs, marching and protesting. We were aware of the ramping up of the war before much of the rest of the country, and we were out there on the front lines.

JOHN GRAY, trustee 1961–2006: A lot of institutions and government bodies were adopting resolutions in favor of, or not in favor of, the war in Vietnam. The Reed Board of Trustees concluded that it was a matter of individual expression and not a position for the institution to take. I believed strongly in that.

WILLIAM WIEST, psychology professor 1961–1995: People were divided over that stance. I don't think there was that much disagreement among the faculty as a whole as to the wisdom of the Vietnam War. Everybody thought it was very foolish. But there was a strong feeling among many not to make political statements as an institution, because that was thought to be stepping outside of the bounds of what the institution was about.

JOAN RUDD '69: Sometime in the fall of '66, there was an anti-Vietnam protest on campus in Eliot Circle. It was mostly students, except for Howard Waskow, a young literature professor. I used to babysit for Waskow and his wife. They had a perfectly normal middle-class home. During the protest, we were barricading Eliot Hall, and the police were called in. Howard Waskow was doing passive resistance, and I watched as the police picked him up on a platform and carried him away to a patrol car as though he were on a funeral bier. He was taken downtown and booked. That really made an indelible impression on me. I had been to his home, and here he was, literally putting his body on the line.

STEVEN WOOD '66: I didn't make it through Reed. I left because of draft resistance. It was difficult, especially given my family background, to do that. I was at Reed for just a couple of years, but it lit in me some sparks that remained important for the balance of my life. One was the courage to take a relatively unpopular stand.

CHAPTER 23

Calligraphy

What Reed was really good at as a culture was analysis, taking things apart. Lloyd Reynolds was putting things together, and that was the difference.
　—Michael McPherson '68

I received lab reports calligraphed. Beautiful! You can't imagine a lab report written, the entire thing, in beautiful script.
　—Bert Brehm, biology professor

For thirty-five years, no single class held more Reed students enthralled than the calligraphy course started by art professor Lloyd Reynolds in the 1940s. Reynolds was viewed by some as a guru more than as a professor, inspiring generations of self-confessed disciples since his arrival at Reed in 1929. A polymath, Reynolds moved from teaching eighteenth-century literature and creative writing to teaching art history, and then to teaching graphic arts and calligraphy. He was given to synthesizing various cultural and religious traditions in the style of writer and mythologist Joseph Campbell. In 1954, the college temporarily suspended him from teaching for his refusal to answer questions by the House Un-American Activities Committee regarding his involvement with the Communist Party.

When the new chemistry building was completed in 1948, Reynolds took over the former chemistry lab in the attic of Eliot Hall for his graphic arts workshop, a course in the history and evolution of calligraphic and typographic letterforms. Calligraphy became one of the college's most popular courses. Championed as the "peoples' art," it dominated the aesthetic sensibilities of the campus for more than three decades, recognized as one of Reed's refined but quirky qualities. As taught by Reynolds, calligraphy transcended the study of handwriting and provided a prism through which to view Western and Eastern humanities.

By the mid-1950s, Reed College had become a center of the mid-century calligraphy revival in America. It would be the training ground for a number of prominent type designers and typographers of the later twentieth century.

The graphic arts workshop in the early 1960s, with Lloyd Reynolds (upper left) and (clockwise) Mary Scherbatskoy '63, Lucille Borgen '65, Bob Charlton '61, Donald Rudy '62, Stephanie Hoyer '65, Stanley Kan '64, and Angela Lane '65.

JAKI SVAREN '50: By the time I got around to taking calligraphy, it was because I was madly in love with Lloyd Reynolds. I don't think anybody could be in the same room with him for ten minutes without being madly in love with him. His autobiography was simply this: "I inhale, I exhale, hallelujah! Just break it all down to the basics—breathe in, breathe out, and stop fretting about all the rest of this stuff."

In introducing people to art, Lloyd was trying to open them up to their own potential, every single person, as he was not particular in picking his successes. Everyone had the potential to be a success. The letters in calligraphy were a way of getting people to open, an easy way to sneak it up on you: "You *can* do this. This is simple. Right here. Now you can move beyond that, because now you know what a counter is." Then, before you know it, you have these terms that all of a sudden apply to everything, not just to calligraphy.

Lloyd had the magical ability to make each person feel that they were the most important person in the room. He didn't have a bunch of special disciples who got special treatment; at least I never felt that way. When he would lecture, he would look at you and you were it, you knew that the whole talk was for you. He made me feel special—"You are the one. You are the one. You are the one."

He could do that to a whole room full of people. It was just a magical ability. He could talk to you on this level or that, or he could talk to children. Whoever he was with he gave that same feeling to. I don't think you can take that apart anymore than you can really take apart a poem. He just . . . was.

CHUCK BIGELOW '67: Lloyd conveyed a grand vision of writing. Those who thought calligraphy was a quaint, ornamental frivolity saw it merely as penmanship. Lloyd saw it as civilization.

LLOYD REYNOLDS, art professor 1929–1969: Letters fascinated me ever since I found their power and beauty when I was five years old. Living in a poor farming community in eastern Washington, we had no electricity and no plumbing, but we did have books. I was always drawing, and letters were a favorite subject. When I was a graduate student in English at the University of Oregon, William Blake, John Ruskin, and William Morris became my mentors. All three hated commercialism and industrialism, and valued art, literature, and book making.

In the spring of 1934 I ordered Edward Johnston's *Writing and Illuminating and Lettering*, thinking that it was probably just another book of alphabets. I shall never forget that May afternoon when I read the author's preface and the first two chapters. It was like a bolt of lightning. Here was the insight I had been seeking—the only logical approach was the historical one. Learn to cut reed and quill pens and write your way through the history of the alphabet! For

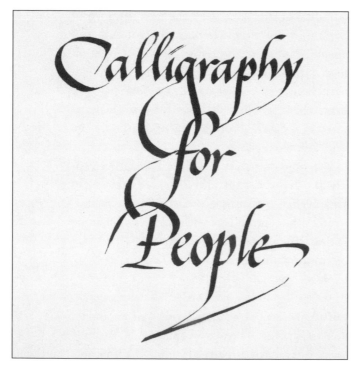

Calligraphy by Lloyd Reynolds.

the next few years I devoted almost all my spare time to paleography, studying alphabets chronologically, pen in hand.

As I acquired skill with the edged pen, the college offices asked me to write out bulletin board notices. Students saw the work and asked me to teach them the skill. For more than ten years I taught informal, non-credit classes. In 1948 it became possible to teach a year-long course on the history of alphabetic communication, with a laboratory. We met for three hours each session twice a week. The first hour was lecture, the rest studio work with the edged pen or printing types on a huge Washington-Hoe hand press we set up. Ever since coming to Reed I had taught creative writing, and students began to write out their original poems or to print them on the press.

A former student of the great calligrapher Arnold Bank suggested that we bring Bank to Portland for a series of lectures, which we did. Our efforts were approved and encouraged. To my great delight, I was asked to teach a night class in the Museum Art School at the Portland Art Museum. That, along with summer sessions at Reed College, made it possible for me to work with interested primary and secondary school teachers. We found that skill in Italic cursive handwriting encouraged literacy. By the mid-1950s, all the high schools and most of the elementary schools in Oregon offered Italic as an art project. In the secondary schools, year-long courses in calligraphy were common.

PHILIP WHALEN '51: I was always in Lloyd's creative writing class, writing all the time, taking stuff to show him. He seemed to get a kick out of what I wrote, and just kept encouraging me to write more. That was very valuable.

Lloyd always said that he was not popular at Reed because he thought people ought to do things. You were not supposed to just sit around and think or speculate about things all the time. Get up and do something. He felt that this made him very unpopular in this heavily academic institution. Of course, he could do academic things perfectly well. But he felt sort of out of step with the institution.

GARY SNYDER '51: Charlie Leong '53, a Chinese-American G.I., came into our world and provided quick, short teachings, like how to do brush calligraphy. He taught me the basic moves of Chinese characters and how to grind ink. Charlie was already a fine calligrapher in Chinese. Then he took up calligraphy with Lloyd Reynolds and made himself into a marvelous calligrapher of chancery cursive. Lloyd looked at that and said, "Well, if you can learn to do chancery cursive, I can learn to do Chinese characters." So he got Charlie to teach him how to grind the ink and hold the brush, and how to cut linoleum blocks of calligraphy for use in printing.

CLYDE VAN CLEVE '55: I was surrounded by people from Phillips Exeter and other prep schools who were much better prepared for scholarly work than I was. The graphics workshop became kind of a haven, a hideout place to escape the toughness of the academic world. It was not that I didn't care for the academic work, but if you had a tendency or a desire to make an object rather than manipulate an idea, there was no real substitute for that, whether it was with letterforms, lines of type, printed broadsides, or books. That all had great appeal to me.

In his teaching, Lloyd never got on anybody's case directly, but he was always very good at pointing out the things you should avoid. The student got a very clear picture of what he called the "path of virtue."

BILL GUNDERSON, Reynolds colleague: The path of virtue is to be direct. Do not try to get fancy. The fundamental forms will be so beautiful if you do them well that you do not need to worry about making them better—at least in the beginning. Don't retouch, because the tendency to retouch never works. You can eliminate glitches, but then when you start out you will think you can fix it later. No. Just start over again.

One of Lloyd's students made a large steel thunderbolt that Lloyd liked to exhibit. The student was about ready to leave Reed because he felt that he was only getting concepts. So Lloyd told him about a blacksmith that he knew and sent him down to do some work with him. The student became very enthused and made Lloyd a thunderbolt. The last time I heard of this fellow he was going over to Japan with a scholarship to study the Japanese style of metalwork.

CONNIE CROOKER '69: Lloyd would often talk about the symbol of the thunderbolt, and how the thunderbolt annihilates and illuminates simultaneously.

JERRY CASE '59: Lloyd struck me as generally unhappy, especially with the failure of people to take up the political messages he inserted into his teachings. Most of us, while sensitive to Lloyd's feelings, felt that much of his orientation was anachronistic and harkened back to a period that tended to view socialism as utopian and necessarily good. There was no question, though, about his love of books and crafts. He seemed to feel that anything mass-produced was, ipso facto, degraded or worse. William Morris was part of his pantheon and he used to talk at great length about the fundamental societal need for individual creativity.

MICHAEL MCPHERSON '68: Lloyd's graphics arts class was basically the history of the world through the prism of calligraphy. He usually came into class very grumpy, and would begin by chewing everyone out for our pathetic attempts at, well, pretty much everything. Then he would start class by talking about a particular typeface or a particular calligraphic style, and the digressions would build on the digressions until by the end of class he was practically giggling. Within a five-minute period Lloyd would quote the Upanishads, the Tao, the Old Testament, the New Testament, and then Mao Tse-tung possibly, all in the same paragraph. Meanwhile, everyone in the class was having a minor satori.

Lloyd was not a rigorous thinker. He was a Joseph Campbell type who took what he needed in order to communicate what was useful to him, to his life, and also to his practice. His will to synthesize ideas would often overwhelm his sources. He would start to talk about Blake, and you'd get really excited, and then you'd go read Blake and wonder, "Boy, where is the magic?" It was more that he saw Blake through Zen Buddhism and through Taoism and through his own experience of life, so that Blake's work became something more than just the original source.

After his talk, there would be a break in the class, and then you would come back and start working. Lloyd would do a demonstration on the board and explain each stroke and what the sequence was and why it was important that you do it in that sequence. Then people would spend the next two hours just working, while he walked around and looked at people's work. The thing about what he told us about our work was that I always felt like I knew he was right, I just couldn't see it. Then you'd practice and you would suddenly see something and you would think, "That's what he meant when he said 'never look at the stroke you're making, only look at the counter form.'" Once you understood it, you knew it emotionally and tactilely.

What Reed was really good at as a culture was analysis, taking things apart. Lloyd was putting things together, and that was the difference.

DOROTHY HURT DEHN '61: By the time I entered Reed in 1957, there were so many people that wanted to take Lloyd's graphic arts workshop that, as a freshman, I was not permitted to en-roll. Because of the demand Lloyd held an open lab on Saturdays. He was on campus six days a week, sometimes seven. He was able to communicate his joy and enthusiasm so well. Most of us didn't dare miss a class because that might be the one where the real secret came together.

STEVEN HEROLD '63: I didn't take his class until my senior year. You couldn't. It was so popular they rationed you. Seniors got precedence because they would never have another chance, then juniors and sophomores if there was room.

CARTER WEISS '66: Calligraphy was an everyday art. You wrote stuff every day, but you could make things that were little works of beauty. It didn't require a lot of fancy equipment, and setup was very easy. Every Reedie could afford the modest kit for calligraphy—the nibbed Osmoroid fountain pen, special paper, and fountain pen India ink.

LLOYD REYNOLDS, art professor: In the spring of 1958 the Portland Art Museum asked me to organize a huge calligraphy exhibition. Most of the items came from the Newberry Library in Chicago, the Morgan Library in New York, and the Hofer Collection at the Houghton Library at Harvard. The exhibition and the catalogue proved to be more of an innovation than I realized, and "everyman's handicraft" acquired publicity and prestige.

JANE HOWARD MERSEREAU '42: When it got to the point where Lloyd was getting an awful lot of publicity for his calligraphy, there was a certain amount of sour grapes among other faculty members. I've always maintained that people are as jealous of publicity as they are of money. It only got worse when Oregon's governor, Tom McCall, whose sister and brother had attended Reed, made Lloyd Calligrapher Laureate of Oregon in a ceremony at the Portland Art Museum.

Father Edward M. Catich chiseling Roman letters into the slate panel above the entrance to Eliot Hall, 1962.

CARTER WEISS '66: Reynolds had an unexpected artistic soulmate, Father Edward M. Catich, a teacher at St. Ambrose College in Davenport, Iowa, and the world's greatest living authority on the inscriptions on the Trajan Column in Rome. His finding was that these magnificent letters were painted freehand on stone with a flat, edged brush, then incised with chisels. That explained the serifs—those thin strokes at the ends of the letters.

In the early 1960s Father Catich came to Reed for a visit. A high point of the visit came when Catich made new signage for Eliot Hall and the dormitories of the Old Dorm Block. He used a brush, and drew beautiful freehand Roman letters from memory on slate panels. Through his union ties, Lloyd Reynolds knew a handful of people in the building trades whose fathers or uncles had taught them rudiments of older skills like stone cutting. They incised these panels with chisels, following Catich's freehand, just like the Roman craftsmen who cut the Trajan Column. As a final step the incised letters were gilded with gold paint.

STEVEN HEROLD '63: In the mid-1960s when they moved the graphic arts lab out of the attic of Eliot Hall to the arts studio, there was something just not right about it. Before that it was like Hogwarts from Harry Potter—we were in this magical place, practicing this magical skill that only the initiated knew about, and it was just wonderful, a warm sort of sharing thing. Magical little toys and types—things that you did with your fingertips—being brought out of drawers. Lloyd was a kitten all of his life. Everything was a wonderful new toy to discover. He played with it and then he showed it to others.

We were sitting one day talking. I was working on some scholarly articles on Renaissance scribes, and he was showing me some samples of people in Portland who were exemplifying that style. I made some comment like, "But they're not in scholarship anymore. These are housewives. Good hands, but. . . ." "Oh," he said, "Don't you *ever* say that! Those 'mere' housewives are greater than you by far! Look at the work they're doing here with the pen. What do you think their attitudes are?"

There is something that happens when people start finding letterforms—you get the magic in you, it transmits, and you just go crazy. There was something about calligraphy that lent itself to disciples. All the great teachers had them. Lloyd had them. People bowed at his feet and worshipped and loved him.

CARTER WEISS '66: Peter Norton '65 was a disciple. Peter came from a modest family background, and worked his way through Reed doing calligraphy. You could later see the Reynolds Italic in Peter's signature on the computer manuals for his Norton Utilities.

How does one work one's way through Reed doing calligraphy? The tradition of the times was that every college event was announced by a calligraphed banner, written on large pieces of butcher paper about three feet by ten, and hung

in the Commons. Reynolds' disciples would make the banners on commission. Every organization budgeted for this expense—maybe five dollars per banner at the time. Sometimes a student would commission a banner for something personal, like a birthday or passing the junior qual. Part of this was a function of the architecture. The old Commons, now the Student Union building, had two balconies where the banners were hung upon the railings. An official student group rotated the banners to phase out the ones that everybody had seen.

LUCINDA PARKER MCCARTHY '66: I did a whole lot of calligraphing of banners and signs and posters for all kinds of events, which were hung in the Commons. They were beautiful, but we thought nothing of it. It was just something we did. I made all my spending money that way,

Calligraphed banners hanging on one of the Commons balconies in the early 1960s.

between fifty and a hundred dollars a month. I took the first two years of humanities where you had to write a five-to-ten-page paper every week. I couldn't type, so I calligraphed all my papers. Nobody ever complained.

JOHN LAURSEN '67: I remember walking into Commons on February 14 one year and seeing this banner that was just absolutely beautiful. It was adorned with hearts and flowers, framing exquisite calligraphy that read, "Happy V. D."

BERT BREHM, biology professor 1962–1993: Calligraphy was part of the real flavor of the institution. It just tasted good. You saw it everywhere around you. It was not something that you admired on occasion; calligraphy was part of everyday life. It was great. There would be these little calligraphed signs hanging on the trees, which Lloyd called "weathergrams." I received lab reports calligraphed. Beautiful! You can't imagine a lab report written, the entire thing, in beautiful script.

I told one student, "I can't believe what I am seeing. I would love to be able to keep this." And she said, "Fine, but if I ever need it will you send it to me?" One day she called me up and said, "Can you please send that lab report to me? I'm applying for an art fellowship and I would like to use it as part of my application."

LLOYD REYNOLDS, art professor: In the early '60s, a profound change in Western society appeared. Many people became aware of the faults in our commercial, technological culture. They were tired of being only spectators and consumers. "We have hands, not paws." We can make things, not just push buttons. We might not need electric toothbrushes, electric can openers, pencil sharpeners, and shoe polishers. We can use our hands. In writing something, we might use a pen and ignore the electric typewriter. Instead of boredom, we might find joy in the making.

RICHARD BURG '67: There was a small group who were freshmen in 1963, a couple of them from my dormitory, who all got involved in visual or graphic arts. Sumner Stone '67 who majored in math, became the first type designer at Adobe Systems. Chuck Bigelow '67, an anthropology major, became a type designer of world renown. John Laursen '67, a political science major, became a book designer and typographer who puts words into metal and stone for all kinds of civic projects. There was something about our experiences in the '60s, and Lloyd Reynolds' influence in particular, that resulted in some people finding a way to live that was entirely different from what Reed's focus on academics might have led them to.

SUMNER STONE '67: I took the beginning calligraphy class on Italic. It was a magical experience that affected my whole life. Intellectual things were the things that were valued in my childhood and upbringing. Lloyd provided me with a pathway to *make* things. In retrospect, I realized that I was a maker of things. And that was a great gift.

My impression was that Lloyd had epiphanies. One day he talked about seeing a blade of grass push up through the concrete. I had the feeling that rather than having a philosophy, he had these mystical experiences that he took very seriously, and that were the basis of him finding resonance in other places. It didn't really matter where. He was looking for other people talking about things in religions and in spiritual writing, such as Blake, that he'd experienced himself.

LLOYD REYNOLDS, art professor: In 1968, Oregon Educational Television Service asked me to make a series of twenty half-hour programs on Italic handwriting and calligraphy. In the following seven years, the entire series was broadcast some fourteen times, and then re-taped in the 1970s in color.

BILL GUNDERSON, Reynolds colleague: I was watching Lloyd's public television show on calligraphy. He was making ampersands. He would do one and he'd go "Wowwwww!" He'd groan. I said "That guy is having an experience here with this ampersand! I can't believe it!"

JOAN RUDD '69: There was almost a complete absence of acknowledgment of the spiritual on campus. Lloyd Reynolds was my first introduction to Eastern thought. He would tell us things like, "Go out and be the tree. Study the tree. Don't just draw the tree." In calligraphy class he would talk about discipline and regular practice. The only time I could find to do calligraphy practice with that sort of intentionality and focus in my shared dorm was to get up at four in the morning each day. Calligraphy was a meditative practice in itself.

PATRICK MCMAHON '69: It wasn't just that Reynolds could bring things together, he could blow things apart too. One day in his freshman art history class he was showing a slide of a painting of a horse. "You can't see this horse if you think about it," he said. It was the first time I had ever heard an alternative to the rational thought process, and it infuriated me. It was a barrier. I couldn't imagine looking at this picture about a horse without thinking about it. Another time he put a pumpkin on the reserve shelf in the library for us to look at. I sat in front of that pumpkin for twenty minutes, and the details started to come out of it. The pumpkin-ness started to come out of it. It was actually the first pumpkin I ever really saw. I had never heard of anything like this before.

CHARLES RHYNE, art history professor 1960–1997: Lloyd's art history course was the most popular course on campus. He was lecturing to a sizeable part of the student body two or three times a week. He was totally fascinating to listen

to, and completely committed to what he was doing. It was the history of art with Lloyd's critical view of it going through. When artists talk, and Lloyd was basically talking as an artist teaching art history, they're fabulous about the things they like, because they respond terribly well to them. But the things they don't like they're terrible about, because they don't like them. I think the artist's own creative impulse comes from taking a very prejudiced view of things.

STAN WASHBURN '66: Reynolds enjoyed Grand Old Man status at Reed, which had its downside in laziness and indulgence. I didn't notice at first. The popularity and clarity of his teaching made calligraphy an art form shared on a sophisticated and personal level by a huge slice of the college. The large calligraphed banners executed by students to advertise coming events were greeted with a knowledgeable and often heated critique. There were disputes about whether leaving your guide lines unerased was a commendable expression of honesty, or merely a crutch for weak design. It was a subtle point. The dispute however, which concerned the boundary between art and its social context, was substantial.

Reynolds also taught art history, which was a wider, trickier subject. Here he was at sea. Art history is too often taught as social history lite, with the art itself brought on as garnish. Reynolds transcended that. He talked about the art, about the works themselves, and why they have the effect they do. He got this part, the formal part, and he was mesmerizing on the deceptively humble craft of seeing what you're looking at. He talked wonderfully about *The Dying Lioness* from Nineveh, circa 650 BCE—how the lion's dragging, crippled body gathers power from the slanting ground beneath.

But art history also involves the vision that underlies the formal choices. Here he got into trouble. Here he drifted off on bizarre tangents. I remember a perfectly sensible explication of the still center in Chinese landscape morphing into a passionate comparison between the austere wisdom of the Confucian scholar on his mountaintop, and the mindless, consumer-driven culture of contemporary America. The comparison was absurd. The ignorance, vacuity, and self-indulgence of it was patent. The implication—that we were too dumb to notice or too enthralled to question—was offensive.

CONNIE CROOKER '69: Lloyd liked to quote William Morris as saying, "The true secret of happiness lies in the taking of genuine interest in the details of daily life and elevating them like art." He talked about light a lot and the function of light. In one class he said, "The light by which one can see the sun is brighter than the sun." These kinds of things were dripping between all this practical instruction, like, "this is the right counter that you have to do for an 'A,' and you have to arch your 'N' this way." He used to tell us to go and look at the spaces between the blades of grass—don't look at the grass, look at the spaces between the blades of grass. Turns out, that was a very practical piece of advice for calligraphy, it wasn't just about some kind of Zen thing of looking at the world a different way. It was about looking at how lines on pages create spaces rather than simply looking at the line. So everything tied back in. It was often a metaphor for the Italic or the handwriting that we were doing.

It was exciting to just be around that eclectic kind of mind. He used to say, "The only way to keep our culture from continuing its present disintegration is to seek larger unities. Learn to count to one."

LLOYD REYNOLDS, art professor, freshman orientation talk, 1962: Remember, nobody—at least this is my theory—nobody can teach you anything, but you can learn. In a sense you teach yourself. I like the old meaning of educate; it means to draw forth. The teacher is one who is

> FELLOWSHIP
>   is heaven
> & lack of fellowship is hell:
> fellowship is life
>   & lack of fellowship is death:
> & the deeds ye do upon the earth,
>   it is for fellowship's sake
>   that ye do them,
>   & for the life that is in it,
> that shall live on and on forever,
>   & each one of you
>   part of it.
>
>   WILLIAM MORRIS
>   THE DREAM OF JOHN BALL

Calligraphy by Lloyd Reynolds.

an educator; he draws out the students' capabilities. He doesn't put things in, like someone on an assembly line in a factory.

See, our minds are dominated by the factory system, and we think that a lot of the things today are just things you assemble. You don't assemble things that way in college, you grow your field. It has be grown, and grown in an organic way. The instructor can give you hints about gardening in regard to growing your French, or your Greek, your chemistry, or whatever it is. So find out from him the method, because this is most of what you'll learn here at Reed. You'll forget many of the facts, especially if you lose your notebook, in which case, well gee, then where are you?

CHAPTER 24

Dreams of Expansion

One of the original conceptions of Reed College was to have a conservatory, a medical school, a technical school, engineering schools, and an art school, as well as a liberal arts college; an architect's map from 1912 shows all of these built around little quads.
—Nicholas Wheeler '55, physics professor

There was a mass student meeting in which every student received a sticker attacking the academic imperialism of President Sullivan. It read "'Reed is a college that mistakes not bigness for greatness'—W. T. Foster."
—Mark Loeb '65

By the early 1960s, President Richard Sullivan's efforts to grow Reed were paying off. He had successfully leveraged the post-Sputnik boom in funding for higher education, upgrading the living and teaching standards of the faculty, increasing the student body by 50 percent to nearly a thousand students, boosting financial aid, and constructing many new buildings on campus. He had also expanded national student recruitment, and succeeded in lifting student academic performance to its highest levels since the college's early years.

But Sullivan had still larger ambitions. With the growing dominance of government-financed research universities, he saw the influence of the private liberal arts model declining in coming years—especially in the West, where public institutions were more prevalent. A group of local business leaders headed by Reed trustee Howard Vollum '36 approached Sullivan with a proposal to expand Reed into a graduate university to serve the personnel requirements of Portland-area industry. At the time, there existed no graduate program between Seattle and Eugene; Portland State College, established in the mid-1940s, was just starting to gear up for university status. Sullivan decided to back the businessmen's proposal. His decision generated strong student protest, polarized the faculty, and ignited an institutional crisis that would rage for the remainder of the decade.

RICHARD SULLIVAN, president 1956–1967: Reed had a package that maximized all costs: low student-to-faculty ratio, generally small classes, and lower teaching loads. The challenge with growth was that unless you agreed to some changes in the teaching methods, the economic problems for the institution simply increased with additional students. This was in contrast to other institutions, where the incremental parcel of students lowered the average cost per student. But it became obvious to me early on that with the growing demand from the surge in the birth rates there would be great pressures to expand, at least in some gradual fashion.

Over the years Reed had been blessed with an unusually able and dedicated faculty. To preserve and possibly enhance the quality of a Reed education, it was clear that faculty salaries had to be increased very rapidly to keep up with other colleges. Of almost equal importance to some individuals were questions of teaching loads and the opportunity in terms of time and energy to press on with one's research.

RICHARD JONES, history professor 1941–1982, 1985–1986: In the late 1950s Reed was one of a few liberal arts colleges selected by the Ford Foundation to receive broad-purpose matching grants. Faculty improvement claimed first attention. Faculty salaries were substantially raised, a sabbatical program was instituted in 1958, and home mortgages were made available at low interest rates for faculty home buyers. The student-faculty ratio was drastically reduced, even below the college's optimum ten-to-one ratio, ultimately reaching a point of 7.4-to-one.

RICHARD SULLIVAN, president: Reed was getting a good deal less than $50,000 a year from the federal government, largely for peripheral programs that the college would not otherwise have had as part of its curriculum. For the basic program of the college, we were far more dependent upon private contributions.

I was exposed to several strong opinions about the relationship between Portland and Reed College. They boiled down to three points: Portland has never understood Reed College; Portland has never appreciated Reed College; Portland has never really supported Reed College. My own belief was that the weight of historical evidence supported these contentions. Reed was the outstanding example, bar none, of a college that had a very high national reputation, a continuous courtship with the ideal of excellence, and yet only the barest minimum of financial support from its own surrounding community.

Then, in 1961, the college was notified of a $1.4 million, two-for-one matching-grant challenge from the Ford Foundation.

RICHARD JONES, history professor: The Ford grant enabled President Sullivan to explore more ambitious developments. The physical plant, never luxurious in either space or condition, and especially overcrowded in the postwar years, was expanded and updated with the biology building, a doubling of the size of the library, new dormitories, the planned construction of a new dining hall, and a new physical education facility. Student enrollment rose from six hundred in 1955–56 to more than a thousand in 1963–64, while the teaching faculty grew from seventy-five to 113. This enlargement, though, did not proceed in accordance with any plan, and serious questions about the effect of size on the basic character of the college had not been raised.

STEVEN HEROLD '63: President Sullivan was charming and dynamic, and he wanted to have a big, successful school for his career, so he just started pushing the envelope, bringing in new people and new curricula. The trustees would say, "We don't have the money." And he would say, "Then we'll find it. If we start this we will have to find the money."

So there was this great expansion at Reed in terms of getting the college better known, and of getting new buildings and state-of-the-art facilities. The endowment then was around $4.5 million. By comparison, Amherst College, roughly the same size, had an endowment of something like $96 million. You don't get much investment income off of $4 million, so it was tough funding all of this, which was why tuition went up twice during my student years, jumping almost 50 percent—from $1,050 a year in 1958 to $1,500 in 1962.

JOHN GRAEF '60: Reed at the time was probably half the cost of other competitive small liberal arts colleges that were coeducational, like Carleton, Swarthmore, and Oberlin. Some of us felt very strongly that if the school did expand and the tuition went up, the self-selection process for attending Reed would be undermined. Students who might otherwise be able to afford the lower tuition simply wouldn't apply, even if there was financial aid available. We would just screen out a whole bunch of kids Reed would never see.

RICHARD SULLIVAN, president: The most serious problem facing higher education was the question of expansion. There were far more students coming to college for three reasons—one, an increase in the birth rate; two, a higher proportion of students finishing high school and choosing to go on to college; and three, changes in the types of employment for young people in this country—due to automation, management of data, operation of sophisticated machines, and new ways of doing business; all of this increased the retention of students in educational institutions.

It was perfectly obvious that there was going to be a very large expansion in higher education, with most of that expansion favoring public institutions as opposed to private ones. Prior to the war, privately supported and controlled colleges and universities enrolled two-thirds of the students in higher education. By 1958, it was less than half, and shrinking rapidly. There was also pressure from some agencies and the federal government, as well as from state institutions, for private institutions to carry some greater share of the expanded enrollment, in the form of the question, "Well, why don't you consider more expansion?"

In terms of service to society—which was the overall notion that excused Reed's existence—there was the moral question of how can you justify your confidence that a small size is the right size? An institution can become so selective as a result of its arbitrary limit on size that it begins to turn down large numbers of students who are highly qualified to profit from attendance there. Reed was faced with this problem, especially with alumni whose children began to be denied admission because of these complex problems.

By the fall of 1960, college applications and enrollments began a sharply rising slope. Reed started to see the effect already in 1958, as parents' and students' concerns about gaining admission to the college of one's choice began significantly increasing the number of colleges to which a student applied.

It also became clear that the most urgent effect of the population bulge would be a frightening shortage of able college teachers.

TOINETTE MENASHE MALS '71: Prior to the war, a significant proportion of Reed graduates—up to 30 percent—had gone into secondary-school teaching as a career. From its inception, the college had offered a master's degree program, but it was restricted to recent undergraduates who were employed at the college as teaching assistants. There were only eleven master's degrees awarded between 1911 and 1934.

Then the Reed graduate program shifted to focusing on education. The Master of Education program, which included an in-service component and expanded summer course offerings, produced fifty-three graduate degrees prior to 1959. That year, a Master of Arts in Teaching program, or MAT, was started, to prepare highly qualified liberal arts graduates for careers as secondary teachers. By 1964, there were forty graduate students in the program.

In 1966, a Master of Arts in Liberal Studies, or MALS, was created as an extension of the MAT program, for teachers who had received their teaching certificate and had at least one year of teaching experience.

CAROL CREEDON, psychology professor 1957–1991: Reed's interest in the Master of Arts in Teaching program was based on the recognition of the serious national shortage of teachers. It started off in a very promising way. We were able to attract "the best and the brightest" in the entire country; in fact, many of our applicants were fresh from the Peace Corps. Their objective was to generate major social change, and they sought fundamental reforms in education as the path to this goal. They were very committed, and really dedicated. We taught the program in the classic Reed tradition, using conferences.

The MATs were on the firing line in the sense that they were doing their practice teaching as interns in the secondary schools as well as taking an academic load. Most of the schools in Portland, as well as throughout Oregon, were very enthusiastic about our MAT students and eager to have them join their faculties.

Alas, it was not to go on forever. Individuals from the state Board of Education showed up to evaluate the program. We felt put upon, and were not as gracious as we might have been. In our arrogant way we thought there was nothing we had to learn about what we were doing. But every year the evaluators wanted us to add courses that we didn't have, like audio-visual training. To satisfy them, we sent the MAT students across the river to Portland State for these addi-

tional courses. Finally, the MATs were spending more time at Portland State than at Reed, so we shut the program down in 1979, by which time it had awarded more than five hundred degrees.

The MAT students were a great lot, and I thought it was good for Reed to have this "intrusion" from the outside world. I suspect some faculty thought that the program was not sufficiently academic, that it was sort of applied sociology or applied psychology. They may have been right, although I maintained my usual standards.

RICHARD SULLIVAN, president: The general teaching shortage in the early 1960s also raised a question of major policy for Reed—was there an important and useful contribution the college could make by offering expanded graduate instruction? From the evidence, it seemed likely to me that existing graduate schools would not be able to expand enough to meet the demand. Would it be possible for a few institutions like Reed, that had done an excellent job of undergraduate teaching, to successfully add—at least in some fields and without a disruption of present commitments or an unwise diffusion of attention—graduate study?

JIM KAHAN '64: President Sullivan was a very distant person, very much a "suit" from the perspective of students. At one point he said, "We're in deep financial trouble and unless we do something we'll go under." What he proposed was to create a graduate school. The faculty was mostly against it, as were the students. The value of Reed was the direct one-on-one contact with your professors, but if there was a graduate school there would be graduate assistants, and instead of the professors running the conferences the assistants would be doing so, and we thought that would be the end of Reed as we knew it.

RICHARD JONES, history professor: Sullivan invited attention to the possibility that the liberal arts college in the nation at large had passed the point of its greatest influence and value, and that only the dreariness of decline lay ahead unless the college moved in other directions. Furthermore, if Reed declined to accept the obligation to supply the need of the metropolitan area for a quality graduate institution, some other college in doing so would come to occupy Reed's position of primacy, and the college would sink into mediocrity and obscurity.

GEORGE ALDERSON '63: After the war, the Vanport Extension Center had started up in Vanport, a town just north of Portland that was created during the war to house shipyard workers. Its purpose was to help meet the demand in higher education for returning veterans. In 1952, it changed its name to Portland Extension Center and moved into the old Lincoln High School building in downtown Portland. My father, William Alderson, was among a handful of Reed professors hired to teach there as a moonlighting job. In 1955, the school became a four-year degree granting institution and was renamed again, Portland State College. They succeeded in recruiting away several Reed professors. Then, as Portland did not have a graduate school, they started gearing up for that in the '60s.

CAROL CREEDON, psychology professor: I found Sullivan quite difficult—edgy, prickly, and abrasive. He was easily upset by all kinds of things. The issue he presented us with was meeting the needs of the larger Portland community, which meant graduate courses. The faculty's reaction to this proposal was just unbelievably negative. They were appalled at the prospect, as they believed it would dilute the finest undergraduate college in the Western world. I'm sure that upset Sullivan no end.

RICHARD SULLIVAN, president: A number of people long associated with Reed over the years told me that there were some basic values and an atmosphere at the college that provided threads of continuity, and that had persisted despite changes in tangible means of operation. Those values had to do with individual liberty, academic freedom, and the understanding that there would be a sharing of real consultation on matters of policy between administration, the faculty, and, increasingly, with students. They also had to do with the belief that the progress of the individual student was more important than statistics about groups of students.

It was terribly hard for many people to avoid making the assumption that any change that looked like a retrogression in desirable educational practice would carry with it an enormous consequence of effect on those intangible values.

CHARLES SVITAVSKY, English professor 1961–1998: I thought Sullivan was really in touch with the spirit of Reed, and that he understood what the place was about. Whether he had any deep spiritual commitment to Reed or not was another matter. I'm not sure. He knew what he needed to do to make it work effectively, but he never gave me the sense that Reed College was in his heart. He always seemed just a shade detached from the place.

RICHARD JONES, history professor: What Sullivan hoped to do was to become the president of one of the great universities in the country. In order to do that, he felt that it was necessary to be successful at Reed. He wasn't really favorable toward the student attitude and social behavior and things like the dress code at the college. He felt we were too liberal in that respect, and it didn't please him. But he didn't try to do anything about it. It just didn't please him.

By 1963 he had turned down the opportunity to be president of the University of Oregon and some other universities like that. But the kind of institutions that he had his eyes on—Yale, Harvard, Chicago—all had new presidents recently appointed and he hadn't even been nominated as a candidate in any of those searches.

That, I think, was what prompted his decision to support establishing a graduate school at Reed. Initially the graduate school proposal had been made by some folks in town, and Sullivan had been against it, on the grounds that it wasn't possible for Reed to do it effectively without in many ways impairing its undergraduate program. Then a year later, he changed his mind and became a strong advocate of it. Sullivan had appointed Dick Frost, a political science professor at Reed, as vice-president. Frost told me Sullivan had decided that the only way that he could become a candidate for some of these big university positions was to make a newsworthy and important change in the character of the college.

NICHOLAS WHEELER '55, physics professor 1963–2010: The local industrial money was aware that Portland was the largest city in the country without a graduate education program, and that that was a handicap to innovative business development. Howard Vollum '36, a trustee who had started Tektronix, Oregon's largest electronics company, wanted to exert his influence to get such a thing going. After all, one of the original conceptions of Reed College was to have a conservatory, a medical school, a technical school, engineering schools, and an art school, as well as a liberal arts college; an architect's map from 1912 shows all of these built around little quads. The liberal arts college was simply the first step. It turned out to be the last step. But something of the recollection of that survived, so it wasn't so radical for Vollum to say, "Well, why doesn't Reed become Reed University?"

President Richard Sullivan reviews plans for Reed's expansion in the early 1960s with trustee Rudie Wilhelm '37 and his wife, Betty, and trustee Howard Vollum '36.

JOHN GRAY, trustee 1961–2006: Howard Vollum '36 was quiet, thoughtful, always making interesting comments about certain things. When he spoke people listened to him. As a businessman, he was very good, but he also had some excellent ideas about education, and was always interjecting some different thinking.

HUBERT CHRESTENSON, mathematics professor 1957–1990: Howard Vollum '36 and some local business people came to Dick Sullivan in the summer of 1963 with an offer of $3 million to help start a graduate program in the sciences. That summer, a group consisting of one person from each of the science departments and a non-science person from philosophy was called to meet several times with Sullivan. At the end of the summer, Dick asked us to go around the table and vote on the idea. The scientists at that time thought it was a good idea, but I didn't like it. I thought that we would end up being a second-rate university, whereas we were, I thought, a first-rate undergraduate college.

In the fall of 1963, I was sent along with Bill Parker, a physics professor who was in favor of the program, on a week-long tour of colleges and universities, among them the University of Chicago, Brandeis, and Dartmouth, where we thought some insight might be gained. One of the things we discovered was that $3 million was a drop in the bucket for attracting a first-rate faculty and providing appropriate equipment and space for them to work.

At the end of that visit, Bill Parker was saying thumbs down on the graduate school, and that had a lot of influence on the faculty vote. The faculty had a couple of meetings to debate the issue, and then voted it down in January 1964.

JIM KAHAN '64: The faculty could vote yes, no, or neutral on the proposal. Thirty-two were in favor, forty-one were opposed, and eleven were neutral. When the time came to transmit the results to the trustees, philosophy professor Hugo Bedau, who was a paid rapporteur on Sullivan's committee, noted that the neutral votes could be counted as either "not opposed" or "not in favor," and argued that they should be added to the votes "not opposed," which made for forty-three votes not opposed, with forty-one opposed. The day after the faculty vote, the trustees gathered to consider the graduate school proposal.

JOHN LAURSEN '67: Students had a firmly held belief in the virtues of the "old Reed"—a long-standing myth that the college had been much better in the past, and indeed in the recent past, just before they themselves arrived. By seeking to create a graduate school—to move Reed even farther away from its legendary earlier self—Sullivan was in violation of this Reed ethos.

RICHARD JONES, history professor: Students became very hostile toward Sullivan in questions about the graduate school, and they felt that they needed to have some kind of voice in these affairs. Sullivan in turn had begun to reveal attitudes toward proper student behavior that seemed to them not dissimilar from those of former presidents Duncan Ballantine and F. L. Griffin, who both had been willing to expel students for sexual misconduct. An independently conducted national study, which showed Reed students to be unusually sensitive to ethical and moral values, apparently did little to abate his misgivings. Before long Sullivan was confronting a militant student demonstration.

MARK LOEB '65: For many years the student government had been distinguished by inability and incompetence. Under the student constitution adopted in 1919, the Student Council was unable to participate in a number of decisions crucial to the college because the faculty or administration had exclusive responsibility for making these decisions. Even in the area of purely student affairs the Student Council showed itself to be inadequate or inefficient. Deliberations were intolerably long and unproductive. The disposition of a single honor case took more than a month.

In the spring of 1963, the Student Council, resentful of unilateral actions by the faculty in community affairs, dramatically dissolved itself, precipitating the 1963 spring crisis. Subsequent discussion between President Richard Sullivan, vice-president Richard Frost, faculty members, and student leaders led to an agreement to establish a government—the Community Senate—in which students and faculty would meet to discuss and act upon community problems, with students having an equal vote with faculty. It was hoped that such a government would result in a closer-knit community of students and faculty, ending the factionalism, apathy, and to a certain degree irresponsibility that had been displayed by all parties in the past. Student body president Tom Forstenzer '65 drafted a constitution with the counsel of vice-president Frost.

When the students returned in the fall of 1963 and learned that President Sullivan was proposing to establish a graduate school, student leaders asked the student body to approve the community government proposal immediately, in order to give them a status in the power structure leading up to the trustees. There was a mass student meeting in which every student received a sticker attacking the academic imperialism of President Sullivan: "'Reed is a college that mistakes not bigness for greatness'—W. T. Foster."

STEVE MCCARTHY '66, trustee 1988–2009: The notion of a Community Senate made up of faculty and students quickly became absurd because a great deal of what the faculty needed to discuss the students had no business being part of, even though we thought we did. And much of what the students were discussing was so poorly organized and so symptomatic of the belief that we had to invent everything from scratch every year, that it drove the faculty nuts, though some of them were incredibly good-natured about sitting through it. I don't know how they put up with it. It was just endless, with all of these students in a state of dismay over the Vietnam War, the civil rights movement, drugs, and so on.

HUBERT CHRESTENSON, mathematics professor: Instead of going to Reed, the $3 million that local businessmen had earmarked for the grad school became the nest egg for the Oregon Graduate Institute of Technology.

OTTOMAR RUDOLF, German professor 1963–1998: It was the Waterloo of Dick Sullivan. He wanted that graduate school badly.

RICHARD JONES, history professor: The unity for which Sullivan had labored among all constituencies of the college was broken. In marshalling support for a massive change opposed by a substantial number of the faculty, he had used up the good will he had accumulated over half a dozen years. He also quite deliberately sacrificed the role he had long assumed of faculty spokesman to the trustees. As the faculty vote was being taken on the graduate school proposal, he had announced that he would present his own recommendations to the trustees whether the faculty supported them or not.

It was during that year, 1964, when the real severance among the faculty also began. They had been severed on specific issues many times in the past, but that year marked the first time since the administration of Richard Scholz in the '20s that the faculty had been severed in terms of what the objectives and purposes of the college were. During the graduate school discussions, the primacy of a common enterprise among the faculty was revealed to be an illusion. Some members of the faculty acknowledged their strong partiality for graduate teaching and research. Restoration of a college-wide allegiance after that became difficult if not impossible.

With the graduate program stalled, Sullivan became greatly worried about the prospect of financing for the college even as it stood, because a good many things began to happen in the mid-1960s all over the country. The foundation grants were being given less and less to educational institutions and more and more to public problems. The individual donors were being asked for money from many different organizations.

RICHARD SULLIVAN, president: In 1965-66, Reed's budget deficit stood at $1.2 million. That deficit rose from the operating budget, the largest fraction of which went into instruction, the library, and student aid, which meant that it would be both repetitive and increasing unless policies and practices were changed. Our financial situation was not unique. The general nature of our problems was shared by virtually every private college, with the rare exceptions of those few with large accumulations of capital.

I was not convinced that we had overbuilt during our expansion. It was necessary in keeping with the larger size of the college in terms of student enrollments and faculty. However we did have to maintain, clean, and manage more space than we had had before. The financial aid budget had been moving up as well, and was a significant factor in our total fiscal operation. There had been great pride in the tradition at Reed in keeping the doors open to students with high ability and good motivation, regardless of family economic circumstances.

Although Reed's supporters gave more during this time than ever before, we simply did not raise enough money soon enough to do the basic things that needed to be done. Our reach just exceeded our grasp. Encouraged by a $1.4 million Ford Foundation challenge grant and by our success in raising matching funds, we made too many financial commitments too fast, beyond our continuing, year-in-year-out capacity to sus-

tain them. We gambled in stating our aspirations and then prayerfully trying to find the money. It was my responsibility and no one else's. I was overly optimistic about financial support, and, in the last analysis, imprudent.

MARVIN LEVICH, philosophy professor 1953–1994, provost 1972–1979: Dick Sullivan would come to me with his recommendations, and it was clear that I was against them. But he never allowed policy disagreements to affect his sense of you. With a couple of exceptions—Dick Sullivan being one—almost every president I've known at Reed has been in one way or another a tragedy, a complete disaster.

The thing about Reed College presidents is that, on the whole, they try to put their stamp on the institution by affecting it, so they think, for the better. And usually the ideas they have to achieve that goal are bad, sometimes very bad, and they in general brook no disagreement on that subject. Almost all the ways that they want to put their stamp on the institution are reckless, ill-prepared, and a guarantee for failure.

RICHARD JONES, history professor: Sullivan formed a committee of forty-two faculty members, students, and some administrative personnel, known as "the Committee of 42," to examine various scenarios to deal with the deficit. He selected Marvin Levich to chair it.

RICHARD SULLIVAN, president: I asked the Committee of 42 to consider what the effects would be on Reed's practices, atmosphere, and tradition of different combinations of changes that might put the college on a sounder financial footing. I suggested a number of variables for the committee to consider, ranging from the size of the college, through the breadth of the curriculum, various student-faculty relationships, working conditions and policies, to a number of intangibles, such as atmosphere of the college, intimacy, and other factors.

I did not suggest any firm plan for them, although in my convocation speech of September 1965 I did purposely suggest one concept as an example of the most extreme possibility of an emerging Reed—a three-college concept, each with a separate student body of seven hundred and faculty of sixty. Each college could be distinctive in its own way. One could be the traditional Reed, a college of about 750 students. Another could be a college of arts and creative work. The third could be a college of social sciences, which would primarily train students for civic positions and things of that sort. Many students and faculty felt I was committed to such a plan, although I tried to make clear that it was just one concept, which might broaden the financial base and yet maintain certain values which Reed considered to be important.

All things considered, I came to favor the dynamic approach of an orderly, planned increase in the student body over a period of time, coupled with some tuition increases, enlarging both the number of students and total tuition income at a considerably faster rate than we would plan further growth of faculty and increases in student aid. While this approach would not wholly cure our deficit problem in a year or two, it did provide a long-range and cumulative solution that had fewer disadvantages on educational and social policy grounds.

RICHARD JONES, history professor: The faculty agreed to raise the student-faculty ratio to twelve-to-one as something to be retained until the financial condition could be improved. That target, as it turned out, remained in place through the 1990s.

But there remained evidences of unpleasantness on campus. One had to do with the building of the sports center. A former trustee, lumberman Aubrey Watzek, gave money to Reed for a new gymnasium. Watzek had himself identified the sports center as a pressing need for the students and faculty. Student advice was consulted at every stage in the planning of the building, but the students got the impression that this was part of Sullivan's design to change Reed into a more conventional kind of place, developing an entirely different sort of student body. That wasn't true, but there was virtually a riot at the time of the dedication of the new gymnasium. Watzek, a sensitive man, was hurt by the demonstration.

Sullivan lost his temper and got really furious with the students. Later, he felt very badly about having done it, since with him, self-control was a cardinal virtue. During the open meetings of the Committee of 42 his tenseness throughout the discussions became apparent, and he came very close to losing his temper at times. I think it was that kind of thing that ultimately caused him to resign in January of 1967. The job that he took upon leaving, as president of the Association of American Colleges in Washington, D.C., was an opening that had been sitting on his desk for a long time. I think he just decided that things were getting too unpleasant for him at Reed. He later went on to the Carnegie Foundation, where he eventually became the foundation's chief financial officer.

In the years that followed, none of Sullivan's major predictions proved to be accurate. The extreme shortage of Ph.D.s he had so confidently forecast had become within four years an actual surplus. The supposed availability of ready money to provide for new educational enterprises turned out to be an illusion. Even as Sullivan was resigning, foundations were already diverting their resources toward objectives other than education and research. Government grants likewise would soon wither. As to the decline Sullivan predicted for the liberal arts college, within a dozen years its potential for constructive influence on American education appeared to be as great as, if not greater than, ever.

PART FOUR

PART FOUR: THE CULTURAL WARS, 1967–1988

The Cultural Wars, 1967–1988

I once declined the presidency of Reed College because of my limited capacity for patient leadership.

—David Reisman, author of *The Lonely Crowd*

Two of the critical developments upon which higher education's rapid expansion during the Cold War was built—general education and the scientific model of academic research—began to erode in the stormy intellectual and political climate of the mid-1960s. Compulsory general education programs—such as the Great Books program and "Western Civ," both developed between the two world wars—provided students with a general understanding of the major events, great people, and great ideas in Euro-based civilization, during a time when Americans envisioned themselves as partners with European democracies in a great struggle against Communism. The Western Civ narrative became, as historian Gilbert Allardyce has noted, the "history of freedom," serving as something of a benign cultural ideology in a pluralist nation that viewed itself as mounting a moral defense of Western civilization.

Likewise, the idea of value-neutral scientific research—the formulation of limited hypotheses subject to empirical verification—also reflected something of an antipathy to ideology, aside from that of forming a common moral defense during the Cold War. Between 1950 and 1970 government expenses for higher education rose from $2.2 billion to $23.4 billion. Research for purposes of pragmatic public policy in the social sciences and national security in the natural sciences flourished. The idea that scholars could provide neutral research to government-funded agencies allowed researchers to skirt any political implications in their work.

In the mid-1960s, the civil rights struggle and the Vietnam War changed all that. In this new political context, the model of disinterested research supported

The Eric V. Hauser Memorial Library, 1972.

by state funding—especially in the social sciences, but even to some degree in the natural sciences—came under political and philosophical criticism. Moreover, the Great Books and Western Civ courses were singled out as inextricably ethnocentric, racist, imperialist, and sexist—an obstacle to achieving diversity, multiculturalism, and broader forms of understanding.

The upheavals of the 1960s projected cultural and minority issues into the center of American life, triggering changes in American scholarship that would work their way through the humanities and social sciences in the coming decades, and ushering in a new era of cultural identity politics. Most immediately, Western Civ courses across the country were, in the words of Allardyce, "decommissioned like old battleships." In the "do your own thing" spirit of the times, a large number of faculty members felt it nonproductive to restrict the education of young people with a prescribed curriculum. The free-electives curriculum, pioneered one hundred years before by Charles Eliot at Harvard, was viewed as being more responsive to students' interests and individual abilities, and therefore more relevant to the times.

On the Reed campus, the cause of relevance was taken up by a cadre of young faculty members, who came to be called the "Young Turks." Surprised by what they viewed as an insular and overly traditional environment at Reed, they led an effort to return the college to William Foster's original model of an electives or "cafeteria-style" curriculum, proclaiming that their primary responsibility was to teach students, not subject matter. They were opposed by the "Old Guard," largely comprised of faculty who had joined the college in the 1940s and '50s. As with most political battles at Reed, the struggle focused on the crown jewel of the college's prescribed curriculum, the humanities program, first introduced in the 1920s by Foster's successor, Richard Scholz.

In many ways, the curricular battle between the Old Guard and the Young Turks echoed the earlier faculty fight between the Foster and Scholz forces in the 1920s. Faculty leaders at that time had resolved the conflict in the wake of Scholz's death in 1924 by adopting a compromise solution with two values in mind: self-protection and frugality. They rejected both William Foster's social activism and Richard Scholz's internationalism—believing that these approaches had exposed the college's academic freedom to outside attack—in favor of a new mission of serving the life of the mind. Going forward, the pursuit of critical thinking for the sake of critical thinking had come to be viewed at Reed as a defensible position for mitigating potential political skirmishes about the content of what was being taught.

The chronic lack of an adequate endowment at Reed reinforced the insularity of this approach. Out of financial necessity, the faculty decided to focus on doing one thing well, which was providing a limited curriculum that balanced the breadth of a general education program with the depth of a specific discipline of study, beginning with the freshman humanities program and ending with the senior thesis. The faculty's adherence to this focus was enhanced by a spirit of self-reliance and independence. Student tuitions paid most of the bills and faculty covered many of the administrative jobs, leaving the college's mission largely protected from outside funding interests, particularly those of the government.

For members of the Old Guard in the 1960s, the college's near-death experience over academic freedom at the hands of McCarthyism a decade earlier had served as a baptism by fire. On the one hand, it reinforced their commitment to maintaining the college's non-ideological approach—any overt political orientation of the curriculum placed the institution's academic freedom at risk in a politically charged external environment. On the other hand, it exposed the college's growing reliance on government funding for research and subsidized tuition in the form of the G.I. Bill. The government's related demands for loyalty oaths and political allegiance was another side of external relevance that threatened academic freedom.

Accordingly, in the mid-1960s the Old Guard viewed calls by the Young Turks for political and cultural relevance in the curriculum as a major threat. They also argued that Reed lacked the financial means to offer the broader free-electives curriculum that the Young Turks proposed and still maintain the quality of the college's historic outcomes. Without the focus of a core curriculum, they believed Reed would lose its ability to do one thing really well, which was providing students with an excellent and distinctive liberal arts education.

The curricular battle at Reed raged for four years, intensified by the political and social turmoil of the late 1960s nationally, and climaxing in a conflict over instituting a Black Studies program. During those years, the college floundered in deep financial crisis without strong presidential leadership. Following Richard Sullivan's resignation in January of 1967, the president's office was held by three interim appointees and one short-term president, a law professor named Victor Rosenblum.

By the time Paul Bragdon, a New York lawyer, assumed the presidency in 1971, the Old Guard had prevailed in the curriculum war, but the college was on the verge of bankruptcy. Over a term that lasted seventeen years, Bragdon successfully put Reed on its first truly sound financial footing and renewed the modernization process begun earlier by Richard Sullivan, although in a more financially prudent manner. The Old Guard's curricular victory overshadowed the college's educational development for the next two decades, as Reed proudly took an iconoclastic stance against the prevailing trends in higher education by retaining its compulsory humanities program. Changes to the college's core curriculum during that period were largely incremental.

A larger threat to the ethos of the Old Guard came from the professionalism of young faculty members joining their ranks in the 1970s and '80s. In the rapid expansion of higher education during the 1950s and '60s, the number of Ph.D.s had nearly quadrupled. Then, in the mid-1970s, the heady expansion of the academic market suddenly collapsed. Student deferments, which had driven many young males to college during the Vietnam War, ended; the United States fell into an economic recession; and the economic value of having a college education began to fall.

Many young scholars who had expected to be employed at major research universities became candidates instead for jobs at liberal arts colleges. They brought with them the professional mode and expectations they had acquired in graduate school, which included defining their scholarly achievements in terms of research and peer-reviewed publication. Prior to that time, a large number of the faculty at Reed, where teaching took primacy over publication, did not have doctorates. There was also a shift in the principal allegiance of the new faculty members away from the institutions in which they taught, and toward their specific disciplines. In 1969, 70 percent of professors nationwide reported feeling loyal to their institution; twenty years later, in 1989, only 40 percent would profess such loyalty. At Reed, these two developments were inadvertently supported by a corresponding professionalization of the college's administration under Paul Bragdon, which relieved faculty of many of the administrative duties they had previously held. That freed up time for faculty research and writing, while at the same time reducing their involvement in college operations.

In the eyes of the Old Guard, both developments threatened the faculty's hold over of the direction and values of the institution.

CHAPTER 25

"The '60s, Pretty Much as Advertised"

Those were the "question authority" days. Not that those days ever end at Reed.
  —Steve Engel '68

In a community like Reed, where being fringe was the norm, people really had to work to get to the outer edges. It was tough.
  —Sandy Osborne Lillie '70

After a year and a half under two interim presidents following Richard Sullivan's resignation in early 1967, Reed welcomed a new president, Victor Rosenblum, in the fall of 1968. A professor at Northwestern University School of Law, Rosenblum was a graduate of Columbia University and Columbia Law School. He had received his Ph.D. in political science from the University of California at Berkeley, where he had studied under Peter Odegard, a former Reed president in the mid-1940s. From Odegard, Rosenblum had formed an image of Reed as an institution dedicated to great teaching and learning.

He arrived on campus with plans of taking Reed's model in the sciences—in which upperclassmen were instructed on a one-on-one basis and were able to have their own laboratories—and applying it to the humanities and social sciences. The trustees welcomed his efforts to renew the academic mission of the college in this way by generously agreeing to cover the annual operating deficit for two years, during which time they launched a new endowment campaign.

These efforts, however, were quickly overshadowed by dramatic changes underway on the American political and cultural landscape. The student revolt at Columbia University in the spring of 1968 quickly spread to campuses across the country, fueled by America's escalating involvement in the Vietnam War, race riots in major cities, and the assassinations of civil rights leader Martin Luther King, Jr., and presidential candidate Robert Kennedy. These developments, together with the flowering of the boundary-breaking hippie movement, were bringing radical social change to Reed College.

President Victor Rosenblum in his office in 1969.

OTTOMAR RUDOLF, **German professor 1963–1998:** After Dick Sullivan left the college as president, his vice-president, physics professor Byron Youtz, stepped in as acting president from 1967 to 1968, and did a very good job. Unfortunately, he left to become a founding professor at Evergreen College in Washington state. Ross Thompson, the financial vice-president, then stepped in as interim president in the summer of '68.

RICHARD JONES, **history professor 1941–1982, 1985–1986:** Following an earlier failed presidential search, Victor Rosenblum was chosen as Reed's new president. Some of us on the search committee objected to his appointment because we were told by people who had worked with him that, although he was a wonderful guy with all the right kinds of attitudes and ideals, he didn't have the stamina to stand up against anybody and that he'd just give in. As it turned out, that was the way things worked out with Rosenblum at Reed. The ultimate effect was that student de-

mands for change—and demonstrations on behalf of it—became very extreme and serious.

VICTOR ROSENBLUM, **president 1968–1970:** I came out to the college as a big spender. Reed was running a deficit with an endowment of about $4 million, but upon my appointment, the trustees announced a new $12.2 million campaign to increase the endowment and make the college less reliant upon meeting its annual deficit with annual fund drives. Of the new funds, $2 million were to go to new classrooms and offices and to a new theatre auditorium. The trustees also generously agreed to cover the projected deficit for the next two years during the fundraising effort, while Reed brought its expenses in line.

JOHN GRAY, **trustee 1961–2006:** We were primarily a board of local business people. Several of us had to dig deep and make some major contributions to help the college stay alive. There was a general agreement that faculty job cuts were what had to be done to end the deficits. The faculty also made sacrifices in agreeing to receive no salary increases.

VICTOR ROSENBLUM, president: I immediately had extensive disagreements with the vice-president of finance and former acting president, Ross Thompson, who wanted to save money. We battled intensely, but we had the warmest personal friendship. Collegiality, I felt, was one of the great riches in life. It is not built on the identities of positions, but on the richness of association and the mutualities of stimuli that people provide to one another intellectually, along with underlying cores of mutual respect. That was the atmosphere I sought to establish at Reed.

EARL METHENY '73: Rosenblum was a communitarian democrat, and that was the sort of atmosphere he expected to find at Reed. People at Reed, though, were really more libertarian. Soon after he arrived, Rosenblum along with various other people conducted a series of talks in Commons on birth control. It turned out that he was a vehement anti-abortionist guy. In fact, years later, after leaving Reed, he was featured in an article in *Newsweek* magazine that named him as the leading legal architect of the incremental approach to nibbling at the edges of *Roe v. Wade*. This was a guy who was very skeptical of individual rights.

AMELIA ROSAMOND HARD '67: Reed students of my generation were all very distinct and unashamed individuals, each doing what they wanted to do academically, socially, morally, politically, physically, and sartorially—in every conceivable way. That atmosphere was very important to me because I had been a very good girl growing up in Beverly Hills—a good student, very obedient, and a predictable kind of person. I needed a little permission to loosen up a bit, and Reed gave me that.

JACK DUDMAN '42, math professor 1953–1985, dean of students 1963–1985: Although students remained about the same over the years, they were much more influenced than they realized by the tenor of the times. When I was a student in the late 1930s, we were approaching World War II, and students got politicized by the choice between intervention and isolation. After the war, in the 1950s, it seemed to me that students became more inner-directed and less political, concerned primarily with their own personal advancement, much like society in general.

During the Vietnam War, with the threat of being drafted, students again became political in reaction to the national mood over the war. Also in the general cultural movement of the 1960s, students were reacting to the pressures of being exploratory in terms of lifestyle, drug use, and sexual activity. They were a very different bunch from how they had been prior to that time. During the 1960s and '70s, students displayed an unusual amount of curiosity, inventiveness, and willingness to try things. They were very challenging of institutions, and challenging of accepted ideas.

JOHN LAURSEN '67: We came to Reed in the 1960s on a rising economic tide and naïvely thought that it was an upward trajectory, that things were going to continue to get better. Figuring out how you were going to make money or whether you should go to graduate school was not the driving principle for anybody I knew. What we got from the college was: "This is what you need to know in order to be a thinking human being." That was a tremendous gift.

RICHARD LEVINE '70: One of my housemates famously finished writing his thesis and never handed it in. At that time and place, having a bachelor's degree was not thought to be a particularly noble accomplishment—nor a useful one, for some people.

TERRY MILLER '73: I came to Reed expecting to find good company in scholarship. Instead I found a lot of intelligent hippie kids who didn't live up to community expectations, but instead pursued selfish intellectualism and solipsism. They didn't seem to know what they were doing, or to take their studies very seriously. Many Reed people affirmed themselves by negating the system.

THEANO MOURATIDES PETERSEN '73: I was a real "sex, drugs, and rock-and-roll" hippie, and political too, which my mother and father did not approve of. So was my boyfriend, a twenty-one-year-old ex-navy fellow who was going to school on the G.I. Bill. We drove our little Volkswagon across the country from Miami to Reed. There were a lot of hippies on campus when we arrived. At first, I was like, "Yes, this is great! This is fun! We're all peace and love." I enjoyed that aspect of it, but academically, almost from the beginning, I did not feel comfortable. I wasn't really in the mood to buckle down. My mind was in other places. I was learning to bake my own bread, sew my own clothes, live off the land, and experiment with many substances. We were marching; we were protesting. I was interested in just about anything other than being in school.

STEVE ENGEL '68: Those were the "question authority" days. Not that those days ever end at Reed. One of our enduring negative impacts—and I don't say this with pride—was a 1967 nude swim-in at the beautiful new Aubrey R. Watzek Sports Center—known to the students as the "Sports Palace." There was some bogus thing about it being a protest along the lines of, "They should have put this money into new library stuff." But it was really that we were going to get naked and jump around in the swimming pool.

ALAN DEAN '41, trustee 1973–1998: Aubrey Watzek was an older gentleman with old-fash-

ioned attitudes toward society and its values. He had been a Reed trustee back in the 1930s and '40s, and then they had appointed him an honorary trustee for life in 1966. In the 1960s he had given money to Lewis and Clark College for a new library and to Reed College for a new gymnasium.

DELLANNE MCGREGOR '70: I was working one day as a lifeguard. Suddenly, all of these people came into the pool area nude, and jumped into the pool. Jerome Barta, the physical education professor, came running up to me and asked, "Why are there boys in the pool with no swimming pants?" He was very apologetic and tried to shield me from witnessing this terrible thing. "Don't worry," he said, "I'll take care of it."

STEVE ENGEL '68: After about thirty-five of us had splashed around nude in the pool, we tried to get back into the gym. But Jerome Barta had locked us out of the locker room. It was snowy that day, and we had to traipse outside naked through the snow, and find another way back into the sports center.

MARK MCLEAN '70: I was in a folk-dancing class in the gym. Somebody came to the class and had this rather urgent conversation with the dance instructor, who told us, "We all better leave because there's a near riot happening at the swimming pool." Being kind of a slowpoke, I turned off the lights and was ready to leave when I heard hammering on the door to the outside. I opened the door, and a whole bunch of guys came running in with no clothes on. Then there was more hammering on the door. I opened it again, and this time a whole bunch of women came running in with no clothes on.

STEVE ENGEL '68: Jerome Barta stood there in the gym as all this flesh paraded by him, saying, "What are you doing?! What are you doing?!"

Dan Mathews '70 said, "It's just us!" Barta said, "No, it's not just you!"

We then decided that it was a great time to do our equivalent of how many people can you get into a phone booth, only with the sauna. We managed to crowd twenty-seven people into the sauna. After awhile, Dean Jack Dudman, in his dear, gentle way, opened the door, looked in and tenderly said, kind of sadly, "Do you think that was enough?" With that, we all left.

GARY STONUM '69: I was editor of the student newspaper at the time. We were at the printers and a thousand or so copies of the next issue of the *Quest* were coming off the *Sellwood Bee*'s antique press. Suddenly, Dean Jack Dudman telephoned, asking for me. He said that he was worried about reactions in Portland to the picture we were running on the front page of the unclad bathers. My co-editors and I agreed to wait until Dudman personally came down to appeal to us. Dudman was pretty much the last guy you would expect of advocating censorship, but advocate he did. He wanted the issue destroyed. I refused to do that, but agreed to censor the article if we were able to clearly announce that it had been censored. The first page was run back through the printer and the entire page overwritten with black ink. It was then distributed that way.

As it happened, no one noticed that the front page story on the swim-in had a jump to page three, where enough information remained that the *Oregonian* newspaper went after the college with the story anyway.

ALAN DEAN '41, trustee: Aubrey Watzek promptly withdrew his name from the building, resigned his honorary trustee post, and cut Reed out of his will. A few years later, when he had finally cooled off and was about to update his will, at a time when Reed was in real dire straits, he died. So all of his money went to Lewis & Clark College rather than to Reed.

CAROL CREEDON, psychology professor 1957–1991: When I asked students how they could have endangered the college in this way, they just laughed. They thought I was getting very excited about something that was not important. They couldn't see why they or I should be concerned about a town-gown conflict.

JOAN RUDD '69: There was a real moral vacuum at the time, and it was scary for a lot of people. The traditional Reed penchant for "free love, atheism, and communism" was very much in vogue. The free love stuff led to confusion for a lot of people. Atheism was okay as long as you actually cared about your fellow human beings, but sometimes doing what you want harms other people. The communism thing was just plain silly. I had lived on a socialist kibbutz. I had an idea of what socialism was. But "communism" at Reed was always a kind of tongue-in-cheek thing.

SUZY FOX '73: There was an ethos in which poverty was a good thing. It would have been a disgrace not to be poor. Living in Reed houses off campus we did various things to eat. Being a scrounger in the Commons was part of that, as was getting our veggies from the big dumpster bins behind the Fred Meyer supermarket. We always cooked horsemeat, because it was much cheaper than buying steak.

The one thing I am ashamed of is that we all went on food stamps. We were so convinced that we were poor. But going on food stamps was not cool, especially since they were provided by the government that we abhorred. I didn't realize until much later that most of my buddies were from quite wealthy, upper-class families.

DAVID LIPSON '69: Nicky Heyer '67 was, I believe, the first scrounger in the Commons. He had this knack of charming people. He would say sweet nothings while devouring pork chops off the plates of freshman girls. He taught us all scrounging, at least those of us who lived off campus and who could feed ourselves by hanging out by the discharge area in Commons where students returned their trays after eating. You couldn't just steal. You had to be given.

GLENN ERICKSON '72: One of the attractions of Reed was that if you sent your child there they would be among the children of the cultural elite in the nation. When I got to Reed, I realized that many of my friends had parents who were millionaires and multimillionaires. So I didn't feel that I was one of the financially privileged students at the school by any means. There were also a lot of students who weren't necessarily that talented themselves, but were children of celebrated artists and writers. A great number of people in my class had well-known parents.

SUZANNE GREENFIELD GRIFFITH '66: I was a working-class student at Reed and the first in my extended family to attend college. When I got there, I felt like everybody else knew the secret code, and I did not. I had no idea what college was about. It was really quite a surprise when I discovered that among all my good friends I was the only Reed student whose parents had not attended college. My mouth dropped open over some things, like the student in my literature class who had to attend some event and was complaining about having to fly to San Francisco to buy clothes. I asked him why. He said, "That's the only Brooks Brothers on the West Coast."

LINDA HAMMILL MATTHEWS '67, trustee 2005– : When I started at Reed in 1963, we were still in the beatnik era, and everybody was wearing black. If the girls had straight hair they parted it in the middle and wore it long. Then, during my sophomore year, people showed up on campus in these flamboyant clothes, all colors, with necklaces and who knows what, and—wow. It

was such a spectacle. It seemed to me that people had a lot of social confidence to pull off these acts. Suddenly there was this psychedelic image that showed up on campus.

KEITH MARTIN '73: My first impression was that Reed was like a zoo for weirdoes. I shared a dorm room in Doyle with three other guys. One, Peter Cattan '73, was the son of a bra manufacturer in Puerto Rico, and he had a pet monkey with him. Gene Schlossberger '73 was a not very tall Jewish boy from back East who was an opera singer, so he loved to sing opera arias. The third roommate was very religious and would say the rosary before he went to bed. So I had one guy praying, another guy singing opera, and the third guy playing with his monkey.

LARRY KUEHN '66, MAT '68: We brought the writer Tom Wolfe to campus as our senior speaker at graduation in 1966. Some people thought it was outrageous because he represented a whole different side of the intellectual world from that of the traditional academic who was usually brought in each year. Wolfe had just published his first book, *The Kandy-Kolored Tangerine-Flake Streamline Baby*, which was a collection of essays that showcased what he called "New Journalism." We greeted him with a big sign at the airport that said, "We loved *Look Homeward, Angel*." Wolfe sent me a letter after his visit that said, "All I've been doing since I got back to New York is raving about Reed College."

MARK MCLEAN '70: When I came to Reed in '66, the first thing I heard walking into the dorm was Frank Zappa's "Help, I'm a rock!" from his album *Freak Out!*, played on two different stereo systems a fraction of a second out of synch. To me, it was stratospheric! Later, in the record library, someone was playing music by the Velvet Underground not through the regular speakers, but through a really big horn-shaped

Charles Bigelow '67.

public-address blaster with a bizarre paint job. Somebody was sitting on a table with his head stuck into the speaker.

SUZY FOX '73: The dances were all acid-rock music. They would clear off the tables in the Student Union, and it would be real dark. Then the blue lights and strobes would start up with the music.

DAVID PERRY '73: It was a crazy time, an era of "anything goes." The Northwest writer Ken Kesey and his Merry Pranksters visited. Carlos Castaneda spoke on campus. Richard Alpert, or Ram Dass, as he was then calling himself, came and lectured, as did Abbie Hoffman, who had just published a book called *Steal This Book*.

PAUL BIGMAN '73: One fall we came back to campus and found that they had put up locking gates in the dining room to stop students from getting in when it was closed. I and some other people thought it was an outrageous violation of trust. So, we got ahold of the keys to the dining room and went in during the middle of the night and removed the framework that the gates locked into.

I was chair of the Judicial Committee at the time. The next morning at freshman orientation, when I got up to explain the Honor Principle, one of my housemates walked in with the framework for the gates, and I said to the freshmen, "Now, this is an example of a violation of the Honor Principle by the administration."

DOUGLAS UHLINGER '72: Our attitude at the time was anti-establishment. Any corporation, any business was seen as fair game for shoplifting or for whatever. This manifested itself at the Reed College bookstore. They were getting shoplifted right and left by Reed students. To defend itself, the bookstore instituted a policy of asking students to place their bags in the shelves at the entrance to the bookstore.

That kind of procedure later became universal, but it was unusual at the time. The request enraged a small percentage of the population. They felt this was a violation of the Honor Principle, that Reedies should be trusted, that they shouldn't have to check their bags anywhere.

GLENN ERICKSON '72: I don't know whose idea was the Bookstore Eight, but one day at a certain hour, eight of us—six men and two women—went into the bookstore, but instead of just taking off our book bags, we took off everything we were wearing and put our clothes in the storage shelves. Then we went into the bookstore and walked around for five or ten minutes—time flies when you're naked in the middle of a bookstore—then put our clothes back on and left. It probably would not have amounted to anything but a blip on the radar, except that the daughter of the governor of Oregon was in the bookstore at that time, and she was very upset to see naked people and so made a protest to the appropriate authorities.

Nudity, though, wasn't anything controversial on campus. To see some girl or boy or a group of people sitting totally nude in the coffee shop, or in a room in Eliot Hall, didn't turn anybody's head in that era, because there were a lot of people who were taking acid or psilocybin or mescaline, and then taking their clothes off and running around the campus. It was considered somewhat antisocial, but only minimally.

MAURICE ISSERMAN '73: The Living Theatre was one of the best-known avant-garde theatre companies in the United States at that time, and notorious for their nudity on stage. They came to Reed in February of '69 and did three nights of their schtick, including their famous *Paradise Now* production. It was very wild. Like the circus had come to town.

SANDY OSBORNE LILLIE '70: The Living Theatre was trying to involve the audience and shock them, at the time a new concept for theatre. But the Reed people were ahead of them. Before they could even get going, people in the audience were stripping off their clothes. Their act didn't really work in the Reed context, which was both funny and telling. In a community like Reed, where being fringe was the norm, people really had to work to get to the outer edges. It was tough.

PAUL BIGMAN '73: One of the student senators was Garrick Beck '71, whose parents, Julian Beck and Judith Malina, were the co-founders of the Living Theatre. Garrick had had a strange upbringing and as a consequence had some strange attitudes. At a meeting of the Community Senate regarding the rules of intervisitation between men and women in the dorms, at which President Rosenblum was in attendance, Garrick and a bunch of his friends abruptly stood up and stripped naked. Garrick, who was scrawny and

Garrick Beck '71 (right) at a Community Senate meeting in 1969 with Dean Jack Dudman, President Victor Rosenblum, and Professor Howard Waskow (standing).

had long hair, walked over to Rosenblum, who was a nice enough guy but incredibly stuffy, and said, "Victor, we've got to get naked and talk."

SUZY FOX '73: When we arrived we were told that there were only two rules for living in the Old Dorm Block. One was that there were hours after which men had to leave our rooms. The other was there could be no smoking of any sort given that it was an old building. After these admonishments there was a competition among the young women to see how many professors and male dorm advisors one could sleep with or smoke dope with inside the Old Dorm Block. Those were the two hard and fast rules.

ROGER PORTER, English professor 1961– : The mid-to-late 1960s were pretty wild. There was no resistance on the part of the institution to faculty-student dating, and a number of people did that; there were a number of marriages that came out of that phenomenon. It wasn't as if everybody was involved. But it was not looked down upon. I certainly understand the dangers for the abuse of power. No question. But we didn't think of it that way in those days. You had to exercise whatever ethical judgments you were capable of making on your own, because there was no taboo about faculty-student dating.

THOMAS DUNNE, chemistry professor 1963– 1995: One chemistry student set out, as a matter of policy, to have sexual relationships with as many of her teachers as she could; she felt she could learn better because of that closer contact with the professors. She just felt it made things more alive for her. I don't think she was particularly trying to grub out good evaluations. I had a relationship with her, but that was after she graduated. She told me then that while she was a student it had come to the attention of her father, who was a lawyer, that she was having a fairly intense relationship with a history professor, and

her father was quite upset. She told me that what she said to him was "Daddy, knock it off. He did not seduce me. I seduced *him*."

KATIE POOL '71: When I arrived at Reed in 1966, women had to sign out of the dorms in the evening, and be back in by eleven. One of my jobs was opening a window at night so that my roommate could crawl in through it after curfew. Within four years, in 1970, everyone was voting on instituting twenty-four-hour intervisitation and coed dormitories. By the time I graduated in 1971, we had couples cohabiting in the dorms.

REED COLLEGE STUDENT HANDBOOK, 1974: Intervisitation hours in recent years have gone the way of marijuana laws and Community Senate legislation for dog control, i.e., rendered ineffectual by lack of enforcement. Once a reality, intervisitation existed formally to comply with Oregon's recently relaxed cohabitation law, which stated that a man and woman not joined in matrimony could not spend more than eighteen hours together in the same room. Dig it. There used to be a women's signout system, also, before the advent of liberation and personal mace. And all the doors of women's dorms used to be locked every night at two AM.

DELLANNE MCGREGOR '70: I went to Reed a virgin, which when I got there I found was a shocking thing. Sexually, I was far behind the eight ball, and it was embarrassing. I had not gone anywhere near that threshold up until that time, and then all of a sudden it seemed something that I needed to shed very quickly or else I was going to be a social pariah. I dug out an engagement ring that I had borrowed from my mother's jewelry box before I left home. It was from a failed fling she had had. I stuck it on my finger and went down to Planned Parenthood, where I lied and said I was engaged and that I was going to need to go on the Pill. Thank God for Planned Parenthood. It probably saved me a lot of hell.

Constance Crooker '69: One woman I knew got pregnant, and, since legal abortion wasn't available, her parents flew her to Japan, where she could have one that was nice, safe, and clean. It seemed unfair, given that other women were having to find back-alley abortionists and then getting butchered.

Matthew Kangas '71: It was before the Stonewall riots in New York City, so a lot of us were not fully aware of our own sexuality. My girlfriend later turned out to be a lesbian and I turned out to be gay. At the time, we didn't even know it. There were no gay rights, gay community, or gay awareness, but people were out. It just wasn't that articulated or organized. You could adopt kind of an assimilation and tolerance strategy. But despite that acceptance there were students who were more deeply conflicted and remained closeted.

Victor Friedman '70: When it came to free love, it was all straight. Being gay wasn't part of being a hippie. Gays were ostracized or pitied. I had a lot of personal resistance to being gay, too. I felt obligated to be straight, and I was trying to change myself. It was the early beginning of women's liberation on campus, but because I was trying so hard to be straight, I was of course a male chauvinist.

Joan Rudd '69: I went to a boys' kegger over in the cross-canyon dorms. This one guy was very drunk and kept making very crude passes at me. I wasn't at all interested, but I recognized that there was something else going on with him besides just lust. So I just sort of let him lean against me, and I petted his head, his shoulders, and his back like he was a dog, for quite a long time. Finally he calmed down and fell asleep. Later, he

tried to kill himself. Dean Jack Dudman asked me to come see him in the infirmary. I said, "I barely know the guy." Dudman said, "Well, he's named you as one of the two people who he wants to come see him."

Some of the pressure towards drinking and sexual activity had nothing to do with either. It had to do with the emotional needs of the students, and this huge lack of emotional support on campus, with its sink-or-swim mentality.

Pat Musick '73: We had a primal scream night sometime deep into the semester when, at a designated time, anyone who wanted to participate would just scream at the top of their lungs as loud as they possibly could for as long as they could. It was a nice release.

Molly Uffelman Stafford '66: There weren't school-sponsored events that had alcohol, but the student dorm advisors could declare the dormitory social room a private room, and then it was okay to have alcohol there. They often did the rum runs because they were the only ones who were over twenty-one and who could do the purchasing.

A lot of the big parties were off campus. There would be a sign up in Commons—a beautifully calligraphed sign—that said something like, "Tap Dancing at the Faucet." That meant there was a keg party going on at the student house called "the Faucet," where there was a big faucet sign for a plumbing store on the ground floor.

Carter Weiss '66: Drugs were not a dominant presence. We knew what drugs were, but they were not at Reed. Sex and booze, yes—Rainier Ale was a favorite because of its higher alcohol content than beer—but not drugs. The beatnik thing of 1957 to 1959 was long gone. The hippies and "flower power" of 1967 were yet to come. Reedies were fascinated with a mountain-man-lumberjack-motorcycle-Pendleton-shirt chic.

There was lots of talk about Reedies who had gone off with Ken Kesey to do legendary things, but nobody knew what they had done. Of course, Reedies bolted to San Francisco and Berkeley at every break, just like Americans rushing to Paris during Prohibition.

Drugs came very suddenly in the fall of 1965. Mary Jane was everywhere. Zig-Zag rolling paper appeared in the bookstore. The drugs of choice that first year were LSD and speed. Everything was psychedelic. I did not know what "psychedelic" meant. I was shamed. People I had known for four years, and whom I thought I knew well, were suddenly consumed with the love of drugs. All those interesting conversations we had had in Commons were replaced with chatter about "good trips" and "bad trips." And endlessly retold boring drug stories. I was in my second year as a dorm daddy, and I was appalled. I had a private meeting with the deans where we tried to make sense of the "great transformation." In retrospect the old Reed trinity of "communism, atheism, and free love" was giving way to "drugs, sex, and rock 'n roll." Note the common denominator.

SANDY OSBORNE LILLIE '70: Campus started erupting in the spring of '66 when people began taking acid. Personally, I was never really interested in drugs, but I recognized that people were having tremendous spiritual experiences with them and were achieving a different level of understanding. It wasn't so much that I felt pressured to fit in, but I did feel that I didn't want to miss out on what other people were describing, and so I didn't. It was an incredibly powerful and very spiritual experience that took me a long time to integrate.

DELLANNE MCGREGOR '70: When I came to Reed in 1966 I didn't smoke cigarettes. I didn't so much as drink a beer. My first experience along that line of any kind was taking LSD in the fall of '66. LSD was not illegal then; that wouldn't happen until 1967. Harvard psychology professor Timothy Leary was conducting what he called "acid tests" around the country. At the beginning it was approached more as a spiritual journey. We also had mushrooms, psilocybin, and mescaline available to us on campus. They had all been used by the Native Americans as part of spiritual rites, and were seen in the context of the journey Aldous Huxley laid out in his book *The Doors of Perception.* We read up on how to prepare yourself for an acid trip. It was a big deal that you planned for, determining whether or not to have a guide. It wasn't a party drug. That was what marijuana was for.

MARK MCLEAN '70: For a number of us, social interactions were really difficult. The social connections and ritual interactions surrounding marijuana were almost as important as the high itself. It didn't make us any smarter and it didn't give us any capabilities that we didn't have before, but it kind of lubricated and freed up what was already there.

LIZ FINK '67: The college had this scene going on in front of them and they had no idea how to deal with it. It wasn't just drugs—the same thing was happening with the music and the whole culture. The faculty and the administration were just blown way. They had no concept of what was happening on the campus.

ANN SHEPARD '23, recorder 1926–1942, dean of women 1943–1950, dean of students 1950–1968: It was pretty funny to observe sober and anxious academics discussing the subject of LSD with fanatical devotees. It reminded me of a wise and experienced woman who said that one shouldn't expect to combat emotional arguments with intellectual arguments. It seemed to me that that was just exactly what we were in the middle of doing, and that we could find no other tool.

Who can say what effect the use of drugs may have had? I saw enough bad results to make me see them as genuine dangers. And yet I didn't feel sure that law enforcement was the successful answer. I was old enough to remember very well that national prohibition did not work at all well and actually created a new set of problems rather than solving any.

MAARTEN ULTEE '70: Timothy Leary came to Reed in the spring of '67. The room was packed with people and there was smoke in the air and a certain buzz and excitement. Leary appeared dressed in a white Asian robe. He sat on a platform in front of the fireplace and spoke in a very soporific voice. He talked quasi-scientifically about a two-billion-year-old life cycle locked inside our body's cells, a two-billion-year-old genetic code that needs to be decoded. To open our minds to new ways of thinking, we needed to drop out of the system, turn on with LSD, and tune in. "God isn't somewhere out there!" Leary said. "He's inside you! Inside every cell!"

DAVID LIPSON '69: At the end of his talk, Leary took questions. From the floor, someone asked, "I've heard that a woman on an LSD trip can have two hundred orgasms. Is this true?" Andrea Stapley '69, known to us privately as "Andrea Shapely," was sitting right next to the stage. Leary leaned over and whispered into her ear. Andrea whispered back into his ear, and then Leary sat up and said, "Yes, and they're all blue."

ANN SHEPARD '23, dean of students: Some young people were in search of something spiritual which they did not find in the heavy, exacting pressure of the college's program. A good many were looking for something religious that they termed "spiritual," and a number of them turned to one or another of the Oriental religions. I was much less concerned when they actually engaged themselves in one of these rather

rigid disciplines than I was by the withdrawal of a student who simply wanted to drift about while "finding himself." Zen may have seemed sort of "far out," but genuine Zen was a very exacting discipline and by no means an encouragement to self-indulgent, do-nothing behavior.

JAMES MCGILL '70: The Beat poet Allen Ginsberg came in the spring of '67 and presented his long, epic poem, "Howl," in the outdoor Cerf Amphitheatre. He recited it all from memory. It was just mind-blowing watching this big, sweaty guy carrying on like he was Homer presenting the *Iliad*. He recited half of it with his eyes shut, as though he was in a trance like a shaman. It was like, wow.

RICHARD LEVINE '70: They put Ginsberg up in my dormitory, Woodbridge. Sam Schrager '70 and I knocked on his door, and the three of us had a marvelous discussion. "Oh you're interested in Zen," he said. "Do you know who Gary Snyder is?" And we both said, "Oh yeah." Snyder was another Beat poet, who had graduated from Reed in the early 1950s. Ginsberg took a letter out of his book bag that he had just received from Snyder. It was written in what some people at the time called "Reed writing"—a version of Italic calligraphy, as taught at Reed by Lloyd Reynolds. The last line of the letter said: "I long to walk with you again in the woods of our lands, dear comrade. Yours, Gary."

Gary's message fell right in with all my enthusiasm for what Zen was about, which is fraternity. During the winter break in January 1969, myself and a few other Reed people drove down to the Zen monastery at Tassajara in the mountains above Big Sur. When we left Tassajara a few weeks later, we invited a young Japanese Zen teacher there named Kobun Chino to come up to Reed. Later that month he showed up to give a meditation instruction and a little talk about Zen in Lloyd Reynold's graphic arts studio. Not

Andrea Stapley '69 and Timothy Leary during his talk at Reed in 1967.

long after that, Lloyd went down to visit Tassajara and lecture there.

PAUL BIGMAN '73: In 1966 there was a pagan feast at the end of classes, at which they had a huge quantity of meat being cooked over an open flame. That nauseated the vegetarians, especially when people started ripping off bloody hunks of meat. Then they brought in a bathtub and a bunch of watermelons, and people ran and got all the liquor they could, which they poured into the bathtub with the broken-up watermelons. Andrea Stapley '69 walked up wearing a bathrobe, slipped off the robe, and climbed into the tub. People passed out straws and everybody sat around drinking all this mixed alcohol out of a bathtub with a naked woman in it.

MARK MCLEAN '70: The pagan feast was part of something they called St. Cecilia's Day Festival of the Arts. After a couple years, Linda Howard '70 decided that that event had been way too poorly planned. She was right. So she staged a Renaissance Fayre, which was popular in those days. It was very laid back. The Society for Creative Anachronism would show up and beat the daylights out of each other with their rather strange forms of armor. Crafts type people would sell stuff that they made. It was a bit of a community event, because we would invite the neighbors from Eastmoreland and other parts of Portland to come in.

JAMES MCGILL '70: At the Renaissance Fayre there was a living chessboard, which pitted the faculty against the students. The students won handily. History professor T. C. Price Zimmermann provided a translation of a letter of indulgence, which someone had done a very nice job of calligraphing, silk-screened copies of which he sold to the students. Zimmermann also dressed up in a monk's robe and led a group of flagellants in the big Renaissance Fayre parade.

Holy Hubert, a schizophrenic, Bible-pounding fundamentalist, would also show up, trying to convert Reedies to "the true way." He was incredibly bright and well read. Jim Mirel '69, who later became a rabbi, would take him on. Those were some of the most mesmerizing religious debates I have ever seen, just really hardcore theological arguments. Holy Hubert was clearly a street wacko but with amazing mental chops. He really loved Reed. "This is the only place," he said, "where I can go and actually talk to people who know something."

LARRY KUEHN '66, MAT '68: We used to talk about there being two Reeds, the "Woodrow Wilson" Reed and the "Paul Goodman" one. One was the Reed of Woodrow Wilson Fellowship scholars, and the other was the Reed of community activists and political activists that Goodman, a sociologist and anarchist, represented.

SUZY FOX '73: We thought we were revolutionaries, an idea that philosophy professor John Mepham was very intolerant of. He considered us the elite in the ivory tower, playing at being Che Guevaras in Portland. He called us "Dickensian liberals," which was like a slap in the face, but it stayed with me.

MAURICE ISSERMAN '73: I had this romantic ideal of college being a place where you go to classes, and then you go out to the barricades and the red flag is flapping over your head, and tear gas is wafting through the air, and you're kissing your beautiful left-wing girlfriend while defying the gendarmes. It turned out when I got to Reed that it wasn't really like that. It was a grave disappointment. The world was more complicated

The Maypole dance at the first Renaissance Fayre, in 1969. Chemistry professor John Hancock, center, plays the bass recorder.

PART FOUR: THE CULTURAL WARS, 1967–1988

than I thought. The science students had a different experience from those of us who were lollygagging around in the humanities. They were taking organic chemistry, or working in the labs, or feeding the nuclear reactor, none of which left a lot of time for overthrowing the state.

If you put all of the students who were politically involved into a room together, maybe there would have been a hundred of us. Then there were twelve hundred others who to my mind seemed appallingly uninvolved, apolitical, wanting to "free their minds instead," as the Beatles song went. They just didn't seem eager to join us on the barricades. Among them, of course, there were hippies. While we all listened to the same music, ingested the same drugs, and had generally the same attitudes about all kinds of things, some of us were more than hippies, we were also radicals, and wanted to change society. A lot of kids at Reed said, "You know, that's too heavy. Don't lay that trip on me."

DAVID PERRY '73: It was a time of turmoil in the country. Martin Luther King and Bobby Kennedy had been assassinated in 1968. The Stonewall riots by gays in New York City took place in 1969, as did the rock concerts at Woodstock and Altamont.

MARGE GOLDWATER '71: Nobody quite had their bearings. I went to my faculty advisor one day for advice about my future: "What should I do after graduation?" He was dressed in a pinstriped shirt with love beads. He said, "How should I know? I may be a mailman next week."

GLENN ERICKSON '72: Those years, from 1968 through 1970, were a watershed for the transition from the old American left to the New Left, from modernism to postmodernism. The New Left broke out in Europe in '68, first with the revolt in Prague, and then in Paris, with students and workers joining together. It came to American campuses as part of a single movement where cultural politics—women's liberation, black politics, and ecology—would become the new issues, instead of the class struggle and entitlement programs for the poor.

That was happening at Reed. A new leftist comprehension of the world was emerging that was no longer a Marxist left, but a Nietzschean left. It didn't matter if Nietzsche himself was a rightist. Cultural values—feminism, ecology—came to be projected by the will of a group. People of this new persuasion destroyed Hubert Humphrey's presidential aspirations at the Chicago Convention in 1968. They called it "a generation of protest." But 5 percent of the youth at the time were sufficient to go out on the streets and provide the numbers to change things.

SUSAN BRODY '71: The Vietnam War radicalized some students on the Reed campus. There were a few protests on campus, but the big ones were downtown in the Park Blocks, near Portland State. I participated in a couple of those. I felt it was an important thing to be doing, but I didn't know if it was really making a difference. For some people the war was a major disruption in their lives. It was a very immediate concern for the men that if you left college then you lost your college deferment. There were debates on campus about why college students should get special treatment, which raised equity issues.

CONSTANCE CROOKER '69: Instead of honoring those poor young suckers who had done their duty when they got drafted—they went like sheep to the slaughter—we included them as part of the bad guys. We thought, "Well, they could have done what all our friends are doing, finding a way to duck and dodge and get out of the draft." We didn't even know how classist and racist that was. They were the Blacks and Hispanics and people who couldn't get college deferments or any other excuse to avoid the draft.

TOM WEISS '68: I came to Reed out of the navy. There was an atmosphere on campus that sometimes made me feel as though I was a product of the military machine. Alan Lewis '68 was another ex-military student. One day Alan and I were standing in line at Commons, listening to students talk about all the military baby killers and mother rapers in Vietnam, when suddenly this woman in line collapsed in front of us. I had been trained in the navy as a hospital corpsman, so I jumped right in to help her as did Alan, because that's what we were trained to do. Nobody else did a thing.

ELLEN KNOWLTON JOHNSON '39, recorder 1945–1962, registrar 1962–1981: There was a time during the Vietnam War when the draft board was saying, "We will draft everybody who doesn't have a grade point average above 'X.'" We had some sympathetic faculty saying, "I'll give them all As." Others felt that we could not change our standards even under these conditions, but they also said, "we will do everything else that we can."

PETROS PANAGOPOULOS '71: Up until the spring of 1968, you could still get a student deferment if you went on to grad school after college. Then suddenly that was no longer the case, and it kicked off the push among many young men to either leave the country or do something dramatic to get yourself out of the draft. Many of the senior men at Reed were working actively to get to Canada to avoid being drafted.

LANCE MONTAUK '71: Before heading downtown for my draft physical, I obtained a pair of high rubber boots, the kind fishermen use to go into deep water, that came up way above the knees. I got two cans of paint, one turquoise, the other orange. I covered my legs with oil to protect them, then I put the paint in the boots and put them on. I asked a friend to write "Fuck the Army" on my back with a magic marker. Then I put on an old army surplus jacket and went down for the draft physical.

When time came for the physical part of my examination, the first thing I took off was the boot that was filled with orange paint, but nobody could tell, because all they initially saw was that my foot was orange. There were a bunch of people around, and they just stood there. So I kicked the boot over and all of the orange paint spilled out on the floor. There was this ghastly silence in the room. I then took off the other boot and kicked it over. The turquoise paint from that boot swirled into the orange paint from the other, making this pretty vortex of color on the floor. The doctor walked in the room, looked at me and said, "Stop what you're doing. I want everyone to freeze."

It was federal property, so I was arrested by the U.S. Marshals. The doctor first ordered them to clean the paint off my legs. They wouldn't let me clean them myself. So, these poor guys had to clean my legs. It was really touching, almost like a reverse biblical myth kind of thing. Then the doc examined me. He noted that I'm extremely myopic. "Why did you do all this?" he asked. "You would have been deferred from the draft because of your eyesight."

I refused to accept a plea bargain, and so they charged me with a felony and sent me to federal prison for a few months.

PAUL BIGMAN '73: I turned eighteen in August of 1968 and publicly refused to register for the draft. Sometime in '69, the FBI came to our house and arrested me early in the morning. I got one of the best draft lawyers in Portland, Gerry Robinson. We challenged the constitutionality of conscription, but Robinson also argued that the FBI had violated my First Amendment rights because the only reason that they knew that I hadn't registered was because I was public about it, and they shouldn't have been able to rely on that.

Students rally in the Student Union—formerly the Commons building—in opposition to the military draft, 1968.

Robinson was also the lawyer of Oregon Senator Wayne Morse, who was one of the two members of the U.S. Senate to vote against the Gulf of Tonkin Resolution in 1964. The day we were leaving Robinson's office to go to the federal building for trial, he said, "Just a minute, there's somebody here who wants to talk to you first." Wayne Morse walked in and said, "I just want to tell you how proud I am to meet you." That made me feel a little better, a little less intimidated.

The trial didn't go my way, though, and there was an appeal. On appeal, the national ACLU took my case because they viewed conscription as unconstitutional. We lost the appeal, and I did two years of community service, taking a leave of absence at Reed and working down in Woodburn, Oregon, with migrant workers. With the arrogance of youth, I then wrote a letter to the judge stating that I believed sentencing on draft cases was biased along race and class lines, with poor people, in particular poor black people, getting much longer sentences, and that I was going to continue working with the migrants but not accept it as probation. My sentence was then changed to two years in prison.

Meanwhile, the judge, Robert Belloni, a decent liberal guy, was under huge pressure from his family over draft cases. Shortly after I went to jail he held a press conference, and said essentially, "This is bullshit, I'm not sending kids to prison for opposing the war anymore for longer than 120 days." He then reduced my sentence to 120 days.

When I came back to Reed from my leave of absence a friend of mine told me I should run for the Community Senate, which I had served on as a freshman and sophomore. I said, "You're crazy. I've been gone two years, nobody knows who I am." He said, "No, Paul, everybody knows you. You're a cultural hero."

CHAPTER 26

Defending the Citadel

Reed used the term "mission," which I always thought had a theological ring to it, and as though there was some truth to that notion of a divine, sanctified—if not Platonic—sense of itself.
　　—Roger Porter, English professor

If you want immediate benefit, there are plenty of ways to get it. Going to college is supposed to be the only thing that you'll get in life that will be of enduring benefit.
　　—Marvin Levich, philosophy professor

President Victor Rosenblum's ambition to advance Reed's educational program was met largely with indifference by the faculty, who were preoccupied with a growing internal battle over the core curriculum. With a number of American colleges dropping general education requirements in favor of a free-electives curriculum, Reed's adherence to its humanities-based curriculum was being challenged by a group of junior faculty known as the "Young Turks." The Young Turks felt that Reed's curriculum was overly intellectual, failed to respond to students' interests, and lacked relevance for the times.

Reed's faculty leaders, known as the "Old Guard," viewed themselves as guardians of the college's prescribed curriculum, which sought to balance the breadth of a general education program with the depth of focus provided by immersion in a specific discipline. This generation of faculty had developed a hypersensitive vigilance around the college's mission of critical thinking for the sake of critical thinking during the anti-Communist witch hunts of the 1950s, when Reed's cherished academic freedom had come under ferocious attack by political forces. Now, in the politically charged climate of the mid-1960s, they heard in the Young Turks' calls for "relevance" echoes of the McCarthy era.

Comic relief in the faculty's ideological war was provided by a charismatic rogue professor, James Webb, who, in the carnivalesque spirit of the times, moved his classes off campus to a salon setting he called "The College in Exile."

BILL PECK, philosophy professor 1961–2002: In the early 1960s, Reed got a number of young faculty members from Berkeley whose political opinions were pretty far to the left, and what I would call very romantic. Their views were quite different from those of a lot of the older faculty members, who I thought of as un-political people, but who, in the midst of a hot situation, reacted defensively because they wanted to retain what they were used to. They didn't want any of this foolish young stuff. I had a lot of sympathy for them, but they were just sort of blank conservatives—there was no discussion with them on the topic of change. Meanwhile, in colleges across the country, English literature departments were leading the attack on the canon. At Reed it was taken up by students and young faculty members in the freshman humanities course. They wanted to go a lot further in putting new stuff into the curriculum than most of us were used to, or had ever thought of.

STEVE HEROLD '63: Rex Arragon came into our first humanities class and said, "We're studying the *Iliad*. You'd better know what it's like." He took out the *Iliad* and started chanting it in ancient Greek. I couldn't understand a word, but as he was reading, warriors rose up and fell down, the dust came through the room, and when he was done, there was silence for about the space of a minute.

JACK DUDMAN '42, mathematics professor 1953–1985, dean of students 1963–1985: The humanities had been run by Rex Arragon since 1924. When Rex left in 1962, history professor Dick Jones accepted responsibility for it, and he became a big and very effective proponent of continuing the tradition at Reed. Then, when the humanities curriculum was challenged by younger faculty members, he viewed that as a terrible personal threat.

CHARLES SVITAVSKY, English professor 1961–1998: Political problems at Reed—and indeed educational and economic issues as well—all had their strongest manifestation in the freshman humanities course.

Longtime professor of history and humanities Richard Jones leading a class in 1970.

The faculty lounge in Eliot Hall, with professors Douglas Herron, Charles Svitavsky, Richard Tron, Marsh Cronyn, Nicholas Wheeler, and Maure Goldschmidt.

I will never forget my first humanities faculty meeting. It was in the old faculty lounge on the second floor of Eliot Hall. Members of the faculty sat in chairs along the walls of the room. The leaders of the humanities program—Rex Arragon, Dick Jones, and Marvin Levich—sat in the interior and did most of the talking. Most people just sat there in sullen silence. Later, I went around to half a dozen different faculty members and asked, "What's going on here?" They said to me, each in almost exactly the same words, "If you think this is bad, you should have seen what it was like a couple of years ago."

Jones and Levich ran the humanities course with an iron fist. They had a model of what they thought the course should be, and they felt it was their responsibility to articulate it.

JON ROUSH, English professor 1964–1970: As a new professor, I loved teaching the freshman

humanities course but thought that the way the course was constructed was a pedagogical disaster. It was impossible for the students to do the course in any way except very superficially. They were seriously challenged even to complete all the required reading, let alone to have time to think about it.

This was some of the most exciting literature, philosophy, and art that anybody had every produced, and yet nobody had the time to get interested in or passionate about it. Nobody had time, really, to explore. It was a shame to spend a year mostly looking upon the humanities course as a marathon.

ROGER PORTER, English professor 1961– : The new professors, who quickly became known as the "Young Turks," were quite appalled at the tremendous toll the intensity of Reed took on its students, and tried to loosen up the curricular requirements and make some real changes in terms of atmosphere. There was an impetus to have students gain a more independent sense of what they were doing at Reed, and to have them structure their own courses more freely than they were then allowed to do. The heyday of the '60s was coming on, and at Reed the Young Turks were leading it.

ELISABETH DEARBORN '68: The group of students I hung out with felt close to the Young Turks. There was just a sense of human warmth all through those guys. Some people gravitated to philosophy professor Marvin Levich's intense intellectual inquiry and to the climate of behaving like a piranha, where we were all being taught to eat each other up in our conferences, proving that the others were wrong and obliterating them in some way. I had no heart for it. In the intellectual intensity that was so characteristic of Reed, I felt like the rest of me stayed outside the door. The climate did not allow for a profound kind of integration to take place between the intellect and the heart.

JON ROUSH, English professor: The four-year attrition rate was about 40 percent when I started in 1964. By the late 1960s it had risen to about 68 percent. A lot of the faculty saw that as a badge of honor: it showed what a rigorous, tough school Reed was, that students really had to have a lot of mettle to make it through. The younger faculty saw that as a problem. We knew that the school was failing its students. It's not that they were looking for some kind of paternalistic institution, but they were certainly looking for a richer and more whole life than the alienation and isolation they were finding at Reed.

ANN SHEPARD '23, recorder 1926–1942, dean of women 1943–1950, dean of students 1950–1968: My role as dean was not to serve as a disciplinarian, but to be useful in any way I could: to listen,

if students wanted a listener, to help them find information they needed, to help them work out the answers rather than to supply them ready made. One of the great virtues of being a non-disciplinary dean always seemed to me to be a greater freedom in stating my own opinions and feelings than perhaps I could have if I were required to sit on the bench handing out penalties. We existed not in loco parentis but as resources a student might use if he or she wished to do so. One of the things I learned to avoid most carefully was the role of mother substitute. When students trusted me it was because they thought my judgment was objective, because they felt I might help them to shape their own decisions, but never, I believed, because they saw me as a surrogate mother.

DEBORAH ROSS '68: I experienced the college as very caring. The two deans, Jack Dudman '42 and Ann Shepard '23, were wonderful. I felt the same kind of care from some faculty members and the students around me: a sense that we were extraordinary people put in a pressure cooker and everybody was rooting for us to succeed. The endless work and the absence of grades threw you on your own resources in terms of deciding when enough was enough—when do you turn off a lamp and go to sleep? There was never a point where you were done. There was always more to do. If you were driven by guilt or a sense of inadequacy, then there was just no end to it.

The French poet Paul Valery famously said that a poem is not so much completed as it is abandoned. The Reed experience encouraged us to develop that internal barometer. At some point you had to turn in your senior thesis.

SUZANNE WONG SCOLLON '69: There was a woman student in our freshman year who was in the library day and night. She wasn't back in the spring semester because she had committed suicide during the break. I decided right then that nothing is worth that. I wasn't going to care about grades, I was just going to be there to learn.

JAMES MCGILL '70: Sociologically, Reed did not have very good support systems. We started out freshman year with about a sixty-forty ratio of male-to-female, but by senior year it was easily two-to-one male-to-female. It was not exactly a macho environment, but it was hands-off as far as the administration was concerned. As long as you showed up and did your work they didn't care what you did the rest of the time. That seemed to be harder on the female students, because women were more comfortable having a support network, whereas guys were kind of oblivious to that and willing to just blunder along.

THEANO MOURATIDES PETERSEN '73: I was part of the early women's movement at Reed. It was a nucleus of ten or twelve people. We held consciousness-raising groups in the social room in Anna Mann dorm. It was very intense. We spilled our guts about everything to do with being women. A salient issue for women at the time was that the men always seemed to take over the seminars. As women, we often found it very hard to get a word in edgewise. We discovered in comparing notes that many of us felt like second-class citizens in the seminars and found it very hard to compete on an equal footing with the men. They were just so much more aggressive, and often so much more confident.

MARK MCLEAN '70: I had grown up in an environment in which a man opened doors for women and carried their bags. At Reed, about half the time this was considered in some way demeaning and requiring retaliation, and then the other half of the time expected. I did not know which half I was dealing with, although sometimes both were expected of me simultaneously. I would barely say more than "hello" to any female

male on campus without getting read a manifesto, usually a fairly hostile one depending on who was reading it. It went something like, "I am liberated and these are my demands. We're going to do this and not this. Don't mess with me!"

LIZ FINK '67: College was one of the most abusive, sexist experiences that I have ever had, and not because of the students but because of the faculty and the administration. The sexism that existed on this campus was beyond profound. There were almost no women teachers. One of them, Gail Kelly '55 in anthropology, hated women and tortured them. For me, it was a procrustean bed that took me years to recover from.

LESLIE SCALAPINO '66: Gail Kelly had incredible fashion sense, and sewed her own high-fashion clothes. I liked her tremendously despite the fact that she was so disbelieving in women's abilities, which was just uncalled for. I found the male teachers to be non-sexist, and very supportive in trying to recruit different women students, including myself, to go to graduate school. In my senior year I received a Woodrow Wilson fellowship for graduate school thanks to the efforts of my thesis advisor, English professor Donald MacRae. He and a group of professors from other colleges in the Northwest banded together and challenged the Woodrow Wilson people that if the fellowship didn't go to some women, they were going to announce publicly that the fellowship board was gender-discriminating.

BRUCE LIVINGSTON '65: Gail Kelly '55 was my advisor. Our age difference wasn't that great, but she was referred to as the "Iron Maiden." A real tough cookie. As thesis time was approaching, she called me aside one afternoon at the end of class: "Mr. Livingston, a word please." "Yes, Miss Kelly?" "I have just looked at Mr. Weisner's thesis"—Tom Weisner '65 was the hero of the department—"Judging from the state of his thesis, I dare not imagine the state of yours. By five o'clock this afternoon, I would like to see you at my house with your typewriter and all your notes, and you will stay there until your thesis is finished."

So, I lived there at her house for the next four days. On the third day of being incarcerated, I was upstairs working away, and I heard this knock on her front door and looked out. There was a cluster of my cohorts standing outside. Miss Kelly opened the door, "Yes?" "Miss Kelly, can Bruce come out and play?" "Not yet."

MARJORY FRANKLIN LUXENBERG '66: At Reed it seemed like there was one value: academic achievement. It didn't matter how pretty you were, or how witty, or if you could play a lot of instruments. It was extremely single-minded. They posted the SAT scores of the freshman class. It wasn't by name, but you could see which range you fell into.

Anthropology professor Gail Kelly '55 in the mid-1960s.

There was a wonderful psychiatrist associated with Reed named Dr. McKinley. When I had depression, I went to him and he prescribed dexedrine for me. I took one dexedrine a day the last three years I was at Reed. That got me through without being suicidal. From the day I graduated, I never took another dexedrine again.

CAROL CREEDON, psychology professor 1957–1991: After entering Reed, many of my advisees were certain that there had been a serious admissions error on their behalf. As time went by, they became more convinced than ever that they were unworthy, and that the mistake would be discovered at any moment, and they were counting on my not giving it away. They were absolutely convinced of this, and miserable with this false discovery of theirs. I told them that they were far from unique, that in fact the Reed norm was very close to where they were.

JEREMY BRECHER '67: I was already in Students for a Democratic Society when I came to Reed, and I started the SDS chapter there. SDS had roots extending back to the labor movement at the turn of the century. It was just starting to take off as a student activist group following the issuance of its manifesto, the Port Huron Statement, in 1962. One of the things SDS had going initially was a university-reform project.

At Reed, four of us—Betsy Dearborn '68, Ann Jenkins '67, Ruth Meyer '66, and I—decided to draft something for that project. The report was a critique of the social aspects of Reed's educational model. What it focused on was the tension-producing results of combining extremely rigorous academic demands with individual freedom and self-direction, and the resulting isolation and alienation that led to on campus. The Reed environment demanded productivity and conformity in the academic sphere, coupled with a complete lack of support for the rest of people's lives. We referred to it as the "Reed syndrome." I sent the report off to one of the national leaders of SDS, Paul Booth. He wrote back and said, "Well, it's a good report for university reform, but we're not interested in reform anymore." SDS had moved on to resistance.

ELISABETH DEARBORN '68: Because of my participation in the SDS report, the dean of students, Jack Dudman, asked me if I wanted to travel east with him to attend a conference at the Institute for Policy Studies on student unrest. The conference brought together representatives from a hundred different colleges and universities, plus educators from around the country involved in setting policy. There were major questions about where education should be going, with growing interest in experiential education, community-centered education, and things that were not about scholarly academic life but about lived life, none of which were being addressed at Reed.

It might be, if you look at the history of change, that disruption precedes change. But at Reed it didn't seem to be necessary to unseat the philosophy of education that the college was centered around, and that I personally found deeply formative of my understanding of history and culture. But when that educational philosophy was carried and so profoundly embodied by people like philosophy professor Marvin Levich, it was hard to create a dialogue that generated change.

JON ROUSH, English professor: There were a cadre of us who had been active in the Free Speech Movement at Berkeley. We came to Reed already thinking a little bit politically. My perception was that the Reed faculty, collectively, had a very narrow definition of intellectual life as preparing students for graduate school, with hopes that maybe some of those students would go on to be professors just like them. Our group had a more holistic idea of what the intellectual life should be. Although we were all serious scholars and all treated our scholarship

very seriously, we were also concerned about the question of relevance.

MARVIN LEVICH, philosophy professor 1953–1994, provost 1972–1979: In the middle of some of the arguments about shaping the curriculum, what we did at Reed was identified as being irrelevant. There was something wrong with our society, and the question was what was the curriculum at Reed College doing about it?

I just didn't think of college education like that. The whole question was: "Relevant to what?" I can see there are some things I do think about that way. If I take an aspirin and my headache goes away, that's why I take an aspirin. But I don't think of an education as the pill you need to swallow so your headache will go away, and that seems to me to be something at the heart of the idea of irrelevance. The thing about education, as some people have pointed out, is that once you begin thinking about the immediate objectives to be achieved by a liberal arts education you lose, in fact, the reason for there being such an institution at all. If you want immediate benefit, there are plenty of ways to get it. Going to college is supposed to be the only thing that you'll get in life which will be of enduring benefit.

JON ROUSH, English professor: Marvin Levich really cared deeply. He cared about teaching and education. Cared about philosophy. Cared about the humanities course. Cared a lot about Reed. That had a lot to do with his power, because it was so clear that he cared. People stopped and listened when Marvin talked. I think he and Dick Jones saw themselves as the defenders of what was best about Reed. He saw us as a threat to that. There were times when he just infuriated me, because I thought he was being close-minded and manipulative, but I never did not like him.

The conflict was only accidentally generational. There were those among the young faculty

Longtime philosophy professor Marvin Levich in his office in the 1970s.

who were very much on the traditional side of things. At the root of the debate there was a different perspective about education. I don't think either view was tremendously coherent. I heard a lot of arguments on both sides that were intelligent and coherent, but you couldn't say there was a coherent educational philosophy on either side. It was a tragedy that we could not meld those two forces and get some dialectical resolution that produced something better than either side was striving for. Because I think most of us recognized each other on the other side. It wasn't black and white. It was just that we made it black and white. That was, for me, the real tragedy because there was a serious opportunity to be creative. But there was just not any fertile ground.

ROGER PORTER, English professor: The emotional and intellectual energy at Reed was almost entirely directed towards teaching the students. I had a feeling that it was an ingrown faculty, that people were not moving out into the world. They weren't publishing. In fact, if you published at that time it was thought to be a sign that you were not taking your teaching seriously enough. I both appreciated the emphasis on the classroom and also distrusted it a bit, as I think it was responsible for some of this ingrown feeling and the taking of what I thought were minutiae of policy so seriously that it created a potentially hostile atmosphere within the faculty.

MASON DRUKMAN, political science professor 1964–1970: In 1965, a group of us younger faculty started CRAP—Committee to Reform Academic Practice—to think about what might be a better approach at Reed. The group included Howard Waskow and Will Baker in English, Kirk Thompson in political science, and Stephan Michelson in economics. We gave ourselves that name as a kind of self-deprecating reference to what we were doing. But the senior faculty seemed to feel very threatened. The fact that we spoke up, and didn't realize that junior faculty members were expected to keep their mouths shut for the first year or so, caused quite a furor.

MARVIN LEVICH, philosophy professor: I had a big debate on curriculum with Mason Drukman. I had developed the view that education had the dual drive of trying to teach something specialized and something general, and that there were ways in which the Reed curriculum answered to both desiderata; that is, in the humanities course—and in certain of the other courses—there was an emphasis on what could be called the "colligation" of courses, built together and attacked in a certain way. Then when a student became a major, his junior and senior year became more and more a matter of specialization, which I thought was a good thing.

Mason had the view that education should be determined by the attitude or preferences of the student. It was what has been called in the literature the "cafeteria style" of education: you simply put out all the platters and decide which students are going to be eligible for what. I thought that was really a chimerical idea.

ROGER PORTER, English professor: Reed used the term "mission," which I always thought had a theological ring to it, and as though there was some truth to that notion of a divine, sanctified—if not Platonic—sense of itself. There was almost a kind of Calvinistic quality about it at the college. That seemed okay for a time, but it wore after a while. There are no surprises when people are on missions. It certainly creates the sense that there are heretics—that there are people who do it the right way, and there are people who don't, and that those people who don't do not belong. Reed was not a place that easily countenanced diversity.

HUBERT CHRESTENSON, mathematics professor 1957–1990: Sudden growth was the major factor in the split between the Young Turks and the Old Guard in the '60s. Within a couple of years the student body had grown from a thousand to almost thirteen hundred students, and

the faculty with it. A smaller student body, with a smaller faculty, would have made for better communication and perhaps not so much of the bad feelings we had. It certainly was not pleasant.

ROGER LAW, artist-in-residence 1968: I found Reed College in 1968 to be the most contentious atmosphere I had ever worked in. It was a minefield of backbiting and sniping, a bit like being in *Who's Afraid of Virginia Woolf?* You would go to some old guy's house for dinner with people who had tenure, and they would get drunk and be incredibly rude about people. Dinner never arrived until two in the morning because everybody got so drunk, and then when it did arrive it was all burnt. It was quite a tough environment.

NATALIE DELORD, wife of Jean DeLord (physics professor 1950–1988): The Faculty Wives Club, which in the 1960s became the Faculty Women's Club, had a very distinct role at the college in the 1950s and '60s. They organized all the college affairs—the Christmas party, the Easter party, the potlucks, the annual faculty picnic each fall—at a time when the college was really poor. The women in the club would also sponsor faculty members who were new to the college, and help with those little things that are so important when you move into a completely new community.

MARJORIE GWILLIAM, wife of Frank Gwilliam (biology professor 1957–1996): The Faculty Women's Club also hosted teas that were given for each faculty meeting. The wives provided cookies and sat at either end of a long table with coffee at one end and tea at the other, which they provided to the faculty members before the meeting. There was a sophisticated ritual about this that history professor Rex Arragon's wife Gertrude, the "hostess with the mostest," had originally started in the 1920s when members of the faculty were at odds with each other.

Beginning in the 1960s, some of the younger faculty wives coming in had careers of their own, and they thought it was an antiquated thing to be identified only as a wife. So in the Faculty Women's Club it began to be only the older women who were doing things.

BARBARA RHYNE, wife of Charles Rhyne (art history professor 1960–1997): Sometime in the early 1970s there was a flap that because we were the Faculty Women's Club we shouldn't be pouring tea and coffee at the faculty meetings. After that, things fell apart.

BECKY POLLOCK, librarian 1957–1987: I was told that the earlier faculty had decided that they were never going to have very much money, and given that, they wanted to make sure to do a few things well. When I was at Vassar, they put up new courses and new programs at the drop of a hat. At Reed, it would be easier to get a constitutional amendment passed in the U.S. Congress than to get a new course passed. The faculty stuck very carefully to academic standards.

MARVIN LEVICH, philosophy professor: When you're in a small liberal arts college you cannot hope to include a curriculum that reflects in subjects anything approaching Stanford or Harvard. So the question is, what should be the basic curriculum of the college? Should it have twenty-five courses in philosophy? The answer is "No." It should contain in philosophy, for example, the rudiments of what one thinks people have to know in that subject.

The same is true of most of the subjects. If a college is to have a subject, there's no point in its just dipping in the pool. It should have a subject that reflects basic learning in a certain area. For example, if we were to give Arabic Studies, we should have enough people in the area to reflect a department of Arabic Studies. Then we would face the question of what department should we

reduce if we add a new department? The matters of debate over curriculum really amounted to small cheese, because there was not too much available to move around.

ROGER PORTER, English professor: Reed faculty members overall were very liberal. In fact, several of the most conservative faculty members in terms of academic politics, like Marvin Levich, were strong backers of liberal presidential candidate Eugene McCarthy and third-party politics in those days. On campus though, personal politics and the institutional politics in the faculty were totally different things. It was true around the country in general that a lot of the people who had been courageous in arguing for academic freedom during McCarthyism in the 1950s became the people most afraid that the students and the leftist faculty were the greatest threat to American education since Joseph

A member of the Faculty Women's Club serving tea at a Reed reception in the early 1960s.

McCarthy. In fact, there was a great deal of sentiment expressed by some of the older faculty that anybody who wanted to make changes at Reed was using "McCarthyist" tactics.

RICHARD JONES, history professor 1941–1982, 1985–1986: After Dick Sullivan left Reed in early 1967, it became clear that the admission office wasn't operating properly. In 1968, acting president Byron Youtz, who sympathized with the younger faculty, got a new admission director named Benjamin McKendall. McKendall was someone who was strongly in favor of Reed being a real free-swinging place, and insisted that he was going to change the nature of Reed College by changing the admission policy. The admission office became a hotbed of agitation for radical change with apparently the full approval of the acting president. This had a lot to do with some of the real disappointment for students when they got to Reed.

BERT BREHM, biology professor 1962–1993: I was always one of the first lecturers in the introductory biology course, and so had the opportunity to chat with students on an informal basis soon after they first came to the college. It became clear that the director of admission and his staff were not representing the college accurately. The institution was *not* promoting social change and activism and allowing students to design their own independent curriculum.

ERIC OVERMYER '73: Some of the freshman kids coming in were radical, and immediately started to buck against the strictures and requirements of the humanities program. There was a lot of talk about how relevant it might or might not be. They were asking Reed to not be Reed, and that just wasn't going to happen.

MAURICE ISSERMAN '73: I came in as a freshman in 1968 very much wedded to the idea that the world was in upheaval, and that it was my job to help realize the millennium. I made pretty big demands on freshman humanities in that it seemed so irrelevant. In fact, as part of Students for a Democratic Society on campus, I led a movement to abolish it.

We were very consciously fighting against the "old Reed." We thought the place had gone stodgy, and had become precious. There was a strong conservative voice in the faculty at the time, and the conservatives saw all of us as a grave threat to the ethos of Reed College as they'd known it. Philosophy professor Marvin Levich, history professor T. C. Price Zimmermann, and a younger faculty member, history professor Jon Westling '64, who later went on to be president of Boston University—they all despised us. There was not a lot of rational discourse between factions on campus, which was too bad, because they were smart guys. If we could have stepped away from the issues at hand, we would have probably found we had a good deal more in common with each other than was apparent at the time. In a way we were being very "Reedish"—really questioning, challenging, and being obstreperous. But we weren't always right.

It gradually dawned on me that you can't really hold Thucydides and Plato responsible for not having abolished slavery in Greece in the third century before the Christian Era. The world was more complicated than that. So, despite myself, I was learning a tremendous amount. Within a year or so I stopped thinking that everything had to be about the revolution to be valid or important or interesting. Some things could be about just life, and thoughts, and people, and ways of viewing the world. The next year I voluntarily signed up for sophomore humanities because I wanted to go further.

BILL PECK, philosophy professor 1961–2002: All over the country there was a fierce backlash against what I would call left-wing "romanticism," which was becoming more and more anarchic, sometimes tending toward violence. I was a student of romantic anarchism because it was part of German thought of the nineteenth century, which I taught. But I could hardly believe that I was listening to it in person from people I had to deal with from day to day. I was just horrified.

ROGER PORTER, English professor: Between 1968 and 1970, things were heating up in the outside world—particularly around Vietnam, with the Tet Offensive and the mining of Haiphong Harbor, then the bombing of Cambodia, and finally the killings of four student protestors at Kent State. There were a number of faculty members who were very distressed at the reluctance of Reed to really engage with those issues. Routinely after each major event in the outside world, there were demands from students for a moratorium on the war. There was huge resistance on the part of some of the faculty to cancel classes for those kinds of things, or to allow students any time to demonstrate, to march, or canvass public opinion off campus or on.

A junior faculty member in the history department, Jon Westling '64, stood up during a debate on the floor of the faculty about a Vietnam moratorium and said, "If I could stop the war in Vietnam by calling off my classes for even one day, I'm not sure I would do it, because too many other values in Western culture might go down the drain." It was probably the single most stunning sentence I've ever heard uttered on the floor of the faculty.

JOHN POCK, sociology professor 1955–1998: The thing about Reed College is that it was such a small place that everything got magnified. It was a place where people spent a lot of time examining their navels and thought that they were so goddamn important that it was going to make a difference in the world. It didn't. It wouldn't. It

couldn't. The so-called "ivory tower" is a good thing because, from its origins, it was a sanctuary from which you could sit and criticize the society out there and then run back and be protected.

Can you effectively separate the academic part of this business from the political and moral parts of your life? I thought that they should not be mixed. Should an institution like Reed take a position on some political event or on some political situation? Again, my answer was "No."

I believed very deeply that public policy should be based on evidence and research. But there's a tricky translation. It's like the difference between physics and engineering. You have to be able to translate, because once you get out into the "real world," that world is a multiplicity of variables that are going all sorts of different ways. Whereas in a research context, whether you're a physicist, or a biologist, or whatever, you're selecting out only one little sector of something to see how that works. That is never going to work over there in the real world, but it may throw some light on the real world.

PATRICK MCMAHON '69: One day English professor Jim Webb walked into class, went to the blackboard, and wrote on it "Fuck Pock," referring to sociology professor John Pock. They were involved in some vicious argument.

ROGER PORTER, English professor: Jim Webb was probably the most charismatic, outrageous faculty member in my time. He had a cult following at Reed. He had a glass eye, and came to the college around 1965 trailing myth: that he had been in the RAF, that he was a fighter pilot. He taught Victorian literature, and he was a total carnivalesque presence. He took nothing seriously. I don't mean that he wasn't a serious teacher, but everything was grist for the mill of his satiric personality. He was very smart, but he was clearly undermining everything, including himself. The last thing that Jim ever exhibited, though, was cynicism. He was a kind of innocent who was fascinated by everything in the world, and would turn all of it into a joke. There was an enormous irreverence in Jim, but I don't think he was ever indifferent. He irresistibly aestheticized everything, turning everything into style.

JIM WEBB, English professor 1965–1971, Reed Union, "Where Are We Going?" 1968: I am representatively the faculty nigger. I embody the liberalism of my colleagues. I take my job seriously. I don't like drinking. I got myself conscientiously drunk. My performance is sl-sloppy. My elocution slurred. I feel good about it. I intended to write out carefully everything that could, or should, or would be said. I didn't get it done. I discovered that life becomes progressively complicated. Last year I lived in a world of tomorrow. People came up to me and made suggestions, and

English professor Jim Webb as a bishop in the human chess game, 1967.

I said tomorrow would be a good day. This year I suggested the day after tomorrow. Tomorrow is full. It will take three or four years possibly for me to get to the point where I say "Uhh, we must get together sometime."

You see what I'm saying? I'm well aware that this is probably going to be one of those years where I come on very messianic. I have a gospel too. I don't mean fanatic—that's pretty extreme. That's beyond the boundary. I will be fanatic one year or the other, but not yet. Chastity and continence. Right now it's messianic. We all have a chance for innovation. We are caught in structures. We exist in departments.

CONSTANCE CROOKER '69: Jim Webb had some kind of weird, negative magnetism. He didn't smile. He didn't hug. He was like a mystery man, with his dark glasses on. You couldn't see what he was projecting or thinking or anything. It was like some Zen blank thing, and he would allow himself to be that. People would gather around him and make him what they thought he was. It was an Andy Warhol type of thing.

RICHARD BURG '67: Webb started a venture called "The College in Exile," which was held in soirées at his house in Eastmoreland on Sunday nights. People referred to it as parallel to an Edwardian salon. There was always a large crowd there, with people smoking dope and drinking espresso, and sometimes there was food. It was a delightful place to go, because it was always interesting, no matter what was going on there.

LANCE MONTAUK '71: Webb's house was very small and intensely decorated. The overall impression was of a Victorian atmosphere. There was this kind of mind-boggling array of things on the walls—tapestries, paintings, small drawings—all nicely framed in a wide variety of ways. All the windows were covered with fabric of some kind, so once you were inside the house, you were cloistered and insulated from the external world. The lighting was subdued and soft, with lots of candles and lava lights.

Webb had taken out the ceiling in part of the house, and put in a loft with a cell of welded steel bars and a door. You had to use a ladder to get to it. The cell was certainly kind of exotic. Was it Marquis de Sade, or was it André Gide? It was a little oddity, or more than a little odd maybe.

ANDREA STAPLEY '69: I started going to the Sunday night soirées and sort of got taken into the intimate circle right away. My father had died earlier in the year. He was a mad poet, just like Jim, so it was just totally natural for me to fall into a relationship with Jim. One day I told him that I needed to align myself with him, and to do so I needed to have a personal relationship with him, which he took me up on. I didn't know what I was getting into. I thought he would just be a boyfriend because it seemed right for me to have a faculty boyfriend at that point. I had already been the centerfold for the *Quest* newspaper in my sophomore year and had kind of put myself out there as a sex object. But he wouldn't let me just leap into bed with him. He put me through my paces and he made it a seduction, which he was very brilliant at. He really turned it into an expanded consciousness experience.

Then, I was his girlfriend. I knew he was gay, and I knew that some of his boy friends were his lovers too. The guys kind of let him have me for an amount of time. I thought I would marry him. But then he kicked me out in the spring, because I had to work on my thesis and he had other things to do. I was devastated. I didn't really learn how to think until Jim took me in hand. I legitimized him for a season, enhanced his image. So in that sense he used me, but I was there. I offered myself. So I was in it.

HOWARD RHEINGOLD '68: The salon at Jim's home wasn't a den of drug iniquity. It was where

people went to talk about ideas. The boundaries between the personal, between Socrates and Tim Leary, between the stylistics of literature in the Middle Ages and Marshall McLuhan talking about media—these were all mixed together. A lot of boundaries were dissolved. You might think of boundaries as being this taboo stuff of teachers having sex with students, but it was also about if you're going to come over on a Sunday night, be prepared to talk about what was on the reading list in humanities this week. Not like that was an assignment, but that was the norm. It was okay to be intellectual.

DAVID PERRY '73: One day, close to graduation, Webb printed up fake diplomas and put everyone's name on a diploma with a letter that said, "Those of you who were here for a diploma can leave now, since you have a diploma. Those of you who want to get an education can stick around."

ROGER PORTER, English professor: Webb was an enormous threat to the college, because Reed took itself very seriously. When Jim didn't get tenure, he put copies of the letter that announced his not getting tenure on the trees all over campus. He then refused to come to campus during his termination year. When he was teaching sophomore humanities, he gave lectures from home by walkie-talkie. In that last year he held classes in his home, one of which, Victorian Aesthetes and Poets, met from eleven at night until six in the morning. It began with the smoking of joints. The other course, Socialists and Visionaries, met from six in the morning until nine. It began with a mandatory hour of calisthenics. It was a total Bacchanalian thing.

JON ROUSH, English professor: There was one point at which Jim Webb taught his class with a bullhorn from across Woodstock Boulevard. He was prone to that kind of gesture, and great at it.

CHAPTER 27

Student Revolt

Black people are different. We come from a culture with its own history and language, and must face a different environment than white people do after graduation. Reed does not answer this need.
— Reed College Black Student Union

I simply felt that the college would just be wagging the tail of whatever emerged as the current notion of blackness, and that the curriculum should not be dictated by the latest political winds of what constituted blackness.
— Marvin Levich, philosophy professor

Identity politics began to assert itself on college campuses in the late 1960s with requests for the inclusion of programs such as Women's Studies and Black Studies. At Reed, that manifested in demands by the campus Black Student Union for the creation of an independent Black Studies Center. Backed by a number of junior faculty, this demand became a flashpoint in the battle already raging between the Old Guard and Young Turks over the relevance of Reed's curriculum. The issue further escalated after the Black Student Union stipulated that the center be initially staffed and administered outside of the faculty's customary oversight, and then staged a takeover of the administrative offices in Eliot Hall.

ELLEN KNOWLTON JOHNSON '39, recorder 1945–1962, registrar 1962–1981: In 1964, Dick Sullivan had received a grant from the Rockefeller Foundation—which it provided to six other colleges as well—to bring a good number of black students to campus under their Minority Group Program. Some of the faculty approved, but some didn't because several of the candidates were not really prepared for Reed. It was

very difficult for some of those students when they arrived—some of the faculty would make the effort to give them remedial work, and others were not about to. By the fall of 1968, there were thirty-five black students enrolled at Reed.

CALVIN FREEMAN '69, MAT '70: My freshman year there were eight black students on campus. By my junior year there were thirty-five black students on campus, a highly diverse group of African-Americans from all different kinds of backgrounds, all different levels of political education and political skill.

The relationship between black students and Reed was tense. The eight of us there my freshman year were probably among the strongest academically in our high schools. Reed had reached out to us. By my junior year, there were students—and I can say clearly that there were no students admitted to Reed who were not incredibly bright—whose public high schools had not prepared them in any way at all for life at Reed. Some struggled with the freedom there and with being in a predominantly white environment for the first time. The Reed faculty was just totally clueless about what it meant to have thirty-five black students on Reed's campus. There were also no black faculty members until my last year. There were acculturation issues, both on the part of the school and on the part of the kids coming in, that needed to be attended to.

RICHARD JONES, history professor 1941–1982, 1985–1986: Recipients of the Rockefeller awards were expected to be fully assimilated into the campus society, and to benefit from the same curriculum and maintain the same academic standards as other students. But assimilation into the Reed society ceased to hold any attraction for most of them. They could not avoid recognizing that no blacks held positions on the faculty or in the administration. The curriculum contained no courses dealing with the special concerns of black citizens or with the history of African culture. Attention in courses to the American black population was, as they perceived it, limited to points of contact with the white majority.

Similar issues were springing up on campuses across the country. The usual stance of black students was militant, their rhetoric not that of discussion but that of demand.

CALVIN FREEMAN '69, MAT '70: A deputy district attorney came on campus to talk about the demonstrations and civil unrest occurring at the time in Detroit, Los Angeles, and other large cities. He made the "I am not a racist" comment, and then continued to say, "Whether you're black, white, or"—at which point he looked at a fair-skinned African-American woman and said—"yellow." That was the button that got pushed. It's difficult to explain what made that a catalyst. I have no idea if he was referring to Asian Americans when he said "yellow"—at the time Reed did have Asian students—but the key point was that a large group of students felt it to be offensive. It was that feeling of offense that sparked action, the way that emotions can be charged up without a cognitive catalyst.

After that session we went to a dormitory room, talked about it, and decided to charter a Black Student Union at Reed in the spring of 1968. I was elected its first president. Most of us, including myself, were fairly politically naïve in terms of mounting a movement and developing an action-based strategy for change. The new black students coming in during my senior year brought a lot more expertise in that area.

MARY FRANKIE FORTE '71: I came to Reed on a scholarship from the Rockefeller Minority Group Program, and was involved in the Black Student Union on campus as the secretary. It was a hectic time. We had meetings upon meetings about pressing for a Black Studies program at Reed. It was very hard for all of us. My mother was extremely fearful. "Are the police going to come on campus? Are you going to get arrested? Don't get involved." I said to her, "Mom, it's too late. I am already involved."

CALVIN FREEMAN '69, MAT '70: It was also the time of the rise of the Black Panthers, who had a small but active chapter in Portland. Meanwhile, the militancy of the Students for a Democratic

Society, created primarily by white students, was rising on a parallel track, but with very little coordination or cross-fertilization with African American students and our form of militancy.

MAURICE ISSERMAN '73: There had been a chapter of Students for a Democratic Society at Reed since 1964, and some of the veterans of previous years were still around, but for the most part the SDS chapter, which had about three dozen members, was almost entirely freshman, plus a few transfers, including Stevie Moskowitz '70, who had been at Columbia the previous year and had been involved in the leadership of the Columbia Strike before being thrown out. At age twenty, he seemed a very wise, very seasoned, and very charismatic revolutionary leader.

The fall of 1969 was a big year for anti-war protest, and those of us in SDS at Reed were involved along with many other Reedies in a succession of moratoriums and mobilizations that drew thousands of protesters into Portland's streets.

GLENN ERICKSON '72: Our dorm daddy, the student advisor in our dorm, was one of the Black Student Union leaders. We all looked up to him because he was everything that we boys wanted to be: mature, handsome, strong, articulate, intelligent. And on top of that, he was black. Since the great majority of the parents of Reed students were from the left, the opportunity of having a black man play this role was very difficult to resist.

One day I was walking behind lower Commons when a black girl ran up to me, crying. She said that she'd been attacked behind the Old Dorm Block by a man who had broken her glasses. I went off in pursuit of this fellow, who turned out to be a thirty-five-year-old man who had escaped from a mental institution. I got two campus cops and we tackled him, and took him to the little campus police cabin attached to the Commons. Then suddenly six or seven black male students burst into the police cabin, knocked the two campus policemen down, and beat the man senseless. Those guys were all taken to student honor court, and expelled from Reed. My dorm daddy was one of them.

ARTHUR LEIGH, economics professor 1945–1988: I was on the Educational Policies Committee, chaired by history professor John Tomsich. We met with a delegation of the black students and agreed to include more material about black people in the history courses, and more black authors in the literature department, but not to add new courses.

Then some of the black students went to a conference at Howard University, and came back with demands that were just totally incompatible with Reed's procedures and traditions and values. Among other things, there were demands for separate courses on Black Studies. That wasn't so bad, but the worst of it was the demand that we have a black faculty that was to be judged in terms of appointment, promotion, and tenure using a different procedure and by a different set of people from all the rest of the faculty, because they said they didn't trust the Faculty Advisory Committee to do what they wanted done or to do it properly.

To me it was unthinkable and amazing that anybody would consider discriminating between people in terms of deciding personnel decisions based on race. But there were people on the faculty, a very active and vocal minority, who supported that idea. The rest of us opposed it. Of all things, this would, in the long run, injure the minorities far more than it would help them.

ROGER PORTER, English professor 1961– : Certain programs around the country were very much a product of identity politics in those days, politicizing the issues not so much in terms of action in the community, but mostly in terms of raising concerns that were important to the students who would be taking these courses. Women's Studies programs were also just beginning in some places.

RICHARD JONES, history professor: On the Black Studies question, there was some similarity to the business of McCarthyism in the 1950s with the changes in the character and programs of the college that were being proposed. Back in 1953–54, Reed's board president and many of his trustee associates had felt that the college's primary need was for strong leadership to overturn domination by the Faculty Council, which they felt gave expression to the faculty majority's narcissistic concentration on its own peculiar set of values. In the late 1960s, it was the people who were in favor of Black Studies who wanted it to be something that they controlled, rather than just something that was part of the college curriculum.

ROGER PORTER, English professor: There was a feeling on the part of a number of the faculty that they were being invaded somehow by forces that seemed absolutely determined to undermine the integrity of the college. The resistance was fierce. It was passionate. There was absolutely a schism in the faculty. One way to define the split was to say that some people wanted an involvement in the community and in the world that would not undermine the intellectual integrity of the institution, and others wanted the ivory tower version of things, the college as a place apart from the world.

REED COLLEGE BLACK STUDENT UNION, preamble to letter of demands, November 22, 1968: Reed is actively recruiting black students. They bring us here, force us to study the culture of our oppressors (Europe and America), and then neglect our own contributions to civilization. Black people are different. We come from a culture with its own history and language, and must face a different environment than white people do after graduation. Reed does not answer this need.

MARVIN LEVICH, philosophy professor 1953–1994, provost 1972–1979: In early December 1968, the faculty suspended classes for a two-day forum. The topic of the forum was the appropriate relationship of students, faculty, and administration in decision making. It was generated by our awareness of what was going on nationally and by other things locally, including the activities of the SDS, the Black Student Union, and the particular row about the humanities course. The hope was that Reed might be the exceptional college in which issues of this kind might be adjudicated by dialogue rather than by confrontation.

SUZY FOX '73: There was a sense among some students that any professor who wasn't radical and wasn't protesting against the war and the draft and gung-ho on supporting things like the Black Student Union was reactionary and hopeless. That was one of the more disgraceful aspects of it. Marvin Levich, who taught philosophy and was a staunch defender of the Greeks and the classics, was the scapegoat for this. During one of Levich's humanities lectures a dog came up on stage, lifted his leg, and peed on him. A lot of people in the audience cheered. That was how extreme it was.

CALVIN FREEMAN '69, MAT '70: On December 11, 1968, the Black Student Union took a decidedly more activist turn. It didn't leave me behind, but essentially I was just not equipped to deal with that level of activism and didn't have the skill in community organizing. Some of the new black students that year did. We upped the level of our demands for Black Studies with a concept paper on what that should look like, and then took over the second floor of the administration building, Eliot Hall.

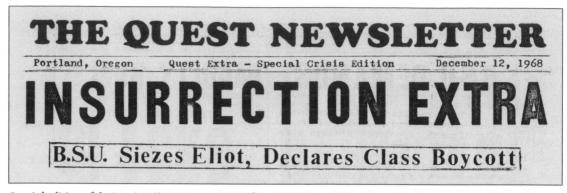

THE QUEST NEWSLETTER

Portland, Oregon   Quest Extra – Special Crisis Edition   December 12, 1968

INSURRECTION EXTRA

B.S.U. Siezes Eliot, Declares Class Boycott

Special edition of the Reed College Quest, *December 12, 1968.*

TERRY WINANT '71: My boyfriend was spending the night in the math library, which was on the fourth floor of Eliot Hall, a very common thing for us to do. I got a phone call from him there at seven o'clock in the morning. "Good morning," he said, "I'm in liberated territory."

MAURICE ISSERMAN '73: I was involved with organizing white support—picketing outside Eliot Hall, delivering food to the building, organizing a class boycott. Down in the Sports Palace there were huge mass meetings and people arguing back and forth about the meaning of the takeover and the Black Student Union's demands.

Those of us in SDS were junior partners. They didn't tell us they were going to take the building. We very much wanted to be accepted by them. They welcomed our support, but I don't think they took us seriously. They were ably led and had a great deal of unity amongst themselves. They sort of talked the same talk we did, in revolutionary jargon, but they knew what they wanted—a Black Studies program. They weren't just out to make the revolution. They had clear demands.

ALEXANDRA HOPE YODER '71: I was among those who occupied the second floor of Eliot Hall. It was all a very civilized sort of encounter. We were just in there doing trivial things. Sitting at the president's desk and eating a half-gallon of ice cream from the Fred Meyer supermarket and

talking in a very calm way with people from the administration.

JAMES MCGILL '70: It was all very amicable. People would bring the protestors notes from the classes that they were missing. Both faculty members and students would bring them food. I've talked to people who were at other schools where things were much more contentious. At Reed, it was like a non-event. I was up there one day chatting with a friend when the alumni director, Florence Lehman '41, came walking up. "I need to get something in my office," she said. "Oh, okay. Fine." She walked in, got her stuff, and walked back out. No problem. It was one of my introductions to surrealism.

JACK DUDMAN '42, mathematics professor 1953–1985, dean of students 1963–1985: It was a period in which people were burning college buildings, hauling guns into Columbia University, waging enormous physical fights at Berkeley as black students argued for a greater degree of autonomy. Yet Reed managed all that with just an absolute minimum of violence. People fought with their mouths a lot, but not with their fists. That struck me as remarkable and greatly to the credit of the place.

SHELDON HOCHHEISER '73: I was shocked, and enormously upset. I was there to get an education, and here were these people disrupting my education. I had no sympathy for their cause. There was this whole attitude among young people at the time that all authority was evil. I didn't share that attitude at all. I expected that these professors, these educational experts, were there to teach me stuff. I did not want to set up my own ashram or my own curriculum. To a large extent, I hung out at the time with other science majors like myself, although I was so upset that I seriously looked into transferring. What I came to realize was that there was no place I could have gone at the time that was not dealing with the same problems.

ARTHUR LEIGH, economics professor: President Rosenblum was much too soft. He failed to provide the firmness that we needed. He was even going along with some of the protestors' demands, which were kind of outrageous, like having a separate system for deciding on personnel decisions based on race, and having separate courses in Black Studies. The phrase, "the black experience," came out frequently.

BILL PECK, philosophy professor 1961–2002: President Rosenblum didn't want to force the issue. He didn't want everything to go up in flames. It was just a sit-in. They were not violent. Some of us argued for finding a middle way. I got up on the faculty floor and argued vociferously against students taking over buildings, and against the faculty canning students because they had been in demonstrations. I argued both points because I was against the college taking a stand politically on anything. But in those days it was hard to make yourself heard if you were in the middle or trying to be reasonable.

VICTOR ROSENBLUM, president 1968–1970: Trying to run a committed educational institution at a time when the nation was being split apart by a war that was both futile and savage meant that people would often see in actions that were taken at Reed parallels to what was going on in the Nixon Administration at that juncture.

So it was not at all unusual to have great ranges in intensities of opinion, but, in retrospect, it seems to me that what was unusual was that we

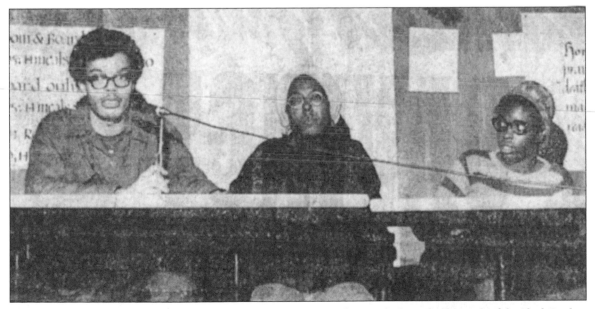

Calvin Freeman '69, MAT '70, Eva Griffin '70, and Patricia Mapps '70 speak about the demands of the Black Student Union at a student meeting, December 11, 1968.

didn't have acts of violence on the campus. I certainly didn't solicit sit-ins, but I thought that the sit-in was itself a manifestation of educational dissonance, and that what we needed was to get to the heart of the educational problem, and the educational need, and the educational gap, and that as long as there was no violence on the campus, we could have a setting in which discussions could proceed and some kind of alternative plan be worked out. There were a few in the community who viewed the sit-in as an act of violence that required the presence of the police on the campus, but that idea was emphatically opposed to my own thinking.

MARIAN FURST '72: The Black Student Union takeover of Eliot Hall lasted a week. A lot of my classes were cancelled. The occupation itself was kind of an inconvenience. I just went about my business.

VIRGINIA OGLESBY HANCOCK '62, chemistry associate 1963–1980, music professor 1991– : I was teaching in the chemistry department on the edge of the campus during the takeover of Eliot Hall, kind of out of the loop. We just went on doing our jobs. I was angry at the people who were disrupting everybody's lives.

MARVIN LEVICH, philosophy professor: The faculty met every day, week after week, trying to resolve this issue of Black Studies. It was really an incredible period of time, given the intensity of the meetings and given the expression of views, and it seemed that these meetings would never end.

VICTOR ROSENBLUM, president: One gap in my leadership was that I did not adequately signal to the faculty that I thought we ought to establish a center for the study of black-related issues. There were members of the faculty who felt that, had I communicated that position earlier, then they would have found it easier to support it. One of the great values of the Black Studies Center was that it was not to be simply a support vehicle for black students, it was to be a vehicle for enhancing the breadth of Reed's education, to take us

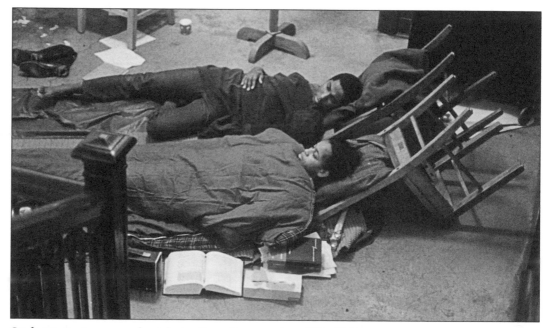

Student protestors camped out during the 1968 occupation of Eliot Hall.

PART FOUR: THE CULTURAL WARS, 1967–1988

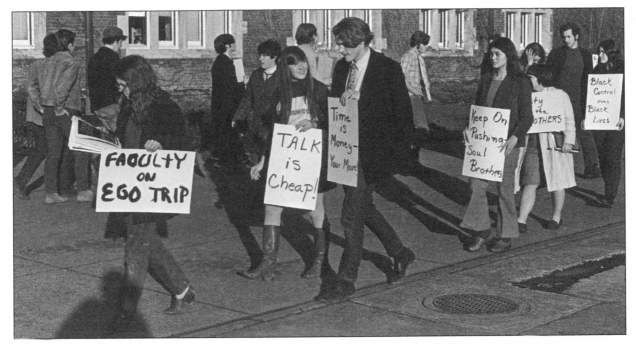

Students march in front of Eliot Hall in support of the occupation by the Black Student Union.

from one way of looking at the world and help us in perceiving the world's variegated cultures.

THOMAS WORCESTER, "Black Studies at Reed," *SALLYPORT* magazine, July 1969: Some white students, acting independently in support of the Black Student Union position, conducted a sit-in in the Portland office of Rudie Wilhelm, secretary of the Board of Trustees, on Wednesday, February 26. Five students were arrested, but charges were dropped after they promised not to sit in at other trustees' offices. On Thursday, February 27, several white students took control of President Rosenblum's office, and remained there until Saturday morning, March 1, when the students left the office following accusations that they were hindering the establishment of a Black Studies Center.

ROGER PORTER, English professor: The issue of Black Studies at Reed culminated in a faculty meeting on March 4, 1969. The final issue was whether there would be an autonomous Black Studies Center, autonomous in the sense that the faculty hiring would be done outside the normal channels of the Faculty Advisory Committee, and the curriculum would be decided outside the normal channels of the Educational Policies Committee. The faculty meeting in which that vote took place was very strange because while emeritus professors do have votes on the faculty, they never come; but the conservative faculty recruited every single emeritus faculty member alive, and suddenly at this faculty meeting you saw twenty people that you had never seen before. That provided a lot of the votes for the other side. But they lost, sixty to fifty-four.

MARVIN LEVICH, philosophy professor: It was a very close decision. It was my view that the faculty voted for this issue just so it would go away. It voted for peace, and I think that was not the right vote. I voted against the decision. I thought the issue was that the very nature of the term "Black Studies" meant that it was going to be politically determined. Because what was black yesterday became something different from what was black today, and in almost every week there was a more and more radicalized version of what constituted Black Studies, and what sort of thing should be admitted in it, and I was against that because I felt it linked in an explicit way the politics of Black Studies to the nature of what would be included in the curriculum.

For example, there was a time when Martin Luther King was thought to be "black," and in one way or another developed the views associated with blackness and the view associated with black politics. Then it became clear that in the view of major people in the black movement, he was no longer "black." He was a "Negro." So the distinction between being "black" and being a "Negro" was a distinction made in political terms. It was not a distinction of ethnicity. It was not a distinction of complexion. It was a distinction as to whether one carried with one the proper notion of "blackness." I simply felt that the college would just be wagging the tail of whatever emerged as the current notion of blackness, and that the curriculum should not be dictated by the latest political winds of what constituted blackness.

CHARLES SVITAVSKY, English professor 1961–1998: Before the Black Studies program actually began, there was a summer session for all the students to help prepare them for the experience at Reed in the fall. I taught an English course that summer. Most of these students were weak in writing and reading, so we spent the summer session working on that. I don't know if we were terribly successful, but nonetheless it was a very positive experience.

In the fall, when the program began, they really wanted to have at least one class in which they were all together, and wanted me to be the instructor. So for the only time in my life I had a freshman humanities class of all black students. It was a good class. They were friendly and happy,

and by and large they worked reasonably hard. But I don't think I ever overcame my sense that these kids would never be regular Reed students. They just didn't have the kind of background and education that would make them very successful in a straight Reed College program.

MARVIN LEVICH, philosophy professor: I called several people around the country, trying to get their advice on the matter. One of the issues that was raised for me was that if you're going have a program in Black Studies, you're not going to get professors who are any good. I was told that if a person is really committed to Black Studies, then he'll be teaching in a black college; and if he isn't teaching in a black college, then he will go to one of the most prestigious institutions in the country—Harvard, Princeton, Yale—which at that time were just wild to get people in Black Studies. Reed, I was told, would end up with a person of no consequence.

VICTOR ROSENBLUM, president: I'm very proud of the fact that the faculty did take the action of approving the establishment of a Black Studies Center. Then, when we had it, the problem was turning it into something that was viable. Again, there were limited resources. I was able to get one of the trustees to volunteer some funding for a couple of years. Even with limited resources we got a group of people who were concerned about education and about integrating these educational ideas into our traditional campus operation.

CALVIN FREEMAN '69, MAT '70: Reed ended up hiring an African-American professor, Bill McClendon, as director of Black Studies, and also an African-American professor of English, Michael Harper, who was a poet and who wrote a terrific poem that was the liner note for a John Coltrane album. But they didn't invest in a Black Studies professor the way that they would invest

President Victor Rosenblum at Reed trustee Rudie Wilhelm's office during the student sit-in there.

in, say, a new economics professor, or even a new art professor. It was pretty much a slapdash recruitment. "Who can we get in here right away?" Although I'm not sure how happy we would've been at the time with a slower process.

BILL BERNHARDT '60: Bill McClendon was already well-known to many of the Reed faculty as the former proprietor of Portland's best-known jazz club—the Rhythm Room—and for his active role as a spokesman for the Oregon NAACP. He organized the first attempt to bring knowledge of the black experience in America into the public-school curriculum in the Northwest. His cordial manner and infectious sense of humor won over even those teachers who most resisted his point of view.

CHARLES SVITAVSKY, English professor: Some black people from the Portland community did some of the teaching for the Black Studies program. Some Reed faculty also taught courses. But generally speaking, they were definitely watered down. Some of the black students saw it that way, and resisted taking Black Studies. They were very serious students and, generally speaking, probably better prepared than their colleagues. They did reasonably well, and a number of them graduated with regular Reed degrees.

VICTOR ROSENBLUM, president: We really needed to have a continuing infusion of funding to be able to do the recruiting that would bring cadres of the best black students to the school. The Rockefeller Foundation declined to provide more funding after five years, on the grounds that their mission was to try to get something going, and once they got it going the institution itself needed to look to other sources in order to be able to continue the operation. Well, schools like Reed were not in a position to get those other sources, which left something like the Black Studies Center dangling on a cliff.

MARVIN LEVICH, philosophy professor: After a few years, the Black Studies program just sort of collapsed of its own weight. History dictated what principle did not.

CHAPTER 28

Faculty "Purge"

Reed was viewed as a faculty-oriented, faculty-dominated institution, with a system of faculty representation that perpetuated an oligarchy of mandarins. I really disagreed with all that.
    —Victor Rosenblum, president

It was an ongoing, death-by-a-thousand-cuts kind of thing, so systematic that many of us left the academic life.
    —Jon Roush, English professor

In the midst of the pitched battle over Reed's curriculum, the Young Turks and a group of student supporters sought to develop their own alternative educational programs at Reed. One result of that effort was Paideia, a four-week period between Christmas break and the spring semester, during which students had the opportunity to engage in academic and creative projects for credit, outside the formal curriculum. The offerings ranged from breadbaking, metalsmith jewelry, and filmmaking, to the plays of Samuel Beckett, survival training, sensitivity groups, and the study of the *I Ching*. Another manifestation was a proposed new college called the "Learning Community," conceived in reaction to Reed.

Adding to the curriculum upheavals of the time was Reed's ongoing financial struggle. The trustees' efforts to launch a major fundraising campaign proved unrealistic, given the turbulent climate at Reed and elsewhere in higher education. The Faculty Advisory Committee, looking to avoid what it termed "drastic surgery to the educational program," and also hoping to restore the strong bonds of a smaller college community, voted in the summer of 1969 to decrease the student body from almost thirteen hundred students to nine hundred. As a cost-cutting measure, the committee also agreed to allow the student-faculty ratio, at that time close to ten-to-one, to revert to the standard of twelve-to-one set at the beginning of the financial crisis three years earlier. Together these two moves would result in a dramatic reduction of the faculty ranks.

362

JAMES MCGILL '70: There was a very heated debate between the liberal arts people and the science people regarding Paideia, with the science faculty being quite vehemently against wasting academic time on such an unquantifiable concept. In fact, during Paideia most of us scientists were just working in the lab.

REED COLLEGE BULLETIN, "Paideia at Reed," **August 1, 1968:** "Paideia," a word from the freshman humanities course, means "training physical and mental faculties to produce an enlightened mature outlook, combined with maximum cultural development."

Two students who submitted the original proposal for Paideia, or Unstructured Independent Study, Richard Mollica '68 and Michael Lanning '71, said that "academics should be a part of education but not the definition of it." Dean Jack Dudman and numerous faculty members feel that Paideia will cut attrition by staving off the alienation that develops when students devote all their time to classroom pursuits.

MASON DRUKMAN, political science professor 1964–1970: Paideia gave older faculty more time off to work on their own stuff, so they went along with it. Otherwise, they hated the idea of it, particularly since academic credit was being given for it.

ROGER PORTER, English professor 1961– : It was during a trip that English professor Howard Waskow and political science professor Mason Drukman made together to a conference on alternative education at Antioch College that the germ of the idea for the Learning Community sprouted. Antioch in those days was starting to have branch campuses in various places, loosely affiliated with the home campus in Yellow Springs, Ohio. Together with English professor Jon Roush, Waskow and Drukman began developing a model for an alternative institution.

Then, at the recommendation of President Sullivan, Roush served for two years at the Carnegie Foundation as one of its officers in higher education, recommending distribution of funds to various institutions. In that role, he had experience with a variety of programs, particularly with programs involving social change.

A number of us had begun meeting, and there were all sorts of suggestions, some having to do with buying a group of houses in town, some having to do with a country location outside the city—something roughly like a commune. There was an attempt to see if we could try to have a kind of alternative wing at Reed, but we quickly realized the utter impossibility of that.

VICTOR ROSENBLUM, president 1968–1970: The formation of the Learning Community was talked about openly on campus. It was being organized within the framework of those who found the college simply too rigid—that its curriculum was too prescriptive and that, given whatever strengths Reed had, it was not sufficiently open or sufficiently communitarian in the sense of encouraging the community to prescribe the course of study. Reed was viewed as a faculty-oriented, faculty-dominated institution, with a system of faculty representation that perpetuated an oligarchy of mandarins. I really disagreed with all that.

Essentially, to me, the Learning Community represented the desire not of trying to be a variation on what they considered to be the inadequacies of Reed as much as it was a communitarian venture. I think the aspirations were wonderful aspirations, very much to be admired. Indeed, it seemed to me that one of the reasons that they didn't want to have a concrete curriculum was that they wanted the spontaneity of community.

RICHARD BURG '67: The Learning Community really got launched in the summer of '68 with a

PAIDEIA
MCMLXXIII·

Wed., Jan. 3

12:00 noon - Yoga - org. meeting in S.U. - R. Friedland

6:00 "Civilization" film series begins - E 314

7:30 Psychology film festival begins - E 314 - panel discussion -

Thurs. Jan. 4 -

10:00 AM - Yoga - each day at this time

11:00 - Sewing, etc. - Holly Pence E 204

1:00 Art of Northwest Indians Gray Pedersen - E 117 Future meetings TBA

2:00 Outing Club Paideia org. meeting - Marji Ure - Ski touring meeting afterward - Talbot Bielefeldt

3:00 Batik - George Lappas, et al. Art Dome

7:30 Psychology film #2

9:00 Utopia - Dan Bullock E 203

Fri. Jan 5

11:00 Linoleum cuts and woodcuts - J. Carl Friedmon - Woodstock 1.

12:00 - Cable TV, David McMahon E 117

1:00 Silkscreen printing - WD 1

2:00 Open dance class in Studio Mon. through Fri. -

3:00 Etching - WD 1 Batik - Art Dome

4:30 Ethnic dancing - Wendy Robinson & Debbie Yadoff - Women's Gym

6:00 "Civilization" #2

TBA - Film Board film

Sat, Jan 6

TBA - Film Board film

8:30 PM - Social in SU

Sun. Jan. 7

7:00 PM - Dinner in Anna Mann for Alumni and students interested in Public Service Law -

Mon. Jan 8 -

11:00 AM - Auto Mechanics: Basics org. meeting - Robert Fields & Rick Samuels E 314.

1:00 Massage - org. meeting in s.u. R. Friedland.

2:00 Graphic Arts Seminar Mitch Evans - E 209A

6:00 "Civilization" #3

7:00 Sufi Dance - org. meeting - Winch Soc. Room - Lin Bennet -

7:30 - Psychology film #3

Tues. Jan. 9 -

11:00 Film Making

1:00 - 3:00 - Gregorian Chant with Mr. Palladino - E 117

4:00 Improvisational Theatre David Glanvill - E 211

7:30 - Psychology film #4

9:00 Utopia seminar - E 203

Wed., 10th

11:00 Swimming - Rena Bornstein & figure diving - Ted Ferwerda: org. meeting at the pool -

1:00 Photography - Allan Back - Winch Soc. Room

2:00 - Motorcycle mechanics - Steve Burks - E 209

Wed, Jan 10, cont.

4:00 - Leatherworking - Valeri Hagenback - E 117

6:00 "Civilization" #4

7:30 Psychology film #5

Thurs. Jan 11

1:00 - Offset printing - Carlos de la Huerga & Tom Rabe - Blackhouse

1:00 - 3:00 Gregorian Chant - E 117 cont. on Tuesdays & Thursdays

4:00 Improvisational Theatre E 211 cont. on Tuesdays & Thursdays

3:00 Batik in Art Dome cont. on Tuesdays & Thursdays

7:30 Psychology film #6

9:00 Utopia seminar - E 203 cont. on Tuesdays & Thursdays

Fri. Jan. 12

11:00 swimming & figure diving at pool - cont. on Wednesdays & Fridays

6:00 "Civilization" #5 E 314

TBA - Film Board Movie

Sat. Jan 13

TBA - Film Board Film.

9:00 Social in S.U. -

Sunday, Jan 14

7:00 2nd dinner in Anna Mann for Alumni & students: "The B.A. as a Terminal Degree."

Mon. Jan. 15 (Events not previously mentioned)

SEE PAGE TWO -

Page one of the schedule for Paideia—Unstructured Independent Study—during winter break, January 1973.

big convocation of Reed faculty members and their families, together with a handful of other academics from around the country, at Jon Roush's ranch in western Montana.

Eighteen months later, back in Portland, we held meetings during Paideia with potential students, of which probably 60 percent or more were Reed students or Reed dropouts. What evolved was something along the lines of a "contribution" model. Students would contribute what they could, and faculty members would take out what they needed. It was very much a kind of Marxist approach.

OTTOMAR RUDOLF, German professor 1963–1998: I belonged to the Old Guard. The Young Turks wanted to start a "Learning Community," and I just didn't believe in it. We were already a community. The same thing with the Black Studies Center. I didn't believe in that either. We could have courses in Black Studies, but we didn't need a program.

Reed was a community, and a community is one. It was primarily a matter of educational principle. The Young Turks would have destroyed the college, in my judgment. Many of them were good teachers. Jon Roush in particular was an honorable man. But they were very politically inclined in terms of the larger social context. The Old Guard were not political in that same sense.

When some of the Young Turks came up for tenure decisions was when it started to get bad. The Faculty Advisory Committee, which made those decisions, was mostly made up of the old conservatives. Richard Jones in history was always voted in, as was Marvin Levich in philosophy. They were good, but when it came to judgments on tenure, they were very tough on people. Representation on the Faculty Advisory Committee became a bone of contention with the Young Turks, so they came up with a slate to vote in their people.

NICHOLAS WHEELER '55, physics professor 1963–2010: Slating meant that somebody would tell all the colleagues in his camp how to vote, so that their votes didn't cancel one another or didn't become redundant, and so had maximum impact. The conservative side was most adept at this. Like in national politics, the Democrats are scattered and canceling each other out, and the Republicans fall behind some character who creates a snowplow. So the conservatives pretty effectively controlled elections at Reed.

HUBERT CHRESTENSON, mathematics professor 1957–1990: I was on the Faculty Advisory Committee in 1968 when we were slating, and I hated it. One day I was walking with chemistry professor Arthur Scott, who had served as interim president of Reed during the Second World War, and he said that years before he had been complaining to F. L. Griffin, one of the founding faculty members, about slating, and that Griffin had said, "Don't worry about it. We've done it for years." In other words, it was a Reed tradition.

CHARLES SVITAVSKY, English professor 1961–1998: Aristotle was absolutely right when he said that in any political conflict the left and the right will, as a first matter of business, eliminate the middle. There were not many of us who were in the middle, and we were forced to choose up sides. My sympathies were more with the Young Turks, though some of the extreme positions taken there had no more appeal to me than the extreme positions of the conservatives.

FRANK GWILLIAM, biology professor 1957–1996, provost 1979–1982: There were meetings and secret cabals, which was distressing, because I thought we were actually determining whether the institution was going to survive or not. As a member of the Faculty Advisory Committee at the time, I was on the conservative side, for keeping the institution the way it was.

RICHARD JONES, history professor 1941–1982, 1985–1986: Respect for tradition was not counted a virtue among the proponents of the open college. Liberation from tyranny and injustice, freedom for novel experimentation, and a curriculum addressed directly to the interests and tastes of the day were their objectives. To their adversaries their rhetoric seemed indistinguishable from the current mode of demand, and their academic politics appeared to afford no room for compromise.

Response to them was not infrequently characterized by intolerance. A few faculty members who had always been proud to be reputed champions of academic freedom spoke of the controversy as a war, with victory as the only acceptable outcome.

SUSAN BRODY '71: Students aligned themselves with one subset of the faculty or another based on the different philosophies espoused by the faculty members with regard to area-based courses such as Black Studies, Women's Studies, and changes to the humanities curriculum. Discussions of curriculum change were happening all the time.

CHARLES SVITAVSKY, English professor: There were more people body-count-wise on the left than on the right, yet only one person on the Young Turks' slate was elected, and that was Jon Roush, who was on leave that year at the Carnegie Foundation for the Advancement of Teaching and wasn't there. It was a marvelous irony that all the members of the left had their own individual agendas and were not really willing to support a group. They could not unify around any group of people.

OTTOMAR RUDOLF, German professor: The slating was just devastating to the health of the faculty. We hated each other after that. It was awful.

MASON DRUKMAN, political science professor: Things became quite factionalized, and then people started losing their jobs. George Fasel, who had come to Reed in 1963 to teach history, had been promoted very fast to acting vice-president under acting president Byron Youtz. Fasel was seen as a fair-haired boy, a very effective teacher, and a committed guy. But then he became a very close friend of mine, and through guilt by association he was fired. I think they thought of him as a traitor. That's what it came to—the Faculty Advisory Committee was wreaking vengeance.

ROGER PORTER, English professor: Among something like twenty-six new faculty members hired for the humanities course between 1967 and 1971, only one person was kept on and given tenure, and that was Peter Parshall in the art department. The humanities course was a kind of graveyard. What was as important as your classroom teaching was the way you performed at meetings and the allegiance and loyalties that you showed to the course.

JON ROUSH, English professor 1964–1970: There were ten people elected to the Faculty Advisory Committee, and I was the only non-tenured member of the committee at the time. Some members began to see me as their envoy to the radical side. I tried to do that in an honest way. I really tried to report to them what I thought was going on, what I thought they ought to know, not betraying any confidences, but trying to bring them along. That year was the year of the purge, when many of my friends on the faculty lost their jobs. Some of those I could understand—maybe they were qualified for tenure, maybe not. But some of these people were tremendously qualified.

Political science professor Kirk Thompson was one. His scholarship was superb. He had published a paper on Rousseau's *Social Contract*.

Marvin Levich said that it was more of an opinion piece than a piece of scholarship, and it really hadn't deserved to be published in a journal. We set aside time at the Faculty Advisory Committee for a debate between Marvin and me on the merits of Kirk's paper. Although it was a real debate, I don't think Marvin had any interest in my view. It was a show trial. He was manipulating the committee, trying to set up a situation where it looked as if we had all done the due diligence that we should do.

ROGER PORTER, English professor: If Kirk Thompson, who had the most scholarly bent and the most meticulous of intellectual attitudes among the younger faculty, could not get tenure, then nobody from that group was going to get it. We were outraged because we felt that his denial of tenure was a profoundly political decision. In a very visceral way, we felt the utter shocking un-rightness of that, a quite palpable sense of injustice.

GALE ROHDE '73: The student newspaper came out with a list of a whole bunch of professors who had been fired, many of them our favorite ones. We didn't know at the time that it might have been for financial reasons at the college. But it seemed to me like a big motivation for a tuition boycott as a form of protesting that action. It was quite powerful and had the administration very scared, but eventually some of those favorite professors who had been fired argued for ending the boycott, saying that they thought it could destroy Reed.

MAURICE ISSERMAN '73: President Nixon invaded Cambodia on April 30, 1970. On May 1, SDS organized a protest in downtown Portland with maybe two hundred people. Three days later there was the shooting of four students at Kent State by the National Guard. The next day there was a national student strike. Something

like five hundred colleges and universities went on strike, some in places that had no history of radicalism—Catholic colleges, Southern universities, the Merchant Marine Academy. ROTC buildings were being burned to the ground. Buildings were being occupied.

KEITH MARTIN '73: The day the students were shot at Kent State, my literature professor, Robert Michael, stood up on the table and stomping his feet, said, "How can we be in class when the National Guard is killing people at Kent State?"

DAVID PERRY '73: The college cancelled exams and classes and we had a series of teach-ins on the Vietnam War. The whole college basically shut down for most of a week. It was pretty traumatic.

PAT MUSICK '73: The political situation in the country in 1970 was such that the Nixon Justice Department decided to send delegations to eight high-level colleges around the country, Reed being one of them, explaining what the Justice Department was really doing and that it wasn't so corrupt after all. Before getting to Reed, the delegates had been boycotted by students at one of the other colleges, and had had pot smoke blown in their faces at another. But at Reed, we gave them a party. We called it "Ramsey Clark Day," since Clark, the former attorney general under Lyndon Johnson, was speaking out at the time about things that the Justice Department was not interested in.

SHELDON HOCHHEISER '73: The Justice Department lawyers were greeted at the Rose Manor Inn motel by two dozen Reed bikers who gave them a motorcycle escort to the campus. When they arrived, we had the "Reed College High School Marching Band"—made up of flutes, garbage can lids, and other assorted instruments—playing something resembling "Hail to the Chief."

Reed's welcoming contingent as seen from the Justice Department motorcade, spring 1970.

Several Reed women, dressed as cheerleaders, were leading the crowd in cheers that spelled out "J - U - S - T - I - C - E." People dressed as clowns were jumping around their car. The lawyers held workshops for the rest of the day, during which there were costumed wrestling matches and vendors going through the audience hawking popcorn. The lawyers had no idea how to react; it was unlike anything they had encountered on their other stops.

ROGER PORTER, English professor: After President Nixon's bombing of Cambodia, a group of five faculty members put out a broadside declaration in which they said that the Reed faculty would be more concerned by a firebombing of the Reed library than they would be by the death of fifty thousand North Vietnamese. That was admittedly hyperbolic, but the declaration was taken by a lot of other faculty members as literally a call to firebomb the library. That night, a group of professors sat up in their offices in the library all night watching for terrorists. It was

insanity. All of those people who had signed that declaration were among those fired.

RICHARD JONES, history professor: Partisans of the losing minority not unnaturally thought of those associates whose appointments were not renewed as victims of a political purge. Promotion and the award of tenure to two of the leading critics of the traditional structure, and non-renewal of the appointments of some of its supporters, did little to modify belief in the unfairness of the majority who dominated the Faculty Advisory Committee.

MASON DRUKMAN, political science professor: I was surprised that I got tenure, since everybody else was getting fired. Vic Rosenblum took me for a drive to tell me, and in the process told me what the Faculty Advisory Committee's criticisms were of one of my upper-division classes, which I did not take kindly to. It seemed a kind of left-handed way of getting tenure.

The Learning Community was still aborning.

I announced that I would be willing to resign from my position at Reed to be the administrator for the Learning Community. I didn't know what my future was going to be, or really how much I was putting my family at risk, but in the back of my mind I thought that I could always come back. I had just had my first book published, and I thought I was enough of a hotshot that I could get a job somewhere. The reality was that the academic market was narrowing considerably, though I was unaware of it at the time.

JON ROUSH, English professor: I decided that Reed wasn't going to be receptive to my ideas about teaching. I can't point to any particular instance, but it was an ongoing, death-by-a-thousand-cuts kind of thing, so systematic that many of us left the academic life. It wasn't that we wanted to be at some other college, it was that, in various ways, we were all traumatized. The fact that so many of us reached that decision, not all for the same reasons, but for various reasons, tells you something about what a pressure cooker Reed was.

JOHN LAURSEN '67: In 1969, the Learning Community received a $50,000 grant from the Carnegie Foundation and satellite accreditation from Antioch College. Kirk Thompson, Jon Roush—these professors were the ones I most respected from my Reed days, and, fresh out of graduate school, I was involved from 1969 to 1970.

It was just very sad. Essentially, this group of Reed faculty members, who had been meeting for two or three years and talking about their desire to create a new school that was not Reed, either did not understand or else could not come to terms with the fact that they had two distinctly different, radically opposed visions. One half saw Reed as having ideals that it did not live up to, and they wanted to re-create a better Reed. The other half wanted an anti-Reed, an institution that would not have such high standards,

and would not be in any way selective—that is, not "elitist." Until there was the Carnegie money and accreditation with Antioch at stake, either nobody recognized that these were two quite different aspirations, or else the stakes weren't high enough for anybody to confront that division.

Almost as soon as it began, it fell apart.

JON ROUSH, English professor: Once there was no longer a common enemy, we just had each other.

NICHOLAS WHEELER '55, physics professor: The odd thing was that these people in the Learning Community were the most in touch with the blue-collar people of the streets. I'm not saying that they were Marxists, but they were certainly not elitists, and yet many of them went on to build expensive restaurants locally that were the pride of Portland, places like Indigene, the Wood Stove, L'Auberge, and Genoa. The world is full of ironies.

DAVID PERRY '73: Convocation in 1969, my freshman year, was held in the sports center. Three students walked in, one holding a Viet Cong flag, one banging on a garbage lid with a wooden spoon, and one carrying a cream pie. They walked up to the front of the assembly where the president, Victor Rosenblum, was standing, and said, "All hail, Vic Rosenblum!" Then they tossed the pie at him.

Dr. Rosenblum decided at the end of that year that he liked teaching law better than being president of Reed College. He resigned and returned to Northwestern.

VICTOR ROSENBLUM, president: It wasn't that it was anybody's fault, but I thought I was coming to Reed to be one of the world's great spenders. Instead, I got myself into a situation, although I did not want to believe it, in which there were the same kinds of fiscal constraints at Reed that my old mentor Peter Odegard had encountered as president of the college back in the 1940s. The notion of needing to cut the budget was really very alien to my thoughts. But it turned out that in conjunction with the other ferments on campus at the time, aspirations for a significant fund drive were simply unrealistic. The trustees realized that, and I had to realize it, and in doing so I also realized that I was the wrong person to be a budget cutter at the school—that to do the kind of cutting necessary required that I cut out my own dreams and aspirations. Rather than do that, I chose, for one of the few times in my life, to resign. I really hated resigning—though I think it was the right and necessary thing to do at that point—because I loved the school.

ALAN DEAN '41, trustee 1973–1998: There were about three or four times in the history of Reed that we took a good professor and made him a poor president. Victor Rosenblum was one.

GLENN ERICKSON '72: "I come not as a man on a horse," President Rosenblum said in his first speech to the students when he arrived. But then he rode out a short time later.

RICHARD JONES, history professor: Ross Thompson, the financial vice-president, was appointed acting president for 1970–71 after Rosenblum left, reprising a role he had held just prior to Rosenblum's arrival two years before. Thompson acted precisely in the same way as E. B. MacNaughton, who had taken over from Peter Odegard in 1948, not as an educator or someone determining what education should be, but as one who gave effective administrative execution to what the faculty and students wanted.

MATTHEW KANGAS '71: Ross Thompson had been the CEO of Litton Industries before coming to Reed. A lot of people disliked him. He was a corporate executive, and not a good fit for the college. Jim Webb, who was finishing up his last year teaching English, had a billboard put up on McLoughlin Boulevard in Portland with a picture of Thompson, and text that asked, "Would you buy a used college from this man?"

English professor Jim Webb's billboard on McLoughlin Boulevard mocking acting president Ross Thompson.

CHAPTER 29

Rising from the Ashes, Again

It was intimidating and a little bit scary that the faculty could come to such a donny-brook of irrational discussion.
    —Ray Kierstead, history professor

My goodness, whatever made me think that I should be so arrogant to believe that I could be successful in this context?
    —Paul Bragdon, president

In 1971, for the third time in its sixty-year history, Reed College faced financial insolvency. As had been true of the political crises sparked by the First World War in 1919 and by McCarthyism in the 1950s, the political upheavals of the late 1960s pushed the college's vulnerable financial model nearly to the breaking point. Highly dependent on tuition income, Reed found itself trapped in a death spiral as student enrollment began rapidly dropping much faster than the faculty had anticipated in proposing to reduce the size of the student body to nine hundred.

Into this challenging environment stepped a new president, Paul Bragdon. A graduate of Amherst College with a law degree from Yale, Bragdon had worked in the reform movement of New York politics and as a press secretary to the mayor of New York City. He left public service to become vice-president for public affairs at New York University, and had also been the director of the President's Task Force on Priorities in Education. Bragdon, however, did not have any managerial or fundraising experience, nor did he have any direct experience working with a community of students and faculty, particularly one emerging from an intense internecine war.

NICHOLAS WHEELER '55, physics professor 1963–2010: In the four years after President Dick Sullivan left in 1967, we saw presidents come and go in very rapid succession—Byron Youtz, then Ross Thompson, then Victor Rosenblum, and then Ross Thompson again. Various people, interstitial terms. The college was in financial and political stress. There were some very colorful figures coming and going among the faculty, which itself was torn asunder by its various reactions to what was going on in the students' minds.

BERT BREHM, biology professor 1962–1993: The financial situation in 1971 was dire in some people's minds. I actually heard a group of senior faculty say during a coffee break, "Well, maybe the best solution is to divvy up the endowment, shut the doors, and let everybody go home."

GEORGE JOSEPH '51, trustee 1972–1980: As president of the alumni board in 1971, I was appointed to the committee to find a new president. Three of us—trustee Harold Hirsch, philosophy professor Marvin Levich, and I—went to interview a fellow named Paul Bragdon at New York University on a hot day in July. Paul said, "I think Reed is an interesting proposition but my friends all say I'd be a fool to go there because it's broke, and it may not open its doors this September. Is that true?"

Harold Hirsch, who was short, leaned forward in his chair so that his feet could touch the floor, and said, "That's just not true. There are a dozen people in Portland, each of whom would give Reed a hundred thousand dollars right now if they knew of the importance."

At this point the story varies. Paul claims that both Marvin Levich and I nodded in agreement. We were actually shaking our heads vigorously, "No." When we left the interview, the three of us didn't even have to talk. All we said was, "We don't need to see anybody else."

PAUL BRAGDON, president 1971–1988: In addition to going bankrupt, the rumor mill also had it that Reed's faculty was irresponsible and that no president could possibly survive there.

Shortly after I became president, Reed's financial vice-president, Ross Thompson, who had been appointed acting president when Vic

Rosenblum resigned, left the college. He was succeeded in the business manager's role by Lloyd Peterson, a conscientious, hard-working person with strong character. Lloyd came to me one day and said, "In eighteen months it's all over unless something happens to change this situation. That will be when the investigation begins about how all this came about."

That was a very sobering thing to hear. The college was very dependent on tuition income, which meant that it was dependent on the number of students who came and then stayed. Historically Reed had had a very small applicant pool, and a less favorable retention rate than a lot of other institutions. Because of budget constraints at the college, the admission office had been in effect dismantled. The person directing admissions was a young faculty member, and he was dependent on random travel by faculty members for recruitment visits to high schools around the country. In my first few months in the job, I also discovered that the rumors about Reed had very much hurt our efforts to gain foundation support. The Ford Foundation and others I approached all said, "We have not given money because the place is such a mess."

NANCY BRAGDON, wife of Paul Bragdon: Paul and I got off the train in August of 1971 and came to see the house in Eastmoreland that we had bought sight unseen on the recommendation of Reed's chairman, John Gray. John wanted us to live fairly close to campus. Paul used to joke, "But not a stone's throw away."

John was then a developer of large resorts, and he had already brought in a man to start remodeling the house in order to accommodate plenty of people when we entertained. The house was just a mess. The doors were all boarded up except for a side door. We came inside and went into the garage. Somebody had spray painted "Fuck you" on the inside of the garage door. Later, when we went to get permits for the remodeling, the immediate neighbors objected violently. One neighbor went to the City Council and said that we were turning the house into a pleasure palace to entertain people from Reed College. We had major vandalism to the house throughout the remodeling process. It was horrendous.

WILLIAM GATES, economics professor 1971– 1972: There was a quality of joylessness at Reed. It seemed to me to be very pervasive in the faculty and to have quite negative effects on the quality of academic life. I could scarcely believe it, but a surprisingly large number of my Reed colleagues seemed to have lost their sense of humor, and even lost sight of the possibility that there can be real joy in the intellectual life and that the great world outside has beauty and excitement, despite a good deal of trauma and sordidness.

PAUL BRAGDON, president: Not coming straight out of the academic track was quite a risky thing both for me and for the college. Also, I had never really had any management experience. Before I came to Portland I had read Burton Clark's book *The Distinctive College*, which addressed the history of Reed as well as the histories of Antioch and Swarthmore up until 1960. It was a cautionary tale at best, describing Reed's financial difficulties through the years, the divisions in the college, and the fact that there had been lots of acting and interim presidents. After stepping into the Reed presidency I re-read the book and thought to myself, "My goodness, whatever made me think that I should be so arrogant to believe that I could be successful in this context?"

CHRIS LOWE '82, history professor 1991–1996: Bragdon came into higher education through politics, which meant that he was used to dealing with people from a wide variety of social backgrounds and constituencies. At Reed, he dealt pretty effectively with the faculty, leaving them a large realm of autonomy, and established

good relationships with the kinds of people he needed to raise money from. That included people from Oregon industries that had been involved in extraction of natural resources, transportation, timber, and technology. He also built up the alumni relations.

He was not a "hail fellow, well met" kind of person, but he was quite genial, and non-confrontational. Slow to anger, he was able to deal with academic personality foibles by shedding them like water off a duck. Bragdon was a patient man with a long-term vision for addressing the big structural issues facing the college, and he was willing to take the time to talk to people and try to work things through.

CHARLES SVITAVSKY, English professor 1961– 1998: The faculty conservatives had won the curricular battles so decisively prior to Bragdon's arrival that the faculty leftists basically disappeared, went underground, or shut up. But the battles had taken their toll. Fatigue does not adequately describe the condition of the faculty at the time. It was more a sense of total defeat. Paul Bragdon was very skillful in establishing and maintaining an environment that was fundamentally non-political for quite some time. Whether that was good or not good, I'm not sure.

DOROTHY DAVENHILL HIRSCH '52: I called him "the Sphinx" when I was serving as president of the alumni association. Paul Bragdon was a person who did not speak his mind. He listened. I just liked him.

JACK DUDMAN '42, mathematics professor 1953–1985, dean of students 1963–1985: Paul Bragdon was a very complicated, very private man, without much openness or friendship with faculty members. He played things pretty close to the vest all the time. He was a very articulate man, but one who used his verbal abilities as kind of a screen that protected him in exchanges with other people. For many faculty and many administrators he was difficult to work with because it was hard to enter into easy conversation with him. He was kind of distant and correct in his dealings with the faculty, but suspicious of antagonism when he sensed it, and so he operated in ways that tended to minimize it.

PAUL BRAGDON, president: Reed had a very critical cultural environment. Stanford, for example, was a culture of love. Although there were many people who were probably unhappy at Stanford, the culture was one of how great and wonderful Stanford was. Not at Reed. The bright students there tended to be critical and turned their criticism on themselves and on the institution, with many of them hoping that the institution would be the one place in society that was perfect, or that came close to living up to everything it said it was, or to what they had looked for in it. Finding both the people and place falling short of that standard, even the best students, and the ones you might say were the best adjusted, adopted a critical posture.

I arrived at Reed immediately following the major faculty split that had taken place. The college was infected with fatigue, weariness, and skepticism. The students were influenced by both that attitude and by the general culture of the time. There had been so many failures in the country—and there would soon be even worse ones like the Nixon Watergate scandal—that doubt was cast on the legitimacy and trustworthiness of institutions and also of the people who were associated with them in leadership positions.

CHARLES SVITAVSKY, English professor: When I walked into class in the morning in the 1960s and said, "Good morning," the students wrote it down. When I walked in and said "Good morning" in the 1970s, students would say, "Oh, I

don't know about that; it doesn't seem that good to me." They questioned almost everything I said.

LAURA LEVITON '73: I became aware of Paul Bragdon's competence in my sophomore year. He had invited Daniel Patrick Moynihan to be the convocation speaker. Moynihan had been serving then as an advisor to President Nixon on urban affairs, and had earlier released his famous and controversial "Moynihan Report," which essentially said that expansion of welfare programs were turning black families into matriarchies, weakening the ability of black men to function as authority figures, and leading to a disintegration of black urban life.

Bragdon's choice was opposed by a lot of the radicals on campus who didn't like Moynihan. As it turned out, Moynihan was indisposed and couldn't make it to Reed. At convocation Bragdon just laid into the radicals. And man, they deserved it. You could tell there was a new sheriff in town.

RICH PARKER '75: There was a takeover of Eliot Hall in early April of '72 in response to the resumed bombing of North Vietnam and the mining of Haiphong Harbor. Just before it happened, there was a meeting of most of the student body in the Commons. The topic was, "Shall we take over one of the buildings?" We took a vote, and the idea was voted down four to one. Then the 25 percent who had voted for it went off and had their own vote. They came back and said, "It's unanimous! Let's go take it!"

PAUL BRAGDON, president: The student sit-in was a crisis, particularly for me as a new president trying to weigh the various interests and not have students harmed or hurt, and just wanting to find a way to end it. One night during this emergency situation I was sitting up late at home, and at two in the morning the doorbell rang. It

Provost Marvin Levich and President Paul Bragdon conferring at a meeting in the Commons during the student takeover of Eliot Hall in 1972.

was a Reed student, who came in and wanted to discuss why this was happening. He had been studying existentialism and reading Camus. To my mind I saw this student as a person whom Camus sent to talk. I thought, here is an intellectualization of this experience.

There was a negotiating committee and I met them in the morning in the physics building. The first thing that one of the students said, in a very nice voice, was, "I hope this hasn't inconvenienced you in any way," adding that the sit-in had nothing to do with me personally. I didn't know how to take that. Was he saying it in just a straightforward way or was it some sort of Marxist comment that great historical forces were moving and I just happened to be there?

At the time, there was an ice-cream parlor and hamburger joint up the hill on Woodstock, Davidson's, that was quite a student hangout. I said to my wife, Nancy, and the children, "Let's go up to Davidson's to get away from this." We went up there and some of the student ringleaders of the sit-in were there. They bought us our dinner.

ED McFARLANE, **controller and assistant treasurer 1973–1978, vice-president and treasurer 1979– :** When I came to Reed in 1973, the college was technically bankrupt, and managing sort of hand-to-mouth. The annual operation budget was probably somewhere in the range of $2 million to $3 million, and the endowment was down to $4.4 million. It was a tough time.

ERNEST BONYHADI '48, trustee 1971–1995: The board of trustees hadn't done such a prudent job of managing Reed, going all the way back to the 1930s and '40s. They kept the college alive obviously, but they did a lot of foolish things like selling off the land holdings the college had received in downtown Portland from Amanda Reed's estate. Every time Reed was short in the annual budget, they'd sell off a piece of land. When I joined the board in the early 1970s, in order to pay the bills we sold off a piece of prime downtown real estate for the new Hilton Hotel.

MARSH CRONYN '40, chemistry professor 1952–1989, provost 1982–1989: At the time, the money thrown off from what little endowment Reed had was being used to pay off debt instead of helping to cover operating costs. That was a hairy situation. Not to mention that the endowment hadn't really grown since the founding of the college, and in fact had eroded.

ERNEST BONYHADI '48, trustee: The college was in debt a couple million dollars to the Reed Institute, which was the original legal entity created by Amanda Reed's will, with Reed College being the adopted business name. The college had essentially borrowed the money from its own endowment to cover its operating deficits. It was just absurd. I was a lawyer. Paul Bragdon and I talked about it, and decided that the note was meaningless and ridiculous. We had the Board of Trustees write it off.

PAUL BRAGDON, president: When I arrived in 1971, economics professor George Hay chaired a faculty and student committee, which developed what was popularly called the "Hay Report." That report reaffirmed the historic mission and goals of the college, and set forth a new plan to achieve financial stability and help assure the future at Reed. It settled the issue of student body size, which had been under discussion for a cou-

ple of years, setting a target of 1,080 students and ninety faculty members, at the twelve-to-one student-faculty ratio that had been set back in the mid-1960s.

Many of the basic recommendations of the Hay Report remained in place long after the emergency conditions that had led up to it had passed. George Hay himself later agreed to take on the position of chief financial officer and treasurer when Lloyd Peterson left in 1976. He continued for several years in that position, and was prominent in the successful evolution of the modern college at Reed.

FRANK GWILLIAM, biology professor 1957–1996, provost 1979–1982: Faced with financial crisis, Bragdon brought some of the college's greatest benefactors into the fold. Some of them were on the board already, but they had not been the kind of supporters that they would become. They saw new hope for the place in the things that Paul was doing, and they believed that Reed was going to make it. Along with the foundations, they began to put money into the college.

PAUL BRAGDON, president: The change began when I visited the Mellon Foundation in New York City. Their new president, Nathan Pusey, had recently departed from the presidency at Harvard. He asked me, "Are you still taking very able, ambitious young people from the Northwest, and raising their aspirations and giving them confidence in what they can do in life?"

I said, "Yes!" Although I didn't think that was as true as it once was, but certainly the students who made me the happiest were those who fell in that category. Those who had gone to fine suburban high schools and good private schools would probably have done well wherever they went. But there were other people who, if they'd gone to another college, might not have broadened their horizons or begun to know what they might do and achieve. Those were the students who were going to live different lives than they might have if they had not come to Reed. To me, that was where we added our value.

After I got back from my visit to the Mellon Foundation, I got a check in the mail for about $250,000. That was our first restoration to the A-list of foundations.

MICHAEL LEVINE '62, trustee 1984–2002: Paul was, in a sense, a perfect fit. He became an ambassador to the local community, and an enormously successful one at that, coming to be, along with his wife, Nancy, part of the Portland establishment. Paul took the college off of life support and gave it a new presence in the community.

DAN GREENBERG '62, trustee 1975– : It was through four people on the board that the college managed to get through that dark period: Howard Vollum '35; John Gray, who along with his wife, Betty, gave unstintingly and in the most unselfish manner you could ever imagine; Ed Cooley, a really wonderful old friend of John Gray; and Dick Wollenberg. They were all, ex-

cept for Howard, local businesspeople who were not alumni of the institution, but who had taken an interest in helping it survive during very difficult times.

RICHARD P. WOLLENBERG, trustee 1962–2005: I got acquainted with Reed originally on a recruiting trip to the campus for my company, Longview Fiber Company in Washington state, but wasn't able to hire anyone. That was when everybody seemed to be going to grad school after Reed. But I was impressed with the college. I realized it was a quality institution that was unique in the Pacific Northwest, and highly unusual in the United States. It was strong in mathematics and science, which, when combined with its broad liberal arts program, made a major contribution to the development of generalists, which were needed as much as specialists. Reed developed both. They were producing well-educated people who could not only think well but also communicate well.

PAUL BRAGDON, president: The turning point was a challenge gift made in 1975 by Jean and

Trustees Richard P. Wollenberg and John Gray, with Betty Gray.

Howard Vollum '35. Howard had been a trustee, but not a very active one. The fact was, he and his wife, Jean, were at the time somewhat disaffected from Reed. A key figure in bringing them around was our chairman, John Gray, a very low-key person and not a flamboyant sales type. He just stuck at it until they said, "Well, we'll try this and see what happens."

Howard Vollum felt that no institution should be totally secure and that all of them should have to continually prove themselves; therefore, he didn't believe in endowment. The Vollum Challenge offered Reed a considerable number of shares of Howard's electronics company, Tektronix, based on the ability of various constituencies—trustees, alumni and other sources of giving—to rise to certain levels and meet certain milestones over a five-year challenge period. It was thrilling because it was a stretch for every constituency. Sometimes it would be at the eleventh hour, just before the close of the college year, that the final milestone for the period would be met, but we did it.

The Vollum Challenge helped build confidence, both in the institution and in people such as the trustees, that things could be done at Reed. It wasn't a school hopelessly mired forever in poverty and uncertainty and insecurity.

ARTHUR LEIGH, economics professor 1945–1988: Overall, Paul Bragdon's administration was one of greater tranquility and greater progress than Reed had known in decades. But there was opposition to Paul, people who didn't like him, though most of us did.

FRANK GWILLIAM, biology professor: During his first year Paul could see very clearly that he wasn't going to be able to do the things that he had to do and still keep track of the academic side of the institution. Marvin Levich was a very highly regarded member of the faculty. He had been chairman of the search committee

that brought Paul to Reed, following which he and Paul got to be good friends. After checking with other people, Paul appointed Marvin to be Reed's first provost.

THOMAS DUNNE, chemistry professor 1963–1995: It was a cunning appointment, because Marvin was apt to be the senior faculty member who might cause the greatest trouble to the president. Instead, the position absorbed Marvin, and he was benched, essentially, as a full, active, potentially hostile faculty member.

PAUL BRAGDON, president: It would have required a change to the bylaws or the constitution to create a dean of faculty, but there was a provision for vice-presidents. So rather than confront the dean issue frontally, I created a position of vice-president and provost with the thought that this person would work full-time on academic affairs.

During my tenure, the position was occupied by three different people—philosophy professor Marvin Levich, who was the longest in service with seven years, biology professor Frank Gwilliam, and chemistry professor Marsh Cronyn '40. Each of them worked very hard and made major contributions.

But they were all products of Reed—some of them had been undergraduates as well as faculty members—and it was very difficult for them to understand what the full role of a dean-like person would be. And, perhaps, difficult for their colleagues to accept them in that role.

MARVIN LEVICH, philosophy professor 1953–1994, provost 1972–1979: Bragdon thought I was bright and industrious, and at the time regarded me as one of the stars of the faculty. But I hadn't mastered the art of administrative mendacity; that is, to say one thing and mean another. So I don't think I was terribly effective in the role of vice-president and provost. I was innocent of what would be involved in doing it. It seemed to me that it was proper for the college to have someone like a dean of faculty to represent the faculty in terms of educational policy and evaluation of faculty, but the position changed more to representing the views of the president to the faculty. That was not my objective in life.

DELL RHODES, psychology professor 1975–2006, associate dean of students 1990–1991: Marvin Levich was a very outspoken and intellectual eccentric, who loved the college first and foremost. He had very strong principles, which he enunciated clearly, if at great length, about the internal workings of the college and its relationship to the expectations and standards of the external world. Of particular concern was the sense that the college was moving towards becoming a business, and that this threatened the purity of the academic mission. A lot of what he said influenced my opinion, and that of many of my peers, about what the college could and should be like. We identified him as being the spokesperson for positions that we held dear about what the college was.

MARIAN FURST '72: At one of his humanities lectures, Marvin Levich walked in, put his briefcase down behind him, went up to the lectern and proceeded with one of his "number-of-sentences-you-could-count-on-one-hand" orations. One of my friends actually counted how many sentences he used in that one-hour lecture—it was six. All very eloquent and each a very long paragraph.

OTTOMAR RUDOLF, German professor 1963–1998: Marvin was a debater. You could never really get a word in edgewise with him. We all respected his mind and his debating skills, but that was not enough in the role of provost. He and history professor Dick Jones worked hand-in-hand to undermine Paul Bragdon. They were both very powerful, and wanted to run the show. You couldn't go against them, really.

DELL RHODES, psychology professor: Among other things, Marvin was a central champion of strong faculty governance and of faculty participation in financial and political decision making. He believed that the college was defined first and foremost by its faculty, such that the faculty ought to be making decisions about how the college was run, and that this included having a major voice in decisions that impacted the financial health of the college. The administration conceded that the faculty was the backbone of the college, but believed that the faculty's responsibilities have to do with the classroom and the curriculum, i.e., with managing the academic program.

PAUL BRAGDON, president: The strong view was that the Faculty Advisory Committee ran the college. It may have been the case that at some points in the history of the institution that the committee, either under that name or some other name, did assume the policy-making and administrative role. That was not the case when I came.

When the faculty said that they were "running the college," it really meant that they were running the most important aspect to faculty members, namely their own compensation, promotions, and tenure decisions, which was not uncommon. And, under the faculty constitution, the faculty did share with the president responsibility for curricular and educational policy. As far as institutional matters though, they did not run any of those things. They provided helpful counsel and advice when asked, or when matters were brought to them for that purpose.

OTTOMAR RUDOLF, German professor: After the finances began to stabilize in the mid-1970s, Bragdon pushed the faculty to rethink the educational principles of the institution. For the first time during my tenure, we debated important educational principles such as the requirement system, including humanities and the science requirements. Bragdon forced the faculty to come to grips with some things that we didn't really want to look at.

PAUL BRAGDON, president: In the late 1970s, an outside accreditation review of the college and a self-evaluation grant from the Northwest Area Foundation offered an opportunity for us to see where the college was overall and where the departments were individually. My suspicion was that the report would say that the faculty as a whole was not considering educational issues, and that for a small liberal arts college, particularly one with the integrated tradition introduced by the Scholz curriculum in the 1920s, it was too heavily departmentalized. Both of those threads could in fact be distilled from looking at the report as a whole. Indeed, one of our outside observers indicated that the departments at Reed were more balkanized than at UC Berkeley.

RAY KIERSTEAD, history professor 1978–2000: I had taught in directed studies at Yale, which had the same purpose as Reed's humanities but was configured in a vastly different way. I didn't think there was one way of teaching humanities that was sacrosanct. The accreditation review made some recommendations for the humanities program. A committee was formed to rethink humanities, and came up with a new plan. It looked like a fairly impressive and well-thought-out program, but it was different from what was being offered at the time.

PETER STEINBERGER, political science professor 1977– , dean of faculty 1997–2010, acting president 2001–2002: Up until that time, the first semester of freshman humanities had been this intense, dense consideration of archaic and classical Greece. The second semester was split between three tracks: the High Middle Ages and the Renaissance, simply the Renaissance, or England in transition from the fifteenth to the seventeenth century. This variety was really fun and interesting but also deeply unsatisfying, because there was not enough time for in-depth consideration of any of those different periods. To address that, the committee recommended breaking the course up into three completely separate full-year tracks. There was a perception, rightly or wrongly, that doing so would make it better for the faculty to teach.

When this proposal came to the floor of the faculty, it set off a deeply and profoundly contentious and unpleasant debate. Faculty members in those days were much more willing to say things on the floor of the faculty with much more candor, and articulate their anger with much more clarity and vehemence. They were more inclined to argue that this or that point of view was "un-Reed-like." That was a basic term of art in those days. To be un-Reed-like was to be intellectually suspect.

RAY KIERSTEAD, history professor: It was intimidating and a little bit scary that the faculty could come to such a donnybrook of irrational discussion. But it seemed to fit with the stories that I was picking up about the curriculum battles in the late 1960s and early '70s. I could tell that they were still burning in the minds of older faculty members.

OTTOMAR RUDOLF, German professor: I could not believe the proposal to break up the humanities faculty and have them teach three different courses. I believed in the canon, period. I made a counter-motion that freshman Humanities 110 should remain one course, and always start with the Greeks—"the Rudolf motion," as it came to be called. The humanities and literature people teaching the course lined up against me, but

History professor Owen Ulph with German professor Ottomar Rudolf, late 1970s.

all the scientists supported me, and my motion passed, defeating the new plan. The first semester focused on the Greeks; the second semester focused on Rome and the Middle Ages.

ROBERT KNAPP, English professor 1974– : Creating a single unified syllabus was helped along by a grant Dick Jones requested from the National Endowment for the Humanities, which enabled the creation of a new course that would bridge the materials chronologically between Ancient Humanities, the freshman course covering Greece and Rome, and Modern Humanities, which was then the sophomore course covering the eighteenth to the twentieth centuries.

The new course, for the first half of the sophomore year, dealt with the Renaissance through the late seventeenth century and was called Early Modern Europe. Modern Humanities became the second-semester sophomore course, and was changed to extend from the French Revolution to the middle of the twentieth century. The result was that we had a freshman syllabus that ran from Homer to Dante, followed by the second-year syllabus from Dante to Voltaire and then almost to the present.

JACQUELINE DIRKS '82, history professor 1991– : The debates over curriculum continued in the late 1970s and early '80s, but the focus on content shifted to sometimes featuring emergent feminist theory, especially in literature. I was enmeshed in feminist politics on and off campus, and also profoundly shaped by the feminist scholars and scholarship I was able to find, as were many of my peers. In the winter of 1979, English professor Jane McLelland organized a symposium of feminist writers and academics featuring Mary Daly, Gayatri Spivak, Tillie Olsen, Susan Griffin, and Patricia Meyer Spacks.

Mary Daly, a former nun turned radical theologian at Boston College, gave a lecture on her essentialist theories of the patriarchal repression of female spirituality. It was quite out there, especially at Reed. The first questioner to leap to his feet when Daly finished was religion professor Robby Segal. Daly electrified the hall by telling the rest of Reed what some of us already knew: "I don't take questions from men." The discussion became quite heated after that.

ROBERT SEGAL, "Letter to the Editor," *REED COLLEGE QUEST*, **February 16, 1979:** The response of the audience was, to me, as damning as the talk itself. The audience, which, to be sure, was by no means limited to members of "the Reed community," applauded not merely her ravings generally but most of all her blind dismissal of learning and scholarship.

The issue is not the propriety and worth of either feminism itself or the symposium, for which Jane McLelland deserves much credit. The issue is the propriety and worth of a ranting, bigoted, ignorant fool being supported in any way by Reed College.

BARBARA PIJAN '79: The Feminist Symposium was indeed life-transforming. During one pressure-cooker week, I suddenly saw the world through a brilliant new prism of "gender." The deep moral problems like greed and hatred now seemed imminently solvable. That was exhilarating. The born-again feminist society, purified of life-killing patriarchal religion, would be freed of domination, exploitation, war, and crime. It would be creative and wildly sensual, yet peaceful, safe, and healing. It was heady stuff.

RICHARD JONES, history professor 1941–1982, 1985–1986: When Bragdon realized after three years that the faculty could not be expected to generate initiatives on educational policy or suggestions for attack on general college problems, he prodded the Educational Policies Committee to conduct a review of the perennially unsatisfactory course-requirement structure and recommend remedial improvements.

Instead, the faculty made it clear that they did not consider an attempt to relate curricular requirements to fundamental principles to be worthy of their professional attention. The

committee's disappointment was as profound as that of the president. The focus then turned to restructuring faculty governance.

PAUL BRAGDON, president: I had hoped that the accreditation report would have sort of a Hawthorne effect, where the thing being studied modifies its behavior simply in response to the fact that it's being studied, and that would lead, initially at least, to a new burst of energy and enthusiasm to examine the larger issue of what the best possible education could be for students coming to Reed College. Instead, what we ended up with was largely procedural or structural reforms relating to the two committees that evaluated the faculty and the budget on one hand, and educational programs and curricula on the other.

RAY KIERSTEAD, history professor: I chaired the subcommittee on restructuring faculty governance. It took at least three years of endless negotiation and consensus building, facing all the obstacles that Reed professors can throw in your way to make life difficult for you. The old Faculty Advisory Committee had been a smaller body of usually ten old guys, who just ran the place as they wanted.

The new structure opened up more opportunities for more faculty members to play a major role in the college. It was meant to subvert that notion of one single elected body that did everything. It wasn't actually instituted, however, until the year after Paul Bragdon left the college.

ROBERT REYNOLDS, physics professor 1963–2002: Up until the change in the late 1980s, faculty governance resided in two bodies—the Educational Policies Committee, which had responsibility for educational policy, and the Faculty Advisory Committee, which had responsibility for personnel and fiscal kinds of decisions that the college was making. They were replaced by two new committees: the Committee on Advancement and Tenure, and the Committee on Academic Policy and Planning.

CHARLES SVITAVSKY, English professor: As time went on, the college was growing and becoming more complex, and it needed a broader, more structured administration.

PAUL BRAGDON, president: Reed was becoming engaged with the outside world in a way that it never had been before. That engagement required professional skills, and no president had them all. You really had to have a financial and business officer as well as somebody who was concerned with the development of the college—with fundraising, public relations, and government relations.

MARSH CRONYN '40, chemistry professor: Presidents are supposed to be fundraising. They start messing with the internals, and it just soaks up all their energy and time. It's two different jobs, and they just can't do it emotionally and physically. Previous Reed presidents started out by letting the faculty take care of things, but once they put their foot in the water, they got sucked in and that became a problem for them. Paul Bragdon, on the other hand, took a whole raft of things out of his office, delegating them to vice-presidents.

RICHARD JONES, history professor: Most of the whole business of determining what the policies should be, or how they should be given effect, came to be determined by management. That's what you had all those vice-presidents doing. In the old days a faculty member at Reed had to devote a good deal of his time and energy to the college's problems in general and to its overall welfare. But not anymore.

For faculty members, the emphasis shifted to pursuing your own special problem, instead of pursuing the problems related to what might be good for the general college program. That became something that fit in very much with what was generally going on all over the country, and with the way that people were being trained for faculty positions. The kind of informal interaction that constantly took place with regard to intellectual matters stopped, because the bulk of the faculty became concerned primarily about what affected their own careers.

PAUL BRAGDON, president: In student services, development, public relations, and the business and development side of the college there were expansions, no question about it. We always did surveys to benchmark ourselves against other colleges, and on a comparative basis we were still not spending the money and didn't have the people that similar institutions had. All of those additions were done grudgingly with a view to doing the essentials but trying not to make administrators a central feature of the college. They served a support function and were not intended to build up a bureaucratic stance that makes you sort of an entity unto yourself. The faculty continued to do administrative things in admissions and development. It was valuable and appreciated.

KONRAD ALT '81, trustee 2010– : Bragdon turned his attention, as he very properly should have, to raising money. But on campus that manifested itself as a clear sign that this guy wasn't so serious about students and faculty, that his priorities were elsewhere, and that "elsewhere" was a place that very few students understood. We saw these new buildings springing up that we didn't ask for—Vollum Center, which housed faculty offices, classrooms, and a large auditorium, and the studio art building—which seemed to be an outgrowth of efforts to appease major donors. They weren't part of any academic need that we could identify.

RICHARD JONES, history professor: We were concerned that if we didn't go along with the things Bragdon wanted, if we opposed him, he was going to resign probably, and that would cause all the trustees to resign. I did not think that Paul Bragdon was an educator, nor that he really understood, or was committed to, the nature of the college.

PAUL BRAGDON, president: From the day I arrived there was talk of an "old" Reed and a "new" Reed. There was always a suspicion that somebody wanted to change something that was a distinct jewel into something that was perhaps another institution. I had gone to Amherst College as an undergraduate, and some people would say, "He wants to turn Reed into another Amherst." Well, I didn't, but the fact was that if I had wanted to, I couldn't have done it. Each institution has its own history, its own culture, and its own traditions. You cannot impose your will upon it or even nurse things in a certain direction.

EDWARD SEGEL, history professor 1973–2011: Paul had, for better or worse, and a little of both perhaps, a group of faculty who he was very close to personally, including Larry Ruben and Frank Gwilliam in biology, and Ottomar Rudolf in German. It was a kind of "kitchen cabinet," and sometimes that caused problems in that it led to some resentment. On the other hand, it did mean that he had some sense of faculty sentiment.

CHARLES SVITAVSKY, English professor: The thing that was outstanding about Paul Bragdon was how deeply committed he was to Reed, and how well he understood the nature of the place and tried to preserve it. His wife, Nancy, was equally committed to Reed, and very involved in the institution. They were a marvelous pair, and entertained us more than any president before or after. They occasionally hosted a dinner, but usually had hors d'oeuvres and drinks at their home. It would be a faculty-wide invitation.

LENA LENCEK, Russian professor 1977– : Paul Bragdon snatched Reed from the brink of disaster and put it on a solid footing. He introduced a system of accountability that stood the college in good stead going forward, and he reëstablished its credibility with the East Coast establishment and with funding sources. He really performed a Herculean task in moving Reed out of one league into another. Bragdon was a real mensch.

CHAPTER 30

The Cultural Shift

With the Republicans in power, President Reagan was flattening everything in his way. It felt kind of hopeless, so Reed drew in on itself.
  —Matt Giraud '85

Some people were sort of hippies. But the girls I hung around with were into punk. We all had punk haircuts and we'd wear Converse shoes and ripped, New Wave T-shirts. My roommate had dyed blue hair. We were tough punk girls.
  —Becky Chiao '85

The 1970s and early 1980s brought noticeable changes in the Reed student body. With America rocked by energy shortages, unemployment, inflation, and political scandals—most notably Watergate—a mood of political ambivalence and skepticism pervaded the times. Yet, while students showed less engagement in the sort of large-scale political activities such as civil rights and the anti-war movement that had characterized the idealistic 1960s, the rising dominance of conservative politics in the country continued to be challenged by social movements that grew out of the activism of earlier generations: the anti-nuclear-power movement, opposition to American intervention in Central America, the many developments in the world of feminist politics, the evolution of the gay rights movement, and organized opposition to apartheid in South Africa.

Student life also began to be affected by the overall conservative shift in America, especially as the Reagan Administration began to tie federal funding for student aid to new public policies, including registration of college males for the military draft, adherence to a federal drinking age of twenty-one, and the "war on drugs."

While Reed students had traditionally taken pride in their self-reliance, the Bragdon administration's focus on accountability meant that the college was increasingly seeking ways to bring more consistency and stability to student life. For some that signaled an increasing encroachment on student autonomy.

CARLETON WHITEHEAD '41, alumni director 1952–1958, college relations administrator 1959–1983: By the 1970s and '80s students no longer thought of themselves as being part of a new movement like they did in the earlier decades. A special identity hung over the college when I was a student in the 1930s, in which we all felt like we were creating something new and different, something much better than what had previously existed. People thought of themselves as part of a special group, and with that identity came both obligations and responsibilities. We called ourselves "Reedites," which meant more than just being a student at Reed College—it meant being a part of this special movement.

While the character of the students changed remarkably little over the years—the change being largely geographic, with more students coming from outside the Northwest, and more affluent students arriving—they referred to themselves as "Reedies," not "Reedites." There was something lost in that change that I felt a little sad about.

JACK DUDMAN '42, math professor 1953–1985, dean of students 1963–1985: The national mood changed after the Vietnam War was over in 1975. It seemed to me that during the late 1970s and '80s students were again making choices, like they had in the 1950s, that would optimize their own gain, looking out for their own interests, but not very socially concerned. I found that kind of disappointing.

But the national mood was a lot less challenging, too. While students didn't necessarily change a great deal, the milieu in which they operated did. When the society around them was sort of self-serving and personally concerned, as it was during the Reagan era of the 1980s, then students were likely to take on that coloration.

MATT GIRAUD '85: Reed was a pretty apathetic place at the time. I have no idea why, but my guess

is that with the Republicans in power, President Reagan was flattening everything in his way. It felt kind of hopeless, so Reed drew in on itself. There were some people who were political during that time, but nothing really awakened the whole campus. There was a long lull.

JACQUELINE DIRKS '82, history professor 1991– : The argument that the noble 1960s ended when "cultural politics" somehow displaced "real" politics overlooks the fact that civil rights activism continued into the 1970s, as black candidates ran for office and won. The same may be said of women's rights activism, especially if one looks at the mobilization to pass the Equal Rights Amendment, which was reintroduced in 1970 and narrowly missed being ratified in 1982, and at organizing for reproductive rights. The *Roe v. Wade* decision was handed down in 1973, and legal abortion clinics were established soon afterward.

KONRAD ALT '81, trustee 2010– : There were a few students who were interested in the whole issue of apartheid and divestiture in South Africa. That issue didn't really gather momentum for a number of years, but there were people beginning to talk about it. There were students who were interested in gay rights and women's rights. There was a group that was very involved in the pro-choice movement. An abortion clinic in downtown Portland got protested by the pro-lifers every Saturday and there was a group of Reedies who went down to stage counter-protests. Nuclear power and the construction of nuclear power stations in Washington state was a reasonably big issue, as was reinstatement of selective service.

PAUL BRAGDON, president 1971–1988: I entered higher education during the search by independent institutions for governmental support, whether state or federal. The Pell Grants, which

Reed students protesting against the testing of nuclear weapons during the Reagan Administration, 1986.

provided funding for low-income students, were passed by Congress in 1965 in what was otherwise a rather adverse climate for higher education in terms of finances and support. But with that kind of support came the burgeoning statutory and regulatory and bureaucratic things that were increasingly impinging on colleges. Conservatives were right when they said, "If you accept this support, there will be a price tag."

ROBERT REYNOLDS, physics professor 1963–2002: Registration for the draft, which had ended in 1973, was resumed in 1980. A congressman named Gerald Solomon pushed through a bill that required all male students to register for the selective service with the condition that if they did not register, they couldn't receive financial-aid funds. That caused disturbance among the faculty.

KONRAD ALT '81, trustee: I was the student body president at the time and I reached out to the student body presidents at Portland State

University, Lewis & Clark College, the University of Portland, and one or two other schools in the area, and we put together a press conference and made a joint statement, and then organized some demonstrations in downtown Portland opposing the new draft.

LISA STEINMAN, English professor 1976– : I put together a resolution that we refuse federal funds, so we would not be tied to the federal regulation, which caused a great deal of debate in the faculty. It was voted down.

PETER STEINBERGER, political science professor 1977– , dean of faculty 1997–2010, acting president 2001–2002: The Solomon Amendment was a rallying point for faculty. There might have been questions about to what extent we should actually resist it, but there was pretty strong support on the faculty to resisting in any way we could. The college could not just turn its back on federal grants, so the arguments were more questions about tactics and what was possible than about basic underlying values—how to balance principle versus practicality.

ROBERT REYNOLDS, physics professor: Carl Stevens '42, who had taught economics since the mid-1950s, was known as the father of baseball mediation for devising the so-called "final-offer" model of arbitration, which famously ended a baseball strike and then went on to be used successfully in a number of other situations. In the final-offer model an arbitrator in a dispute simply chooses one of the disputing parties' proposals without trying to craft a resolution. Its purpose is to encourage the parties to arrive at a settlement by introducing uncertainty into the arbitration.

Carl's background as a mediator turned out to be helpful in crafting a resolution to the Solomon Amendment matter from the point of view of the college. The students just went ahead and registered for the draft and got their financial aid, or they didn't. But the college didn't stand in the way of their getting financial aid as a matter of principle.

KONRAD ALT '81, trustee: You would think at a place like Reed you might have people who were interested in food banks or tutoring kids in the inner city or that sort of thing. There was very little of that. The school was very weak in terms of that kind of outreach.

There was also remarkably little in terms of electoral politics. There weren't any serious student organizations supporting Jimmie Carter or Ronald Reagan in the 1980 presidential election. A student group called "Reds for Reagan" was anything but a conventional campus political group.

BARBARA LITT '82: Reds for Reagan was kind of like street performance. Other people could not be sure what they were doing, or whether they were friendly or not.

JIM QUINN '83: We went to the Portland airport, where Ronnie Reagan was doing a brief campaign stop, and unfurled a giant banner that read "Reds for Reagan," chanting:

Marx, Lenin, Stalin, Mao—
Reagan, Reagan, now, now, now!

Two, four, six, eight—
Smash the liberal welfare state!

JOHN NEUMAIER '83: There were a couple of Republicans in my dorm, but they were very smart and eloquent. One guy, though, might have been a monarchist. His father was in the State Department, and he had grown up around the world, and spoke with a British accent. I'm not sure if it was a real accent or not; there were several people at Reed who had fake British accents. Patrick would make these very traditional conservative cases—conservative in the sense of "John Locke had it just right." He got along really well with Ed Segel, who taught British history. Segel was quite conservative but open to discussion, and would teach texts that he absolutely disagreed with because they were good discussions and concepts. That would never happen in most places.

KEN BELSON '87: During the 1984 presidential election Scott Giese '86 conducted a straw poll on campus in which the Democratic candidate Walter Mondale beat Ronald Reagan by a thirteen-to-one margin. The day after Reagan's reelection, some students organized a protest and marched from the library to the traffic circle outside Eliot Hall with these mock ICBM missiles, in mourning over the continuation of the Reagan era.

About half a dozen guys who were the Young Republicans on campus showed up wearing blue blazers with red ties. They were hooted and hollered at. People called them all sorts of nasty stuff. I thought to myself, "Those guys are more open-minded than the guys in the majority."

PETER GUSS '78: Reed was a very white place with a fifty-fifty balance of men and women. There were a tremendous number of Jewish kids, one or two black students, and a few Asians. It was mostly just white middle-class or upper-middle-class kids from the New York area, the West Coast, and a smattering of other places.

NANCY SLOTE '75: I had grown up in an upper-middle-class community in Scarsdale, New York. At Reed I met people for the first time who had to work their way through college. I was in this enviable position of having my entire tuition and room and board, along with an allowance, paid for by my parents. So meeting people who were trying to make ends meet was a whole new experience.

BARBARA PIJAN '79: The class thing was very intense for me. I was raised in Chicago with the blue-collar lifestyle pretty much stamped on my brain. That Reed was filled with kids from Philadelphia's Main Line, Chicago's North Shore, and various elite international circles, was utter hell. They had money in their pockets and unflagging self-confidence despite the normal adolescent depression and study anxiety. It pissed me off.

The biggest problem facing working-class kids at Reed was self-isolation. In my freshman dorm, about a third of the students already knew each other through prep school or summer camp, and the others seemed to have comparable easy-to-understand backgrounds. Nobody could figure out where I was coming from, so I stopped talking.

My freshman year I hit the conceptual barricade of Europe. Where I grew up in Chicago, Europe was "the old country." It was dirty, poor, stupid, and nobody would ever want to go back there. I got to Reed and Europe was the pinnacle. It seemed that everybody had summered in France and toured exquisite museums. Most people read French and German.

JOHN NEUMAIER '83: For one or two of the years I was at Reed there were no black students at all. I was embarrassed by that. How, I wondered, could we consider ourselves to be liberals when we were living in this completely racist context? I wrote a letter to Paul Bragdon complaining that we are being disserved by the lack of diversity, because the campus environment was not representative of the real world. After that, Paul Bragdon periodically sent me copies of memos that had to do with the efforts the college was making to attract black students. But being such a Reed booster I didn't stop to wonder why a black student wouldn't want to come to Reed.

RON HUDDLESTON '87: In the early 1980s there was a reënergized effort to get more diversity on campus. There were five of us admitted in 1982, the first time that there had been a substantial number of people of color admitted to Reed since the days of the Black Student Union in the late 1960s. We were given a certain amount of money from the Student Caucus, which we used to buy a membership in the National Association for the Advancement of Colored People. Our primary activities were having that membership and encouraging the administration to recruit more black students. But, to be honest, it was five black freshmen, trying to acclimate ourselves to Reed.

Our group held our first meeting in one member's dorm. Some of us were a little late getting there. One of the five members then wrote a note saying, "The black people on campus obviously can't tell time. Until they learn, I'm withdrawing my membership." So, all of a sudden, we were down to four members. Then we had a problem with another member who announced that she was really a white person in a black body. At that point, we were down to three members. There was a quorum of the Black Student Union every time Mike Mercy '87 and I got together for a beer.

WILLIAM ABERNATHY '88: Spanish professor Bob Johnston maintained that one of the reasons that Reed didn't have a diverse student body was because of scrounging. For him scrounging was essentially a money thing, a very ostentatious display of poverty on the part of people who really didn't need to scrounge, because they could afford to pay.

In the Commons there was a passage leading to the slop window where people would discard their food trays after eating. Scroungers would stand along the wall and as people walked past, ask, politely, if they were done with something on their tray. If someone said "Yes," the scrounger would pluck it off the plate and eat it. On a big night, there would be maybe twenty scroungers. For me, the motivation was definitely free food, as I was in a needy financial position.

RORY BOWMAN '90: I was the first in my family to go to college, and didn't have much money. Some of the other scroungers were there, like me, out of economic necessity. Others were trust-fund kids who thought it was a fun place to hang out, and a neat thing to say you'd done. The interaction was fine. There wasn't any class resentment, partially because people didn't know who was who. It was very amicable and collegial.

WALL STREET JOURNAL, VICTOR ZONANA, "Freeloaders Ambush Paying Customers at College Mess Hall," April 8, 1982: Princeton's thirteen exclusive eating clubs date back to the nineteenth century. Harvard's periodic food fights have their antecedent in a 1789 student rebellion against moldy butter. Less venerable, but also worthy of note, is Reed College's scrounging.

LESLIE SQUIER, psychology professor 1953–1988, dean of students 1955–1962: At Reed, you didn't have to bring a new fall wardrobe of "in" clothes in order to feel comfortable on campus. There was always a minority of students at Reed who liked to be seen as different, and that difference extended to different ways of behaving, different ways of dressing. If you can't do that when you're at that age, when will you? So it seemed to me an appropriate part of establishing one's identity, of trying out other ways of being. That's one way that we grow. Not only those of us who do it, but those of us who see it, because it makes us realize how conformist we are to be doing the things we do.

GREG CLARKE '88: My friends and I came from prep school. When we started at Reed we dressed the way we had in prep school—Top-Siders, khakis, and Polo shirts or button down oxford shirts. That was the prep school uniform. But not at Reed. Reed was shoes optional—even in the rain—and torn jeans. There was definitely a hippie ethos: "We don't care what society thinks, so we don't care how we dress." At the same time, it was not as clear-cut as that, as there was a bit of conformity to it. It was more like you kind of had to be alternative to fit in.

RON HUDDLESTON '87: In 1980 *The Official Preppy Handbook* was published. It defined a group of prep schools and colleges and essentially a lifestyle that adhered to an upper-middle-class way of life, including the way people dressed. Some of us at Reed adopted that dress. There was some irony in it, obviously. But I think it was also an attempt for those of us of from middle-class backgrounds to reach up one level of the economic strata and so establish ourselves as upper middle class. And for those who were already upper middle class and had gone to fine New England prep schools, I think it was a way of separating themselves from the culture of Reed in saying "We're going to buy into the Establishment." We went to dance socials sometimes in coats and ties. We wore Dockers—casual khaki pants—along with Izod Lacoste shirts, moccasins, and other apparel that were part of this signature look.

PETER MARS '82: It was the birth of the Sony Walkman, which was the first personal stereo device. You could put a cassette tape in this machine with headphones on and walk around listening to music. That was new.

JACQUELINE DIRKS '82, history professor: The late 1970s boasted a new cultural politics, one that included punk rock. For me the punk icon was Patti Smith. When she played a gig in Portland she was interviewed by KRRC, and at the behest of the Reedie interviewer, Patti Smith called my dorm to wish my roommate a drunken happy birthday. I happened to answer the phone—I actually spoke with Patti Smith!

BECKY CHIAO '85: Some people were sort of hippies. But the girls I hung around with were into punk. We all had punk haircuts and we'd wear Converse shoes and ripped, New Wave T-shirts. My roommate had dyed blue hair. We were tough punk girls.

A lot of the girls were bulimic. I had already been bulimic before and kind of was out of that. But breakfast was all-you-can-eat. So we would eat all this food, and then go in the bathroom and throw up. Most of my friends smoked cigarettes. We were being like tough, old, broken-down women, even though we were just these young eighteen-year-old girls.

JOHN NEUMAIER '83: Reed was very tolerant of unconventional behavior, and very intolerant of conventional behavior. When I was a dorm advisor I had a guy in my dorm who transferred into Reed from Texas. He explained that he had chosen to come to Reed because it was the best, and he felt that he would be able to make the most money later because of this excellent education. That careerist thinking immediately put Reedies off. He was quite conservative—just worshipped Ayn Rand—and smart but socially very inept. He'd explain how girls at Reed just didn't

dress right, and that they ought to be wearing nice tight jeans like the girls back in Texas. That would alienate everybody, but he just didn't get it. Reed was very intolerant of him, and it was painful to watch it play out. He lasted a semester.

LESLIE VICKERS-JONES '83: Our responsibilities on the Student Activities Board were running the monthly dance socials—booking the band and buying the beer. We did about eight socials a year and some of them would have a theme, like Halloween or Mardi Gras. We also provided "sunny day" kegs of beer. If it was a glorious day, we would get a keg going out on the front lawn. It was a spontaneous, word-of-mouth affair.

RANDY LATHROP '80: The sunny day keg was a holy grail. When I was on the student Funding Circus, the sunny day keg was first on the list. There was one year when we didn't have any sunny days. It was like, "Oh my God, we have excess funds: what should we do?" So we had a "rainy day commiseration" keg.

KEN BELSON '87: The Reagan cultural agenda was sort of all-pervasive in the country at the time, and places like Reed were on the outs. There was a move, thanks to Nancy Reagan, the President's wife, to tie federal funding of financial aid to making sure that the new federal drinking age of twenty-one was enforced.

CHRIS LOWE '82, history professor 1991–1996: When I came to Reed in 1977, the student socials there would be beer kegs and dancing all in the same place. When I came back in 1991 to teach at Reed, they had what was called the "beer garden." It was a lot like a frat party. There were a lot of people packed inside drinking beer, and no room to do anything else. It was really hot and sweaty, and closed off to anyone who did not meet the drinking age of twenty-one years old.

MELA KUNITZ '87, alumni relations staff 1990–1994, 2003– : Dance socials were called "meat markets." If you wanted to be picked up you could be picked up. They featured a whole bunch of really bad beer, and then maybe one big jug of apple juice that would run out very fast. Security was pretty loosey-goosey. There would be people at the doors who would ask you funny questions like "'Book of Ships' in the *Iliad*—what chapter is that? Name some of the ships." They'd try to screen you to make sure you were not, say, a "Clevie," which is what we called students from nearby Cleveland High School.

KONRAD ALT '81, trustee: There was a crazy intensity to the socials. People really needed to blow off some steam. They just came in and cut loose in a big way. It was almost a little scary.

Students at a costume dance social, 1986.

JOHN NEUMAIER '83: Klaus Heilmayr '82, who spoke with an artificial German accent, would be dancing around in a weird Scheherazade costume. My dorm advisor, an upperclassman, used to put a skirt on for the socials, although I don't think he was a cross-dresser. There were a couple of people who would always take their clothes off and dance around, like this one very quiet and seemingly inhibited Japanese student. You'd bump into him dancing and realize that this naked guy with tennis shoes on didn't want his feet to hurt.

BECKY CHIAO '85: There was a lot of open-mindedness and tolerance for different types of people. Not necessarily in terms of racial or economic diversity, but in terms of being open to kind of weird people, as compared to high school where there was a more banal social hierarchy in which the freaks or the geeks were not at the top. I appreciated meeting and getting to know people with personality quirks, even though I was troubled by what seemed to be a large number of people with depression and other disorders.

PAUL BRAGDON, president: Many students who came to Reed were people who felt alienated from schools and other institutions of society. They thought they were coming to a place that would be congenial for them, and by and large it was. On the other hand, some of them expected a perfection at Reed that could not be found in any human institution and became somewhat disillusioned and critical when it didn't measure up to that impossible standard.

CHARLES RHYNE, art history professor 1960–1997: Reed didn't face the very important test of being able to discuss ideas with people who were representative of other points of view. Outside speakers with very strong alternative positions didn't get a serious hearing at Reed. People invited as speakers were often known by some faculty member, who either had had them as a professor, or had done some work with them outside and respected them. That in-built kind of culture had some disadvantages. In a sense, the things that made the college so distinctive and good were also liabilities in certain ways.

The campus climate was so opposed to established religion that if somebody happened to be a practicing Catholic, or a Muslim, or whatever they might be, they wouldn't get much support at Reed. In fact, they might get some negative responses. The same was true of politics when it came to more conservative points of view.

RICHARD COIT '76: My first week at Reed I met some very interesting people. It was a time when born-again Christianity was fresh, exciting, and sort of counterculture. In a place like Reed with its reputation for atheism, communism, and free love, it really felt like a different sort of take. I thought, "This is the place to be a born-again Christian!"

So I plugged in with the evangelical Christians of Reed, and we started the Reed College Christian Fellowship. We got a prayer room in Doyle and would meet weekly. It was like a spiritual transformation for me.

MARK MCLEAN '70: There were some things that didn't go quite so well with the Reed College Christian Fellowship. For one thing, almost half of the group were Messianic Jews, which was really hip two thousand years ago. Some of their families, however, were not at all pleased about that. One of the women went home for spring break, and when she came back she reported that her family had in fact declared her dead.

KONRAD ALT '81, trustee: A group of Christian students wanted to invite a pro-life speaker to campus. They came to the Student Caucus to get our blessing to use a college facility for the event. There was quite a level of controversy about it.

The room we were meeting in was packed with people listening to the arguments on both sides of the issue. I wasn't a Christian and I wasn't pro-life, but these were perfectly decent students and they were doing something they believed in and I didn't feel good about saying "No" to them. There was no good outcome there. It was just awful.

STEVEN FALK '83, trustee 2007–2011: Robert Segal, who taught religion, was a guy who I was convinced was in his heart of hearts a rationalist and perhaps an atheist, but if you took that position in the class, he would very compellingly argue you down using Christian or other theology, forcing you to focus your own argument and test your own philosophy. He was brilliant. His class literally changed the way I viewed religion.

PATRICK PRUYNE '83: Holy Hubert was a televangelist who used to visit campus. He would come with his thumb-eared Bible and stand in front of the Student Union and tell students it was time to get saved. One day, somebody went and fetched Robby Segal for a theological debate with this Bible thumper. They set up a chalkboard outside in front of the Student Union to keep score as to who got the winning points. Somebody showed up wearing just a loin cloth and carrying an eight-foot-tall slapdash crucifix. A bunch of students tied him to the cross, and hoisted him up right behind Holy Hubert while the debate was going on.

BECKY POLLOCK, librarian 1957–1987: It took me awhile to discover that Reed students had a very subtle sense of humor that rested on the unexpected. One April Fool's Day I came to the library to discover that the front door was blocked by an eight-hundred-pound chunk of ice. In the spring of 1983 the water fountain in the library lobby was taken out, leaving a hole about forty inches wide by forty inches tall. One evening there appeared in that cavity about seventy-five rubber dolls under a sign that said "Water Babies." I was very impressed that some of the students knew Charles Kingsley's nineteenth-century fairy tale of the same title. Even the graffiti showed a certain amount of class. In the men's bathroom at the front of the library one student reproduced *The Last Supper* on the wall. The art department asked that it not be painted over for at least a year because it was that good.

Susan McLucas '72: The day senior theses were due time stopped and everybody marched in parade formation from the library to the registrar's office between four and five o'clock to turn theirs in. It was such a wonderful pageant. There was one guy who was actually still typing his thesis as his friends carried him and his typewriter along to the registrar's office. As we were marching in the thesis parade, the sophomores showed up with their own parade, which they called the "feces parade," having been supplied with feces by someone who worked at the Portland Zoo. Everything was scientifically labeled: "giraffe dung," "elephant dung," and so on.

Leslie Vickers-Jones '83: Renaissance Fayre weekend, which was kicked off each year with the thesis parade, was sort of homemade. There was a giant maze on the front lawn, fireworks, and skydiving, with students parachuting onto the front lawn from airplanes, and a naked slip-'n-slide. Softball was big. The feast was initially a potluck, and then became the big "meat-o-rama" roast down in the canyon in which they roasted in entire cow. That in later years turned into the annual "meat smoke" tradition.

There were dance socials both Friday and Saturday nights. Some people had their thesis orals Monday morning, so Saturday was the big day. If you were going to do hallucinogens but once in your life, it would most likely be Saturday of Renn Fayre.

Laura Nix '89: Some friends who were into this ritual ceremony gave me my first acid, in liquid form, to take at Renn Fayre. Everybody was clapping and passing it around like fairy dust. Then they said "Oh, Laura. We're really sorry, but we kinda messed up. We did the math wrong and we meant to give you one hit but we gave you ten. You're going to be fine and we love you, and we're going to make sure that somebody is with you the whole time." And I'm like, "What!!!" What are you talking about!?" I was freaking.

Then it hit me like a train. I realized that I had no resistance to it and that if I fought it I wouldn't win. So, I just had to hand myself over to this experience and roll with it. I went on this journey through Renn Fayre that was quite intense. My friend Paula took me to the feast across the canyon, where we sat and ate turkey legs with naked people who were sitting in this huge pot of lentils. Then Paula took me into this bathroom where these naked women had put up blacklights and were painting themselves with glowing fluorescent paint.

We walked outside and someone came up to us with a sign that said, "Dental floss, anyone?" So we sat and flossed our teeth. Around the corner, in the archway of one of the dorms, there was this group of guys with saxophones just doing these noise walls of sax music. From there we went to the Ferris wheel, which I stayed on for a long time. The Toy Patrol heard I was tripping hard and they gave me all these toys, which I was going crazy over. The Karma Patrol, who were these people who went around making sure that everybody was okay, kept checking in on me. I was like, "Yeah, I'm okay. I'm having a good time."

It just kept going! There was this great five-minute performance of an entire Shakespeare play in the Student Union. Then I went and watched the movie *The Wizard of Oz*. After that, I entered the huge maze out on the lawn for some time. Later, there was a group of people in one of the dorm libraries reading poems aloud from Gertrude Stein's *Tender Buttons*. That was beautiful. I didn't sleep all weekend but I never felt endangered. It was just kind of a magical mystery world. Everywhere you turned somebody was doing something creative and fun.

WILLIAM ABERNATHY '88: The flagellation parade during Renn Fayre was one of those traditions that had died out and I decided that it was worth reviving. The first flagellation revival parade was just me and three other guys marching along in front of the thesis parade, whacking

The thesis parade departing Eric V. Hauser Memorial Library, spring 1986.

Tournament of "knights in armor," Renn Fayre, 1980s.

ourselves on the back with chains and shouting: "Oh, I have work to do! I shouldn't be out here! I should be staying in and studying!"

LAURA NIX '89: Leslie Hemstreet '88 started a women's chorus that would sing really hilarious women's songs. There were these small, round, glow sticks that you could put in your mouth, and when you opened it they made your whole mouth light up in green in the dark. One year at Renn Fayre, I took ten of us in the chorus and staged a performance with the glow sticks called "the Glow Opera," and everybody loved it.

For the next Renn Fayre I got way more glow sticks and attached them to the members of a marching band, who marched around the campus in the dark like glowing pied pipers, leading everybody down to the outside Cerf Amphitheatre, where we did a reprise of the glow-stick chorus singing "Hallelujah" from Handel's *Messiah.* Then we had some dancers come out wear-

ing these long glow strings and dance while the marching band played behind us and the chorus sang out front.

DAVID HOLINSTAT '78: At Renn Fayre every year chemistry professor John Hancock used to do an outdoor show called "The Magic of Chemistry," with all sorts of exploding powders and smoke at the end. The first time I saw the performance there were little fireworks and lots of smoke and then, all of a sudden, underneath the podium Hancock was using, and much to his surprise, the Doyle Owl appeared. Then, just as suddenly, it disappeared. As it turned out, it was taken down into the heating tunnels underneath the college. A lot of people then dove down into the tunnels after it.

LESLIE VICKERS-JONES '83: I was never quite drawn to the Doyle Owl. Maybe it was a guy thing. At the thesis parade the Owl made a showing in the back of a pickup being driven across the front lawn. The driver was the man who later became my husband. People were flinging themselves at the truck and tried to climb into it as it was driving along. It amazed me, because I never understood the attraction.

BRIAN RUESS '87: We got word that a group called the "Society for Creative Anachronism" was going to be bringing in the Doyle Owl via helicopter during a softball game at Renn Fayre. On the day the helicopter showed up, a whole group of us got in a Datsun pickup driven by Dave Conlin '88, and came blazing across the field where it had landed. Half of the guys jumped out of the pickup with fire extinguishers—the water-only kind—blasting everybody down, while the other half of the guys grabbed the Doyle Owl. We tossed it in the back of Dave's pickup, and we all jumped in the truck and took off up the hill. We then proceeded to take the Owl all around Portland.

ANGEL DAWSON '83 (Reed thesis): To possess the Doyle Owl was a coveted position, but simply to touch it was also an honor. There was a prestige in knowing and being able to tell stories about the Owl, whether they were eyewitness accounts or repetitions of stories heard from someone else. The Owl was shown in order to cause a commotion and to be captured so that possession of it transferred to a new group of people. Gaining the Owl was usually a heroic feat—either one of physical action or craft and cunning, oftentimes both—that was undertaken as though by a raiding party of warriors. Honor, prestige, superior status, and charisma were all conferred upon those who possessed the Owl.

BECKY POLLOCK, librarian: Part of the Reed ethos was to be in the library. One of the things unusual about Reed's library was that it was a "live-in" library. That was totally different from any other place that I had ever been. It was the place to go, which is why the front hall was

President Paul Bragdon chats with Amy Kurland '78 and Orrin Wang '79 outside the original entrance to Hauser Library, 1978.

always noisy. Students would come in and talk to their friends, and then grab their professors as they came through to discuss things. Intellectual talk was the students' idea of social fun. A good many of them preferred discussing Plato to playing football.

JACK SCRIVENS, physical education professor 1961–1999: The majority of students did not want to have to take physical education. There were some who had gone through private schools that didn't have P.E. programs. They were often the ones who jumped into playing ultimate Frisbee or hackysack. The ones who did get involved in physical education participated in what we called "club" activities—soccer, fencing, squash, tennis, and basketball. If we won, great. If we didn't, that was great too. The majority of the students I coached were the more well-rounded ones, who really wanted to learn something like squash or handball. The others, who were taking things like hackysack or ultimate frisbee, were often the ones who fell by the wayside and didn't fulfill their P.E. requirement, and so didn't graduate.

CHRIS LYDGATE '90, alumni magazine editor 2008– : When they told us to get our two-year P.E. credit out of the way while we were underclassmen, I just blew it off. I thought to myself, "Aw! They can't really be serious. Once you've done your thesis surely they wouldn't withhold the degree from you." But I came to find out they damn sure would. For my final P.E. class, I took ballroom dancing at Portland State University.

JACK SCRIVENS, physical education: Jerry Barta, Pearl Atkinson, and I all joined the P.E. department between 1955 and 1961.

Pearl's forte at Reed was international folk dancing, which was really big on campus during the 1950s and '60s. In the early 1970s, the interest in folk dancing started to dwindle, as people started asking for modern dance classes and instruction in African dance.

Jerry, who headed up the department, was very versatile. He had played basketball in college at the University of Portland, and then played pro baseball until he hurt his arm and started teaching. He was the type of guy who really enjoyed being around students. If there was a Super Bowl game or baseball championship, anybody could come over to his house and have pizza and soft drinks and watch the game with him.

ROBERT REYNOLDS, physics professor 1963–2002: Reed's football program was discontinued right after I came to Reed in 1963. German professor Ottomar Rudolf was coaching the soccer team at the time, and I started following their games. Reed had a small complement of international students who had enough experience to be among the leaders of the team. They were competitive, and made a very good showing for themselves, competing with places that had tens of thousands of students registered.

Then, in the 1980s and '90s men and women's rugby became popular. The women's rugby team had a favorite yell:

Girdle bra, girdle bra—
Support, support, support!

The opposing rugby teams didn't know what to make of that.

THE OREGONIAN, STEVE DUIN, "Where Sports are Secondary," May 24, 1987: In collegiate circles, there is Reed and there is everywhere else. Sport is no exception. In the Renaissance Fayre softball tournament, the championship game once matched two carefully named teams of philosophers: Illusion vs. Reality. Illusion won in extra innings. Reality at Reed is still trying to make a comeback.

To the outside, disbelieving world, Reed is where the phone rang when E.T. called home.

Co-ed rugby practice in front of the Old Dorm Block, 1980s.

What Reed is is kept relatively safe behind the shroud of what the college might be: a haven for drugs, liberals, and the bacchants who pour out of the library every night for their pagan rituals.

Sorry, but except for the liberals and the library, you've got Reed College wrong again. "At Reed, you're so busy with academics, sports are a relief," said Winship Boyd, a dancer and swimmer. "I jump into the pool to get away from academics." Others dive into lacrosse, weightlifting, rugby, and water polo to meet Reed's strenuous physical education requirement for a degree: three semesters. . . .

The college's casual approach to sports doesn't make for undefeated seasons, but gentle solace waits on the other side of that diploma.

"I think it's all summed up," Mike Mercy said, "in that old Reed cheer: 'During the race we may eat your dust, but when we graduate, you work for us.'"

In truth, not that much dust is consumed at Reed. If the squash team can find a foe, it can usually beat one. The men's lights more than pull their own in crew. The rugby team dominates small colleges in the area; it's also reputed to be the house champion in the lager wars at the Produce Row Café.

They play a good game at Reed rather than talking one. Spartan heroics rarely intrude on the Socratic dialogue. There are no cheerleaders, no press clippings, no debate on athletes getting paid, no toilet paper in the trees when Illusion wins in the bottom of the twelfth.

CHAPTER 31

Rude Girls

We tried to be enlightened men and throw off the mental shackles of our parents and grandparents and generations before us. Women were equal.
— Chris Lydgate '90

Guys didn't have cars. They didn't take you out. They didn't pay your way. There were no flowers, love letters, jewelry, or phone calls. God, it used to just frustrate the hell out of me!
— Stephany Watson '82

The rising conservative reaction on cultural issues in the 1970s and '80s did not deter the continued evolution of the 1960s' conflicts over race and sexuality. America became a society more tolerant of racial, religious, and sexual difference than it had been during the years of the great postwar boom. The emergence of sexual liberation in the 1970s took on an openly provocative and confrontational political style in feminist circles, and among gay-rights activists who shifted to a more radical agenda following the Stonewall riots of 1969 in New York City. During this time of changing sexual norms, women kept moving into the workplace, sexuality was no longer confined to marriage, and the subterranean world of gay and lesbian life continued to move into the open.

On the Reed campus, these changing cultural mores were most evident in the rising trajectory of the feminist movement.

LESLIE VICKERS-JONES '83: Reed was pretty heterosexually focused, although there was a Gay and Lesbian Student Union that was kind of small and in the corner. There were plenty of folks who slowly came out over the years and were not negatively received but sort of not understood. Some of that was societal at the time.

KONRAD ALT '81, trustee 2010– : There were a couple of dozen students at most in the Gay Student Union. They were not a militant group, really more of a mutual aid society than anything else. They were trying to promote the notion that people should be comfortable being out. They had pretty broad support from the student body, and held an annual cocktail party in the Anna Mann social room, which was among the best-attended student events of the year. Whereas other student events served beer, they served mixed drinks.

RANDY LATHROP '80: The Gay Student Union cocktail party was a big social event. Everybody went. One year, Ronnie Geller '78, a wild man, was running for student body president on the anti-Christ platform, against Jenny Camper '79, a hardcore lesbian in shit-kicker boots and jeans. The two of them decided that they would stir things up at the Gay Student Union cocktail party. The place was packed with a couple hundred people. Ronnie, who was renowned for getting outrageously drunk and doing outrageous things, started yelling at Jenny, using very rude language. And she was yelling back at him. No one knew that this was contrived, except the two of them. The next thing you know, Jenny picks up this big butcher knife and starts screaming, "I'm going to whack your lousy balls off!" Then Ronnie Geller was running through this crowded cocktail party, screaming away as if his life was ending, with this crazy lesbian following him with a butcher knife, both of them candidates for student body president.

There was always a beginning-of-school party at Ronnie's student house off campus. It was an old Portland house. They were anything-goes parties. One time they started to run out of beer. Ronnie had this old Volvo. He went driving off in his Volvo to get some beer. When he came back, he drove right up the steps of the porch and crashed the car into the house. He got the beer out of the car, and the party went on.

D. D. WIGLEY '77: There was a costume party at the St. Patrick's Day dance one year, with lots of people in green. The winner that night was Jenny Camper '79, who came clad entirely in Band-Aids with a large Telfa pad between her legs. She won a bottle of liquor, and then got in the tub, soaked, and had her friends peel the Band-Aids off because you could never do that to yourself, it was just too painful.

Jenny Camper was also the person who one night towards graduation covered Eliot Hall entirely with helium balloons in big arcs, all the way around, top to bottom. Each balloon had the word "money," "power," or "fame" written on it. Jenny announced that she was hoping to levitate Eliot Hall.

PETER GUSS '78: Being homosexual was not an issue at Reed. Nobody held it against you. In fact, for freshman women, lesbianism was kind of chic to try. There appeared to be a number of women who were lesbians for a year or two during their freshman or sophomore years, and then said, "Okay, I'm through with that."

JANET RUSSELL '78: The prevailing theory among women was that you didn't want to buy into the oppressive patriarchy, and one way to not do that was to have lesbian relationships.

BECKY CHIAO '85: There was a certain style that was prevalent among Reed women of not shaving our legs or under our arms. We were not trying to be girly or conform to standard ideas of female beauty. We had issues around having spaces for women only, which turned on feminism and exclusion. There was a Women's Center, or "Womyn's Center," and questions about whether men could come into it.

MELA KUNITZ '87, alumni relations staff 1990–1994, 2003– : The Women's Center was the social room of the MacNaughton dorm. It was a pretty skanky place. There were weekly meetings, and a lot of people would get together in between and conduct kind of support groups. There was lots of discussion about how you spell "women," whether it should be spelled "m-e-n" at the end or "m-y-n." There was some anti-male feeling, but it definitely felt like a safe place, and somewhere you could go once a week and not feel academic pressure.

Annie Lionni '79: I was hassled by other women in the sports center because I shaved my legs. I was also hassled in the student house that my boyfriend and future husband, Peter Guss '78, and I lived in because I made dinner in the evenings for Peter and myself. Peter was a great cook, and he did a lot of cooking for me, too. I felt that choice was really what was at stake here, not whether I was cooking or shaving my legs. It had to be my choice.

Barbara Pijan '79: There had been a series of temperance-style, feminist sing-along rallies at the Saturday night music venue known as "the Coffeehouse." Hosted by humorless Reed women in baggy pants, they seemed way too serious. My housemate Stacey Fowler '80 and I cooked up an alternative women's Coffeehouse performance with Stacey on bass guitar and me in a tight, sea-green taffeta prom dress and three-inch heels. We sang Tammy Wynette's truck-stop classics "Stand By Your Man" and "D-I-V-O-R-C-E." In 1980 that was culture-war comedy. We brought down the house.

Stephany Watson '82: I liked my history classes but they were very much dominated by a few super-history-jock guys who were going after their Ph.D.s. It was a really male-centered environment. The European Diplomatic History course that Ed Segel taught reminded me of guys playing with little plastic green army men. A real G.I. Joe kind of culture. Those guys were the top students and they were always in the really good classes, which made those classes awfully tough to be in. They were interrupters, and sort of hostile toward things that women would say. It would just go on, a constant background noise, always happening, particularly in the history courses.

Barbara Pijan '79: I wrote the first explicitly academic-feminist thesis at Reed. It was an ontological argument for the existence of a uniquely female spiritual experience based in the physical, social, emotional, intellectual, and spiritual conditions of female life. My thesis adviser, John Kenney, in his first semester at Reed, was horrified at my sources: Mary Daly, Adrienne Rich, and Simone de Beauvoir. He promised to fail my "garbled rant" as being no excuse for a thesis.

At the oral defense of my thesis, the committee observed that my citations included only primary texts. "Where is the opinion from the literature?" they asked. "There really isn't any," I answered. "It's really too new," I said. "I have designed my own argument." My thesis advisor rolled his eyes, then looked around the room. "Insufficient research," he said firmly. "Unfortunately, I cannot approve it." He lit a pipe and leaned back in his chair, awaiting approval of this verdict from his like-minded peers.

"I think this thesis is very interesting," said philosophy professor Bill Peck. "It is creative, reasonably well-organized, and properly cited. But more important, it is original." Then he turned to my thesis advisor. "Mr. Kenney, you have not been at Reed for very long. You might have the wrong idea about Reed theses. Here we encourage seniors to do original research. We are not concerned so much with the content as with the method. We want proof that our seniors know *how* to think, but we do not tell them *what* to think. It does not matter what sources Ms. Pijan has chosen to use, so long as her sources can be located. It matters how she has constructed her argument. It matters that her data support her conclusion. It matters that the effort shows logical consistency and some degree of independent thought. This sort of original work is exactly what the Reed thesis is all about."

JACQUELINE DIRKS '82, history professor 1991– : For our commencement, my class chose a pioneering historian of women's experience, Gerda Lerner of the University of Wisconsin. She was also president of the Organization of American Historians at the time. Her example influenced my choice of profession.

CHRIS LYDGATE '90, alumni magazine editor 2008– : In several of my conferences, the most articulate, intelligent, and smartest comments came from women, so that was a good education for me. The difference between a man and a woman in the class didn't hold up for a split second when you were discussing Aristotle. It just didn't come into it. We rejected labels because we didn't want to be stereotyped, but I would say that, overall, we tried to be enlightened men and throw off the mental shackles of our parents and grandparents and generations before us. Women were equal.

MELA KUNITZ '87, staff: My political science courses were skewed towards male students. There would be sixteen men and four women. In political philosophy the professor came off at times as somewhat sexist. We'd be reading Aristotle or Rousseau, and he would often turn to one of the women to get the "female perspective." I very much hated that.

It wasn't equal in the academic environment, and we had to prove ourselves. There was a bias that if you were a woman you weren't necessarily going to go into education or academia or even into the job world—that you might go off and get married, then get some kind of half-assed job and have children. The great majority of females that I went to Reed with did not go into academia.

But our concerns at the time were not so much about the gender ratio within academia, as they were about trying to make campus safe in terms of sexual assault and harassing behavior, and get-

A student recruiting for the campus Women's Center, early 1980s.

ting things like night buses to transport women safely home after dark and emergency phones placed around campus.

BECKY CHIAO '85: Aerbo was a dog that belonged to Ricky Boney '82. There was a picture on the front page of the student newspaper, the *Quest*, of someone performing oral sex on the dog, and it was called "Aerbo-lingus." That became this feminist thing that the women were really mad about. It was perceived as saying that Reed women were dogs.

KONRAD ALT '81, trustee 2010– : The *Quest* published a series of pieces that were generally viewed as quite offensive to a lot of the women on campus. Just degrading and humiliating. There was debate as to whether it was more important to support having a healthy community or to back the First Amendment rights of the *Quest* editors to publish whatever the hell they wanted.

I and some others who were on the community side of the question ran for the Student Caucus and captured a majority of seats. We cut off funding for the *Quest* at our first meeting, and then basically shit-canned the *Quest* editors and appointed new ones. It was a total power play and very controversial at the time.

ABBY RICHARD '84: Partly in reaction to the offensive *Quest* issues that year, myself and a collective of six women started a newspaper called *The Rude Girl Press*, named after a ska record. The idea came from Jackie Dirks '82. We put out an issue and, when it hit, everybody was talking about it. I got some very interesting notes in support of it from professors such as John Pock.

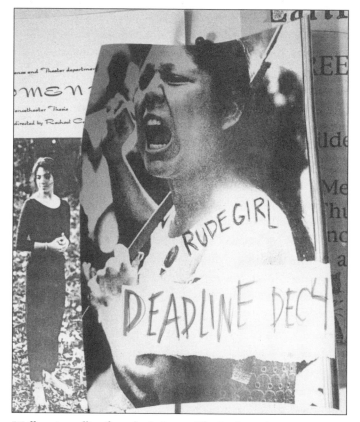

Wall poster calling for submissions to The Rude Girl Press, *1980s.*

JOHN POCK, sociology professor 1955–1998: I deliberately selected out women to develop or encourage. If I had a choice between a male and a female, I would encourage the woman over the male. It was fairly easy for a bright male to make it in just about any area, but it was still difficult for a woman to make it, at Reed and at any other place. They were confronted with a lot of very subtle kinds of discriminations. Women in academia still had to cope with things like marriage and boyfriends, in a way that boys didn't have to. A number of women that I had had as students elected not to get married, or once they were married, not to have children.

LESLIE VICKERS-JONES '83: *The Rude Girl Press* understandably came from a fairly angry place. They were excluding men from taking part. There were two guys who truly wanted to participate. One of them went on after graduation to teach Women's Studies somewhere. Somebody brought an honor case against the Student Caucus and me as student body president for funding an exclusionary group. Everybody understood the issues on both sides, and there just wasn't a clear, easy answer. It was awkward. The solution was that we wrote a letter of apology in the *Quest*.

WILLIAM ABERNATHY '88: There was a lack of rigor in a lot of the feminist analyses that were being bandied about. It definitely had a sort of girls-versus-boys flavor to it that was not focusing on the real issues. You've got someone who's maybe had sex three times in her life lecturing you about the imperial nature of the phallus. I'm not in a great position to criticize because I was certainly not an enlightened, new-age kinda guy. I'm sure there were plenty of legitimate grievances that women had at Reed, but that didn't mean that it was appropriate to call someone a "potential rapist" just because he was a guy. That was a juvenile sort of feminism lite.

RORY BOWMAN '90: What drew me to feminist meetings on campus was trying to be a good person. The issue was central to people I cared about. But it was difficult to be a man who was sympathetic to feminism. There was a whole discussion on campus over whether men could be feminists, and what role they had in the feminist movement.

In the fall of '86 we started a group called the "Reed Men's Circle." Basically, it was men who wanted to make sense of feminism but understood that the place to do that at Reed was probably not with women. That later became part of a group of men and women called the "Rape Awareness Project," which was designed to encourage better sexual communication and greater awareness of what rape was and the importance of consent around sexuality.

WILLIAM ABERNATHY '88: The feminist Andrea Dworkin came to campus, and a lot of women who read her new book at the time, *Intercourse*, thought men were inherently evil and sex was inherently oppressive. That was very hostile. I could respect that. We all have to work through a period of hostility in our youth, I certainly had mine, and if that's the form it takes, then great. But I felt threatened by it, in that it was an argument that as a man you preëmptively could not win.

That is not to say that all Reed men were good and charming and honorable to women by any stretch. I don't think I was honorable. But if someone accused you of being an oppressor, you spent the rest of the discussion not arguing the merits of the case but trying to redeem yourself. I had people actually tell me to try to redeem myself.

RON HUDDLESTON '87: The dorms were coed, and so were the bathrooms. The urinal was exposed so girls would actually witness you standing there peeing.

STEPHANY WATSON '82: My dorm, Griffin, was coed. There were two single-sex dorms, Ladd and Winch, which was funny just because of their names. But there was no big deal about a co-ed dorm. It wasn't like being in a hyper, sexually charged environment. It was more like being at camp. We were always in each other's rooms or sitting in the long halls of the dorms they called the "Asylum Block"—Foster-Scholz and MacNaughton.

BARBARA PIJAN '79: There was a "black list" in the women's bathroom. The list specified men by name and crime. Crimes were often merely lack of virtue, e.g., "selfish," but no less awful for being normal male traits. After the criminal had been advertised for awhile, other lovers might add further complaints against the named vermin, or, rarely, defend his actions or lack thereof. Occasionally someone would post thanks for having been forewarned, or regret for not having seen the warning before jumping in.

JERI JANOWSKY '78: Student health services handed out birth-control pills in giant cartons. The sex scene seemed to be more active in freshman and sophomore years, with lots of experimenting around. In your junior and senior year you had to actually get serious and study. There was lots of trading around. I had a roommate my freshman year whose boyfriend would stay in our dorm. Each morning I would go out and say, "Hi, George," and then, oh, it was not George, it was Sam. Oh, and then it was not Sam anymore, but someone else.

STEPHANY WATSON '82: People had lots of partners. It was just pretty accepted, although there were also a lot of people in long-term relationships, like I was. I really felt that the men were in charge in relationships. The women were more interested in having a boyfriend-girlfriend relationship, but for the men it was more just having sex. The guy I dated most of the time would just periodically take off and go sleep with somebody else, and I'd hear about it from someone. Other women I know had the same experience, that it was just sort of a smorgasbord for the guys.

There was a counterculture ethos that everybody was trying to practice. Guys didn't have cars. They didn't take you out. They didn't pay your way. There were no flowers, love letters, jewelry, or phone calls. God, it used to just frustrate the hell out of me! It was so strange that that whole traditional ritual, that way of relating between men and women, was just kind of turned off at the time. It wasn't being practiced.

KONRAD ALT '81, trustee: A typical date would be going to see a movie in downtown Portland and maybe dinner at a place called Hamburger Mary's, or perhaps Papa Haydn's near the college in Westmoreland, which had great desserts.

BECKY CHIAO '85: It was a very hedonistic time: have sex, party, just have fun. We weren't necessarily monogamous, nor did we worry about testing and safe sex. AIDS hadn't yet become a big concern.

People believed the worst possible thing that could happen was that you would get pregnant; that was the life-ruining thing to fear and avoid. I think that was an overreaction to the earlier generations' situation where women could only be moms. There was just one girl who had a baby that I was aware of. But I'm sure plenty of people got pregnant and had abortions.

FRANK GARCIA '85: I met my wife, Kim Helweg '85, at Reed, and we got married in our sophomore year. It was very unusual at the time to get married, and people used to point us out on campus and say, "There goes the married couple."

GEORGE HAY, economics professor 1956–1983, vice-president 1973–1980, acting president 1980–1981, assistant to the president 1981–1983, "Memorandum for the Community," September 2, 1980: Under recent interpretations of Title IX of the Education Amendments of 1972 and of Title VII of the Civil Rights Act of 1964, concerning the question of sexual harassment in faculty-staff-student professional relationships, I am obligated to inform you of institutional policy against such harassment and to notify you of grievance mechanisms in place at the college.

JOHN PECK '88: Faculty members having relationships with students was sort of frowned upon and very publicly debated, but still happening. There was an honor case filed by some male students against their professor for sexual discrimination. They claimed that they couldn't sleep with the professor and get a better grade like some of the female students could.

DAVID CONLIN '88: The pool of students who were dating or having sex with each other was relatively small. There were a lot of people who were busy with schoolwork. Of course everyone knew everyone's business throughout campus. What inevitably would happen is that at the end of your four or five years at Reed, you'd be standing around talking to some people and realize that you had spent intimate time with like three of the five of them. Then, in about 1986, people started becoming aware that HIV/AIDS was an issue. That really did put the brakes on everything.

WILLIAM ABERNATHY '88: From the end of '86 on, it was all condoms and safe sex. We had a student AIDS czarina who put up posters: "Practice safe sex or you'll be like Tyrannosaurus Rex!"

CHAPTER 32
Self-Reliance vs. "Neo-Nannyism"

As a student, you wanted to live in a consequence-free zone, but looking back I can see that some of that behavior might be construed as enablement.
　—William Abernathy '88

Reed had sort of a social Reaganism in which people could do whatever they wanted to without consequences or without having to heed some responsibility that they had to others or to the community as a whole.
　—Paul Bragdon, president

One of the primary initiatives of the Bragdon administration was addressing a lack of accountability in various areas. Having financially stabilized the college in the 1970s, Paul Bragdon turned his focus in the early 1980s to improving student life on campus. For seven decades, student life at Reed had been left largely to the responsibility of the student body. This was in line with William Foster's belief that intellectual freedom was best cultivated in an environment that resisted unthinking conformity to imposed social and moral expectations, and instead emphasized self-reliance as the basis of independence both individually and across the community. Accordingly, the dean of students office had functioned purposely as more of a reactive form of assistance on campus, leaving the center of gravity for student life to student autonomy.

Matched with the intensity of Reed's academic rigor, the consequences of this laissez-faire approach to student life were high. Student attrition had averaged more than 50 percent during the school's first seventy years, much higher than at peer colleges. The affliction among students of what might be called "imposter syndrome"—a fear that one is not as smart as other students—had been a source of depression and anxiety for many decades. These outcomes, matched with Reed's idealistic valuing of self-reliance and non-conformity, created a cultural dilemma—students wanted to be treated like independent adults but at the same time wanted to be supported in a non-paternalistic manner by the college.

ERIC PESETSKY '84: Reed had the only student-run nuclear reactor in the country. There was a conflict between Carol Creedon, who was the most senior psychology professor, and Michael Hay, who was director of the reactor in the '80s, over Hay's statement that one didn't have to be a science major to work on the reactor. "Our highest-scoring applicant," he said, "was a psych major, of all things." Carol Creedon was outraged that he would attempt to minimize a fellow scientific discipline like psychology. Although the psych department counted themselves as one of the sciences, they weren't accepted by chemistry, biology, and physics in that regard.

STEPHEN FRANTZ, director, Reed reactor, 1993–2011: Most people were underwhelmed when they saw the reactor. It's the size of a washing machine, and not very intimidating. Yet, over the years, hundreds of students had received a license to operate the reactor. For some of them, it has been their defining experience of Reed. None of them became nuclear power plant operators. That's not the track Reed students were looking at.

MARTIN RINGLE, chief technology officer 1989– : I was always amused by the fact that Reed ranked fourth in the nation in the number of its students who went on to earn doctorates in computer science, because we didn't have a computer science program or department.

In 1985 Reed had hosted a conference—"Computing in the Liberal Arts"—subsidized and supported by Apple and with a stellar cast of characters, including Bill Gates, the co-founder of Microsoft. That conference cemented Reed's reputation as a real hotbed of innovation. Reed was among the earliest to say that it was going to distribute Apple computers to all of its faculty and all of its students. It didn't, but everybody went away believing that it would. As a result, the notion of saturation—that computing was

everywhere at Reed—grew very quickly, outstripping the reality, and became one of those self-fulfilling kind of prophesies. Because the reputation was so big, students and faculty came to Reed to do things with technology.

In the 1980s and '90s there were a handful of "Research I" universities—Harvard, MIT, Carnegie Mellon, Stanford, Dartmouth, the University of Michigan, the University of Wisconsin—engaged in computing. When they would get together, Reed was the only small private liberal arts college that would be invited to sit at the table. Whenever we opened our mouths, everybody sat up and listened.

MARIANNE COLGROVE '84, computer and information services staff 1986– : Computing at Reed had an awful lot to do with Richard Crandall '69, who taught physics. He created this space on campus called the "Development Lab," or the "D Lab," which was a place where students and some faculty members could get together without any real structure or curricular framework, and delve quite deeply into computer science, and develop all kinds of interesting software. He also spearheaded the whole computing master plan and the concept of a unified approach to computing, and got Reed involved in the Apple University Consortium for doing academic software development. He left Reed to work for Steve Jobs '76 at NeXT, the company that Jobs started after leaving Apple in the 1980s; and then, when Jobs returned to run Apple, he went to work there.

BECKY CHIAO '85: Reed activities were all student-run. If someone wanted to do something, like start a bike co-op, they would get the money—assuming people voted for their project at the student Funding Circus—and buy a lot of tools and set up a bike co-op. That year the bike co-op would be really good. But when the person who started it left school and no one took over,

Professor Richard Crandall '69 and Steve Jobs '76 at the 1991 Reed convocation.

everyone would forget it was even there. Student activities were all kind of ad hoc, but they gave some people good skills. Especially students who were in charge of running things like orientation week for incoming freshmen.

STEPHANY WATSON '82: The lore was that sometime in the '60s the students had wrestled responsibility for running freshman orientation away from the administration. In the summer before my senior year I became director of orientation, with an office in Eliot Hall and a $10,000 budget. I got paid to plan a week of academic and social activities, and to get people into their dorms. The previous orientation director, Mark Srere '81, sat me down, turned over his files, and said, "Don't fuck this up. This is really important. You have a sacred duty to do a good job, so the administration doesn't take it back from the students."

ROBERT REYNOLDS, physics professor 1963–2002: There was never anything that provid-ed institutional memory for student organizations, other than what one student generation might happen to write down and pass along to the next.

LESLIE VICKERS-JONES '83: Activities were funded from student body fees at what was called the "Funding Circus." Groups would sub-mit a budget to the Student Caucus. Students would then vote on their top ten student organi-zations, and then the Caucus would meet for one long, hellish Saturday and start doling money out to various groups based upon who had the most votes.

Each organization would have some amount of time to plead their case. It was a very long and messy process with a lot of hard feelings when it was all finished and done. Every different orga-nization had their own account at the bank and their own checkbook. The student body funds were audited for the first time in the early 1980s by the accounting firm Deloitte Touche. It was a mess.

KONRAD ALT '81, trustee 2010– : There were these wonderful things going on around campus because students were making them happen. It was really empowering to me. In my mind, events had always just been things that happen to you—you didn't make them happen. I quickly came to realize that at Reed you could create your own events.

Steve McGeady '80 and Ann Kosobud '80 had started a weekly concert called "the Coffee-house," presenting nationally known folk musicians in the Student Union. In my sophomore year I took over running it. Suddenly I had this opportunity to interact directly with folk musicians whose albums I'd been buying. I went out of my way to really promote the concerts, and we had a packed house almost every Saturday night.

LESLIE VICKERS-JONES '83: The coffee shop at the time was attached to the north end of the Student Union toward the Reed canyon. It was open from first thing in the morning to midnight, and it was always loud. There was a great jukebox, along with a pool room, and fairly large booths that held a good number of people. Then there was an area of smaller tables away from the noise, where you would see people either deep in conversation or doing some studying. It was always full of smoke.

MATT GIRAUD '85: In 1985, Mike Magrath '84 and I started a student-run café called "the Paradox," in the Student Union building. There was an unused part of the building that had been an art gallery and writing center back in the early 1980s. We turned the space into a café with the blessing of the woman who ran the college's nearby coffee shop, then operated by the food-service corporation Saga. We had a tacit agreement that we'd serve coffee but nothing that competed with Saga's business. Coffee culture

The Student Caucus Funding Circus in the Student Union, early 1980s.

was not yet ubiquitous in Portland, but being snobby Eurocentric Reedies we thought, "Let's bring a taste of Europe to Reed College," even though we didn't really know what that was.

There was the usual reactionary response Reedies have to things that are new—the café was a business and therefore part of "the Man." But by the second year, the Paradox Café started to become redefined as an institution. We spent some time trying to figure out how to integrate it into the student body bylaws in such a way as to strike a balance between autonomy and accountability, and not operate on student consensus, which, while admirable, rarely seemed to produce anything of any lasting value.

RORY BOWMAN '90: A big blow to student autonomy in the 1980s was the loss of the Reed College Bookstore, which was a cooperative owned by the student body. In the late '80s, the operating rights of the bookstore transferred over to the college.

RICHARD ABEL '48: When I was a student, the Reed College Co-op was open four hours a day, selling textbooks, school supplies, cigarettes, candy, ice cream, and pop. I became manager in my sophomore year. In 1950, after I had graduated and gone to Berkeley for graduate school, history professor Dick Jones called me up and said, "The bookstore's a mess." He asked me to come back to run it. The bookstore grew and prospered, until finally I had taken over the entire basement of the old Student Union building for the operation.

In 1954, the Portland public library and the University of Oregon library came to me to sell them books. I went to the Board of Trustees, because even though the Student Council owned the bookstore as a not-for-profit entity, at the end of the day it was the board that was legally responsible. They agreed to allow me to sell books to the other libraries, and also to start a

for-profit corporation, Reed College Bookstore, Inc., wholly owned by the Reed College Co-op. After that, the operation grew and grew, supplying scholarly and scientific books to many universities and libraries.

Then, in 1959, the IRS put out a series of draconian regulations about not-for-profits earning money, and the Board of Trustees said to me, "We're going to shut down the Reed College Bookstore. It's too dangerous." By this time, we were about a $750,000-a-year business. An agreement was struck in 1961 that allowed me to move the for-profit Reed College Bookstore, Inc., off the campus, change the name to Richard Abel and Company, and pay Reed the net worth of the corporation. I lined up Dick Ehelebe '49 to run the remaining on-campus bookstore co-op as the full-time manager.

MARVIN LEVICH, philosophy professor 1953–1994, provost 1972–1979: While Dick Ehelebe '49 didn't manufacture bookselling the way Abel had done, there was an allegiance to the bookstore as an academic adornment of the college. They may not have been very good at it, but the fact that they were very good or very bad was no longer a matter of very great importance.

Then, in the 1980s the administration proposed to take possession of the bookstore from the student body, so that it could be run efficiently like every other business of the college. I argued that when it became simply a tool of the administration, it would be dealt with as any other tool of the administration—that is, to make a profit—and that it would simply descend into the condition of other kinds of administrative instruments, becoming like any other bookstore in America, filled with pennants and sweaters, but no longer having a big stock of books. And that was the result of it.

MICHAEL LEVINE '62, trustee 1984–2002: For the trustees, it was a no-brainer. We weren't hostile to the students, but it was clear they couldn't manage it and that the college was financially on the hook. It's like your kid out driving your car, not his. It was important that the bookstore did its job. It was important that it paid its bills. But it was in terrible financial shape, and likely to function better once it was run professionally.

For students it was mainly a symbolic thing. It was a piece of their turf that they cared deeply about. In the same way the faculty didn't think the administration should run the school, the students didn't think the administration should run the bookstore.

Paul Bragdon, president 1971–1988: I would characterize the Reed student body as generally ahead of their peers in intellectual and academic things, and that is what most of them had distinguished themselves with through high school. In that context they were presented at Reed with a rather structured curriculum, with a lot of requirements imposed upon them, and an apprenticeship relationship in which they were most competent and perhaps most mature. But in the social area, where many were not as competent as many of their peers, they were left almost totally alone. It was the area where they needed support the most.

Leslie Squier, psychology professor 1953–1988, dean of students 1955–1962: There was a peculiar tradition at Reed of student independence, not as an organized group, but as individuals. The individual had to stand on his own and achieve on his own. That was a feature of the college that was admirable but at the same time unfortunate, in the sense that the academic enterprise is a cooperative one. In a college where much of the teaching is done in conference style, it's important that there be cooperation rather than aggressiveness and competitiveness in academic endeavors. I don't think the latter was the general tone at Reed, but it was the tone that

some students adopted. In those cases it was likely that the person saw him or herself as competitive, isolated, and at war with everybody else.

Robert Knapp, English professor 1974– : History professor T. C. Price Zimmermann used to say "Reed gets its claws into you." There was the sense that not only did one identify with Reed, but it was a place with which one had relationships that were disturbingly familial in character. There was, for example, the grievance of failed response to love that's proffered.

From a psychological standpoint one might not call it a healthy relationship to have with an institution, but it was healthy insofar as it promoted the sense that ideas mattered, and that the way in which people talked about ideas mattered, and that the way in which people govern themselves mattered.

Jack Dudman '42, math professor 1953–1985, dean of students 1963–1985: There's no doubt that the student culture was formed in a demanding, intense, difficult environment. Students seemed to take pride in some of those difficulties rather than in trying to reduce them. They were proud of the fact that they had survived in a difficult and relatively unsupportive environment. Economics professor Carl Stevens '42 used to claim that student culture at Reed was passed on, inculcated in the newly arrived students by the older ones, and that if you really wanted to change the nature of the college, what you would have to do is close it down for a few years and then start up again, in order to put an end to this intense, perpetuated student culture.

Nicholas Wheeler '55, physics professor 1963–2010: During the difficult years of the early 1970s, music professor Fred Rothchild got the idea to utilize an inconspicuous green, wooden hut down at the Cerf Amphitheatre overlooking the Reed lake for informal meetings. He got authorization to install a pot-bellied stove, and "the Shack," as it was called, became a cozy place in the evening that students and faculty would go to. A dozen or so people would be sitting in there around the stove talking, typically intensely, about all kinds of things.

CRAIG LINDAHL-URBEN '75: Faculty members would sit in the Shack in the evenings until midnight, listening to the students' stories of whatever was going on for them at Reed. I got to know the president, Paul Bragdon, and just about every senior faculty member. A couple of them would show up each night.

KONRAD ALT '81, trustee: By a wide margin I was the most academically serious person I knew in high school, and even at Reed I was a little bit of a freak in my study habits. But there were other people that were kind of out there with me. I wasn't alone. And there were lots of people who would've liked to be out there with me. They just weren't quite as disciplined or they couldn't get by with as little sleep as I could. I felt like my attitudes toward academia were really valued and very much in sync with the community.

STEVEN FALK '83, trustee 2007–2011: I was so oriented toward the work that I broke into the library one morning at four AM through an open window because I needed to reference a book. Where else do people break into the library because they can't wait to look something up?

PETER MARS '82: Occasionally I would attend courses where I just didn't understand anything that they were talking about. I would come out thinking, "Oh, my God." I wanted to do the work, and I threw myself into it as hard as I could, but at the same time I was drowning in books and in papers that needed to be written. I didn't have much of a social life at school. I was just working.

JANET RUSSELL '78: Reed was a pressure cooker. Some of the students were troubled when they came. Some of them felt that they had nowhere to turn, and so came apart for one reason or another, and left.

LESLIE VICKERS-JONES '83: There was very little counseling. The campus was so insular that most students had a group of friends for support, but it was also very possible for people to not have that, which meant that there just wasn't much safety net there. If you lived on campus there were the dorm parents—older students who managed the dorms. I was a dorm parent. We didn't receive a whole lot of training, nor did we have counseling experience. There was a rape by somebody from off campus in the dorm where I was dorm parent at the beginning of the year. We also had a student who was just going off the deep end. Here I was, twenty-one years old, with this whole dorm of new students, primarily freshmen, trying to get them back on track and feeling good about being at Reed. It was hard.

ALICE STEINER '74, trustee 2005– : I was okay with the academics but I was uncomfortable enough with the social atmosphere that I applied to transfer to another school. I was actually sitting on my trunk out in front of Eliot Hall, waiting for the railroad express guy to come and take me to this other school, when Dean Jack Dudman '42 came out and asked me, "Where are you going?" I told him, and he said, "You can't leave Reed." I was so amazed that someone cared, that I stayed.

STEVE JOBS '76: Jack Dudman '42 was one of the heroes of my life because Jack Dudman looked the other way when I was staying on campus without paying. He looked the other way when I was taking classes without being a formal student and paying the tuition. And oftentimes, when I was at the end of my rope, Jack would go

Dean of students Jack Dudman '42, 1978.

for a walk with me and I would later discover a twenty-dollar bill in my tattered coat pocket following that walk, with no mention of it from Jack, before, during, or after.

PAMELA MATSUDA-DUNN '78: Dean Dudman was our "Wolf," the character in the Quentin Tarantino film, *Pulp Fiction*, who comes in during a crisis and takes care of everything. If you had a problem, you went to him. He would very discreetly take care of it.

WILLIAM ABERNATHY '88: As a student, you wanted to live in a consequence-free zone, but looking back I can see that some of that behavior might be construed as enablement. Someone

putting in fairly superhuman efforts to smooth out situations and make it so that you didn't end up in jail or in detox somewhere, might not be actually doing you a favor.

DAVE KEHOE '82: A bunch of us working at a Portland research firm donated our time to do a market-research project for the college. We surveyed all the students about their healthcare needs. I was assigned to compile the answers to the mental-health questions. The first response I read said, "I'm so depressed. I'm the only one here's who's not smart enough. This work is too hard. I can't do it. Everyone is smarter than me. I get so depressed at night and so lonely, and they don't have any counselors on campus after five o'clock." I picked up the next one, and it was exactly the same thing. In all twelve hundred responses everyone essentially said that they were the only one who wasn't smart enough, and who couldn't do the work.

ROBERT REYNOLDS, physics professor: I served as acting dean of students for one year in the late 1970s, while Jack Dudman '42 was on sabbatical. There were a number of things about the operation of the dean's office that I thought were extremely admirable. One was that students really felt warmly connected to the office and very supported by it. For some reason everybody in the office was kind of encouraged to function as a counselor. We had a psychiatrist and two people who were psychiatric social workers, but they were being supplemented by total amateurs.

The connection between the dean's office and the infirmary was more open than seemed medically proper to me, in that the two talked about medical problems that specific students were having. Added to that, the college physician was prescribing amphetamines for students as study aids fairly routinely. And nurses were authorized to dispense Valium, at their own discretion, to students. The result was essentially that the infirmary was a source of chemical as well as emotional aid to students who were feeling for some reason depressed or beleaguered.

LESLIE VICKERS-JONES '83: Dr. Dana had been at the infirmary forever, and while people had complaints about him, the Health Center had a very homey feel. It felt to me like when you were at camp and you went to the infirmary. There was an informality that I think most people liked, except if you ended up with something more complicated.

DELL RHODES, psychology professor 1975–2006, associate dean of students 1990–1991: One of the very first things Bob Reynolds did

in his role as acting dean of students was to address the faculty on the topic of amphetamine use among students. The college physician at the time came to a faculty meeting to explain his dispensation of amphetamines out of the infirmary, and he proceeded to do two things in his rationalization. One was to point the finger at the faculty, claiming that the whole problem was our fault because we assigned too much work, and suggesting that if we would back off from the heavy work assignments, then students wouldn't need to stay up all night, and there would be no need to confront the issue of prescribing dexedrine.

The second thing he said was that dexedrine was not an illegal drug. I pointed out that although prescribed dexedrine was not illegal, it was illegal to pass prescribed dexedrine on to somebody else, and to prescribe amounts of the drug that were in excess of those needed for an acute situation. Dexedrine over-prescription by the infirmary stopped after that.

PETER GUSS '78: Every college at the time had a drug culture. There was a variety of drugs, really interesting drugs. There was a lot of knowledge about drugs, and a lot of curiosity about drugs. They were kind of the lingua franca of college students at the time. And as with religion and dressing, there were always the groups of people who didn't smoke dope, didn't drink beer, didn't do anything.

ROBERT CLARK '79: The campus was kind of split on drugs. I had had a pretty party-hearty high school experience and so when I got to Reed I was done with it, and really interested in my studies. There was a big split between people like me who said, "Sorry, I've moved on in life," and other people who were just going nuts.

LESLIE VICKERS-JONES '83: Drinking was primarily beer. Every once in a while we had a toga party and got some awful spiked punch, but that was the exception. There wasn't that kind of incredible frat-party binge drinking like on other campuses. Pot was smoked anywhere. At one point Dean Jack Dudman '42 issued a letter to the community suggesting that it really needed to be scaled back, in that it could affect Reed's finances and legality. We were offended that he dare say such things, but for a little while people didn't smoke pot in the coffee shop.

BECKY CHIAO '85: People took a lot of drugs in my freshman year. There was a lot of acid and mushrooms, and then all these new designer drugs people were starting to invent, like MDA, which later came to be called "ecstasy." Certain drugs were tolerated, but other drugs were looked down on. Methamphetamine, or speed, was seen as a problem, as was cocaine, because some people couldn't afford it and would get into debt. It was a little difficult to get drugs. You had to know the right people. As a girl, I'd have to ask some guy where I could get them.

ADAM PENENBERG '86: I was a dorm parent, which was really wonderful. I was a little older than other students, and I had had a life before Reed, which helped too. Basically, my role was making sure that no one in the dorm got hurt. There was a lot of self-policing to keep hard drugs off campus. There were times when people would bring heroin in and we would get some dorm advisors together and head over to meet them and say, "Listen, get that shit off the campus. We're not judgmental or anything, but this attracts police and all sorts of bad stuff, and we're not going to let it happen."

JOHN NEUMAIER '83: There was no intravenous drug use that I was aware of. A few people at Reed would get into academic trouble with drugs, and alcohol too. It was very unusual. The word was that the nurses in the health center had

informants who would tell them what was going around. Their primary concern was for people's safety. If there was word of something bad on campus, the college would step in. So there was this sense that drug use was being monitored in a very distanced way. As long as there weren't severe outcomes, and as long as you didn't bother other people, things would be tolerated. That was where the Honor Principle came in.

WILLIAM ABERNATHY '88: My view and understanding of the Honor Principle was strictly an interpersonal thing. "I will not hurt you or discomfort you or embarrass you." The institution was not in my opinion a person and my definitions were very fluid around what my activities were and should be. I didn't view it as an honor issue if there was no person individually being hurt. But I eventually got called on this when I became very incensed at someone stealing ether from the chem lab to get high with. That was totally unconscionable, and a violation in my mind of the Honor Principle.

LESLIE VICKERS-JONES '83: The Honor Principle was discussed in a way that was distinct from or removed from actual honor cases. We would talk about it with each other and remind each other that we were supposed to be living by it, but some of that would become theoretical pretty quickly. The threat of an honor case wasn't something that really existed. There weren't many honor cases.

PAUL BRAGDON, president: Ironically, the prevailing political views at Reed at the time reflected some of the things that were going on in society at large during the Reagan Administration, where the focus was increasingly on individualism and on individual rights, without reference to the community or the needs of the community as a whole. Reed had a sort of social Reaganism, in which people could do whatever they wanted to without consequences or without having to heed some responsibility that they had to others or to the Reed community.

There were a few students who were aware of the weaknesses or the vulnerabilities of the system and they were quite skillful in manipulating it. In fact, if they were charged with a breach of the Honor Principle, it was not uncommon to see them put the persons who had called them on that breach on the defensive, making them the "bad guys." It was a form of sophistry. But at its best, I knew many students who cherished the Honor Principle because to them it was posing a constant challenge to or test of their own personal conscience and the appropriateness of their actions.

ROBERT REYNOLDS, physics professor: Students were being somehow encouraged by their interactions with the dean's office to think of the faculty as an adversary—that the faculty was overworking them terribly, and since they were getting so little positive reinforcement from faculty members in those days, that it was kind of hopeless. That led to a low morale situation on campus for some time. When my duties as acting dean were over, I prepared a long report in which I outlined my concerns about the dean's office.

CHRIS LOWE '82, history professor 1991–1996: There was a kind of mystique to the idea that a combination of things led to certain positive outcomes at Reed, including the high proportion of students who went on to graduate school, and the willingness of students to engage in a high level of work that created a different kind of student culture from that of most colleges. Just why exactly they worked, nobody was quite sure, but they were reluctant to monkey with the basic building blocks—the humanities program, the thesis, the junior qualification exam, the small classes, the conference system, and the deëmphasis of grades—too much.

At the same time, there were things that were problematic. The attrition rate was a problem. The questions of what did the Honor Principle mean, and how should student life be organized, were problems. Those issues spilled over into the academic side of things to some extent, in that if students' lives were difficult or chaotic, it would obviously impinge on their ability to function academically. It was not an accident that one of the places where Bragdon pushed his administrative initiative was in institutionalizing student services on a much larger scale. His idea was to provide a more stable platform for student life, which would support the academic machine. But that came into conflict with aspects of the way that the college culture had been working.

PAUL BRAGDON, president: My own concept of the deans' operation was that you don't just respond to the problems that students have, you think of the environment in which they are operating and how that can be improved for them. As an imperfect metaphor, it's the difference between having a "Health and Wellness Center" as opposed to a "First Aid Center," where you're just responding to emergencies. Both things are important, but one represents a comprehensive, coordinated approach, while the other is vitally important but narrowly focused.

I spent a year studying the situation with the Faculty Advisory Committee, including having the dean of Swarthmore come in and evaluate the office. Everybody concluded that we really did have to make changes. We then started the search for a vice-president for student services. I knew that decision would change things forever for me. In fact, I thought I might not survive it.

OTTOMAR RUDOLF, German professor 1963–1998: Bragdon's problem was that he couldn't get along with the dean, Jack Dudman '42. The two of them didn't like each other. Students, on the other hand, loved Dudman. He was a beloved dean, but he was not a dean who could crack the whip. Dudman always sided with the students.

CHRIS LOWE '82, history professor: If you didn't get on with Jack Dudman '42, there wasn't that much in the way of an alternative. At times, his personalism could be a kind of paternalism. But when Dudman was effectively pushed out— he remained at the college for a couple of years, but not as dean—there were a lot of students who were very upset. They saw the new student-services structure as a different kind of paternalism, and a less personal one that was sort of infantilizing and against the ethos of students being treated as adults. There was a lot of faculty support for that point of view as well.

PAUL BRAGDON, president: Reed was generally an anti-authoritarian, skeptical, questioning environment. There was only one authority that carried weight with students, and that was that of the faculty. What faculty members said and did, and how they said and did it, you would find reflected in the students' attitudes. That went beyond the mentor relationship in the classroom or outside the classroom. It was that they were the respected ones—all other figures were criticized. Of course, teachers were criticized for their teaching as part of evaluation, but nevertheless, faculty were the authority figures and their word and attitudes did count with students. A willingness of faculty to speak out on some problematic things and practices on campus would have a marvelous effect in achieving overdue change.

LARRY LARGE, vice-president of college relations 1982–1987, 1992–1999: There were those who said that we shouldn't create "neo-nannyism," a term that I believed was coined by anthropology professor Gail Kelly '55. She was not convinced that the college ought to invest in auxiliary services for students, that instead every-thing ought to be focused on their intellectual and cognitive development. Other members of the faculty agreed with her.

RORY BOWMAN '90: With the creation of the vice-president of student services there was a tendency toward the professionalization of that office, which meant treating the students more as consumers who were to be matriculated and run through like cattle in a chute, more like passengers on a cruise ship than members of a monastic order. Cruise-ship management, or what was called by some "neo-nannyism," does not want to develop student autonomy or to develop student abilities. Under the guise of improving retention, they tried to attract a different kind of student, people who were less iconoclastic and more conventional and could thus be run through a system that was designed to make them even more conventional.

PAUL BRAGDON, president: It was certainly not "nannyism" to want to give appropriate help to suffering individuals. I always felt that there was not the awareness and sensitivity necessary in reading admissions files to identify the implications of some forms of behavior.

It's one thing to admit a feisty kid who is an individual, an upstreamer, an independent thinker, a nonconformist, a rebel, or an eccentric. Reed wants and gets a lot of them. But in some cases there were warning signals that the behavior was not just that of an independent or rebellious type of personality, but that it connoted something else.

EDWARD SEGEL, history professor 1973–2011: The complaint from some faculty about neo-nannyism was a typical, frankly parochial viewpoint from the Old Guard. They tended to have a very narrow view of Reed, and had real difficulty in seeing the college in the broader context of what was going on in higher education. They were bent on keeping Reed's uniqueness, which was not necessarily a bad idea, but to them that uniqueness was very classical, very traditional.

PAUL BRAGDON, president: I don't think that some of those who opposed the change realized that after nightfall the campus was a student ghetto, and a lot of what was going on—some of it dangerous, some not—was not a very desirable environment in many ways. There wasn't the interaction there used to be among all elements of the community. The faculty was dispersed, not living on or near the college campus as they once had. They were all much more engaged in their professional work, both in preparation for teaching and in other scholarly and intellectual work, than in the past.

And while it was clear to me that some institutions had gone overboard in providing services for students, turning into sort of a luxury camp as a competitive status thing, I thought some of the human support services being extended on other campuses for students were desirable and necessary in the current society. It was more a case of, "Where do you draw the line?"

SARA NICHOLS '83, trustee 2008–2009: In my junior year, 1982, the college hired a professional administrator named Paula Rooney to the newly created position of vice-president for student services. That was the worst thing you could be at Reed, a professional administrator.

She was a dynamic, smart, interesting, single woman in her late thirties, from Colgate University back East. A lot of the women faculty members were really happy to have her there, because she was such a powerful woman, and it was a very male-dominated environment. But for us, the students, Paula Rooney became a universally reviled figure who was emblematic of everything that people didn't like about what was changing at the college at the time. She became a lightning rod.

LESLIE VICKERS-JONES '83: Paula Rooney was more formal both in her dress and in her manner than what Reed was used to. As student body president, and someone who was very involved in trying to make things work around Reed, I certainly saw value in what she was doing and bringing to the college, and I learned a lot from her. But since I was fairly close with her I was seen as a little bit suspect by other students.

RORY BOWMAN '90: Reedies had the sense that we are sui generis—we're our own thing. Any outsider was considered inherently inferior, and so any outsider who told us what to do was asking to be smacked down psychologically, socially, even physically. At some point, students were so unhappy with Paula Rooney that some of them broke into her office and trashed the place.

WILLIAM ABERNATHY '88: I and another angry young man decided that we should go into Paula's office late one night and throw paper on the floor. The only thing we could round up at that hour was recycling-bin paper. It was a juvenile and stupid thing and I regretted it as soon as I was inside her office, but once you get going on something like that it's very difficult to say "Oh! This is wrong!" We left a note that said, "Stop the monkey business. If you violate the Honor Principle you aren't welcome to its protections."

It was a terrible, terrible thing to do and it really violated a lot of the ethos of the place in ways that I did not yet understand. I was nineteen at the time and, as is often the case with nineteen-year olds, I felt like I knew everything. I thought I was sort of an avenging angel, but it was just a stupid thing to do. Someone honor-cased me, and I did some perfunctory community service, but it was no compensation.

SARA NICHOLS '83, trustee: There was a campaign to drum Paula Rooney out, to get rid of her. She had a chip on her tooth that she said she had gotten at Kent State during the anti-Vietnam demonstrations. People were circulating a rumor that it was from the kickback of a rifle. Because I was a Student Caucus member and one of ten extroverts in my entire class, I was placed in a position of having to deal with Paula Rooney on a lot of things. She would call me into her office and ask, "Why do the students hate me so much?"

The culmination of the anti-Paula Rooney sentiment was when somebody collected thousands of toothbrushes and spelled out "Surrender Paula" across the lawn on a huge scale.

MELA KUNITZ '87, alumni relations staff 1990–1994, 2003– : The turning point for Paula Rooney was a dance social in Commons. People were dancing to one of the marimba ensembles popular in Portland at the time, when suddenly there was this explosion and glass was flying everywhere. When they turned up the lights, people were bleeding.

KURT OPPRECHT '85: A fellow named Matt was developing a flash powder. It was a white powder that exploded with a very low flashpoint at a very low temperature. Matt was there sprinkling his powder up on the copper-lidded structure that used to be in the center of Commons, and then lighting it and setting off this huge wall of flame like at a rock show. Then the fire department showed up on campus, driving their trucks toward Commons. People said to Matt, "You've got to knock this shit off."

Matt had the flash powder in a glass jar. He had just dumped some of it onto a table to light. So he started scraping it back into the glass jar, at which time, due to the friction of doing that, it exploded, blowing a six-inch hole through the plywood wall beside the table and sending glass shrapnel everywhere. There were ambulances called. Six people went to the hospital with various injuries, mostly glass in their arms and faces, and one person had an eye injury.

WILLIAM ABERNATHY '88: After those injured had been pulled out, they started the music back up, and nice and slow got people back into a good mood. Then Paula Rooney showed up. Poor Paula. She was trying to be the responsible grownup in charge of the madhouse. She got up on the bandstand and basically told people that the beer truck outside was closing, and that they needed to wrap things up.

MELA KUNITZ '87, staff: Up until then it felt—and maybe this was my illusion—that the student community kind of led itself, and that the staff only interceded when very necessary. But the incident at the social suddenly shifted to Paula Rooney saying in essence, "I am staff. I am stopping this social. You've been bad. Go home." It was kind of horrific in the way it was dealt with. It's not like the head counselor was there to help folks. Instead it was scary, really scary.

WILLIAM ABERNATHY '88: It was not so much what she did—I can see that it was necessary for her to be able to control things—but how she did it. She acted in unilateral executive fashion without consensus. Of course, in an emergency situation consensus was rubbish, but we had these various ideals of everything being democratic and us being involved with everything and not wanting to be administered to. We wanted to be self-sufficient in all things.

RORY BOWMAN '90: After that, they intimidated Paula Rooney until she resigned because she was afraid for her safety. History professor David Groff was made the acting dean until a permanent replacement named Susan Crim, a very well-intentioned woman, was hired.

PAUL BRAGDON, president: Paula Rooney did a very good job of pulling student services together—so much so that, when she left, the heads of the different offices within student services were strong advocates of continuing the coordinated approach she had implemented. She had a lot of support among students, and she also had her share of adversaries, some because of opposition to change from the old order, and some because she was a direct and straightforward person in all circumstances.

FRANK GWILLIAM, biology professor 1957–1996, provost 1979–1982: I was never terribly impressed with student politics and governance at Reed, but it was a learning experience for them, and I suppose it was necessary. I watched it with amusement sometimes, and at other times with some irritation. At larger institutions, of course, student government had an almost professional quality, staffed by people in departments of political science who addressed governance.

MARSH CRONYN '40, chemistry professor 1952–1989, provost 1982–1989: In the late 1980s we eliminated the Community Senate, which had been established in 1963. Prior to 1963, the students had the Student Council and the faculty had the Community Affairs Committee, which I served on for years. In those days, as a faculty member, you were talking one-to-one with students, but you represented the faculty and they represented the student body. The Community Senate structure wasn't like that. The students elected their representatives, as did the faculty. But the Senate soon became a toothless tiger, just a place for students to vent their frustrations about things that they wanted to see done, because faculty on the Senate were not representing a constituency with policy. They were just dealing with things that came from the students.

WILLIAM ABERNATHY '88: The Community Senate was half students and half faculty, with one tie-breaker faculty member running it. The faculty had their own separate government. Students had a funding body called the Student Cau-

cus. It was a subaltern body to the Community Senate, responsible for spending the student activity fees, without the ability to form a political consensus or articulate an official student body position. The Community Senate itself was very unwieldy, not to mention that it was broken. It could not come to resolution on anything.

CHRIS LOWE '82, history professor: In 1989 the new community constitution split up not only the Community Senate, but also other joint bodies. The Judicial Board, which had been a joint body of students and faculty that adjudicated Honor Principle violations, became a student-only body. The Community Senate was split into the Student Senate on the one hand, and the Community Affairs Committee of the faculty on the other. Nobody on the faculty wanted to be on that committee because either you were dealing with the efforts of the administration to get control of stuff in the student body that the students were pushing back against, or you were on the dog poop subcommittee, spending hours and hours talking about the recurring issue of what to do about dogs on campus.

JOE ROBERTS, mathematics professor 1952– : When, in 1987, the faculty wrote a new constitution that got rid of the Community Senate, they placed things more under faculty and administrative control than they had been under the existing constitution. That document clearly stated that in order to make the kinds of changes that were being proposed, they had to be approved by the student body, which initially voted against the new constitution.

Ultimately, in December of 1989, a revised version of the new constitution was negotiated and approved by both the faculty and the student body. After its adoption, students were in a much less dominant position in terms of community governance than they had been with the Community Senate.

CHAPTER 33

The End of the Barony

When I first came to Reed some of the old faculty barons took me aside and warned me that I was publishing too much. Bad thing.
— Peter Steinberger, political science professor

Reed was a place that was in some way divided deeply within itself between its allegiance to traditions of the past, and its curiosity and desire for experimentation.
— Lena Lencek, Russian professor

Beginning in the mid-1970s, a new generation of professors began arriving at Reed, many of whom would ascend to faculty leadership positions during the following decades. Unlike the Young Turks, whose departure at the end of the 1960s had left a noticeable gap in faculty succession, this new faculty cadre did not challenge the relevance or the framework of Reed's core curriculum. In fact, by the early 1980s, a number of prestigious colleges such as Harvard and Stanford that had adopted free electives in the mid-1960s were returning to core curricula. What the new faculty members did bring to Reed was a new sensibility that was less insular, less combative, and more inclusive than that of the Old Guard. They were interested in participating in the larger academic community beyond Reed through research and publication, while still maintaining their dedication to the primacy of teaching.

The transition from the Old Guard to this next generation of faculty leaders would slowly unfold throughout the 1980s. Although these changes occurred during a relatively calm period for Reed, major fault lines were developing beneath the surface, exacerbated by the pressure of shifting cultural forces. One of those forces was evidenced by an increase in the number of women on the faculty. While women had comprised 22 percent of the faculty in the college's first decade, rising to 30 percent by 1940, they accounted for a mere 10 percent in 1965. By 1990, women made up 26 percent of the faculty, and over the next two decades their numbers would increase to 40 percent.

PETER STEINBERGER, political science professor 1977– , dean of faculty 1997–2010, acting president 2001–2002: In the early 1980s, when Paul Bragdon started professionalizing the administrative staff, some of the old faculty barons were giving him pushback, and this created some real tensions within the faculty and the college. Philosophy professor George Bealer got into a shouting match with Paul and other members of the faculty during a faculty meeting. It was very unpleasant.

I was elected to the Faculty Advisory Committee immediately after getting tenure. Marvin Levich, who by then had relinquished his role as provost, was also on the FAC. An issue arose that had to do with the percentage of the budget that was being spent on so-called "administrative" items as opposed to "instructional" ones. Marvin gave it to Paul Bragdon pretty hard. Paul seemed to take what Marvin said very personally and gave it back to Marvin equally hard, and at great length. When he finished, we just sat there. Maybe it was only a minute and a half, but it felt like half an hour. Nobody said a word. It was like an episode from the Twilight Zone. That long silence really brought to the surface the tension between what Paul was doing and what some members of the faculty, particularly the so-called "Old Guard," were thinking. Some of these people were arguing that we were getting away from the foundational ethos of Reed, and becoming too much like other institutions.

MARVIN LEVICH, philosophy professor 1953–1994, provost 1972–1979: I felt that during his regime Bragdon was very protective of the administration and increased it considerably. A good many ills, if the college has any, were caused by what he did in his administration.

CARLETON WHITEHEAD '41, alumni director 1952–1958, college relations administrator 1959–1983: Within the boundaries it had established early on, Reed did a great deal of innovation and creative programming, but it was not a compulsive experimenter. That distinguished it from many colleges, particularly those that had followed trends of the late 1960s that had since come to be seen as rather faddish. During that time, thanks to members of the Old Guard, Reed had stuck by its basic principles and its fairly structured, conservative academic program.

CHANGE magazine, BARRY MITZMAN, "Reed College, the Intellectual Maverick," September 1979: Though a foolish consistency may be the hobgoblin of little minds, Reed's reasoned stubbornness may be its greatest strength. The college's administrators and faculty seem to think so. They see the reaction elsewhere to 1960s laxity as a reaffirmation of Reed's uninterrupted rigor. They see Harvard's widely publicized new core curriculum as a return to what Reed has been doing all along. They see Antioch's foundering as a cautionary tale, demonstrating the dangers of headlong institutional experimentation.

ROBERT KNAPP, English professor 1974– : The intellectual style and integrity of the college promoted a very healthy—though sometimes disorienting –belief among the student body that no subject was off limits. One of the things that I first noticed coming to Reed after my eight-year stint at Princeton was that, although Reed students were not brighter than Princeton students, and probably didn't come from better educational backgrounds, they didn't know their own limits. They didn't have the sense of needing to stay within boundaries. That was central to Reed's "Reed-ness," if you will.

That of course had all kinds of implications for the relationship of the institution to the larger world, and to the way in which Reed has been able to maintain itself as things changed on the national educational scene.

PETER STEINBERGER, political science professor: They were the "barons" of the faculty when I first arrived, and they were extremely impressive, very smart, but very intimidating and very tough. I feared them. In many cases I admired the fact that they were not only committed to the ethos of the college, but they also understood and lived it. They lived the idea of rigor and of quality and of seriousness: "If you're going to come to Reed and screw around, get out. That's not what you're here for. You're here to study and study hard and to enjoy it while doing it."

They included Maure Goldschmidt '30, whom I replaced in political science, Dick Jones in history, Marvin Levich in philosophy, Gail Kelly '55 in anthropology, Marsh Cronyn '40 in chemistry, and Larry Ruben in biology.

The idea embraced by these faculty members was Foster's original founding idea: that this would be, to the degree possible, a place free from the usual kinds of nonsense one finds at many other colleges—the intercollegiate athletics, the fraternities, the sororities, the grade grubbing, the grade inflation. This barony both articulated that idea and embodied it. They were really smart people and they didn't suffer fools gladly. They called a spade a spade and this was in many respects good for me. You couldn't get away with shoddy thinking. You couldn't get away with a shoddy argument.

PAUL BRAGDON, president 1971–1988: Sometime in the mid-1970s there was a shift in the faculty. With departures and retirements, we began to have younger people, who, because of changes in society and changes in the people going to graduate school, were different from the faculty that had preceded them. Women became a definite presence on the faculty in terms of numbers during that time and, generally, I was pleased with what I saw happening.

EDWARD SEGEL, history professor 1973–2011: When I came to Reed from Berkeley in 1973, I

Biology professor Laurens Ruben teaching a conference on the lawn, 1980.

was quite firmly out of the closet. I wasn't quite sure how to deal with it at Reed, but it turned out that some of my Berkeley students had friends at Reed, and had told them, "There's a gay professor coming. Look out for him." So the gay students knew about me before I arrived. Reed was always, so far as I've been aware, quite hospitable that way.

JUDY TYLE MASSEE, dance professor 1968–1998: When I arrived in the late 1960s, there were something like eighty-three men on the faculty, and seven or eight women. The faculty was an old boys' club, and the majority of faculty hiring that was done at that point was by men. Title VII of the 1964 Civil Rights Act did prohibit discrimination in employment on account of sex, but that didn't mean that a woman's curriculum vitae would be looked at the same as a man's. The first faculty meeting I went to was an incredible eye-opener. When I walked into the meeting I was asked to leave by one of the faculty leaders, Marvin Levich, because he thought I was a student and was invading the sanctum of the Reed College faculty. I said, "Well, I'm on the faculty." He just gave me this strange look and turned around and walked away.

RAY KIERSTEAD, history professor 1978–2000: The attitudes of many of the men hired at Reed in the late 1930s, '40s, and '50s were those of that era. I noticed that some of the faculty titans seemed uncomfortable around intellectual women. The great exception to the rule was Gail Kelly '55, who inspired respect, awe, and terror in all who knew her.

When I arrived in 1978 there had already been appointed a contingent of very active female faculty, including Doris Berkvam, Leila Falk, Lisa Steinman, Dell Rhodes, Lena Lencek, and Christine Mueller. They represented only a small fraction of the faculty, but through example and advocacy they had an important influence on the

Chemistry professor Marsh Cronyn '40 with Kelly Kenison Falkner '83 in the chem lab, 1982.

changing college culture, while, at the same time, the older generation of males was retiring. In the early 1980s another cluster of women appeared, including Ellen Stauder, Maryanne McClellan, Gail Sherman, and Sharon Larisch. Anyone who chaired faculty searches then realized that the general academic demography was shifting fast, and that Reed would follow the trend. The gender composition of the humanities staff shifted dramatically in those years and that, in my opinion, had something to do with the survival of the humanities program at Reed.

CHARLES SVITAVSKY, English professor 1961–1998: In 1976, we finally got around to hiring a woman in the English department, Lisa Steinman. The hiring that followed in the early 1980s brought Gail Berkeley, Ellen Stauder, and Nathalia King, until by the time we got to the end of the '80s, it was women who were running the department. I felt that, eventually, it was very

Russian professors Asya Pekurovskaya and Lena Lencek, 1978.

similar to having all males run it. The women were running it from a woman's point of view, really leaning in the direction of female colleagues, just as in the past we had always leaned in the direction of male colleagues.

LISA STEINMAN, English professor 1976– : I was very aware there were very few women faculty when I came, and even fewer tenured women faculty. You couldn't help looking around and thinking that that might be because women in academics were not being taken seriously, or because the women being hired were being hired by people who weren't thinking of them as serious colleagues. That was certainly the case then, but it changed over the years to the point that almost half of the faculty members were women. And certainly from my perspective, they were among the strongest, smartest, and most articulate faculty members. The women were not there to fill any quotas. They were part of what was keeping Reed College being Reed.

LENA LENCEK, Russian professor 1977– : Lisa Steinman, for me, set the benchmark for

what an ideal professional profile of a woman at Reed would be like. I marveled at her ability to be a productive scholar, artist, teacher, and administrator.

But even after the number of women admitted to the faculty increased, there was still the continuing existence of gendered enclaves and networks of alliances and affiliations. That's the nature of human beings and societies. As far as a subculture of women faculty, we didn't have quite as formalized a structure for socializing as the male faculty members had. Most of my personal interactions with women on the faculty that were not connected with academic things had to do with child-rearing issues, things such as how to persuade the institution to be more child friendly in terms of providing child care. I believe I may have been one of the first Reed woman faculty members to get maternity leave.

Meanwhile, there were places where men on the faculty gathered to do their collegial, competitive male bonding, networking, and power-base building, all of which is part of the art of politics in any institution. There was a group of men that played poker, which was a very sexist kind of thing, and then there was the lunch-time basketball, also a kind of bastion of the boys. That meant that there were consequences in terms of my ability to maneuver for potential gains in my department. In that respect, I relied on my male colleagues in the department to do the work of campaigning for whatever concessions we needed.

PETER STEINBERGER, political science professor: In my first couple of years the basketball team was also the informal "Frankfurt School of Critical Theory Study Group." The basketball players would be reading Max Horkheimer, Theodor Adorno, or Karl Korsch in between shooting baskets. I played basketball with them, and in the locker room, in between talking about the game, we'd talk about Jurgen Habermas's latest stuff.

JACK SCRIVENS, physical education professor 1961–1999: Most of the faculty members with whom I was in contact were into tennis or squash. Charles Svitavsky, in the English department, Bob Reynolds in physics, Peter Steinberger in political science—all those guys loved squash. I would rig up a match between the faculty and student squash teams and bring in some food and have a Saturday afternoon of squash and hot dogs.

BILL PECK, philosophy professor 1961–2002: The 1960s had been a boom time in higher education. It was just the right time to be coming into the teaching profession. There were lots of jobs, and salaries kept going up—although at Reed salaries still remained pretty small. Nobody had a Ph.D. when they got their first job; they were still working on it. I dare say that most of the faculty at Reed did not have a Ph.D. when I arrived. Marvin Levich, who was the senior member of the philosophy department, a crackerjack philosopher, and a well-known guy

with many publications, never got a Ph.D. You were evaluated on what kind of a thinker you were, not on the basis of credentials.

Starting in 1970, the academic market began to clamp down. There were suddenly fewer openings and an over-abundance of available teachers, and it became harder and harder to get a job. With that tightening of the job market, credentials came to make more and more of a difference. You had to have a Ph.D. or be right on the brink of getting one.

VINCENZ PANNY, German professor 1963–1984: Reed professors very often went back to campus after going home in the evenings. I went back in the evening to open the German language lab for students. That was hard on family life. I wasn't home that much, and so my wife, Ann, was there alone with the kids. Then I would be up early the next morning because I had an eight o'clock class. It was masochism to have that morning class on top of everything else.

ROBERT KNAPP, English professor 1974– : In the late 1970s, when President Bragdon was making an effort to raise faculty salaries, some professors began getting nasty letters of complaint from alumni. In their view, Reed's faculty had always been distinguished by a kind of idealism that was not compatible with getting a high salary; that complete dedication to teaching students didn't require this kind of additional reward.

LAURENS RUBEN, biology professor 1955–1992: Within the biology faculty there was a good deal of hostility to changes in the department in the late '50s and '60s regarding taking on research, in part from many of the old-timers who had been through the very high teaching loads of the Depression, and who had not, themselves, been involved in research. They felt that research was not appropriate because it would draw students out of the classroom. Of course, our classrooms in biology were our laboratories, so that attitude wasn't quite appropriate for us; nevertheless, there was a good deal of concern among some of the non-science faculty that we were really looking out for ourselves and our own futures and our own professions rather than paying adequate attention to our students. I didn't think that was at all true. We in biology felt it important to provide appropriate role models for our students by being "teacher-scholars"—professors who were both teaching and doing research.

Physics professor Byron Youtz, who was acting president in 1967 and '68 after Dick Sullivan left, was the first president to state clearly that there was an expectation that every faculty member would be involved in a certain amount of professional research. After that, the notion

began to grow at Reed that the members of the faculty should be involved in their professional fields, and should involve students in their professional fields. This was especially true during the mid-1970s and the 1980s when tenure-track jobs were really very scarce around the country, and we were able to hire a lot of folks who might otherwise have gone to universities instead of coming to a small college.

DELL RHODES, psychology professor 1975–2006, associate dean of students 1990–1991: Many of the older faculty members whom I strongly admired were not particularly interested in having a major impact in their designated field outside the college. Although some of them did have such an impact, that wasn't their pri-

Professors Lisa Steinman, Robert Knapp, and Peter Steinberger, late 1980s.

PART FOUR: THE CULTURAL WARS, 1967–1988

mary goal. Their primary goal was the pursuit of scholarship in the context of teaching students.

That stance began to shift beginning with my generation of faculty members. We were a transition generation that included several superstars who were gifted teachers as well as gifted scholars, and who gave their all to the college. Among them were Lisa Steinman in English, Bill Ray in French, David Griffiths in physics, and Peter Steinberger in political science. These people and others continued to view Reed College as first and foremost a teaching institution, gave a lot to the college in terms of governance, and also managed to have national reputations as publishing scholars. Professors of that earlier generation, such as Gail Kelly '55 in anthropology and Nicholas Wheeler '55 in physics, were incredibly productive scholars, but they were not sending their work out for external review and consumption.

Peter Abrahams '77: Some of the best teachers almost never published. For example, I don't know of anything that physics professor Nicholas Wheeler '55 ever really published, except his self-published, calligraphed course materials or textbooks, of which there were something like twenty-five volumes. Yet he was certainly an inspirational teacher for everybody who had him.

Peter Steinberger, political science professor: When I first came to Reed some of the old faculty barons took me aside and warned me that I was publishing too much. Bad thing. If you are publishing too much that means you're not spending enough time with your teaching. That seemed to me whacky. There were aspects of the demeanor of the faculty barony that I didn't admire so much. They were perhaps a very inward-looking group, who felt that Reed had it right and nobody else did. That is a gross overstatement and I'm painting with a fairly broad brush here, but a lot of these people weren't all that actively involved in larger scholarly communities outside of Reed College.

The other model certainly was the mini-university or research college model, which many of Reed's peer institutions adopted. According to this model, the fundamental job of the faculty member was to do research. But a liberal arts college can only be a great institution because of great teaching. It can't be a great institution because of world-class scholarship. That doesn't happen at small colleges. There are exceptions for individual faculty members, but Nobel Prizes are not won at Reed, or Amherst, or Pomona, or Oberlin. They are won at big places like Chicago, Stanford, and Harvard.

Lena Lencek, Russian professor: The senior faculty were absolutely terrifying when I arrived. They seemed to constitute a club that communicated telepathically. In the faculty meetings I was mystified generally by the references in the discussions. They were very impassioned, and involved dredging up and referring to precedents that seemed to be familiar to the speakers but were completely unknown to me. That was a little bit intimidating.

And they all spoke so eloquently. There was Marvin Levich in philosophy, who spoke in tremendously ornate paragraphs, and Owen Ulph, a history professor, who, because he was a rancher as well as a scholar, spoke in earthy anecdotes as opposed to the arcane, philosophical, abstracted vocabulary of some of his colleagues. All of them seemed to be titans of certitude.

Paul Bragdon, president: I thought that there was a harshness in the relationships between the senior and junior faculty members, not universally, but it was a noticeable aspect of the college. It could be symbolized by the humanities course, which was usually quite a hurdle for a junior faculty person. The story was told that before I came to the college, when a junior or

Psychology professor Dell Rhodes with students after class, 1978.

non-tenured member of the faculty lectured in humanities, the senior faculty would sit in the back row, and if they were not taken with the lecture, their newspapers would snap open.

LENA LENCEK, Russian professor: I did understand very early on that Reed was a place that was in some way divided deeply within itself between its allegiance to traditions of the past, and its curiosity and desire for experimentation. It was always trying to find a good balance between these two poles: the conservative, the static, the fear that by deviating from the origins we would lose our specific identity—and, at the same time, the awareness that knowledge has to be elastic and accommodate the present and have an eye to the future. That tug of war between the past and the future was clearly one motif of Reed's ethos.

There were times that the faculty meetings were sites for sort of ceremonial combat in debating movement to or from one pole or the other. Men took a lot of pleasure in all kinds of posturing and rhetorical one-upmanship that had little to do with the issues at stake, but much more to do with the pecking order.

EDWARD SEGEL, history professor: In my first two or three years at Reed, there were frequent meetings of the History and Social Science Division. Among the four Old Guard members of the division—John Pock, Dick Jones, Maure Goldschmidt '30, and Gail Kelly '55—there would be such poison, such animosity generated into the atmosphere, that frankly I wondered what kind of snake pit I had wandered into. Sometimes it was against one another, sometimes against their colleagues, or the faculty as a whole, or the administration. It was a very unpleasant scene.

John Pock had extremely high academic standards, but sometimes the standards seemed to

PART FOUR: THE CULTURAL WARS, 1967–1988

be so high as almost to become nihilistic, although that sounds like a contradiction.

DELL RHODES, psychology professor: Sociology professor John Pock fit the mode of the "cranky" professor. By "cranky" I mean edgy, outspoken, and possessing a mode of teaching that does not conform to the warm and fuzzy "you're-always-right" style currently prevalent in education. The latter claims that it's not good to criticize students. You should always provide a lot of supportive feedback; maybe then you can indicate a couple of things that could be improved, but always softened with praise, implying that everybody's thinking is above average. The "cranky" professors did not agree with this philosophy. Their mode of teaching was one in which, if the faculty member thought that your point was not worthy, you, and usually everyone else in your conference, knew what they thought.

When critiques were offered in a public and fairly edgy fashion, many students, sometimes correctly, viewed the process as not sufficiently supportive. And that style of teaching was demonstrably hard on some students. Students who liked the cranky professors were often students who saw through their gruff style, and who got excited by the material and the intellectual challenge, while respecting, but perhaps not particularly liking, the faculty member.

BECKY CHIAO '85: John Pock was a scary figure. I took his year-long introduction to sociology class. He was known for seeing the class as a social entity, and trying to use that as an example of what sociology was like. He would give the class all the same grade with some minor variation; some might get a C-minus, others a C-plus. He decided that our class was a "bad" class. The two serious, "good" students told the rest of us that he had said to them, "You should drop this class because the other people aren't good." That made me feel bad. I don't think he ever really knew my name or recognized me, even though there were only eight people in the class.

RAY KIERSTEAD, history professor: I was hired to replace Owen Ulph in history. He lived in his office in the library much of the time, and kept a sleeping bag there, which he would pull out of a drawer. He was eccentric and idiosyncratic, kind of a western cowboy. He had been a French historian when he was a young man, then became mainly interested in western history. He actually owned a ranch and did ranch work. He had a coterie of students who admired the style, the eccentricity of the man. But he was a difficult man to know, really, because he was so eccentric. I went to one of his final humanities lectures out of homage. He gave one of the most incoherent lectures I'd ever heard in my life, rambling and walking around on stage.

Sociology professor John Pock, 1974.

CHRIS ALDEN '81: Owen Ulph was a seriously cantankerous and cynical teller of yarns from his cowpoke days, but a very engaging teacher. His opening line in our humanities conference was "All of you are guaranteed a B-plus already, so only attend the class if you are interested in participating." We went on to have a very stimulating year.

Ulph was unafraid of confrontation with the powers that be at the college. We had the impression that he was in a constant condition of dispute with the administration.

DAVID CONLIN '88: Anthropology professor Gail Kelly '55 was deeply schooled in British social anthropology and knew the British social anthropologists incredibly well. She didn't like me very much, but I certainly admired her knowledge and her understanding of her subject, even though I was afraid of her. She had a British affectation in her speech, and once told me that she was to be called "Miss Kelly," because anthropologists in the British tradition are called "Miss" and "Mr." They would never be called "Gail" or "Professor Kelly." She called her students by their last names. "Mr. Conlin," she said once, "you are anti-intellectual." I didn't know it at the time, but that was code for something akin to being a fascist.

LEE BLESSING '71: Kenneth O. Hanson, who had taught English since the mid-1950s, was the poet on campus. Ken was from Idaho, and very involved with ancient Chinese literature. He was this sort of marvelous Zen creation—a wonderful poet and extraordinary human being, formal, very quiet, and very contained. He was extremely intellectual and you were always afraid that his critical eye would fall upon you. I had a conference with him for a paper I had written, in which he said, "I have only one criticism, and it is fundamental." The conference went downhill from there.

JOHN PECK '88: Kalesh Dudharker, who had taught political science since the 1950s, had been involved in the independence movement in India, but in a much more radical manner than Gandhi was. He taught comparative Communist systems. In one of our early classes, he started asking questions and it became obvious that no one had done the reading. We were all just trying to bullshit our way through. Dudharker just stood up, and said, "I'll see you all next week. I hope you're prepared then." Then he just walked out. It was so humbling and embarrassing. After that, the course improved immensely because people actually did read the readings.

When we showed up for our final exam, he said, "I have one question for the final. For three hours you can write on the following topic. Compare and contrast the Yugoslav Revolution and the Chinese Revolution." That was the question. For three hours of writing! I was like, "Wow, that's pretty serious."

TONY FISHER '80: In the economics department the heroes of the age were Art Leigh and Carl Stevens '42. Art Leigh was blind, more or less, and had to have readers who read the papers that you wrote, so that he could think about them and assign a grade. Because Art was blind, when he would lecture on and on about some subject in class, people would put their heads down on the tables, resigning themselves completely. There was a large couch at the back of the classroom that people would crash on. But he was a wonderfully revered professor, and once you figured out that all you had to do was listen and absorb everything he said—when he sent you off to take your final exam, forget about what was in the textbook and just go with what he taught you—then you'd be able to respond correctly, and he would give you an A.

KEN BELSON '87: I took a seminar on labor economics with Carl Stevens '42. In the conference

Longtime economics professor Carl Stevens '42 in his office, 1980s.

he would sit there and say "What do you think?" And we'd have to just jump in. Carl employed the Reed professorial ethic, to shut up and let students battle it out. Then, at some point in the fifth or sixth week, somebody asked, "Are we going to have to write a paper?" Carl said, "Yeah. Here's what you do. You get an idea. You type it up and you run a staple through it. Give it to me around Thanksgiving." And that was it. That was the entire instruction from Carl Stevens. His priorities were correct from my perspective: first learn something interesting, and then learn how to debate about it.

GLENN ERICKSON '72: The idea of having small classes of twelve to fifteen students, where the professor was only kind of a guide who didn't impose his will or his interpretation, was a quick and efficient way of refining intellectuals. Students taught each other. The professor was there like a referee; when the ball went out of bounds, he'd take it and throw it back onto the field, and the students would continue to play with it. The

class was only as good as the quality of the other students. So if you had all these brilliant students in the class, they raised the bar for each other. They prepared their work outside of class, then learned to have the courage of their convictions in class to stand and deliver. And then to put it all together in term papers, not copied from books, but of original thought, teaching you that you can form an opinion and defend that opinion about a topic.

ROBERT KNAPP, English professor: The most important curricular development in the history of the college was clearly the humanities program. It established a certain kind of intellectual style by demanding that people confront texts and traditions and institutions that are foundational to the way in which we think and organize our lives today. At the same time, no one addressing those topics was an expert in the whole area. The consequence of that was that it leveled the playing field, so that both faculty and students were in the position of having to confront and make sensible arguments about things that ought to be part of the common heritage, whether or not they really are, and to do so on a basis where every argument can be challenged—where nobody can just pull out the particular expertise to say, "Well, I just happen to know the answers to more of these things."

One was always in the position of discovering that freshman had insights that were new, and not just because they were coming at it from a naïve perspective, but because they were smart people who were reading these texts and seeing things in them that you yourself may not have seen. This combination of amateurism and professionalism—the professionalism having to do with knowing how to address a field of study, knowing something about the kinds of question you ask, knowing something about the kinds of answers that make sense—is what made the humanities program successful.

JOHN POCK, sociology professor 1955–1998: Everybody had a different version of the Socratic method used in the conferences. The instructor's job was to engage everyone. So you always answered a question with a question, and you didn't just sit there being an umpire to some kind of debate. In talking about a text, say, it wasn't the student's opinion but the text itself that was discussed. You wanted the student to take a position about whatever was being discussed in that text and make it his or hers. The demand was very heavy on the students to do the discovery of the issues, and to analyze and examine a line of argument. It wasn't a matter of the teacher sitting there and doing a mini-lecture on something.

That was my strategy, and my way of teaching. It just drained me. I would end the day completely exhausted, because it took a lot of energy out of me. It wasn't something that students necessarily enjoyed. Some of them became very hostile about that. I had students who walked out,

saying, "Look, I'm spending a lot of money on the tuition here. I didn't come here to hear these other students. I came here to hear you talk."

STEVEN FALK '83: I took a class from Richard Fox in American intellectual history. Each week we were assigned to read a major work of nonfiction that was three or four hundred pages long. Fox had this theory that you couldn't comprehensively discuss a complex work like that in an hour-and-a-half class session, so he held one class a week that lasted three hours. You spent the week reading the assigned book, and then three hours each Tuesday discussing it. If you hadn't read the book, there was just no faking it. It became almost like a survival of the fittest. There were only four other people in the class as the semester progressed, all of whom were really serious about the subject, and it was just fabulous. We'd get in such fantastic discussions that at the end of class none of us could believe that three hours was up, and neither could Fox. He would say, "Let me call my wife. She's making hamburgers." We'd go over to his house and the conversation would continue over dinner.

MARVIN LEVICH, philosophy professor: I had won an award from the Danforth Foundation for being one of the ten best teachers in colleges and universities in the country, but I had no idea of what was involved in good teaching. I'd never thought of it. The only thing I could think of in terms of good teaching was that you had a problem that you asked students to pursue, and then you talked at it as if everyone in that class were a professional, as though they were your equals. That was a method of teaching that made some people uncomfortable, but in a lot of cases it was amazing how—if you expected the best from the students—how many of them would, in one way or another, fulfill your expectation. I thought that any other method of teaching was coddling the students.

CHAPTER 34

Putting the Arts in the "Liberal Arts"

There were not a lot of places on campus where Reedies could collaborate and figure out how to work with people as opposed to just working by yourself.
—Kathleen Worley, theatre professor

Reed offered perhaps the best calligraphy instruction in the country. . . . None of this had even a hope of any practical application in my life. But ten years later, when we were designing the first Macintosh computer, it all came back to me, and we designed it all into the Mac.
—Steve Jobs '76

From the early days of William Foster's administration, applied arts such as the-atre, dance, studio arts, and creative writing were largely viewed at Reed as ex-tracurricular activities, and only nominally incorporated into the formal cur-riculum. For some faculty members, applied arts strayed too much toward craft or pre-professional training, and were seen as having no place in a liberal arts environment devoted to the life of the mind. Even critical or historical views of art were for decades pushed to the margins of academic study.

A series of presidents, beginning with Dexter Keezer in the 1930s, champi-oned the arts at Reed as an important counterbalance to the college's intellectual intensity. They were joined over the years by a handful of teachers who persisted in promoting as robust an arts program as possible at Reed under the circum-stances. In the mid-1980s, following the successful completion of the first major fundraising campaign in the college's history, Paul Bragdon made growing the arts at Reed a top priority.

BILL NAITO '49, trustee 1974–1996: Reed College had always had financial problems of one sort or another. At times they had been worse than others. In the early 1980s, the Seventy-Fifth Anniversary Campaign was launched, with the goal of raising $45 million. It was an attempt for once and for all to put the college on sound economic footing, and get over that constant, nagging problem of not having enough bucks. Most of the money was to go toward an endowment that would generate income toward meeting wages and operating costs, so that the college would not have to rely so much every year on tuition income and annual gifts.

PAUL BRAGDON, president 1971–1988: The endowment had grown from the low point of $4.4 million in 1971 to something over $16 million by 1981. Even so, it was still a very small endowment, partly because funds from the Vollum Challenge of 1975 to 1980 had not been for the endowment. The Seventy-Fifth Anniversary Campaign changed that. Originally set for $45 million, it ended up by its conclusion in 1988 coming in at $65 million. That helped to raise the endowment from $16 million to $67 million, which then grew very significantly to $125 million and higher, just by the returns it was getting of 30 percent a year. One of the key figures in that effort was the chair of our investment committee, Walter Mintz '50, who later chaired the Board of Trustees.

MICHAEL LEVINE '62, trustee 1984–2002: Walter was a financial genius, a Wall Street legend, and so whatever funds Paul Bragdon was able to raise, Walter over the years turned into a very big pile of money. Of course, the way this works in the world is that when people see your pile of money is becoming bigger, they're more willing to contribute to it. They're no longer worried that the college might go bankrupt. They're no longer thinking, "This is the gang that can't shoot straight." Walter was an extraordinary money manager, and he was chairman of the investment committee. He gave a fair amount of money to the college just as a gift, but, in a sense, he gave more money to the college than anyone because of how he grew the endowment. That's not to take anything away from Howard Vollum '36, John Gray, or Dick Wollenberg. They gave very generously, but Walter was extraordinary.

RICHARD P. WOLLENBERG, trustee 1962–2005: Reed, unlike the half a dozen or so comparable schools in the East with which it was frequently compared, did not have a large constituency of people with inherited wealth. We did not have a lot of alums who were in a position to do major things financially for the school. As a result, the endowment was comparatively small on a per-capita basis. I felt, though, that we had a moral obligation on the board to maintain Reed's standards in any way we could. They had to be the highest we were capable of producing, because that was Reed's essential niche in the educational spectrum. At the same time, the trustees had a strong feeling that they had to be fiscally responsible. We could not mortgage the future in order to take care of the present.

THE OREGONIAN, ROBERT LANDAUER, "Reed Refuses to Accept a World of Mediocrity," May 1, 1983: Universally acknowledged as a "steeple of excellence" in American higher education, Reed is a rare institution. . . . Because it seeks so much (all students participate in an honors curriculum) and because its students so regularly meet the challenge, the college continually affirms the ideal that much will be accomplished when much is expected. Reed's ability to perpetuate that tradition offers hope and encouragement for American education at all levels.

RICHARD JONES, history professor 1941–1982, 1985–1986: In the mid-1960s, the college had raised the target student-faculty ratio to twelve-to-one to temporarily address its deficit. While the financial condition of the college greatly changed in the 1970s and '80s, that money all went to things other than the educational program, and consequently there wasn't any shift in the student-faculty ratio.

By 1989, the increase in tuition income was about five times what it had been in 1970. The faculty salary schedule, however, had only doubled by 1989 over what it was in 1970, which meant that that tremendous increase in tuition income was not going mostly to the educational program. That was perfectly clear, also, in looking at the size of the administrative and faculty staffs. In 1970, the ratio of faculty members to administrative staff members was about two-to-one. By 1989, it had reversed, to more than two-to-one administration staff to faculty.

ED MCFARLANE, controller and assistant treasurer 1973–1978, vice-president and treasurer 1979– : The running of a college campus became more complicated from the time I started working at Reed in the early 1970s.

First, there were a lot more rules and regulations. To manage those sorts of requirements you needed more professional staff to interrelate with the outside agencies that dealt with those issues. Next, there were third-party demands on institutions, a very visible one being the Americans with Disabilities Act. Making facilities and programs available to individuals who possibly couldn't have accessed them before was an expensive thing to do. There were also liability issues. Educational institutions were being sued much more than they had been. That meant legal bills and higher insurance rates. Thirty years before nobody even gave a second thought to the cost of healthcare benefits for employees. By the 1990s, this had become a very expensive benefit, along with retirement funds. The whole technology explosion also meant that every institution was spending millions on installing, running, and housing that technology. With declines in funding from federal and state governments, there was also more need to provide financial aid to students.

For Reed specifically, in the '70s there was very little in support structure for student services. Over the years, that changed as this huge student support structure was created in terms of the health and counseling departments with a lot more deans in the student services operation. There was also an increase in the areas of academic support and career services, neither of which existed back then. All of these were just added-on costs, most of them not directly related to the educational mission of the college.

PAUL BRAGDON, president: Once I knew that the Seventy-Fifth Anniversary Campaign was going to be successful, I turned my attention to trying to get money for things that were not part of the campaign. One was to expand study and exploration of other cultures and incorporate that more into the curriculum. Elizabeth Ducey, who was a very independent-minded, progressive, local donor, was very interested in Asia and Asian studies, and enthusiastic about providing money that gave us an opportunity to develop the curriculum in that direction. Given Reed's location on the Pacific Rim, that seemed to make sense.

We were fortunate too, that a generous gift from Ed and Sue Cooley enabled the college to strengthen art and art history in the curriculum and to build and establish an art gallery. These additions were not part of the campaign, but they addressed a concern of many, including myself, over strengthening the creative side of the college. That effort had begun in the early years of my tenure, with John and Betty Gray's gift to provide a studio art building.

CHARLES RHYNE, art history professor 1960– 1997: In many ways the development of the art department at Reed followed parallel developments of other colleges around the country in incorporating art and music into the academic curriculum. The classical educational position was that art wasn't intellectual enough, that music and art, dance and theatre, were all sort of extracurricular things. Even when they did become part of the curriculum, there remained a subtle attitude of not letting them in too far because they were not very intellectual.

Reed was particularly extreme in not fostering art. In my first two years at the college, in the early 1960s, you couldn't major in art. There wasn't an art department. It was me and Lloyd Reynolds. We also had visiting artists, usually a local artist for a semester or a year, because they were cheap and available. There were people on the faculty, such as Rex Arragon in history and Kaspar Locher in German, who were interested in art but didn't have an academic training in art history.

Lloyd taught the art history class, but his main love was calligraphy. He was somewhat of a self-taught art historian just as he was a self-taught calligrapher. He originally came to Reed to teach English literature. That was how he got the calligraphy course into the curriculum in the late 1940s, positioning it as being about writing, and so got it in as a literature course. I'm sure if he had first offered it as an art course, people would have said, "That's a studio art course," and probably not accepted it.

PETER PARSHALL, art history professor 1971–2000: In the humanities program, which was sort of based on literature and history, it was fair to call marginal the status that the visual arts had. For me it was not a question of resistance so much as it was the difficulty of managing this sort of thing, and doing it in a congenial way. It takes a kind of literacy that requires a great deal of time to acquire.

CHARLES RHYNE, art history professor: When Lloyd Reynolds retired in 1969, I took over the introductory art history course and also started teaching an advanced art history course. That was an important event in the history of the art department, as it then led to students wanting more courses, and theses.

My approach to art history was quite different from Lloyd's, much less of a survey. But a lot of what I admired most in Lloyd I also just nat-urally tried to include in my teaching, because I always believed that enthusiastic response to things is important. So it wasn't like two completely mutually exclusive approaches to teaching art history at all. But it was a generational change, and I just happened to come along at that stage. I was brought up as an art historian. He wasn't. I was brought up as a careful, systematic researcher. The only area in which I saw him as systematic was in calligraphy, where he was systematic and creative at the same time, exactly the combination I admire. I came along at a stage when the whole discipline of art history had finally started to emerge at the undergraduate level, and the kind of split that existed at Reed between the approach in Lloyd's era and the one in mine were not that different from what occurred elsewhere.

PETER PARSHALL, art history professor: One of the wonderful things about objects is that they keep sitting there and looking back at you. I always resisted the post-structuralists' conviction that language is consciousness and that all experience is textual, partly because of the difficulty I had trying to figure out how to turn an object into text. There is something about the material permanence of objects that definitely separates them out from other forms of humanist creations. It makes them a very special and stimulating center of the teaching problem, but a difficult one and a specialized one. But then, people don't mature intellectually by memorizing data. They mature by looking closely at something that's complex and provocative.

PETER MARS '82: Reed had just completed the brand new studio art building when I was a student. The old art building had just been a little geodesic dome, and another small building where they had a couple of potters' wheels. It was very low key. The new art building was revolutionary for the school. I spent a lot of time there, all hours of the day and night, just painting and sitting around talking to other artists. In the process I found out that I really loved it, and that I had an immediate intuitive understanding of the language of art. I had been a science major up until that point, but I had kind of an epiphany that art was where I needed to be, that that was my calling. Here I was, this kind of geeky science guy, and all of a sudden this other area of my brain just opened up.

CHARLES RHYNE, art history professor: The whole arts program at Reed began to change dramatically in the late 1980s and early '90s, thanks to a fabulous grant in 1988 from two trustee couples, Ed and Sue Cooley, and John and Betty Gray, of $4.7 million specifically for art history and its place in the humanities. That may very well have been the largest donation for art history at any liberal arts college in the country. They also endowed a new exhibition space, the Douglas F. Cooley Memorial Art Gallery, named

for the Cooleys' son. Thanks to that grant, Reed came to have a first-rate art department in every way.

LARRY RINDER '83: Reed was the perfect environment for me, because the kind of work that I was interested in at that time was collaborative and interdisciplinary, work that was not really beholden to any artistic tradition or methodology. Being at Reed offered a great opportunity to collaborate with students who were physicists or computer engineers, and who were able to bring some kind of technical capacity or image or idea into the hybrid mix that would somehow turn into a performance. These were very open-ended experiences of sound and light and image and music and gesture that I was working with.

The depth of knowledge and sensitivity and intelligence that I got from my collaborators at Reed was vastly greater from what I got at the School of Visual Arts in New York City, where I went to study between my freshman and senior

The geodesic dome, shown here in the late 1960s, was for a long time the home of studio arts at Reed.

years at Reed. People there were basically just channeled into one kind of activity in art making. There was not a huge value placed on becoming a more well-rounded person or having tangential thoughts and experiences.

KATHLEEN WORLEY, theatre professor 1985– : There was a real kind of intellectual competition that happened at Reed, but there were not a lot of places on campus where Reedies could collaborate and figure out how to work with people as opposed to just working by yourself. In theatre, you can't do anything alone. Even with a monologue or developing an audition piece, you can't really fully commit yourself to doing it while standing outside yourself and watching it at the same time. You need an outside eye that you trust, and the way you come to trust an outside eye is to have been in the situation in which you've been able to observe other people's works and other people's criticisms of work. There's this old thing about "Acting is reacting." If we don't see that human transaction happening, it's like watching corpses on stage, and nobody cares. You have to work together on just that simple level.

That discovery of the collaborative process was important for a lot of students. Most of the people who came to theatre from the sciences came because they wanted to relate to people in a completely different way from the way they had in the sciences. They wanted some kind of creative outlet.

FRANCE GIDDINGS '69: Seth Ulman taught a course at Reed in Oriental theatre, a world I knew nothing about at all. I would walk out of class and just be bouncing, full of all these incredible connections. The whole thing became like this volcano of creative energy that was just so precious for me. He had that impact on students in a way that we truly loved and were grateful for.

ERIC OVERMYER '73: There was not much of a theatre department at Reed in the early 1970s. Seth Ulman, who had run the department for a very long time, was an intimidating, imposing sort of Old Testament figure. He offered classes in such odd things as Japanese Noh theatre. He also offered a film course in which he showed very boring films by the Danish film director Carl Dreyer, famous for such films as *The Passion of Joan of Arc*. It was tough.

Ulman's own productions, such as Maxim Gorky's *The Lower Depths*, tended to be long and tortured. He just squeezed every moment, wrung it out like a rag.

JUDY TYLE MASSEE, dance professor 1968– 1998: In the spring of 1969, there was a dance-theatre student, Nina Wiener '69, who wanted to do an interdisciplinary thesis in art-dance. In the dance and art world at that time, this was going on everywhere. Merce Cunningham was working with Jasper Johns and Robert Rauschenberg. Still, it was really hard getting permission for a student to do a combined thesis. Nina, who went on to become a well-known dancer—including working with Twyla Tharp—was the first one.

The theatre, such as it was at that time, was in the old Student Union, where Vollum Hall now is located. Nina did her dance production. Then, later that night, I got a phone call that the theatre was on fire. I got in my car and drove over to campus, and watched the theatre burn down. I joked to Nina that she went out in a blaze of glory.

LEE BLESSING '71: After the old theatre burned down, Seth Ulman, who was running the theatre department, was very eager to get a new theatre building. He had designed his own octagonal theatre space and worked very hard to get Reed to let him go out and get the funding. But he encountered a lot of resistance from the administration.

Theatre professors and staff Cara Carr, Kathleen Worley, Max Muller, and Craig Clinton, 1996.

KATHLEEN WORLEY, theatre professor: There was a major effort on the part of chemistry professor Marsh Cronyn '40 and Seth Ulman to raise money so that we could actually get a decent building. The college, though, resolved that it would only build what it could pay for with the insurance money from the fire, and Cronyn was forced to return all the money he had collected from alumni.

LEE BLESSING '71: We all looked at the new building and said to ourselves, "It's designed for when Reed gets rid of theatre. Then they will have a really good warehouse."

KATHLEEN WORLEY, theatre professor: Seth Ulman resigned when he saw the building. Larry Oliver, who took over the theatre department after he left, was really interested in starting a conservatory of some kind, and began bringing in guest directors and guest actors. That's how

I originally came to Reed, as a guest actor. But eventually, through his ambitious conservatory program, Larry ran up something like a $40,000 debt for the college. He took his conservatory and moved it downtown, where it became the Portland Conservatory Theatre Company.

PETER GUSS '78: Larry Oliver was a very educated guy, and had an intellectual attitude toward theatre. When I went to graduate school I found that that clearly separated Reed from other places. Other students had done a lot of musicals in their college, but not many of them had read Chekhov or the German playwright Frank Wedekind or others whom we routinely read and talked about at Reed.

KATHLEEN WORLEY, theatre professor: When Craig Clinton came to run the theatre department after Larry Oliver departed in 1978, he brought with him a designer from Carnegie

Tech named Warner Blake. Warner redesigned and built, with student help, the upstairs theatre and changed the configuration of the downstairs theatre.

JOHN PECK '88: I had a work-study job at the Reed theatre helping build sets. We'd go dumpster diving for construction materials, which was a way to save costs. Craig Clinton was very into that. "Oh, God, see what two-by-fours you can find," he'd say. "Chicken wire. Anything you can come up with. Go get it, guys!" We would borrow a college vehicle and go out looking for stuff around town.

JUDY TYLE MASSEE, dance professor: It was difficult for dance to make use of that theatre because it had no scenic shop. It had a tiny little costume-design shop. And the enrollment in theatre soon got to the point that they needed the theatre full-time for the theatre thesis productions. So we continued to have our dance performances in what I referred to as the "Judy Massee portable dance theatre," which consisted of an incredible design of freestanding folding sets and a portable lightning system that could create a stage space in an open setting like the gym.

KEITH MARTIN '73: Most of the kids who came to Reed were not athletic and were so out of touch with their body it was like a chasm. Judy Massee had a way of making dance interesting. She had worked with Martha Graham, who is really the mother of modern dance, and was very smart and good at teaching a sense of kinetics to people who had great brains and totally gimpy bodies. Her classes got huge.

JUDY TYLE MASSEE, dance professor: In the mid-1950s, when I was in high school in Portland, there was an organization at Reed called the "Dance Events Committee," run by a group of women that included Cornelia Cerf, the daughter of longtime literature professor Barry Cerf.

Professor Judy Massee, leading a dance class in 1970.

They brought modern dancers to Reed to teach classes that were open to the public. I discovered that they were bringing in Charles Weidman, the father of American modern dance, to conduct master classes. The freedom of the movement that he was doing was mind-boggling to me. I loved every minute of it. It was an epiphany. I decided that I wanted to be a modern dancer.

Tricia Brown, who taught at Reed in 1959 and 1960, was responsible, I believe, for getting academic credit for dance in the Division of the Arts. Other dance classes were given physical education credit, but not academic credit. During Reed's accreditation review in 1976–77, I asked Martha Hill, who had danced in Martha Graham's first company and gone on to create the dance department at Bennington College, to come out and review the Reed dance department. She evaluated the department very positively, but she also mentioned many things that it needed. The day that she was to go back to New York, she had an exit interview with President Paul Bragdon and the provost, Marvin Levich, in the president's office. I was waiting outside Eliot Hall to take her to the airport. When she came out there were tears in her eyes. She walked down the steps to meet me and said, "Judy, I could weep. They are so cold. So thoughtless." I know she wasn't referring to Paul Bragdon. There was a whole faction of people who thought dance was a useless subject.

KEITH MARTIN '73: The last year I was in Portland, Judy Massee and I started a summer dance program at Reed with maybe sixty or seventy students. Within three or four years we had four or five hundred students on campus, and I was flying out my teachers from Juilliard to teach in the program. Judy's husband, classics professor Richard Tron, helped us run the program. It was great fun. By 1983, when the program ended, we had almost five hundred students taking workshops, coming from New York and Europe.

JUDY TYLE MASSEE, dance professor: Dance went from being thought of as a very frivolous activity among many of the faculty when I arrived in 1968, to being accepted by everyone in the Division of the Arts, and considered by a majority of the faculty as a very acceptable, academically strong area of study that the college could be proud of. Reed was really considered the school in Oregon with an incredibly strong dance department. It was a hugely exciting time. But I was told that no one in dance would ever be tenured. It was just so desperately unfair. They never gave me tenure in the thirty years I taught at Reed. That was because of the prejudice against dance.

LISA STEINMAN, English professor 1976– : Things that looked like hands-on practices of art—studio arts, theatre, dance, creative writing—rather than critical or historical views of art, didn't have departments at Reed. There were some older professors for whom that was a kind of principle. That is to say, the arts didn't seem like they were "liberal arts."

Philosophy professor and provost Marvin Levich was someone I had a number of arguments with about this. Faced with that skepticism, I was forced to talk about why the arts belonged at a liberal arts college, and to articulate the reasons why I thought, for example, that would-be writers should know something about the history and practice of their craft outside of their immediate circles. And why I thought people who were historians or even critics of, say, poetry, might have more insight into what they were talking about if they were in a situation where they had to do some practice. I found myself telling my colleagues what it was that one did in creative writing courses, why they weren't just craft or pre-professional but could be part of a liberal arts education, which I firmly believe they are. It was the case that the people whose minds I couldn't change finally retired.

ERIC OVERMYER '73: There was a tradition of having writers around at Reed. The Beat poets Philip Whalen '51 and Lew Welch '50 came to visit. There were also readings from other visiting writers, such as Phillip Levine and Ralph Ellison, and Northwest poets such as William Stafford and David Waggoner. I took a poetry class with English professor and noted Northwest poet Kenneth O. Hanson, who was friends with Robert Peterson, another wonderful poet, who came to Reed to be a visiting writer-in-residence from 1969 to 1971. Bob Peterson was very much a mentor to me.

LEE BLESSING '71: Robert Peterson was my thesis advisor. He taught me more about writing, and how to be a writer, than anyone I've ever known. What I responded to most in his poetry was its insistence that life, while disappointing at nearly every turn, remains somehow always lovable—that the sad, ironic twists in our lives must never wholly distract us from the infinite happiness of having been invited to the party at all. What Bob saw as the gift of moral complexity in the world, and the opportunity it affords us all to learn and grow, is something of which I am forever mindful. The skill that he spent so much time trying to teach me was simply how to embrace yourself.

LISA STEINMAN, English professor: Things like poetry readings were not subsidized by the college until the 1980s. Up until then, there was no money for visiting poets and writers. The tradition was that faculty members would fundraise among ourselves to pay for writers to come and give readings. We would give the money to Reed and ask them to write a check so it didn't look like we were just doing charity.

There had been a part-time position for a visiting writer-in-residence position at the college going back to the early 1960s with such writers as James Dickey and Galway Kinnell. They would come to Reed for a two-year appointment. In the mid-1980s, I took it on myself to ask every year for a full-time creative writer. Once we eventually got that, then I asked every year for two full-time, tenure-track creative writers. It took twenty years, but finally that was approved.

PATRICIA MUSICK '73: The calligraphy studio was a refuge for me. There was the kind of discipline that we were talking about in the "academic" courses, whereas in the art courses at that period of time it was all about expressing yourself. In calligraphy there was a right way to do it, to always go back to the basics, but as taught by Lloyd Reynolds, and by Robert Palladino, who succeeded him, it was also a vehicle for teaching, an approach to life that embodied an attitude and a philosophy. It wasn't just a "craftsy" thing.

CHARLES RHYNE, art history professor: The calligraphy course was an absolute model of artistic expression, and also an understanding historically of what you were doing, going into some depth in an area of the teacher's expertise. Lloyd Reynolds was an absolutely remarkable human being, and his work in calligraphy was internationally important. I've saved every letter he wrote me, because they're just unbelievably beautiful as well.

ROBERT PALLADINO, calligraphy professor 1969–1984: In the late 1960s I was living in a Trappist monastery in New Mexico, teaching myself calligraphy. Some of Lloyd Reynolds' calligraphy students came out to the monastery and met me. They told Lloyd about me, and eventually he came out and spent a whole day with me. The fact that Lloyd picked me, a priest, to be his successor at Reed when he retired in 1969 was rather significant, especially since I had been a Trappist monk for eighteen years. He wanted someone who could understand that there was more to art than just drawing pictures, and more to calligraphy than just drawing letters.

At Reed, I taught letterforms, so that students would know how to write, and then I taught them that, whenever you write, write something worth reading. Lloyd had taught the same thing. I used to lecture for one hour and do studio art for two hours. Lloyd loved to talk, and would sometimes lecture for three hours. Calligraphy was the most heavily enrolled elective class on campus. Most of the students were science majors, and almost none of them were art majors.

SUZANNE PARDEE '83: Robert Palladino was a very spiritual man. He had a real sweetness and an uplifting presence to him.

SAMUEL FROMARTZ '80: My mother, Mitziko Sawada '51, had taken calligraphy from Lloyd Reynolds when she was a student at Reed. She had Lloyd's calligraphy book at home, which I liked to look at growing up. When I got to Reed

I took calligraphy with Robert Palladino in my freshman year, which turned out to be quite fortuitous, because it became a very lucrative work-study program for me during my next three years at Reed, calligraphing posters for display in Commons and little leaflets distributed for various events.

ROBERT PALLADINO, calligraphy professor: Steve Jobs '76, who co-founded Apple computer, came back to Reed in the early 1980s and consulted with me about Greek letters for a type font. I don't know if he ever used my Greek letters, or if he just used them as a starting point, but we had a good time. He was educating me about what a computer was. I didn't have the foggiest idea of what he was talking about at the time.

STEVE JOBS '76: Reed offered perhaps the best calligraphy instruction in the country. I learned about serif and sans-serif typefaces, about varying the amount of space between different letter

Professor Robert Palladino teaching a calligraphy class, 1982.

combinations, about what makes great typography great. It was beautiful, historical, artistically subtle in a way that science can't capture, and I found it fascinating.

None of this had even a hope of any practical application in my life. But ten years later, when we were designing the first Macintosh computer, it all came back to me, and we designed it all into the Mac. It was the first computer with beautiful typography. If I had never dropped in on that single course in college, the Mac would never have had multiple typefaces or proportionally spaced fonts, and since Windows just copied the Mac, it's likely that no personal computer would have them.

ROBERT REYNOLDS, physics professor 1963–2002: I served as chair of the Educational Policies Committee in 1984, the year that calligraphy was removed from the list of courses offered for academic credit. That wasn't our initiative. The Division of the Arts was solidly behind it, in spite of the importance calligraphy had played in the college for many years and the fact that it was very popular on campus. There was a sense that, as a graphic art, what was seen as a fairly limited activity was not sufficiently intellectual to be worth full academic credit.

ROBERT PALLADINO, calligraphy professor: The excuse for getting rid of me was to extend the sculptor in the department to full-time. He was half time and I was half-time, so they decided to combine the two into a single full-time position. He was teaching modern art, and I was teaching historical art. The head of the art department at that time wanted as much modern art as possible.

I happened to read the faculty minutes when they decided to get rid of calligraphy. One of the art historians said that it didn't fit in with the modern art department. That it was something from the past. It was sad, because the students

themselves—at least half of the student body—requested that they keep it. The faculty said they were going to keep it as a non-credit course, but that only lasted one more year.

BERT BREHM, biology professor 1962–1993: Palladino was very upset, not just by the decision, but by how it was done. They never spoke to him about it one way or another. On the day the proposition was being discussed by the faculty, he wrote a long letter in beautiful script, but he said that, emotionally, he just couldn't deliver it. So I read Palladino's letter out loud at the faculty meeting. There was surprisingly little discussion on the faculty floor after I read the letter, before they brought up the proposal to eliminate the calligraphy program for a vote. What in the world were they thinking? They threw away the thing that Lloyd Reynolds made the college famous for.

PAUL BRAGDON, president: The elimination of calligraphy—and with it Bob Palladino—was one of the biggest disappointments of my presidency. Indeed, I regard it as a defeat. I understand why the art department wanted to augment its program in core areas of art and art history, but I believe that in making the decision the faculty gave insufficient attention to the history and place of calligraphy at Reed and to the significance of calligraphy to large numbers of students at a college with very limited offerings in courses combining discipline and knowledge, on the one hand, and the value of the opportunity for creativity and an aesthetic experience on the other. Adding force to my conviction is the role of legendary professor Lloyd Reynolds in bringing calligraphy to the fore for those at Reed, and indeed his leadership in fostering the art in Oregon, the Pacific Northwest, and elsewhere. On balance, the college and the students were the losers in sacrificing calligraphy from the academic program.

CHAPTER 35

The Fight over Divestment

I thought that it would be the thin edge of the wedge, that once you had one kind of demand for divestment, that would open the door for others to use the college's endowment as a political weapon.
—Edward Segel, history professor

Politicization was unavoidable, and neutrality very difficult to achieve.
—Sam Danon, French professor

In 1971, following student protests over the inclusion of Black Studies at Reed, the college adopted, as part of what was called the "Hay Report," a set of operating principles, one of which was that the college would avoiding taking positions on political issues that did not directly affect the college or higher education. In doing so, the faculty, administration, and trustees had sought to affirm that Reed would remain a home for the independent thinking and diversity of opinion that they felt to be the foundations of academic freedom.

This principle was put to the test in the mid-1980s during the nationwide controversy over apartheid in South Africa, amid calls for the college to divest from its investment portfolio the holdings of any company doing business in that country. At the time, an estimated 25 percent of the college's endowment was invested in blue-chip stocks of companies such as IBM and Ford that were operating in South Africa.

Faced with similar demands, a number of American institutions had adopted a screen for their investment portfolios called the "Sullivan Principles." Developed in 1977 by Reverend Leon H. Sullivan, an African-American with corporate board experience, the Sullivan Principles called for U.S. companies doing business in South Africa to establish a set of guidelines for promoting racial equality in their employment practices there. In the mid-1980s Reverend Sullivan, noting the intractability of the South African government, repudiated these principles and argued instead for divestment.

ADAM PENENBERG '86: There were college protests all over the country: "Don't invest in South Africa." At Reed we had a group of twenty to twenty-five students who were very involved in the issue and really believed it was morally right. Chris Phelps '88, who later ran for governor as a Socialist Party candidate, and Nathan Keene '88 were the two big names among the activists, who called themselves the "South African Concerns Committee."

DAVID CONLIN '88: Keene and Phelps held a big anti-apartheid rally, but it turned into kind of a farce because the invitation that went out was to come and protest whatever you wanted. There were hundreds of protesters on campus, protesting discrimination against gay people, discrimination against women, nuclear weapons, the Contras in Nicaragua, and all kinds of stuff. Many of these issues didn't have any relationship to Reed College. One Reedie was marching around with a big sign that said, "Bad Things Are Wrong."

RON HUDDLESTON '87: A lot of the political uproar at Reed seemed to be posturing, to be imitating what students thought the 1960s had been like. That's why you got these loose statements like "Bad Things Are Wrong." There was no civil rights movement or Vietnam War anymore. Instead, there seemed to be a great deal of focus on telling the administration what to do, but not exercising change in one's individual life. For instance, why tell the administration to sell their Coke stock when you still buy Coke?

There was one black student on campus actively involved in the divestiture thing, but the other four of us weren't motivated in that direction. One of the leaders of the divestiture movement told me at one point that I wasn't really black, and I was offended. He was a white kid. I felt that there was a certain hypocrisy in fighting for the rights of blacks in South Africa when blacks in Portland were so disadvantaged, and when there were almost no blacks on our campus.

CHRIS LYDGATE '90, alumni magazine editor 2008– : In November 1985 a group of students occupied President Bragdon's office on the second floor of Eliot Hall, shutting themselves in for two or three days. It was the first takeover of a building on campus since the late 1960s. They couldn't use the stairs, so they sent supplies in and out through the window using buckets tied to ropes. How they worked the bathroom situation I have no idea.

MARSH CRONYN '40, chemistry professor 1952–1989, provost 1982–1989: The weekend of the occupation, Paul Bragdon was off giving a talk someplace in the East. Before he came back, the dean of students and myself set up a public meeting Sunday morning to address the protesters' concerns. While they vacated the president's office to attend this meeting, we had the janitor do his work in there and then lock the door. When Paul Bragdon came in Monday morning, nobody was there.

JOHN PECK '88: The level of grassroots organizing on campus was really heightened and very focused. I imagine it would have been like that in the anti-war movement during the '60s, a similar feeling on campus as though everyone was involved in it or affected by it to some extent.

In my dorm we all voted to paint one big letter on each of our windows, spelling out "D - I - V - E - S - T - N - O - W" across the face of the dorm. Everyone coming down Woodstock Boulevard would see this huge "DIVEST NOW." In Eliot Hall, we went in at night and taped pictures of black people's faces all over the floor. When the administrators came in the morning they basically had to walk over black people to get to their offices. That caused a huge reaction. We got the janitors to open up all the classrooms during the night so that we could place signs over the clocks in each classroom that said, "Five minutes to midnight. Time to divest now."

Because Reed was a private school, its investments, unlike those of a public school, were not a public record per se. Thankfully we had friends on the Board of Trustees who gave us the information we needed. They basically said "We're willing to support you if you bring this up as an issue at the trustee meeting." And we did.

HARRIET WATSON, director of public relations 1984–1991, vice-president for public affairs 1991–2002: We had one meeting of the Board of Trustees where students came in and "took over" the space. They were lying on the floor. People stepped over them. It was a tense time. All relevant arguments were represented at the board. There were smart, caring, responsible, committed people who disagreed passionately on these matters. Richard Danzig '65, who would later be Secretary of the Navy, was an alumni trustee who was elected to the board by alumni on the platform of divesting all holdings in South Africa.

ERNEST BONYHADI '48, trustee 1971–1995: We had a number of board members who were for divestiture. They were liberal purists, I would say. Dick Wollenberg, the chairman, was just ranting at the board meeting because he was a libertarian, and politically to the right of Attila

A 1985 student demonstration outside Commons, demanding divestment from South Africa.

the Hun. Nevertheless, he had given lots of money to Reed. He was fuming about the people who wanted divestiture, when trustee Tom Bruggere got up and said, "Mr. Chairman, if you think that all those who disagree with you on this issue should get off the Reed board, that is a very illiberal position. It really is not right. I think you should apologize to the board." Wollenberg sat silent for about a minute. Then he got up and he said, "You're right, and I want to apologize." Now, that took guts. That was a classy thing.

RICHARD P. WOLLENBERG, trustee 1962–2005: Someone once stated that there should be only one agenda item for a board of trustees: "Should we fire the president?" If the answer is "No," adjourn. If "Yes," form a search committee.

DAN GREENBERG '62, trustee 1975– : There were two really solid groups on the board: those who believed that this was a way of changing social policy in this country, and those who believed that making a social issue like the South African situation a part of the way we managed our money would seriously affect our ability to grow the endowment. Worse than that, once you take on one social issue and you make that an important part of the institution's investment policy, where are you going to draw the line?

ERNEST BONYHADI '48, trustee: I was very much against divestiture. My reasons were not just academic or abstract. I happened to have friends in South Africa who were not racists, such as Helen Suzman, who was a liberal member of the South African parliament. Helen wrote several letters to me, which I used on the Reed board in arguing that divestiture by governments—it was government policy that the U.S. Treasury wouldn't buy South African securities—was fine. It was good policy. But divesting of multinational corporations working in South Africa, like General Motors or Ford, could be a

setback in helping to close the racial divide or to kill apartheid. Some of these companies had to get rid of their subsidiaries down there. They sold them to local management, and that local management didn't have the clout that a foreign multinational corporation had in dealing with the apartheid government.

EDWARD SEGEL, history professor 1973–2011: The faculty was split. Motions in favor of divestment came up among the faculty and were defeated by a small margin. I personally was opposed to it because I felt that it was divestment on political grounds and I thought that it would be the thin edge of the wedge, that once you had one kind of demand for divestment, that would open the door for others to use the college's endowment as a political weapon. I didn't like that. I would much prefer to keep academic institutions as neutral as possible.

MARVIN LEVICH, philosophy professor 1953–1994, provost 1972–1979: I was among the faculty members who thought that we should divest of South African stocks. I thought the issue had risen so sharply that the college could make a minor effort to divest.

PETER STEINBERGER, political science professor 1977– , dean of faculty 1997–2010, acting president 2001–2002: The issue was not whether apartheid was a good thing, because nobody in American politics argued that it was. The real question was: "What's the best way to get rid of apartheid?" And that seemed to me a political question, and I didn't think Reed should take a stand on that political question.

A core principle of the institution was its commitment to academic freedom, and academic freedom requires, among other things, an institution that is open and that institutionally does not ally itself with any particular points of view, whether they are religious, philosophically controversial, ideological, or political. For an institution to take such stands has, in principle if not in fact, a chilling effect on the openness of discourse on campus.

The mini-version of that is that I didn't take political stands in my classroom. When I did, my students knew that I was playing devil's advocate for one view or another, that fifteen minutes later I might play devil's advocate for the other view. My hope was that many of my students left class not really knowing what my deep political views were, because they were irrelevant.

SAM DANON, French professor 1962–2000: Whether the board of trustees decided to invest or to divest in companies doing business in South Africa, it inevitably took a political stand. Politicization was unavoidable, and neutrality very difficult to achieve. Invoking the principle of academic freedom on moral grounds when there was no danger in sight is not enough. Hiding behind it when problems arise is, perhaps, to endanger the principle of academic freedom itself.

JOHN POCK, sociology professor 1955–1998: I talked to just a very few people about divestment, largely because it was part of a course I was teaching on organizations and corporations. I tried to explain to students how modern corporations work, and how they are capitalized. Some students seemed to infer from that that I didn't believe in divestment, which was true although I didn't say that outright, and bombed my house. They threw two cherry bombs into my mailbox—which was a mailbox embedded in the wall of the house—and blew up the whole side of my dining room wall.

I left it that way for a long time. It was a rather disappointing thing for me to accept that Reed students would do that. We would have people over for dinner and show them what Reed students were capable of.

BRET FETZER '87: There was an element of priggishness to the student protests. Which is not to say that the protestors weren't passionate about what they were doing, but there was a kind of self-righteousness about their protesting that was perhaps different from earlier times. It seems as though in the 1960s it was a more honestly narcissistic rebellion in some respects. Whereas, in the 1980s you suddenly started getting a sense of moral righteousness to it, in which the spirit of revolution began to be married with another deeply American strain of moral rectitude that led to things like Prohibition. A sense that there was a right way for the world to be.

At the time, the term "politically correct" was just coming into use, and it was first viewed as an insult, a mocking term for people who were trying to impose some kind of larger moral superstructure around things that people thought. Then, within five years, people wanted to be politically correct. There was a big sea change.

PETER GOODMAN '89: A number of U.S. corporations that had operations in South Africa had adopted the "Sullivan Principles," which had been enunciated ten years before by an African-American minister, Reverend Leon H. Sullivan, as a way to help assess whether a company doing business in South Africa was acting in complicity with apartheid or working to counter apartheid. Reverend Sullivan had then renounced his own policies and had essentially said that these principles will not get us there, that they will not end apartheid, that at this point we just simply need to have the international community not invest in South Africa.

In the winter of 1986 the South African Concerns Committee on campus managed to get the Board of Trustees to take a vote on whether the college should divest from companies invested in South Africa. The committee held a series of teach-ins around campus. They did an excellent job of organizing the students in anticipation of what was about to happen—either the trustees would decide to divest altogether, or they would refuse to divest, or they would say they were going to divest from all companies that were not in compliance with the Sullivan Principles. Only the first option was acceptable to the protestors. Choosing to adopt the Sullivan Principles was viewed as pure tokenism, but which the trustees were going to spin as addressing the protestors' demands.

MICHAEL LEVINE '62, trustee 1984–2002: It all came to a head one trustees' weekend in January 1986, with student demonstrators outside. Students were allowed into the Board of Trustees' meeting room for a while to sort of stand as silent witness so they could see how important we thought all this was. I was then sent off by Paul Bragdon to draft a statement. A few changes were made to it, but that became the college's policy statement on political matters going forward.

DAN GREENBERG '62, trustee: In the end, the board ended up with a policy of real wisdom, which was that you can't invest in a way where social issues govern what you're going to be doing. There were consequences to taking that stand with the students and with some of the faculty, given that feelings ran strong.

CHRIS LYDGATE '90, alumni magazine editor: On Saturday, January 25, 1986, Paul Bragdon emerged from the trustees meeting in Vollum Hall holding a piece of paper. He stood on the steps before a crowd of students. "You're left with a messenger with the possible fate of all messengers delivering a message from other people," Bragdon began. There were boos and jeers at this. Then he read the trustees' decision —they had rejected divestment. They were going to adopt the Sullivan Principles.

This was not taken well by the mob of students outside. Chris Phelps '88 seized the micro-

phone and said, "Even as I speak, my comrades in Eliot Hall are securing the doors. We've taken over Eliot and we're not going to leave until the trustees change their mind." It was the most dramatic moment you could imagine. There was pandemonium. No one knew what was going to happen next. That began the second occupation of Eliot Hall. They shut the entire building down and no one could go in or out.

PETER GOODMAN '89: To be perfectly honest, I don't even know that I grasped what we were doing, but all of a sudden Chris Phelps '88 and Nathan Keene '88 were saying, "If you're concerned about this, if you're outraged, follow us into Eliot Hall." So, I became part of the rabble. There were a hundred-plus of us in there and we ended up staying for six days, negotiating with the administration. We operated by a consensus process, which was absolutely fascinating and maddening and inefficient. We were crashing for two or three hours at a time on these mattresses that we laid out in the classrooms.

The first couple of days we were like heroes. I was one of three or four people picked to go to a social that was held in the Student Union with some South African band and speak to the students. It was like a rally asking for people to support us, and people were supporting us. They were sending us food and drinks and telling us, "Way to go!"

Obviously a hundred students at Reed College were not going to solve the problem of apartheid in South Africa. We were aware of the fact that at some of the Ivy League campuses there were similar actions taking place, and so we did understand that we were operating in a much larger context. We wanted to keep the pressure on, and capturing media attention, which we initially got, was key to the deal.

Then, when classes started on Monday and we were still in there, a real backlash began. All of a sudden we became like the registrar, because

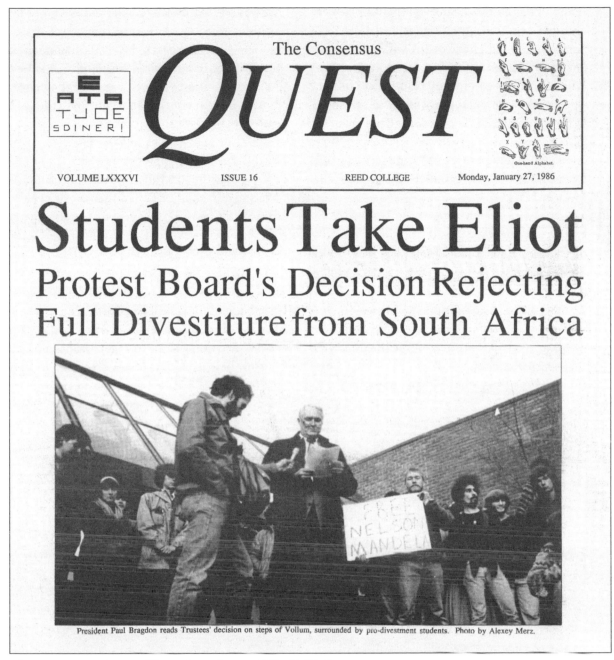

The Consensus

QUEST

ATA TJOE SDINER!

VOLUME LXXXVI   ISSUE 16   REED COLLEGE   Monday, January 27, 1986

Students Take Eliot
Protest Board's Decision Rejecting Full Divestiture from South Africa

President Paul Bragdon reads Trustees' decision on steps of Vollum, surrounded by pro-divestment students. Photo by Alexey Merz.

The Quest *announcement of the student takeover of Eliot Hall in January 1986.*

we had to sit down and figure out where all the classes that were normally held in Eliot Hall could be held, and then posting this stuff outside. Some of the students were really annoyed with us: "This is outrageous. Who are you to decide to interfere with our education?"

MATT GIRAUD '85: The first Eliot Hall occupation had been a pretty noble enterprise and the people who ran it, ran it pretty well. Subsequently, when they tried it a second time, it was a disaster for various reasons. They were trying to run it on a consensus model but they couldn't

CHAPTER 35: THE FIGHT OVER DIVESTMENT   453 really agree on much. Everything took forever and it turned into just this exhausting ordeal. Some people got a little drunk with their power and swept up in the drama of leading the rebellion, which you can hardly blame them for. But that sort of undercut for other Reedies the purity of the idea. We were trying to get Reed to not invest money in this repressive regime—a worthy enough goal, but because of the personal dynamics and because of the group dynamics it became more muddy.

PETER GOODMAN '89: After six exhausting days, we accepted a deal to come out of the building in exchange for the creation of some dubiously empowered study committee on which we would have representation, which would continue to follow up with the trustees on some expanded divestment strategy. Then life went back to normal.

It was one of those rare experiences where you are just completely immersed in what you're doing—and, between sleep deprivation and belief and the hundred other people all living in close quarters, it was a very powerful experience. Months later there was an honor case brought against all of us for the occupation.

JOHN PECK '88: The question posed in the honor case was: "Who are you to restrict our right of access to our office or our computer lab? You're saying this is for the greater social good, but it's not." A lot of intellectual time and energy went into debating all of that.

It made the Honor Principle very much a vibrant living idea. People took it seriously and talked about it all the time. The word "discomfit" was part of the debate. What constitutes discomfit? Did not being able to get into your office for a few days cause you discomfit?

The student occupation of Eliot Hall over the issue of divestment from South Africa, January 1986.

LARRY LARGE, vice-president of college relations 1982–1987, 1992–1999: The board made a hard but calculated decision. It had a rationale for it. The decision got a lot of local publicity, and a certain amount of national publicity. I think it was counter to the image of Reed in the community of higher education. They would not have predicted that Reed would decline to divest.

CHRIS LYDGATE '90, alumni magazine editor: The trustees didn't change their minds, so the issue continued to convulse the campus. People didn't go to classes for weeks at a time. At the end of that year came the third occupation, which was the nastiest. A group of students took over the Faculty Office Building, later called Greywood, which then housed the development office. This time the administrators were much tougher with them.

MARSH CRONYN '40, chemistry professor: They were in there several days. The college cut off electricity and plumbing and so these kids had candles in what was a crummy old wooden army-surplus building. Then, what started to get kind of hairy was that people were coming on to campus who had nothing whatsoever to do with Reed, and joining the protest. At that point, we just decided to end it.

Paul Bragdon, the dean of students, and I made arrangements with the head of security, and at about three in the morning—while the student protestors were snoozing—we reached inside with a broom handle to unlatch the barricaded door, and walked in. Paul had alerted the Portland police, and so a policeman came in with us. He politely said, "We've got a car outside and I would appreciate it if you would just come out. Of course, if you choose not to, we have also arranged for that."

They all walked out except for one guy who was the organizer. He went limp and refused to move. The police just lifted him up and carried him out. He was yelling, "Police brutality! Police brutality!" The *Quest* editor, who was there on site, said, "Hey, good show there! Good show!" They took everybody up to the Safeway parking lot and released them on their own recognizance. Nobody was arrested, although they wanted to be, to make a big issue.

Meanwhile, the students of the Judicial Board had declared them in violation of the Honor Principle and revoked their status as students. The protestors did not have enough student body support to change the mind of the Judicial Board. A couple of the leaders of the divestment movement simply left the college and got their degrees elsewhere.

PETER GOODMAN '89: The opinion on campus seemed to be really negative against both the occupiers and the tactic of having them arrested. The administration had just recently taken over the student-run bookstore, and a bunch of us were really angry at the president of the student body and his vice-president for having secretly cut that deal with the administration without getting any student consultation.

I had been elected to the Student Caucus on a kind of hard-line position of "Let's challenge the administration." So I organized a candlelight vigil march over to Paul Bragdon's house in Eastmoreland with three or four hundred people. It was a moment of real old-fashioned campus activism; it seems a little silly now, but it was real to us at the time.

WILLIAM ABERNATHY '88: When you looked at a group of homogeneously white kids surrounding the president's house with candles, singing "We Shall Overcome," you either needed a strong stomach or a good sense of irony about you. It was a time when I went from being an earnest angry young man to being a cynical angry young man, and it no longer suited my metanarrative to be a "divestnik." In the long run the divestment movement was on the right side of history, but for me personally I just couldn't abide the kind of sanctimony that hung around it. So, I distanced myself from it and was critical of it. That had as much to do with the personalities involved as it did with anything else.

CHRIS LYDGATE '90, alumni magazine editor: During the divestment protest, those of us on the editorial staff of the *Quest* believed that fundamentally it was our job to be as objective and as fair as we could, and report the facts that would be the basis for further discussion. We ran an editorial saying "Divest," so people knew where we stood, but we struggled not to let our own attitudes color our reporting.

At the end of the year there was an election for a new *Quest* editor. A group of the students who had occupied Eliot Hall ran for the position. Their criticism of us was that we had been *too* objective. They felt that we had been insufficiently supportive of the occupation, thus indicating that we were bankrupt morally and didn't deserve reëlection. They won the election by a margin of five or six students.

DELL RHODES, psychology professor 1975–2006, associate dean of students 1990–1991: There was a period of time in the mid-1980s when a lot of things that should have been happening were not happening, largely, it seemed, because of a group of senior male faculty members. These things included the transition from a drug-liberal campus to a campus that needed to toe the line set by state and federal laws, from a campus in which there were almost no women faculty members to a campus in which there were a significant number, from a campus in which things such as parental-leave policies for faculty and staff were nonexistent to a campus in compliance with mandated external laws on the matter, and from a campus in which there was no explicit sexual harassment policy

to a campus that had one and had actually implemented it.

During my years on the Faculty Advisory Committee, beginning in 1982–83, and certainly in 1985–86, these issues were brought up, but there was no one willing to take them on and work seriously to solve them. The harassment issue, for example, was on the table, and there were women faculty members and a couple of the men who were trying to make things happen, but their efforts seemed to lead nowhere. To some extent it was institutional inertia. There were a lot of things that needed to be changed, but Reed remained in a bit of a bubble as the world changed around us, both because we were a small private liberal arts college, and because we were in a frontier town in Oregon, instead of in Boston or Chicago or New York City.

Meanwhile, the sociology of the faculty was changing. There were more families with both parents working, meaning that faculty members could no longer count on having a spouse at home to take care of the kids. Many younger faculty members had to leave campus at four or five in the afternoon to pick up the kids, to go home and have dinner with the kids, to help the other working spouse. In addition, the housing costs in the Eastmoreland neighborhood were outrunning the ability of regular professors to afford homes near Reed, so faculty members had longer distances to travel to get home, which meant less time on campus.

Paul Bragdon was virtually lecturing us about the effects of these changes, and some of my faculty colleagues seemed to find his lectures offensive. He was very aware of the things that needed to be changed, but he seemed to be standing back more than trying actively to overcome the inertia of the institution. He seemed to be allowing a group of individuals whom he trusted to manage the college. In retrospect, I understand why he trusted them, but they were not the faculty members who were going to move forward on these social issues. It was a very frustrating time, because important things just were not happening.

LAURENS RUBEN, biology professor 1955–1992: Generally, the faculty was pleased with Bragdon's appointment and for some years was very cooperative. It was only later on that there were certain individuals who decided they were unhappy with the way things were going and who began to give Paul and the rest of us a hard time. But aside from that, when you consider the size of the problems when Bragdon came in and the condition to which he brought the college—I don't mean just fiscally, but educationally as well—we went through a lot and came out winners.

Paul converted the place into a professional academic institution by giving us an infrastructure of professional administrators who knew what they were doing. If you have an inadequate infrastructure, you're going to have an institution that suffers from that. Some of the faculty members didn't appreciate the process, but it had to happen. I don't think we lost faculty governance, but, certainly, there were personal losses. There's no question that the sense of family disappeared. Yet the changes gave us opportunities to think about other ways of having Reed College go. It was all part of the enlargement and the professionalization of the college.

DAN GREENBERG '62, trustee: Seventeen years is a long time to be a college president. If you do your job right, you create enemies over time. Paul Bragdon stayed a much longer time than most people, and longer than he probably wanted because he felt a responsibility to protect the institution, and felt that he still had some things to do in that respect. But at some point, the challenge simply isn't there in the same way it was before. You've done most of what you are able to do, and at that time it's really appropriate to give up the reins and let somebody different, with new energy, take over.

PAUL BRAGDON, president: I became aware that whatever attention had once been paid to what I was saying—for example the need for review and renewal as a constant in curricular matters—nobody was paying much attention to it any more. A fresh voice may be more effective saying some of the same things in a different way or addressing other things that were important. Also, the five-year fundraising campaign for Reed had come to a successful conclusion. I knew that I wouldn't be around for another five-year campaign. We had begun planning for the next steps, and it was time for others to pursue the stated goals.

My final day as Reed's president, in June 1988, brought a genuine surprise and a pleasant one at that. Joe Brooks, the amazing jack of all trades who kept Reed's facilities and equipment going, came out of retirement for the morning and appeared next to my driveway bright and early in the morning in an all-too-familiar utility vehicle. I walked over and clambered in. Off we went to the main entrance of Reed.

Lined up on the roadway to Eliot Circle and around the circle were all of Reed's vehicles from power mowers on up, members of the staff, some faculty members, and friends. My wife, Nancy, and I were escorted to the east stairs of Eliot Hall, and the parade began. A day in the life of Reed, a fine one, and not usual at all. I can't think of a better ending.

PART FIVE

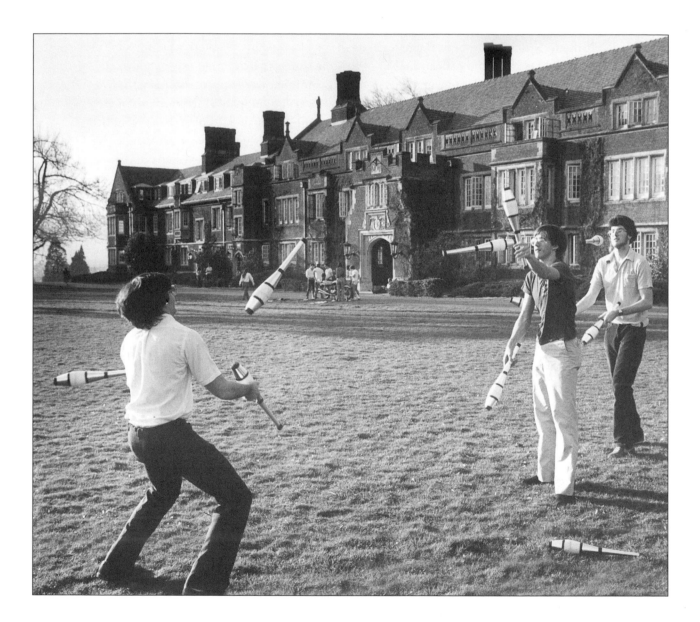

Part Five: Radical Traditionalist, 1989–2011

RADICAL TRADITIONALIST, 1989–2011

The curriculum has given way to a marketplace philosophy: it is a supermarket where students are shoppers and professors are merchants of learning.
  —Association of American Colleges, February 1985

Beginning in the mid-1980s, Reed College found itself contending with an increasingly competitive field of private liberal arts colleges. The tremendous growth in higher education since the Second World War had largely favored public colleges and universities. In 1950, the 2.5 million students enrolled in colleges and universities had been split almost evenly between public and private schools. By 1990, only a third of the country's fourteen million students were enrolled in private colleges and universities. While public schools grew by becoming more accommodating during this period, most elite private colleges became more selective.

That selectivity had its roots in the reforms instituted by Charles Eliot at Harvard in the late nineteenth century. To save the private liberal arts college from irrelevance during the rise of the research university, Eliot made obtaining a college degree a prerequisite for Harvard's professional schools. Prior to that, students pursuing such fields as medicine and law did not bother with undergraduate degrees. Other universities soon followed Eliot's lead, making liberal arts colleges the gateways to high-status professions and establishing them as an elite type of education, often favoring students from privileged families. It wasn't until after the Second World War, with the creation of the G.I. Bill and the adoption of such standardized tests as the Scholastic Aptitude Test (SAT), that the private liberal arts colleges became more of a meritocracy. While quotas for Jewish students and male-only restrictions remained in place at many of the top private schools until the 1970s, more students were able to gain entry to these elite gateways based upon tested competency and graded ability in high school, regardless of family background or financial means.

Students juggling on the lawn in front of the Old Dorm Block, late 1980s.

In the 1980s and '90s, selectivity among elite private colleges became increasingly complicated by the rise of consumerism and materialism in the broader American culture. During the Reagan era, with its exaltation of free-market economics, the notions of brand value, quantitative assessment, and price as an indicator of quality became major considerations for students and parents in selecting a college. To compete in this new, market-based environment, private colleges engaged in higher spending and investment to enhance their appeal; this, along with other factors, led to rapidly growing operating costs.

To some degree, the increased competition was intensified by a shrinking pool of applicants. Between 1976 and 1993 the number of high school graduates declined from 3.2 million to 2.5 million. As colleges spent more to attract and keep students, the bigger schools held the advantage. Large research and doctoral universities with average enrollments of more than eight thousand students were better able to spread the cost of improvements in facilities, student services, and administrative structure than were small liberal arts colleges, whose enrollments averaged a mere thirteen hundred students. Small private colleges faced another challenge in the 1990s as public universities began to copy the liberal education model by installing honors colleges within their large institutions and, thanks to their economies of scale, were able to charge students only a fraction of the fees asked for by private colleges. The greater financial capacity of the universities also increased the competition for promising young professors, undercutting the drawing power of prestigious schools such as Reed that for decades had subsisted upon genteel poverty among the faculty.

Reed and its peer schools had also employed a low-cost approach to admissions marketing, relying for decades upon longstanding relationships with high school or prep school networks for student referrals. Now they had to compete for quality applicants with glossy brochures, marketing consultants, and elaborate pricing and discounting policies borrowed from the airline industry, gauged on a student's ability to pay and a college's capacity for providing financial aid. The targeted admissions pool itself was relatively small. Out of fourteen million college students nationwide in 1990, total attendance at small, liberal arts residential colleges numbered a quarter of a million. For those schools considered, like Reed, to be selective in their admissions, total enrollment was only a hundred thousand.

In this increasingly competitive marketplace, the gap that separated well-endowed, elite colleges with strong brand identification, such as Amherst, Swarthmore, and Williams, from those that were less known and less well endowed, began to widen. A handful of wealthy colleges set the standards on class sizes, faculty reputations, course loads, scientific facilities, gymnasiums, and performing arts facilities, using their financial resources to subsidize improvements in their educational programs. They exercised considerable discretion over who they admitted, generously distributing financial aid to broaden their racial and ethnic diversity, and, in some cases, awarding merit aid to students who would enhance their demographic mix but who were not necessarily in need of financial assistance. Accordingly, their selectivity increased. At Harvard, for example, a private, undergraduate college, the acceptance rate in 1940 was 85 percent; by 1970 it had dropped to 20 percent, and by the first decade of the twenty-first century it was down to 6 percent. In the emerging consumerism of higher education, top-tier colleges were able to maintain the primary market distinction that Charles Eliot had prescribed a hundred years earlier, that of providing a broad liberal arts education. Their graduates, emerging from among the best and most well-rounded students in the liberal arts pool, were always welcome at the top graduate and professional schools.

The next two tiers of liberal arts colleges, less affluent and less prestigious in brand value, were, however, more prone to the changing demands of the consumer market. In 1966 more than 80 percent of college freshmen polled said that the purpose of college was to develop a meaningful philosophy of life; by 1990 that figure had dropped below 50 percent. Conversely, pursuing a college degree for the purpose of being financially well off was cited in 1966 by 45 percent of freshman; by 1990 more than 70 percent reported that as their goal. Some of this shift undoubtedly was related to the rapidly rising costs of higher education during the late twentieth century—and to the related debt that many students were forced to incur. While the major part of student aid in the 1960s had been outright grants, by the 1990s it had switched to student loans. These economic changes contributed to students and their parents becoming consumers of education, utilizing the techniques of comparison shopping to determine the best "product." The percentage of American graduates majoring in traditional liberal arts disciplines fell from 38 percent in 1971 to 25 percent in 1995, forcing many small liberal arts colleges in the third tier—those unable to be selective given their relative lack of both wealth and high brand value—to transform themselves into schools offering pre-professional training rather than courses of free-standing intellectual interest.

The rise in student consumerism also brought with it an increased narcissism. Charles Eliot had introduced the free-electives curriculum at Harvard in the late nineteenth century as a means of infusing relevancy into the classical, prescribed curriculum of the antebellum college. One hundred years later however, free electives at many campuses had devolved into a curriculum of almost "anything goes." Liberal arts colleges established with the mission of promoting self-discovery, critical thinking, and the exploration of values, found students instead wanting to focus on occupational skills or the pursuit of personal interests, including such ephemeral knowledge as current events and pop culture. This trend, along with demands for courses in disciplines such as gender studies and ethnic studies as a consequence of the rise of multiculturalism and identity politics in the 1980s and '90s, created challenges for small colleges. Meeting new curriculum requests was usually a zero-sum game—additions in one required subtractions in another.

While a handful of such large, prestigious institutions as Harvard and Stanford attempted to buck the electives trend by returning to a core curriculum in the 1980s, Reed College simply stayed its traditional course, continuing to anchor responsibility for its core curriculum with its faculty, not its students. Reed, however, was not able to avoid the rising investments in security and administration required by new public policies that linked federal funding for colleges with the enforcement of strictures against underage drinking, illicit drug use, and sexual harassment. In addition, a national increase in the treatment of depression and attention deficit disorder with new prescription medications meant that more students were arriving at college with clinical profiles, requiring greater spending on student health services, counseling, and other support amenities.

As "brand value" became more important in the consumer culture, college-ranking guides began to wield enormous influence over the public's perception of the comparative worth of colleges and universities. To establish or maintain a competitive edge, many schools began to change their educational policies, inflate student grades, and quietly skew the data they provided to college-guide services in an effort to positively influence their place in the rankings. Under these conditions the growing stratification between first-tier and second-tier liberal arts colleges began to accelerate, with those colleges in the second tier becoming vulnerable to straying from their liberal arts missions in order to meet more utilitarian consumer demands.

At Reed, applicants had traditionally been viewed as largely self-selecting from a small but academically qualified pool, and therefore limited in number. In the early 1980s the college was admitting up to 85 percent of applicants. Final selectivity was, in a sense, administered after a student's admittance, as indicated by the college's high average attrition rate of more than 40 percent. As a culling mechanism, though, the system was emotionally brutal, and it tended to weed out a number of strong students for reasons other than academic performance. High attrition was also costly to the college, given the direct and indirect costs of finding qualified replacements by reaching deeper into its limited applicant pool. In the costly and competitive environment of higher education, Reed's low graduation rates placed it in jeopardy of falling academically into the newly endangered second tier of liberal arts institutions. The college's middling tuition pricing in the 1980s already reflected a second-tier position.

Beginning in 1989, that situation changed. Over a four-year period, Reed increased its tuition fee by 60 percent—from $11,000 to $18,000 per year—placing it among the top tier of elite liberal arts colleges in terms of price. Paradoxically, the price hike helped increase applicant demand, as it raised the college's perceived value. That perception was in turn supported by visible improvements to the college, made possible in part by the increased tuition income and in part by substantial growth of the endowment through savvy investments in a rising stock market. A successful $100 million fundraising campaign in the late 1990s furthered Reed's ability to claim a respectable, although still moderately endowed, position among top-tier colleges.

With improved finances, Reed was able to expand its recruiting efforts for new students while also reducing its high attrition rate, thanks in part to the construction of new dormitories, which expanded the proportion of students who lived on campus, and also to an increase in social and academic support services. In addition, investments were made toward returning the college to its historic ten-to-one student-faculty ratio, from the twelve-to-one ratio that had been adopted during the financial crisis of the mid-1960s. Faculty members were added in areas that expanded the curriculum, including interdisciplinary studies and a program in Chinese humanities. New funds also spurred a building boom on campus, resulting in new laboratories and classrooms, as well as a new auditorium. While Reed's relatively modest endowment still hobbled the college in such competitive areas as financial aid and the recruitment of ethnic minorities, its tolerance of difference served to foster greater diversification with sexual minorities in the emerging LGBTQ—lesbian, gay, bisexual, transgender, and queer—movement. Finally, in a bold decision that reinforced its iconoclastic reputation for academic integrity, Reed became the first top-tier college to voluntarily withdraw from participation in the country's leading college ranking service, published by the news magazine *U.S. News & World Report*.

Still, Reed being Reed, all of this transformative change would first have to be preceded in the early 1990s by a civil war among the faculty and a rift between some of the faculty and the president that together would propel the college into a major financial and governance crisis.

CHAPTER 36

Civil War

The administration was pushing a line that would have severely compromised the intellectual integrity of the college as a whole.
    —Robert Knapp, English professor

Members of the Old Guard were screeching like gored elephants.
    —Edward Segel, history professor

During his seventeen-year reign as president, Paul Bragdon had rescued Reed from financial disaster, dramatically increased the endowment sixteen-fold, expanded the curriculum by adding Asian studies, enhanced the arts, transformed student services, modernized the administration, and overseen a period of stability unprecedented in the college's history. Yet, a combination of factors ranging from a generational change in faculty leadership, to cultural changes in higher education, to the Reagan Administration's use of public policy to drive cultural changes on college campuses, left Reed with a host of underlying tensions.

Into this potentially volatile environment stepped a new president in 1988, James Powell, fresh from the presidency of Franklin and Marshall College in Pennsylvania. Southern-born, he had attended Berea College in Kentucky before earning his Ph.D. in geochemistry from MIT, after which he had taught at Oberlin College. Powell, a crusader for science education, arrived at Reed with the goal of safeguarding its accomplishments rather than changing its direction. His personal approach, however, helped raise the internal stresses at the college to the level of institutional turmoil, setting off a divisive battle among the faculty.

RAY KIERSTEAD, history professor 1978–2000: Jim Powell had had some severe problems at Franklin and Marshall College in Lancaster, Pennsylvania. He changed the fraternity system in some way, either challenging it or abolishing it. There was a lot of unrest on campus, and it turns out that he wasn't a beloved figure there. Of course, in the Reed context, a president who confronted fraternities was heroic.

The search firm that brought Jim Powell to

our attention passed along a request to Monford Orloff, a trustee who was chairman of the search committee, that Jim didn't want anyone going on campus to check him out. Nor were we to receive letters from within the Franklin and Marshall community. It was assumed that Powell did not want it known at Franklin and Marshall that he was on the market. Rightly or wrongly, the committee accepted this condition because Powell was vouched for by a set of very distinguished national academic figures, including Paul Bragdon, who knew him as a fellow member of an association of college presidents.

We could see a record of accomplishment for Powell, who, like the other two top candidates, went through very rigorous interviews. In the end he was the consensus candidate. The science faculty members were delighted to have a scientist as president. He had strong trustee support. On the search committee, there were three faculty votes against him, including mine. Retrospectively, we should have found out what was cooking on the Franklin and Marshall campus.

FRANK GWILLIAM, biology professor 1957–1996, provost 1979–1982: At his inaugural speech, Powell said, "I come to Reed not to change it but to preserve it." And then, as soon as he got the reins, he tried to change it. Powell, it turned out, was a control freak. He wanted to have his hands on everything. He had some good personal friends on the faculty and on campus, but he was not a people person, and didn't seem to be able to attract people to his way of thinking in a graceful manner, as Paul Bragdon before him had been able to do. He was authoritarian, and more of a manager and an attempted manipulator than a person who brought people along with him.

DELL RHODES, psychology professor 1975–2006, associate dean of students 1990–1991: Whoever was hired as president following Paul

President Jim Powell, early 1990s.

Bragdon's lengthy presidency was bound by circumstances to have a short tenure. He was a sacrificial lamb. But, given that, Jim Powell was a particularly unfortunate choice. When Powell came, he took on a lot of the issues that had not been addressed in Bragdon's final years—such things as sexual harassment, drug policies, hiring more women faculty, parental leave, and other policies that reflected social changes in the faculty—with a vengeance, and not very diplomatically.

ALAN DEAN '41, trustee 1973–1998: One of the first things Powell did was send a letter out to the trustees requesting that they not talk to students or faculty members without going through him. But, under the Reed constitution, the trustees *are* the college. The president is somebody we hire to be our chief executive. There wasn't a trustee on the board that wasn't offended by the letter. No trustee complied with it.

LAURENS RUBEN, biology professor 1955–1992: When Powell made his public performances, going out to speak to groups, he had all the right language. He was good. But when it came to dealing with the faculty it just didn't seem to work. I kept a record. Sixty-eight members of the administrative staff, out of maybe a hundred plus, resigned, were fired, or retired just to get out of Reed, during Powell's first couple of years.

THOMAS DUNNE, chemistry professor 1963–1995: Jim Powell decided that he didn't want inside people at high levels in his administration. He wanted his own people. So he conducted a nationwide search for the position of provost, which had been occupied by Marsh Cronyn '40 in chemistry. The winner of the national search for provost was a guy named Doug Bennett. Bennett was a straight, honest person, but because of the mechanism by which he came to us, lots of people were not willing to give him adequate respect. He was kind of doomed on arrival, painted with the label of being "Powell's man."

MARSH CRONYN '40, chemistry professor 1952–1989, provost 1982–1989: As the departing provost, I had looked at the structures of about fifty college administrations, and ours looked—on paper at least—just like a lot of the others. We had one faculty committee on personnel and another on curriculum. But at Reed those committees were elected by the faculty, not appointed by the president or provost as they were elsewhere, and charged with advising the president, not just with rubberstamping his decisions. Reed's provost served as the chair of the two faculty committees, but didn't get a vote. Whatever the vote, the provost was bound to honor the decision of the faculty committee.

Whenever I went to meetings of administrators from other colleges and described what I did as provost, they would look at me kind of funny and say, "But you're just a clerk."

DELL RHODES, psychology professor: The new provost, Doug Bennett, was an educational philosopher. He believed in certain kinds of principles, and liked to debate such things. A Quaker by heritage, he was as far from being a dictator as one could imagine. He was very much, as the Quakers are, a community consensus person.

DOUG BENNETT, provost 1989–1993: As I was preparing for my first set of interviews with the faculty, one of the things that really struck me immediately was a missing generation of professors. There was almost nobody who had arrived in the very late 1960s or early 1970s still on the Reed faculty. That just stunned me. It wasn't until later in my first year that I began to understand that the conflicts that had burst out in the college in the late '60s and early '70s had led to a number of tenure decisions that sent people on their way, or led other young faculty to say, "My future is not here."

The faculty on the older side were—not completely, but virtually—all men. The faculty who arrived after 1975, which is when hiring picked up again, were a somewhat more gender-balanced mix. It was still a very Caucasian group. I knew right from the beginning that one of the things to deal with would be to work on the composition of the faculty. I was very concerned about that missing generation.

DYLAN RIVERA '95: Doug Bennett was a champion of diversity in the curriculum. He felt as though the faculty was too entrenched in the old ways of doing things. He also believed that Reed needed to take sexual harassment and drug use among students on campus really seriously. That appeared to rub a lot of Reed professors the wrong way. They saw him as an outsider and maybe as an intellectual lightweight.

EDWARD SEGEL, history professor 1973–2011: Within perhaps a year of Jim Powell's arrival the college had to come up with a much stricter alcohol and drug policy, because Congress had passed the "Drug Free Schools and Communities Act." That meant things really had to tighten up in order for the college to continue receiving federal funds for financial aid. For many students, this was the end of the good old days, in which, for example, on warm sunny days a pickup truck would come to campus with a keg of beer that would be heartily welcomed by all. They couldn't do that anymore. Whenever there was a student function where alcohol was served, it had to be in a segregated area and students had to show their ID.

ROBERT MACK '93: The record for emptying a "sunny day" keg was eighteen minutes. Picture a churning mob of forty or fifty people, each with a cup, all reaching toward the center spigot, and once somebody gets their cup full of beer, they run off inside to their dorm and back to work!

As pressure from the authorities increased, people who were under twenty-one and who still wanted to consume alcohol had to go underground. They couldn't do it openly any longer in the presence of the community, so they ended up going in their closet and drinking a bottle of Jack Daniels before going out to a campus event. That made the situation worse. When people were drinking in the open, you looked out for friends as you hoped they would look out for you. But if people were drinking in private, nobody knew what they had been consuming, or how much.

BRET FETZER '87: The student handbook, written by students, included an entire section about drugs, called "Tips for Trips." It was actually very thoughtful and informative, with suggestions like, "Drink lots of water and take vitamins," as well as extremely funny. I personally was in favor of articles of that kind because, if students were going to take drugs, it was better that they be well-informed about what they were

taking. That was much more likely to prevent bad drug experiences than anything else.

Then William Bennett, who was the U.S. Secretary of Education at the time, and later the White House drug czar under President George H. W. Bush, publicly pointed to the Reed student handbook as an example of "decadence and moral decay" on college campuses. We all thought that was quite hilarious.

IGOR VAMOS '90: In 1989, William Bennett, the White House's drug czar, mandated that federal aid money to colleges would be cut off if they didn't comply with the new Drug Free Schools and Communities Act. It seemed to us like sort of an invasive civil-liberties issue. The policy didn't require piss tests, but as a political form of protest we staged a prank where we put urine sample cups in everybody's mailbox with these little code names and numbers. We instructed students that to comply fully with mandates coming down from the federal government they had to submit a urine sample directly to the president's office. It was all to send a clear message to President Powell of what we thought about his adoption of the policy.

PETER BRAY '94: A panic ensued over the urine test, especially among freshmen like me. Fortunately I caught on soon enough. But I did pass by the president's office on Sunday and saw stacks of the cups, replete with urine.

DOUG BENNETT, provost: There was not a functioning student conduct system at Reed. Susan Crim was the dean of students the year I arrived. I asked her, "Give me an example of something for which the college visited some consequence upon a student last year for some conduct issue. Anything." And she said, "I don't think there were any." "How about the year before?" I asked. She couldn't think of one. By now there was this incredible silence in the room. I said, "How far back do you have to go since the college ever visited any consequence on a student for any misconduct of any kind?" She said, "Well, I guess it was when students occupied a building and we had to call the police." At that point I realized that there wasn't a functioning conduct system—that the college had slipped into a kind of laissez-faire attitude toward student conduct.

ALEX GOLUB '95: We weren't necessarily anti-rules, but the entire idea at Reed was that the framework and rules should be created by the students. So to have the administration do something like say, "You should not do extremely illegal and extremely dangerous drugs," seemed really inflammatory to us.

GRAHAM JONES '97: In the Student Senate, we were trying to hash out the language of the drug and alcohol policy, rewriting documents that had been written by the college's lawyers who were getting paid hundreds of dollars an hour. It was a problem so much bigger than whatever we were going to hash out, because it involved laws that we didn't have any influence over. I could see that tying federal funding to prohibitions on the use of alcohol and drugs was creating many unnecessary social, cultural, and political conflicts over issues that didn't really matter that much. In the end, I just became very disillusioned by the whole thing.

PETER STEINBERGER, political science professor 1977– , dean of faculty 1997–2010, acting president 2001–2002: I was very unsympathetic to the interest in drugs and alcohol among the student body. That was one of the things about Reed that has never resonated with me. I was deeply involved in the new drug and alcohol policy, and wrote some central parts of it. I thought it was a good policy. First of all, it committed the college to being in compliance with the law. I don't think we had any choice. Second, it did so

not by saying that all drugs are the same or that all drug use is the same. It made what I regarded as sensible—difficult, arguable, complex, but sensible—distinctions between different kinds of drugs and different kinds of drug use so that to be in possession of distributable quantities of heroin was not the same as to be in possession of a can of beer, and indicating that the college would respond in different ways to different kinds of circumstances.

JON PETERSON '93: I really didn't think that it was appropriate for Student Services to get involved in people's choices that were their own responsibilities about how they wanted to live their lives. When I was student body president I worked on getting the drug policy more tied in with the Honor Principle, making sure that the student Judicial Board would resolve drug cases, rather than the administrators.

ROBERT KNAPP, English professor 1974– : For good reasons and bad reasons, a lot of students were not willing to consider a violation of something like the drug and alcohol policy an honor violation. If someone was selling drugs in the dorm, the tendency was to live and let live. That's kind of a perverse adaptation of John Stuart Mill's notions about how what you do affects only you, and doesn't injure me.

But it was clear that selling drugs injured the whole community. If you can't get members of the community to acknowledge that then you're in a peculiar relationship to the law at large. But I would much rather try to thrash it out on the level of conversation and making arguments about why it matters that policies against distribution are upheld, than to have a member of the administration be in the position of bringing cases to the student Judicial Board.

Of course, what happens then is that that body evolves from being a student-only Judicial Board to being a board that is partly staffed by administrative people. At least that's the way in which things have gone at almost every other institution. But if you go in that direction, you erode students' commitment to the institution, and it becomes more something that people just try to get around.

RORY BOWMAN '90: When I was a community safety officer on campus in the 1990s, I thought my job was to make sure that everyone led a fairly temperate life and got the help they needed if they had a drinking problem or whatnot, by suggesting to them or to their friends that they get counseling at the Health Center. I argued that, if we treated the drug and alcohol policy as a matter of public safety, temperance, and health, we would have less trouble with dealers, less trouble with overdoses, and a better understanding of the health aspects of the problem, meaning that we could take better care of the students. And the students would in turn take better care of each other if they trusted us. I very much lost that battle. The school started hiring a number of former cops as community safety officers, and they took a punitive war-on-drugs sort of approach.

NIC WARMENHOVEN '96: Jim Newhall was the doctor at the Health Center. He also maintained a part-time medical practice outside of Reed as a reproductive health doctor whose practice included performing abortions. In the mid-1990s a militant anti-abortion group published his name online among a list of doctors, making them targets for violence. But what made him controversial and difficult for the administration to deal with related to the new drug and alcohol policy. Newhall saw student drug use as a medical issue and wanted to treat students and work with their issues of addiction or unhealthy behavior. He probably didn't respond in all the ways that the college would have wanted him to, and so he was fired rather suddenly.

DELL RHODES, psychology professor: Jim Powell pushed very hard on the need for a clear drug and alcohol policy. He hired as the new dean of students Jim Tederman, who, as far as I was concerned, walked on water. Tederman was perfect for the job of managing the transition from a dean of students office that didn't do much to one that had to take on responsibility for enforcing drug and alcohol policies and getting the student Judicial Board to toe the line or else have its functions taken out of students' hands. He was a straight shooter, an honest cowboy. You might disagree with him, but you could never come to the conclusion that he was jacking you around.

MARY CATHERINE KING, health services director 1994–1997, associate dean of students 1997–2003, dean of students 2003–2007: Students of that era had been so completely on their own, so autonomous, and then Jim Tederman entered the scene to take charge of Student Services. Cowboy boots and jeans were Jim's standard attire. Students were sometimes intimidated and a little frightened of him. He could be a commanding presence. You didn't mess with Jim. And yet, he was so caring and so kind. He had had experience in another private, liberal arts school, Grinnell College, and he also had social work in his background, so he could think both administratively and clinically when he needed to.

He did his work with a lot of finesse, but, boy, that had to be a rough era for him, because there were several suicides during that time. I think he suffered tremendously with all of that. Not to mention that people were continuing to question whether we even needed Student Services. He was a gift to the campus, ultimately.

DOUG BENNETT, provost: Jim Tederman and I had a lot of searching conversations about student community life. We took to meeting once a week with my associate dean of faculty, Ellen Stauder, and Betsy Emerick, the dean of first-year students. The four of us would sit and talk about students in academic difficulty or students in social mayhem of one sort or another. It was really the first time in a long while that the academic side of the house and the community life side of the house had talked with each other routinely. It was a good thing to do.

STEVE MCCARTHY '66, trustee 1988–2009: It became an interesting social science issue: how do you change the culture of a place? Most institutions are incredibly resistant to change. Plus, Reedies are very smart, and very quick to smell a rat. The normal college cookbook solutions were absolutely non-starters with them. It had to be done in ways that were honest.

DELL RHODES, psychology professor: There were a number of trustees in the late 1980s who were proponents of the college expanding the reach of student services. They were very concerned about safety nets for students, both with respect to drug use on campus and with respect to academic performance and the high attrition rate at the college. Some of those trustees were very influential in pushing for the expansion of the student services office. Some of the faculty, however, were wont to refer to the expansion of student services as "neo-nannyism." There was even a little demonstration in which a bunch of folks walked around the quad wearing diapers.

DOUG BENNETT, provost: I was accused at one point of "neo-nannyism." I thought it was just hilarious. I think what they wanted was for the college to really have nothing to do with student life outside the classroom. And anything that went on outside the classroom amongst students, or between faculty and students, was not the college's business.

VIRGINIA OGLESBY HANCOCK '62, chemistry associate 1963–1980, music professor 1991– :

Once it became economically unfeasible to buy a house close by campus—given the rising real estate values in the 1980s and '90s—it changed the culture, particularly with the younger faculty, of students being in and out of faculty members' houses and in and out of their lives. It became much more of a situation for professors in which, "During the day I'm on campus, and when I go home to someplace across town, I'm gone." It didn't provide for the same kind of familial interaction.

RORY BOWMAN '90: Historically, student activities had been run by the Student Senate. The new Office of Student Services was an entire group of basically activity directors who tried to program activities for the students, who would then choose among them like on a cruise ship rather than generate them themselves. The students were no longer creating their own culture.

Students who worked for the student activities office were more like interns and less like entrepreneurs. The old system whereby people would come up with ideas and be given money to succeed or fail marvelously without any adult supervision had created more dynamic events and a greater sense of student autonomy.

DYLAN RIVERA '95: A male student was accused of rape in 1991. He was honor-cased and it was publicly known that he was accused, and many people on campus assumed that he was guilty. Part of the story was that there had been a one-night stand, and sometime after the fact the woman decided she had been raped. The question debated on campus was: "Is it possible to say way later that something was forced or to call it 'rape' when it may have been considered or indicated to be consensual at the time?"

HEATHER FRYER '89: There were two things going on. One was the expectation of a sort of radical gender egalitarianism, like "This is Reed and we've got this figured out." Then, underneath that, there was also a suspicion that we don't have it figured out, and so, as this really tight network of women, we're going to believe in gender egalitarianism and live it out, at least on the surface, but where it's broken down we've got each other's backs. It was a difficult time for women, who were very wary and distrustful of the reality behind the rhetoric. I imagine it might have been really tough also to be a man at that time.

RORY BOWMAN '90: When you're eighteen, nineteen, twenty years old, that simplistic sort of political ideological fundamentalism around feminism was very strong and very empowering for the people who were on the right side of it, and very confusing and intimidating for the people who were theoretically on the "wrong" side,

but weren't what we would call "perpetrators." As a man there was a lot of soul-searching.

ANJA LARSON '92: Women staged "Speak Out" events on the lawn in front of Eliot Hall. Many of them shared their most intimate personal sexual stories over a public address system broadcasting across the lawn. For those people who were willing and able to participate, it was a very powerful thing. Some women had terrible stories of being raped, for instance while traveling in Europe as naïve students.

MOLLY FRANKS '97: At a Speak Out women could get up and say whatever they wanted about the violence of discrimination they had experienced or express something about being a woman. There also were "Take Back the Night"

At Speak Out events in the 1980s and '90s women students publicly gave voice to their experiences with abuse and discrimination.

marches that were a part of Women's Week every year. Women walked around campus chanting and singing, placing stakes in the ground at different places where they had experienced violence or discrimination, and telling their stories. There was a men's candlelight vigil that happened at the same time. A group of men would stand in Eliot Circle and hold the vigil while the women marched around campus.

DYLAN RIVERA '95: At the Speak Out no rebuttal or discussion was allowed. It was like: "This is what happened to me. This was my experience, and therefore the expectation is that it will be affirmed and acknowledged." The organizers made it clear that a woman who claimed to be abused and made this public at the Speak Out couldn't be held responsible if it was slanderous.

PETER GOODMAN '89: It almost felt like the Cultural Revolution in China, in that there wasn't room for competing views, and people would be shouted down if they spoke up. There was something of a social fear that ruled at Reed at the time, that you would be caught not conforming to the dominant view.

REBECCA MCLAUGHLIN '90: Students at the time were taking more ownership of their own sexual behaviors than they had in the past, honor-casing each other for sexual harassment. Professors' sexual relationships with students also appeared to most people to be a really disproportionate power relationship. Women started honor-casing male professors who slept with female students.

LENA LENCEK, Russian professor 1977– : It was a difficult and divisive time because it raised very troubling issues for the college, having to do with personal integrity and with the jurisdiction of the institution in personal life. It was also part of the larger social climate at the time, which turned on national concerns about gender issues, power, and the role of sex in the classroom.

When I first came to Reed, there was a culture of interactions between faculty and students that was much looser. There were anecdotes and evidence of relationships between faculty and students. There were professors who married their students. That was not considered deviant or destructive. One trusted that the faculty acted responsibly. That all drastically changed in the 1980s. There was a complete sea change in the levels of social acceptability of behaviors that had been fairly standard, not only for Reed College, but for many academic institutions.

The trigger points came from several things. One was that a larger number of young women were hired for the faculty who brought their awareness of the inequalities in the marketplace to campus. Second, there was a generation of young women students who were also sensitized to these issues and who were not afraid to speak out when they felt themselves to be discriminated against, and who used or saw the college experience as an opportunity to find a voice and to put themselves into life, into the world, through their work rather than through their ability to manipulate sexual stereotypes.

What helped move that forward was the arrival of Jim Powell, who was willing to legislate these attitudes and to put some muscle behind them.

BILL PECK, philosophy professor 1961–2002: Powell was behind it, but he wasn't the only one. There were several strong-minded women on the faculty who thought that the male faculty members better toe the line and not fool around with the students.

DELL RHODES, psychology professor: I was serving as part-time associate dean of students in December of 1990, when Jim Powell called me into his office and said that a situation had arisen that he hoped I would be willing to help with. The gist of it was that an accusation of sexual harassment had been made in a letter from a faculty member to the Committee on Advancement and Tenure, or CAT, about a junior faculty member who was being considered for tenure that fall. The process of normal faculty review was not the appropriate channel for dealing with this accusation, but our system for handling complaints against faculty members was in sufficient disarray at the time that it wasn't entirely clear what the appropriate channels were. As president, Powell had to approve any tenure recommendation before it went to the Board of Trustees, and he felt that he would be unable to pass judgment on a recommendation to the trustees without knowing more about the situation.

Powell asked if I would be willing to serve on a two-person investigative team, along with a female attorney. In January of 1991, the attorney and I traveled to several locations to interview former students who had been identified as individuals who might have something to say about whether this particular faculty member engaged in harassing behaviors towards female students. We collected our materials and put them together into a report.

Powell informed the CAT that he had authorized an investigation, that a report would be forthcoming, and that it would go to them, the CAT, to determine whether it was to be forwarded to the Appeals and Review Committee only by Powell or by Powell and the CAT. The Appeals and Review Committee, which was made up of both faculty and trustees, needed to have enough time to consider the report before Powell was legally bound to forward his tenure recommendation to the trustees in April. In other words, things needed to be done in a timely fashion.

ROBERT KNAPP, English professor: I was a member of the so-called "CAT from Hell," which took the view that a decision to award tenure was separate from a decision to review someone's behavior, and that there was an extant process for reviewing behavior, specifically the grievance procedures in the constitution, which ultimately led to dismissal.

We had been aware for some time that our grievance procedure was not sufficiently fine-grained—that there needed to be a procedure that was more accessible and that allowed for intermediate outcomes, because the existing procedure seemed to allow only for the outcome of dismissal. There had been a judicial review committee at work on these kinds of proposals for institutional practices, but it hadn't completed its work when this crisis occurred.

DELL RHODES, psychology professor: Our report, forwarded to Powell in late January or early February, said that there was sufficient evidence for the possibility that sexual harassment had occurred and that the case needed to be properly vetted through the college's judicial procedure, meaning that it should go to the Appeals and Review Committee.

Instead of moving rapidly, the Committee on Advancement and Tenure sat on our report and initiated its own investigation. It also violated expectations of the confidentiality of CAT procedures by releasing to the faculty at large—with the accused's permission—a moderately detailed summary of what was going on. CAT did not make its decision about forwarding the harassment report to the Appeals and Review Committee until it was too late for that committee to unroll its own investigation in a timely fashion before the April trustees meeting.

RAY KIERSTEAD, history professor: The vote in the CAT was one vote in favor of the president's position and all the other votes in favor of granting tenure to the person. The feeling was that you had to have some kind of policy of disciplinary action in place if you were going to do anything about it. The accusation wasn't really a clear-cut case of assault or rape or anything like that. The person in question denied the impropriety of his behavior, rightly or wrongly. So that became the constitutional issue, whether this was a matter that rose to a level that would cause you to deny a person tenure.

Dell Rhodes, psychology professor: Powell was put on the spot. Despite the recommendation in favor of tenure from the CAT, he submitted a negative recommendation to the trustees, who accepted it. Meanwhile, in March of 1991, Jim Powell had been offered a job at the Franklin Institute, a science museum in Philadelphia, and he knew he was leaving. So this sensitive matter was being handled by a lame-duck president as his final act at the college.

Some of us on the faculty believed firmly that the way the CAT was behaving during the sexual harassment investigation was unconscionable. When the committee elections came around in the spring of 1991, a group of us got together and put forward a slate of candidates for the CAT in an effort to prevent the most serious offenders on the CAT from being reëlected. The slating was successful. All seven of the people who were elected to the CAT were from the slate.

Peter Steinberger, political science professor: The perception was that the CAT was dominated by the "Old Guard," and not sufficiently sensitive to the particular kind of issue raised in the tenure case. There was also a perception on the part of some members of the faculty that members of the Old Guard were being elected to the CAT for no very good reason except simply inertia. Since I was getting elected to the CAT in those years, I guess I was one of them.

When the election results came out, they were pretty surprising. New people were elected. I don't think that was a bad thing. Very good people were elected. But then the fact of slating came

out shortly thereafter, when one member of the faculty who had been contacted about voting for the slate ratted them out. If that hadn't happened, I'm not sure people would have known.

Well, my goodness gracious, all hell broke loose. Because the tradition, unwritten, completely unwritten, was that we didn't politic at Reed College. Slating was not a violation of any written rule, but it was, arguably, a violation of the unwritten tradition, the perceived unwritten tradition. We didn't organize. We didn't run for the CAT. We didn't organize to elect people to the CAT. We voted as individuals, independently, for other individuals based upon our individual views, not on what this person's particular politics, so to speak, were, but who this individual was, and what their qualities were as a colleague, as an intellect, and as a good member of this "guild" that we called the faculty at Reed College. So the perception by some members of the faculty was, "Oh, my God! This is a savage break of good faith."

Edward Segel, history professor: Prior to that election, slating had not been done at Reed for many years. There were a number of extremely contentious, angry faculty meetings. A couple of things impressed people like myself who were trying to maintain a position in the middle of this argument. On one hand, members of the Old Guard were screeching like gored elephants. They were very loud, very noisy, but they really did not have a strong case. On the other hand, the young progressives, including many women faculty members, had a better case, but they didn't make it well. It was quite clear in the many faculty meetings held on the issue that there was more oratorical ability on the conservative side than on the progressive side. The whole thing was really very nasty. Many scars were made.

Dell Rhodes, psychology professor: Three or four of us who had been identified as leaders

English professor Ellen Stauder teaching a conference, late 1980s.

of the "slaters" were targeted for venomous attacks by various male members of the senior faculty. There was nothing that forbade slating, but it was not okay with the old boys. According to them, it was an unacceptable political action.

I was one of the primary targets. Another was Ellen Stauder, professor of English and a part-time associate dean of faculty. Both of us had half-time administrative appointments. We were attacked mercilessly as being pawns of the administration. However, no one else in the administration was involved in this. Some of the senior faculty who attacked us at that time quit speaking to me. Some did not speak to me for several years. It was very, very unpleasant.

PETER STEINBERGER, political science professor: It was by far the worst time I ever experienced at Reed College. It was awful. And it was devastating to the college. Horrendous. It set us back years, and tore the faculty apart. And it trickled down to students. Enrollment dropped, because students were aware of what was going on. It had a negative effect on the academic program, because it was so distracting to faculty

members. Students knew that members of the faculty weren't talking to each other and were pissed off at each other, and it was a horrible, horrible situation. It was really a civil war, and I found it very unpleasant.

DELL RHODES, psychology professor: Many of the things Powell did were unavoidable for any person coming in as president at that particular time, and a couple of the things he did were actually courageous in terms of how quickly he moved forward and the stands he took. He came down hard on the drug and alcohol culture. That needed to happen, and he got the ball rolling on the enforcement aspect. We also got a sexual harassment policy passed after his presidency, and, after much debate about the faculty judicial system, our documents moved towards their ultimate form.

What was at issue was less what he tried to do than the style in which he tried to do it. He wasn't interactive enough. He liked to close himself in his office and communicate by email, at a time when that wasn't yet done by most. He really had difficulty talking to people, particularly if they were opposing him in any way. Personality-wise, he was just not the best choice. Still, the changes to the college under his administration, as uncomfortable as they were, were absolutely necessary. He basically came in with the mop and the bucket and cleaned up after a period of time in which it was impossible to move some difficult issues forward due to a combination of institutional inertia and good-old-boyism.

FRANK GWILLIAM, biology professor: At his last commencement, Powell castigated the faculty for being afraid of the "C word," by which he meant "change."

DOUG BENNETT, provost: After Jim Powell departed, Bill Haden, the vice-president of college relations, was appointed acting president. To help identify issues the next president needed to address, the Board of Trustees brought in a team of three consultants who were pretty distinguished people in American higher education—Bob Atwell, who had been president of the American Council on Education and president of Pitzer College; Elizabeth McKinsey, the sitting provost from Carleton College; and Stephen Weiner, the executive director of the Western Association of Schools and Colleges and a former provost and dean of Mills College.

AT REED magazine, "Report of Visiting Consultants," September 5, 1991: We found Reed College to be a deeply troubled institution. The underlying pathology has been unaddressed for many years. Jim Powell did not cause the problems now facing the college, nor will his departure help solve any of them.

ROBERT KNAPP, English professor: Two of the three consultants had served previously on the Western States accreditation group—chaired by Jim Powell—which had visited Claremont-McKenna. The consultants came back with a re-

port that essentially condemned the faculty as being dysfunctional and the institution as not at all being up-to-date in its way of dealing not only with harassment issues but also with student life, and with faculty governance.

They recommended revising the constitution to establish a system where the president would have a completely independent voice in tenure decisions. They also recommended strengthening the role of the dean of faculty. In essence, they proposed transforming Reed's governance system into something that looked a lot more like the governance system at most other colleges and universities in the country.

AT REED magazine, "Report of Visiting Consultants," September 5, 1991: The pure intellectual ethos of the college, which quite consciously rejects concepts such as education of the whole person or cocurricular dimensions of college life, is out of sync with the realities young people face today—substance abuse, broken families, changing gender roles and expectations.

DYLAN RIVERA '95: The consultants' report was a massive indictment of student life at Reed. The student body president at the time, Jon Peterson '93, regarded the whole report as an affront, a big offense, a misunderstanding of what Reed was about, and an attempt to justify more parental-type oversight and a growth in Student Services and administrative control of student life.

JON PETERSON '93: We looked at the administration encroaching on what we believed to be the students' rights and liberties, and we saw some parallel between what we were going through and what the faculty was going through. The administration was also trying to corporatize the faculty, to make a curriculum that would compete better in what they believed to be the market for higher education. The real problem was that we felt as though the administration was seeking a corporate rebranding of the school, and that all these policies they were instituting really dovetailed back into this point, from the increases in the bureaucracies down to the drug policies and the curriculum.

ROBERT KNAPP, English professor: One issue the consultants objected to strenuously was the peculiar role of the president at Reed. The president is simultaneously a member of the faculty and a member of the Board of Trustees, and serves as the faculty's representative to the board. What this means in practice is that, if the president does not have the kind of relationship with the faculty that enables him or her to responsibly represent the faculty to the trustees, he or she cannot remain in office. It doesn't take a vote of no confidence, it simply takes a sense of responsibility and a sense of understanding what one's real role is as a bridging figure between the board and the faculty.

The consultants wanted us to get rid of that aspect of the constitution. A group of rogue members of the CAT from Hell—John Tomsich in history, Sam Danon in French, Steve Arch and Maryanne McClellan in biology, and me—put together a rebuttal to the consultants, objecting to their conclusions and recommending that the faculty reject them, which they did by a very substantial margin, ending the most important constitutional crisis since the firing of Stanley Moore in the early 1950s.

COMMITTEE ON ADVANCEMENT AND TENURE, "Memorandum," August 31, 1991: The report issued by the consultants is a whitewash of the Powell presidency at Reed, which blames the senior faculty for driving him out of the college. It is difficult to resist the inference—based on these consultants' prior acquaintance and working relationship with him—that Mr. Powell recommended these two administrators, knowing full well what they could be expected to say.

STEVE MCCARTHY '66, trustee: The initial search firm hired for the presidential search was linked to the consultants who had issued the report. They apparently felt, going in, that they had a duty to correct Reed's errant ways, and the consultants' report manifested this attitude. I chaired that search, and felt that we needed a certain kind of skilled help and not another irritation from our search consultant. We parted company with them partway through the search, and retained another firm that actually *liked* Reed. They were very helpful. The search statement—laying out what we were looking for in a new president—was a product of the Reed search committee as a whole, as it should have been. There was no intellectual pathway from the consultants' report to that statement. The contrary was probably more nearly the case.

DYLAN RIVERA '95: One big reaction on the part of the trustees to the consultants' report was the establishment of the Gray Fund. John Gray, a longtime board member and supporter of the college, with his wife, Betty, established a $2 million endowed fund to support student life. The committee created to initiate it included students, faculty, and staff. I joined the committee as a student member, and became the chair. Our plan for the Gray Fund was to have a variety of big, infrequent events and smaller-scale, more frequent activities, to enrich students' lives and get them out of the library for a few hours.

The political environment on campus at the time, though, was very charged with suspicion of Jim Tederman and Student Services. A student group called the "Guerilla Theatre of the Absurd" put on a protest during meals in the Commons during Parents Weekend. They had students dress up in black with armbands that read "SS" for "Student Services," and goose-step two-by-two in this lockstep formation around the Commons, as though they were police patrolling to make sure no one was misbehaving.

CHAPTER 37

Benevolent Dictatorship

What we had seen during Powell's administration in the early 1990s may have been the last big battle for the faculty-led college.
   —Karen Perkins-Butzien, assistant to the dean of faculty

There was this fear about selectivity, and the loss of what I considered to be the myth of self-selection.
   —Chris Moses '02

As had been true in previous periods of institutional turmoil at Reed, specifically during the struggle with McCarthyism in the 1950s and the curriculum battles in the late 1960s, the faculty governance crisis during Jim Powell's presidency led students to flee the college. The exodus, exacerbated by a national economic recession, precipitated a drop in tuition revenue and plunged the college into a new financial crisis.

In 1992, Steven Koblik came to Reed as its thirteenth president. A scholar of Swedish history, Koblik had been a faculty member at Pomona College for more than twenty years, and just prior to coming to Reed had served for three years as dean of faculty at Scripps, a college for women in the Claremont Colleges. He had earned a B.A. from the University of California at Berkeley, an M.A. from the University of Stockholm, and a Ph.D. from Northwestern University.

Koblik's main priority was to address the financial crisis, and then to set about healing the faculty rift created during the Powell administration. He was able to make a significant change in the roles of the two elected faculty committees, empowering both of them, as representative bodies, to make decisions without a vote of the full faculty. This change significantly improved the efficiency of faculty governance, as it meant that a number of issues no longer had to be debated among the entire faculty. But it also contributed to the faculty as a whole being less engaged in the overall administration of the college, an effect that was reinforced by faculty members' increased interest in their own research.

During a dramatic upswing in the stock market in the early 1990s, the college's endowment, under the management of trustee and future board chairman Walter Mintz '50, soared from $116 million in 1992 to $349 million by 2000, augmented by a successful $100 million fundraising campaign. The money helped Koblik fund a new building boom on campus not seen since the Sullivan administration in the early 1960s, and to expand the ranks of the faculty in an initiative to officially return the college to its original ten-to-one student-faculty ratio. A concentrated effort was also made to increase the student graduation rate, which rose from 66 percent in 1991 to 75 percent in 2001.

STEVE MCCARTHY '66, trustee 1988–2009: We gave Steve Koblik a list of the things that were broken at Reed, and basically said, "Please come here and fix these things." And, in short order, he did so, brilliantly. In an odd way it was easier because the things that needed to be fixed were so glaring. Koblik, though, really understood Reed intuitively. He was very bright and very verbal, but he could also be kind of a bulldozer when necessary.

STEVEN KOBLIK, president 1992–2001: In accepting the job I was fully aware that there were difficulties in the faculty, although I didn't know exactly what they were, and that there were financial difficulties, although I was not told the full extent of those difficulties until just before I arrived. The students were leaving in droves. Between the first and the second semester of President Powell's last year, Reed had lost almost 150 students, which was an extraordinary economic blow to the college.

Reed had had to lay off 8 percent of the staff just before I arrived. That was very difficult and traumatic. I gave both the staff and the faculty six weeks to give me ideas to balance the budget, as I wasn't going to sustain a deficit. I had the chief financial officer, Ed McFarlane, run open seminars, and I had a suggestion box and got lots of ideas. As my contribution in this context, I volunteered to raise more money than had been put into the budget. Because of a variety of factors, by mid-winter of my first year we knew that the economic crisis had passed and that we were fine.

The most important problem that I confronted when I became president was restoring among the faculty and the student body a sense of purpose and mission and a capacity to move ahead, to make Reed what they both wanted Reed to be.

LAURENS RUBEN, biology professor 1955–1992: Koblik was such a people person that it didn't matter whether it was students, faculty, rich guys, poor guys, he could interact well with everybody. He spent a lot of time taking faculty members out to lunch to get to know them better, or meeting with them for a beer after classes. There was nothing standoffish about Steve. He was a big person, and I don't mean just physically. He came at you full on, and he impressed you. He certainly impressed me. He had a sense of what he wanted the mission of the college to be, and he saw to it that it came out that way. He did a lot of arm twisting to make sure that the college stayed strong.

HARRIET WATSON, director of public relations 1984–1991, vice-president for public affairs 1991–2002: If a member of the faculty was unhappy with Steve, he didn't triangulate. He would get out of his office, walk over to the person's office, and say, "Let's take a walk, and talk."

He just dealt with things head on and was able to move the school forward in some very meaningful ways. People thought it was going to take a decade before the rifts from the Powell era were mended. Within a year of Steve's arrival, there was a civility again that was quite remarkable.

DYLAN RIVERA '95: During the first week of classes Koblik had an ice-cream social with each dorm group in turn, over at the president's house in Eastmoreland. You're having ice cream with the president, and he just wants to talk with you about whatever you want to talk about, and take questions and just be kind of casual. It was like, "Wow! This guy is not a stuffed shirt."

Then you learn a little bit more about, oh, he's married to a Swedish wife, he's into the Social Democratic Party in Sweden, which is really the vanguard of liberalism, and he really gets the liberal quasi-socialist politics that resonate with Reedies. This guy was sort of like one of us, but he could look good in a suit and raise millions of bucks. Until then, it never occurred to a lot of students that it might be possible to call the president by his first name, whereas they were used to calling the professors by their first names. That was really a great breakthrough that served Koblik well.

DELL RHODES, psychology professor 1975– 2006, associate dean of students 1990–1991: Steve was wonderful, but he was a Teflon president. It was very hard to get a purchase on him. He was a benevolent dictator at a time when the faculty had just had a major bloodletting and needed a period to disarm, and he did an excellent job in that role.

Faculty meetings prior to Koblik's arrival had been exercises in performance art as much as anything else. There were skilled rhetoricians on the faculty, and a good deal of what happened in faculty meetings was the endless rehashing of points, some of which needed to be made, but they were often made again and again in rather lengthy oratorical presentations. Documents that came to the faculty for approval were shredded on the basis of where commas should be and the choice of words, as well as on underlying principle.

KAREN PERKINS-BUTZIEN, assistant to the dean of faculty 1988– : Koblik had an ability to shut the faculty up in these meetings without them taking issue with it. It was just his manner, his way of communicating, sort of like the jester. He ran the faculty meeting in a way that didn't lend itself to extensive discussion. People didn't know what had happened until it was too late. There was a vote taken at the first meeting he held, and the faculty had made a decision without a discussion and a battle. And no one seemed to notice.

HARRIET WATSON, vice-president for public affairs: Steve Koblik was wonderfully consultative, though he would say that it wasn't a participatory democracy; somebody had to make decisions.

STEVEN KOBLIK, president: I insisted that everybody in the community get far more information than had normally been the case—either at Reed or at any other college institution—because of my own understanding, which developed from studying Sweden. One of the clear secrets to Sweden's success as a modern industrial state was the fact that it operated in a very open fashion, making information readily available to almost anyone who wanted it on almost any topic, and making a real attempt to develop consensus in the decision-making process.

Now, in a college where different constituents within the community have different responsibilities, "participatory" cannot mean a full egalitarian democracy. But if "participatory" means that each of the constituent elements has a right to understand what's going on, and also to be able to reflect on that and to offer advice to whichever groups have the responsibility for making the decisions, then yes, I believe in the participatory system.

I had a very high tolerance for different viewpoints. In fact, I had been raised to make arguments that were radically opposed to each other about the same issue with equal conviction, to the point where most people would not be able to recognize what I really believed—presuming of course that I *had* any belief. The benefit to that approach over time is that you begin to understand the complexity of an issue, and are patient enough to wait until it becomes clear that certain options are more attractive than others. So the consensus of a group comes both in terms of reaching a particular solution, but also in accepting a process in which people felt comfortable with their input, and feel comfortable with the decision even when it isn't the decision that they might have preferred.

DELL RHODES, psychology professor: One of the main things Koblik did was empower the two elected faculty committees—the Committee on Advancement and Tenure, or CAT, and the Committee on Academic Policy and Planning, or CAPP—at the expense of the faculty as a whole. He said that these elected committees should have the ability to make decisions about the things in their domain, and that while the faculty as a whole should be informed of those decisions, they should not necessarily be asked to approve them.

After that, faculty meetings moved towards being primarily informative—"Here's what happened in the meetings of your committees," or "Here are the latest policies we've agreed to." Occasionally discussions happened in faculty meetings, but increasingly the faculty abnegated responsibility for serious discussions of principled issues to the committees.

At the time, the faculty was sick of endless debates and the interpersonal intensity those de-

President Steven Koblik meeting with students, including Tim Solomon '96 (left) and Robin Tovey '97 (center), mid-1990s.

bates often generated, and they were more than happy to let decisions get made, and to return to the classroom and to their scholarship. And for a few years it was, overall, good in terms of getting things done. But after that, the pendulum needed to move back towards a system of principled discussion, on occasion at least. And it didn't.

KAREN PERKINS-BUTZIEN, assistant to the dean of faculty: One of the things that I felt had made Reed great was the desire to get down and dirty with ideas and discussions and be forced to hammer things out, so that you ended up with the best possible result. Prior to the conflicts of the Powell administration, faculty members did have their hands in the administrative elements of the college. In the years that followed, they tended to be less involved. Apathy became a trend among the faculty with regard to who ran the college. What we had seen during Powell's administration in the early 1990s may have been the last big battle for the faculty-led college.

MARVIN LEVICH, philosophy professor 1953–1994, provost 1972–1979: The general attitude of the faculty in the 1990s was reflected in what one faculty member said at an emergency meeting we were called to. "You know, I don't want to mess around with this," she said. "I've got my work to do."

ROBERT KNAPP, English professor 1974– : Reed's kind of forum democracy of faculty governance had been quite crucial for the college's identity, and yet it became increasingly harder to maintain for two primary reasons. One was the growing dependence on federal funding. The more one is dependent on federal dollars the more careful you have to be on a whole range of things. The college's ability to resist federal incursions into our notion of academic freedom was a consequence of this dependency. The 1980 Solomon Amendment, requiring male stu-

dents to register for the draft to maintain federal funding, was also an aspect of that, and the drug and alcohol policy adopted in the early '90s was another.

The second reason was the pressure to professionalize among the faculty, which made it less likely that faculty members were willing to just stand up and debate. They didn't want to take the time to come to faculty meetings. They were less ready to feel that their identity as an intellectual was at stake in an assault on the institution, because of course their identity was not exclusively that of a member of the institution. It was as a member of the academic profession at large.

ROBERT REYNOLDS, physics professor 1963–2002: When Jim Powell was president he explicitly introduced the notion that publication should play a more important role in faculty advancement and evaluation than it had prior to that time. In some respects that was helpful, but its explicit overt emphasis made younger faculty who were interested in getting tenure feel that they should be putting all of their energy into publication and teaching, leaving the governance aspects to take a back seat. That's largely because they were coming from institutions where the faculty was not involved in the governance of the place.

During my own second year at Reed, I got assigned to the Public Affairs Board, a joint student-faculty committee responsible for bringing visitors to campus for purposes of stimulating awareness of public affairs. That was a minor responsibility, but it made me realize that faculty members were expected to do things that had to do with the larger life of the community. Later, functions like that were taken over by the expanded administration.

DELL RHODES, psychology professor: The teaching mission of the college didn't seem to have the same vocal proponents that it had when I started. I took the option of teaching large numbers of students, being very involved in campus events, and focusing on "community service" in campus governance over a long period of time. Some number of people continued to follow that model, but the "get grants and publish your books" role models were much more visible. Furthermore, several faculty members began to be away from the college a lot, doing research. Most were on campus enough to meet the "residence rule," but their primary contributions to the college were their reputations as scholars. While there should be a few individuals contributing at that level, their visibility and the acknowledgments they received made young faculty members feel that they all had to become that kind of scholar, too.

ROBERT KNAPP, English professor: If you look at the set of people in the generation that joined the faculty in the 1970s and early '80s, not a one of us had published significantly until we got tenure, and nobody published a book until after they'd gotten tenure. You'll also notice that every one of those books has clear evidence within it of influence from the effects of teaching at Reed—from having to explain oneself to people not in one's field, to having to confront various kinds of problems of interdisciplinarity, to feeling obliged to get at the conceptual heart of a problem rather than just do something that is on the edge of where the field is moving at any particular moment in time. That now changed.

LAURENS RUBEN, biology professor: Doing research keeps your mind active and keeps you in the mode of asking questions, answering questions, and constantly honing your own analytic skills. That puts you in a better position then to teach students these things. At another level, you are a role model and your students are being encouraged to follow a research paradigm in teaching and so as students they see what that

role model is like. The teacher-scholar model is ideal for a place like Reed, because we encourage our students to think about graduate school and about professional school.

PETER STEINBERGER, political science professor 1977– , dean of faculty 1997–2010, acting president 2001–2002: I felt that we should resist both the teaching model and the research model, and develop a third way of understanding that at Reed we were there to teach and train young minds. That was what made us who we were. But you can't do that unless you, yourself, as a faculty member, are modeling scholarly behavior. We were not trying to produce scholars. We were trying to produce people who enter the world with a scholarly mindset, with a cast of mind that is critical, that is intellectual, that is conceptual, that thinks about things.

In order to teach students to do that we ourselves had to be scholarly, and that meant we had to engage in scholarship. The rubber hit the road when we evaluated the faculty members. We were not interested in the quantity of scholarship. We were not even that interested in the prestige of the publications. We were interested in the quality of the publications even if they were relatively few in number, and we were interested in examining the degree to which the scholarship, assuming it to be outstanding, actually manifested itself in positive ways in the classroom.

That was different from what the life of a faculty member was at an Amherst, a Pomona, a Williams, a Wesleyan, where things were much more oriented towards the kinds of outside, professional, publication-oriented activities that would be characteristic of a large college.

STEVEN KOBLIK, president: Because of the difficulties that had occurred during the two years prior to my arrival, some of the faculty thought Provost Doug Bennett was wonderful and some thought Doug was terrible. My own view was that I needed to move on. So I asked Doug if he would consider retiring out of that job, which he did, because he was a wonderful person and understood what I needed to do. That decision was unfair to Doug, because I didn't give him a chance to show what he could do. But I needed to ground that position as a deanship in the faculty constitution, and not simply as the administrative vice-president and provost position that it had been.

Doug Bennett, provost 1989–1993: When Steve Koblik told me that he wanted me to end my term of service as provost, I wasn't a tenured member of the faculty. I couldn't stay at Reed. When Jim Powell had offered me the job, he said that Reed had never tenured anyone from the outside directly on arrival, but we could work on that after I arrived. Well, we never did. That would not be the case at any other institution of higher education I know of. You wouldn't bring a chief academic officer from the outside and not tenure them. That put me at risk.

Steven Koblik, president: The Reed faculty wouldn't countenance anyone from within the faculty becoming the first constitutionally based chief academic officer. The hostilities that existed before I came continued at a level that made it impossible to select somebody inside. Another person from outside the faculty, Linda Mantel, who was really a pleasure to work with—an extraordinarily generous human being, and smart—served in the position for three years. It was only after Linda retired in 1996 that Peter Steinberger, who taught political science at Reed, was elected in the next search process. By that time the faculty had moved to a point where you could appoint an internal candidate.

Alex Golub '95: Peter Steinberger was a very strong personality. As far as I could tell, he hat-

ed actually assigning any work in class. He just wanted us to read Plato and talk about it. To appease the administration, we had to write a five-page paper at the end of class, the topic of which was, "How does language function as the horizon of a hermeneutic ontology?" Extreme jargon aside, it was sort of shocking that he was asking people who were twenty years old to answer that question, and equally shocking that, by the end of the class, we could do it.

Peter Steinberger, political science professor, dean of faculty: The main job of the dean was to support the faculty, to put faculty members individually and collectively in a position where they could do what they wanted to do as effectively as possible—and to function to the degree possible as a lubricant between the faculty and the president, to help the faculty talk to the president and the president talk to the faculty. And that was it. That was the whole job.

That said, faculty members had all kinds of different views about all kinds of different things they wanted to do. They were very contradictory. Some of the faculty felt we should do "X." Others thought we should absolutely not do "X." So pulling that all together was a big job. I had a tremendous amount of help, but it took up big chunks of time.

Steven Koblik, president: Peter Steinberger was a spectacular dean and a first-rate scholar and teacher. He and I often disagreed, but we were able to have good arguments. We developed a deep respect for one another. It was clear who was the dean and who was the president, and in terms of faculty matters, obviously Peter had the last say, and in terms of college matters, I did.

At one point I decided, rather unexpectedly, that we had developed enough financial capacity that we could add fifteen faculty positions. This was a huge increase in the faculty, and it would move the student-faculty ratio closer to ten-to-

Long-serving trustees Dan Greenberg '62 and Walter Mintz '50 in the late 1990s.

one. It was about twelve-to-one at the time. I told Peter that I was ready to try to do that, and asked him how he was going to go about adding the positions. He said, "I want to run some open discussions with the whole faculty, and I will lead those discussions. And I want to discuss what principles the faculty should use in adding positions. And then once the faculty approves the principles, we'll ask everyone in the community — faculty, students, staff—to make any recommendations for new positions based on those principles."

He looked at me and said, "What do you think?" And I said, "I think you're out of your mind. That is the most complicated process I've ever heard in my life." And he said, "I can do this." And he did.

KARL HITTELMAN '58, trustee 1990–1994: It happened to be a terrific time in the stock market in the early 1990s, and Reed's endowment just exploded. There was a sense of relief at the college since that took some of the financial pressure off. It was wonderful that a member of Reed's Board of Trustees, Walter Mintz '50, who later became the board chair, was a leader in the development of hedge funds, and that there were others on the board who could also do that kind of magic with investments.

LARRY LARGE, vice-president of college relations 1982–1987, 1992–1999: During the Bragdon years we operated through a lens of, "We've got to figure this out, we've got to get this place stabilized. It's too good to mess up." The focus was on building the endowment.

Then, in the Koblik period, we got this new generation of students, and a new set of opportunities. When we launched the $100 million capital campaign in the 1990s, the question was, "How do we take this campaign and design it in a way to make a distinguishing statement about the distinctiveness of the institution?"

NIC WARMENHOVEN '96: Steve Koblik was great at raising a crap-load of money. And building. He built! He took a lot of teasing from students, that all he cared about was buildings, not students, which of course was not true. But definitely, the face of the campus changed quite a bit. Koblik really took on improving the physical plant.

STEVEN KOBLIK, president: One of the things going on nationally was that an enormous amount of money was going into improving the quality of facilities. What we were seeing was changing the nature of the competition for really good students. The Reed campus was, by comparison, really shabby. The facilities were quaint and they were "old Reed," but they were beat up and rundown, and not particularly attractive. We needed to do something about them.

Much of what we did in the '90s was related both to attracting students to Reed and to keeping them there. The re-doing of the dining facilities and the creation of Kaul Auditorium were very much in that vein. There was some unhappiness that Kaul Auditorium was a music venue. The dance faculty and the theatre faculty were not happy, because they were working in inadequate facilities. That decision was mine. I wanted to make sure that what we did was good, and therefore I didn't want an auditorium that met everybody's needs and nobody's needs simultaneously, and I opted for music.

Also, students were wanting to be on campus and there weren't enough beds for them. So we also added a whole variety of new residence halls on the Reed campus. The internet was just taking off and we could provide access on campus, but not to off-campus students. The chemistry department had gotten a big new building just before I got there and the biologists were envious. So we built a spectacular new building for biology. We also added a computer science building to meet the needs of the growing interest in computer science at Reed. And then we expanded the art building because of growing demand in that area.

When I came I had promised I wouldn't build any more buildings before meeting our human needs, but I managed to deal with both the human needs and the building needs. So it was a good run.

JESSICA LEE PATTERSON '96, art professor 2009–2010: What I liked most about the "old" Reed was the grunginess of it. Everything was grimy and covered with graffiti. I loved it! Aesthetically, I didn't care for a lot of the new buildings going up on campus. I understood why they had to do it, because as they kept raising the price of tuition they had to make it look more fancy and collegiate for the parents paying the bills, but I missed all those old spaces that were very much student spaces and felt very comfortable for us.

JEREMY STONE '99: When I arrived at Reed in 1995 it was a dirty, alternative, fun place where you could do whatever you wanted. By 1999, it was a very different place. The school started changing the appearance of the physical structures. They also set out to change the culture at Reed. The way the school marketed itself changed. Reed made a concerted effort to become competitive with other top-tier liberal arts colleges. As a result, the student body was also changing.

RICHARD JONES, history professor 1941–1982, 1985–1986: Starting in the 1980s the emphasis had shifted to selling the college to potential students, rather than relying on the kind of word-of-mouth and general knowledge that used to pass around about Reed's unusual quality and distinction. Of course, that was not just true of Reed College, it was true of what was going on generally in higher education. The emphasis was really on student success of a particular type, not conceived of in terms of being a member of a community in which you are stimulated in a kind of way that you wouldn't be in most other places. The new emphasis for the student became focused on his or her individual performance.

THOR PRICHARD '97: The admissions material just seemed to be this huge farce. There was no way that the Reed depicted there was really what Reed was like, because there were always pretty, airbrushed pictures with perfect students. It almost made me feel like I shouldn't be there because it was too pretentious. But when I visited as a prospective student and stayed overnight in the dorms, I came upon one of the student handbooks, this sort of unofficial guide to Reed and its culture, published by students. It was, bar none, the best admissions material ever, with articles on topics like "the law and your arse," "the good, the bad, and the ugly of recreational drugs," and "the power of patchouli when correctly used." It was perfect, unfiltered, and authentic.

GRAHAM JONES '97: There was definitely an ambient perception on campus in the 1990s that Reed had been, for a long time, a kind of bastion of bohemianism and counterculture intellectualism, and that it was going to become somehow engulfed by a kind of stultifying ethos of middle-class aspirations. When I first got to Reed, most of the people that I looked up to had been enrolled at Reed off and on for six, seven, or even eight years. They were just hanging out in Portland and doing all these crazy things. But by the time I left, most people I knew were in and out in four years, and on to internships and graduate or professional school.

JEFF PARKER, economics professor 1988– : In the 1970s and '80s, during Paul Bragdon's administration, Reed was in the second tier of selective liberal arts colleges in terms of tuition fees. Our tuition in 1988–89 was $11,240, while the tuition level of our aspirational comparison schools was thousands higher. President Powell established a policy of raising tuition by $2,000 per year for three years, bringing us up above $18,000 and into the middle of our aspirational peers, such as Carleton, Oberlin, Swarthmore, Haverford, Amherst, and Williams. That big increase in tuition was also accompanied by expanded financial aid. At the same time, he increased faculty salaries, after finding that our salaries were below the level of the schools with which we wanted to compete.

DAN GREENBERG '62, trustee 1975– : We were able to begin benchmarking Reed for the first time against other colleges, thanks to the hiring of Jon Rivenburg as director of institutional research, a position that my wife, Susan, and I had funded at the urging of Paul Bragdon before he left the college.

JEFF PARKER, economics professor: The size and quality of Reed's applicant pool grew during the years of tuition increases. However, to attribute the growth in admissions to the price increase would be risky and probably wrong. Many other variables changed along with tuition price. Additional resources were spent wisely on improvements in faculty and staff support, expansion of the library, upgrading of dormitories and food services, and other changes that improved the quality of the Reed experience in both highly visible ways and less visible ones. Reed also increased the aggressiveness with which we targeted prospective students.

CHRIS MOSES '02, admission staff 2003–2005: There was this fear about selectivity, and the loss of what I considered to be the myth of self selection. Certainly some of the objective criteria for selecting students, whether SAT scores or class rank, went up. It was not done in a way that was meant to change the character of the institution, but to respond to the unspoken pressure that was coming from faculty who were frustrated with having crappy students. They wanted really smart students, and it was annoying to them when a third of the kids couldn't make it academically for one reason or another.

ROBERT MACK '93: Reed historically had taken chances on admitting people, myself being one. While that may have been an inherent risk for the retention rate, that risk also created the character and color of the campus that allowed for spontaneity, change, and newness. For example, in physics there are controls. But you can't have something that's very predictable and at the same time is responsive and adaptive to new things. To some degree you need response instability. To get that you've got to take chances.

So, to the extent that the administration began pushing for guaranteed graduation, with students going straight through by the book, they were sacrificing something.

DAN GREENBERG '62, trustee: Reed always gloried itself on the notion of having people outside of the normal boundaries, people who, aside from being smart, had arcane interests or who had led lives that were not necessarily completely normal, and who would bring a little vim and vigor, add some piss and vinegar to the place. That was a really important part of what the college was. To preserve Reed's independence and to give the college future vitality, I and a couple of other trustees began to put some serious money to work in the admissions area. We realized that we needed to have a much broader cross-section of people in the way of applicants to choose from in filling the college with the sort of "ideal" Reed student, and not be totally dependent on just a small group of people. It's my perception that the student body has not changed all that much in the fifty years since I graduated. And that is something really beautiful to behold.

JON PETERSON '93: We viewed Reed as a very Darwinistic environment. The fact that a lot of people didn't make it through Reed was part of what Reed was about. If you didn't like it, you should go someplace where everybody got As and everybody got to graduate.

JON RIVENBURG, director of institutional research 1988–2011: Reed had been studying the issue of high attrition for twenty years. Back in 1973, music professor Fred Rothchild had issued a report that looked at attrition between 1960 and 1972 in relation to student SAT scores. He found that Reed wasn't only losing weak students, it was also losing students with perfectly acceptable and wonderful grades. In 1975 there was another document, the Pitzer Report, which compared Reed with a group of nineteen other liberal arts schools, including Stanford and Princeton. The results were quite embarrassing. Stanford was graduating 80 percent of its students in four years, Princeton 70 percent, and Reed about 25 percent.

In the 1980s Gary Conner, a Reed registrar, did some amazing analysis on student attrition with a psychology thesis student, David Harris '84. They found that a number of students left Reed because of dissatisfaction with the social environment. Most of the literature on retention spoke to the fact that improved retention was highly correlated with residential community.

ED MCFARLANE, controller and assistant treasurer 1973–1978, vice-president and treasurer 1979– : When I came to the college in the early 1970s, about 50 percent of the student body was able to live on campus. Thirty years later, after the college dramatically increased the capacity of the on-campus beds with five new dormitories, that was up to almost 70 percent. We found that for students who lived on campus not only was the retention rate higher, but they also performed better academically. So, becoming more residential helped strengthen the academic program.

LARRY LARGE, vice-president of college relations: The millennial student generation—those students born after 1982—brought a different culture to the college and a different set of expectations from their parents. There was more focus on residence halls, and more attention to issues related to student life, such as security, health and counseling services, and technology. These were all things that drove up the cost of operating the college and therefore the price of tuition, and reinforced the need for an increase in financial aid.

JOHN POCK, sociology professor 1955–1999: As the tuition fee went up, a different type of student was showing up, one that was less intellectually risk-taking. I felt a very distinct change in the student body toward more consumerism or entitlement. They wanted to know something, to be taught something for their money. They certainly didn't go for my Socratic conference techniques. They wanted information, and I felt sorry for them, because they were increasingly more ignorant of things in general than the students had been before.

They also struck me as being less prepared - they exhibited very poor writing skills and they also couldn't read properly. If you asked them what they thought the main thesis was of a paper they were reading, they couldn't figure it out. They certainly weren't the kinds of students I was familiar with. They seemed to behave as though they were entitled to something filling up their notebooks.

FRANK GWILLIAM, biology professor 1957–1996, provost 1979–1982: Some older faculty members thought the student body had deteriorated, but I didn't. It changed, but that had a lot to do with the surrounding world. In my earlier years at Reed, the students had been a lot more intense about their academic interests, really sort of submerged in them. There was less of that in the 1990s. It was not an absolute change in character; rather, it was a change in students' willingness to subject themselves to the discipline of the academic program entirely. For ex-

ample, I didn't feel that the quality of the students' dedication to the thesis experience was quite as intense as it had been when I first came, although there were exceptions to that. In some ways that was probably more healthy. It seemed to me that students did more things that were fun than they had before.

ROGER PORTER, English professor 1961– : I didn't think that Reed fundamentally changed over the decades. Reed was one of those places that had really done one thing very well—taking students who were very interested in and excited about their work, and making them enormously focused on the nature of academic study and on becoming independent and self-reliant intellectuals. That was the hallmark of the institution. The faculty was very good, but there are good faculties at lots of places. I don't think there were very many student bodies with the kind of dedication and the tremendous sense of involvement in their work that Reed students had.

PETER STEINBERGER, political science professor, dean of faculty: During my first year at Reed, one of the things that struck me was that the place was not driven by pre-professionalism. Here was a place that thought there was something to be said for the notion of scholarship and intellectual engagement as being intrinsically rewarding—things that hopefully produce good extrinsic rewards, but are not done solely for ulterior purposes but because we just love doing this stuff. That's pretty good for certain kinds of people with certain kinds of needs and ambitions and interests, but might not work so well for others. For certain kinds of families, pre-professionalism is really an important thing, and ought to be an important thing.

MARTIN RINGLE, chief technology officer 1989– : When I came out to Reed to be interviewed for a job by the president at the time,

Jim Powell, he offered to interview me early one Sunday morning while jogging around Eastmoreland together. When we got to the campus, Powell said, "Would you like to see the library?" I asked, "Is it open Sunday morning at seven o'clock?" He said, "Oh, yeah."

We went into the library, and what I saw were bodies everywhere, people who had apparently been there all night long. I didn't know what was going on. I didn't realize that senior theses were due the following week. One groggy fellow woke up and I asked him what his thesis was on. When he started telling me, all I could think was, "Boy, this doesn't sound like an undergraduate thesis." I had directed senior theses at various places and had sat on dissertation committees for graduate students. This sounded like at least a master's or maybe a doctoral thesis.

By the time we left the library I was impressed with the dedication and the passion—some might call it the obsession—of the Reed students that I'd encountered. I was then the chair of the computer science department at Vassar College. It was a very good school, but I never felt that the students at Vassar were there because of a burning and intense desire to learn.

PANCHO SAVERY, English professor 1995– : I had experiences at Reed where I walked into the classroom and found the students already talking about the subject we were studying. I sat down and they just kept talking and talking. I sat there for fifty minutes and did not open my mouth once. To me, that was the paradise of teaching. I couldn't imagine that happening anywhere else.

A student studying at his thesis carrell in the Hauser Library in the mid-1990s.

Jessica Lee Patterson '96, art professor: I took for granted that the classes at Reed were very discussion based and that people actually talked. It wasn't until graduate school that I began to see that this might not be ordinary for an undergraduate institution. Although Reed classes actually felt very similar to my graduate seminars at UC Berkeley, they weren't anything like the classes that we were teaching the undergraduates there. I realized that at Reed you got a taste of the graduate school experience.

John Pock, sociology professor: Historically, Reed was under-bureaucratized, which led in part to the perennial problem of the high dropout rate, as there was virtually nothing on the non-academic side for the students to do. Steve Koblik was a big blowhard. He was too noisy and too activist for Reed. But he was instrumental in increasing the non-academic bureaucracy of the college. He conducted a big study on student life in 1993.

Jon Rivenburg, director of institutional research: One thing students talked about in the study in terms of attrition was depression. Reed then increased its health and counseling services, with broader participation across the student body and more counselors available for students to discuss issues that might be bothering them.

Mary Catherine King, health services director 1994–1997, associate dean of students 1997–2003, dean of students 2003–2007: The first episode of psychosis in a person often occurs between ages eighteen and twenty-five. It could be schizophrenic, it could be bipolar, it could be drug-induced, but it's psychotic. Those are the times when major depression is likely to happen. The incidence of this was much higher than I realized, and not just at Reed, but at other colleges also. I was giving papers around the country at the time on psychopharmacology and

became aware that this was a huge national issue at colleges across the board. At Reed, we quadrupled the number of medical leaves the first year I came. There were far fewer people flunking out because we got them out on a medical leave, and then they would come back and finish up once they had cleared.

The other thing happening was that a whole new set of anti-depression drugs, serotonin reuptake inhibitors, or SSRIs, had just become available, and it suddenly became possible to treat students on campus and keep them going to class and being successful. Because of the rise of the SSRIs and other medications, more students arrived already on them. In fact, parents would call me and say, "My student's applied to Reed. This is their clinical background. Is it possible for them to be treated on campus?" That became part of the family decision about whether or not the student would go to Reed. I saw it as a way to bring some of the best students to campus and to keep them.

Aaron Hoffnung '93: The Reed ethos supported the independent, depressed, pained, existential passage; it even exalted it. It was cool to be depressed and brilliant, and to bump into trees because you didn't know how to relate to anyone. I often wondered if all of that openness for intellectual exploration –that curiosity in questioning yourself and things around you— or even the social rebellion that forced you to rethink paradigms in your social interaction, was a disservice to a lot of students who were not organized enough or were focused on other parts of their development. I had a friend at Reed who never saw the light of day. He studied at night and slept during the day, and sort of prided himself on being a recluse. But he wasn't happy.

Mary Catherine King, dean of students: Sometimes the real challenge was, do we treat it or do we feature it? Some students were like,

"Well, I'm this way, and I like the way I am." Were we looking at eccentric? Were we looking at a touch of outrageous? Were we looking at a developmental thing along the lines of, "This too shall pass"? Or, were we looking at a real problem that needed addressing? If you consider bipolar illness, you could be hypomanic at Reed and it might really serve you well. You might not have a lot of friends some days, or there might be some bodies along the highway, but you could have a brilliant thesis and march through life.

THOMAS DUNNE, chemistry professor 1963–1995: By the 1990s we had reached a point where there were regular review sessions before examinations. That was not done when I first came to Reed in the 1960s. It was a tougher place then. Exams would come and it was up to the students to take care of their own preparation. But by the '90s we were into an era of greater concern about students who might be struggling. I held review sessions before chemistry exams. I was known for giving fairly demanding exams, so the room was always pretty full, and it was active with students asking questions.

JON RIVENBURG, director of institutional research: We also used to lose most students between sophomore and junior year, over what one might call "junior qualifying exam anxiety." Every student was required to take an exam at the end of their junior year before being admitted to their senior year. The faculty considered the issue. There was much discussion about sophomore seminars and different things to help students understand that the junior qualification exam was really a diagnostic, and not the sorting mechanism that they may have thought it was.

LAURENS RUBEN, biology professor: In earlier times, as part of the junior qual in biology, we used to give an oral exam that followed the written exam, so that we could expand on what we thought were weaknesses or strengths within the written exam, if we were so inclined. One year the students decided to come into the oral exam wearing a tuxedo, only it was one tuxedo for everybody. There were about twelve or thirteen students. As they came out they changed out of the tuxedo and handed it to the next person to put on. We had guys as large as football players in size and then people where the sleeves hung over their hands and the legs were all bunched up around their shoes. It was absolutely hilarious.

MARY CATHERINE KING, dean of students: There are certain subgroups that are found at a higher percentage at private liberal arts schools. Parents whose children have disorders like Asperger Syndrome, or high-end autism, often don't want them going to big state universities because they tend to have so much trouble socially. Reed may have had a higher rate of bipolar disorders because there's a subset of bipolar that's correlated with high IQ—you see many well-treated attorneys, physicians, and scientists, for example, with bipolar disorders. If it's treated, people stay very bright, very functional, and very competent.

I watched a huge group of students at Reed and over time I began to see a pattern with some of them. They were so bright that they would have compensated for years with an undiagnosed learning disability or attentional issue, and then got to Reed and found out that they had a problem. They would feel as though at any moment they were going to be discovered for not being very smart. I don't think Reed had a higher percentage of such individuals, but at larger schools like state universities they had more students who were likely to have been diagnosed earlier and already used to things like tutors and medication and quiet rooms. The subset that came to Reed had often not been diagnosed.

CHAPTER 38

Thinking Out of the Box

One of my favorite things about Reed was the constant, spontaneous expressions of creativity that just came out of nowhere.
—Lena Phoenix '90

There was a reaction against earnestness. Let's be ironic and detached: that was the thing in the '90s.
—Nic Warmenhoven '96

Student life at Reed in the 1990s was marked by increased attention to multiculturalism, feminism, and gay rights. After a burst of campus activism over sexual and gender rights in the late 1980s and early '90s, sexual mores at Reed began evolving toward the sex-positive movement rising in the broader culture. This movement celebrated and promoted open sexuality, making no moral distinctions among different types of sexual activities. Sex-positivity was also incorporated on campus into third-wave feminism, which challenged many of the notions of second-wave feminists from the 1970s and '80s with regard to ideas about oppression and empowerment.

The strain of wacky, subversive humor that had long characterized the Reed community took on new expression in the 1990s. Unlike the earnest protests that had marked the 1980s, activism over geopolitical or cultural issues among students shifted to creative pranks and demonstrations of direct action, designed to generate publicity with playful twists of ironic distancing. Clever and sometimes bizarre or madcap Dadaist expressions of intellectual jest became a common occurrence at Reed.

CHRIS MOSES '02, admission staff 2003–2005: I was always surprised by those people who were so afraid that things were going to change at Reed. To my mind, the fear pointed to a real insecurity about the power of the institution to shape people. It certainly changed me a hell of a lot over the four years I was there. But institutions change really, really slowly. So the fear that the tradition, curriculum, faculty, and nature of the institution didn't have enormous staying power always surprised me. If anything, I thought the place was changing far too slowly, for instance, with things like diversity.

PANCHO SAVERY, English professor 1995– : There was only one other black faculty member at the time I came to Reed, which I thought was pretty appalling. I was led to believe that in hiring me, Reed was making the first step in a long process to make the college much more diverse than it had been up to that time. I found out, after I got tenure, that I was the first tenured black professor in the history of the college. That just completely amazed me, and did not make me happy. It was clear that, for whatever reason, the faculty had not been doing a very good job in terms of recruiting minority faculty members.

Students demanding greater ethnic diversity on campus, 1990s.

PETER STEINBERGER, political science professor 1977– , dean of faculty 1997–2010, acting president 2001–2002: Faculty diversity had been one of our less successful endeavors. The faculty was strongly supportive of the initiative, but we were not successful in doing it. I'm not sure the lack of success was entirely our fault.

My opinion was that Reed should continue to pursue diversity in the student body and in the faculty, not for social-justice purposes, since I didn't think that Reed successfully pursuing diversity would aid social justice, but because diversity was good for the academic program. That was because it brought multiple perspectives, multiple voices, and multiple ways of thinking. It's always good for monologues to become dialogues.

MOLLY FRANKS '97: There were a bunch of different organizations on campus that were focused on different subcultures within Reed— the Latino Student Group, the Jewish Student Group, the Black Student Group, and the Asian Student Group. All of those groups were part of the new Multicultural Resource Center, which itself also organized events. We developed a workshop that we took to different groups on campus to have dialogues on class, race identity, and oppression.

There were plenty of students who were resistant to the work of the Multicultural Resource Center. They either felt that it was a waste of time or that people were too sensitive or were overreacting. There were people who would write letters to the *Quest* newspaper protesting reverse discrimination and stuff like that.

ROBIN TOVEY '97, alumni relations staff 2003– : As a student with a visible physical handicap, I had people respond to me in a helpful and genial way, yet it was clear that some of the ADA stuff was new territory for Reed. Steve Koblik declared that staff and faculty should do whatever it took to prepare for my arrival in my freshman year. Widening the aisles in the bookstore for my wheelchair was one that sticks with me. Eliot Hall hadn't yet installed an elevator at that time, so when the day came for me to turn in my thesis, four of my staff friends from Student Services carried me up to the third floor and through much of the thesis parade in my portable wheelchair. I felt quite triumphant—and a bit like Queen Victoria on her sedan chair.

REBECCA LAVE '93: Reed was in some ways the most gender-neutral place I've ever been. Many of the ways in which women were expected to defer to men in the general society were muted. But the subtle, underground forms of prejudice that remained were perhaps harder to combat at a place like Reed, where arguments based in emotional responses were completely dismissed in favor of logical rigor.

My humanities conference was one of the most relaxed and yet exciting classes I ever took at Reed, but, despite an equal male-female ratio, out of the five people who spoke regularly I was the only woman. That was the norm for all of my classes. This became especially noticeable when I began taking upper-division classes in philosophy, my intended major. Confronted with classes in which the male-female ratio was eight-to-one if you were lucky, and with a group of male students who consistently used metaphors about rape and masturbation, and who referred to the conferences as "penis-dueling," and with professors who only seemed to fuel the testosterone level, I shut up.

ALEX GOLUB '95: Obsession, virtuosity, addiction, and performance seemed central to the group that I ran in. It was basically a masculine kind of thing about control and mastery. It took the form of, "I know more about Theodor Adorno than you do. I've read everything by this guy. I haven't just read the commentary; I've read the

Schopenhauer in the original German." In the off-campus Reed house called "Force 10 from Navarone," it took the form of obsession with sports scores. Reedies who lived there obsessively read nineteenth-century Germany military theory and constantly watched *Sports Center* on TV. Somehow those two things were united.

At one point everybody was taking extra-strength Tums because they were drinking tons of coffee and chain-smoking, and always having problems with their stomachs. It was a weird mix of focus on academics and punk rock attitude. There were also the remains of hippiedom still circulating in Oregon, which was definitely all about not getting worked up and being extremely mellow. We found those people pathetic and gutless. For example, Bear Wilner '95, who I thought of as a good friend, organized a drum circle. We were just like, "Fuck! What could be more fucking ridiculous? Getting in touch with nature?! These people are just fucking deluded! Hey, you got any Tums?" That was the way things were.

CHANTAL SUDBRACK '97: There was sort of a pervasive gutter hippie culture when I arrived on campus. A gutter hippy was somebody who didn't bathe and who had really knotty hair. I came from a background where general hygiene was of the utmost importance. I was just completely horrified.

MIRIAM POSNER '02: Gender was constantly and heavily under scrutiny because we had a lot of women who had grown up as the children of second-wave feminists. I got the sense that many women of previous generations thought that we believed the job was done and that we didn't understand the contribution that, for instance, second-wave feminists had made to our lives.

That certainly wasn't the case for women of my generation in the late 1990s. Our priority was not only insisting on the importance of thinking about gender and sexuality but insisting on new possibilities for women and insisting that gender could be malleable and that things could change for women. We were also interested in finding ways to inject some humor and some self-reflection and some fun into feminism.

MOLLY FRANKS '97: For several years the local group Stopping Violence Against Women came to Reed during Women's Week to show their graphic pornography slide show. They talked about how they considered pornography and prostitution to be forms of violence against women that perpetuated a misogynistic, woman-hating culture. That was the legacy I had come into. But over the time that I was at Reed, the thinking among students shifted from that view of pornography and prostitution to one that perceived them as having a potential for empowerment and agency, with women doing sex work by choice in a way that they felt good about, or women engaging in pornography or creating erotica in a way that wasn't disempowering to women.

For example, when I got to Reed a group of people facilitated these dialogues with first-year students that they called the "Rape Awareness Project." It was about avoiding sexual violence in your intimate relationships when you were a Reed student. Later we changed the name of that project to "Sex at Reed" so the focus was not just "Rape is bad. Don't do it," but "How do we have safe, loving, consensual sexual interactions? What is it that we want out of our sex lives, and how can we work for that?"

THOMAS BURNS '98: There was no such thing as dating. Like everything else at Reed, hooking up was super intense. There was no ramp-up time. If you got to the point where you and another person were into each other, usually you went from zero to a hundred in twenty-four hours. Then, things usually crashed at about the same speed at some point down the road.

KAREN SAPPLETON '97: There were a couple of potential sexual assault cases. Most schools would have had the administration solely handle that. At Reed, those cases were largely left to the students on the student Judicial Board to figure out, and their findings were sent up to the college president to review and make a decision about. There were student-wide discussions on the issue. It was just a really incredible experience, in my mind at least, that students had so much opportunity to have their own input and say in how something like that was taken care of. For the most part, the students did a very good job with it.

ROBERT MACK '93: Reed Arts Week, or "RAW," was an event held in early spring each year. One year the theme of RAW was "Really Awesome Women." Here we were, a bunch of fairly testosterone-crazed beer-drinking men, feeling unable to participate because we weren't female. Somehow that drew us into Christianity, and we decided to form the Feminist Christian Brotherhood, which was a group of painfully ignorant men who really wanted to participate and get along and help out, but were just too dumb to be able to do anything.

During RAW we created a float on the back of a 1984 Nissan truck that was a chapel in the classic evangelical sense, with a lower deck and an upper deck and a pulpit at the center. We got Preacher Tom, an itinerant preacher who often showed up on campus, to stage an old-fashioned Southern revival on our float. Then we dressed up in tight, slinky dresses under our regular clothes, with the idea that once the revival got going, we'd tear off our outer clothes, revealing ourselves to be women in a sort of conversion ceremony.

None of us, though, had heard Tom's speech beforehand. As we were standing in the crowd during the revival, waiting to rip off our regular clothes, Tom started to go off the reservation as it were, saying things like "Look, women don't start wars. Men start wars. Women don't rape. Men rape." People were cheering, and there started to be a lot of back-and-forth call and response between Tom and the crowd. Tom just kept building it up, going on about all of the bad things that men do and the good things that women do. There were tears in people's eyes. It was an amazing moment of monocracy, in which a whole group was captivated by his every word and he was in control.

KAREN SAPPLETON '97: There was a Muslim woman who was very offended by a man who was often sunbathing stark naked on the front lawn. Given their schedules, almost every time she would walk by there, there he would be, naked. At other colleges her complaint would have gone to the school administration to sort out, whereas at Reed it went straight to the student Judicial Board.

The issue was his freedom versus her rights. The way they handled it was to strike a compromise: he was allowed to exercise his right to lie naked on the front lawn at certain times on certain days of the week, which were times that she would not encounter him. If he was willing to make that concession, then she couldn't complain about his nakedness. In this way, both of their rights were respected.

THOMAS STRONG '94: From 1990 to 1995 identity politics became huge, especially gay or queer-inflected gender-identity politics. As part of that, some of us adopted this kind of queer pose and decided we were going to be these radical sex activists, breaking down all the norms and hierarchies and barriers—sexual liberationists but in a queer way, which was a bit different from the hippie sexual liberation that may have previously occurred on campus. Queer sexuality was more playful, more fabulous, not like any of the stereotypes one might have about hippies.

It was kind of pop and campy, not rooted in the sense of nature per se but more about the fun of artifice.

ROBIN TOVEY '97, staff: Although Reed struggled with recruiting minorities, the college made genuine efforts to support varieties of diversity beyond ethnic and racial classification. Among my classmates, there were more non-traditional-age students and more who were comfortable talking about being first-generation students or receiving financial aid than there had been historically.

Moreover, there was positive recognition of LGBTQ—lesbian, gay, bi-sexual, transsexual, and queer—issues. The student group Queer Alliance made it cool to acknowledge sexual identities all along the spectrum. On a lighter note, a small group of students called for taking pride in their countrified roots with the Rural Student Union, staging a hoedown complete with plywood farm animals.

MOLLY FRANKS '97: The Queer Alliance on campus organized events, creating a safe space for students to explore sexual orientation and gender identity. Coming Out Week was a chance for people to articulate their identity more clearly. We took photos of the group, and then displayed the photos in the Paradox Café on campus for a month each fall. My thesis advisor said to me, "I saw your picture in the Paradox, and it was really nice." It was a way of having who you are be acknowledged.

THOMAS STRONG '94: Embracing radical queer difference and gender nonconformity, Andrew Leavitt '93 and I founded, along with some other Reed students, Queer Nation Portland. Nationally, Queer Nation was a group of queer activists that started up in 1990 in response to prejudice and violence against gays and lesbians. It came out of ACT UP, an advocacy group for people living with AIDS. The main activity of our chapter in Portland was selling stickers, which kind of took over the Reed campus for a long time. One of my all-time greatest accomplishments was creating a sticker that read "Fuck your Gender," which was a pun on several levels. We also staged events around Portland, such as "Take Your Love to a MAX," which was a giant kiss-in in which we took over an entire train on Portland's MAX light rail system.

CHRIS TARNSTROM '95: A conservative Christian group calling itself the "Oregon Citizens Alliance" sponsored a variety of anti-gay initiatives in Oregon, basing its support for the initiatives on the Book of Leviticus in the Bible, which states certain rules. That inspired a rallying on campus to expose an appliance salesperson up the street who had literature from this group displayed in his shop.

Our approach was to call for the implementation of the rest of the rules in the Book of Leviticus. We marched up the street from campus under the banner, "Family Alliance for God," or "FAG," to the appliance shop, where we held a rally.

After the rally, as the parade of Reed folks was walking back towards campus along the downhill slope of Woodstock Boulevard, a truck with a great big wood chipper pulled up. Three big, burly, angry men got out of the truck and grabbed some large tree trunks from the back and made a heave-ho into the wood chipper as a threatening gesture. Unfortunately, they forgot to put on the brake, so the truck and the wood chipper continued going down the street without a driver. Two of the guys ran after it, leaving the third guy standing there empty-handed amidst all these FAG folks.

In keeping with its focus on the Book of Leviticus, FAG later extended its protests to barbershops that would trim sideburns, and oyster bars in which people might eat shellfish.

MOLLY FRANKS '97: I did an independent project with my thesis advisor in psychology, Kathy Oleson, surveying students on sexual orientation. About a quarter of the students identified themselves as being something other than heterosexual, which was way higher than in the broader U.S. community. But not all of those one in four identified as "queer." It was more like "I'm not exclusively heterosexual."

KAREN SAPPLETON '97: At Reed there was no reason why we had to play into the stereotypical roles of being women and men. Some of my girlfriends cut their hair and dressed in a more masculine style, not as an indication that they were lesbian or anything, but simply because they wanted to. And vice versa, there were guys who used to wear skirts all the time. One of them also had a Mohawk haircut while he was wearing the skirts, and that was just so unique to me. Eventually I came to understand it, but it meant having to think out of the box.

LENA PHOENIX '90: One of my favorite things about Reed was the constant, spontaneous expressions of creativity that just came out of nowhere. There was a spiral staircase that went from Commons down into the mailroom area on the floor below. Sometime during the night someone spray-painted extremely meticulous and accurate DNA sequences on every single stair. It was brilliant.

STEVEN KOBLIK, president 1992–2001: I loved it when Reed students would come in and say they wanted to do something that I thought was outrageous, rash, undoable. It may not have anything to do with what they were being asked to do in the classroom, but it did reflect what Reed was about—taking risks, reaching beyond the normal, being willing to be successful or unsuccessful, and recognizing that the ride is the best part of the experience.

ROBERT MACK '93: In science everything was cold and cut and dried, just yes or no. It was kind of boring, which was why a lot of people didn't like it. So we wanted to have something within the realm of science that people could really get excited about with the kind of passion and emotion that the softer disciplines had.

Nitrogen emerged as the unsung hero, and the more research we did into it, the more that just became obvious. Nitrogen is an inert molecule or compound, and two nitrogens stick together very solidly. The three pairs of electrons that they share geometrically is a very stable shape, like a pyramid. It's a fundamental building block of chemical relations. It is also eighty percent of our atmosphere. Hemoglobin's absorption of oxygen is greatly assisted by nitrogen in the atmosphere. Finally, nitrogen is the workhorse of a plant's growing cycle, in which it carries things from the soil up to the leaves, then goes back down and gets more.

We announced the establishment of Nitrogen Day I in the *Quest* newspaper "to preserve spiritualism and awe while rationalizing and deconstructing the world around us." Chemistry professor Tom Dunne and other faculty members gave speeches about nitrogen at the event.

BEAR WILNER-NUGENT '95: The joke was that nitrogen is so ubiquitous that you can do anything and say it's about nitrogen because you're breathing nitrogen, and there's nitrogen in your food and your drink. There were innocent pleasures at the event like spontaneous nitrogen haiku contests and people wearing shirts with the nitrogen box from the periodic table on them, and doing handshakes with the triple bond. It was a surrealist holiday run by scientists.

GRAHAM JONES '97: The spirit of play and the lunatic energy on campus were really wonderful and inspiring. What made Reed such an exciting place were things like Chunk 666, which was a

Members of the bicycle group Chunk 666 at Renn Fayre in the 1990s.

group of men and women—a lot of them math majors—who built outlandish bicycles and tricycles, often defying natural laws such as gravity. They would stage these bizarre rallies around the campus or the local neighborhoods, that were kind of like very silly performance art. Karl Anderson '95, Chunk 666's founder, concocted a whole mythology around it, publishing a hundred-page manifesto.

AMY BOGRAN '89: A classmate who had transferred from a school on the East Coast came up with the idea of starting "Midnight Theatre," similar to something he had seen back East, based on the Elizabethan sense of theatre, with a lot of audience interaction. The first one was held outdoors in the Cerf Amphitheatre, with people presenting various acts. Michael Corrigan

Actors in the 1997 version of the "Hum 110 Play," including, in the foreground, classics professors Wally Englert, David Silverman, and Nigel Nicholson.

'89 was the MC. A group of us rented a boat and ferried him across the Reed lake with a torch to light our way, like Vikings arriving. Corrigan then did a presentation of Shakespeare's *Hamlet*, telling the entire story, very rushed and chaotic.

GREG LAM '96: I directed the first version of the "Hum 110 Play." The premise was that a student had not gone to freshman humanities all year and needed to catch up. In a parody of Humanities 110, the gods sent Homer from the heavens to drag him through the humanities syllabus in one night. The play became an annual Reed tradition, featuring classics professor Wally Englert and others professors as regular performers.

LUKE WEISMAN MIRATRIX '96: Greg Lam '96 was also famous for his extremely abridged version of the *Iliad*, which was: "Shit happens, then your armor clatters thunderously. Such was the battle of Hector, breaker of horses."

IGOR VAMOS '90: Phil Bender '91 and I formed a club called the "Guerilla Theatre of the Absurd" and sought funding from the student body to do "interventions" around campus, different weird actions, theatrical things that were surprising or unusual. A lot of the stuff was just meant to disrupt the regular flow of things.

Portland had renamed Union Avenue, which ran almost the length of town, as Martin Luther King, Jr., Boulevard. That commemoration was sort of a hot-button issue for racism and racial-justice issues, and set off a big public debate in Portland. There was a huge amount of support for a kind of reactionary movement to return the street back to its original name.

Greg Haun '90 and I came up with a plan to change this other street in Portland, Front Avenue, to "Malcolm X Boulevard." We meant to illustrate that in a political continuum there is always a more radical edge. And if that more radical edge sort of scares people a bit, then maybe they'd be a little bit more willing to adopt the softer, middle ground. You don't know where the middle is until the edges are defined. Our point was that Martin Luther King, Jr., would not have achieved the level of popularity that he had back in the 1960s without there being a Malcolm X.

Front Avenue was another long street, so there were all different kinds of signs to make: regular green ones, and black ones for the historic district. We printed hundreds of them. We also made highway directional signs that were twelve or fourteen feet wide with letters a foot tall. We hung up the street signs for Malcolm X Boulevard overnight all along Front Avenue. We didn't come out in the media, we just called ourselves "Group X."

NIC WARMENHOVEN '96: The Guerrilla Theatre of the Absurd did things like switch the voice boxes in talking Barbie dolls with those in talking G.I. Joe dolls and then return them to the stores. So the kids would buy a G.I. Joe doll that said, "Let's go paint our nails," or buy a Barbie doll that said, "Let's kill the enemy."

THOMAS STRONG '94: Direct action was the model of early-1990s activism—staging events, being in the public eye, trying to raise awareness or make public intervention—as opposed to, say, writing to your legislator or working behind the scenes. It was very much about visibility and generating discussion.

ROSE CAMPBELL '96: "Eat Bugs for Money" was an event that was put on by me and my friend Alexa Harcourt Green '96. Alexa's brother had the idea. He threw it out there, like, "Wouldn't it be funny if you ate the bugs and it would be like *Name that Tune*, but instead of bidding up to buy something, you would be bidding down. How little money would it take for you to eat a bug?" We were like, "Oh, yeah! That's a great idea."

We launched it at Renn Fayre our sophomore year. Our original idea was that maybe somebody would eat a cricket for five dollars. Little did we know how very little money people would eat large amounts of bugs for. It was like a mob mentality where people get into situations in which, for that particular instance in that particular group, the norms of social behavior become completely different. People do things that they would not normally do, myself included. After that first year, Eat Bugs for Money took on a life of its own, becoming the biggest event at Renn Fayre.

BEAR WILNER-NUGENT '95: Eat Bugs for Money consisted of several qualifying rounds, during which contestants bolted down crickets, mealworms, ladybugs, and other relatively innocuous beasties, and then elimination play intensified in the semifinals, which were dominated by the official mascot species of the event, a type of cockroach known as the "blaberus." "Eat the blaberus!" was an early slogan. The favorite final-round bug was definitely the profoundly well-appendaged and thick-carapaced giant Madagascar hissing cockroach, and during that round the entire crowd went, "Hiss-s-s-s."

GREG LAM '96: The Guerilla Theatre of the Absurd morphed in the early 1990s into the "Guerrilla Theatre of the Hors d'Oeuvres," led by Nic Warmenhoven '96 and Thomas McElroy '97. A lot of their pranks had to do with food. At one of them they dressed as waiters and served food in the library to protest the new "no food or drink" policy. At another, they got some portable hot plates, tables, and a kitchen setup that turned the library lobby into a full-service, late-night café.

NIC WARMENHOVEN '96: There was a Portland personality named Tom Peterson, who ran an empire of furniture stores. He was kind of this small-scale tacky capitalist guy, who everyone knew because he used his face in all his advertising on billboards and in newspapers and on TV.

Given all the new building going on around campus, we cooked up this idea of getting Tom Peterson to come to Reed to hand over a giant check for the dedication of a new classics building, which was ridiculous because classics only graduated three or four students a year, and didn't need a building. I met with Peterson and told him that we wanted him to come and do the groundbreaking, dig a hole with a shovel, hand over the check, cut the ribbon—the whole thing. He looked at me and said, "So this is a total sham, right?" I said, "Yeah." And he said, "Oh, yeah. I'd love to do it."

We posted pictures of Tom Peterson everywhere on campus. The people at the physical plant set up a little stage for us on the lawn of Eliot Hall. One of my friends built this giant plywood Tom Peterson head with a moveable mouth that functioned like a oracle—you could walk up and ask questions of the Tom Peterson head and it would answer you.

At the mock dedication, a couple hundred people gathered. Tom Peterson came and gave this like ten-minute complete bullshit speech about Agamemnon and Achilles and the Greek heroes and how he'd been influenced by all these guys in his rise to the top. We got classics professor Wally Englert to come out and accept the check. It was total hilarity. At the end everybody in the crowd was like, "Well, all right! I guess we're starting work on the new classics building!"

JON RIVENBURG, director of institutional research 1988–2011: A local auto dealer named Scott Thomason had a motto for his dealerships that went, "If you don't come see me today, I can't save you any money." Thomason had huge banners around town with his motto and his face printed on them. One year, during the week that prospective students were on campus, the Guerilla Theatre got one of Thomason's banners, substituted President Koblik's face on it, strung up strings of flags like you see at auto dealers, and then started parking cars in front of Eliot Hall, including President Koblik's car. There were actually people coming from Woodstock Boulevard thinking that this was real, that Reed College was having a used-car sale. They almost sold Koblik's car that day.

NIC WARMENHOVEN '96: The Guerrilla Theatre of the Hors d'Oeuvres picked a Friday in April that was the busiest for visits of "prospies"—prospective students—and their parents, and that also coincided with a Board of Trustees meeting on campus, to stage an action that played off of the South Africa divestiture controversies of the 1980s.

We demanded that Reed divest all of its assets in Canada, because Canada was secretly behind global warming, planning to turn all of their tundra into fertile cropland. We put up posters that read "Reed out of Canada Rally" with big Xs over maps of Canada. On the Friday the prospies came, we gathered about two hundred people in front of Eliot Hall. I was talking through a bullhorn, ranting about the Canadian warming machine and how the college was supporting this indirectly by investing in all these companies that did business with Canada. We burned a Canadian flag and smashed bottles of Canadian beer, working the crowd into a fervor, chanting:

Fifty-four–forty or fight!
Divest!

and:

We're here!
We're queer!
We don't need your Canadian beer!

Then, together we stormed into Eliot Hall and marched up to President Koblik's office, insisting that we would occupy his office until the college divested from Canada.

JON RIVENBURG, director of institutional research: I was with the investment committee of the Board of Trustees during the protest, and they were asking, "What's going on outside?"

NIC WARMENHOVEN '96: Not that many years before, divestment from South Africa had been a real issue at the college. Now we were brazenly staging this mockery of it with the protest over divestment from Canada. It says a lot about how the era evolved. There was a reaction against earnestness. "Let's be ironic and detached"—that was the thing in the '90s.

STEVEN KOBLIK, president: There was a pervasive tolerance of difference among the students that was so ingrained in the Reed culture that it allowed small, minority values to sometimes dominate other value systems. To address

that you had to try and build social and personal bridges across groups of young people who didn't necessarily have the tools to do that themselves.

I spent a lot of time talking publicly about the Honor Principle, because Reed won't survive as Reed if the student body will not enforce—not just honor, but *enforce*—the Honor Principle. In a very permissive society, which is what our society had become, students were less and less willing to do that, and that really caused problems for everybody. It threatened the college as I loved it, because for awhile it was much easier for the college just to establish rules and principles and enforce them, which was not the way Reed had historically wanted to do it.

DIANA BURKHART '97: In the mid-1990s they installed an electronic alarm system for the books in the library. Prior to that, people oper-

Terrance Tso '98 walks by the "Reed out of Canada" rally in front of Eliot Hall in April 1995, with Nic Warmenhoven '96 at the megaphone, Bear Wilner '96, Joel Revill '97, and Joshua Webb '97 unfolding the flag, and Michael Braun Hamilton '97 and Eric Eschen '95 holding signs.

ated on the Honor Principle in checking books out. Until then though, every time I went to the library I could never find the book I was looking for because somebody had stolen it. That changed with the alarm system.

CARL STEVENS '42, economics professor 1954–1990: The Honor Principle was long recognized as a fair-weather system. It worked best in those situations where, in a sense, it was not really needed—that is, in those situations in which individuals tended strongly and naturally and on their own, so to speak, to comport themselves in accord with the principle. The enforcement mechanism was never taken seriously. Under that mechanism, if there were widespread defections from the Honor Principle, the students were converted into a community of snoops and tattletales—not an attractive prospect, most would agree.

Reed's concept of the Honor Principle was a source of community common law. But there is a general principle or rule in the law of torts that states, in effect, that if A inflicts harm on B, that is possibly actionable; but A may be excused if the harm she inflicted on B was an unavoidable consequence of A's pursuit of her own legitimate self-interests. This, of course, led to the various absurdities in the Honor Principle's application on campus about which we all complained.

LAURENS RUBEN, biology professor 1955–1992: In 1955, my first year at Reed, there was a plagiarism case, and F. L. Griffin, the mathematician who was the acting president at the time, threw the student out. There wasn't any question about it. I admired that. I thought, "Hey! This Honor Principle really works." I always depended on it. I never thought to stay in my classroom when I handed out an exam, and I often gave take-home

exams, even exams that students wrote their own questions on. For many years students in embryology would be graded on the quality of the questions, as well as on the answers they gave. If it hadn't been for the Honor Principle, I just couldn't have done any of those things.

In the 1990s, as the internet became available, it became far too easy for people to cheat, in that they could find and copy things on the internet that before would have been very difficult to discover. That bothered me a lot. If the Honor Principle no longer worked in the classroom, that meant it was really broke.

ANGELINA CLARKE '04: Economics professor Noelwah Netusil used to do an experiment to teach her students game theory. It was a series of games that basically pitted the communal good against individual instinct. If everyone decided to go for the communal good, each person got four cents on the dollar. But if one person decided to spoil it all, that person got twenty dollars out of the pot and the others got nothing. Based on economic theory, at some point someone should spoil the whole situation for everyone and just take the money and run.

Noelwah ran this test on students over a series of years, and to very perturbing results. Reedies did not spoil the game. They consistently voted for the communal good, and consistently played the game—even with strangers at Reed who they didn't know—in a way that the communal good was upheld. Everyone got happily richer and richer, based on this completely equitable system. Noelwah took these results to economics conferences and tried to present them. People didn't believe her that at Reed the Honor Principle had so permeated the lives of the students that they actually were defying the laws of economics to do what was in the common good.

CHAPTER 39

Gutsy Iconoclast

Since its founding, Reed had fought against the larger currents of higher education. The current got more intense in the time I was at Reed, as the larger culture changed.
  —Peter Steinberger, dean of faculty

Higher education isn't a commodity like cars or refrigerators. There aren't twenty-five colleges in this country that are the best for everyone.
  —Steven Koblik, president

In the mid-1990s, a new generation of senior professors stepped into leadership positions at Reed, in effect the third generation of faculty leadership since the college's founding. They brought with them a culture of greater inclusion and egalitarianism among the ranks, as compared to the faculty oligarchies of past generations. While the humanities program remained a political battlefield in terms of responding to evolving intellectual and academic trends, gradual changes began to emerge within the framework of Reed's curriculum, including the incorporation of gender and ethnic perspectives. Most significantly in this decade, a fully staffed Chinese humanities program was introduced at the college.

The 1990s also saw a further increase in America of consumerist attitudes toward higher education. This trend was perhaps best exemplified by the rise of college rankings by various services, the most popular of which was the province of the news magazine *U.S. News & World Report*. The criteria upon which their rankings were based tended to disfavor an educational model like Reed's. In keeping with its contrarian nature, Reed made the risky decision to stop participating in the *U.S. News* rankings.

ROGER PORTER, English professor 1961– : Reed was a self-conscious institution, which is not to say that it had an inferiority complex. If anything, Reed tended to have a superiority complex. But there was something of a fear that things would fall apart if they were not held on to with great rigor and attention. In many ways Reed was like a family. It had all the potentials for squabbling and for dysfunction. It had that family quality of demanding a certain kind of loyalty, which I personally found very hard. It was a rare place in a way, a fragile butterfly in some respects, but not as fragile perhaps as people believed it was. They felt there was a need to protect everything. That's like a family, isn't it?

STEVEN KOBLIK, president 1992–2001: Unlike many liberal arts colleges at the time, Reed alumni of the 1930s and 1940s would still recognize the college they had attended. They would recognize what was going on in the classroom. They would recognize what the faculty was trying to accomplish. The faculty members themselves would have a sisterhood and a brotherhood with the faculty members of that earlier era. They wouldn't agree, but they would understand each other and understand where they were.

From my perspective, that was one of the most exciting things about Reed. The question that I felt everyone involved at Reed needed to reflect on was, "How do you continue to do that so that it works for every new generation of students and faculty?"

MARVIN LEVICH, philosophy professor 1953–1994, provost 1972–1979: There is something built into any institution such that for a certain period of time a lot of fairly good things can happen to you—"He's a great teacher." "He's a great leader of the faculty"—and then, after a time, things change. You don't sense it in yourself, but you sense it in terms of the attitudes of people toward you. There's a feeling that you might not be what you were once, so you just decide to retire and get out.

At the moment you achieve emeritus status at Reed, you become a nonentity. You find it strange when you go to the library and somebody looks at you and says, "Who are you?" You feel like saying, "I've taught at this institution for fifty years."

ED MCFARLANE, controller and assistant treasurer 1973–1978, vice-president and treasurer 1979– : You had more generalists in teaching when I started working at the college in the early 1970s. A faculty member in physics then could probably teach every physics course. That wasn't so true thirty years later. The physicist probably couldn't teach another physicist's class because it had become so specialized. That required more resources to find somebody to fill the gap when a particular faculty member was gone. All of that put pressure on the financials of a small institution.

PETER STEINBERGER, political science professor 1977– , dean of faculty 1997–2010, acting president 2001–2002: Since its founding, Reed had fought against the larger currents of higher education. The current got more intense in the time I was at Reed, as the larger culture changed. There was more movement toward fragmentation, toward the balkanization of disciplines through specialization and departmentalization. Reed went down that road more than I would have liked. Pretty tough, though, to resist.

LAURENS RUBEN, biology professor 1955–1992: The sciences became a world of specialties. With equipment so varied and specialized, and the jargon so different from specialty to specialty, it was very hard to carry on a professional conversation with colleagues. Across the college there came to be an expectation, derived from the people within the departments, that at least some of their time should be spent in scholarship and in improving their own professional standing. It changed the character of the faculty the college sought. It changed the relationship between professors and students. It gave much more depth to the capacity of the faculty to direct theses and direct students in intellectual activities in their professional field. All in all, that was the most significant change in my time at the college.

LAURA NIX '89: I had some reservations about the conservatism of the Reed curriculum, but there was value in keeping it limited because of the intensity that such focus brought. At other schools I have attended, where there was a much more liberal view towards what could be taught, it was clear that people just didn't have the chops. They couldn't reason as well. They couldn't put together an argument as well. There was something about being in Reed's small-conference style of teaching that really helped me understand how to talk to people, how to argue with them, and how to sort out differences of opinion. It was really rare, in other schools, to be in an environment where you were both encouraged to do that and taught how to do it.

ROBERT KNAPP, English professor 1974– : The centrality of the humanities program to the college was not just propaganda. There is something about the effort, not just to provide a shared intellectual experience, but to provide a shared intellectual experience that drew on materials that are central to the way in which people think, because one way or another you can root contemporary ways of thinking in the ancient world. You can see historically the development of problems in the interaction between peoples that are akin to problems in the interaction between peoples today. That effort, from a multidisciplinary perspective and with a kind of enlightened amateurism, produces a way of thinking that generalizes into all kinds of other work.

Freshman humanities also served as the core for a model of the way in which people from different backgrounds, different disciplines, and different departments interacted and felt a shared sense of intellectual community—a shared sense of the responsibility to be able to explain things to one another, and a shared resistance to over-specialization. When I went to a chemistry thesis oral exam, and the student was able to engage with my questions, however

Chemistry professor Pat McDougal with a student in the chem lab, 1990s.

naïve they may have been, and explain his or her chemistry thesis to a complete non-science outsider in a way that really made sense, I took that as being an effect ultimately of the kind of thing that we tried to do at Reed.

THOMAS BURNS '98: There was often a lot of tension in the classroom, but that was sort of the price you paid for having so many people who felt strongly about what they were studying. Where else can you go where everybody cares that passionately about Herodotus or black holes in space?

CHRIS LYDGATE '90, alumni magazine editor 2008– : At Reed you would break down problems to their most elementary fundamental aspects and then build them back up again, in the process coming to understand what really truly made them work. I had one friend who was taking Math 110. His final exam was to prove that one plus one equals two.

DYLAN RIVERA '95: Among some students there was loyalty to the Reed curriculum and to having a very macho conference environment that was this contest of ideas, where we were reading the original texts of Marx and Engels and Hegel, dealing with the big ideas and none of this namby-pamby, trendy, minority stuff.

CHRIS MOSES '02, admission staff 2003–2005: Pancho Savery's course on African-American studies was not itself all that politically charged. But sometimes Pancho himself would become implicated in questions and issues of affirmative action. It was certainly a very live issue, and there was a lot of vocal dissent on campus that characterized diversity as being all about political correctness.

PANCHO SAVERY, English professor 1995– : In a meeting of the diversity committee on campus, I made what I thought was a very uncontroversial statement, that part of our job as teachers was to help prepare our students to go out into the real world, and inasmuch as the real world was becoming increasingly multicultural, we, in a completely white environment, were not sufficiently preparing our students to go out and deal with real-world issues. One of the people on the committee responded by saying that that was one of the most dangerous things he had ever heard in his entire life. My interpretation was that for this person that was somehow bringing politics into the classroom.

CHARLES WU, Chinese professor 1988–2002: Political correctness was something that was one of the dominating concerns among student activists and some faculty in the 1990s. I appreciated the basic spirit behind it, coming with the rise of feminism, racial and multicultural sensitivity, and the debate over the canon, because I was absolutely for social equality and for basic concepts of human caring. But I had reservations about just playing with the language without changing the substance. For instance, one of my students talked about the handicraftsmanship of a work of art but she used the word "handicraftspersonship," which was quite a mouthful. There was that kind of linguistic game going on at the time.

LAURA NIX '89: Because Reed didn't have a Women's Studies program, it was very hard to make it part of your academic life. We had feminist professors but we didn't really have people spending focused time talking about feminism. You could bring up critiques in class and start to learn how to bring that viewpoint to a discussion, but you didn't have a structured course that really taught you how to do that well. Professors were more apt to welcome those viewpoints in literature classes than they were in the social sciences. That's probably why most of the women

History professor Jacqueline Dirks '82, second from right, chatting with students in the 1990s.

feminists at Reed were English literature majors. In a lot of classes it was really an uphill battle. One professor actually told me that my particular take on a subject was "shrill."

MIRIAM POSNER '02: Jackie Dirks '82, a professor of history and American studies, was a role model for a lot of us, because, while she was a fantastic professor, she really resisted being maternal. It was important to us to have this example of a woman who was successful and didn't trade on gender explicitly in order to succeed. She taught a course on the way that consumerism influences the identities that we build. That was meaningful to me.

Anthropology professor Charlene Makley was also really influential for a lot of women. Her course on gender and sexuality demonstrated that gender was different all around the world, so what we might have felt were natural categories for women and men to fall into didn't necessarily hold in other times and places.

DYLAN RIVERA '95: Elizabeth Wingrove '84, a professor in the political science department, was a great feminist political theorist. She could lead you through a feminist thesis in almost any discipline. The class I was in had about fifteen students and I was the only male. As opposed to exploring the political aspects or political philosophy of the work, a lot of the class got stuck on delving into questions like "Are men and women different at birth, or are they socialized to be different?"

Wingrove's classes to me represented a way that Reed could incorporate diversity into its curriculum. A lot of students were dead set on "We've got to have a department on me; otherwise I'm not being acknowledged adequately. It's just dead white men." I never thought that was realistic. Reed was very much a place for generalists and for the basic academic departments. To establish a whole Women's Studies or Black Studies or Latino Studies department could take five or ten professors that would each equal the size of the English department. I just didn't see that happening financially for the college. It was a big-school solution at a small school.

CHARLES WU, Chinese professor: With regard to the issue of the male-dominant canon, I appreciated the rediscovery of women poets and women artists conspicuously lacking in the canon, but to categorically write off the male-dominant tradition was, I thought, ahistorical, because we would not have reached the present state of consciousness of the Other without the initiation of those who made it into the canon in the great tradition of the Renaissance, including Romanticism and all that.

The names all seem to be male, but their ideas should cross gender boundaries. As an English major, my major author was Shakespeare. When I saw people dubbing Shakespeare a "dead white male" poet, I couldn't accept that. Of course he had the limitations of his era, but he did his best to present the human condition as it was in his time, and also to give his work long-lasting universal value.

JOHN PECK '88: There definitely was a lot of tension in the curriculum. There were some attempts to bring in more of what are called "sub-altern" voices—people who are not the elites speaking. I took several anthropology classes from Gail Kelly '55, who had this air about her that caused some people to call her the "Dragon Lady." She had done her fieldwork in Ghana with the Ashanti elites, and was interested in diversity as a way to study things, but she also definitely believed in the canon of the Western classics. I had huge debates with her about diversifying Reed's curriculum by bringing in Asian studies, African studies, and Latin American studies.

JOHN POCK, sociology professor 1955–1999: Students have always periodically been dissatisfied with having to study the classical curriculum, which is centered on the works of, as they say, the dead white European authors. They want relevance. In the late 1960s some at Reed felt that the college should respond to the interests of students, whatever they might be at that particular time. That was a precursor to the kind of entitlement and consumer orientation that students brought to higher education in the early twenty-first century.

That approach presented what I believed was a danger to the integrity and the mission of higher education: focusing on Western culture. Western culture was the core of modernization. There was hardly anything that was not the result of the Western Enlightenment period, the Industrial Revolution, and so on. Studying China or other civilizations didn't contribute anything except in a comparative sense to what I would regard as the higher education of students, because those cultures were all responding to—and were sometimes the creatures of—Western culture, for good or ill.

ROBERT KNAPP, English professor: One of the things that changed in the humanities faculty was the increasing influence of junior and middle-rank faculty members. In part that was because a number of the senior faculty were people who were acculturated in the 1960s, and who had a much stronger sense of egalitarianism than was the case with the generation of faculty that preceded them. History professor Ray Kierstead probably was the person who had the most influence over the humanities in the 1980s and '90s. Ray had a very broad sense of humanistic education and an unusual ability to bring people together and help them, not through direct manipulation, but through setting an example, such as giving lectures that were simultaneously expansive and focused.

STEVEN KOBLIK, president: I was enthusiastic about development of a Chinese humanities program at Reed. I thought that initiative, which President Paul Bragdon had begun in the late 1980s, was a good one. China was an appropriate focal point, in that the intellectual traditions of that culture and civilization were every bit as challenging, and offered as much opportunity for rigorous study, as the Western tradition. I thought it was important for our students to be able to pursue other civilizations with the same kind of rigor with which they pursued the study of Western civilization.

MARSH CRONYN '40, chemistry professor 1952–1989, provost 1982–1989: In the late 1980s, Elizabeth Ducey, a longtime supporter of the college, had donated funds from her estate toward establishing an Eastern Studies program at Reed. The faculty discussed which "Eastern"— Japanese or Chinese—choosing finally to focus on China since it was the more ancient culture,

having then spread to Korea and Japan. They decided to create two faculty positions in Chinese literature and language. At the same time, the history faculty had a position in the Middle Ages that they had been unable to fill. Ray Kierstead, who was in charge of the search, agreed to extend that search to find an Eastern historian.

Then, by sheer serendipity, Sue Cooley, wife of trustee Ed Cooley, made a very generous grant to Reed, which financed the addition of two new appointments in art history. One of those positions went to our start-up Chinese program. All of these bits and pieces came together to create the Chinese humanities program.

ROBERT KNAPP, English professor: By the early 1990s there was a sense that the Humanities 110 syllabus that we put together in the early '80s was just too baggy and extensive. A group of us went off on a retreat and came up with a new

Members of the faculty in the Chinese program: Charles Wu, Doug Fix, Denise Hare, and Hyong Rhew.

A humanities class with English professor Pancho Savery, late 1990s.

center-periphery model that started with the Greeks and ended with Augustine's *Confessions*. It incorporated a good deal more of the Roman materials than we had included in the past, with Livy, Seneca, and Cicero, as well as Virgil, Tacitus, and Biblical materials. It was the first time that we had gotten a significant section focusing on Judaic materials, too.

PANCHO SAVERY, English professor: My second year at Reed I had to give my first humanities lecture. I chose to give it on Herodotus, and to talk about Herodotus in connection with Martin Bernal's book *Black Athena: The Afroasiatic Roots of Classical Civilization*. Bernal argued that Greece was heavily influenced by the many cultures around it, and that a lot of Greek ideas, religious practices, uses of language, etcetera, were derived from those other cultures. In fact, Herodotus himself said that all of the Greek ideas

about religion came from the Egyptians. So, the question I raised in my lecture was: "If Herodotus says that the Greeks got all their ideas about religion from the Egyptians, then why aren't we reading something in this course from the perspective of the Egyptians?"

I ended up giving that lecture every year for fourteen years. Absolutely nothing changed in the curriculum. The Egyptians were never added to the humanities syllabus. It was very frustrating. I presented a concrete proposal to the humanities staff to change the syllabus. I said that we needed to look at the Persians from the perspective of the Persians; we needed to look at the Egyptians from the perspective of the Egyptians. People pretty much unanimously voted it down. They considered it to be too radical.

PETER STEINBERGER, political science professor, dean of faculty: The world of higher education in the 1990s became dominated by the scourge of constant assessment, usually quantitative assessment. "How much are students learning?" "How can we assess how much they are learning?" "To what extent are the students receiving added value?" All of these various kinds of economic and economistic scientific models were developed for judging whether schools are doing a good job or not. I thought they were awful.

When you think about assessment, especially quantitatively oriented assessment, it is a homogenizing endeavor. It reduces education to a single kind of template. That's not what we were at Reed. It's not what we did. All of this assessment garbage was very anti-intellectual, and very skeptical of the professionalism and expertise of faculty members. They wanted to quantify things. They wanted hard data. We didn't do that at Reed. We provided *real* assessment. The junior qualifying exam was an obvious example.

In the political science department we used to have a sit-down junior qual with four questions. Students had the whole weekend to do it. They wrote the answers and then submitted them to the department secretary. She would give them to us. We would read them anonymously. After we had read them, we'd gather for breakfast at the golf course across the street and we'd go through the quals one by one, assessing them, evaluating them. The quality of writing, the quality of thinking, whether the student has absorbed the materials, etc. When we were all done, we'd open up the envelope and match up the quals with the individual students.

That's evaluation. That's called reading a paper like a professional and making a kind of a professional judgment about what a paper is. The junior qual was a diagnostic device. It was a fine way by which we evaluated how much our students were learning. It was similar with the senior thesis and with all our classes at Reed, including Humanities 110. The student came in

and you would have your paper conference. That means I would sit down with each of my students and go through the paper line by line, marking it up for grammar, for language, for style—but also for substance, for argumentative structure. That's what real assessment is.

JOHN POCK, sociology professor: The attorneys and the physicians that Reed College produced from that training were unique, usually the kinds of people who were considered mavericks in their professions. Most of them were peculiar in that they asked peculiar kinds of questions, and didn't behave themselves in a traditional manner. Their questions were peculiar because they were fundamental. It was a question of balancing the subject matter against the analytic skills that are involved in, say, taking a novel apart. What's the structure of reasoning? What's the knowledge claim that the author is making? What's the evidence that the author is producing? It's not something that you are just born with. You have to work at it.

A lot of students came to Reed not understanding that—that what we were providing was the transmission of a set of techniques about how to think, and about how to always answer a question with a question. If you can't come up with a new hypothesis or a new question at the end, you're done. You're dead.

RAY KIERSTEAD, history professor 1978–2000: Because it reflects disinterested scholarship, good teaching often confronts and subverts one of the cherished principles of the modern world, egotism, and the worse perversion of that principle, narcissism. Good teaching also does battle with another of modernity's ugly children, formlessness. The best teachers, in my experience, have been enlightened professionals in their fields. They have been craftsmen whose classroom teaching has been controlled by craft discipline.

The axioms of this discipline are simple, but severe. Learning is the product of hard and difficult work. Rigid rules of evidence govern scholarly work. Exactitude of expression is the necessary corollary of scholarship. Insight and capacity for critical thought are the rewards of often painful and frustrating labor.

Peter Steinberger, political science professor, dean of faculty: I was playing golf one day with Steve Koblik. We were on the fourth green at the Eastmoreland Golf Course, and talking about *U. S. News & World Report*'s college rankings. It was something I'd been thinking about for a long time. I said, "Steve, what you should do is forget about *U. S. News & World Report*. Don't cooperate. Don't participate. Ask them not to evaluate us. Ask them not to rank us. Just forget about it. We don't need it. It's not doing us any good. It's doing us harm. It's a lousy thing as it is. Let's forget about it."

Steve went ballistic. "You're out of your mind," he said. "We can't do that. It would kill Reed College." Then, maybe two days later, I get this phone call and it's Steve and he says, "You know, that's not a bad idea."

Steven Koblik, president: I sat in my office for a while and thought about our conversation. I had been involved in discussions about the *U. S. News & World Report* college rankings earlier, when I was dean at Scripps College. I had met the editors in Washington, D.C., and like virtually everyone else had decided they were a necessary evil. I didn't really think much more than that, other than that the rankings were stupid.

I asked Bob Mansueto, the dean of admission, to come to my office. I said, "Bob, what would happen if we pulled out of *U. S. News & World Report*?" He said, "Can I have a month to talk to my staff?" A month later he came back to me, and he said, "Steve, we've talked about it and we think it doesn't really make any difference either

way." So I talked to the faculty committees and they were very enthusiastic, as was the Student Senate. The trustees were positive, although worried that I might be working outside a box that we needed to stay inside of.

I wrote a letter to *U. S. News & World Report* telling them to drop us out of the rankings. They immediately responded in a rather ugly tone and threatened to sue Reed College. Well, when you do that to me, my tendency is to respond with at least equal aggression, if not more. Immediately I was on my horse, charging around my office saying, "I'm going to get those bastards." We responded by telling them, "Go ahead and sue us. We'd be happy to discuss this in court and besides, we might sue you for something."

Peter Steinberger, political science professor, dean of faculty: There were lots of schools that were cheating on the data that went in the *U. S. News* rankings. There were different ways to report data, and different ways to calculate data. So there was the problem of unreliable data. The formula for ranking was a horrible formula, but there was no such thing as a good formula, so you're working with pseudo-scientific ratings.

For example, one data point was selectivity in admissions. The ranking was based on the idea that the fewer you admit, the more selective you are. Makes sense, right? But if you are selecting a small number of students from a very big applicant pool you might be way less selective than if you are selecting a larger number of students from a smaller but very strong applicant pool.

At that time, in the mid-1990s, Reed's acceptance rate was down to 55 to 60 percent. When I first came to Reed in the mid-1970s it had been 85 percent. Later, in the 2000s, it went down to 31 to 35 percent. But at the time we were accepting say 60 percent of students from a small but tremendous applicant pool, and there were other places, much weaker schools, that were accepting 35 percent of their applicants from a much bigger applicant pool. You could see that their SAT scores were two hundred points lower than our SAT scores. Some of the students they were accepting couldn't get into Reed. They were much less selective, but it didn't show up in the formula. Just the opposite.

There was also a fear—and the fear was a reality—that colleges that were buying into the *U.S. News* industry had begun to make academic decisions not for academic reasons but to move themselves up in the rankings. I had seen it happen at very good colleges and universities. For example, the percentage of faculty members with Ph.D.s was a big point to *U.S. News & World Report*. Some places wouldn't hire a person without a Ph.D. because it would lower their percentage. At Reed, we would hire faculty members who were a year or two years away from getting a Ph.D. We made sure that the Ph.D. was going to happen, but if the young faculty member was spectacular and it appeared that he or she was going to be a great teacher-scholar, that was good for Reed, because we got these people who might go other places once they got their Ph.D.

The last point was that the very idea of a single quantitative rating of colleges was stupid. It was like rating religions, or rating churches, or rating great novels or poems. Trying to rate a college is like that. A college is a big, complex, culturally specific kind of thing. You can't rate these things on a single scale because it's a category mistake.

ROLLING STONE magazine, STEPHEN GLASS, "The College Rankings Scam," October 16, 1997: *U.S. News & World Report* punished Reed College. They gave it the lowest possible score in nearly every category. The school plunged to the bottom quartile. No other college had dropped so far, so fast.

STEVEN KOBLIK, president: Now, whatever one thought of Reed College, no one thought it de-

served to be at the bottom with a bunch of goose eggs. *U.S. News & World Report* did Reed College an enormous favor by dropping us to the absolute bottom of their rankings. The immediate response was that Reed suddenly attracted enormous media attention for all the right reasons. We became an institution that college counselors all over the country were excited about, because they hated the ranking system as much as we did.

Suddenly Reed was a player at the national level in a way that it had not been since the 1950s and early 1960s. That was just a side effect that was extraordinarily beneficial to the college, but not one that we had anticipated. Later, when I had contact with the magazine's editor, who was a very good guy, he said, "Boy, did we make a mistake by giving you a platform with all those goose eggs."

NICHOLAS CHURCH '95: The *U.S. News & World Report* decision gave Steve Koblik a lot of credibility among the student body, because it demonstrated that he understood something fundamental about Reed: that it was unique and that it wasn't measurable in that way. Steve was standing up for a principle of academic integrity, and being unruly. There was something really very Reed-like about that act, and it gave Steve a lot of street cred. It was an important act.

STEVEN KOBLIK, president: No other liberal arts college dropped out of the *U.S. News & World Report* college rankings when we did. Most of my presidential colleagues said to me privately, "Steve, I'd love to do what you're doing but my board won't let me," or "My faculty is against it." What they really were saying was that it was a changed environment and, although they hated it, they had to change with that environment.

Well, we didn't like it at Reed, and we didn't do it.

Epilogue

I hoped that Reed College would continue to stand staunchly—and if necessary, stand alone—for whatever Reed College considered right.
    —William Foster, founding president

What has held this college together from its beginning, during the periods when it has gone through some really remarkable catastrophes? It has been an acceptance on the part of faculty, students, and alumni that Reed College stands for something that is different—not just different to be different, but different because it means something. In other words, this place has been committed to an ideal. That commitment has carried it through the dark days when it was suggested that the college ought to fold up, liquidate, or combine with some of the local independent colleges, and change from a scholarly place with scholarly ideals to a vocational school, lessening its standards, and certainly lessening its liberal point of view.

The commitment to the Reed ideal held and has been maintained, but at some considerable cost, and not a material one altogether. The hard world of realism, cynicism, and skepticism gets a great laugh when somebody with a dream, an ideal, a vision, a hope, falls flat on his face. The aspiration to be different, which was part of the founding of the college, did not mean that the college would ever become a haven for irrational idiosyncrasies. That was never contemplated.

The difference lay in the fact that the college had seriousness of purpose and was confident in the capacity of students to be mature, and of faculty to be wise, and that all together they would be comrades of a quest for learning.
    —Dorothy Johansen '33, history professor 1934–1969, archivist 1969–1984

Reed was like a kendo dojo, where you practice sword-fighting with bamboo swords. It gave me the tools to hold my ground in any territory.
    —Gary Snyder '51

The commencement procession emerging through the Old Dorm Block sally port, 2009.

Reed College entered the twenty-first century well-ensconced among the top tier of liberal arts colleges in the country, and in its best financial shape since opening in 1911. Steven Koblik, who had led Reed since 1992, stepped down in 2001 to become president of the Huntington Library in Southern California. On the whole, he left the college richer, healthier, more civil, and better positioned to respond to the changing academic environment than it had been when he arrived.

After a one-year interim presidency filled by the dean of faculty, Peter Steinberger, Colin Diver became Reed's fourteenth president in 2002. Diver's tenure, which would span the next ten years, ending with the college's centennial year in 2011–12, was historic if only for one simple reason: it was the first presidential transition in Reed's history not marked by a major financial or governance crisis. Diver, a graduate of Amherst College and Harvard Law School, had worked in the Massachusetts governor's office for ten years before entering academia. He taught at Boston University and Harvard's Kennedy School, and served for ten years as dean of the law school at Penn State prior to arriving at Reed.

During his tenure, Diver confronted a series of challenges in maintaining Reed's standing among liberal arts colleges. To attract quality students and faculty, top-tier schools were stepping up their investments in a number of areas: improvements to campus facilities and student amenities, the diversification of their student bodies so as to provide environments that would foster cultural literacy and competence, the expansion of curriculums to add specialization, a focus on globalism both on campus and through study-abroad programs, the creation of new interdisciplinary programs to bring together methods and materials from more than one area of study, and the introduction of new technology into the classroom, including online learning. Finally, to expand their socio-economic diversity, wealthier schools implemented need-blind policies that covered the full financial needs of the most disadvantaged students, and, for students from middle-class backgrounds, offered programs that converted student loans to grants.

Meanwhile, during the first decade of the new century, college expenditures continued to spiral upward largely as a result of rising costs in financial aid, health care and other benefits, maintenance of facilities, and compliance with new governmental regulations. In an effort to defray these expenses, many colleges turned to filling teaching positions with non-tenure-track and part-time adjunct faculty. Between 1999 and 2009, the number of adjunct faculty at private colleges increased 46 percent, compared to 16 percent for tenured faculty. Even so, the cost of tuition at elite private colleges continued to rise faster than the rate of inflation. Between 1990 and 2008, tuition fees at private four-year colleges grew by 50 percent, adjusted for inflation. Despite an even greater increase in private colleges' average financial aid provided per student, which rose from 27 percent to 42 percent of average tuition cost during that same period, the escalating sticker shock elicited calls for accountability from both the public and the federal government.

Reed kept pace with the pricing of its peer schools, raising annual tuition from $33,000 in 1999 to almost $43,000 for the 2011–12 academic year. Adding in room and board, that made the total cost for a year at Reed almost $54,000. During this period, the college doubled its spending on financial aid, exceeding the growth in tuition price. As of 2011, 55 percent of Reed students received aid, with an average award of $36,000. However, when pitted against schools with much larger endowments, Reed fell short of becoming fully need-blind—admitting all accepted students without regard for their financial capacity—and found itself facing the increasing likelihood that the wealthiest colleges, especially those well funded by research grants and contracts, would someday virtually eliminate undergraduate tuition.

Many aspects of Reed's distinctive model of academic rigor continued to be challenged by the consumer-based approach to higher education. The growth of online learning, readily adopted as a solution to reducing overhead costs by a number of colleges with tightly structured programs targeted at career preparation, ran contrary to Reed's highly participatory, small-conference approach. Grade inflation also became rampant among colleges as students and their families increasingly looked for quantitative validation of their tuition investment. Between 1990 and 2010 the rate at which the grade of A was issued rose by almost 40 percent; at the end of this period, A had become the grade most commonly awarded. By contrast, Reed's 2010 average grade point average of 3.2 on a scale of 4.0 remained consistent with that of the previous three decades. In those thirty years only nine students graduated from the college with perfect 4.0 averages.

In addition, the growing popularity of off-campus internships and community service, which stressed experiential learning as an academically relevant means of career preparation, worked against an environment that was dedicated solely to intense academics. Most troublesome, perhaps, to Reed's reputation during this time was the oversupply of Ph.D.s in the academic market. For a college that had long prided itself on having one of the highest percentage of graduates going on to obtain doctoral degrees, Reed was challenged to re-conceive of itself as having a purpose more various than professional academic reproduction. The college's expanded engagement with its alumni underscored this necessity, as it revealed that just 24 percent of Reed graduates pursued careers in education, while the largest percentage went into business and industry. Meanwhile, the number of pure liberal arts colleges—those issuing at least 40 percent of their degrees in the liberal arts—declined from 212 in 1990 to 137 in 2009, as many institutions were forced to respond to market demand, evolving their curriculums toward professional degree programs.

Colin Diver set out to address these and other developments during his administration by broadening Reed's admission process, expanding the diversity of its faculty and student composition, and improving the quality of student life on campus. By the end of his tenure the pool of prospective students held more than three thousand qualified applicants—twenty years earlier it had been just eighteen hundred—increasing Reed's selectivity and putting an end to its myth of self-selection. Just 28 percent of applicants were accepted in 2011, as opposed to 55 percent a decade before, yet average SAT scores held steady at nearly 1400. The proportion of minority students at Reed rose from 14 percent to 26 percent, while first-generation college attendees remained a consistent 11 percent. The number of international students tripled—now amounting to 7 percent of the student body—following trends at other private colleges and universities. Faculty diversity, however, continued to be a challenge, although by 2010 the percentage of women on the faculty had risen to a historic high of 40 percent.

The college built several new dormitories and purchased nearby apartment buildings, increasing campus residency to 70 percent of the student body. Diver also continued to expand student services and academic resources designed to help students better cope with Reed's intense academic environment, including the establishment of a tutoring center for writing, science, quantitative skills, and statistics. Thanks to these and other efforts, the number of students graduating in four years rose from 60 percent in 2002 to a historic high of 70 percent in 2011, with a total of 80 percent graduating within six years.

In 2009, Reed launched a $200 million funding campaign, the largest in its history, to coincide with its centennial in 2011–12. The college's endowment, which had climbed from $350 million in 2000 to a peak of $456 million in 2007, was brought down to $329 million by the stock market crash of 2008. Thanks in part to new gifts made to the Centennial Campaign, the endowment stood at $400 million in early 2012. In addition to expanding financial aid and adding new tenured faculty positions, the campaign also funded construction of Reed's first-ever performing arts center, which broke ground in 2011. Diver recruited to the Board of Trustees a majority of members who were Reed alumni, marking a shift from the small group of local and regional business and industry leaders who had stewarded the board for most of the college's history. In 1998 Walter Mintz '50 became the first Reed graduate to chair the board, a tradition continued by succeeding chairs Dan Greenberg '62 in 2002 and Roger Perlmutter '73 in 2010.

President Diver's tenure was not, however, without controversy. As at other colleges, student use of drugs and alcohol remained a serious issue. The availability of dangerous and addictive narcotics, particularly methamphetamine and opiates, and the growing abuse of prescription drugs such as oxycodone affected many campuses. Diver's administration sought to create a more effective system to combat substance abuse with increased enforcement, treatment, and educational initiatives. In the midst of this effort, the death of two students from heroin overdoses drew the attention of prosecutors and the local media, who took aim at the college, particularly during the annual three-day Renn Fayre celebration following the conclusion of classes in the spring. In 2011, a nationwide controversy erupted over sexual assault on college campuses, bringing unfavorable media focus to Reed's use of a student judicial board for such cases, which had been in place since the late 1980s. At the request of students and faculty members, adjudication of sexual assault and harassment cases were thereafter assigned to a trained committee comprising both student members of the Judicial Board and college staff. Despite these controversies, Reed's relationship with the Portland community began to change for the better, as Portland completed its metamorphosis from a provincial western city into an exemplary American metropolis known for its urban planning, ecological sustainability, and artisan culture.

In the sphere of academic governance, Diver crossed swords with the faculty over two contentious matters. The first occurred when the president, a devout Episcopalian, initiated a spiritual-listening project on campus in an effort to support student faith practices, raising strong opposition from faculty members concerned about undermining the college's nonsectarian charter. A second controversy erupted when Diver, struggling to fill two faculty positions in the highly competitive field of economics, approved compensation offers that exceeded the common faculty pay scale. In opposition, three-quarters of the faculty voted in 2011 to preserve the egalitarian ethos of pay equity, underscoring their belief that Reed's academic excellence was fostered primarily by the fact of it being a community undertaking, and that a differential, market-driven salary structure would undermine the successful pursuit of this shared effort.

As student enrollment at Reed grew from 1,389 in 2002 to 1,474 in 2012, Diver added twenty-eight full-time faculty positions, provided more sabbatical opportunities for faculty members to pursue individual scholarship, and brought the student-faculty ratio to 10.2-to-one, very near to founding president William Foster's original goal of ten-to-one. While the college retained its commitment to the primacy of teaching, younger faculty members expressed interest in reworking Reed's curriculum and pedagogy in ways more hospitable to their intellectual training and personal research, and more responsive to student interests. This was reflected in changes to the mandatory freshman humanities program, which in 2010 was revised to address such concerns as multiculturalism and the exercise of global power by examining subaltern relationships to the dominant cultures of the Greco-Roman eras. Homer's *Odyssey* was substituted for the *Iliad* as the opening text in the course, establishing a travelogue framework that circumnavigated the Mediterranean world and incorporated material from the Egyptians and the Persians. Also, in keeping with interdisciplinary trends in higher education, a major in environmental studies was added in 2010 to the eleven other interdisciplinary majors offered at Reed.

Meanwhile, students at Reed maintained the creative, insouciant sense of humor that had distinguished the student body since its earliest days. Reed's mascot, the large cement lawn ornament known as the Doyle Owl—originally stolen from an Eastmoreland neighbor's yard in 1919—made a notable appearance in 2010, trundled forth from the sally port of the Old Dorm Block encased in a massive block of ice. The resulting contest lasted seven hours as teams struggled back and forth with the chilly prize, some attempting to defrost it, others simply bent on wrestling it into a getaway vehicle as quickly as possible.

The Doyle Owl wasn't the only tradition that managed to deeply engage the hearts of those drawn to a college that originally sought to be "neither hampered nor hallowed by traditions." Reed's founding president, William Foster, did establish one tradition, that being an uncompromising academic devotion to the pursuit of truth. Foster believed this pursuit, framed in a unique set of rigorous practices and an equally unique belief in student freedom, to be the basis of the "ideal college," continually providing renewed vitality to the liberal arts while preparing its graduates to be self-reliant in the ever-widening dimensions of the modern world. Over the decades, this tradition, along with self-selection, socialization, and a protective insularity, worked powerfully to create a Reed "type," one marked by intense intellectualism, social nonconformity, and unconventional creativity. While a number of students rejected or were scarred by their experience in Reed's demanding, almost monastic setting, others—graduates and nongraduates alike—embraced it almost as though it were a secret cult.

As became clear quite early on in the college's development, however, Foster's design of the ideal college came with a set of inherent paradoxes. Those paradoxes, which arose from Foster's intended outcomes and the principled means he set down for achieving them—intellectual freedom, academic rigor, and egalitarian democracy—were the inevitable source of ongoing internal tension within the college. They also made Reed a target of dislike and contempt among many of those in the outside environs who were not so intellectually or progressively inclined. For the members of the early Reed community the only way forward was to work with these paradoxes while struggling to preserve the college's fundamental principles. This quest, hard fought at times over a century of ferocious internal and external battles, resulted in four financial and political near-death experiences for the college in the twentieth century, and remains a formidable challenge to the Reed community in the twenty-first.

The most acute difficulty the college faces has to do with the viability of the liberal arts themselves. The global recession of the late 2000s placed major stress on the economic model of elite liberal arts colleges, most of them built on "artisanal" cost structures, lacking efficiencies of scale. Their ever-rising tuition fees—and the related debt loads they imposed upon many students—stirred a national skepticism about the utilitarian value of their diplomas for graduates entering a tight job market. For many colleges this call to accountability sparked an identity crisis. Some of them, having followed the herd in chasing the latest trends of consumer demand, had strayed far from their original missions and found themselves vulnerable to the ever-changing winds of public opinion.

Not so, Reed College. Born during a similar crisis in the liberal arts one hundred years ago, Reed has maintained its distinction by conservatively focusing on doing one thing well: training students in critical thinking. As William Foster made clear, such training depends on a heightened level of creative tension that resists the comforts of status quo thinking. At Reed, ideally no idea or assumption goes unchallenged, but is instead tested in a pervasive environment of argument and discussion. In its intentionality, this Socratic training is naturally drawn to the dynamic ground of disruption, sometimes self-manufactured, in which important ideas and values are examined and debated. This attraction has been ritualized at Reed in an annually revived spectator sport of sorts known as the "spring crisis," in which an unpredictable event engulfs the entire community in a fierce debate over such principles as academic freedom, participatory democracy, self-determination, personal liberty, or Reed's non-codified Honor Principle. The dialectic that unfolds is not always about two opposites seeking a unified reconciliation—indeed, in many cases there is no reconciliation—but is rather, as John Dewey described, a matter of looking at the classic dialectic process from the other end: the inevitable physical and moral tension of a unity attempting to embrace opposites in its growing understanding.

That sense of unity—of knowing one's primary mission—has allowed the Reed community over the past century to successfully weather various social and political trends. It has also provided a means of adapting the college to various developments in higher education—the progressive education movement in the 1910s, the general education programs between the two world wars, scientific methodology in the 1950s, political relevance in the 1960s, theories of structuralism and deconstruction in the 1970s, the cultural wars in the 1980s, political correctness in the 1990s, and ideological bias in the 2000s—without losing its focus. Where other liberal arts colleges may have faltered by holding too loosely to their missions, Reed, when it did falter, did so by holding too tightly. During such times in the college's history, a stubborn resistance to change set in, which, while preserving the practices shown to be successful in delivering on the college's mission, stifled the vitality necessary for adapting that mission to an ever-changing world.

As Reed College moves forward into its second century, its central challenge remains the same: to balance the strength of the college's founding ideals and historical educational model with a pragmatic responsiveness to demands of the present day. That task—and its reward—are only fitting for those who take up William Foster's call to be comrades of the quest.

The Reed Oral History Project

In a very real sense, the Reed Oral History Project had its genesis in 1934 during a renovation of the attic in Eliot Hall, when a packet of Simeon Reed's business and private papers was discovered beneath the floorboards. Dorothy O. Johansen, a 1933 Reed College graduate, had just returned to Portland with a master's degree in medieval history from the University of Washington, and was working at the college as a graduate assistant. Reed's president at the time, Dexter Keezer, offhandedly said to her, "You're a medieval historian; you have some study in that. Why don't you catalogue these papers?" Johansen proceeded to prepare a short history of the institution, based on Simeon Reed's papers, for the college's twenty-fifth anniversary in 1936.

She also began, with funding from the Works Progress Administration, to write the history of Simeon Reed's Oregon Steam Navigation Company. That effort involved interviewing people who had known Reed while he was alive, including his nephew's son, Simeon Winch, who was then a trustee of the college. Winch subsequently lent Johansen the money to return to the University of Washington for her Ph.D. in American history, specifically the history of the Pacific Northwest.

Doctorate in hand, Johansen returned to teach history and humanities at Reed. In the 1950s she authored, with Charlie Gates, the popular Northwest history *Empire of the Columbia*. In 1959, she received a grant from the Ford Foundation to write a history of Reed College, and began interviewing, both in person and by mail, many of the figures who had participated in establishing the school. Johansen retired from full-time teaching in 1969 and became the college's part-time archivist, in which position she continued to work on her history of Reed.

By the time I went to work for her as a student at Reed in the late 1970s, she had succeeded in writing much of the first decade of that history. Working next door to the Reed chapel on the second floor of Eliot Hall, in a small archives office filled with stacks of old papers and small index cards each containing a particular fact or insight jotted down in her cursive script, Johansen had rewritten the book's opening chapters many times, trying to get the story exactly right. She impressed upon me that those early years at Reed had laid the foundation for all that followed. When Dorothy Johansen died in 2001, her manuscript remained unfinished, ending in 1919.

The impetus for the formal launch of the Reed Oral History Project occurred on a sad note in 1995. Deborah Ross '68, chapter representative of the Southern California Reed Alumni Chapter, received a call from an attorney for Virginia Mackenzie '16, an alumna from Reed's second graduating class. Mackenzie had excelled at Reed, and immediately following graduation had been appointed a lecturer in classics at the college. In 1918 she left Portland and sailed to Japan, where she spent the next forty years teaching and serving as principal of a Presbyterian missionary school. Mackenzie's attorney now informed Ross that his client, having just celebrated her hundredth birthday, was anxious to share her memories of early Reed with the college. Ross contacted alumnus and radio personality Barry Hansen '63—aka "Dr. Demento"—who agreed to drive out to the assisted living facility in the San Gabriel Valley where Mackenzie resided to interview her. When Hansen reached her, however, Mackenzie's mental health had deteriorated to the point that all she could manage upon meeting him was a smile.

This experience led Ross, a noted author and storyteller, to raise with the Reed Alumni Association the importance of interviewing aging alumni before their stories were lost to time. With the support of then alumni director Marianne Brogan '84, the alumni board appointed a committee—Nancy Stewart Green '50, Mort Rosenblum '49, and Sheldon Hochheiser '73—to pursue the idea of organizing an alumni oral history project. In 1997 I joined the committee, becoming its chair and the volunteer director of the project.

We set the goal of interviewing 275 alumni in ten years. I conducted the first interview in 1998 with Gary Snyder '51, who suggested that we consider assembling a book of the oral histories for the college's centennial in 2011. Snyder also provided the project with its rallying cry: "Get the stories before they're gone."

Volunteers who were archivists and oral historians or public historians were recruited from among Reed alumni. Gail Kurtz '82, a professional oral historian in Berkeley, agreed to design the project and train alumni volunteers as interviewers. Lauren Lassleben '75, an archivist at UC Berkeley's Bancroft Library, one of the two key centers of oral history in the country, joined the project as its national coordinator, recruiting and managing coordinators for most of the regional alumni chapters, and screening potential interviewees. Malca Chall '42, a longtime oral historian, also at the Bancroft Library, provided advice, as did Chris Lowe '82, a historian and former Reed faculty member. AT&T archivist Sheldon Hochheiser, along with oral historians Michael O'Rourke '66 and

Laura Ross '98, MALS '06, contributed their professional services, expanding the project to include interviews with retired faculty members, trustees, and administrators. In 2002 Gay Walker '69 was appointed librarian of special collections at the Reed library; she created a system for archiving the interviews and also contributed significant personal time to the project as a volunteer. Professional storyteller Cricket Parmalee '67 joined the effort in 2004, adding another dimension by hosting storytelling sessions at alumni gatherings around the country.

For the first six years, the work was financed solely by alumni contributions, with Lauren Lassleben, Gay Walker, Gail Kurtz, and Cricket Parmalee comprising the core volunteer team. By 2005 the volume of activity had begun to overwhelm the project's volunteer capacities, and, thanks to the generosity of Hugh Porter, Reed's vice-president of college relations, the college provided a grant to increase the budget. One of Oregon's foremost oral historians, Donna Sinclair, was hired as part-time manager of the oral history project, and the duties of Reed library archives assistant Mark Kuestner were expanded to give support for Gay Walker in coordinating research and archiving the interviews. When Sinclair moved on in 2008, oral historian Cynthia Lopez stepped in as project manager.

Over the years, 125 alumni volunteers were trained and deployed to conduct interviews. Alumni chapter coordinators included June Anderson '49, Julia Chamberlain '04, Becky Chiao '85, Kristen Earl '05, Nancy Green '50, Brie Gyncild '91, Robert Hadley '53, James Kahan '64, Lauren Lassleben, Miriam Moore '98, Richard Parker '75, Cricket Parmalee, David Perry '73, Pat Pruyne '83, Barbara Carter Radin '75, Laura Ross, Barbara Weeks Shettler '50, and Chantal Sudbrack '97. Alumni director Michael Teskey provided critical support, as did a series of Alumni Association presidents that included Sally Brunette '83, Sheldon Hochheiser, Pat Pruyne, Steve Falk '83, David Perry, Konrad Alt '81, Tony Fisher '80, Rachel Hall Luft '95, Sandy Blake Boles '90, and Erik Speckman '91. An online extension of the project, "Reed Stories," was developed under the direction of alumni director Teskey and alumni relations coordinator Robin Tovey '97, and launched in 2008 with Joanne Hossack '82 as its national volunteer coordinator.

The Reed Oral History Project has been an extraordinary community endeavor. Over thirteen years more than fourteen hundred people were interviewed, far exceeding the initial goal. This total included almost four hundred alumni, faculty members, administrators, and trustees who were interviewed individually, and more than a thousand people who participated in forty-six group interviews conducted at class reunions and thirty-four storytelling sessions held at alumni chapters around the country. In addition, dozens of legacy interviews conducted between 1935 and 1992—primarily by Dorothy Johansen '33 and Blake Nebel '92—were transcribed and added to the collection. Taken together, these oral histories provided the basis for the creation of *Comrades of the Quest*.

Acknowledgments

Comrades of the Quest is the culmination of many years of interviews, research, and distillation that depended on the help and support of a considerable group of people. They included, foremost, those who volunteered their oral histories, and more than a hundred volunteers who traveled the country as "story catchers" to collect and archive them. As anyone who has been involved in a large-scale volunteer effort knows, a project of this nature relies upon a high level of individual commitment for its success. I am very grateful to all of those involved in the Reed Oral History Project who wholeheartedly gave of themselves to generate the source material of this book.

For the daunting task of excerpting and editing the interviews into discrete stories, I was fortunate to have a trusted and discerning team—Laura Ross '98, MALS '06, Simon Woodard '10, Cynthia Lopez, and Donna Sinclair. Susan West provided invaluable professional editing, helping me work through the challenges of the narrative model and deftly trimming the book down to a manageable size. At critical junctures in the process I turned to a first circle of readers—Jackie Dirks '82, Sam Fromartz '80, Ray Kierstead, Chris Lowe '82, and Chris Lydgate '89—each of whom provided constructive feedback, insights, and historical perspectives that helped shape the manuscript's narrative flow. I am indebted to all of them for their wisdom, patience, and generosity.

This book was brought to fruition thanks to the close collaboration of four individuals with whom I began planning the project a decade ago, each of whom brought to the task great personal dedication and a unique set of talents. Laura Ross served as my trusted and diligent right hand, assisting with organizing the content and conducting interviews to help close historical gaps. Gay Walker '69, special collections librarian at Reed, together with her resourceful assistant, Mark Kuestner, provided expert help with research, image access, and fact-checking. Working with Gay and Mark was a delightful experience of continual discovery, in which long-buried and sometimes forgotten fragments of history repeatedly emerged from deep storage within the college archives, expanding the scope of the project far beyond what I had originally imagined. And I very much appreciate the many hours of hard work Gay dedicated to proofreading and to assembling the bibliography, notes, and index. Finally, I am grateful to John Laursen '67 for the book's graceful design and typography, which give elegant visual expression to the contrasting narrative styles of oral history and introductory text. John also produced the book and worked closely with me on selecting the photographs; he made valuable editorial suggestions at every stage of design and production, constantly challenging and pushing me over the entire course of the book's development to reach for a higher standard of quality. The rigor and care with which he and the other members of the team approached this project are highly exemplary, I believe, of Reed College itself.

I want to express my gratitude to Oregon State University Press, including in particular acquiring editor Mary Braun and associate director Tom Booth for believing in the book and navigating it through the publication process, and managing editor Jo Alexander for her careful review and thoughtful editorial comments. Thanks also to PSU historian Carl Abbott for his close reading of the manuscript, to Joanne Hossack '82 for copyediting assistance, to Laurie Lindquist for help with research, to Sumner Stone '68 for generously donating a customized version of his Cycles typeface, and to my good friend Jack Stauffacher for his early advice on the look and feel of the book. The unflagging support provided over the years by Reed alumni relations director Michael Teskey and his staff—Mela Kunitz '87, Robin Tovey '97, and Todd Hesse—in many ways both large and small, was critical, as was the hospitality of Colby Westhead at the Parker House.

In conceiving of the narrative format of this volume, I am indebted to Peter Kann, whose *Comrades and Chicken Ranchers*, an oral history of the community of radical Jewish chicken ranchers in my hometown of Petaluma, California, suggested an innovative way to portray the story of the Reed community. I am also grateful to Gary Snyder '51 for his encouragement, and to Reb Anderson, who taught me the value of listening to others' stories and to my own.

During the course of its gestation this project took on added poignancy with the deaths of a number of those who had shared their oral histories, some of whom I had interviewed personally. As the years passed, what had begun as a celebratory project for the college's centennial took on an unforeseen theme of transience, underscored by the unearthing of the long-forgotten voices of people captured in taped interviews decades ago or in unpublished memoirs and letters. The desire to ensure that their stories would live on gave me fortitude as I worked to bring the book to completion.

Last, I wish to thank Laurie Szujewska for her great patience, wise advice, and wonderful sense of humor, all of which helped to carry me through this journey.
—John Sheehy '82
March 2012

Notes

Page 1: The epigraph by Burton Clark is from page 168 of *The Distinctive College*.

INTRODUCTION

Page 3: The David Starr Jordan quotation is from his speech, "At the Laying of the Corner-stone of the Dwelling Hall," from "Occasional Addresses," *Reed College Record*, no. 8 (December 1912), 25.

The *Quest* quotation is from an unsigned editorial, *Reed College Quest*, vol. 1, issue 1, June 16, 1913, 2.

The phrase "communism, atheism, free love" was cited as being attributed to Reed following the First World War in interviews with alumni from the 1920s and 1930s. It was also referred to by Reed's board chairman, E. B. MacNaughton, in his "Statement," at the Conference on Educational Problems on the Occasion of the Inauguration of President Dexter Merriam Keezer, May 15–17, 1935.

Page 4: *The New York Times*: "Where College Boys Prefer to Study Baseball," April 15, 1917, section M, 5.

The *Saturday Evening Post*: "School for Smart Young Things," Richard L. Neuberger, October 25, 1952, 36.

Time magazine: "Colleges. A Thinking Reed," December 28, 1962, 38.

The Princeton Review: The Best 361 Colleges, 2006, 30.

Page 6: Statistics on college attrition levels are from Douglas Bennett, "Retention and Attrition at Reed: A Status Report."

Page 9: Comments on history and memory are informed by Margaret McMillan, *Dangerous Games: The Uses and Abuses of History*.

The Ralph Waldo Emerson quotation is from Emerson, *Essays: First Series*, Charleston: BiblioBazaar, 2008, 13.

Pages 9–10: The Leslie Stephen quotation is from Max Hastings, "Drawing the Wrong Lesson," *The New York Review of Books*, March 11, 2010, 41.

Page 10: The Alessandro Portelli reference on memory is from Betsy Brinson, "Crossing Cultures: An Interview with Alessandro Portelli," *Oral History Review*, vol. 28, no. 1 (Winter/Spring 2001): 108.

The Portelli quotation is from an interview with Portelli by Alexander Stille, "Prospecting for Truth in the Ore of Memory," *The New York Times*, March 10, 2001, section B, 9.

"History-telling" is from Portelli, *The Battle of Valle Giulia*, Madison: University of Wisconsin Press, 1997, 6.

The definition of collective memory is from Maurice Halbwachs, *On Collective Memory*, edited and translated by Lewis A. Coser, Chicago and London: University of Chicago Press, 1992, 27–28.

The Eric Hobsbawm quotation is from Hobsbawm, *The Age of Empire: 1875–1914*, New York: Vintage Books, 1989, 3.

Page 11: The Jorge Luis Borges quotation is from Scott Russell Sanders, "The Power of Stories," *The Georgia Review* 51 (Spring 1997), 115.

Part One: The Radical Upstart, 1911–1920

Introductory Essay

Page 15: The Woodrow Wilson quotation is from John Axtell, *The Making of Princeton University*, Princeton, New Jersey: Princeton University Press, 2006, 239.

Pages 15–16: The discussion of the pragmatist movement is informed by Louis Menand, *The Metaphysical Club: A Story of Ideas in America*.

The discussion of college developments in the nineteenth and twentieth centuries is informed by Louis Menand, *The Marketplace of Ideas*; and by Steven Koblik and Stephen R. Graubard, editors, *Distinctly American: The Residential Liberal Arts Colleges*.

Page 16: The Simeon Reed quotation on "useful industry" is from William G. Robbins, *Education, Arts, and Letters: Establishing a Framework for Learning*, the Oregon History Project, Oregon History Society, http://www.ohs.org.

The discussion of early Portland history is informed by E. Kimbark MacColl, *The Shaping of a City: Business and Politics in Portland, Oregon, 1885 to 1915*.

Pages 16–18: The background on early Reed history is from Dorothy O. Johansen, "History of Reed College."

Page 17: The discussion of Charles Eliot's reforms at Harvard is informed by Hugh Hawkins, *Between Harvard and America: The Educational Leadership of Charles W. Eliot*; by Bruce A. Kimball, *Orators & Philosophers: A History of the Idea of Liberal Education*; and by Frederick Rudolph, *The American College & University: A History*.

Page 18: The William Trufant Foster quotation is from Foster, "Specializing in the Humanities," 1.

Chapter 1

Page 19: The William G. Eliot quotation is from a letter dated 13 January, 1881, quoted in John Frederick Scheck, *Transplanting a Tradition: Thomas Lamb Eliot and the Unitarian Conscience in the Pacific Northwest, 1865–1905*, 366.

Page 24: The excerpt from Thomas Lamb Eliot's letter to Simeon Reed is from Earl Morse Wilbur, *Thomas Lamb Eliot, 1841–1936*, Portland, Oregon: The Greenleaf Press, 1937, 91.

Chapter 2

Pages 31–32: Ralph Hetzel's remarks prefaced his address at Reed College's "Portland 1915 Conference," and are from Dorothy O. Johansen, "History of Reed College," 86.

Chapter 3

Page 36: The Jean Wolverton Petite excerpt is from Johansen, "History of Reed College," 84.

Page 37: The excerpt from William Foster's opening day speech is from Johansen, "History of Reed College," 85.

Chapter 4

Page 66: The 1920 *Griffin* excerpt is from "The Houses," and "Looking Backward."

Chapter 5

Page 76: The March 2, 1917, *Morning Oregonian* excerpt is from "Reed Pledges Its Loyalty to Wilson" and "Reed College and Peace."

Part Two: The Golden Age, 1921–1945

Introductory Essay

Page 88: Background on the development of Western Civilization courses between the wars is from W. B. Carnochan, *The Battleground of the Curriculum*, 68–90; from Lionel S. Lewis, "Introduction to the Aldine Transaction Edition" of Alexander Meiklejohn, *Education Between Two Worlds*, ix; and from Robert Maynard Hutchins, *The Higher Learning in America*, 105.

The Matthew Arnold quotation is from Carnochan, *The Battleground of the Curriculum*, 64.

Pages 88–89: Details of the goals of the Scholz curriculum are from Richard Scholz, "President R. F. Scholz," in the Association of American Colleges, Commission on the Organization of the College Curriculum, *Unifying the Liberal College Curriculum*, 30–40.

Pages 89–90: Background on the general education movement is from Menand, *The Marketplace of Ideas*, 23–43.

Chapter 6

Page 91: The Richard Scholz quotation is from the *Quest* article "President Richard Frederick Scholz—The Man and His Program," 4.

Page 92: The Richard Scholz excerpt is from the *Quest* article "President Richard Frederick Scholz—The Man and His Program," 4.

Page 103: The Alexander Meiklejohn excerpt is from Meiklejohn, "President Alexander Meiklejohn," in the Association of American Colleges, Commission on the Organization of the College Curriculum, *Unifying the Liberal College Curriculum*, 11–23.

CHAPTER 7

Page 106: Comments on Reed's institutional development are informed by Clark, *The Distinctive College*, 117.

CHAPTER 8

Page 116: Comments on and details of Reed's institutional development are informed by Clark, *The Distinctive College*, 116–124.

CHAPTER 10

Page 138: Statistics are from Reed College, "Self-Study Report, Impact of the College: The Coed"; from the registrar's records, 1915 through 1959; from Dexter Keezer, "A Letter to the Alumni from the President," 5; and from "Reed Graduates Appraise the College," *Reed College Bulletin*.

CHAPTER 11

Page 154: Background on Reed student life is informed by Clark, *The Distinctive College*, 135.

Page 173: The January 18, 1939, *Quest* excerpt is from "Keezer Seeks to Keep Reed in Original Path, Report Says," 3.

The February 1, 1939, *Quest* excerpt is from "Men's Athletic Policy," Ernest Ehinger, 1.

PART THREE: THE NATIONAL COLLEGE, 1946–1966

INTRODUCTORY ESSAY

Page 197: Details of the G.I. Bill are from Louis Menand, "Show or Tell," 106.

Pages 197–198: Details of student enrollment in the 1960s are from Menand, *The Marketplace of Ideas*, 63–68.

Page 198: Details of student accomplishments are from Neuberger, "School for Smart Young Things."

The John Dewey quotation about the Great Books program is from Carnochan, *The Battleground of the Curriculum*, 88.

Pages 198–199: The discussion of Arragon and the humanities is based in part on the Rex Arragon interview in June 1970.

Page 199: The discussion of Reed students' majors is based on the registrar's records from 1915 to 1959.

The discussion of McCarthyism, President Sullivan, and the student body are based on *Time* magazine, "Colleges: A Thinking Reed", on *Look* magazine, Sam Castan, "Reed College: Portland's Academic Gadfly"; and on Neuberger, "School for Smart Young Things."

The discussion of research in academia is informed by Clark, *The Distinctive College*, 228.

The discussion of graduate programs is informed by Menand, "Show or Tell," 106.

CHAPTER 17

Page 217: The discussion of the new faculty cadre is informed by Clark, *The Distinctive College*, 153.

CHAPTER 18

Pages 232–233: The introductory essay to Chapter 18 is informed by Lionel S. Lewis, Cold *War on Campus*, 70–72; and by Richard Norton Smith, *The Harvard Century: The Making of a University to a Nation*, 195–197.

Page 233: The Richard Jones excerpt is from "A Reed Union on Academic Freedom," 25–27.

Pages 240–241: The excerpt from *The Oregonian's* interview with Duncan Ballantine is from the article "Reed College Board Silent on Plans After Meeting," Wilma Morrison, 1.

CHAPTER 19

Page 244: The introductory essay to Chapter 19 is informed in part by Clark, *The Distinctive College*, 163, 165.

CHAPTER 20

Page 256: The introductory essay to Chapter 20 is informed in part by Clark, *The Distinctive College*, 135, 142.

Page 261: The Bob Charlton excerpt is from "Discourse: Does Reed Stifle Creativity," 30–32.

Chapter 22

Page 284: The introductory essay to Chapter 22 is informed in part by Clark, *The Distinctive College*, 166.

Chapter 23

Page 297: The Chuck Bigelow excerpt is from Todd Schwartz, "The Dance of the Pen," 2.

Part Four: The Cultural Wars, 1967–1988

Introductory Essay

Page 317: The David Reisman quotation is from Nardi Reeder Campion, *Over the Hill, You Pick Up Speed*, Lebanon, New Hampshire: University Press of New England, 2006, 120.

The discussion of the mid-1960s academic climate is informed by Gilbert Allardyce, "The Rise and Fall of the Western Civilization Course"; by Peter N. Stearns, *Western Civilization in World History*, 15–16; by Menand, *The Marketplace of Ideas*, 74; and by Daniel Bell, *The End of Ideology*.

The discussion of education expenses and scientific research is informed by Thomas Bender, "Politics, Intellect, and the American University, 1945–1995."

Pages 317–318: The discussion of political criticism is informed by Menand, *The Marketplace of Ideas*, 77.

Pages 319–320: The details of Ph.D.s are from Christina Elliott Sorum, "New Problems in the Humanities," 247.

Page 320: The discussion of economic threats is informed by Menand, *The Marketplace of Ideas*, 68.

The details of the shifts in faculty allegiance are from Sorum, "New Problems in the Humanities," 247; and from Ernest Boyer, *Scholarship Reconsidered*, 56.

The statistics on faculty allegiance are from Menand, *The Marketplace of Ideas*, 122.

Chapter 25

Page 324: The Terry Miller excerpt is from "Discourse: Drop Outs," 32.

Chapter 27

Page 355: The preamble from the Black Student Union and the Marvin Levich excerpt are both from Thomas K. Worcester, "Diary of a Confrontation: Black Studies at Reed," 15–16.

Chapter 30

Page 385: The discussion of the 1970s and 1980s is informed by Kim Phillips-Fein, "1973 to the Present," 176–189.

Chapter 31

Page 400: The discussion of the 1970s and 1980s is informed by Phillips-Fein, "1973 to the Present," 177, 184.

Chapter 35

Page 450: The Richard Wollenberg excerpt is from "Profile of a Trustee: Richard P. Wollenberg," 2.

Part Five: Radical Traditionalist, 1989–2011

Introductory Essay

Page 459: The Association of American Colleges quotation is from the Association's Project on Redefining the Meaning and Purpose of Baccalaureate Degrees, *Integrity in the College Curriculum: A Report to the Academic Community*, 1.

The details of student enrollment are from the U.S. Department of Education, National Center for Education Statistics, *Digest of Education Statistics*, 2008 (NCES 2009-020), table 190; and from Michael McPherson and Morton Owen Shapiro, "The Future Economic Challenges for the Liberal Arts Colleges," 48.

The discussion of Charles Eliot's reforms is informed by Louis Menand, "Live and Learn," 76.

Page 460: The details of high school graduates are from McPherson and Shapiro, "The Future Economic Challenges for the Liberal Arts Colleges," 47.

The details of private versus public costs and enrollments are from Paul Neely, "Threats to Liberal Arts Colleges," 44.

The details of admission rates are from McPherson and Shapiro, "The Future Economic Challenges for the Liberal Arts Colleges," 47–50.

Pages 460–461: The details of acceptance rates are from Menand, "Live and Learn," 76.

Page 461: The details of the economic changes in college attendance are from Neely, "Threats to Liberal Arts Colleges," 30, 35–37.

The details of majors and third-tier schools are from McPherson and Shapiro, "The Future Economic Challenges for the Liberal Arts Colleges," 49.

The details of the free-electives curriculum are from the Association of American Colleges, *Integrity in the College Curriculum.*

Page 462: The discussion of student health needs is informed by Neely, "Threats to Liberal Arts Colleges," 32, 37.

CHAPTER 37

Pages 478–479: The introductory essay to Chapter 37 is informed by "An Interview with Steve Koblik," 7.

CHAPTER 38

Page 493: The discussion of sexuality in the 1980s and 1990s is informed by Astrid Henry, *Not My Mother's Sister: Generational Conflict and Third-Wave Feminism.*

CHAPTER 39

Page 505: The Steve Koblik quotation is from Harriet Watson, "*U. S. News and World Report* Hat Trick," 25.

The discussion of the 1990s and college rankings is informed by Harriet Watson, "Reed Rank(le)s *U. S. News and World Report,*" 28–29.

EPILOGUE

Page 519: The details of grade inflation are from Jeffrey R. Young, "Professors Cede Grading Power to Outsiders—Even Computers."

The details of Reed grades are from "Grades at Reed."

Details of the supply of Ph.D.s are from Menand, *The Marketplace of Ideas,* 154.

The details of Reed graduates' careers are from "Life After Reed."

Page 520: The details about female faculty numbers are from Ellen Stauder, "A Historical Snapshot of the Reed Faculty by Gender."

Page 522: The details of the icy Owl fight are from "The Reed Almanac," 35.

The discussion of Reed's demanding nature is informed by Clark, *The Distinctive College,* 236.

Page 523: The discussion of movements in higher education is informed by Mark Bauerlein, "A Solitary Thinker."

Credits and Permissions

QUOTED MATERIAL

Pages 19–21: Excerpts from the oral history of Simeon Reed reprinted by permission of the Bancroft Library, University of California, Berkeley.

Pages 91, 92, 94, 97–98, 104: Excerpts from the article by Clarence Ayres, "Scholz of Reed," reprinted by permission of *The New Republic.*

Page 103: Excerpt from the April 7, 1924 *Morning Oregonian,* copyright © 1924 The Oregonian. All rights reserved. Reprinted with permission.

Page 105: Excerpt from the July 24, 1924 *Morning Oregonian,* copyright © 1924 The Oregonian. All rights reserved. Reprinted with permission.

Pages 106, 108: Excerpt from "Retro Santanas!" copyright © 1925 The Harvard Crimson, Inc. All rights reserved. Reprinted with permission.

Pages 118, 138, 141–142, 164–165: Excerpts from Mary Barnard's *Assault on Mount Helicon* reprinted by permission of Elizabeth Bell.

Pages 125, 158, 163, 172: Excerpts from Thomas Lamb Frazier's *Between the Lines* reprinted by permission of Delphine and Richard Frazier.

Pages 127, 129–132, 134, 137, 156–157, 158–159, 163–164, 171, 172–173, 176, 177, 179–180, 181–182, 186: Excerpts from pages 28–30, 35–39, 50–51, 61, 71–83, 85–92, 99–101, 142–143 from *The Light That Flickers* by Dexter Merriam Keezer, copyright © 1947 by Harper & Brothers; renewed copyright © 1975 by Dexter M. Keezer. Reprinted by permission of HarperCollins Publishers.

Page 128: Excerpt from "Prex Dex," copyright © 1935 Time, Inc. All rights reserved. Reprinted with permission.

Page 166: Excerpt from "Nomination," copyright © 1936 Time, Inc. All rights reserved. Reprinted with permission.

Pages 175–176: Excerpt from the *Eugene Register-Guard* reprinted by permission of the Register-Guard.

Page 176: Excerpt from "Husky Reed," copyright © 1939 Time, Inc. All rights reserved. Reprinted with permission.

Page 186: Excerpt from Dexter Keezer's "Guest Editorial" in *College Management* reprinted by permission of *College Planning & Management Magazine.*

Page 204: Excerpt from "Shelley by Moonlight," copyright © 1947 Time, Inc. All rights reserved. Reprinted with permission.

Page 220: Excerpt from "Reed's Choice," copyright © 1952 Time, Inc. All rights reserved. Reprinted with permission.

Pages 240–241: Excerpt from *The Oregonian,* October 2, 1954, copyright © 1954 The Oregonian. All rights reserved. Reprinted with permission.

Pages 241–242: Excerpt from "Reed Tries Again," copyright © 1954 Time, Inc. All rights reserved. Reprinted with permission.

Pages 280–281: Excerpt from "Students: The Free-Sex Movement," copyright © 1966 Time, Inc. All rights reserved. Reprinted with permission.

Page 398: Excerpt from *The Oregonian,* May 24, 1987, copyright © 1987 The Oregonian. All rights reserved. Reprinted with permission.

Page 427: Excerpt from an interview with Vincenz Panny reprinted by permission of the Oregon Historical Society.

Page 436: Excerpt from *The Oregonian*, May 1, 1983, copyright © 1983 The Oregonian. All rights reserved. Reprinted with permission.

PHOTOGRAPHS

Uncredited photographs are from the Reed College archives in Special Collections at the Reed College Library.

Page 14: William Trufant Foster surveying Crystal Springs Farm by Beaver Engraving Company.

Page 22: Simeon and Amanda Reed's Portland house by Isaac G. Davidson.

Page 48: Faculty group by Angelus Photo Company.

Page 61: Campus Day by Angelus Photo Company.

Page 73: Downtown Portland waterfront by Benjamin Gifford, courtesy of the Oregon Historical Society, bb007945.

Page 78: Foster reviewing troops by Columbia Commercial Studio.

Page 80: Reconstruction Aides by Hill Studios.

Page 86: Eliot Hall circa 1921 by Benjamin Gifford, courtesy of the Oregon Historical Society, bb007925.

Page 101: Commons from the 1922 Reed College *Griffin*.

Page 102: Daydodgers by Hicks-Chatten Engraving, from the 1923 Reed College *Griffin*.

Page 110: Portraits of L. E. Griffin, A. A. Knowlton, and F. L. Griffin courtesy of Colin Herald Campbell '33.

Page 111: Portraits of Charles McKinley, Rex Arragon, and E. O. Sisson courtesy of Colin Herald Campbell '33.

Page 115: 1930s library courtesy of W. Boychuk.

Page 118: Portrait of Barry Cerf courtesy of Colin Herald Campbell '33.

Page 119: Portrait of Victor Chittick courtesy of Colin Herald Campbell '33.

Page 120: Women of House A from the 1928 Reed College *Griffin*.

Page 129: Portrait of Dexter Keezer courtesy of Colin Herald Campbell '33.

Page 156: Prentiss Lee and Mary Kuylaars courtesy of Mary Jackson Gibson '39.

Page 174: Emilio Pucci skiing from the 1937 Reed College *Griffin*.

Page 175: Coxswain Mary Elizabeth Russell from the 1941 Reed College *Griffin*.

Page 190: Portland stockyards during the internment of Japanese-Americans courtesy of the Oregon Historical Society, bb002208.

Page 193: World War II Army Meteorology Program cadets courtesy of Colin Herald Campbell '33.

Page 204: Students at Breitenbush Lake courtesy of Les Ordeman of the *Oregon Journal*.

Page 216: Students at 1414 Lambert Street courtesy of Gary Snyder '51.

Page 219: "School for Smart Young Things," 1952, courtesy of the *Saturday Evening Post*.

Page 220: Duncan Ballantine courtesy of Arlen Quan '54.

Page 225: Students in the Hauser Library courtesy of Gwil Evans '61.

Page 227: Reed coffee shop from the 1947 Reed College *Griffin*.

Page 230: Student archers by Photo-Art Commercial Studios, from the 1947 Reed College calendar.

Page 236: Lloyd Reynolds at the 1954 HUAC hearings courtesy of the Oregon Historical Society, bb004581.

Page 265: Boar's head procession by Edmund Y. Lee, from "To acquaint you with Reed College," a Reed College flyer circa 1955.

Page 266: Barry Hansen at KRRC by Steve Doob '63, courtesy of Barry Hansen.

Page 270: Doyle Owl from the 1967 Reed College *Griffin*.

Page 278: Student couple courtesy of Wyn Berry.

Page 282: Outdoor concert from the 1967 Reed College *Griffin*.

Page 289: Reed football team from the December 1951 *Sallyport*.

Page 298: Lloyd Reynolds' "Calligraphy for People" by Dan Kvitka, for the 2011 exhibition "Lloyd Reynolds" at the Douglas F. Cooley Memorial Art Gallery, Reed College.

Page 305: Lloyd Reynolds' "Fellowship" by Dan Kvitka, for the 2011 exhibition "Lloyd Reynolds" at the Douglas F. Cooley Memorial Art Gallery, Reed College.

Page 327: Charles Bigelow from the 1967 Reed College *Griffin*.

Page 333: Allen Ginsberg from the 1967 Reed College *Griffin*.

Page 337: Student rally in the Student Union from the 1968 Reed College *Griffin*.

Page 350: Jim Webb from the 1967 Reed College *Griffin*.

Page 356: *Quest* masthead from the *Reed College Quest*, December 12, 1968.

Page 357: Dissident students speaking at a student meeting from the *Oregon Journal*, December 12, 1968.

Page 358: Occupation of Eliot Hall courtesy of Stephen S. Robinson '72.

Page 359: Students protesting 1968 courtesy of Stephen S. Robinson '72.

Page 361: Victor Rosenblum in Rudie Wilhelm's office courtesy of Stephen S. Robinson '72.

Page 364: Paideia schedule from an insert in the *Reed College Quest*, January 1973.

Page 370: Jim Webb billboard of Ross Thompson from the 1971 Reed College *Griffin*.

Page 387: Anti-nuclear protest courtesy of Larry Clarkberg '87 from the 1986 Reed College *Griffin*.

Page 392: Costume dance social from the 1986 Reed College *Griffin*.

Page 395: 1986 thesis parade by J. Quarles, from the cover of *Reed* magazine, October 1986.

Page 403: Women's Center information table courtesy of Tom Cobb '92.

Page 404: Poster for *Rude Girl Press* courtesy of Tom Cobb '92.

Page 414: Portrait of Jack Dudman by Clyde Keller, from the *Reed College Bulletin*, September 5, 1978.

Page 424: Class with Laurens Ruben on the lawn by Helen Fernandez, from the *Reed College Bulletin*, September 5, 1980.

Page 428: Lisa Steinman, Robert Knapp, and Peter Steinberger courtesy of Carole Archer.

Page 439: Geodesic dome courtesy of Wyn Berry.

Page 441: Theatre professors and staff by Owen Carey, from *Reed* magazine, May 1996.

Page 445: Robert Palladino by J. Moon, from *Reed* magazine, August 2003.

Page 449: Divestment protest by S. Eugene Thompson from *Reed* magazine, Spring 1986.

Page 453: *Quest* front page from January 27, 1986.

Page 454: Student protest in Eliot Hall from the 1986 Reed College *Griffin*.

Page 471: *Quest* front page from April 17, 1989.

Page 494: Protest over lack of diversity courtesy of Lisa Currier.

Page 499: Chunk 666 bicyclists courtesy of Paula Barclay.

Page 503: Reed Out of Canada rally courtesy of Reed Student Services.

Page 507: Pat McDougal and student courtesy of Rex Ziak.

Page 509: Jacqueline Dirks with students courtesy of Rick Rappaport.

Page 511: Chinese humanities faculty by Carole Archer, from *Reed* magazine, February 1994.

Page 512: Pancho Savery and class courtesy of Rex Ziak.

Page 516: 2006 commencement courtesy of Reed Public Affairs.

Bibliography

BOOKS AND PERIODICALS

Reed College publications can be found in Special Collections at the Reed College Library.

Alden, Chris. Untitled letter to the editor in "Letters." *Reed* magazine 83 no. 4 (November 2004): inside front cover.

Allardyce, Gilbert. "The Rise and Fall of the Western Civilization Course." *American Historical Review* 87 no. 3 (June 1982): 695–725.

The American Mercury magazine, "The Life and Times of Reed College," Stewart Holbrook. (October 1950): 477.

The Association of American Colleges, Commission on the Organization of the College Curriculum. *Unifying the Liberal College Curriculum.* New York: The Association of American Colleges, 1923.

Association of American Colleges, Project on Redefining the Meaning and Purpose of Baccalaureate Degrees. *Integrity in the College Curriculum: A Report to the Academic Community.* Washington, D.C.: Association of American Colleges, 1985.

Ayres, Clarence. "Scholz of Reed." *The New Republic* 40 no. 516 (October 22, 1924): 197–199.

Barnard, Mary Ethel. *Assault on Mount Helicon.* Berkeley: University of California Press, 1984.

———. "Gargoyles, Phantoms, Baudelaire." *Reed* magazine 79 no. 5 (November 2000): 11.

Bauerlein, Mark. "A Solitary Thinker," *The Chronicle Review*, May 20, 2011: section B, 6–10.

Bell, Daniel. *The End of Ideology: On the Exhaustion of Political Ideas in the Fifties*, rev. ed. New York: Free Press, 1962.

Bender, Thomas. "Politics, Intellect, and the American University, 1945–1995." In *American Academic Culture in Transformation: Fifty Years, Four Disciplines*, edited by Thomas Bender and Carl E. Schorske, 17–54. Princeton, New Jersey: Princeton University Press, 1997.

Bernhardt, William. "Letters: A Tribute to William McClendon." *Reed* magazine 76 no. 4 (August 1997): 48.

Berry, Frances. "Editorial." *Reed College Quest* (December 9, 1924): 2.

Blessing, Lee. "Accidents in a Moral Universe." Reed College commencement speech, 2001. *Reed* magazine 80 no. 3 (August 2001): 20–22.

Boyer, Ernest L. *Scholarship Reconsidered: Priorities of the Professoriate.* San Francisco: Carnegie Foundation for the Advancement of Teaching, 1990.

Carnochan, W. B. *The Battleground of the Curriculum.* Palo Alto: Stanford University Press, 1992.

Chait, Richard P., and Zachary First. "Bullish on Private Colleges." *Harvard Magazine* (November/December 2011): 37–38.

Clark, Burton. *The Distinctive College.* New Brunswick, New Jersey: Transaction Publishers, 1992.

Coleman, Norman. "The College as Community." Inaugural address, June 11, 1925. *Reed College Bulletin* 4 no. 3 (July 1925): 1–14.

———. "President Coleman speaks." *Reed College Quest* (February 24, 1925): 1–2.

Crowley, Robert. "Art as Avocation at Reed." *Sallyport* 30 no. 1 (January 1971): 14–17.

"Discourse: Does Reed Stifle Creativity?" *Sallyport* 30 no. 1 (January 1971): 27–33.

"Discourse: Drop Outs." *Sallyport* 29 no. 4 (February 1970): 30–32.

Ehinger, Ernest. "Men's Athletic Policy." *Reed College Quest* 27 no. 19 (February 1, 1939): 1.

Eugene Register-Guard, "Get 'em together!" (June 8, 1941): page unknown.

Forstenzer, Tom. Untitled letter to the editor in "Letters." *Reed* magazine 86 no. 5 (November 2007): 5.

Foster, William Trufant. "The Ideal College." In William T. Foster, *Administration of the College Curriculum*. Boston: Houghton Mifflin Company, 1911, 337–340.

——. "Reed College and the Truth." *The Pacific Unitarian* 24: 106.

——. "Specializing in the Humanities," *Reed College Record*, no. 13, January 1914.

Fox, Betty Jean Perry. Untitled letter to the editor in "Letters." *Reed* magazine 79 no. 2 (May 2000): inside front cover.

Fox, Ron. "Fowl Tales." *Reed* magazine 83 no. 3 (August 2004): 57.

Frazier, Thomas Lamb. *Between the Lines*. Oakland, California: Regent Press, 2001.

Friedrich, Franz. Untitled letter to the editor in "Letters." *Reed* magazine 88 no. 3 (August 2009): 3.

"Grades at Reed." *Facts About Reed*, Institutional Research, Reed College, 2011, http://www.reed.edu/ir/ir_internal_web/grades.html.

Harvard Crimson, "Retro, Santanas!" (January 10, 1925).

Hawkins, Hugh. *Between Harvard and America: The Educational Leadership of Charles W. Eliot*. New York: Oxford University Press, 1972.

Henry, Astrid. *Not My Mother's Sister: Generational Conflict and Third-Wave Feminism*. Bloomington: Indiana University Press, 2004.

"The Houses." Reed College *Griffin* (1920): 50.

Hutchins, Robert Maynard. *The Higher Learning in America*. New Haven: Yale University Press, 1936.

"An Interview with Steve Koblik." *Reed* magazine 80 no. 3 (August 2001): 4–9.

Johansen, Dorothy O. "Historical Aspects of Student Activities." *Sallyport* 25 no. 2 (Winter 1963): 9–12.

Keezer, Dexter. "Guest Editorial." *College Management* (March 1970): 46.

——. "A letter to the Alumni from the President." *Reed College Bulletin* 13 no. 4 (November 1934): 1–24.

——. *The Light that Flickers*. New York: Harper and Brothers, 1947.

——. "To the Alumni of Reed College." *Reed College Bulletin* 13 no. 4 (November 1934): 3–24.

——. "Where Are the Able Women Teachers?" *Journal of the American Association of University Women* (April 1938).

"Keezer Seeks to Keep Reed in Original Path, Report Says." *Reed College Quest* 27 no. 17 (January 18, 1939): 3.

Kierstead, Ray. "What is Good Teaching?" *Reed* magazine 57 no. 9 (April 1979): 12–13.

Kimball, Bruce A. *Orators & Philosophers: A History of the Idea of Liberal Education*. New York and London: Teachers College Press, 1986.

Koblik, Steven and Stephen R. Graubard, editors. *Distinctly American: The Residential Liberal Arts Colleges*. New Brunswick and London: Transaction Publishers, 2000.

Lave, Rebecca. "Letters." *Reed* magazine 72 no. 4 (August 1993): 2.

Levine, Michael L. "Friends of Lenny Ross, '63, Establish a Memorial Scholarship." *Reed Campaign Bulletin* (Winter 1986): 4.

Lewis, Lionel S. *Cold War on Campus: A Study of the Politics of Organizational Control*. New Brunswick, New Jersey: Transaction Publishers, 1996.

"Life After Reed." *Facts About Reed*, Institutional Research, Reed College, 2011, http://www.reed.edu/ir/ir_internal_web/grades.html.

Loeb, Mark. "Peaceful Co-Existence . . . Reed Style." *Sallyport* (November/December 1964): 24–27.

"Looking Backward." Reed College *Griffin* (1920): 89–91.

Look magazine, "Reed College: Portland's Academic Gadfly," Sam Castan. (March 27, 1962): 88.

MacColl, Kimbark. *The Shaping of a City, Business and Politics in Portland, Oregon 1885 to 1915*. Portland, Oregon: The Georgian Press Company, 1976.

MacNaughton, Ernest Boyd "E. B." "Statement by E. B. MacNaughton." Conference on Educational Problems on the Occasion of the Inauguration of Dexter Merriam Keezer. *Reed College Bulletin* 14 no. 4 (November 1935): 3.

MacRae, Patti. "Basking in Glory: the Thesis Parade." *Reed* magazine 77 no. 2 (May 1998): 34 and inside back cover.

McMillan, Margaret. *Dangerous Games: The Uses and Abuses of History*. New York: Modern Library, 2010.

McPherson, Michael, and Morton Owen Shapiro. "The Future Economic Challenges for the Liberal Arts Colleges." In Steven Koblik and Stephen R. Graubard, eds., *Distinctively American: The Residential Liberal Arts Colleges*: 47–75.

———. *Education Between Two Worlds*. New Brunswick, New Jersey: Aldine Transaction Publishers, 2006.

Menand, Louis. "Live and Learn." *The New Yorker* 87 no. 16 (June 6, 2011): 76.

———. *The Marketplace of Ideas*. New York: W. W. Norton & Company, 2010.

———. *The Metaphysical Club: A Story of Ideas in America*. New York: Macmillan, 2002.

———. "Show or Tell." *The New Yorker* 85 no. 17 (June 8, 2009): 106.

Miller, Beatrice Olsen. "Under the Green Tiles." Reed College *Griffin* (1922): 11–18.

Mitzman, Barry. "The Intellectual Maverick." *Change* magazine 11 no. 6 (September 1979): 38–43.

Morning Oregonian, "Academic Freedom." (June 30, 1915): 8.

———, "Dr. Meiklejohn Here." (April 7, 1924): 6.

———, "One of America's Great Colleges Will Soon be Founded in Portland," Thomas Lamb Eliot. (January 1, 1910): section 3, 4.

———, "Pacifists are Put Down as Traitors." (February 28, 1917): 16.

———, "President Scholz, Reed Chief, Dies." (July 24, 1924): 7.

———, "Reed Co-Eds Tell Taste in 'Hubbies.'" (February 28, 1916): 10.

———, "Reed College and Peace." (March 2, 1917): 11

———, "Reed Pledges Its Loyalty to Wilson." (March 2, 1917): 5.

———, "Too Much Socialism Hurts Reed," H. H. Ward. (March 3, 1917): 11.

———, Untitled letter to the editor, S. M. Mears. (March 3, 1917): page unknown.

Munk, Michael. "Oregon Tests Academic Freedom in (Cold) Wartime: The Reed College Trustees versus Stanley Moore." *Oregon Historical Quarterly* 97 no. 3 (Fall 1996): 262–354.

Neely, Paul. "Threats to Liberal Arts Colleges." In Steven Koblik and Stephen R. Graubard, eds., *Distinctively American: The Residential Liberal Arts Colleges*: 27–45.

Neuberger, Richard L. "School for Smart Young Things." *Saturday Evening Post* 225 no. 17 (October 25, 1952): 36, 95–101.

Odegard, Peter. "As the Twig is Bent." *Reed College Bulletin* 26 no. 1 (November 1947): 4–15.

The Oregonian, "Reed College Board Silent on Plans After Meeting," Wilma Morrison. (October 2, 1954): 1.

———, "Reed Refuses to Accept a World of Mediocrity," Robert Landauer. (May 1, 1983): 110.

———, "Where Sports are Secondary," Steve Duin. (May 24, 1987): 85.

Oregon Journal, "Dr. Foster's Move is Not Unexpected." (December 19, 1919): 1.

Peters, Lon. "Unleashing the Imagination: The Collegium Musicum is as Unique as Reed." *Reed* magazine 80 no. 2 (May 2001): 20–21.

Phillips-Fein, Kim. "1973 to the Present." In *American History Now*, edited by Eric Foner and Lisa McGirr, 176–189. Philadelphia: Temple University Press, 2011.

Portland Journal, "Dr. R. Scholz, Reed College Chief, Is Dead." (July 23, 1924): page unknown.

Portland Telegram, "Why Dr. Foster Failed." (December 23, 1919): page unknown.

"President Richard Frederick Scholz—The Man and His Program." By the Students of Reed College, July, 1924. *Reed College Quest*, special issue (July 1924): 1–6.

"Profile of a Trustee: Richard P. Wollenberg." *Reed* magazine 60 no. 12 (July 1982): 2.

"The Reed Almanac." *Reed* magazine 90 no. 4 (December 2011): 30–47.

Reed College Student Handbook, 1974.

"Reed Graduates Appraise the College." *Reed College Bulletin* 11 no. 1 (January 1932): 5.

Reed, Simeon Gannett. "The Last Will and Testament of Simeon G. Reed." In *A Selection of Wills*, edited by Albert L. Grutze, 42–43. Portland, Oregon: Title and Trust Company, 1925.

"A Reed Union on Academic Freedom." *Sallyport* 25 no. 1 (Fall 1962): 22–28.

"Report of Visiting Consultants Preparatory to Conducting a Search for a New President at Reed College." *At Reed* magazine 3 no. 3 (September 5, 1991): 1–4.

Rolling Stone magazine, "The College Rankings Scam," Stephen Glass. No. 771 (October 16, 1997): 93–94.

Rosenbaum, Robert. Untitled letter to the editor in "Letters." *Reed* magazine 80 no. 1 (February 2001): 52.

Rudolph, Frederick. *The American College & University, A History*. New York: A. Knopf, 1962.

Scheck, John Frederick. *Transplanting a Tradition: Thomas Lamb Eliot and the Unitarian Conscience in the Pacific Northwest, 1865–1905*. Ann Arbor: University Microfilms, 1970.

Scholz, Richard. "President R. F. Scholz." In the Association of American Colleges, Commission on the Organization of the College Curriculum, *Unifying the Liberal College Curriculum*: 30–40.

Schwartz, Todd. "The Dance of the Pen." *Reed* magazine 82 no. 3 (August 2003): 2–9.

Segal, Robert. "To the Editor." *Reed College Quest* (February 16, 1979): 2.

"Senior Statistics." *Reed College Annual* (1915): 57–59.

Shepard, Ann. *Yours Sincerely, Ann W. Shepard: Letters from a College Dean*. Portland: Reed College, 1978.

Short, Jessie May. "Women in the Teaching Profession." *Reed College Bulletin* 18 no. 2 (April 1939): 19–33.

Sisson, Edward O. "Reed College: 1939." *Reed College Bulletin* 18 no. 2 (April 1939): 7–18.

Smith, Brewster. Untitled letter to the editor in "Letters." *Reed* magazine 86 no. 5 (November 2007): 3–4.

Smith, Richard Norton. *The Harvard Century: The Making of a University to a Nation*. Cambridge: Harvard University Press, 1986.

Sorum, Christina Elliott. "New Problems in the Humanities." In Steven Koblik and Stephen R. Graubard, eds., *Distinctively American: The Residential Liberal Arts Colleges*: 241–264.

Stearns, Peter N. *Western Civilization in World History*. New York: Routledge, 2003.

Sullivan, Richard, and Thomas K. Worcester. "Sullivan—Eight Years Later." *Sallyport* 26 no. 3 (November/December 1964): 10–15.

Thompson, S. Eugene. "Wrestling with Divestment Questions." *Reed* magazine 65 no. 1 (Spring 1986): 2–4.

Time magazine, "Colleges: A Thinking Reed." 80 no. 26 (December 28, 1962): 42–43.

——, "Husky Reed." 34 no. 23 (December 4, 1939): 59.

——, "Nomination." 28 no. 20 (November 16, 1936): 113.

——, "Prex Dex." 26 no. 20 (November 11, 1935): 53–54.

——, "Reed Tries Again." 64 no. 16 (October 18, 1954): 113.

——, "Reed's Choice." 59 no. 24 (January 16, 1952): 49.

——, "Shelley by Moonlight." 49 no. 7 (February 17, 1947): 81.

——, "Students: The Free-Sex Movement." 87 no. 10 (March 11, 1966): 78–79.

Van Cleve, Jane Clapperton. "Four Women of Different Generations." *Reed* magazine 72 no. 1 (February 1993): 14–15.

Wall Street Journal, "Freeloaders Ambush Paying Customers at College Mess Hall," Victor F. Zonana. 199 no. 68 (April 8, 1982): 1.

Walsh, James. "We Hear from Reed's Rhodes Scholars." *Reed* magazine 72 no. 2 (May 1993): 26–32.

Watson, Harriet. "Reed Rank(le)s *U.S. News and World Report*." *Reed* magazine 74 no. 6 (November 1995): 28–29.

——. "*U.S. News and World Report* Hat Trick." *Reed* magazine 76 no. 5 (November 1997): 25–26.

Worcester, Thomas K. "Diary of a Confrontation: Black Studies at Reed." *Sallyport* 29 no. 1 (July 1969): 10–32.

——. "Size and Solvency: The Reed Dilemma." *Sallyport* 29 no. 3 (November/December 1969): 3–5.

Young, Jeffrey R. "Professors Cede Grading Power to Outsiders—Even Computers." *The Chronicle of Higher Education* 57 no. 43 (August 12, 2011): 1–5.

UNPUBLISHED MATERIALS IN THE REED COLLEGE LIBRARY

Unpublished materials listed here can be found in Special Collections at the Reed College Library, unless otherwise noted.

Alderson, George. "Reminiscences of Reed College." February 6, 2003, manuscript, Alumni Files.

Arragon, Reginald Francis. "Then, Now, Future." March 1968, Portland, Oregon, audiotape and transcript, Faculty Files.

Bennett, Douglas. "Retention and Attrition at Reed: A Status Report," January 3, 1992, General Files.

Bernat, Harry. June 5, 2004, pre-meteorology manuscript, Oral History Project Files.

Black Student Union. Cover letter to list of demands, November, 1968, General Files.

Bragdon, Paul. Email to Bert Brehm, June 23, 2008, printout, General Files.

Coleman, David C. "A Biography of Norman Coleman, Reed's Third President." March 1, 2000, manuscript, Oral History Project.

Colie, Carole Calkins. "Carole Calkins Colie '54." Manuscript, Oral History Project.

Dawson, Angel. "The Doyle Owl: A Study of Ritual at Reed," bachelor's thesis, Reed College, 1983.

Dolph, Cyrus. Letter to William Trufant Foster, June 19, 1913, Trustee Papers.

Douglas, Paul. Letter to Dorothy O. Johansen, September 9, 1959, Johansen Papers.

Ehrenreich, Barbara Alexander. "For the Love of Learning: Reed's Centennial Conference." March 19, 2009, Washington, D.C., transcript, Alumni Files.

Felts, Josephine. "Glenn Chesney Quiett—a personal memoir." 1973, manuscript, Alumni Files.

Foster, Bessie. Letter to Dorothy O. Johansen, January 15, 1959, Presidential Files.

Foster, William Trufant. "Campaigns of a Crusader," 1950, autobiography, typescript, Presidential Files.

———. Letter to Lindsley Ross, December 31, 1912, Scrapbooks.

Gates, William. In "Comments with Respect to the Quality of Student Life," by Paul Bragdon and Colleagues, March 24, 1977, 5–6, typescript, General Files.

Griffin, Frank Loxley. Autobiographical audiotape and transcript, Faculty Files.

———. "Presidential Responsibility at Reed College, A Statement Prepared for the Information of Several Friends of the College." November 1955, Presidential Files.

Hastings, Hudson. Letter to William M. Ladd, June 3, 1920, Faculty Files.

Hauck, Arthur. "The Service of Reed College to Portland," bachelor's thesis, Reed College, 1915.

Hay, George. "Memorandum for the Community." September 2, 1980, Presidential Files.

Helms, William. "A Boy's Life in the Old West and Following Years." 1979, memoir, typescript, Reediana.

Howes, Cora. Undated letters, Alumni Files.

Jobs, Steve. Stanford University commencement speech, June 12, 2005, transcript, Alumni Files.

———. "Remarks." Reed College convocation speech, August 27, 1991, transcript, General Files.

Johansen, Dorothy O. "Anecdotes and History of Reed." September 1968, Portland, Oregon, transcript, Oral History Project.

———. "History of Reed College." 1984, typescript, Johansen Papers.

———. "History of Reed Ideals." September 6, 1962, Portland, Oregon, transcript, Johansen Papers.

———. "Talk on Reed College." September 1970, Portland, Oregon, transcript, Oral History Project.

———. Letter to Harry Beal Torrey, February 28, 1959, Faculty Files.

Jones, Richard. "A History of Reed College." 1982, manuscript, Archives.

Keezer, Dexter. Letter to Dorothy O. Johansen, March 17, 1976, Johansen Papers.

Leigh, Robert. Letter to A. A. Knowlton, February 7, 1921, Faculty Files.

———. Letter to Charles McKinley, February 28, 1934, Faculty Files.

———. Letter to William T. Foster, December 13, 1919, Faculty Files.

Lyman, Lloyd. "Simeon Gannett Reed: A Preliminary Biographical Study," bachelor's thesis, Reed College, 1948.

———. Letter to Bessie Foster, September 24, 1954, Presidential Files.

Markus, Lois Shoemaker. "Reminiscences of Reed College." 2009, memoir, typescript, Alumni Files.

McKinley, Charles. "Richard F. Scholz—an educational leader." Address at the Reed College Memorial Chapel Service, September 16, 1924, Presidential Files.

———. Letter to Richard Scholz, September 6, 1921, Presidential Files, Faculty Council.

Menashe, Toinette. "A Brief History of the Master's Programs at Reed College (1911–1994)," January 1994, typescript, General Files.

Merriam, Harold. Letters to Dorothy O. Johansen, April 21, May 25, 1959, Faculty Files.

Nace, Robert. "In Life My Only Comfort in Death." Memoir, typescript, Reediana.

Ogburn, William. Letter to Dorothy O. Johansen, March 10, 1959, Faculty Files.

Perrow, Elsa Gill. "50th Anniversary Reunion, Autobiographical Sketch." 1965, Alumni Files.

Reed, Amanda Wood. "Last Will and Testament of Amanda Wood Reed." July 28, 1904, document with manuscript entries, Reed Papers.

Reed, Simeon Gannett. Dictation of autobiography, before 1895, BANC MSS P-A 130, Bancroft Library, University of California at Berkeley, copy, Oral History Project Files.

Reed College. "Self-Study Report. Impact of the College: The Coed." (1953): 71–81, General Files.

Reed College Board of Trustees. "Resolution." May 23, 1981. Trustee Files, President's Office, Reed College.

Reed College Faculty, Community Affairs Committee. "Report." 1960–61. Faculty Files.

Reed College Registrar. Records, 1915 through 1959. Registrar's Office, Reed College.

Reed College Student Council. "Minutes." May 31, 1912, Governance Documents.

Reynolds, Lloyd J. "Autobiographical Notes." 1977, manuscript, Reynolds Papers.

Ross, Lindsley. Letter to Dorothy O. Johansen, June 19, 1958, Alumni Files.

Shepard, Ann. Letter to Barbara Morris Dickey, November 18, 1949, Faculty Files.

Sisson, Edward O. Letter to Dexter Keezer, October 19, 1941, Presidential Files.

Stauder, Ellen. "A Historical Snapshot of the Reed Faculty by Gender." Academic Affairs Committee, Board of Trustees Meeting, October 1, 2010, General Files.

Stevens, Carl. "Memo to the Faculty." September 22, 1989, typescript, Faculty Files.

Stonum, Gary. Email to Special Collections, March 2, 2011, printout, Alumni Files.

Strasser, Judith J. "Reed College. A Study in Educational History," bachelor's thesis, Reed College, 1966.

Sullivan, Richard. "Portland and Reed College." Speech to the City Club of Portland, December 14, 1956, typescript, Presidential Files.

———. "Reed College: Potential, Problems, Policies." Reed College convocation speech, September 25, 1958, typescript, General Files.

———. "Report to the Ford Foundation from Reed College." August 18, 1964, typescript, Presidential Files.

———. "The Sputniks and American Education." Speech to the Northwest Electric Light and Power Association, September 19, 1958, Sun Valley, Idaho, Presidential Files.

———. "The State of the College." Reed College convocation speech, September 16, 1965, typescript, General Files.

Torrey, Harry. Letter to Katherine Kerr Riddle, March 7, 1958, Faculty Files.

———. Letter to Dorothy O. Johansen, February 8, March 5, March 7, 1959, Faculty Files.

Washburn, Stan. Email to James Kahan, October 2007, transcript, Alumni Files.

Watson, Sally. "Who Me?" Manuscript, Alumni Files.

"Where Are We Going?" Reed Union with panelists Marvin Levich, Kirk Thompson, Jim Webb, and Nicholas Wheeler, September 30, 1968, transcript, General Files.

Wood, Arthur. Letter to Dorothy O. Johansen, June 3, December 23, 1959, Faculty Files.

Woodard, Simon. "'The Evil of Sex': Reed College and Progressive Social Hygiene in Oregon, 1911–1920," bachelor's thesis, Reed College, 2010.

REED COLLEGE ORAL HISTORIES

Transcripts are in the Oral History Project Files in Special Collections at the Reed College Library.

Abel, Richard '48

Abernathy, William '88

Abrahams, Peter '77

Abramson, Paul '52

Adams, Stephen '61

Akerman, Clement, economics professor 1920–1943

Alderson, George '63

Allen, Keith '83

Alt, Konrad '81, trustee 2010–

Arragon, Reginald Francis "Rex," history professor 1923–1962, 1970–1974

Ashby, James B. '00

Averill, Katherine '50

Bailey, Maida Rossiter, librarian 1912–1918, advisor to women 1936–1937, dean of women 1937–1942

Barnard, Mary Ethel '32

Barr, Dugan '64

Barta, Janet, wife of Jerome Barta, professor and director of physical education, 1956–1988

Bauer, Mary Russell '43

Beck, E. Patricia '44

Belson, Kenneth Jon '87

Bennett, Douglas, provost 1989–1993

Benveniste, Jack '43

Bergman, Abraham '54

Berleman, Rosemary Lapham '48

Bernat, Harry AMP '44

Bernhardt, Nancy Nomland '55

Bernhardt, William '60

Bigelow, Anita Lourie '67

Bigman, Paul '73

Blau, Harvey '63

Blessing, Lee '71

Boals, Vera Ruth '79

Bogran, Amy '89

Bol, Morris '58

Boles, Sandy '90

Bonyhadi, Ernest '48, trustee 1971–1995

Bowman, Rory '90.

Bragdon, Nancy, wife of Paul Bragdon

Bragdon, Paul, president 1971–1988

Brau, Ben '93

Bray, Peter '94

Brecher, Jeremy '67

Brehm, Bert, biology professor 1962–1993

Brockway, Thomas '21.

Brody, Susan '71

Brown, Elizabeth Ann '40

Brownell, Barry '43

Buchanan, Charles '58

Burg, Richard '67

Burkhart, Diana '97

Burns, Carol '62.

Burns, Thomas '98

Campbell, Colin Herald '33

Campbell, Rose Relevo '96

Carson, Arthur B. '40

Carter, Charles Conrad '46

Case, Jerry '59

Casseres, David '65

Chall, Malca Kleiner '42

Chiao, Becky '85

Chittick, Victor L. O., English professor 1921–1948

Chrestenson, Hubert "Hugh," mathematics professor 1957–1990

Church, Nicholas James '95

Churchill, Jack '49

Clark, Elmer Bailey "Jiggs" '42

Clark, Robert '79

Clarke, Angelina '04

Clarke, Gregory Laurence '88

Coad, Thomas '42

Coit, Richard '76

Colgrove, Marianne '84, staff 1986–

Colie, Carole Calkins '54

Colton, Hattie Kawahara '43

Conlin, David '88

Conviser, Richard '65

Cooke, Katharine Baker '41

Creedon, Carol, psychology professor 1957–1991

Cronyn, Marshall William '40, chemistry professor 1952–1989, provost 1982–1989, vice-president 1983–1989

Crooker, Constance '69

Cushing, John A. '67

Cutrell, Sandy '63

Danzig, Richard '65

Davies, Kathleen Bucklin '67

Dean, Alan '41, trustee 1973–1998

Dearborn, Elizabeth '68

Dehart, Ella, Reed family friend

Dehn, Dorothy Hurt '61

DeLord, Natalie, wife of Jean DeLord, physics professor 1950–1988

Dick, Gale Jr. '50

Digby, David '57

Dirks, Jacqueline '82

Doolan, Roy '58

Drukman, Mason, political science professor 1964–1970

Dubnoff, Zachary '91

Dudman, Jack '42, mathematics professor 1953–1985, dean 1963–1985

Dunn, Pamela Matsuda '78

Dunne, Thomas, chemistry professor 1963–1995

Eames, Patricia '50

Edlin, Dorothy Moore '56

Eliot, Henrietta, wife of Thomas Lamb Eliot, trustee 1904–1924

Emerson, John '69.

Engel, Steve '69

Engeman, Richard '69

Engstrom, Dale AMP '44

Erickson, Glenn '72

Eveland, J. D. '64

Falk, Steven '83, trustee 2007–2011

Falkenhagen, Jane Willson '37

Fernea, Elizabeth Warnock '49, public relations staff 1950–1954

Fernea, Robert '54

Fetzer, Bret Lee '87

Fink, Liz '67

Fisher, Tony '80

Forte, Mary Frankie '71

Fox, Suzy '73

Franks, Molly '97

Freeman, Calvin '69, MAT '70

Freer, Christian '36

Friedman, Victor A. '70

Fromartz, Samuel '80

Fryer, Heather '89

Furst, Marian '72

Garcia, Frank '85

Gibson, Wallace '66

Giddings, France Bennett '69

Giraud, Matt '85

Gladstone, Herb, music professor 1946–1980

Gleysteen, Laura Tunnell '40

Goldberg, Shirley Peterson '45

Goldwater, Marge '71

Golub, Alex '95

Goodman, Peter Simon '89

Gordner, M. Jeanne Hansen '46

Graef, John '60

Gray, John, trustee 1961 2006

Green, Donald '54

Green, Nancy Stewart '50

Greenberg, Dan '62, trustee 1975–2011

Gregory, Chilton '60

Griffith, Suzanne Greenfield '66

Gunderson, William, colleague of Lloyd Reynolds

Gunterman, Joseph F. '34

Guss, Peter '78

Gwilliam, Frank, biology professor 1957–1996, provost 1979–1982

Gwilliam, Marjorie, wife of Frank Gwilliam

Hagen, Erica '99

Hanchett, Suzanne '62

Hancock, Virginia Oglesby '62, chemistry assistant 1963–1980, music professor 1991–

Hansen, Barbara Serrell '62

Hansen, Barry '63

Hansen, Kristiana '96

Hard, Amelia Rosamond '67

Hart, Gilbert '51

Hastay, Helen Wheeler '39

Hathaway, Loline '59

Henderson, Almalee Stewart '47

Hendrickson, Carroll '42

Hepburn, Carol '75

Herold, Steve '63

Hirsch, Dorothy Davenhill '52

Hittelman, Karl '58, trustee 1990–1994

Hochheiser, Sheldon '73

Hoffnung, Aaron '93

Holinstat, David '78

Holzer, Elizabeth Hines '29

Hood, Cordelia Dodson '36

Hopwood, S. Blake '31

Horsfall, Robert '63

Huddleston, Ron '87

Humphreys, Michael '64

Hunt, Melinda '81

Hyla, Adam Holdorf '97

Isserman, Maurice '73

Jackets, Vera Smith '28

Jacob, Harry '54

Jambor, Harold A. "Jim" '35

Janowsky, Jeri '78

Johansen, Dorothy O. '33, history professor 1934–1969, archivist 1969–1984

Johnson, Arlien '17

Johnson, Ellen Knowlton '39, physics staff 1942–1945, clerical assistant and recorder 1945–1962, registrar 1962–1981

Jones, Graham '97

Jones, Lyle Vincent AMP '44.

Jones, Richard, history professor 1941–1982, 1985–1986

Joseph, George '51, trustee 1972–1980

Judkis, Melvin H. '39

Kahan, James '64

Kangas, Matthew Arvid '71

Kehoe, Thomas David '82

Kierstead, Ray, history professor 1978–2000

Kim, Helen Kyong '89

King, Mary Catherine, director of health services 1994–1997, associate dean of students and student health services 1997–2003, vice-president and dean of student services 2003–2007

Kirby, William '65

Kirsch, William '50

Knapp, Robert, English professor 1974–

Koblik, Steven Samuel, president 1992–2001

Krisch, Patricia Leavey '59

Kristof, Ladis '55

Kuehn, Larry M. '66, MAT '68

Kunitz, Mela Susan '87, alumni office staff 1990–1994, assistant director of alumni events and programs 2003–

Labovitz, Margaret Churchill '30

Ladd, Mary (Mrs. William Mead), daughter-in-law of William S. Ladd, Simeon Reed's business partner

Laing, Ron '56

Lam, Greg '96

Lamb, Cara '66

Langston, Peter '68

Large, Larry, vice-president of development and college relations 1982–1987, executive vice-president 1992–1999

Larson, Anja Stephanie '92

Larson, Carl '27

Lathrop, John Randy '80

Latourette, Kenneth, history professor 1914–1916

Laursen, John '67

Law, Roger, artist-in-residence 1968

Laws, Priscilla Watson '61

Leaf, Murray '61

Leber, Lewis '50

Leigh, Arthur, economics professor 1945–1988

Leitz, Fred '40

Lencek, Lena, Russian professor 1977–

Lenon, Harlow F. '35

Lenske, Moshe '50, trustee 1992–1996

Levich, Marvin, philosophy professor 1953–1994, provost 1972–1979

Levine, Michael L. '62, trustee 1984–2002

Levine, Richard '70

Leviton, Laura C. '73

Lewis, Esther Dorles '42

Lewis, Fred R. "Dick" '44

Lewis, Gwendolyn '65, trustee 1994–1998

Liebes, Brunhilde Kaufer '35

Lillie, Sandy Osborne '70

Lindahl-Urben, Craig '75

Lionni, Annie '79

Lipson, David '69

Litt, Barbara '82

Liu, Sam B. '36, trustee 1977–1981

Livermore, Arthur '40, chemistry professor 1948–1965

Livingston, Bruce '65

Loader, Jayne '73

Lomhoff, Peter '66

Lovell, Michael '52

Lowe, Christopher '82, history professor 1991–1996

Luxenberg, Marjory Franklin '66

Lydgate, Chris '90, *Reed* magazine editor 2008–

Macaulay, Elizabeth Funge '43

Macaulay, Robert '43

MacCaffrey, Wallace T. '42

Maccoby, Eleanor Emmons '39

Mack, Robert '93

Index

Helweg, Kim, 406
Hemstreet, Leslie, 396
Henderson, Almalee Stewart, 173
Hendrickson, Carroll, Jr., 162
Herold, Steve, 300–302, 307–308, 339
Herron, Douglas, 340
Hetzel, Ralph, 31–32
Heyer, Nicky, 325
Hill, Jim, 114
Hill, Martha, 443
Hines, Elizabeth, *see* Elizabeth Hines
 Holzer
Hirsch, Dorothy Davenhill, 373
Hirsch, Harold, 372
Hittelman, Karl, 485
Hochheiser, Sheldon, 356–357, 367–368,
 526–527
Hodgkinson, Lucy, 147
Hoffnung, Aaron, 491
Holbrook, Stewart, 208
Holinstat, David, 396
Holt, Lamar, 166
Holzer, Elizabeth Hines, 121, 173
Homer, Susan, 264
honor case(s), 68, 80, 272–273, 278, 313,
 404, 406, 416, 419, 454, 470
Honor Principle, 4–6, 40, 57, 67–68, 80–
 81, 100, 154–157, 213, 231, 271–274, 277–
 278, 327, 416–417, 419, 421, 454–455,
 468, 503–504, 523
Hood, Cordelia Dodson, 174
Hope, Alexandra, *see* Alexandra
 Hope Yoder
Hopwood, S. Blake, 124, 172
Horkheimer, Max, 427
Horsfall, Robert, Jr., 122–123, 283
Hossack, Joanne, 527
Houses A, B, C, D, G, H (dorms), 66, 130
House A dorm, 120
House F dorm, 66–67
House F owl, *see* Doyle Owl
House H dorm, 100, 102, 148
House Un-American Activities
 Committee, 233–236, 238, 243, 285, 296
Hovey, Sally, *see* Sally Hovey Wriggins
Howard, Jane, *see* Jane Howard
 Mersereau
Howard, Linda, 333
Howes, Cora, 79
Howl (Ginsberg), 332
HUAC, *see* House Un-American
 Activities Committee
Hubbard, Alfred, 176
Hubert, Holy, 333–334, 393
Huddleston, Ron, 389–390, 405, 448
Hull, Clark, 133
Hum 110 play, 500
Humanities 11, 194
Humanities 110, 500, 511, 513
Humanities 21, 194

humanities program, 90, 95, 98, 118, 142,
 144, 187, 194, 198, 202, 214, 221–222,
 224–226, 230, 260, 282, 318–319,
 338–340, 344, 346, 348, 351, 355, 360,
 366, 379–381, 425, 431–434, 495, 500,
 505, 507, 510, 512, 521; *see also* Ancient
 Humanities; Chinese humanities;
 Modern Humanities
Humphreys, Michael, 290
Hurley, Frank, 188
Hurt, Dorothy, *see* Dorothy Hurt Dehn
Huss, Walter, 291
Hutchins, Robert Maynard, 90, 232

"Ideal College, The," 34
Iliad (Homer), 117, 149, 194, 257, 332, 339,
 392, 500, 521
Imai, Midori, 187, 191
*Impoverished Student's Book of Cook-
 ery, Drinkery, and Housekeepery, The*
 (Rosenberg), 283
Industrial Workers of the World, 76, 108,
 160, 265, 284
Institute for Policy Studies, 344
Institute of International Relations, 169
Intercollegiate Zionist Federation of
 America, 205
International Livestock Pavilion, 189
intervisitation, 104, 156–157, 271–272,
 264, 278, 328–329
intervisitation crisis, 272, 274, 278
Irwin, Helen, *see* Helen Irwin Schley
Isom, Frances, 44–45
Isserman, Maurice, 328, 334–335, 348,
 354, 356, 367
Italic cursive, 298, 302–303, 305, 332
Ivy League, 205, 218, 258, 452
IWW, *see* Industrial Workers of the
 World

Jackets, Vera Smith, 139
Jacob, Harry, 234, 239
Jaeger, Winifred, *see* Winifred Jaeger
 Wood
Jambor, Harold A. "Jim," 116, 123–124,
 172
Janowsky, Jeri, 405
Japan, 107, 164, 183, 188, 194–195, 291,
 299, 330, 511, 526
Japanese Noh theatre, 440
Japanese poetry, 216
Japanese-Americans, 189–190
Jarrico, Bill, 259
Jefferson Street, 36–37, 39, 73
Jenkins, Anne, *see* Anne Jenkins Perry
Jew(s), 99, 143, 145, 189, 202, 205, 283,
 291, 326, 389, 393
Jewish quota, 258, 459
Jewish Student Group, 494
J. K. Gill store, 290
Jobs, Steve, 408–409, 413–414, 435,
 445–446

Johansen, Dorothy O., 8, 24–25, 27–28,
 33–35, 39, 44, 47, 59, 62, 66–70, 73–75,
 80–82, 99, 107, 115, 117, 139, 151, 179,
 204, 217, 224–225, 228–231, 250–251,
 260–261, 269, 280, 517, 525–527
John Reed Club, 234
Johnson, Arlien, 40
Johnson, Carl, 263
Johnson, Ellen Knowlton, 85, 98, 102, 121,
 130, 134, 136–137, 202, 206–207, 222,
 238, 245, 336, 352
Johnson, Hazel, 191
Johnson, Louise, *see* Louise Johnson
 Rosenbaum
Johnston, France, *see* France Bennett
 Johnston Giddings
Johnston, Bob, 390
Jolly Joan, 210
Jones, Alyce, 220
Jones, Frank, 202, 238
Jones, Graham, 468, 487, 499
Jones, Lewis, 55
Jones, Lloyd, 262
Jones, Lyle Vincent, 192, 194
Jones, Richard, 8, 58–59, 81, 97, 107, 111,
 113, 127–128, 211, 220–222, 224, 229,
 239–243, 246–247, 259, 277, 295, 307,
 309–315, 322, 339–340, 344, 348, 353,
 355, 365–366, 368, 370, 379, 381–384,
 411, 424, 430, 436–437, 486
Jordan, David Starr, 3, 30, 52, 76
Jordan, Miles, 260
Jorgenson, Dale, 239
Joseph, George, 203–205, 208–210, 215,
 235, 241, 372
Joyce, Thomas M., 105
Judicial Board, 277, 421, 455, 468–469,
 496–497, 521
Judicial Review Committee, 327
Judkis, Melvin H., 168
Junior qualification examination (junior
 qual), 13, 97, 124, 145, 195, 221, 230,
 255–256, 273, 302, 417, 492, 513
Justice Department, *see* United States
 Department of Justice

Kahan, James, 256–257, 267–268, 275–
 276, 283, 293, 309, 312, 527
Kan, Stanley, 297
Kangas, Matthew, 330, 370
Kanouse, David, 256
Karl Marxmen, 287
Kaufer, Brunhilde, *see* Brunhilde Kaufer
 Liebes
Kaul Auditorium, 486
Kawahara, Hattie, *see* Hattie Kawahara
 Colton
Keele University, 279
Keene, Nathan, 448, 452
Keezer, Anne, 130, 180, 182
Keezer, Dexter, 127–134, 136–137, 154–159,
 163–164, 166, 171–174, 176–186, 201,
 246, 435, 525

Kehoe, Thomas David, 414–415
Kelly, Gail, 342–343, 418, 424–425, 429–430, 432, 510
Kelly, Tom, 203
Kenney, John, 402
Kenison, Kelly, *see* Kelly Kenison Falkner
Kent State, 349, 367, 420
Kerensky, Alexander, 170
Kerr, James B., 27, 87, 92–93, 96, 98, 107, 113–114
Kerr dorm, 130, 269
Kesey, Ken, 282, 327, 331
Kierstead, Ray, 371, 380, 382, 425, 431, 464–465, 473–474, 510–511, 513–514
King, Mary Catherine, 469, 491–492
King, Nathalia, 425
Kinnell, Galway, 444
Kirby, Bill, 267
Kirsch, William, 210
Kleiner, Malca, *see* Malca Kleiner Chall
Kleinholz, Lew, 248, 254
Knapp, Robert, 381, 412, 423, 427–428, 433–434, 464, 468–469, 473, 476–477, 482–483, 507–508, 510–512
Knowlton, Ellen, *see* Ellen Knowlton Johnson
Knowlton, Gertrude (Mrs. A. A.), 121
Knowlton, A. A. "Tony," 50, 95, 98–99, 102, 110–111, 134, 140–141, 147, 187, 201, 222, 249
Koblik, Steven, 478–481, 483–486, 491, 494, 498, 502–503, 505–506, 510–511, 514–515, 518
Kolesoff, Katherine, *see* Katherine Kolesoff Averill
Korean War, 209–210
Korsch, Karl, 427
Kosobud, Ann, 410
Krichesky, Boris, 104
Krisch, Patricia Leavey, 252, 264–265
Kristof, Ladis, 234
KRRC, 266, 391
Kuehn, Larry M., 326, 334
Kuestner, Mark, 527
Kunitz, Mela, 392, 401–403, 420
Kunzig, Robert, 236
Kurland, Amy, 397
Kurtz, Gail, 526–527
Kuylaars, Mary, 156

Labovitz, Margaret Churchill, 125, 141, 160
Ladd, Mary (Mrs. William Mead), 22
Ladd, William Mead, 27–28, 31, 52, 82–83, 99, 107
Ladd, William S., 19–20, 22, 27
Ladd and Reed Farm Company, 39
Ladd dorm, 120, 130, 161, 265, 405
Ladd Estate Company, 28, 30, 37, 73
Ladd farm, *see* Crystal Springs Farm
Laing, John, 185, 207

Laing, Ron, 212, 218, 230–231
Lam, Greg, 500–501
Lamb, Cara, 292
Lamb, Elizabeth, *see* Elizabeth Lamb Tate
Lambert Street, 1414, 215–216
Landauer, Robert, 436
Lane, Angela, 297
Langston, Peter, 253
Lanning, Michael, 363
Lapham, David, 216
Lapham, Rosemary *see* Rosemary Lapham Berleman
Large, Larry, 418, 455, 485, 488–489
Larisch, Sharon, 425
Larkin, Alice, *see* Alice Larkin Steiner
Larson, Anja, 471
Larson, Carl, 123–124, 140–141
Larson, Helen, 140
Lassleben, Lauren, 526–527
Lathrop, John Randy, 391, 401
Latino Student Group, 494
Latourette, Kenneth, 55–56, 61, 63, 69, 95–96
Laursen, John, 268–269, 281–282, 292, 303, 312, 323, 369
Lave, Rebecca, 495
Law, Roger, 346
Laws, Priscilla Watson, 261
Layman, Donald, 226
Leaf, Murray, 288
Learning Community, the, 362–363, 365, 368–369
Leary, Timothy, 331–333, 351
Leavey, Patricia, *see* Patricia Leavey Krisch
Leavitt, Andrew, 497
Leber, Lewis, 214
LeBoutillier, Cornelia, 181–182, 186
Lee, Gilbert Prentiss, 156
Lee, Jessica, *see* Jessica Lee Patterson
Lehman, Florence, 356
Leigh, Arthur, 354, 357, 378, 432
Leigh, Robert, 55, 68–69, 71
Leitz, Fred, 137, 173
Lencek, Lena, 384, 422, 425–427, 429–430, 472
Lenon, Harlow F., 117–118, 124–125, 137, 143–144, 163, 167–168
Lenske, Moshe, 202, 205, 210–212, 226, 263
Leong, Charlie, 226, 299
Lerner, Gerda, 403
lesbian, gay, bisexual, transgender, and queer movement, *see* LGBTQ movement
Lester, Gabriel, 254
Levich, Marvin, 221, 238, 240, 251–252, 294–295, 314, 338, 340–341, 344–348, 352, 355, 358–361, 365, 367, 372, 375, 378–379, 411, 423–425, 427, 429, 434, 443, 450, 482, 506

Levine, Michael L., 251, 258–259, 377, 411–412, 436, 452
Levine, Phillip, 444
Levine, Richard, 323, 332–333
Leviton, Laura C., 374
Lewis, Alan, 336
Lewis, Claudia, 119, 125, 147
Lewis, Esther Dorles, 169, 181
Lewis, Ethelwynne, 159
Lewis, Fred R. "Dick," 183
Lewis, Gwendolyn, 278
Lewis, Josephine, *see* Josephine Lewis Utley
Lewis & Clark College, 138, 148, 206, 324–325, 387; *see also* Albany College
LGBTQ movement, 463, 497
Library, 225; *see also* Hauser Memorial Library
Liebes, Brunhilde Kaufer, 120
Life Among the Lowbrows (Rowland), 46
Lillie, Sandy Osborne, 275, 321, 328, 331
Lincoln High School, 78, 100, 136, 144, 153, 310
Lindahl-Urben, Craig, 413
Lionni, Annie, 402
Lipson, David, 325–326, 332
Litt, Barbara, 388
Liu, Sam B., 121, 144–145
Livermore, Arthur, 166, 170
Living Theatre, 328
Livingston, Bruce, 342–343
Locher, Kaspar, 438
Loeb, Mark, 277–278, 306, 312–313
Lomhoff, Peter, 291, 293–294
Look magazine, 286–287
Lopez, Cynthia, 527
Lourie, Anita *see* Anita Lourie Bigelow
Lovell, Michael, 212–213
Lovin, John, 290
Lowe, Christopher, 8, 24, 373, 391, 417–418, 421, 526
Loyal Legion of Loggers and Lumbermen, 108, 112, 114
Luft, Rachel Hall, 527
Lutz's Tavern, 209, 212
Luxenberg, Marjory Franklin, 295, 343
Lydgate, Chris, 398, 400, 403, 448, 452, 455–456, 508
Lyman, Lloyd, 21–23

Macaulay, Elizabeth Funge, 183
Macaulay, Robert, 183
MacCaffrey, Wallace T., 171
Maccoby, Eleanor Emmons, 132–133, 166
MacDonald, Sandy, 214
Mack, Robert, 467, 488, 496–497, 499
Mackenzie, Virginia, 525
MacNaughton, Cheryl Scholz, 92–96, 98, 103–105, 107, 113–114, 117, 119, 127, 131–132, 140, 156, 160, 164, 178, 180–185, 207

Comrades of the Quest has been designed and produced by John Laursen at Press-22 in Portland, Oregon, during 2011 and 2012. The typeface is Cycles, created by Sumner Stone at Stone Type Foundry. The cover photograph of the Reed College griffin on the Old Dorm Block is by Aaron Johanson. The illustrations have been scanned and prepared for reproduction by Jim Haeger at Revere Graphics, and the photograph of Simeon and Amanda Reed was digitally restored by Phil Bard at Cirrus Digital Imaging. The paper is acid-free Natures Natural. The books have been printed and bound by Thomson-Shore in Dexter, Michigan.